ICSA Study Text

Advanced Certificate in
Corporate Governance

ICSA Study Text

Advanced Certificate in Corporate Governance

Alison Dillon Kibirige
Andrew Hamer

icsa

The Governance
Institute

First published 2019
Published by ICSA Publishing Ltd
Saffron House
6–10 Kirby Street
London EC1N 8TS

Typeset by Frances Rooney

British Cataloguing in Publication Data
A catalogue record for this book is available from the British Library.

ISBN 9781860727870

Contents

How to use this study text

This study text has been developed to support ICSA's Advanced Certificate in Corporate Governance and includes a range of navigational, self-testing and illustrative features to help you get the most out of the support materials.

The text is divided into three main sections:

◆ introductory material
◆ the text itself
◆ reference material.

The sections below show you how to find your way around the text and make the most of its features.

Introductory material

The introductory section includes a full contents list and the aims and learning outcomes of the qualification, as well as a list of acronyms and abbreviations.

The text itself

Each part opens with a list of the chapters to follow, an overview of what will be covered and learning outcomes for the part.

Every chapter opens with a list of the topics covered and an introduction specific to that chapter.

Chapters are structured to allow students to break the content down into manageable sections for study. Each chapter ends with a summary of key content to reinforce understanding.

Features

The text is enhanced by a range of illustrative and self-testing features to assist understanding and to help you prepare for the examination. You will find answers to the 'Test yourself' questions towards the end of this text. Each feature is presented in a standard format, so that you will become familiar with how to use them in your study.

These features are identified by a series of icons.

The text also includes tables, figures and other illustrations as relevant.

Reference material

The text contains a range of additional guidance and reference material, including a glossary of key terms and a comprehensive index.

Stop and think

Test yourself

Making it work

Case study

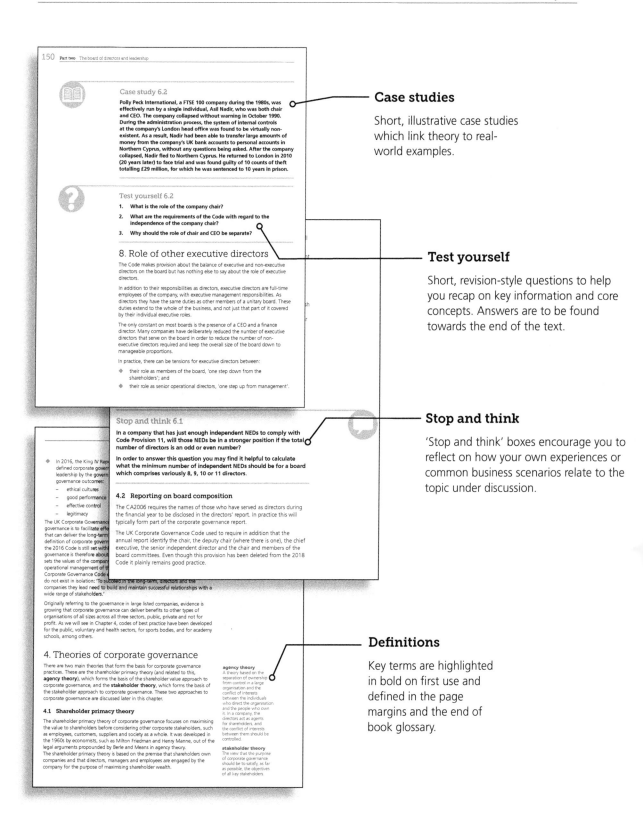

150 **Part two** The board of directors and leadership

Case study 6.2

Polly Peck International, a FTSE 100 company during the 1980s, was effectively run by a single individual, Asil Nadir, who was both chair and CEO. The company collapsed without warning in October 1990. During the administration process, the system of internal controls at the company's London head office was found to be virtually non-existent. As a result, Nadir had been able to transfer large amounts of money from the company's UK bank accounts to personal accounts in Northern Cyprus, without any questions being asked. After the company collapsed, Nadir fled to Northern Cyprus. He returned to London in 2010 (20 years later) to face trial and was found guilty of 10 counts of theft totalling £29 million, for which he was sentenced to 10 years in prison.

Test yourself 6.2

1. What is the role of the company chair?
2. What are the requirements of the Code with regard to the independence of the company chair?
3. Why should the role of chair and CEO be separate?

8. Role of other executive directors

The Code makes provision about the balance of executive and non-executive directors on the board but has nothing else to say about the role of executive directors.

In addition to their responsibilities as directors, executive directors are full-time employees of the company, with executive management responsibilities. As directors they have the same duties as other members of a unitary board. These duties extend to the whole of the business, and not just that part of it covered by their individual executive roles.

The only constant on most boards is the presence of a CEO and a finance director. Many companies have deliberately reduced the number of executive directors that serve on the board in order to reduce the number of non-executive directors required and keep the overall size of the board down to manageable proportions.

In practice, there can be tensions for executive directors between:

◆ their role as members of the board, 'one step down from the shareholders'; and
◆ their role as senior operational directors, 'one step up from management'.

Stop and think 6.1

In a company that has just enough independent NEDs to comply with Code Provision 11, will those NEDs be in a stronger position if the total number of directors is an odd or even number?

In order to answer this question you may find it helpful to calculate what the minimum number of independent NEDs should be for a board which comprises variously 8, 9, 10 or 11 directors.

4.2 Reporting on board composition

The CA2006 requires the names of those who have served as directors during the financial year to be disclosed in the directors' report. In practice this will typically form part of the corporate governance report.

The UK Corporate Governance Code used to require in addition that the annual report identify the chair, the deputy chair (where there is one), the chief executive, the senior independent director and the chair and members of the board committees. Even though this provision has been deleted from the 2018 Code it plainly remains good practice.

◆ In 2016, the King IV Rep defined corporate govern leadership by the govern governance outcomes:
  – ethical cultures
  – good performance
  – effective control
  – legitimacy

The UK Corporate Governanc governance is to facilitate eff that can deliver the long-term definition of corporate govern the 2016 Code is still set with governance is therefore about sets the values of the compan operational management of t Corporate Governance Code do not exist in isolation: 'To succeed in the long-term, directors and the companies they lead need to build and maintain successful relationships with a wide range of stakeholders.'

Originally referring to the governance in large listed companies, evidence is growing that corporate governance can deliver benefits to other types of organisations of all sizes across all three sectors, public, private and not for profit. As we will see in Chapter 4, codes of best practice have been developed for the public, voluntary and health sectors, for sports bodies, and for academy schools, among others.

4. Theories of corporate governance

There are two main theories that form the basis for corporate governance practices. These are the shareholder primacy theory (and related to this, **agency theory**), which forms the basis of the shareholder value approach to corporate governance, and the **stakeholder theory**, which forms the basis of the stakeholder approach to corporate governance. These two approaches to corporate governance are discussed later in this chapter.

4.1 Shareholder primacy theory

The shareholder primacy theory of corporate governance focuses on maximising the value to shareholders before considering other corporate stakeholders, such as employees, customers, suppliers and society as a whole. It was developed in the 1960s by economists, such as Milton Friedman and Henry Manne, out of the legal arguments propounded by Berle and Means in agency theory.

The shareholder primacy theory is based on the premise that shareholders own companies and that directors, managers and employees are engaged by the company for the purpose of maximising shareholder wealth.

agency theory
A theory based on the separation of ownership from control in a large organisation and the conflict of interests who direct the organisation and the people who own it. In a company, the directors act as agents for shareholders, and the conflict of interests between them should be controlled.

stakeholder theory
The view that the purpose of corporate governance should be to satisfy, as far as possible, the objectives of all key stakeholders.

Case studies

Short, illustrative case studies which link theory to real-world examples.

Test yourself

Short, revision-style questions to help you recap on key information and core concepts. Answers are to be found towards the end of the text.

Stop and think

'Stop and think' boxes encourage you to reflect on how your own experiences or common business scenarios relate to the topic under discussion.

Definitions

Key terms are highlighted in bold on first use and defined in the page margins and the end of book glossary.

About the authors

Mrs. Alison Dillon Kibirige is a global expert on corporate governance. She is the Founding Director of AMDK Consultancy & Training Services Limited (AMDK), a business she set up in early 2007, which focuses on improving corporate governance practices in all sectors globally. Her work at AMDK has taken her throughout Africa, the Caribbean, the Middle East and Asia working for organisations across all three sectors, Corporate Governance Institutes, Institutes of Directors and other bodies involved in corporate governance.

Alison has served as a member of boards, committees and industry working groups since the early 1980s. Alison has worked for the IFC/Global Corporate Governance Forum on projects in Africa, Asia and Eastern Europe. She developed the IFC Corporate Secretaries Toolkit and Handbook and a series of workshops for IFC for Directors of Banks in Nigeria and for SME Governance.

She was formerly a member of the ICSA (Institute of Chartered Secretaries and Administrators) UKRIAT Division Committee, the Company Secretary of aBi Trust and aBi Finance Limited, Director of the Leadership Team Uganda Ltd, Chair of ICSA Uganda and a member of the ICSA's Professional Standards Committee.

She is a lawyer and a Fellow of ICSA. Alison was awarded the 2013 ICSA President's Medal for Meritorious Service, the inaugural ICSA Company Secretary of the Year award in 2005 and has also won awards globally for her work with shareholders.

Andrew has worked as a Partner of The Mentor Partnership, a consultancy specialising in company secretarial practice, publishing and training. He writes and lectures widely on company secretarial and legal issues, document retention and document management.

Andrew is the author of two books with ICSA, The Law and Practice of Company Meetings and The ICSA Guide to Document Retention. He is also an Editor of the ICSA's Company Secretarial Practice manual, and its weekly email newsletter.

Acronyms and abbreviations

ABI	Association of British Insurers
ACCA	Association of Chartered Certified Accountants
AGM	Annual General Meeting
AIFS	Alternative Investment Funds
AIM	Alternative investment market
AoA	Articles of Association
BCP	Business Continuity Plan
BEIS	Business Energy and Industrial Strategy
BHS	British Home Stores
BIS	Bank of International Settlement
BITC	Business in the Community
BREXIT	British Exit from the European Union
CA2006	Companies Act 2006
CalPERS	California Public Employees Retirement System
CBI	Confederation of British Industry
CDSB	Climate Disclosure Standards Board
CEO	Chief Executive Officer
CFO	Chief Financial Officer
CIMA	Chartered Institute of Management Accountants
CIPD	Chartered Institute of Personnel and Development
CIPE	Centre for International Private Enterprises
CIPFA	Chartered Institute of Public Finance and Accountancy
CMA	Capital Markets Authority
CNPC	China National Petroleum Corporations

COSO	Committee of Sponsoring Organisations
CRO	Chief Risk Officers
CSR	Corporate Social Responsibility
CS	Company Secretary
DTR	Disclosure and Transparency Rules
DFID	Department of International Development
DJSI	Down Jones Sustainability Indexes
DSEP	Dove Self-esteem Project
DTI	Department of Trade and Industry
E&Y	Earnest & Young
EBITDA	Earnings before interest, taxation, depreciation and amortisation
ECGI	European Corporate Governance Institute
EcoDA	European Confederation of Directors Associations
EEA	European Economic Area
EP&L	Environment Profit & Loss Account
EPS	Earnings per share
EPS	Equator Principles
ESG	Environment, Social and Governance
EU MAR	European union Market Abuse Regulation
EU	European Union
FCA	Financial Conduct Authority
FRC	Financial Reporting Council
FSMA	Financial Services and Markets Act 2000
FTSE	Financial Times Stock Exchange
GAAP	Generally Accepted Accounting Principles
GBP	Great British Pound
GP	Governance Professional
GDPR	General Data Protection Regulation
GHG	Green House Gas
GMI	Global Measures International
GSSB	Global Sustainability Standards Board
HIV	Human immune deficiency virus
HR	Human Resources

HSBC	Hong Kong and Shanghai Banking Corporation
IA	Investment Association
IAS	International Accounting Standards
IBE	Institute of Business Ethics
ICAEW	Chartered Accountants of England and Wales
ICGN	International Corporate Governance Network
ICSA	Institute of Chartered Secretaries and Administrators
IEA	International Energy Agency
IFAC	International Federation of Accountants
IFC	International Finance Corporation
IFRS	International Financial Reporting Standards
IIRC	International Integrated Reporting Council
IMA	Investment Management Authority
IOD	Institute of Directors
ISO	International Organisation for Standardisation
IT	Information Technology
JSE	Johannesburg Stock Exchange
KPIs	Key performance Indicators
LPDT	Listing Prospectus and disclosure and Transparency Rules
LR	Listing Rules
LTIPs	Long-term incentive plans
M&A	Mergers & Acquisitions
MENA	Middle East and North Africa
MSC	Marine Stewardship Council
NAPF	National Association of Pension Funds
NASDQ	Nasdaq
NCA	National Crime Agency
NEDS	Non-executive Directors
NGOs	Non-Governmental Organisations
NIS	Network and Information System
NYSE	New York Securities Exchange
OECD	Organisation for Economic Co-operation and Development

OES	Operations of Essential Services
OHSAS	Occupational Health and Safety Assessment Specification
PBIT	Profit before interest and taxes
PCA	Principle Component Analysis
PCAOB	Public Company Accounting Oversight Board
PDMR	Person discharging managerial responsibilities
PIE	Public Interest Entity
PIN	Personal Identification Number
PIRC	Pensions and Investments Research Consultants
PLSA	Pensions and Life Savings Association
PWC	Price Water Coopers
RCG	Remuneration Consultants Group
RDS	Royal Dutch Shell
RDSP	Relevant Digital Service Providers
RIS	Regulatory Information Service
ROCE	Return on Capital Employed
ROSC	Reporting on Observations of Standards and Codes
SAIL	Single alternative inspection location
SASB	Sustainability Accounting Standards Board
SAYE	Save as you earn
SDGs	Sustainable Development Goals
SEC	Securities and Exchange Commission
SID	Senior Independent Director
SIGMA	Sustainability – Integrated Guidelines for Management
SMEs	Small and Medium Enterprises
SOX	Sarbanes Oxley Act 2002
SRI	Socially Responsible Investment
SYSC	Senior Management Arrangements, Systems and Controls
QCA	Quoted Companies Alliance
TCFD	Task Force on Climate-related Financial Disclosure
TIAA-CREF	The Teachers Insurance and Annuity Association – College Retirement Equities Fund
TSR	Total Shareholder Return

UBS	Union Bank of Switzerland
UKLA	UK Listing Authority
UN	United Nations
VaR	Risk at Value
VCT	Voluntary Counselling and Testing
VMF	Value for Money
VW	Volkswagen
WWF	World Wildlife Fund

Part one

Corporate governance – principles and issues

Overview

Part 1 of this study text examines the nature and scope of corporate governance, its importance to the long-term success of all types of organisations and the role of the company secretary at its heart.

Chapter 1 tries to define the term 'corporate governance' and looks at the different approaches to, and theoretical frameworks for, corporate governance. It describes the four principles of corporate governance: responsibility, accountability, transparency and fairness. It then looks at the corporate governance framework, discussing the differences between the rules-based and principles-based approaches to corporate governance regulation and the difference between compliance and governance. Finally, it looks at the benefits of good corporate governance to an organisation versus the consequences of poor governance.

Chapter 2 looks at how corporate governance has developed in the UK, the laws and regulations that govern it for companies with listings on the London Stock Exchange and for unlisted private companies.

Chapter 3 examines the importance of the company secretary to governance within an organisation. It discusses the role of the company secretary in governance and compliance and as an advisor and communicator. It considers the importance of the company secretary having strong interpersonal skills and commercial and business acumen. It looks at why the independence of the company secretary is essential to good governance and how an organisation can take steps to preserve that independence. Finally, the chapter considers the pros and cons of outsourcing the company secretary role and the challenges of combining it with another role in the organisation such as the in-house lawyer.

Chapter 4 looks at the international aspects of corporate governance, and how other countries have established their corporate governance frameworks. It examines how governance has been adopted outside of the corporate sector in the public and not-for profit sectors. It also discusses the key corporate governance issues facing companies today.

Learning outcomes

Part 1 should enable you to:

- explain the different approaches to corporate governance that are adopted throughout the world;
- understand why there are different approaches to corporate governance globally;
- describe the difference between a rules-based approach to corporate governance and a principles-based approach;
- distinguish between compliance and governance;
- demonstrate the importance of the role of the company secretary within the corporate governance framework;
- explain the importance of applying the principles of corporate governance: responsibility, accountability,

transparency and fairness within your organisation for its long-term success and sustainability;

◆ appreciate the difference between good and bad governance practices, and the impact they have on the performance and long-term sustainability of the organisation;

◆ understand why it is important for boards to consider the impact of decisions on a wider stakeholder group including employees, customers and suppliers — not just on shareholder value

◆ differentiate between the role of the board and the role of management, understanding the importance of the board to the organisation; and

◆ understand why the governance role of the organisation should be kept separate from that of compliance-based roles, for example that of the in-house lawyer.

Chapter one
Definitions and issues in corporate governance

CONTENTS

1. Introduction

corporate governance
The system by which a company is directed, so as to achieve its overall objectives. It is concerned with relationship, structures, processes, information flows, controls, decision-making and accountability to the highest level in a company.

This chapter introduces you to **corporate governance**, what it is and what it is not, why it is important and the consequences of not practising good governance. It discusses the different approaches to, and theoretical frameworks of, corporate governance and how they have developed over the years. It looks at what makes up a corporate governance framework and how this might be implemented in an organisation.

2. The origins of the term corporate governance

English dictionaries define 'governance' as the way that organisations or countries are managed at the highest level, and the system for doing this. Bob Tricker first used the term 'corporate governance' in an article, 'Perspectives on corporate governance: Intellectual influences in the exercise of corporate governance', which was published in a 1983 collection of essays edited by Michael Earl. Tricker had realised in the 1970s that 'governance' was different from 'management' – a topic which had been written about extensively.

The term corporate governance was picked up and used by Sir Adrian Cadbury when he was asked to **chair** a committee established in May 1991 by the Financial Reporting Council (FRC), the London Stock Exchange, and the accountancy profession due to an increasing lack of investor confidence in the honesty and accountability of listed companies. This followed the sudden financial collapses of two companies, Coloroll and Polly Peck, both of which had apparently healthy published accounts. While the committee was in session, there were two further scandals at the Bank of Credit and Commerce International (BCCI) and the Mirror Group News International.

The recommendations from the Committee were published in 1992 in 'The Report of the Committee on the Financial Aspects of Corporate Governance: The Code of Best Practice' (the Cadbury Report) and underpin many of the corporate governance laws, regulations, standards and codes adopted globally today. The topics covered by the Cadbury Report included: board effectiveness, the roles of the chair and the **non-executive directors**, access to independent professional advice, **directors**' training, board structures and procedures, the role of the company secretary, directors' responsibilities, internal **financial controls** and internal audit. We will see later in this book that each of these topics has, over the years since 1992, been developed further as best practice and thinking on the subject has evolved in response to subsequent events to where we are today.

chair
Leader of the board of directors often referred to as the 'company chair' in companies and 'chair' in public bodies and voluntary organisations.

non-executive directors
A director who is not an employee of the company and who does have any responsibilities for executive management in the company.

executive director
A director who also has executive responsibilities in the management structure. Usually a full-time employee with a contract of employment.

financial controls
Internal controls to prevent or detect errors resulting from financial risks.

Case study 1.1

Polly Peck was a UK listed company which was placed into administration in October 1990. Its share price fell 75% from the beginning of August 1990 to 20 September 1990 when its shares were suspended from trading on the London Stock Exchange. The chair and chief executive of Polly Peck was Asil Nadir, a charismatic and hard-working businessman. It is argued that the fact that Nadir was chair and CEO of Polly Peck meant that the concentration of too much power in the hands of one individual may have meant that important decisions were not fully discussed by the board of directors.

Nadir had acquired 58% of Polly Peck in 1980 at a cost of £270,000. Under his management Polly Peck experienced unprecedented growth, with Nadir's investment valued at just over £1 billion by 1990. The growth was achieved through diversification into other product lines and expansion internationally, both of which were deemed to be high-risk strategies by market analysts.

In August 1990, Nadir – frustrated with Polly Peck's low price-earnings ratio, i.e. the relationship between its share price and reported profits

chief executive officer (CEO)
The person who is the head of the executive management team in an organisation.

before dividends (earnings) – announced that he was to bid for the company and take it private.

Five days later he abruptly changed his mind and dropped the plan. This caused the share price to fall substantially. As the company went into administration, it issued a statement stating that a combination of the fall in share price and negative publicity associated with it, had caused the company's liquidity problems.

Nadir had claimed that he could shore up the company with his own personal wealth, which at the time was thought to be about £1 billion. However, it turned out that he and his other companies were in substantial debt. Unfortunately, many of the banks were holding Polly Peck shares as collateral against these loans. Following the collapse, Nadir was charged with theft and false accounting.

3. Definitions of corporate governance

There is no one definition of corporate governance.

In 1984 Bob Tricker stated: 'If management is about running business, governance is about seeing that it is run properly. All companies need governing as well as managing.' Since then corporate governance has been defined in many ways. For example:

◆ The Cadbury Committee (1992) defined corporate governance as 'the system by which companies are directed and controlled'.

◆ The Organisation for Economic Co-operation and Development (OECD) published its Corporate Governance Principles in 1999 (revised in 2004) and defined corporate governance as involving 'a set of relationships between a company's management, its board, its shareholders and other **stakeholders** … also provides the structure through which the objectives of the company are set, and the means of attaining those objectives and monitoring performance are determined'.

◆ In 2004, The New Partnership for African Development (NEPAD) Declaration on Democracy, Political, Economic and Corporate Governance defined corporate governance as being 'concerned with ethical principles, values and practices that facilitate the balance between economic and social goals and between individual and communal goals. The aim is to align as nearly as possible the interests of individuals, corporations and society within the framework of sound governance and the common good.'

◆ In 2015, the G20/OECD issued a new set of corporate governance principles which stated that corporate governance practices should 'help build an environment of trust, transparency and accountability necessary for fostering long-term investment, financial stability and business integrity, thereby supporting stronger growth and more inclusive societies'.

stakeholder
A stakeholder group is an identifiable group of individuals or organisations with vested interest. Stakeholder groups in a company include the shareholders, the directors, senior executive management and other employees, customers, suppliers, the general public and (in the case of many companies) the government. Stakeholders maybe categorised as financial or non-financial stakeholders and as an external or internal stakeholders (depending on whether The in the company) the nature of their interest differs between stakeholder group.

◆ In 2016, the King IV Report on Corporate Governance for South Africa defined corporate governance as: 'The exercise of ethical and effective leadership by the governing body towards achievement of the following governance outcomes:

- – ethical cultures
- – good performance
- – effective control
- – legitimacy

The UK Corporate Governance Code 2016 stated that 'the purpose of corporate governance is to facilitate effective, entrepreneurial and prudent management that can deliver the long-term success of the company'. It refers back to the definition of corporate governance from the Cadbury Report, and states that the 2016 Code is still set within the context of this definition: 'Corporate governance is therefore about what the board of a company does and how it sets the values of the company. It is to be distinguished from the day to day operational management of the company by full-time executives.' The 2018 UK Corporate Governance Code expands the definition, recognising that companies do not exist in isolation: 'To succeed in the long-term, directors and the companies they lead need to build and maintain successful relationships with a wide range of stakeholders.'

Originally referring to the governance in large listed companies, evidence is growing that corporate governance can deliver benefits to other types of organisations of all sizes across all three sectors, public, private and not for profit. As we will see in Chapter 4, codes of best practice have been developed for the public, voluntary and health sectors, for sports bodies, and for academy schools, among others.

4. Theories of corporate governance

There are two main theories that form the basis for corporate governance practices. These are the shareholder primacy theory (and related to this, **agency theory**), which forms the basis of the shareholder value approach to corporate governance, and the **stakeholder theory**, which forms the basis of the stakeholder approach to corporate governance. These two approaches to corporate governance are discussed later in this chapter.

4.1   Shareholder primacy theory

The shareholder primacy theory of corporate governance focuses on maximising the value to shareholders before considering other corporate stakeholders, such as employees, customers, suppliers and society as a whole. It was developed in the 1960s by economists, such as Milton Friedman and Henry Manne, out of the legal arguments propounded by Berle and Means in agency theory.
The shareholder primacy theory is based on the premise that shareholders own companies and that directors, managers and employees are engaged by the company for the purpose of maximising shareholder wealth.

agency theory
A theory based on the separation of ownership from control in a large organisation and the conflict of interests between the individuals who direct the organisation and the people who own it. In a company, the directors act as agents for shareholders, and the conflict of interests between them should be controlled.

stakeholder theory
The view that the purpose of corporate governance should be to satisfy, as far as possible, the objectives of all key stakeholders.

The contrary view advocated by supporters of the stakeholder approach to corporate governance is that shareholders don't actually own the company as the company is a separate legal entity in and of itself. Companies, like individuals, are therefore citizens of the countries in which they operate and should therefore comply with societal norms for that country, which includes complying with all laws and regulations and taking into consideration how they impact other citizens and the environment.

Since the 2008 global financial crisis, the focus by many companies on shareholder primacy as a governance model has come under criticism for the following reasons:

◆ Inappropriate stewardship. It is argued that changes in shareholder structure from direct investment by individual shareholders to wealth invested under management (asset managers, pensions, insurance) has led to what are often referred to as 'ownerless companies', where no single investor has a large enough stake in the company to act as the responsible owner, checking the performance and behaviour of the board and management of the company. Even where the asset managers, pensions and insurance companies group together under shareholder representative bodies such as the Investment Management Association and the Pensions and Lifetime Savings Association (formerly National Association of Pension Funds), their focus tends to be on issues such as executive pay and board composition rather than the decision making of the board and management team.

short termism
This refers to the tendency for company management to take actions that maximise short-term earnings and stock prices at the expanse of the shareholders' objectives of long-term company performance.

◆ **Short termism**, defined by the Kay Report (2012) as both 'a tendency to under-investment, whether in physical assets or in intangibles such as product development, employee skills and reputation with customers, and as a hyperactive behaviour by executives whose corporate strategy focuses on restructuring, financial re-engineering or mergers and acquisitions at the expense of developing the fundamental operational capabilities of the business'. A report in 2016 from Tomorrow's Company, an independent non-profit think tank, found that UK companies were not allocating capital to tackle the major challenges faced by the UK in infrastructure and research and development. Instead companies are choosing to pay out more of their cash to shareholders by way of dividends or share buy-back programmes.

Furthermore, there is evidence that there has been a decline in the average holding periods of shares in both the UK and the US from around six years in 1950 to six months in 2010 (Haldane 2010). It is argued that this demonstrates that shareholders are investing in shares more often as a tradable commodity for short-term gain, with investment in the business itself of secondary importance.

4.1.1   Agency theory

Agency theory was developed in 1932 by Berle and Means, although it has been argued by Letza, Sun and Kirkbride (2004) that Adam Smith in his book the Wealth of Nations (1772) first pointed out the principal–agent relationship between shareholders and directors when he argued that company directors were not likely to be as careful with other people's money as their own. Further work to understand how the relationship between agents and principals played out in corporates was carried out by Jensen and Meckling (1976).

The agent–principal relationship exists when an agent represents the principal in a particular transaction and is expected to represent the best interests of the principal above their own. Jensen and Meckling argued that the agent–principal relationship existed in companies where there was a separation of ownership and control, the shareholders playing the part of the principal and the directors and managers playing the part of the agent. Where separation of ownership and control in a company exists, the challenges associated with the agent–principal relationship also occur. These relate to conflicts of interest and the costs associated with avoiding/managing those conflicts.

Agency conflict

Conflict arises in an agent–principal relationship when agents and principals have differing interests. The main conflict between shareholders and managers is as follows:

◆ Shareholders usually want to see their income and wealth grow over the long term so will be looking for long-term year-on-year increases in dividends and share prices.

◆ Directors and managers, on the other hand, will be looking more short-term to annual increases in their **remuneration** and bonuses.

remuneration
The payment packages offered to top company executives and all executive directors.

Jensen and Meckling identified four areas of conflict:

◆ Moral hazard. A manager has an interest in receiving benefits from his or her position in the company. These include all the benefits that come from status, such as a company car, use of a company plane, a company house or flat, attendance at sponsored sporting events and so on. Jensen and Meckling suggested that a manager's incentive to obtain these benefits is higher when they have no shares, or only a few shares, in the company. For example, senior managers may pursue a strategy of growth through acquisitions, in order to gain more power and 'earn' higher remuneration, even though takeovers might not be in the best interests of the company and its shareholders.

◆ Level of effort. Managers may work less hard than they would if they were the owners of the company. The effect of this lack of effort could be smaller profits and a lower share price.

◆ Earnings retention. The remuneration of directors and senior managers is often related to the size of the company (measured by annual sales revenue and value of assets) rather than its profits. This gives managers an incentive to increase the size of the company, rather than to increase the returns to the company's shareholders. Management are more likely to want to reinvest profits in order to expand the company, rather than pay out the profits as dividends. When this happens, companies might invest in capital investment projects where the expected profitability is quite small, or propose high-priced takeover bids for other companies in order to build a bigger corporate empire.

♦ Time horizon. Shareholders are concerned about the long-term financial prospects of their company, because the value of their shares depends on expectations for the long-term future. In contrast, managers might only be interested in the short term. This is partly because they might receive annual bonuses based on short-term performance, and partly because they might not expect to be with the company for more than a few years.

Agency theory says that companies should use corporate governance practices to avoid or manage these conflicts. Examples of how companies can achieve this are as follows:

♦ The use of long-term incentive share award or stock option schemes based on **total shareholder return** to align the interests of shareholders and management.

♦ Adoption of conflict of interest and **related party transaction** policies.

Agency costs

Agency costs are the costs associated with maintaining the agent–principal relationship. In companies, these costs are:

♦ Bonding costs – the cost of paying directors and executive management.

♦ The costs of monitoring the performance of the board and executive management. These will include the cost of **general meetings** and of the production and distribution of shareholder information such as annual reports and financial statements. It could be argued with the introduction of electronic communications that the cost of the latter has been reduced in recent years.

♦ Residual loss relates to the costs to shareholders associated with actions by the directors and executives which in the long run turn out not to be in the interests of the shareholders, for example a major acquisition or disposal, fraud or foray into a new business line.

Evidence shows that applying good corporate governance practices helps to minimise both the potential for conflict and the costs associated with the separation of ownership and control in corporates.

It is argued that agency theory appears to focus exclusively on maintaining value for the shareholders and this in turn has led to short-termism at the expense of long-term performance as many shareholders are looking for short-term gains. Blair (1995) goes on to argue that 'what is optimal for shareholders often is not optimal for the rest of society. That is, the corporate policies that generate the most wealth for shareholders may not be policies that generate the greatest total social wealth'.

4.2 Stakeholder theory

Stakeholder theory, in direct contrast to shareholder primacy theory, states that the purpose of corporate governance should be to meet the objectives of everyone that has an interest in the company. Individuals and groups that have

total shareholder return
The total returns in a period earned by the company's shareholders, consisting normally of the dividends received and the gain (or minus the fall) in the share price during the period. The returns might be expressed as a percentage of the share value, e.g. the share price at the start of the period.

related party transaction
A transaction by a company with a 'related party' such as a major shareholder, director, a company in which a director has a major interest or a member of a director's family.

general meeting
A meeting of the equity shareholders of a company.

an interest in a company are known as stakeholders. Key stakeholder groups are investors, employees (often represented by unions), suppliers, customers, government, regulators, creditors, local communities and the general public. When making decisions, boards should balance the interests of these different stakeholder groups, deciding on a case-by-case basis which interests should take priority in a particular circumstance. This means that non-financial objectives, such as employee relations or limiting environmental impact, should be considered equal to the financial objectives, such as the return on investment, usually associated with maximising shareholder value.

Stakeholder theory also states that companies should act as good **corporate citizens** when making decisions and carrying out their activities, taking into account the impact these will have on society and the environment. Companies should be accountable to society and should conduct their activities to the benefit of society. This aspect of the stakeholder theory forms the basis for arguments in favour of **corporate social and environmental responsibility** discussed in more detail in Chapter 11.

corporate citizen
A company acting with due regard for its responsibilities as a member of the society in which it operates. Corporate citizenship is demonstrated through CSR policies.

corporate social responsibility (CSR)
Responsibility shown by a company or organisation for matters of general concern to the society in which it operates, such as protection of the environment, health and safety and social welfare.

Test yourself 1.1

1. **What is the main difference between the agency and stakeholder theories?**

2. **How do they affect the objectives of companies?**

3. **How can a company manage conflicts of interest between shareholders and directors and managers?**

5. Approaches to corporate governance

There are four main approaches to corporate governance, the first two of which have as their basis the theoretical frameworks discussed above. These are:

◆ shareholder value approach;
◆ stakeholder approach;
◆ inclusive stakeholder approach; and
◆ enlightened shareholder value approach

5.1 Shareholder value approach

The shareholder value approach to corporate governance states that the board of directors should govern their company in the best interests of its owners, the shareholders. The main objective is to maximise the wealth of a company's shareholders through share price growth and dividend payments, while conforming to the rules of society as embedded in laws and customs. The directors should only be accountable to the shareholders, who should have the power to appoint them and remove them from office if their performance is inadequate. This approach focuses on protecting investors and the value of their shareholding in the company. It was historically adopted in listed companies where there was a separation of ownership and control. However, private companies are now also adopting this approach.

Non-corporates can also adopt an investor value approach to their governance. Investors in not-for-profit and public sector organisations can expect a 'social impact' as value for their investment. For example, in developing economies an investor in private sector agribusiness will expect value for money from the activities undertaken by the organisations in which they invest.

It is argued that a pure shareholder value approach is not sustainable in the long term as companies are not islands and have to interact with different stakeholder groups, the interests of which they will have to consider if they are going to be successful and sustainable in the long run.

5.2 Stakeholder approach

The stakeholder or pluralist approach to corporate governance states that companies should have regard to the views of all stakeholders, not just shareholders. This would include the public at large. When taking decisions, boards of companies should try to balance the interests of all the company's stakeholders.

The stakeholder approach to corporate governance is predominantly adopted in civil law countries, such as France and Germany, and in Japan and China where companies are often required to take account of the social and financial interests of employees, creditors and consumers in their decision-making. This approach is also reflected in the New Partnership for Africa's Development's definition of corporate governance, which states that corporate governance is concerned with achieving a balance between economic and social goals and between individual and communal goals.

Opponents of the stakeholder approach argue that if companies were to take into account all stakeholders' conflicting views, they would never come to a decision. However, there is no direct evidence that one approach is superior to the other in terms of the success of the organisation.

5.3 Inclusive stakeholder approach

The South African King Reports, developed by the Institute of Directors in South Africa, introduced a third approach to corporate governance, the inclusive stakeholder approach. This approach differs in its emphasis from the shareholder value and stakeholder approaches in that its supporters believe that the board of directors should consider the legitimate interests and expectations of key stakeholders on the basis that this is in the best interests of the company. The legitimate interests and expectations of key stakeholders should be included in the board's decision-making process and traded off against each other on a case-by-case basis in the best interests of the company.

In the inclusive approach, the shareholder does not have any predetermined precedence over other stakeholders. The best interests of the company are defined by the Institute of Directors for Southern Africa, King Code of Governance for South Africa 2009, King IV, not in terms of maximising shareholder value, but 'within the parameters of the company as a sustainable enterprise and the company as a corporate citizen'.

The inclusive stakeholder approach reflects African needs and culture. It incorporates the concepts of **sustainability** and 'good citizenship' (**ethics** and corporate social responsibility) into the definition of corporate governance as part of the fight against corruption, poverty and health issues such as TB, malaria and HIV/AIDS. The concepts of ethics and corporate social responsibility are often seen in the shareholder value approach as complementary disciplines.

5.4 Enlightened shareholder value approach

The **enlightened shareholder value approach** proposes that boards, when considering actions to maximise shareholder value, should look to the long term as well as the short term, and consider the views of and impact on other stakeholders in the company, not just shareholders. The views of other stakeholders are, however, only considered in so far as it would be in the interests of shareholders to do so. This differs from the stakeholder and stakeholder inclusive approaches where boards balance the conflicting interests of stakeholders in the best interests of the company.

The enlightened shareholder value approach was introduced in the UK by the Companies Act 2006 (CA2006), which imposed a statutory duty on directors to 'promote the success of the company for the benefit of its members as a whole, and in doing so have regard (among other matters) to:

◆ the likely consequences of any decision in the long term;

◆ the interests of the company's employees;

◆ the need to foster the company's business relationships with suppliers, customers and others;the impact of the company's operations on the community and the environment;

◆ the desirability of the company maintaining a reputation for high standards of business conduct; and

◆ the need to act fairly as between members of the company.

Interestingly, the interests of creditors are not included within this list. CA2006 specifically states that the duty imposed on directors to promote the success of the company overrides any laws or regulations requiring the director to act in the interests of creditors of the company.

There are two main challenges in practice with how the enlightened shareholder value approach has been adopted in the UK. Although directors now have a duty to consider the interests of a wider stakeholder group, there is:

1. No provision in CA2006 to enforce the duty. The only stakeholder with enforcement rights within CA2006 are those for members through a **derivative action**. It could be argued, however, that there is redress for non-shareholder stakeholders through other aspects of law, e.g. employment law, health and safety legislation and environmental law.

sustainability
Conducting business operations in a way that can be continued into the foreseeable future, without using natural resources at such a rate or creating such environmental damage that continuation of the business will eventually become impossible.

corporate ethics
Standards of business behaviour, sometimes set out by companies in a code of corporate ethics.

enlightened shareholder approach
Approach to corporate governance based on the view that the objective of its directors should be to meet the needs of shareholders, while also showing concern for other major stakeholders.

derivative action
Legal action taken against a director by shareholders in the company, alleging negligence or breach of duty.

2. No guidance as to how directors should take other stakeholder interests into account, particularly conflicting ones. Boards, therefore, in reality still focus on shareholder interests only, perhaps as these are the only enforceable ones.

The Companies (Miscellaneous Reporting) Regulations 2018 seek to address these challenges by providing guidance and reporting requirements on how directors are taking into account in their decision making the interests of employees and fostering relationships with customers, suppliers and others. More information on this is provided in Chapter 2.

5.5 Convergence of approaches to corporate governance

Proponents of each of the approaches to corporate governance have traditionally been very protective of their approach, seeing the shareholder value and stakeholder approaches as being diametrically opposed.

However, trends today seem to support convergence of the two main approaches to corporate governance: the shareholder value approach and the stakeholder approach. As we saw in Africa, where many countries follow the common law system, 'in the best interests of the shareholders' is being redefined as 'the long-term sustainability of the company', which appears to resemble more closely the stakeholder approach, rather than being 'in the best interests of shareholders'. This is not seen as at odds with being in the shareholders' best interests.

In civil law countries, pressure is being exerted to give priority to the interests of shareholders. For example, in France, the Marini Report criticised the concept of company interest, since it brought the danger of having management act primarily in its own interests. In Japan, corporate governance principles suggest on the one hand that a balance of various interests must be drawn, but on the other hand that the providers of capital are at the core of corporate governance.

Whichever approach to corporate governance is adopted, one of the underlying issues corporate governance attempts to deal with is conflicts of interest (potential or actual) between shareholders, members of the board as a whole, or as individual members and stakeholders. Directors may be tempted to take risks for short-term benefit whereas shareholders and many stakeholders will be looking to the long term. If a company gets into financial difficulty, directors can usually move on to another company with limited or no financial loss, leaving the shareholders and other stakeholders to suffer the fallout and loss.

Test yourself 1.2

1. **What is the difference between the enlightened shareholder value and inclusive stakeholder approaches to corporate governance?**

2. **Which approaches see boards taking a longer-term view in decision-making?**

3. **Which approaches put shareholders first?**

6. Principles of corporate governance

Despite there being no agreed definition of corporate governance, there are four agreed principles underlying the development of corporate governance. These principles can be found operating to different degrees in all types of organisations whichever sector they are in: private, public or not-for-profit. These principles are:

- responsibility;
- accountability;
- transparency; and
- fairness.

6.1 Responsibility

This refers to a person or group of people having authority over something, and who are, therefore, liable to be held accountable for the exercise or lack of exercise of that authority. Those given authorities should accept full responsibility for the powers that they have been given and the authority they exercise. They should understand what their responsibilities are, and should carry them out ethically with honesty, probity and integrity.

Organisations should ensure that procedures and structures are in place so that people know what they are responsible for and thus liable to account for. This will help people to minimise, or avoid completely, potential conflicts of interest that could arise in the exercise or lack of exercise of their authority. Mismanagement of authority should be penalised, and therefore responsibility goes hand in hand with accountability.

6.2 Accountability

This refers to the requirement for a person or group of people in a position of responsibility to account for the exercise (or not) of the authority they have been given. Accountability should be to the person or group of people from whom the authority is derived.

Those providing accountability should provide 'honest' information and not manipulate facts or 'spin' them to their or their organisation's advantage.

Accountability applies to all the different 'players' within an organisation, whether they are the owners of the organisation, the governing body, the management or the employees. The challenge is in deciding how the person or group of people should be made accountable, and over what time period.

Corporate governance best practice requires an organisation to set out clearly who is accountable for what and over what time period so that an organisation's stakeholders are clear whom they should hold responsible for what. The sophistication of how this is set out will again depend on the size and complexity of the organisation and can range from a few lines to a large manual as the organisation becomes more complex.

accountability
The requirement for a person in a position of responsibility to justify, explain or account for the exercise of their authority and their performance or actions.

6.3 Transparency

This refers to the ease with which an outsider is able to make a meaningful analysis of an organisation and its actions, both financial and non-financial. It also refers to the clarity of process in making decisions and carrying them out. Transparency builds trust between the organisation and its stakeholders: those with whom it interacts or who have an interest in the organisation.

Organisations should:

◆ be open in all of their actions, relationships, processes and decision-making – this includes tenders, recruitment and disclosures about business performance and risks; and

◆ ensure that disclosure is timely and accurate on all material matters, including: the financial situation, performance, ownership and corporate governance. It does not include commercially sensitive information, for example, the Coca-Cola Company would not be required to disclose the recipe for the Coca-Cola drink.

Those interested in the organisation need to know about it in order to make informed decisions when dealing with it. Information disclosure needs to be timely to be of benefit to its recipients. It can be delivered through press releases, market releases, annual reports and an organisation's website.

Organisations should have policies in place about the disclosure of information – what information should be public and what information should be kept secret, who has authority to disclose what information and when, and so on. They should also have a policy and process on how information should be kept confidential once it has been classified as confidential information.

6.4 Fairness

This refers to the principle that all key stakeholders should be treated fairly when decisions are made or actions taken by the organisation. The organisation should provide effective redress for violations, for example to **minority shareholders** when they have been unfairly treated.

Again, organisations should have policies, structures and procedures in place to ensure that the organisation and the people within consider key stakeholder views with justice and avoidance of bias or vested interests. Fair practices should be applied in an organisation's dealings with stakeholders. These dealings should also adhere to the spirit, not just the letter, of all rules and regulations that govern the organisation. An example of this would be where an organisation outsources to lower cost suppliers in emerging or developing markets who achieve the lower costs through less favourable working practices such as sweat shops and child labour. The organisation hopes to benefit through higher profits and the senior executives through higher bonuses.

7. Reputational management

In addition to the above principles, many corporate governance experts now see reputational management as an important issue within corporate governance. We saw above how in the UK, directors now have as part of their **statutory duties** under CA2006 'the desirability of the company maintaining a reputation for high standards of business conduct'.

statutory duties
Duties imposed by statute law.

Reputation defines an organisation as well as the individuals associated with that organisation. A good reputation attracts and motivates employees, customers and investors, and also assists in raising cash. The destruction of a reputation can lead to the end of the organisation. For example, the global accounting firm Arthur Andersen was destroyed in 2002 by the damage of its involvement in the Enron affair in the USA.

Organisations must have structures, policies and processes in place to manage reputational risk. Judy Larkin (2002) identified the benefits of effective reputational management, which can be summarised as follows:

- improving relations with shareholders;
- creating a more favourable environment for investment and access to capital;
- recruiting and retaining the best employees;
- attracting the best business partners, suppliers and customers;
- reducing barriers to development in new markets;
- securing premium prices for products and/or services;
- minimising threats of litigation and of more stringent regulation;
- reducing the potential for crises; and
- reinforcing the organisation's credibility and trust for stakeholders.

8. The corporate governance framework

An organisation's corporate governance framework consists of the following:

- applicable laws, regulations, standards and codes
- organisation's constitution
- structures
- policies
- procedures

8.1 Applicable laws, regulations, standards and codes

In developing the framework of laws, regulations, standards and codes of best practice relating to corporate governance countries have adopted three main approaches:

- rules-based approach

**principles-based code
of governance**
A code based on general
principles of best
governance practice, rather
than detailed rules and
guidelines. A principle of
best governance practice,
rather than detailed rules
and guidelines A principles-
based code may include
some practical provisions
or guidelines, but these are
not comprehensive.

◆   **principles-based approach**

◆   hybrid approach

Rules-based approach

A rules-based approach to corporate governance consists of a mandatory set of laws, regulations, standards and codes. An example is the US, Sarbanes-Oxley Act 2002. Failure to obey in a rules-based system may result in a company suffering sanctions and/or fines. Directors of companies in breach of the rules may also be fined, imprisoned and/or disqualified from holding the position of director for a period of time.

Critics of the rules-based approach argue that it only works where:

◆   the challenges faced by companies under the purview of the regulation are substantially similar, justifying a common approach to common problems; and

◆   the rules and their enforcement efficiently and effectively direct, modify or preclude the behaviours they are aimed at affecting.

The benefits of such a system is that it sends a message out to owners, potential investors and other stakeholders that the country takes seriously their protection from nefarious practices by those managing and overseeing the organisations they are investing in or dealing with. In reality, it is the enforcement of the rules that achieves this and in many countries, enforcement is weak.

Principles-based approach

A principles-based approach to corporate governance comprises a voluntary set of best practices usually contained in a code of best practice. An example of such a code is the UK Corporate Governance Code 2018. These codes of best practice, which were developed originally for listed companies, protect shareholders and potential investors. They are based on the presumption that shareholders will self-regulate the companies within which they invest. The codes being voluntary often adopt a '**comply or explain**' or 'apply and explain' approach, discussed later in the chapter.

comply or explain rule
Requirement for a
company to comply with a
voluntary code of corporate
governance (in the UK, the
UK Corporate Governance
Code) or explain any non-
compliance.

The principles-based approach allows companies and their shareholders to choose which principles and practices of corporate governance they believe are appropriate for their company at a particular time. The approach recognises the need for flexibility due to the diversity of circumstances and experiences within companies, and the fact that non-compliance may, at that time in a company's lifecycle, be in the organisation's best interests. It was also hoped that the approach would restrict the regulatory burden on companies.

For the principles-based approach to work, institutional shareholders have to take a more active role in the governance of those companies in which they invest. It is argued that institutional shareholders, such as pension funds, unit trusts and life assurance companies, hold funds on behalf of many individuals and are therefore investing indirectly on behalf of those individuals. They thus have a responsibility on behalf of those individuals to make sure that the boards of directors of the companies in which they invest are made properly accountable and govern their companies responsibly.

Many business leaders say a principles-based approach, allowing for discretion based on the circumstances of the company, is far preferable to what is perceived as a rigid rules-based approach. They claim that evidence suggests that long-term economic development is best achieved when business leaders are permitted to exercise judgement. However, the catalogue of business scandals over the last 20 years seems to indicate that some sort of regulation may be needed to ensure that good governance prevails in organisations, and stakeholders and stakeholder interests are protected.

Even in the UK, questions are being asked as to whether current market structures, which are very different from those in place in the early 1990s, are still able to regulate listed companies in the way envisaged. The concern is that, with limited resources and time, are UK investors going to be devoting their energies to monitoring the corporate governance performance of UK-listed companies? Evidence has also shown that in addition to time and resource, overseas investors face practical barriers to direct engagement with UK companies. Neither of these developments bode well for a future self-regulating system for the UK market.

Hybrid approach

Many countries are now adopting a hybrid approach to corporate governance combining mandatory laws and regulations with voluntary principles-based codes of best practice. The UK is an example of this. Some elements of corporate governance are contained in:

◆ Laws: company, insolvency, directors' disqualification and disclosure of directors' remuneration.

◆ Regulations: listing authority rules, such as UK Listing Rules and Disclosure and Transparency Rules.

◆ Standards: International Financial Reporting Standards (IFRS).

◆ Voluntary codes of best practices: UK Corporate Governance Code, Good Governance: A Code for the Voluntary and Community Sector.

Many developing and emerging countries struggle with the issue of how to encourage the adoption of good corporate governance practices. The organisations that provide products and services in these countries are often unregulated coming mainly from the public and not-for-profit sectors. Private sector businesses tend to be family owned and smaller in size. Many stakeholders are looking to the media to fill the regulation gap by reporting on good and bad practices of corporate governance. The reality is, however, despite training by organisations such as Thomson Reuters, that many journalists are still ill equipped to fill this role.

The debate continues around the world as to which of the three approaches should be adopted. Whichever route is taken, corporate governance should be flexible enough to allow the leaders of organisations to make decisions that are in the best long-term interests of their organisations, ensuring their success and sustainability. The adoption of corporate governance practices should, also whenever possible, be appropriate to the company's stage of development.

8.2   Concepts of 'comply or else', 'comply or explain', and 'apply or explain'

◆   'Comply or else' refers to a company's obligation to abide with a mandatory rules-based system of corporate governance. Failure to abide with the rules, as we saw above, usually results in some form of sanction for the company and/or its directors.

◆   'Comply or explain' refers to the system whereby a company is asked to comply with a voluntary principles-based code of best practice. Where the company believes that it is not in its best interests to 'comply' with a provision of the code, it is required to 'explain' to shareholders why they have not complied. The company's shareholders and shareholder representative bodies are then expected to assess whether the explanation is acceptable or not. The UK corporate governance code works on the premise of a 'comply or explain' regime.

apply or explain rule
Similar to the 'comply or explain' rule. Companies should apply the principles of a code or explain why they have not done so.

◆   The term **apply or explain** was adopted in the South African King Code III for two main reasons:

–   Firstly, the code, for the first time, applied to all types of entities regardless of their form of establishment or incorporation. These entities under a 'comply or explain' regime would only have had the option of complying or not. As many of the entities were not listed companies, which the corporate governance practices had originally been designed for, it was felt that that regime would put off many entities from adopting good corporate governance. Asking them how they were 'applying' the principles within the code was a less harsh way of reporting on what they were doing as they did not have to give a yes or no answer, they could tell a story of how corporate governance was being adopted in their organisations.

–   Secondly, to avoid a 'mindless response' to the corporate governance recommendations contained within the code. There was a feeling among many stakeholders that the 'comply or explain' regime was leading to companies adopting a tick box approach to corporate governance, adopting the provisions without considering whether they were suitable for their companies or not.

King IV, introduced in 2016, has adopted an 'apply and explain' regime. This regime requires organisations to apply the good governance outcomes set out in King IV and explain how they have done so. King IV says:

'The required explanation allows stakeholders to make an informed decision as to whether or not the organisation is achieving the … good governance outcomes required by King IV.'

King IV goes on to say that it hopes organisations will start to see corporate governance as something that will yield results if thought about carefully giving consideration to an organisation's particular circumstances.

The Wates Corporate Governance Principles for Large Private Companies' were published in December 2018 and adopted an 'apply and explain' approach. Companies adopting the Wates Principles should 'apply each Principle by considering them individually within the context of the company's specific circumstances. They should be able to explain in their own words how they have addressed them in their governance practices.'

Test yourself 1.3

1. **What are the pros and cons of a rules-based approach versus a principles-based approach to corporate governance?**

2. **What is the 'comply or explain' rule for listed companies in the UK?**

3. **How does it differ from the 'apply and explain' rule in King IV?**

8.3   Organisation's constitution

An organisation's constitution is known by many names depending on its country of incorporation and the type of organisation it is. The most common are **articles of association**, bylaws, charters or trust deeds. The constitution sets out how an organisation is to conduct itself within the laws, regulations, standards and codes adopted by the country within which it operates. It usually covers shareholders' rights, including the right for shareholders to share in profits and to attend general meetings and vote, the appointment, powers and duties of the directors and chief executive officer, board proceedings, appointment, powers and duties of the company secretary, matters to do with accounts and audit and provisions for winding up the entity.

articles of association
Effectively the company's constitution, together with certain shareholder resolutions.

8.4   Structures

An organisation should consider the structures that are appropriate to it. This will depend on many things:

◆   the type of organisation it is, for example a listed company, a financial institution or a family-owned business;

◆   the laws and regulations applicable to the type of entity that require certain structures to be in place, for example **audit committees** for banks;

◆   the strategic objectives of the organisation;

◆   the risks associated with the operations conducted by the organisation; and

◆   the people who work for the organisation.

Examples of the types of structures that can be put in place are:

◆   a board with a charter and statement of reserved powers or delegated authorities;

◆   audit committee;

◆   **risk committee**;

audit committee
A committee of the board, consisting entirely of independent non-executive directors, with responsibility for monitoring the reliability of financial statements, the quality of the external audit and the company's relationship with its external auditors.

risk committee
A committee of the board that a company may establish, with the responsibility of monitoring the risk management system within the company, instead of the audit committee. A risk committee maybe established when the audit committee has so many other responsibilities to handle.

nominations committee
A committee of the board of directors, with responsibility for identifying potential new members for the board of directors. Suitable candidates are recommended to the main board, which then makes a decision about their appointment.

remuneration committee
A committee of the board of directors, with responsibility for deciding remuneration policy for top executives and the individual remuneration packages of certain senior executives, for example all the executive directors.

insider trading
Dealing in the shares of a company by an 'insider' (such as a company director or professional adviser) on the basis of knowledge of price-sensitive information that has not yet been made available to the public.

internal control
A procedure or arrangement that is implemented to prevent an internal control risk, reduce the potential impact of such a risk, or detect a failure of internal control when it occurs (and initiate remedial action).

- governance and **nominations committee**;
- **remuneration committee**;
- role profiles for the chair, chief executive officer, non-executive directors etc.;
- executive committee or senior management team; and
- organisational structure including employee job descriptions.

8.5 Policies

Organisations also need to introduce policies to govern how they conduct their operations. The policies to be introduced will again depend on the type of organisation and the sector within which it operates.

Examples of policies are:

- code of conduct or ethics;
- bribery;
- conflicts of interest;
- related party transactions;
- whistleblowing;
- disclosure of information;
- sexual harassment;
- **insider trading**;
- risk;
- IT policies;
- HR including a remuneration policy;
- gifts, entertainment and gratuities; and
- fair competition and business practices.

8.6 Procedures

Organisations also establish procedures and processes to enable them to utilise the resources available to them to operate their business and implement the policies and strategies they have adopted effectively and efficiently.

Examples of procedures and processes are:

- strategic planning;
- business continuity;
- risk management and **internal controls**;
- computer data and security;
- managing information;
- health and safety;
- procurement; and
- recruitment.

Stop and think 1.1

Does the organisation I work for have or need any of the above policies and procedures?

Does my organisation have other policies or procedures not mentioned above?

9. Implementation of a governance framework

In considering the implementation of the appropriate governance framework for an organisation, the company secretary/governance professional should also consider:

◆   the organisation's purpose;

◆   the assimilation of corporate governance practices; and

◆   what constitutes success for their organisation?

9.1   The organisation's purpose

The first thing to consider when implementing a governance framework is the organisation's purpose. An organisation's purpose is the reason the organisation is in business, its raison d'être. Sometimes, it is set out in an objects clause in the company's memorandum of association. If not, the board should ensure that it is defined in the governance documents of the organisation. Knowing the organisation's purpose is very important as everything stems from it: the organisation's vision, mission, strategic goals and governance framework, including risk management. It is only through knowing the purpose of the organisation and focusing efforts and resources on achieving that purpose that organisations can be successful in the long run.

The Chief Executive of Unilever, Paul Polman, stated: 'I have long believed that clarity of purpose is a key enabler in the delivery of sustainable long-term value for all stakeholders.'

If an organisation has clarity of purpose then its employees know what they are working towards, investors know what they are investing in and boards and management know how to focus their resources and manage their risks.

For the company secretary/governance professional, knowing the organisation's purpose helps set up the organisation's governance framework of structures, policies and procedures.

Many will say that the purpose of an organisation is obvious. A private sector company's purpose is to make money for its shareholders, a charity to support a particular cause, a state-owned enterprise to provide services to the public. In reality, the purpose for which an organisation has been set up is not so simple. Companies, for example, are often set up to carry out particular activities described in their purpose. For example,

Lloyds bank states on its website (1 October 2018) that its purpose is:

'Helping Britain Prosper – building a stronger, more responsible business by meeting the needs of people, businesses and communities across the UK.'

Unilever, in its 2017 Annual Report, states its purpose is:

'to make sustainable living commonplace. We believe this is the best way to deliver long-term sustainable growth.'

9.2   Assimilation of corporate governance practices

Based on the organisational purpose, the company secretary/governance professional can advise the board on the appropriate corporate governance requirements for the organisation. The company secretary/governance professional should ensure that the organisation puts in place the structures, policies and procedures required to meet the organisation's specific strategic needs, manage its risks and comply with the appropriate laws, regulations, standards and codes applicable to the organisation. In doing so, the company secretary/governance professional will need to consider the type of organisation and the sector within which it is operating as different laws, regulations, standards and codes will apply. For example, listed companies, in addition to CA2006 will also have to comply with the governance requirements in the UK Corporate Governance Code 2018.

Figure 1.1 explains how the corporate governance framework should be implemented. The lessons learned from previous corporate scandals show that it is not sufficient just to comply with the laws, regulations, standards and codes. More needs to be done to ensure that the structures, policies and procedures put in place are assimilated into the organisation.

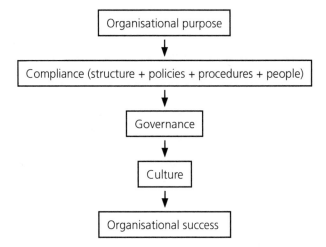

Figure 1.1 An organisation's corporate governance framework

The assimilation of the corporate governance framework into an organisation is what governance is all about. It requires engagement with the people who work for the organisation to create cultures of good practice.

When advising an organisation on governance the company secretary/governance professional should ensure that they are differentiating between compliance and governance when fulfilling their role.

Compliance basically answers the 'what is required' question. It leads to an organisation adopting the appropriate structures, policies and procedures. On its own, it is a pure **box-ticking** exercise. As we will see in the case of Enron (case study 1.2), it was able to tick the box of having a model code of ethics.

box-ticking approach
An approach to compliance based on following all the specific rules or provisions in a code and not considering the principles that should be applied and circumstances where the principles are best applied by not following the detailed provisions.

Case study 1.2

Enron was one of the world's largest power companies when it went into bankruptcy at the end of 2001. In July 2000, its board approved a 64-page model Code of Ethics. Ken Lay, Enron's chair and CEO circulated the new Code of Ethics with a memo which stated: 'Employees of Enron (its subsidiaries and affiliates) are charged with conducting business affairs in accordance with the highest ethical standards.' So, what went wrong? Enron's leadership was not committed to the high ethical standards so neither was its employees. Senior management was rewarded on the basis of high annual earnings and was thus motivated to carry out unethical acts to achieve these earnings. Unethical behaviour became the norm and employees had no incentive to disclose it. Finally, a 'whistleblower' (see Chapter 13) disclosed dubious accounting practices and this led to the share price collapsing. Several senior managers, including two former CEOs and CFO, were convicted of financial crimes.

Governance answers the 'how do we make this effective' question.

The company secretary/governance professional needs to ensure that the infrastructure is appropriate for the organisation, that people are focused and work well together, resources are used effectively, and information flows smoothly. Decisions are then made effectively, and this all contributes to a successful and sustainable organisation. If the infrastructure is not appropriate for the organisation, then the anticipated 'cultures' will not be developed. Those within the organisation will develop their own cultures which, as they are not being managed, often leads to bad practices, such as failure to follow policies, the misuse of resources, breakdown of important relationships, etc. This in turn threatens the performance and long-term sustainability of the organisation.

Stop and think 1.2

When answering questions, are you advising or recommending just compliance — providing the 'what' answer — or are you going on to explain 'how' to make the compliance effective?

In 2016 the FRC published a report, 'Corporate culture and the role of boards: Report of observations', which recognised that rules and sanctions on their own could not deliver productive behaviours over the long term. The report confirmed that corporate culture is increasingly important in delivering long-term business and economic success and aimed 'to stimulate thinking around the role of the board in relation to culture and to encourage boards to reflect on what they were currently doing' with regard to culture in their organisations.

The report highlights the following key observations on corporate culture:

◆ recognise the value of culture;
◆ demonstrate leadership;
◆ be open and accountable;
◆ embed and integrate;
◆ assess, measure and engage;
◆ align values; and
◆ exercise stewardship.

As we will see in Chapter 3, governance requires the company secretary/governance professional to have emotional intelligence skills in addition to the technical skills required for compliance to assist the board in its governance responsibilities.

9.3 Organisational success

As we have seen earlier, if an organisation gets its governance right then it reaps the benefits of success. To ensure that this is happening an organisation should define what its critical success factors are so these can be measured. This will usually be done as part of the strategic planning process. If these critical success factors are not being met the board may have to revisit the governance practices of the organisation, not just its strategic planning.

Test yourself 1.4

1.   **Why is knowing your purpose important for an organisation?**

2.   **What is the difference between compliance and governance?**

3.   **How can a business ensure it assimilates corporate governance practices into its culture**

10. The importance of adopting good corporate governance practices

Corporate governance, however defined, provides a framework for efficient, transparent and accountable decision making. According to the Centre for International Private Enterprises (CIPE), that framework is needed in every enterprise regardless of the size or form of ownership: 'All companies must have a way of reconciling divergent interests, planning for strategy and **succession**, accessing capital, cultivating company image in the community, and ensuring legal compliance. Corporate governance is a key tool for achieving those business goals.'

board succession
The replacement of a senior director (typically the chair or CEO) when he or she retires or resigns.

There is a plethora of evidence that well-governed organisations perform better. The studies, some of which are mentioned below, show that the adoption of good governance practices by organisations leads to:

◆ long-term sustainability;
◆ improved access to external financing, whether through listing or from banks;
◆ lower cost of capital;
◆ improved operational performance;
◆ increased firm valuation;
◆ improved share performance;
◆ reduced risk of corporate crisis and scandals;
◆ effective decision making;
◆ improved oversight, monitoring and evaluation;
◆ succession planning; and
◆ ethical behaviour – an anti-corruption tool.

Examples of studies showing the benefits of corporate governance are:

◆ The McKinsey's Global Investor Opinion Survey 2002 concluded that an overwhelming majority of investors are prepared to pay a premium for companies exhibiting high governance standards. Premiums averaged 12–14% in North America and Western Europe; 20–25% in Asia and Latin America; and over 30% in Eastern Europe and Africa.
◆ The S&P/Hawkamah Environmental, Social and Corporate Governance (ESG) Pan Arab Index which monitors and ranks listed companies in the Middle East and North Africa (MENA) region on ESG issues. The recently issued report on the Index (2017) showed that companies within the Index had outperformed those in its benchmark, the S&P Pan Arab Composite for the past nine years.
◆ In 2007, Derwall and Verwijmeren found that US companies with better governance practices received a lower cost of equity.

Hermes Investment Management, a UK investment firm, after reviewing evidence on the benefits for organisations of adopting good corporate governance practices is of the view that it is not just the governance structure of organisations that lead to better performing companies but the active engagement by the ownership of those organisations with the boards and senior managers that matters. Shareholder relations will be discussed further in Part 5.

There is a misconception that organisations can choose to 'do' governance or not. In fact, all organisations do governance – the question should therefore be, do they want to do it well or badly?

Take the example of a tennis match.

The court dimensions and the rules of the game are set – compliance.

The umpire regulates the match in line with those rules – oversight.

How the players choose to play the game – governance. They can be very expressive like John McEnroe or cool as ice like Bjorn Borg. They choose the type of racket they prefer to play with, the clothes they want to wear, the customs they have before and during the match and the type of game they want to play to win the match. Each player is different, but they are playing the same game.

Stop and think 1.3

Governance is all around us. You even do governance in your own home. Assigning roles, risk managing, decision-making, exercising social responsibility, accountability and so on.
Think for a moment of examples of this in your home.

11. Consequences of weak governance practices

We have seen above that practising good governance brings benefits. Evidence shows that practicing weak governance, on the other hand, leads to:

◆ Failing companies – reflected in many of the corporate scandals of recent years:
- accounting fraud, e.g., Enron, Worldcom. Parmalat;
- lack of knowledge skills and experience on the board, e.g. Barings Bank;
- dominant personalities, e.g. Maxwell, Polly Peck, Tesla and Elon Musk;
- failure to understand and manage risk, e.g. global financial crisis, Lehman Brothers;unethical business practices, e.g. BHS and Philip Green.

◆ Reputational problems:
- unethical business practices, e.g. Volkswagen ('Dieselgate'), Siemens (bribery);

  - lack of transparency and disclosure, e.g. Olympus;
  - poor relationship between the board and shareholders, e.g. Sports Direct;
  - inappropriate remuneration and reward systems for directors and senior executive, e.g. Enron, Carillion.

From a wider economic perspective, weak corporate governance practices can bring:

◆ Excessive regulation – many of the laws, regulations, standards and codes introduced globally have been in response to the scandals that have resulted from weak governance practices. It has meant that regulation in some cases has been reactive to a particular circumstance and although well intended has been poorly conceived. It has been argued by some that each initiative has tended to add to the compliance burden of organisations, especially those listed on stock exchanges. This in turn has led to a compliance culture around corporate governance reflected in the tick-box approach adopted by many. An example of this was the introduction of the Sarbanes-Oxley Act 2002 in the US which led to many non-US companies de-listing from the New York Stock Exchange to avoid having to comply with s. 404 of the act which was seen to be over-bureaucratic, costly and providing little benefit.

◆ Lack of investment in capital markets – evidence shows that investors place importance on good governance practices when investing in companies. A lack of those practices can therefore lead to a lack of investment.

◆ The development of shareholder representative bodies, such as the Investment Association or functions within some of the larger institutional shareholders specifically for monitoring the corporate governance practices of the companies they invest in, e.g. Hermes, CalPERS.

◆ A focus on regulating and disclosing senior executive pay.

◆ The establishment of powerful regulators such as the US Securities and Exchange Commission.

Case study 1.3

Accountancy fraud at Parmalat, an Italian dairy and food manufacturer, led to its collapse at the end of 2003. Forged documents indicated that there was a substantial amount of cash held by one of Parmalat's subsidiary companies, but this money did not exist. Parmalat's internal controls and external auditors failed to uncover the fraud. Several employees suspected wrongdoing but as there was no formal process for raising such issues, no one reported it.

Case study 1.4

On 7 August 2018, Elon Musk, the chair and CEO of Tesla the electric car manufacturer, which is a listed company, tweeted:

'Am considering taking Tesla private at $420. Funding secured.'

This led to the US Securities and Exchange Commission fining Elon Musk and Tesla $40 million as they argued that the social media post had misled and harmed investors who bought shares in the company as a result of the tweet. They also required Musk to step down as chairman for at least three years and for Tesla to appoint an independent chairman to oversee the company.

Case study 1.5

Siemens AG is a German multinational and one of the largest industrial manufacturing companies in Europe. In November 2006, the German authorities revealed Siemens' massive corruption scandal. For about seven years, the company had used illegal funds to pay bribes of about €1.3 billion. The following are examples of some of the bribes paid by Siemens:

◆ In Bangladesh, Siemens paid $5 million to the son of the prime minister to win a mobile phone contract.

◆ In Nigeria, Siemens paid $12.7 million to various officials to win government telecommunication contracts.

◆ In Argentina, Siemens paid at least $40 million in bribes to win a $1 billion contract to produce national identity cards.

◆ In Israel, Siemens provided $20 million to senior government officials in order to win a contract to build power plants.

◆ In China, Siemens paid $14 million to government officials to win a contract to supply medical equipment.

During his arrest, Mr Sekaczek, a sales manager at Siemens at the time, said from 2002 to 2006 he oversaw an annual bribery budget of about $40–50 million. In 2008, Siemens agreed to pay $1.6 billion in fines to settle legal suits brought by the American and German governments.

Case study 1.6

In August 2017, Sports Direct International plc, a UK listed company, lost two of its biggest institutional shareholders, Standard Life and Aviva, for failing to address corporate governance issues which included:

- the dominance of Mike Ashley, the founder and majority shareholder of Sports Direct, who held approximately 60% of the shares of the company;
- the replacement of a weak chair who investors felt failed to counter the power of Mike Ashley, and was being kept in position by Mike Ashley;
- excessive pay rewards; and
- poor treatment of workers.

majority shareholder
A shareholder holding a majority of the equity shares in company and so having a controlling interest in the voting power to remove directors from the board and so can control the board.

12. Governance and management

Bob Tricker, when talking about the difference between governance and management, said, 'whereas management is about running businesses, governance is about seeing that it is run properly'.

The board of directors is responsible for the 'governance' of the organisation: setting up the structures, policies and procedures within which the business of the organisation is conducted and ensuring that they operate effectively. The powers to manage the day-to-day affairs of the company are usually delegated to the CEO and their executive management team. There are two ways this happens:

- The authority to manage is passed to the CEO with the power to sub-delegate as they think fit to either individual members of management or to an executive committee.
- The authority is passed to several executives depending on the nature of their responsibilities. The chief finance officer would therefore receive authorities direct from the board in relation to the financial affairs of the business.

These days the first option is preferred as it allows the board to hold one person, the CEO, accountable.

The board will, however, keep some of the management powers to itself and these are usually set out in the 'Schedule of Matters Reserved for the Board'. Further details on this will be discussed in Chapter 6.

When members of the senior executive are appointed to the board, it is important for company secretaries/governance professionals to arrange an **induction** for them, the focus of which will be on their responsibilities and duties as members of the board. As a director they owe their allegiance to the company and not to the CEO, as they may feel they did as a member of the executive management team.

induction
Process of introducing a newly-appointed director into their role, by providing appropriate information, site visits, meetings with management and (where necessary) training.

Stop and think 1.4

Many employees within organisations see the CEO as all-powerful and the leader of their organisation. This is because they see him more often than the board. In fact, in some organisations, the employees may never interact with the board. Boards comprised of a majority of independent directors are often seen as 'outsiders' and not part of the organisation, which often leads to tensions and mistrust between the board and the employees within the organisation. Who do you see as the leader of the organisation? How could you raise the profile of the board without alienating your CEO?

Chapter summary

◆ There are no agreed definitions or approaches to corporate governance. There is, however, agreement on four concepts of corporate governance: accountability, responsibility, transparency and fairness.

◆ There appears to be a convergence of approaches to corporate governance as organisations realise that stakeholders' interests are important, to differing degrees.

◆ When companies collapse, poor corporate governance is often to blame.

◆ Adopting good governance practices results in sustainability and good performance over the longer term.

◆ There is a growing recognition that reputational risk and the protection of an organisation's reputation are also of growing importance when discussing corporate governance.

◆ Countries adopt corporate governance in different ways through laws, regulations, standards and codes of best practice.

◆ Corporate governance issues differ from country to country and organisation to organisation, so it is important that unique governance frameworks are established dependent on particular circumstances.

Chapter two
Corporate governance in the UK

CONTENTS

1. Introduction

This chapter describes how corporate governance has developed in the UK and its relevance for corporate governance practices today. It examines the legal and regulatory frameworks for listed and unlisted companies. Finally, it looks at recent developments in corporate governance in the UK, including requirements for large private companies to adopt corporate governance principles and the requirement for all companies to report on how they are taking into consideration the interests of employees and other stakeholders in their decision making.

2. History of corporate governance in the UK

Corporate governance scandals are not new in the UK. The first recorded incidents of corporate governance malpractices here occurred in the eighteenth century with the British East India Company and the South Sea Company.

The British East India Company had been established in 1600 by Royal Charter to help merchants and explorers establish trade on behalf of England in the East. The charter granted limited liability to the East India Company investors.

The company rose to global domination in both business and government as it extended its operations from trade to obtain territory. Over the years, the East India Company controlled and ruled territories either directly or indirectly via local puppet rulers, owned private armies exercising power and administrative functions, and monopolised exports of products such as opium and tea. By 1784, the East India Company had become so corrupt that the British government nationalised it through the India Act of 1784.

In 1720, speculators in the stock of the South Sea Company created the South Sea Bubble, an economic bubble where the price of the stock was considerably higher than the intrinsic value of the company. When the bubble burst following acts of insider trading and bribery, it left many in financial ruin. The South Sea bubble led to the passing of the Bubble Act in 1720, which required all joint-stock companies to be created by either Royal Charter or an Act of Parliament. Subsequent changes to the law relating to joint-stock companies led to the creation of the Registrar of Companies (1844), the introduction of limited liability for the investors in joint-stock companies (1855) and other aspects of company law which underpin the current law set out in CA2006. CA2006, in its turn, codified directors' duties, provided for electronic communication with shareholders, enfranchised indirect shareholders and extended the rights of proxies.

In addition to company law, the London Stock Exchange also introduced rules to regulate joint-stock companies, the first being its 1812 rule book which dealt with settlement and default in the trading of stock. In May 2000, the London Stock Exchange lost its position as the UK Listing Authority (UKLA) and was replaced by the Financial Services Authority (FSA), which in turn was replaced by the Financial Conduct Authority (FCA) in April 2013.

Despite all of the laws and regulations, as we saw in Chapter 1, there were a number of high-profile company collapses in the late 1980s and early 1990s which led to the establishment of what became known as the Cadbury Committee. In each case, common themes emerged:

◆   Investors were not kept informed about what was really going on in the company.

◆   The published financial statements were misleading.

◆   External auditors were accused of failing to spot the warning signs.

◆   The companies had self-seeking powerful chiefs, who lacked business ethics.

◆   Board members were unable to restrain management from acting improperly.

◆   Risk management systems were inadequate or ineffective.

Following the publication of the Cadbury Report in 1992, the London Stock Exchange introduced a requirement into its Listing Rules that listed companies should include a statement of compliance with the code of best practice in their annual report and accounts. The statement of compliance required an explanation of where the company had complied with the code of best practice and in circumstances where it had not and an explanation as to why not.

2.1   The Cadbury Report

Board of directors
The Cadbury Committee agreed that the **balance of power** between directors
and shareholders was appropriate, but that there should be more accountability
by directors to shareholders. Control over the company should be exercised
collectively by the board as a whole. There should be no domination by a single
individual. There should be a separate chairman and chief executive, and both
should have clearly defined roles. The board should have reserved matters which
should not be delegated to management. The board should meet regularly and
should monitor the performance of the executive management. Individual board
members should be able to seek professional advice at the company's expense.
This recognised the risk that some directors might not have the necessary
experience or skills in a particular area to play an effective role in a particular
discussion.

balance of power
A situation in which
power is shared out evenly
between a number of
different individuals or
groups, so that no single
individual or group is in a
position to dominate.

Non-executive directors
At the time of the Cadbury Report, non-executive directors were not
common. Those that did exist were major shareholder appointments or former
executives. The Cadbury Committee recommended that there should be
sufficient non-executive directors for their views to carry weight, and most
of them should be independent. Independent non-executive directors should
be able to bring judgement and experience to the deliberations of the board
that the executive directors on their own might lack. Non-executive directors
should be selected through a formal process overseen by a nominations
committee. Recommendations would then be made to the board, who would
formally appoint them. Their appointment would be for a fixed term, and
their reappointment should not be automatic. Although the Cadbury Report
Committee did not set maximum terms for non-executive directors, it did imply
that they became less independent over time.

Executive directors
The Cadbury Committee recommended that directors' service contracts should
not exceed three years without shareholder approval. This was to reduce large
pay-outs for poor performance. At this time, there was not the debate about
directors' remuneration and pay for failure that we see in many countries today.
The Cadbury Committee also recommended that directors' remuneration should
be decided by a remuneration committee consisting wholly or mainly of non-
executives.

The audit committee
The Cadbury Committee recommended that all listed companies should have an
audit committee and set out its remit. The audit committee should comprise at
least three non-executives and should be the main relationship with the external
auditors. Previously the external auditors' main relationship had been with
executive management. The audit committee should also review the interim
and annual financial statements before their submission to the full board for
approval.

A 'going concern' statement
The Cadbury Committee recommended that companies should include a 'going concern' statement in their annual report and accounts. An implication of this recommendation is that before approving the report and accounts, each director is under a personal responsibility to reassure themselves that the company is a going concern and is not on the brink of insolvency.

Internal financial controls
Directors should also report to shareholders on the company's system of internal financial controls.

The Cadbury Report therefore introduced for FTSE 350 companies the requirements for non-executive directors, independent directors, audit, nomination and remuneration committees, evaluation of performance and reports on the internal controls of a company.

2.2   Directors' remuneration: The Greenbury Report

On the recommendation of the Cadbury Committee and due to directors' remuneration becoming a problematic issue in the UK, a committee was set up under the chairmanship of Sir Richard Greenbury to look into the issue. The Greenbury Report, published in 1995, made the following recommendations:

◆   The remuneration committee of the board should decide the remuneration of the executive directors.

◆   The Committee should comprise entirely non-executive directors, so that no executive director has responsibility for setting his or her own or the remuneration of executive colleagues.

◆   Maximum notice periods in executive directors' contracts should normally be 12 months. However, two-year notice periods may be acceptable in exceptional circumstances to entice a key individual to join a board.

◆   Executive pay should not be excessive but remuneration packages should be sufficient to attract, retain and motivate individuals of the required quality. One could argue that this gave remuneration committees carte blanche when setting packages because any package can be justified on the grounds that it was needed in order to attract a person of the necessary calibre.

◆   The concept of performance-related pay being closely linked with the interests of shareholders was introduced. The performance criteria should be relevant, stretching and designed to enhance the business.

◆   Matters for the remuneration committee to consider should include the phasing of any reward schemes, the nature of any **share option** packages and the implications of each element of the remuneration package for payments into the directors' pension plans.

◆   Share option awards should be phased into smaller payments and should not be issued at a discount.

◆   Remuneration committees were tasked with taking a firmer line on payments to directors dismissed for unsatisfactory performance. In practice this was difficult, as outgoing directors could still insist that a company honour its contractual obligations set out in the service contract.

◆ Listed companies were required to disclose information about their remuneration policy and the remuneration of their individual directors in a remuneration report in the company's annual report and accounts.

◆ The chair of the remuneration committee should attend the **annual general meeting** of shareholders each year in order to provide some accountability to shareholders.

annual general meeting (AGM)
A yearly meeting of the equity shareholders of a company. Public companies are required to hold an annual general meeting.

2.3   Hampel Report and Combined Code

In 1996, the Hampel Committee was set up to review corporate governance practices in the UK following the introduction of the codes from the Cadbury and Greenbury Reports. The result in 1998 was the publication of the Hampel Report, which led to the introduction of the Combined Code of Corporate Governance in the UK.

Hampel proposed the introduction of a code based on principles, which would hopefully restrict the regulatory burden on companies. Companies were required to 'comply or explain', explaining why they did not comply with the principles set out in the code. This approach, which recognises the need for flexibility due to the diversity of circumstances and experiences within companies and the fact that non-compliance may at that time in a company's lifecycle be in its best interests, still endures today in the UK and has been adopted in many other countries.

The Combined Code also included, for the first time, principles and a code of practice for institutional shareholders. The aim was to encourage institutional shareholders to take a more active role in the governance of those companies in which they invest. It was argued that institutional shareholders, such as pension funds, unit trusts and life assurance companies, hold funds on behalf of many individuals and are therefore investing indirectly on behalf of those individuals. They thus have a responsibility on behalf of those individuals to make sure that the board of directors of the companies in which these individuals invest are made properly accountable and govern their companies responsibly.

Institutional shareholders should have a dialogue with the companies in which they invest and make their views known, through advisory reports and, if necessary, via their voting practices at shareholder meetings.

The UK Combined Code was updated in 2003 by the Higgs and Smith Reports and in 2006 by the Financial Reporting Council (FRC). The aim has been to strengthen the provisions and disclosures surrounding non-executive directors, to make institutional shareholders more accountable and to give guidance on the role of audit committees and the responsibilities of their members.

The disclosure requirements for directors' remuneration set out in the Combined Code led in 2002 to the amendment of the Companies Act by the Directors' Remuneration Report Regulations. These Regulations were amended in 2013. The requirements introduced in 2013 are discussed in Part 5.

2.4   Internal control: guidance for directors on the Combined Code (Turnbull Report)

The Turnbull Report, issued in 1999, gave directors guidance on carrying out the review of the effectiveness of the company's risk management and **internal control systems** and reporting on it to shareholders required by the UK Corporate Governance Code. The review should cover all material controls, including financial, operational, and **compliance controls**.

In 2005, revised guidance on the Turnbull Report was published. There were few substantive changes but boards were encouraged to review their application of the guidance on a continuing basis and to look on the internal control statement as an opportunity to communicate to their shareholders how they manage risk and internal control. They should notify shareholders, in the annual report, of how any significant failings or weaknesses in the effectiveness of the internal control system have been dealt with.

The Turnbull Report has now been replaced by the FRC's 'Guidance on Risk Management, Internal Control and Related Financial Business Reporting' (Guidance), which was published in 2014. The aim of this guidance was to bring together all of the previous guidance for best practice in risk management: the FRC's 'Internal Control: Revised Guidance for Directors on the Combined Code' and 'Going Concern and Liquidity Risk: Guidance for Directors of UK Companies', and reflects changes made to the UK Corporate Governance Code. It also links the Turnbull guidance on internal control with emerging good practice for risk management reflected in the conclusions of both the FRC's 'Boards and Risk' report, issued in September 2011, and the final recommendations of the Sharman Panel of Inquiry into Going Concern and Liquidity Risk, issued in March 2011.

2.5   Institutional investment in the UK: A review (HM Treasury 2001, updated 2007) (Myners Reports)

Lord Myners chaired working groups which looked into the relationship between companies and **institutional investors** in 1995, 2001, 2004 and 2007. The recommendations from these working groups were incorporated into the UK Combined Code. They included suggestions for improving communications between companies and their shareholders, and urged institutional shareholders to reassess their role as shareholders, especially their role in respect of good governance. Companies were also encouraged to carry out their voting by way of a poll, so that the votes of all institutional shareholders were counted whether they attended a general meeting or not.

2.6   Review on the role and effectiveness of non-executive directors (The UK Department of Trade and Industry 2003) (Higgs Report)

The UK Department of Trade and Industry asked Sir Derek Higgs to set up a Committee to review the role and effectiveness of non-executive directors. The Higgs Report was first published in January 2003 and reviewed in 2006 by ICSA ('Improving board effectiveness'). Revised guidance was published in July 2018

internal control system
A system of controls within an organisations. The system should have suitable control environment, and should provide for the identification and assessment internal control risks, the design and implementation of internal controls, communication and information and monitoring.

compliance controls
Internal controls to prevent or detect errors resulting from compliance risks.

institutional investor
An organisation or institution that invests funds of clients, savers or depositors.

by the FRC to accompany the new version of the UK Corporate Governance Code 2018.

The Higgs Report looked at the role and effectiveness of non-executive directors. Many of the report's recommendations were incorporated into the Combined Code or appended to the Code in the 'suggestions for good practices'.

The Higgs Report concluded that the role of a non-executive director had four elements:

1. Strategy: non-executive directors should constructively challenge and help to develop proposals on strategy.

2. Performance: non-executive directors should scrutinise the performance of executive management in achieving agreed goals and objectives, and monitor the reporting of performance.

3. Risk: non-executive directors should satisfy themselves about the integrity of financial information and that the systems of internal control and risk management are robust.

4. People: non-executive directors are responsible for deciding the level of remuneration for executive directors and should have a prime role in succession planning for the board.

The Higgs Report also introduced the concept of a **senior independent director** and a definition for directors' 'independence'.

The good practices suggested by Higgs have also been adopted by many other countries as the basis for their corporate governance codes and best practices.

2.7   Audit committees: Combined Code Guidance (Smith Report)

In January 2003, the Financial Reporting Council published the Smith Report to give guidance to boards on how to organise their audit committees, and to members of audit committees on their roles and responsibilities. The Guidance was appended to the Combined Code.

The FRC Guidance for Audit Committees was updated in April 2016. It was intended to assist company boards when implementing Section C.3 of the UK Corporate Governance Code 2016, which deals with audit committees and auditors, and to assist directors serving on audit committees in carrying out their role.

The FRC has also provided a Best Practice Guide to Audit Tendering (2016), to assist audit committees looking to put their external audit out to tender.

2.8   Report on the recruitment and development of non-executive directors 2006 (Tyson Report)

Following publication of the Higgs Report, the Department of Trade and Industry set up a task force under the Chair of Laura Tyson, the Dean of the London Business School, to look into the recruitment and development of non-executive directors. The Tyson Report was published in June 2006 and argued

senior independent director
A non-executive director who is the nominal head of all the non-executive directors on the board. The SID may act as a channel of communication between in NEDS and the chairman, or (in some situations) between major shareholders and the board.

that a range of different experiences and backgrounds among board members can enhance the effectiveness of the board. It suggests how a broader range of non-executive directors can be identified and recruited.

Sources of non-executive directors highlighted in the report included:

◆ the 'marzipan layer' of corporate management, just below the board level;
◆ individuals in private sector companies;
◆ individuals in the public sector/non-commercial sector; and
◆ individuals working for business consultancies or professional firms (lawyers and accountants) and retired professional accountants.

2.9 The UK Corporate Governance Code 2010–2016

Following the financial crisis in the UK which came to a head in 2008–09, Sir David Walker was asked to review governance in banks and other financial institutions. His findings led to the FRC instigating a review of the Combined Code. The FRC review concluded that more attention needed to be paid by boards 'to follow the spirit of the Code as well as its letter' and that the impact of shareholders in monitoring the Code could be enhanced by better interaction between the boards of listed companies and their shareholders. The revised code, renamed the UK Corporate Governance Code, was published in June 2010. It encouraged the chair to report personally in their annual statements on how the principles relating to the role and effectiveness of the board have been applied. It also recommended that, in the interests of greater accountability, all directors of FTSE 350 companies should be subject to annual re-election.

The major changes to the UK Corporate Governance Code between 2010 and 2016 are as follows:

◆ Organisations are required to provide information about risks that affect the longer-term viability of the organisation. Investors should assess the statements given by organisations on solvency, liquidity, risk management and viability, and engage accordingly.

claw back
The act of recovering sums paid or withholding payment to directors or senior executives where there has been deemed to be deliberate disclosure of misleading information to increase entitlement to bonuses.

◆ Organisations are required to include within service contracts provisions that will enable performance adjustment or post-vesting **clawback** for executive directors' variable pay (bonuses and long-term incentives) and specify the circumstances in which remuneration committees would consider it appropriate to act by retrieving money paid out to the director under one of these variable pay mechanisms. Remuneration committees are faced with some difficult decisions relating to issues such as trigger events for clawback, how long the clawback risk should last, how to structure variable deferred pay to ensure ability to withhold or recover sums in practice and managing shareholder expectations.

◆ Remuneration committees are responsible for ensuring that remuneration policies must be designed to deliver long-term benefit to the company. Performance-related elements of pay should be transparent and not encourage excessive risk taking.

◆ Boards are obliged, where a significant proportion of votes have been cast against or withheld on any resolution, to try to understand the reasons for the shareholders opposing it. They also need to explain how they intend to engage with shareholders in order to address their concerns.

◆ Boards should avoid 'group-think' and the Code suggests a way to do this is to introduce diversity on to the board. This diversity should consist of not just race and gender, but also skills and experience.

◆ Boards should set the right 'tone at the top' – culture, values and ethics – and lead by example.

◆ Chairs should report in annual statements on how the principles in Schedule A and B to the Code have been applied by the company. Schedule A relates to executive directors' performance-related pay and Schedule B covers the corporate governance arrangements of the company.

The UK Corporate Governance Code was last updated in 2018. More information on the 2018 Code can be found later in the chapter.

2.10 UK Stewardship Code

Corporate governance best practices states that there should be open communications between a company and its shareholders. The UK Stewardship Code, which was published in 2010 and revised in 2012 by the FRC, sets out the responsibilities of the institutional shareholders in this relationship. More information on the Stewardship Code will be provided in Chapter 14.

2.11 The Davies Report: women on boards

The UK government asked Lord Davis to review the current status of women on the boards of the UK's largest companies. Lord Davis' conclusions were published in a report in 2011. It concluded that there was a case for a greater proportion of women on the boards of UK companies, there being only 12.5% female board members on FTSE 100 companies in 2010, as there was evidence that boards with greater diversity were 'more likely to be effective boards, better able to understand their customers and stakeholders, and to benefit fresh perspectives, vigorous challenge and broad experience. These in turn lead to better decision-making.'

The specific recommendations of the Davis Report were as follows:

◆ By 2015, FTSE 100 companies should have a minimum of 25% female representation on their board. This was raised in 2016 by the Hampton-Alexander Report to 33% female representation on FTSE 350 boards by 2020.

◆ Listed companies should disclose each year the proportion of women on their board, in senior executive positions and for the company as a whole.

◆ Listed companies should also establish, and report progress on each year, a policy for boardroom diversity, including measurable policy objectives. The report should include 'meaningful information' on how the nomination committee addressed the issue of diversity in its appointment process for board members.

◆ Companies should consider advertising for board members, as this may result in a more diverse pool of applicants.

◆ A voluntary code of conduct for executive search consultants should be developed to address gender diversity and best practices in searching for and nominating more diverse board members in FTSE 350 companies.

The report rejected the previously held view that a director should be financially literate and have experience of financial responsibilities prior to becoming a director. It was felt that these could be learnt.

Hampton-Alexander Report

The Hampton-Alexander review was established in February 2016 to continue the work of Lord Davis. Its remit was to improve representation of women on FTSE 350 boards and to consider options for increasing the number of women in the executive layer of FTSE 350 companies, thus building a talent pipeline. The Report was published in November 2016. In addition to raising the target for women on boards mentioned above, the Report recommended that the UK Corporate Governance Code be amended to require all FTSE 350 listed companies to include in their annual report and accounts information on the gender balance of members of their executive committees and the direct reports to executive committee members. This amendment was made in the 2018 version of the UK Corporate Governance Code.

2.12 EU Audit Regulations 2014

In 2014, the EU introduced new Audit Directive and Regulations which came into force in the UK from June 2016. The regulations applied to listed companies and included, among other things, requirements for **non-audit work** and **audit firm rotation**.

2.13 2016 Parker Report into ethnic diversity of UK boards

The Parker Report, published in November 2016, concluded that listed companies in the UK did not reflect 'the ethnic diversity of either the UK or the stakeholders they seek to engage and represent'. The Report made three recommendations:

1. Increase ethnic diversity of UK boards.
2. Develop candidates for the pipeline and plan for succession.
3. Enhance transparency and disclosure.

2.14 Relevance of historic corporate governance developments

It is important to understand how corporate governance has developed to be able to advise boards on their governance practices. For example, the requirement for the division of responsibilities between the chair and the CEO is designed to counter the power of one dominant individual who runs the

non-audit services/ work
Work done by a firm of auditors for a client company, other than work on the annual audit, such as consultancy services and tax advice. In the context of corporate governance, the independence of the auditors might be questionable when they earn high fees for non-audit work.

audit firm rotation
Changing the firm of external auditors on a regular basis.

company for their own benefit. If the governance adviser is aware of this, they are able to advise a board wishing to combine the roles what other practices should be put in place to ensure that there is not a concentration of power in one individual. This could be the appointment of a majority of independent directors on the board or of a senior independent director. The board would also have to look at the delegation of authority to the chairman/CEO to ensure that sufficient matters were reserved to the board to ensure effective oversight of the chairman/CEO.

3. UK law and governance

As mentioned in Chapter 1, the UK predominantly follows a principles-based approach to corporate governance through codes of best practice, such as the UK Corporate Governance Code for listed companies. There are, however, aspects of corporate governance in many other parts of UK law, which a company secretary/governance professional needs to be aware of when advising the board, directors or members of the senior management team. For example:

◆   companies laws;
◆   laws regulating the financial markets and financial services;
◆   environmental laws;
◆   health and safety laws;
◆   employment and pension laws;
◆   insolvency law; and
◆   laws on **money laundering** and insider dealing.

Aspects of these laws are discussed throughout this study text when relevant to the topic under discussion.

3.1   Companies law

The main company legislation in the UK is the Companies Act 2006 (CA2006), which includes regulations on:

◆   shareholder rights and voting;
◆   general meetings;
◆   disclosure of information to shareholders including information on directors' remuneration and information required in the annual report and accounts such as in the strategic report;
◆   powers and duties of directors; and
◆   preparation and auditing of the annual financial statements.

The Companies Act applies to all companies registered in the UK. There are, however, different aspects of the companies law which relate to private companies, unlisted public companies and listed public companies.

In recent years much of the legislation introduced by the UK has been as a result

money laundering
The process of transferring or using money obtained from criminal activity, so as to make it seem to have come from legitimate (non-criminal) sources. Companies are often used as cover for money laundering.

EU Directive
An instruction devised by the European Commission and European Parliament. The contents of a Directive must be introduced into national law or regulations by all member states of the European Union.

European Commission
The managing and administrative body of the European Union.

of **European Union Directives**. EU Directives, as the name suggests, derive from the European Union. They are initiated by the **European Commission** and then agreed as legislation by the European Council and European Parliament through a process known as the 'co-decision procedure'. Once agreed, an EU directive has to be implemented by EU states within a certain timeframe. Examples of company law introduced as a result of EU directives are:

◆ requirement to publish a business review;

◆ Shareholder Rights Directive;

◆ requirements to publish corporate governance statement;

◆ requirements to have an audit committee;

◆ requirements to introduce measures that provide for independence and ethical conduct of their external auditors; and

◆ requirements in respect of auditing, including a cap of 70% non-audit work.

Many of these requirements which apply to listed companies already existed in the UK through the provisions of the Corporate Governance Code, however they were voluntary as a company could opt not to comply with them and explain their non-compliance.

Test yourself 2.1

1.   **What relevance does knowing the historical development of corporate governance have for advising on today's governance practices?**

2.   **What type of UK companies can be listed?**

3.   **What is the difference between a public and a private company in the UK?**

Since the introduction of CA2006, several regulations have been introduced. The following impact corporate governance.

The Companies Act 2006 (Strategic Report and Directors Report) Regulations 2013.
These regulations introduced a requirement for companies (excluding small companies) to include a strategic report, rather than the business review, in their annual report and accounts. More information on the requirements can be found in Chapter 11.

The Large and Medium Sized Companies and Group (Accounts and Reports) (Amendment) Regulations 2013.
These regulations brought in new requirements for the reporting of directors' remuneration. More information on the requirements can be found in Chapter 16.

The Companies (Miscellaneous Reporting) Regulations 2018.
These regulations are a response to the government's green paper on corporate governance reforms published in November 2016 and the Department for Business, Enterprise and Industrial Strategy (BEIS) Select Committee inquiry into corporate governance, which reported in April 2017. They cover the following topics:

◆ executive pay

◆ guidance for companies on s. 172 of CA2006 requirements relating to directors having a regard to employee interests and fostering relationships with customers, suppliers and others

◆ corporate governance arrangements for large, privately-held businesses

The new regulations will apply to companies reporting on financial years starting on or after 1 January 2019 so actual reporting by companies on them will be in 2020.

The BEIS has provided extensive guidance on how the regulations should be applied by companies. The guidance is accessible on the BEIS website.

4. UK Listing Regime

Companies which are listed on the London Stock Exchange are required to comply with the rules issued, from time to time, by the UK Listing Authority, which since 2013 has been the Financial Conduct Authority (FCA). The current rules are set out in the FCA Handbook, which comprises the UK Listing, Prospectus and Disclosure Guidance and Transparency Rules (LPDTR).

4.1   UK Listing Rules

The UK Listing Rules require all companies, UK or non-UK incorporated, with a **premium listing** on the London Stock Exchange to comply with the UK Corporate Governance Code or explain their non-compliance in a governance statement in the company's annual report and accounts. The 'comply or explain' regime was discussed in Chapter 1.

Companies listed on the AIM (formerly the Alternative Investment Market), a sub-market of the London Stock Exchange, do not have to comply with the UK Corporate Governance Code. The companies listed on AIM are usually smaller companies, which require a less stringent regulatory regime than that provided by the UK Corporate Governance Code. AIM companies do, however, have to adopt a set of governance standards and most choose to adopt the Corporate Governance Code for Small and Mid-Sized **Quoted Companies** issued by the Quoted Companies Alliance (QCA).

From September 2018, AIM companies are required to set out in a statement the details of a recognised corporate governance code that has been selected by the board, how that code has been applied and, where the company departs from its selected code, an explanation for doing so.

Premium Listing
One of two categories of listing for companies in the UK. Companies with a premium listing are required to meet the highest standards of regulation and corporate governance.

quoted company
For the purposes of the CA2006, a quoted company is defined in s. 385 as a UK company whose equity share capital: has been included in the official list in accordance with the provisions of Part VI of the FSMA (this includes UK companies with either a premium or standard listing whose shares are traded on the main market of the London Stock Exchange); is officially listed in an EEA state (for example, a UK company whose shares are quoted on the Paris Bourse); or is admitted to dealing on either the New York Stock Exchange or the exchange known as Nasdaq.

4.2   Disclosure Guidance and Transparency Rules

DTR 2 Disclosure and control of inside information by issuers
This rule sets out the requirements for prompt and fair disclosure of relevant information to the market. It also gives guidance on aspects relating to disclosure of such information, including the circumstances in which disclosure may be delayed.

The rule should be read in conjunction with the following other regulations which govern the disclosure of information:

market abuse
When an individual distorts a market in the investments, creates a false or misleading impression of the value or price of an investment, or misuses relevant information before it is published. Although it is similar to insider dealing, which is a criminal offence; this is a civil offence under the Financial Services and Markets Act.

◆   the **Market Abuse** Regulations

◆   Part 7 (Offences relating to Financial Services) of the Financial Services Act 2012 relating to misleading statements and practices

◆   Part V of the Criminal Justice Act 1993 relating to insider dealing

◆   the Takeover Code

DTR 3 Transactions by persons discharging managerial responsibilities and their connected persons
This rule sets out the notification obligations of Persons Discharging Managerial Responsibilities (PDMRs) and their connected persons in relation to shares, debt instruments or derivatives of the company. Directors and senior executives are usually classified as PDMRs.

DTR 4 Periodic Financial Reporting
This rule sets out the requirements for the content and publication of a company's:

◆   annual report and financial statements

◆   half-yearly report and interim statements

◆   reports on payments to government

DTR 5 Vote Holder and Issuer Notification Rules
This rule sets out the requirements for holders of shares in a company to disclose the percentage of their holding above certain thresholds to the company. It also sets out the disclosure relating to a company's share capital which are to be made by the company to enable holders to fulfil their requirements.

DTR 6 Continuing obligations and access to information
This rule sets out what continuing obligations the listed company agrees to comply with. The obligations include, among others:

◆   equality of rights of shareholders of the class

◆   exercise of rights by shareholders

◆   electronic communications

◆   information about dividend payments, shareholder meetings, changes in share capital

The rule also sets out the disclosure requirements for listed companies in relation to the continuing obligations.

DTR 7 Corporate governance
This rule sets out the requirements for listed companies to have:

◆ an audit committee
◆ a corporate governance statement in its annual directors' report

5. UK Corporate Governance Code 2018

As mentioned above, all companies listed on the premium market of the London Stock Exchange are required to 'comply or explain' with the latest version of the UK Corporate Governance Code (the Code), which was published in July 2018. The Code has been the responsibility of the FRC since 2003.

The Code sets out good practices to enable boards to:

◆ establish their company's purpose, strategy and values, and satisfy themselves that these are aligned to their company's culture and aimed at achieving long-term success for the company;
◆ consider the practices and processes that need to be put in place to ensure an effective interaction with the company's employees, customers, suppliers and wider stakeholders;
◆ develop effective policies to ensure diversity (gender, social and ethnic backgrounds, cognitive and personal strengths) on the board, within the management team and in the management pipeline; and
◆ ensure that appointments to boards are based on merit and objective criteria to avoid group think.

The 2018 version of the Code includes new requirements for boards to consider the needs and views of a wider range of stakeholders, integrity and corporate culture, diversity and how the overall governance of the company contributes to its long-term success.

The 2018 Code is split into five sections:

1. Board leadership and company purpose: this section concentrates on the role and responsibilities of the board as a whole.
2. Division of responsibilities: this section focuses on the division of responsibilities between the chair and the CEO, the make-up of the board and the role of the non-executive directors.
3. Composition, succession and evaluation: this section talks about the selection and appointment process for directors and committee members. It also outlines the requirements for annual evaluation of the board, its committees and individual members.
4. Audit, risk and internal control: this section focuses on the internal and external audit functions and on the establishment of procedures to

manage risk and oversee internal controls.

5.   Remuneration: this section concentrates on the process for developing and overseeing a remuneration policy for directors and senior executives.

Each section is divided into a set of Principles followed by more detailed Provisions.

Listed companies are required to make a statement in their annual report and accounts on how they have:

◆   applied the spirit of the Principles; and

◆   complied with, or explain why they have not complied with, the Provisions and supporting guidelines for the Code.

The statement should allow shareholders to evaluate the application of the Principles by the company, the actions taken by the company in support of the Principles and the outcome of those actions, and whether a description of how the Provisions and additional guidance has been complied with. The justification for any non-compliance should set out 'the background, provide clear rationale for the action the company is taking, and explain the impact the action has had.' Any action that is timebound should also state the time limit for completion.

The aim of the 2018 Code is to get away from a box-ticking or boilerplate responses. It is hoped that the statements will provide the basis for a positive and constructive dialogue with shareholders. Shareholders, as we saw in Chapter 1, have responsibilities under the Stewardship Code to engage with companies on their corporate governance practices, especially where they have provided an explanation for non-compliance with a code provision.

The 2018 Code applies to accounting periods beginning or after 1 January 2019 for all premium listed companies.

The Principles and Provisions of the 2018 Code will be addressed in detail in the forthcoming chapters.

6. FRC guidance

To assist companies in developing their corporate governance practices based on the requirements of the UK Corporate Governance Code, the FRC has published a series of guidelines

Guidance on Board Effectiveness (2018)
The latest version of this guidance was published by the FRC in July 2018. It is based on the Higgs Report (2003) and the first version of the guidance, which was published following an ICSA review of Higgs in 2011. The primary purpose of the guidance 'is to stimulate boards' thinking on how they can carry out their role and encourage them to focus on continually improving their effectiveness'. The guidance follows the structure of the UK Corporate Governance Code 2018 and covers sections 1–3 and 5.

Guidance on Audit Committees (2016)
This guidance was previously known as the Smith Report. It provides more detailed guidance on the role and responsibilities of audit committees.

Guidance on Risk Management, Internal Control and Related Financial and Business Reporting (2014)
This guidance replaced the Turnbull Guidance which had first been published in 1999 and revised in 2005. The guidance was aimed at encouraging boards to consider how:

◆ to discharge their responsibilities in relation to existing and emerging principal risks of the company; and

◆ to embed risk management and internal control systems into the businesses processes of the company. It introduced the concept of cultures of risk.

Guidance on the Strategic Report (2018)
The 2014 version of the Guidance on the Strategic Report explained the requirements of the Companies Act 2006 (Strategic Report and Directors' Report) Regulations 2013. The revised Guidance has been enhanced to recognise the increasing importance of non-financial reporting.

Further information on the FRC guidelines can be found later in this book.

Test yourself 2.2

1. **What new requirements are included in the UK Corporate Governance Code 2018?**

2. **What is the difference between principles and provisions in the UK Corporate Governance Code?**

3. **Who enforces the requirements of the UK Corporate Governance Code?**

7. Guidance from investors

Institutional shareholders and their representative bodies, such as the Pensions and Lifetime Savings Association (PLSA), formerly the National Association of Pension Funds (NAPF) and the Investment Association, have issued a series of guidelines on corporate governance issues, such as directors' pay and stakeholder engagement for listed companies.

Several of the guidelines were originally published by the Association of British Insurers (ABI). In 2014, the Investment Association took over responsibility for the ABI investment affairs function, hence these guidelines.

8. QCA Corporate Governance Code 2018

As mentioned above, many AIM listed companies adopt as their corporate governance standards the Quoted Companies Alliance (QCA) Corporate Governance Code. The QCA is a body that represents smaller quoted companies.

The QCA Code consists of 10 principles that are similar to the UK Corporate Governance Code for listed companies. They are, however not as rigorous. The 10 principles are:

1. Establish a strategy and business model which promotes long-term value for shareholders.
2. Seek to understand and meet shareholder needs and expectations.
3. Take into account wider stakeholder and social responsibilities and their implications for long-term success.
4. Embed effective risk management, considering both opportunities and threats throughout the organisation.
5. Maintain the board as a well-functioning balanced team led by the chair.
6. Ensure that between them directors have the necessary up-to-date experience, skills and capabilities.
7. Evaluate board performance based on clear and relevant objectives, seeking continuous improvement.
8. Promote a corporate culture that is based on ethical values and behaviours.
9. Maintain governance structures and processes that are fit for purpose and support good decision-making by the board.
10. Communicate how the company is governed and is performing by maintaining a dialogue with shareholders and other relevant stakeholders.

Companies adopting the QCA Code are required to issue an annual statement on how they comply with the QCA Code in their companies and where they depart from it and provide a justification for doing so.

9. Corporate governance and unlisted companies

As mentioned above, the UK Corporate Governance Code applies to companies with a premium listing on the London Stock Exchange. It was designed for public listed companies with a significant separation of ownership and control. Its aim was to protect the investor by ensuring that boards and managers behaved appropriately and were accountable to the company's shareholders.

The owners of private companies are often their managers, so the issue of protecting the investor does not tend to exist. Recent high-profile corporate scandals, relating to large private companies, for example at British Home Stores

(BHS), have raised a different concern to that of protecting the investor for private companies. This is protecting a wider stakeholder group, which includes employees, former employees and suppliers of the company, when things go wrong.

Case study 2.1

In April 2016, BHS went into administration leading to a loss of 11,000 jobs and a deficit in BHS's two pension schemes of up to £571 million. The deficit meant that the 20,000 members of the two schemes would enter the Pension Protection Fund and see their benefits cut by at least 10%.

This followed Sir Philip Green, BHS's owner through his company the Arcadia Group, taking large amounts of money out of the company. For example, in the years 2002 and 2004, extensive dividends amounting to around £423 million were paid to the Green family. In 2005, according to The Telegraph, dividends, rent from BHS stores and loan interest generated almost £587 million for the Green family.

In 2015, Green sold BHS to a former bankrupt with no retail experience for £1.

The UK Pensions Regulator published a report in June 2017 stating that the main purpose for Green selling BHS was to avoid the pension deficit. Green agreed to pay £363 million to rescue the BHS pension schemes.

Green, by making the payment, has avoided disqualification proceedings as a director being brought against him. Dominic Chappell, BHS's purchaser in 2015, and three other former directors of BHS have been informed by the Insolvency Service that disqualification proceedings will be brought against them.

The Government's Green Paper, published in November 2016, raised the issue of extending some of the features of the UK's corporate governance framework to the largest privately held companies.

9.1 The Companies (Miscellaneous Reporting) Regulations 2018

As we saw earlier, the Companies (Miscellaneous Reporting) Regulations 2018, introduced corporate governance arrangements for large private unlisted companies in response to the Green Paper and the BEIS Select Committee inquiry into corporate governance which reported in April 2017.

The regulations provide that large private unlisted companies, defined as those with more than 2,000 employees or with turnover of more than £200 million and a balance sheet of more than £2 billion, will have to include a statement as part of their directors' report stating:

◆ which corporate governance code they are following and how;

◆   if they deviate from their chosen code and explanation as to why; and

◆   if they have not adopted a code, an explanation as to why not and what arrangements for corporate governance have been applied instead.

The statement will have to be made available online through the company's website or another suitable website on behalf of the company.

Some private companies already publish this information, e.g. Dyson, JCB and Pentland, who owns JD Sports Fashion and Speedo Swimwear.

In addition, large private companies will have to provide within their strategic reports, a s. 172 statement describing how the directors have had regard to the matters set out in s. 172 CA2006 when performing their duty under s. 172 to promote the success of the company. More information on the s. 172 duty can be found in Chapter 5.

9.2   The Wates Corporate Governance Principles for Large Private Companies

In June 2018, the FRC published for consultation 'The Wates Corporate Governance Principles for Large Private Companies'. The consultation period ran until September 2018 and the Principles were published in December 2018, with reporting against them being effective for financial years starting on or after 1 January 2019.

The six Principles seek to introduce 'a high-level approach to good corporate governance. This can be applied to any large private company, while allowing sufficient flexibility for the companies to explain the application and relevance of their governance arrangements'. The Principles adopt the 'apply and explain' approach described in Chapter 1.

Principle One – Purpose and Leadership
An effective board develops and promotes the purpose of a company, and ensures that its values, strategy and culture align with that purpose.

Principle Two – Board Composition
Effective board composition requires an effective chair and a balance of skills, backgrounds, experience and knowledge, with individual directors having sufficient capacity to make a valuable contribution. The size of the board should be guided by the scale and complexity of the company.

Principle Three – Director Responsibilities
The board and individual directors should have a clear understanding of their accountability and responsibilities. The board's policies and procedures should support effective decision-making and independent challenge.

Principle Four – Opportunity and Risk
A board should promote the long-term sustainable success of the company by identifying opportunities to create and preserve value, and establishing oversight for the identification and mitigation of risks.

Principle Five – Remuneration
A board should promote executive remuneration structures aligned to the long-term sustainable success of a company, taking into account pay and conditions elsewhere in the company.

Principle Six – Stakeholder Relationships and Engagement
Directors should foster effective stakeholder relationships aligned to the company's purpose. The board is responsible for overseeing meaningful engagement with stakeholders, including the workforce, and having regard to their views when taking decisions.

9.3   IoD Corporate Governance Guidance and Principles for Unlisted Companies

In 2010, the UK Institute of Directors (IoD), together with the European Confederation of Directors Associations (ecoDA) published 'Corporate Governance Guidance and Principles for Unlisted Companies' (IoD corporate governance guidance). Many private companies have selected to follow the IoD corporate governance guidance for their corporate governance arrangements. The guidance is voluntary and seeks to ensure the long-term survival and sustainability of the company as it develops and matures.

The IoD corporate governance guidance recognises that the requirements for good corporate governance will evolve as the company grows and becomes more established. In the earlier years of its existence, an unlisted company may be led by its entrepreneurial founder, who may be both chair and chief executive. Eventually, the entrepreneur will reduce their input to the company, and at some stage will retire. The entrepreneur may retire gradually by giving up their role as chief executive officer and becoming a non-executive chair. For a company to survive, it will have to make the transition from entrepreneurial leadership to a more professionally governed organisation.

The IoD corporate governance guidance is presented as 14 principles of governance, divided into the following two phases:

- Phase 1 principles are universal principles that should apply to all unlisted companies.
- Phase 2 principles apply to large and/or more complex companies, including those that may have plans for eventually progressing to public company and listed company status.

IoD Phase 1 principles
There are nine Phase 1 principles:

- Shareholders should establish an appropriate constitutional framework and governance structure for the company.
- Every company should try to establish an effective board, which should be collectively responsible for the long-term success of the company, including its strategy. An interim step for small owner-managed companies may be to set up an advisory board.

◆ The size and composition of the board should reflect the scale and complexity of the company's business operations.

◆ The board should meet sufficiently regularly to discharge its duties and it should be supplied in a timely manner with appropriate information.

◆ Levels of remuneration should be sufficient to attract, retain and motivate executives and non-executives of the quality required to run the company successfully.

◆ The board is responsible for the oversight of risk and should maintain a sound system of internal control to safeguard the shareholders' investment and the company's assets.

◆ There should be dialogue between the company's board and the shareholders based on a mutual understanding of objectives. Directors need to understand that shareholders should be treated equally.

◆ All directors should receive induction on joining the board and should keep up-to-date and regularly refresh their skills.

◆ Family-controlled companies should establish a system for family governance that promotes understanding and coordination between the family members and establishes a suitable relationship between family governance and corporate governance.

IoD Phase 2 principles
There are five Phase 2 principles:

◆ There should be a clear division of responsibilities at the head of the company between running the board and running the company's business operations. No individual should have 'unfettered powers of decision'.

◆ All boards of directors should have a suitable mix of competencies and experience. No one individual (or group) should dominate decision making by the board.

◆ The board should establish appropriate committees to discharge its duties more effectively.

◆ There should be periodic appraisal by the board of its performance and the performance of individual directors.

◆ The board should present a balanced and understandable assessment for the shareholders of its position and prospects, and there should be a suitable programme for engagement with stakeholders.

Stop and think 2.1

Although the standards of corporate governance may differ between listed and unlisted companies, many of the core principles are the same or similar. Why do you think this is?

Test yourself 2.3

1. **Which corporate governance code(s) applies to:**
    ◆ **UK listed companies**
    ◆ **UK unlisted companies**
2. **What are the arguments for and against the application of corporate governance codes of best practice to large private companies?**

Chapter summary

◆ The historical development of corporate governance is important in understanding how to advise boards of today on their governance practices.

◆ The UK corporate governance framework consists of provisions in law, regulations and principle-based codes. There is no one-size-fits-all, with different types of companies having different codes of best practice. Despite this, the underlying principles of good governance within them are similar.

◆ The 2018 UK Corporate Governance Code includes new requirements for boards to consider the needs and views of a wider range of stakeholders, integrity and corporate culture, diversity and how the overall governance contributes to the company's long-term success.

◆ The 2018 Code requirements and s. 172 CA2006 reporting is driving an expectation that long-term stakeholder interests should be playing an ever-greater role in the decision-making of UK companies. This is replacing the traditional shareholder value focus where creating and maintaining shareholder value, often in the short term, was the aim.

◆ Regulating the corporate governance practices of large private companies was recommended by the UK government following several corporate scandals, such as BHS, that have had a wider societal impact. A consultation process followed, resulting in the publication of the Wates Corporate Governance Principles for Large Private Companies in December 2018.

◆ The IoD published 'Corporate Governance Guidance and Principles for Unlisted Companies' in 2010.

Chapter three
Role of the company secretary in governance

CONTENTS

1. Introduction

This chapter examines why the role of the company secretary is often described as being at the heart of the governance systems within an organisation. It examines the role of the company secretary in governance and compliance and as an adviser and communicator to the board and senior management. It looks at the skills and qualifications needed for an effective company secretary, emphasising the importance of strong interpersonal skills and commercial and business acumen. It looks at why the independence of the company secretary is essential to good governance and considers the steps that can be taken to preserve that independence of the company secretary which is considered by many to be one of the most important in-built internal controls. Finally, the chapter considers the pros and cons of outsourcing the company secretary role and the challenges of combining it with another role in the organisation, such as the in-house lawyer.

2. The company secretary and corporate governance

The role of the company secretary in governance has been recognised as far back as the Cadbury Report, which stated that 'the company secretary has a key role to play in ensuring that board procedures are both followed and regularly reviewed'. Subsequent versions of the UK Corporate Governance Code and the additional guidance published to support it have gone into more detail as to what the role entails.

Historically, the role of the company secretary was only found in common law countries, such as the UK and other Commonwealth countries. In more recent times, the position of the company, board or corporate secretary is being included as an important provision in corporate governance regulations of countries adopting other types of legal systems, such as the Middle East, North Africa and parts of Asia and South America. This reflects the growing recognition of the importance of having a role with responsibility for the governance of the organisation, which as we saw in earlier chapters is essential for the long-term sustainability of an organisation.

ICSA: The Governance Institute state on its website that 'the company secretary is a strategic position of considerable influence at the heart of governance operations within an organisation.'

In an ideal situation, the company secretary should be a confidante and adviser to the chair and other members of the board. They should also be a conduit for information flows and often a mediator or arbitrator between the board, management, shareholders and other stakeholders. This requires an individual with certain skills and experience holding a senior position in the organisation.

3. The requirements for a company secretary

3.1 Companies Act 2006

Section 271 of the CA2006 states that all public companies in the UK must have a company secretary.

Since April 2008, unless there is an express requirement in the company's articles of association, s. 270 of the CA2006 no longer requires private limited companies to appoint a company secretary. Although there is no requirement for private companies to employ a company secretary, in practice many still choose to do so. The important tasks that would normally fall to a company secretary, including shareholder administration and communication, corporate governance and statutory compliance must still be done. In the absence of a company secretary, s. 270 of the CA2006 states that directors must take on this responsibility. This is why many private companies continue to employ a company secretary in order to reduce the administrative and corporate governance burdens which that would otherwise be placed on their directors.

The Wates Principles for large private companies suggests in its guidance that the chair and the company secretary should 'periodically review the governance processes to confirm that they remain fit for purpose and consider any initiatives which could strengthen the governance of the company'. If there is no company secretary, then a company may have alternative arrangements.

3.2   UK Corporate Governance Code 2018

Provision 16 of the 2018 Code, which applies to companies with a premium listing, states:

'all directors should have access to the advice of the company secretary, who is responsible for advising the board on all governance matters. Both the appointment and removal of the company secretary should be a matter for the whole board.'

The FRC Guidance on Board Effectiveness, also issued in 2018, provides further information on what this means in practice.

3.3   ICSA guidance on the corporate governance role of the company secretary

ICSA issued a guidance note in 2013: 'The corporate governance role of the company secretary' which sets out the specific duties and responsibilities of the company secretary for governance. Despite the fact that the UK Corporate Governance Code has been updated since this guidance note was published, it is still very useful in justifying the need for and the value of having a company secretary.

4. The role of the company secretary

The duties of the company secretary can be broken down into four main categories:

- governance;
- statutory and regulatory compliance;
- advising the board and senior management; and
- being the board's communicator.

4.1   Governance

ICSA's guidance note 'The corporate governance role of the company secretary' sets out the following specific duties and responsibilities of the company secretary for governance:

Board composition and procedures
- Establishing a formal schedule of matters reserved for decision by the board and a formal division of responsibilities between the chair and CEO or other layers of management.

◆ Scheduling board meetings, assisting with the preparation of agendas, providing guidance on board paper content, ensuring good and timely information flows within the board and its committees and between senior management and non-executive directors; recording board decisions clearly and accurately, pursuing follow-up actions and reporting on matters arising.

◆ Ensuring that appropriate insurance cover is arranged in respect of any potential legal action against directors.

◆ Ensuring **board committees** are constituted in compliance with the 2018 Code and that the committees have the appropriate balance of skills, experience, independence and knowledge of the company.

◆ Supporting the board and nominations committee on board succession planning and on the process for the appointment of new directors to the board.

board committee
A committee established by the board of directors, with delegated responsibility for a particular aspect of the board affairs.

Board information, development and relationships

◆ Planning and organising director induction programmes which provide a full, formal and tailored introduction to the board and the business. There is a separate ICSA guidance note on the induction of directors.

◆ Planning and organising director professional development programmes to refresh the directors' skills and knowledge.

◆ Arranging for major shareholders to be offered the opportunity to meet new directors.

◆ Facilitating good information flows between board members, the committees and senior management as well as and fostering effective working between executive and non-executive directors.

◆ Establishing and communicating procedures for directors to take independent professional advice at the company's expense if required.

◆ Developing a proactive relationship with board members, providing a source of information and advice, and acting as the primary point of contact with non-executive directors.

◆ Supporting the process for the board to undertake formal annual evaluation of its own performance and that of its committees and individual directors.

Accountability

◆ Financial and business reporting:

  – having a detailed knowledge of, and advising on, the board's responsibility to present a fair, balanced and understandable assessment of the company's position and prospects in annual and interim reports, other price-sensitive public reports, reports to regulators and information required under statute. The company secretary should also ensure that the requirements of the FCA's Listing, Prospectus, and Disclosure and Transparency Rules are met and be aware of the guidance available on these areas.

◆ Risk management and internal control:

– assisting the board in an annual review of the effectiveness of the company's risk management and internal control systems including financial, operational and compliance controls.

◆ Audit committee and auditors:

– ensuring that the audit committee is fully conversant with the 2018 Code principles around corporate reporting, risk management and internal control principles. This should include the relationship with the external auditors, in particular as regards audit quality, provisions of non-audit services, recommendations for appointment and renewal of auditors and putting the audit contract out to tender;

◆ Ensuring the implementation and monitoring the effectiveness of the procedure for staff to raise concerns about possible improprieties in matters of financial reporting or other matters.

Remuneration

◆ Ensuring that the remuneration committee is familiar with the 2018 Code principles and provisions on remuneration, including the provisions on the design of performance-related remuneration for executive directors.

◆ Ensuring that grants of share options and other long-term incentive awards do not contravene the 2018 Code.

◆ Ensuring that the provisions in the directors' term of appointment in relation to early termination are in accordance with the 2018 Code.

◆ Ensuring that non-executive remuneration is determined in line with Code provisions and within the limits set by the articles of association.

◆ Ensuring that all new long-term incentive schemes and significant changes to existing schemes are submitted to shareholders for approval, in accordance with the Listing Rules.

◆ Ensuring compliance with the legal requirements in relation to directors' remuneration, including any necessary shareholder approvals, contributing to the drafting of the directors' remuneration report and ensuring its compliance with the full range of disclosure requirements.

Relationship with shareholders

◆ Ensuring the board keeps in touch with shareholder opinion on a continuing basis.

◆ Managing relations with institutional investors on corporate governance issues and board procedures in accordance with the principles established in the UK Stewardship Code.

◆ Managing the convening and conduct of the AGM in line with statutory and regulatory requirements and the 2018 Code and using it as an opportunity to communicate with retail investors.

Disclosure and reporting
◆ Ensuring that the necessary disclosures on corporate governance and the workings of the board and its committees are included in the annual report. All companies with a premium listing of equity shares in the UK are required under the Listing Rules to report how they have applied the 2018 Code in the annual report and accounts.;

◆ Ensuring that the requisite types of governance information are made available, as required, for example on the company's website.

4.2 Statutory and regulatory compliance

'The corporate governance role of the company secretary' also sets out the following specific duties and responsibilities of the company secretary for statutory and regulatory compliance.

The company secretary normally has full responsibility for Companies Act compliance and, where the company is listed, carries much of the responsibility for compliance with the FCA's LPDTRs. For listed companies, there is also the need to make the board aware of the market abuse provisions of the Financial Services and Markets Act 2000 (FSMA) including, in particular, the responsibility not to release misleading information about the company's financial performance or trading condition, or to mislead the market by the failure to disclose relevant information.

Set out below are the areas of action required to discharge those governance responsibilities which are normally managed or shared by the company secretary are set out below.

Directors' duties
◆ Implementing procedures to help directors discharge their statutory duties as codified under s. 171 to 177 of the CA2006, in particular their specific duties to promote the success of the company taking account of a wide range of stakeholder interests and to avoid conflicts of interest. Guidance on these particular duties is available in the ICSA guidance note, 'Directors' general duties'.

Share dealing
◆ Communicating and implementing procedures for listed company directors and any other 'person discharging managerial responsibilities', as defined in section s. 96B of FSMA (PDMRs) to comply with the Market Abuse Regulations in respect of directors' share dealing;

◆ Establishing and operating procedures for disclosure of dealings in shares by major shareholders and PDMRs.

Protection of inside information
◆ Implementing procedures to comply with the provisions of the Disclosure Rules on the protection of 'inside information' as defined in section s. 118C of FSMA and on the maintenance of **'insider' lists** as required by the Market Abuse Regulations.

insider list
A list of persons in a company who have access to inside information, which listed companies are required to prepare and maintain under the Market Abuse Regulation.

Verification of published information

◆ Implementing a 'verification and approval' process to review and confirm the accuracy of all company statements prior to publication and to authorise their release to the market.

Responsible release of market information

◆ Developing a formal policy and established procedures to make the announcements required under the Listing Rules and the Disclosure and Transparency Rules and, particularly, on the disclosure of inside information so that the company's shareholders and the market generally are kept fully informed.

◆ Ensuring that there is appropriate and timely consultation with the company's brokers and other advisers on the release of significant information about corporate performance and developments whenever the company is in any doubt.

Compliance with continuing obligations under the LPDTRs

◆ Developing and implementing policies and procedures for compliance by the company and its directors of all other aspects of continuing obligations under the LPDT Rules, including the restrictions in relation to class and related party transactions, requirements in relation to notifications of particular events, restrictions and requirements in relation to share issues and share buy-backs, and requirements in relation to the issue and contents of circulars to shareholders.

4.3   Advising the board and senior management

Listed below are some examples of how a company secretary in practice can advise a board and senior management on how the organisation can meet its governance requirements. These examples are discussed in more detail under the relevant topics throughout this book.

Good board practices

Evidence of good board practices that company secretaries should advise are in place are:

◆ There should be clearly defined roles at the board level and delegated authorities from the board to its committees, and to individuals at board level or in senior management. These should be set out in board charters, terms of reference for committees and delegation of authority matrices.

◆ Directors should understand their duties and responsibilities. These should be set out as part of the directors' induction and included in the Directors Manual. Updates and refreshers should be provided as part of the on-going professional development of the board.

◆ The board should be well structured and have the appropriate composition and skills. There should be formal board succession plan based on the organisation's long-term strategic goals.

◆ Directors remuneration is in line with best practice. There should be regular benchmarking against comparable companies followed by a review of the remuneration policy.

◆ Board procedures should be established and maintained. These should be set out in the board charter or in a board manual. The chairman should agree with the board ground rules for acceptable behaviour at board meetings.

◆ An annual **board evaluation** of the whole board, its committees, the chairman and individual directors must take place. There should be a report and findings from the evaluation. An action plan should be created which should be reviewed by the board. It will therefore appear as an agenda item.

board evaluation
The evaluation of the board, board committees, chair and other individual directors carried out by companies.

◆ Board professional development. There should be information sessions whereby management inform the board about different parts of the business, including corporate services. More formal training programmes should also be carried out on topic issues of relevance to the board.

◆ Company secretaries should ensure that board papers include the relevant information in relation to stakeholder impact, and assist reporting by capturing board discussion relating to how having regard to these stakeholders has influenced decision making. More information on this can be found below.

Transparency and disclosure
Evidence of transparency and disclosure that company secretaries should advise are in place are:

◆ A formal and transparent procurement policy and procedure should be in place. This should be reflected in a procurement manual.

◆ A formal and transparent recruitment policy and procedure should be in place. This should be reflected in the human resources policies and procedures of the organisation.

◆ A process is put in place to ensure that all statutory and regulatory disclosures are reviewed by the board. This would be set out in the board charter and also in the disclosure of information policy for the organisation. Evidence could also be agenda items for board meetings discussing such disclosures. Disclosures should also be posted on the company's website.

◆ Information disclosed by the company, both financial and non-financial, should be balanced between the positive and negative. This should be considered at the board meetings and evidence to the fact that it has should be included in the minutes of the board meeting considering periodic reports, semi-annual and annual reports.

Effective control environment

Evidence of an effective control environment that company secretaries should advise are in place are:

◆ An audit committee comprising of independent members with the appropriate skills and experience. There should be a clear term of reference for the committee. The effectiveness of the committee would be assessed annually by and independent evaluation.

◆ The risk management and internal controls systems should be assessed for their adequacy annually by the **internal auditors**. Assurance of its adequacy should be included in the minutes of the board meeting considering the effectiveness of the internal controls which forms part of the 'statement of directors responsibilities' in the company's annual report and accounts.

◆ An internal audit function. Evidence of the existence of an effective internal audit function is the consideration of an internal audit plan and budget for the year being considered by the audit committee, receipt of internal **audit reports** for consideration and an independent evaluation of the function in line with internal audit standards.

◆ If an internal audit function does not exist within the organisation, consideration by the board on an annual basis as to whether there should be one established. Evidence of consideration of whether to establish an internal audit function should be in the minutes of the audit committee and board meetings.

◆ Appointment of an independent external auditor. This is evidenced by agenda items and minutes of meetings discussing the independence of the external auditor, policies prohibiting non-audit work by the company's external auditors and auditor rotation.

Relationships with shareholders and other stakeholders

Evidence of relationships with shareholders and other stakeholders that company secretaries should advise are in place are:

◆ Engagement with shareholders can be evidenced through a well-run annual general meeting, records of face-to-face meetings with major shareholders and the adoption of electronic communications with shareholders.

◆ Engagement with stakeholders can be evidenced by agenda items and minutes of meetings discussing who the key stakeholders for the organisation are. Records of meetings with stakeholders and disclosures on how the interests of stakeholders have been taken into account in decision-making at board level.

Corporate responsibility

The company secretary should share responsibility with relevant specialist functions, if they exist, for ensuring that the board is aware of all of the current requirements with regard to their company's responsibility to stakeholders and the environment. The board should identify what these areas are and

internal audit
Investigations and checks carried out by internal auditors of an organisations, internal auditors of an organisation. Internal audit is a function rather than a specific activity. However the programme of internal audit team might reduce the amount of work the external auditors need to carry out in their annual audit, provided the internal and external auditors collaborate properly.

audit report
A report for shareholders produced by the external auditors on completion of the annual audit and included in the company's published annual report and accounts. The report gives the opinion of the auditors on whether the financial statements present a true and fair view of the company's financial performance and position.

ensure that they are taken into account in its stewardship and oversight of the company.

Evidence of an organisation exercising corporate responsibility that company secretaries should advise are in place are:

◆ Social and environmental issues to be considered and reported on. Agenda items and minutes of board meetings can evidence that the board is considering the social and environmental impact of its activities and decision making, as can social and environment reports against board-approved key performance indicators.

◆ Promoting the long-term view. This can be evidenced by an emphasis on long-term performance incentives for senior executives, as well as the development of a business continuity plan setting out how the organisation intends to stay in business in the long-term. Targets and key performance indicators for the longer-term can also show the board's commitment to the long-term sustainability of the organisation.

◆ Carrying out activities responsibly. Evidence of this is the establishment of win–win partnerships that benefit both the organisation and the society.

Conducting businesses ethically

Evidence of an organisation conducting businesses ethically that company secretaries should advise are in place are:

◆ An ethical culture should be developed based on shared values. This can be evidenced by the board approving a set of values that have been generated by employees. These should be displayed around the organisation's premises and on the company's website. Evidence from strategic planning and minutes of board meetings that the company operates according to these values.

◆ Code of ethics based on the values developed. Integration of the 2018 Code into the company's business practices can be evidenced by the lack of breaches of the 2018 Code. Any breaches should be raised and considered at the audit committee.

◆ Ethical conduct rewarded through the remuneration practices of the company. Remuneration practices should be audited to ensure that they are effective in reducing ethical behaviours.

Board's commitment to corporate governance

Evidence that a board is committed to corporate governance that company secretaries should advise are in place are:

◆ Ensure that the board discusses corporate governance issues on a regular basis. This can be evidenced by agenda items and minutes of board meetings.

◆ Develop a corporate governance improvement plan. This usually comes from the board evaluation process. Evidence would be the plan being discussed at board meetings.

◆ Promote the company as a corporate governance leader with best-in-class corporate governance reporting. A company may want to put themselves forward for corporate governance awards.

The importance of agenda development and minute taking to good governance is apparent from the above evidence which shows that a company is actually practising good governance.

4.4 The board's communicator

The company secretary plays an important role as the board's communicator. This will differ from company to company. However, best practice is that the company secretary should be the person responsible for:

◆ Communicating all board decisions to the relevant member of the management team. Although CEOs often intend to do this, evidence shows that due to their other work commitments CEOs are not very good at doing this in a timely manner.

◆ Managing the disclosure of the board's decision's to regulators and other stakeholders. This is because they understand the requirements as far as content to be disclosed and the importance of timely and balanced disclosure.

◆ Liaising between the board members and senior management on logistics for board and board committee meetings, training sessions, board retreats, board evaluation sessions and other board events.

◆ Facilitating good information flows between the board, individual board members, the committees and senior management that foster effective working relationships between them.

◆ Being the primary point of contact between the non-executives and the company, providing a source of information and advice. Without this, management could be distracted by requests from non-executive directors, some of which may be for the same information. Also, non-executive directors could receive conflicting information or advice depending on whom they speak to. The company secretary can collate the information and/or advice in a format which that is more appropriate for the non-executive directors.

◆ Ensuring that the board keeps in contact with shareholder opinion and that shareholders are briefed on the reasons behind the board's adoption of certain governance practices and decision making.

◆ Ensuring that relevant disclosures on corporate governance and directors' remuneration are made in the company's annual report and accounts and that the annual report and accounts is made available electronically on the company's website.

4.5 Additional responsibilities

Company secretaries have a wide range of additional responsibilities within their role, such as responsibility for insurance, pensions, facilities management, and many other company administration matters. Areas of responsibility differ from company to company.

Whatever the scope of their responsibilities company secretaries are in a unique position as they attend board meetings but are not involved in the actual decision making at the meetings. Company secretaries cannot tell directors what to do, they can only advise. It is argued, however, that they are able to influence the matters discussed at the board meeting through their involvement in agenda drafting, the advice they provide to the chairman and other directors and the relationships they have developed with both the board and senior management. If this influence exists, it does not appear overnight – it takes time to develop and can often depend on the knowledge, ability and personality of the individual.

Test yourself 3.1

1. **Why might a private company appoint a company secretary?**
2. **Why is the company secretary often referred to as a bridge for information, communications advice and arbitration?**

5. The company secretary as the 'conscience of the company'

The company secretary is often referred to as the 'conscience of the company'. This is because, in fulfilling the role as governance professional, the company secretary is often called on to advise the board what the right thing is to do in the long-term interests of the organisation. This often goes beyond what the law and regulations require and so takes the company secretary into the realm of what is known as business ethics.

As the governance professional the company secretary should also speak out against bad governance and unethical or illegal practices, such as if the company secretary discovers that a proposal from management requires the company to pay a bribe to a government official.

In order to be the 'conscience of the company', the company secretary must be independent-minded and also not be under the influence of either senior management, the chair or another individual director.

Business ethics will be discussed in more detail in Chapter 10.

6. The Company Secretary: Building trust through governance

In 2014, ICSA in collaboration with Henley Business School published 'The Company Secretary: Building trust through governance'. The study focused on the role of the company secretary and 'examined the expectations of stakeholders, board dynamics and the interactions of other board members and their views' on the role.

The study found that many company secretaries found that their role was misunderstood and that many of their duties were considered administrative in nature. The importance of what they contributed to effective governance and decision making within the organisation was not appreciated. The company secretary is often in the shadows, orchestrating the board, its interaction with management and other stakeholders.

Stop and think 1.1

Using the analogy of a car, the company secretary would be the oil in the engine. No one sees it but it is essential for the effective performance of the car. If it is not there the car comes to a grinding halt. So too with the company secretary: if the organisation has a professional company secretary working well in their role everything runs smoothly. If not, then evidence suggests boards start to have issues.

The key findings of the report were as follows:

◆ The role of the company secretary is much more than just administrative. At its best, it delivers strategic leadership, acting as a vital bridge between the executive management and the board, and facilitating the delivery of organisational objectives.

◆ Company secretaries are ideally placed to align the interests of different parties around a boardroom table, facilitate dialogue, gather and assimilate relevant information, and enable effective decision making. They are often the only people to know first-hand how the decisions made have been reached.

◆ The skills and attributes of the best company secretaries are closest to those of the chairman: humanity, humility, high intelligence, understanding of agendas, negotiation and resilience.

◆ It is vital that company secretaries have both direct and informal access to board members – executive and non-executive directors, CEOs and chairs.

◆ Maximising effectiveness requires that the company secretary's direct reporting line should be to the chair, and there should be parity of esteem and good team-working between the 'triumvirate at the top' – the chairman, the company secretary and the CEO.

◆ The role is changing: it is increasingly outward-focused (incorporating investor engagement and corporate communications), and not just about internal administration.

◆ ICSA-qualified company secretaries deliver a more rounded governance and board member service than those who have come to the role via other professional routes.

- There is a conflict of interest in the combined 'head of legal (or general counsel) and company secretary' role. The roles should be separate, as they can be incompatible.
- Board members often have a lack of awareness of the ways in which the company secretary supports an organisation in its decision-making. Boards may miss out on making full use of the skills, knowledge and experience at their disposal.
- Company secretaries are often the longest-serving members present at board meetings, and so are a vital repository of company history and culture, and a guarantor of continuity.
- Company secretaries are embedded in the process of making boards more effective; they contribute by observing boards in action and advising on any skills gaps that need filling.
- The breadth of the company secretarial role includes additional responsibilities such as being an officer of the company, chief of staff to the chairman and adviser to the board on governance. Consequently, the secretariat needs to retain independence to rebalance power as required and demonstrate accountability.

7. Qualifications and skills

7.1 Companies Act 2006

Section 273 of CA2006 requires directors of public companies to enlist the services of a secretary, who should:

- Be a person who appears to them to have the requisite knowledge and experience to discharge the functions of the secretary.
- Have one or more of the following qualifications:
    - have been a secretary of a public company for at least three years of the five years immediately preceding his or her appointment;
    - is a member of one of the following seven professional bodies:,
    - the Institute of Chartered Accountants in England and Wales;
    - the Institute of Chartered Accountants of Scotland;
    - the Association of Chartered Certified Accountants;
    - the Institute of Chartered Accountants in Ireland;
    - the Institute of Chartered Secretaries and Administrators;
    - the Chartered Institute of Management Accountants;
    - the Chartered Institute of Public Finance and Accountancy; and
    - is a qualified barrister or solicitor.

7.2 The Company Secretary: Building trust through governance

ICSA's 'The Company Secretary: Building trust through governance' found that many company secretaries come into their role from diverse backgrounds, often as a second or third career. They therefore have a diverse set of skills and experience that they can bring to the role. They have also often held senior positions in organisations and so understand the issues and forces that influence decision making.

The key challenges faced by many company secretaries which were identified in the study were:

◆ being considered traitors by the executive team;

◆ supporting chairs exhibiting poor performance;

◆ acting as the third person in a CEO-chair relationship;

◆ becoming a pivotal contact for unsurmountable problems; and

◆ maintaining independence from other executives and board members.

To overcome these challenges company secretaries, in addition to their technical skills, needed commercial and business acumen and interpersonal skills, which many considered the most important.

7.3 Interpersonal skills

The interpersonal skills considered important for the position of the company secretary are set out below.

Interpersonal skills required by company secretaries

◆ Empathy and relationship management

◆ Respectful, diplomatic and effective communication

◆ Active listening

◆ Bringing issues to the surface, especially those relating to reputational risk

◆ Personal and social awareness

◆ Being able to summarise common concerns and interests

◆ Generating alternative solutions

◆ Respecting confidences

◆ Independent mindset

◆ Strength of personality

◆ Appreciating the views of all parties

◆ Effective team-working

◆ Disagreeing constructively

◆ Emphasising commercially minded approaches

◆ Integrity

Practical skills to manage relationships and tensions

To maintain good working relations and balance any competing tensions between the board, shareholders and management, the company secretary should:

1. Listen actively: demonstrate attention and interest by nodding or using facial expressions. Try not to interrupt a speaker unless the speaker is dominating or going off topic.

2. Establish rapport: encourage speakers to reveal their concerns of interests: Use open-ended questions that begin with words like: Who….? What….? Why….? How….?

3. Be aware of body language: watch for signs of tension.

4. Focus on constructive ideas: build on and contribute constructive alternatives. Avoiding using the word 'but' too often.

5. Stay calm: be polite and avoid using heightened language or tone of voice that adds to or provokes anger.

6. Avoid misunderstandings: paraphrase statements to ensure understanding: 'So if I understand you properly, you are saying that……'

7. Allow others to save face: reframe statements in less confrontational terms to unlock disputes.

8. Know when to close a confrontational exchange: 'I suggest that we continue this discussion later.'

9. Stay neutral: be ready to provide additional information if it helps. Avoid becoming argumentative.

10. Suggest steps to resolve situations.

Source: International Finance Corporation (IFC) Corporate Secretaries Toolkit

7.4   Commercial and business acumen

In 2012, a study by the All Party Parliamentary Corporate Governance Group criticised many company secretaries for not being 'commercially minded' or aware. This they saw as being an important feature of the job especially as they advise the board on governance issues. Governance is more than just compliance – it is how an organisation structures itself to perform effectively and efficiently in the long-term. To be commercially aware, an individual must understand the business they are in and make good practical decisions as a result. In the case of the company secretary this means being able to advise the board on this basis so that they can make the decisions. To be commercially aware you should make sure:

◆   You understand how your company makes money and creates value.

◆   You understand what your company needs, now and in the future, so that it continues to make money and create value.

◆   You have a thorough understanding of your organisation's competitive advantage.

◆   You keep up to date with your industry.

'The Company Secretary: Building trust through governance' highlighted the importance that the majority of company secretaries acknowledged that 'commercial awareness and abilities are critical to ensuring their understanding of what is right for the organisation, what information means and to whom relevant questions need to be passed'.

Test yourself 3.2

1. **Why is it important for a company secretary to have interpersonal skills and commercial and business acumen?**

2. **Name five interpersonal skills a company secretary should have and explain why each one is important to the company secretary in fulfilling their responsibilities.**

8. Position in the organisation

In order for the company secretary to carry out their duties and responsibilities effectively they need to hold a position of seniority within the organisation. It is debated whether they should be a member of the executive team. Some think this compromises their independence. Whether or not they are a member of the executive team, they should attend meetings of the executive team. This will enable them to advise the executive on governance issues arising out of any proposals as they are being formulated. They can also advise on how the board might react to a particular proposal and what questions the executive should be prepared to answer when the proposal is considered by the board. Attending executive meetings also helps the company secretary get an understanding of the executive's positioning and reasons for suggesting the proposal which may help the company secretary if the proposal needs to be 'sold' to the chair. Remember that the company secretary can often fill the role of mediator or arbitrator between the CEO and the chair.

8.1 Reporting line

The reporting lines for the company secretary differ between organisations. Some company secretaries report direct to the chair, others to the CEO or another senior executive. Whatever reporting line is put in place for the company secretary needs to preserve the independence and integrity of the position. We will see later in the chapter that the role of the company secretary is one of the most important inbuilt controls within an organisation and it is important that it is protected.

ICSA: The Governance Institute sets out in its guidance note 'The duties and reporting lines of the company secretary' the following five reporting guidelines for company secretaries, which are based on established best practice in large companies:

◆   The company secretary is responsible to the board and should be accountable to the board through the chair on all matters relating to corporate governance and their duties as an officer of the company (core duties).

◆   As the person elected by the directors to act as their leader, the chair is the person to whom the company secretary should report with respect to responsibilities which concern the whole board.

◆   If, in addition to the core duties mentioned above, the company secretary has other executive or administrative duties, he should report to the chief executive or such other director to whom responsibility for that matter has been delegated by the board.

◆   The company secretary should not report to a director (except the chair) on any matter unless responsibility for that matter has been delegated to that director by the board.

◆   A director who is authorised unilaterally to fix the company secretary's remuneration and benefits could gain undue influence. It is therefore recommended (particularly where the company secretary reports to the chairman on all matters) that decisions on remuneration and benefits should be taken (or at least noted) by the board as a whole or the relevant committee thereof.

8.2   Remuneration

As we have seen above, best practice as set out in the ICSA's guidance note 'The duties and reporting lines of the company secretary' is that decisions on the remuneration and benefits of the company secretary should be taken by the board or by the remuneration committee. This is to protect the independence of the position of the company secretary.

Where a company secretary has a reporting line to the CEO or another director, the views of the CEO or other director can be taken into account by the board or remuneration committee when decisions are taken on the remuneration and benefits of the company secretary.

8.3   Evaluation

It is important for the company secretary to have an annual evaluation. Again, in deciding how this should be done an organisation should consider how it will maintain the independence of the role following the evaluation. Two ways the board could consider when conducting the evaluation of the company secretary are as follows:

◆   The company secretary's evaluation is carried out as part of the annual board evaluation. The external evaluator engaged to carry out the evaluation of the board, board committees and individual directors can be requested to also carry out an evaluation of the company secretary.

◆   The remuneration committee can request management to carry out an independent 360-degree evaluation of the company secretary, the results of which are fed directly back to the committee.

Any recommendations from the evaluation should be reviewed and monitored by the board to ensure they are implemented and that the company secretary receives any training or additional support required to carry out their role more effectively.

As part of King III, the Chartered Secretaries Southern Africa division and the Institute of Directors of Southern Africa developed a company secretaries' evaluation questionnaire template which requires in:

- Section 1: the company secretary to assess themselves against the statutory and governance requirements of their role.
- Section 2: the directors to grade the performance of the company secretary a list of competencies expected of the company secretary.
- Section 3: requests the board to confirm that all of the organisational formalities relating to the role are in place, such as a resolution of the board appointing the company secretary, a policy for evaluating the company secretary, and that the company secretary has received a letter of appointment setting out their statutory and governance roles.

9. Independence of the company secretary

The guidance note 'Appointment of the company secretary' states that:

'Boards have a right to expect the company secretary to give independent, impartial advice and support to all the directors, both individually and collectively as a board.'

It is for this reason that best practice is that company secretaries should be appointed and dismissed by the board as a whole.

9.1 Dual roles

The two main challenges to the independence of the company secretary are caused by:

- reporting lines, (discussed above); and
- dual roles.

In 2012, a study by the All Party Parliamentary Corporate Governance, found that a large number of board members support the trend of a combined role as this was seen to allow recruitment from a broader pool of professionals and also to increase the standing of the position in the company. In FTSE 100 companies, the role of the company secretary was combined 70% of the time, compared with 66% in the FTSE 250 and 59% in the FTSE Small Cap. By far the most common position with which the role of the company secretary was combined was the general counsel or head of legal, ranging from just over 50% in FTSE 100 to 35% in the FTSE Small Cap. The lower down the index, the more likely the role was combined with that of a senior finance role.

If the company secretary role is combined with another role such as that of the in-house lawyer or accountant, care should be taken to see that the governance role is not compromised. A general counsel who is also given the role of the company secretary will often have to take sides in fulfilling their legal role to represent the particular interests of the company. And although they may be complying with the letter of the law and in the interests of management, they may not be acting in the best long-term interests of the company.

This would be inconsistent with the company secretary's governance role which requires impartiality when advising on governance issues. It may also prevent a company secretary from speaking out against bad governance or unethical practices, or proposals that are not in the long-term interests of the company, especially if to do so was costly or against the wishes of the CEO.

The company secretary in their governance role should also be considering the reputational impact of the board's decision. This again may require the board to consider more than just complying with the laws and regulations. An example of this is the recent tax avoidance cases by multinational companies, such as Starbucks, Apple, Google and Amazon. Their accounting policies and practices comply with the law but are not considered 'morally' correct by the media and certain members of the general public.

Case study 3.1

In 2012, Starbucks, known for its strong corporate responsibility and customer service, came under scrutiny for its UK tax payments. In the previous year, 2011, despite making sales of £398 million, Starbucks paid no corporation tax. The company showed a loss in its annual financial statements of £32.9 million due to a charge of £107.2 million of 'administrative expenses' which appeared to represent, in part, royalty fees for UK division franchises.

In a statement, Starbucks insisted that it had 'paid and will continue to pay its fair share of taxes in full compliance with all UK tax laws, as it always has'. It went on to say that Starbucks was considered to be a good tax-payer by UK regulators and behaved in a moral way, balancing profit with social conscience.

The UK public was outraged by Starbucks' comments and started to boycott and protest outside the company's coffee shops. Starbucks' response was to offer to pay, over a period of years, £20 million in corporation tax despite its continued loss making, 'to please its customers'. In a statement, the company said, 'We felt that our customers should not have to wait for us to become profitable before we started paying UK corporation tax.

Test yourself 3.3

1. Why does a company secretary's position need to be one of seniority?

2. How can an organisation maintain the independence of the company secretary?

10. Liability of the company secretary

As an officer of the company, the company secretary may be liable, with the directors, to default fines and other penalties for officers under the Companies Act 2006.

Company secretaries may also be held liable, under the Insolvency Act 1986, for damages awarded by the court in the course of a winding-up of a company if there has been a misfeasance or breach of trust in relation to the company.

A company secretary can, under s. 1157 CA2006 apply to the court for relief in respect of any liability. The secretary will not normally be held liable with directors for any breach of trust or malfeasance committed by them.

It is unusual for a company secretary to be held personally liable for their actions. There is, however, an interesting on-going case involving the Hillsborough disaster where the former company secretary of Sheffield Wednesday football club has been charged with offences relating to his responsibilities for health and safety of the ground. Further details are provided in the case study.

Case study 3.2

On the 15 April 1989, during the 1988–1989 FA Cup semi-final game between Liverpool and Nottingham Forest there was a human crush at Hillsborough football stadium in Sheffield, England. The resulting 96 fatalities and 766 injuries makes this the worst disaster in British sporting history.

The crush occurred in the two standing-only central pens in the Leppings Lane stand, allocated to Liverpool supporters. Shortly before kick-off, in an attempt to ease overcrowding outside the entrance turnstiles, the police match commander, chief superintendent David Duckenfield, ordered exit gate C to be opened, leading to an influx of even more supporters to the already overcrowded central pens.

There have been two inquiries, the Taylor Report (1990) and the Hillsborough Independent Panel (2012) and two inquests, Stefan Popper (1st inquest, 1989–1991) and Sir John Goldring (2nd inquest, 2014–2016) into what has become known as the Hillsborough disaster.

The second coroner's inquest ruled that the supporters were unlawfully killed due to grossly negligent failures by police and ambulance services to fulfill their duty of care to the supporters. The inquest also found that the design of the stadium contributed to the crush, and that supporters were not to blame for the dangerous conditions.

In June 2017, six people were charged by the Crown Prosecution Service with various offences including manslaughter by gross negligence, misconduct in public office and perverting the course of justice for their actions during and after the disaster. One of those charged is the former company secretary of Sheffield Wednesday at the time of the disaster, Graham Mackrell. His role gave him responsibility for the overall control of safety at the club's stadium, Hillsborough. Defects at the ground, including calculations over crowd capacity, allegedly contributed to the disaster.

Mr Mackrell has been charged with two offences of contravening a term of condition of a safety certificate contrary to the Safety of Sports Grounds Act 1975 and one offence of failing to take reasonable care for the health and safety of other persons who may have been affected by his acts or omissions at work under the Health and Safety at Work etc. Act 1974. The case is outstanding.

11. In-house versus outsourced company secretary

Smaller companies often choose to outsource the role of the company secretary. A board, when considering whether to outsource the role or not, may want to consider some of the factors set out below.

11.1 Reasons to outsource

1. To ensure that all of the statutory and regulatory requirements are met by a specialised firm. These requirements are changing regularly in some countries as new laws and regulations are introduced.
2. To reduce costs of employing a person with a specific qualification, especially in a company start-up.
3. To fulfill a requirement to file company documents online, which requires a PIN for security reasons. There may also be a requirement that filings be carried out by a professional firm. For smaller companies, it may be more cost-effective or efficient to outsource the role to a professional firm.

11.2 Reasons not to outsource

1. An in-house company secretary acquires an in-depth knowledge and understanding of the company and its history and also develops relationships with the board and management that an external firm lacks.

2. An in-house company secretary is available at all times to discuss corporate governance issues. A professional services firm may be much slower in providing assistance or responding to questions.

3. A qualified in-house company secretary offers a wide range of services and is able to take on other responsibilities in a start-up or smaller company. For example, ICSA educates people in strategy, risk management, law, and accountancy.

4. An in-house company secretary may provide support that is difficult for an external firm to provide; for example, assisting the chairman to prepare for meetings.

5. An in-house company secretary can truly act as the 'conscience of the company' and has no conflict, in that they do not do other work for the company such as providing legal or accountancy services.

An in-house company secretary can be relied upon to maintain confidentiality. In-house corporate secretaries can in many cases be held liable for any breaches in confidentiality, whereas this may be problematic in cases of an outsourced service.

Where the role of the company secretary is outsourced, the directors maintain responsibility for the duties that should be carried out by the company secretary if one were employed in-house. Therefore, there needs to be oversight of the third party fulfilling the role.

Test yourself 3.4

1. **What are the major challenges to independence of the company secretary?**

2. **Is it appropriate for the company's in-house lawyer to carry out corporate governance responsibilities?**

3. **Explain why companies may not want to outsource the role of the company secretary.**

Chapter summary

◆ The company secretary role is at the heart of governance within an organisation.

◆ The duties of a company secretary can be divided into four categories: governance, compliance, advice and communication.

◆ The company secretary should be appointed and removed by the whole board.

◆ It is important for an organisation to protect the independence of the company secretary by ensuring that they cannot be influenced by individual members of the board or senior management team.

◆ The company secretary is the 'conscience of the company', ensuring that the company always does the right thing.

◆ It is equally important for company secretaries to have interpersonal skills and commercial awareness as well as technical skills.

Chapter four
Other governance issues

CONTENTS

1. Introduction

This chapter looks at the international aspects of corporate governance, how other countries have established their corporate governance frameworks. It also looks at how governance principles and practices has been adopted outside of the corporate sector in the public and not-for-profit sectors. Finally, it considers some of the key issues in corporate governance today around the world.

2. Corporate governance outside the UK

Some countries around the world have based their corporate governance frameworks on the UK model of corporate governance. Others have adopted different approaches. The European Corporate Governance Institute (ECGI) makes available on its website the full text of all of the corporate governance frameworks adopted globally. This chapter cannot go into the details of all of them so the most noteworthy have been selected here.

3. The US and Sarbanes-Oxley Act 2002

As mentioned earlier, the US has adopted a rules-based approach to corporate governance in response to the corporate collapses in the US in the early 2000's, among them Enron and WorldCom, and the stock market collapse following the bursting of the dot.com bubble. The Sarbanes-Oxley Act of 2002 (SOX) was enacted, the Securities and Exchange Commission (SEC) adopted many new rules and the New York Stock Exchange and Nasdaq Stock Market changed their standards governing listed companies.

SOX and its related SEC rules resulted in the following with respect to corporate governance:

◆ The SEC, as required by Section s. 307 of SOX, adopted a rule that required all stock markets to adopt standards in their listing rules governing the composition and functions of audit committees, and the independence of directors. Both NYSE and NASDQ adopted listing rules requiring that companies listed on their markets to have:

  – a majority of independent directors on their boards. Controlled companies, that is, where 50% or more of their capital is held by one individual, a group or another company, were exempted;

  – regular executive sessions of the independent directors, that is where the independent directors meet on their own;

  – an audit committee, compensation committee and a nominating committee; and

  – shareholder approval for all equity compensation plans.

◆ The SEC under s. 208 of SOX, introduced new rules on auditor independence, restricting the non-audit services an auditor could provide to the company, introducing a 'cooling off' period for auditors, audit partner rotation and expanded disclosure by the company relating to its auditors.

◆ Section 101 of SOX introduced an independent, non-governmental board, the Public Company Accounting Oversight Board (PCAOB) to oversee the audits of public companies.

◆ The SEC under s. 302 of SOX introduced requirements for the CEO and CFO to certify the quarterly and annual reports including financial statements filed with the SEC. False certifications under Section 302 resulted in SEC penalties and potential civil liability. Section 309 of SOX added a potential criminal liability for false certifications.

◆ The SEC under s. 404 of SOX introduced requirements for management to:

  – establish and maintain an adequate system of internal controls and procedures for financial reporting;

  – include in the company's annual report a report on the effectiveness of the company's internal controls over financial reporting.

The original implementation of the Section 404 requirement to review the system of internal controls was seen as very draconian and costly, and was blamed for discouraging foreign companies from listing in the US. In 2006, the provisions were reviewed, and the SEC issued new guidance which allowed management more discretion on how the annual review of internal controls is carried out.

◆ The SEC under Section 406 introduced requirements for codes of conduct and ethics governing the CEO, CFO, principal accounting officer or controller, or persons performing similar positions. It did not require a company-wide code of ethics, which has now become common. The New York Stock Exchange and NASDQ, however, did bring in requirements for a company-wide code of ethics, which included directors, officers and employees for companies listed on their exchanges.

◆ Other standards applicable to directors and officers were also brought in by SOX/SEC. These included:

- prohibition of personal loans;

- reporting of trades in the company's securities;

- insider trading blackout periods around the release of material information, such as a company's financial reports; and

- clawback of bonuses and incentive or equity-based compensation where financials have to be restated due to the misconduct of the individual.

◆ Section 806 of SOX created a civil action for employees of listed companies who were subject to retaliation by their employers for whistleblowing.

4. South Africa and the King Codes

The King Committee on Corporate Governance was established in the early 1990s and has issued four versions of the King Code of Corporate Governance in 1994 (King I), 2002 (King II), 2009 (King III) and the latest version (King IV) in 2016. The King Code is the responsibility of the Institute of Directors in Southern Africa (IoDSA). Compliance with the King Code is a requirement for all companies listed on the Johannesburg Stock Exchange.

The King Codes are interesting for the following reasons:

◆ They created and still adopt the 'stakeholder inclusive' approach to corporate governance discussed in Cchapter 1.

◆ Corporate responsibility and ethics form part of the King Code definition of corporate governance.

◆ They are well-established, having been first introduced in 1994 – only two years after the Cadbury Code in the UK.

◆ They provide for a single corporate governance framework in that they apply to all types of organisation, not just listed companies.

◆ King III adopted the 'apply or explain' regime to be followed by the 'apply and explain' regime in King IV, both of which are explained in more detail in Chapter 1.

The South African corporate governance framework is often described as a hybrid corporate governance regime, as some of its provisions follow the principle-based approach, King IV, and others are rule-based, being found in a number of laws that apply to companies and directors, including the Companies Act of South Africa of 2008. In addition, further enforcement takes place by regulations such as the JSE Securities Exchange Listings Requirements.

4.1 King IV

King IV assumes application of the principles set out within it, this is why it has adopted the 'apply and explain' regime. The disclosure is an explanation of the practices that have been implemented and how these support achieving the associated governance principle. The governing body can choose where and how to make the disclosures, which should be publicly accessible.

King IV also aligns best practices in corporate governance to shifts in the approaches to:

◆ capitalism – financial capital to inclusive capital market systems;

◆ reporting – 'silo', that is by capital: financial, human, intellectual, manufactured, social and natural to **'integrated' reporting**; and

◆ capital markets – short-term to sustainable capital markets.

integrated reporting
Reporting on all aspects of the company's activities that have relevance to the creation or loss of value in six areas of capital: financial, manufactured, human, intellectual property, natural and social. Similar to sustainability reporting, but directed at the company's shareholders.

The focus of King IV is on outcomes-based governance. It places accountability on the governing body within an organisation to attain four governance outcomes:

◆ ethical culture and effective leadership;

◆ performance and value creation in a sustainable manner;

◆ adequate and effective controls; and

◆ trust, good reputation and legitimacy with stakeholders.

King IV also introduces a principle applicable to institutional investors.

The King Reports have repositioned corporate governance in South Africa as a method of achieving sustainability of organisations rather than just a method of protecting investors. The integration of corporate responsibility and ethics into the definition of corporate governance is also seen as essential in a region struggling with issues such as corruption, health issues and lack of much needed skills. It is hoped that through this repositioning, more organisations will see the appropriateness of corporate governance to their sustainability with the consequential economic development it should produce.

5. Corporate governance frameworks in Germany

Germany, unlike the UK, South Africa and the US, operates what is called a two-tier board system. It also has a concentration of share ownership in large listed companies. Franks and Mayer (2001) reported that, in 1990, 85% of a sample of 171 large listed industrial companies in Germany had a single shareholder with an ownership stake of more than 25% of the share capital, and 57% had single shareholder who owned more than 50%.

The concentration in ownership would appear, as we will see for China later in the chapter, to give the majority shareholder complete control of the company. This is not the case in Germany, however, as safeguards have been put in place in Germany's Stock Corporation Act, last amended in 2016, to protect the minority shareholders. The Act provides that the **supervisory boards** of large listed companies, that is, companies of with 2,000 or more employees, are elected 50% by the company's employees and 50% by the company's shareholders. The supervisory board is then responsible for appointing and dismissing the **management board**. It is the management board who has responsibility for managing the company. The Act also contains provisions that stop unfavourable contracts being imposed on the company by its major shareholder.

The German Government set up the Cromme Commission to look at the corporate governance regime for listed companies in Germany. The Cromme Code was published in May 2003. It recommended that a maximum of two former executives could sit on the supervisory board of a listed company at any one time. Historically, many executives saw as part of their retirement a place on their supervisory board. The Cromme Code was replaced in 2017 by the German Corporate Governance Code, which applies to all listed companies.

The German Code consists of three types of provisions:

◆   Legal stipulations that oblige the company to follow applicable law.

◆   'Shall' recommendations, which follow the comply or explain regime.

◆   'Should' suggestions, where companies do not need to disclose their deviation from them.

The commitment of companies to corporate governance practices are judged by their application of the 'shall' recommendations.

supervisory board
A board of non-executive directors, found in a company with a two-tier board structure. The supervisory board reserves some responsibilities to itself. These include oversight of the management board.

management board
A board of executive managers, chaired by the CEO within a two-tier board structure. The chair of the management board reports to the chair of the supervisory board. The management board has responsibility for the operational performance of the business.

6. Corporate governance frameworks in Japan

Shareholding in Japan is dispersed and held predominantly by financial institutions and businesses, like the UK and the US. There is therefore a separation of ownership and control, with managers running the day-to-day affairs of the company. However, historically, the corporate governance model in Japan has been more like the European model with management giving a strong priority to the interests of employees rather than the shareholder focus of the Anglo-American corporate governance model. In recent years, it appears that Japan, with its new corporate governance regime, is becoming more market-orientated and adopting its own hybrid approach to corporate governance, which contains elements of both the European and Anglo-American corporate governance models.

The change to a more market-orientated corporate governance regime is predominantly government driven as part of the reforms brought in as a response to Japan's long-running economic problems.

Principles for Responsible Institutional Investors: Japan's Stewardship Code

In an attempt to open the market to foreign investors, Japan issued its 'Principles for Responsible Institutional Investors: Japan's Stewardship Code', in 2014. The Code was updated in 2017. By September 2017, there were nearly 300 signatories in support of the Stewardship Code, the majority of which were domestic investors.

The Stewardship Code comprises a set of seven principles, the aim of which is to provide a framework for institutional investors in fulfilling their stewardship responsibilities with due regard both to their clients and beneficiaries and to investee companies which contributes to the growth of the economy of Japan as a whole. It adopts a 'comply or explain' regime. The principles are:

1. Institutional investors should have a clear policy on how they fulfil their stewardship responsibilities, and publicly disclose it.
2. Institutional investors should have a clear policy on how they manage conflicts of interest in fulfilling their stewardship responsibilities and publicly disclose it.
3. Institutional investors should monitor investee companies so that they can appropriately fulfil their stewardship responsibilities with an orientation towards the sustainable growth of the companies.
4. Institutional investors should seek to arrive at an understanding in common with investee companies and work to solve problems through constructive engagement with investee companies.
5. Institutional investors should have a clear policy on voting and disclosure of voting activity. The policy on voting should not be comprised only of a mechanical checklist; it should be designed to contribute to the sustainable growth of investee companies.

6. Institutional investors in principle should report periodically on how they fulfill their stewardship responsibilities, including their voting responsibilities, to their clients and beneficiaries.

7. To contribute positively to the sustainable growth of investee companies, institutional investors should have in-depth knowledge of the investee companies and their business environment and skills and resources needed to appropriately engage with the companies and make proper judgements in fulfilling their stewardship activities.

6.1 Japan's Corporate Governance Code

Japan's Corporate Governance Code defines corporate governance as: 'a structure for transparent, fair, timely and decisive decision making by companies, with due attention to the needs and perspectives of shareholders and also customers, employees and local communities.'

The Code adopts a principle-based approach based on the G20/OECD Principles of Corporate Governance discussed later in this chapter. It also adopts the 'comply and explain' approach developed by the UK Corporate Governance Code. The Code, which applies to all companies listed on the Tokyo Stock Exchange, was first published in 2015 and revised in June 2018.

Securing the rights and equal treatment of shareholders
Companies should take appropriate measures to fully secure shareholder rights and develop an environment in which shareholders can exercise their rights appropriately and effectively. In addition, companies should secure effective equal treatment of shareholders. Given their particular sensitivities, adequate consideration should be given to the issues and concerns of minority shareholders and foreign shareholders for the effective exercise of shareholder rights and effective equal treatment of shareholders.

Appropriate co-operation with stakeholders other than shareholders
Companies should fully recognise that their sustainable growth and the creation of mid- to long-term corporate value are brought as a result of the provision of resources and contributions made by a range of stakeholders, including employees, customers, business partners, creditors and local communities. As such, companies should endeavour to appropriately cooperate with these stakeholders. The board and the management should exercise their leadership in establishing a corporate culture where the rights and positions of stakeholders are respected, and sound business ethics are ensured.

Ensuring appropriate information disclosure and transparency
Companies should appropriately make information disclosure in compliance with the relevant laws and regulations, but should also strive to actively provide information beyond that required by law. This includes both financial information, such as financial standing and operating results, and non-financial information, such as business strategies and business issues, risk, and governance. The board should recognise that disclosed information will serve as the basis for constructive dialogue with shareholders, and therefore ensure that

such information, particularly non-financial information, is accurate, clear and useful.

Responsibilities of the board

Given its fiduciary responsibility and accountability to shareholders, in order to promote sustainable corporate growth and the increase of corporate value over the mid- to long-term and enhance earnings power and capital efficiency, the board should appropriately fulfil its roles and responsibilities, including: (1) setting the broad direction of corporate strategy; (2) establishing an environment where appropriate risk-taking by the senior management is supported; and (3) carrying out effective oversight of directors and the management from an independent and objective standpoint. Such roles and responsibilities should be equally and appropriately fulfilled regardless of the form of corporate organisation.

Dialogue with shareholders

In order to contribute to sustainable growth and the increase of corporate value over the mid- to long-term, companies should engage in constructive dialogue with shareholders even outside the general shareholder meeting. During such dialogue, senior management and directors, including outside directors, should listen to the views of shareholders and pay due attention to their interests and concerns, clearly explain business policies to shareholders in an understandable manner so as to gain their support, and work to develop a balanced understanding of the positions of shareholders and other stakeholders and acting accordingly.

7. Corporate governance frameworks in China

China's listed companies have a concentrated ownership structure, unlike the UK, US and Japan where ownership and control are separated. The focus of their corporate governance regime is, therefore, on protecting minority shareholders, regulating controlling shareholders and disclosure and transparency.

China follows the **two-tier board** system originating in continental Europe, whereby Chinese companies have:

two-tier board
Board structure in which responsibilities are divided between a supervisory board of non-executive directors led by the chairman and a management board of executives led by the CEO.

◆ a board of directors which is responsible for the management of the company including the oversight from an operational perspective of the management who run the company on a day-to-day basis; and

◆ a supervisory board which is responsible for ensuring that the board of directors and management do not violate laws or the company's articles of association. It is also entitled to inspect the company's financial records.

China's corporate governance framework is rules based and consists of:

◆ Laws, such as Accounting Law (2000), Companies Law 2006, Securities Law 2006, and the Law on State-owned Assets of Enterprises (2009);

◆ Code of Corporate Governance for Listed Companies (2018); and

◆ Listing Stocks and Trading Rules made by the individual stock exchanges.

The Chinese Code, which was first published in 2001, is based on the OECD Principles of Corporate Governance. It was revised in 2018.

The 2000 edition of the Chinese Code contained provisions on shareholders and shareholders' meetings, listed companies and controlling shareholders, directors and board of directors, supervisors and the supervisory board, performance assessment and incentive and disciplinary systems, stakeholders, and information disclosure and transparency. The 2018 version includes greater emphasis on environmental, social and governance (ESG) disclosure, the role of institutional investors as stewards, the accountability of board directors, and board member skills and diversity.

8. Corporate governance frameworks in Scandinavia

Scandinavian law is distinct from other contemporary legal systems which tend to be based on the Anglo-Saxon or German models. Scandinavian law is adopted by five countries: Denmark, Finland, Sweden, Norway and Iceland, known as the Nordic countries. Companies adopting this legal system maintain the one-tier board of directors from the Anglo-Saxon model, but have inserted beneath it a management structure which can be either the CEO on their own or a group of senior executives including the CEO. The management structure is subject to the instructions of the board of directors. A member of the management structure can also be a member of the board of directors but cannot be its chair and they must be in the minority.

unitary board
A board structure in which decisions are taken by a single group of executive and non-executive directors, led by the company chairman.

The liability of the management is for the day-to-day affairs of the company; anything outside of this must be submitted to the board of directors for a decision. Like the **unitary board** of the Anglo-Saxon model, the board of directors in the Scandinavian model enjoys both executive and oversight powers. In the traditional two-tier German model, the executive powers are vested solely in the management board and the oversight powers in the supervisory board.

Shareholders in the Scandinavian model sit above the internal structures of the board of directors and management structure creating a hierarchical system. Only those in the level directly above can appoint and dismiss the members of the body beneath them. Shareholders therefore appoint and dismiss the members of the board of directors and the board of directors appoints and dismisses the members of the management structure.

Share ownership in Scandinavia is concentrated but is not seen as problematic. Scandinavian law supports the supremacy of a dominant majority shareholder, giving them the power to appoint all of the board of directors and as such control the company. This is countered, however, by the potential for a dominant shareholder to be held liable under Scandinavian law for any reckless behaviour in their decision making or where the dominant shareholder is seen to be coercing either the board of directors or management into a particular action for the benefit of that shareholder.

Despite having the same legal systems, the Nordic countries developed their own self-regulating corporate governance codes which had significant differences within them. In 2007, there was an attempt to bring the regulators responsible for these codes together to see if they could be brought closer together in an attempt to help foreign investors understand the Scandinavian model.

9. Corporate governance frameworks in the Netherlands

The Dutch model of corporate governance accommodates both the two-tier German model, which is followed by the majority of Dutch listed companies, and the one-tier Anglo-Saxon model. This is because of the Anglo-Dutch companies, such as Unilever and Shell, that were required by their listings in the UK and the US to adopt a one-tier system. Chapter 5 of the Dutch Corporate Governance Code 2016 applies specifically to one-tier board companies, with the rest of the code focusing on two-tier companies.

Test yourself 4.1

Why have different countries' corporate governance best practices developed in different ways?

10. Governance in other sectors

The recognition that there have been benefits of good corporate governance for the private sector has led to organisations in the public and not-for-profit sectors taking an interest in how they can improve their own governance practices. This has led to the adoption of corporate governance guidelines or codes by these types of organisations.

We saw earlier that since King III, the corporate governance codes in South Africa have applied to all types of organisations. The UK, in contrast, has taken the route of developing different corporate governance codes and guidelines for different sectors within the economy. This is because, although the principles of corporate governance apply in all sectors, the governance challenges are different sector by sector so to ensure that the practices deal with the particular challenges different codes or guidelines are applicable.

Stop and think 4.1

You all do governance in your homes. In what ways do you:

◆   **Allocate responsibilities?**

◆   **Expect accountability?**

◆   **Treat members of the family fairly?**

◆   **Risk manage?**

◆   **Ensure transparency?**

10.1 Governance in the public sector

Corporate governance in the public sector in the UK is based on the Nolan's seven principles of public life, which were developed by the Nolan Committee on Standards in Public life in 1995. The Nolan Committee was set up in response to concerns that the conduct of some politicians was unethical. The Nolan Principles now form the basis of corporate governance codes in the voluntary, as well as the public, sector in the UK.

Nolan's seven principles of public life

1. Selflessness. Holders of public office should take decisions solely in terms of the public interest. They should not do so to gain financial or other material benefits for themselves, their family or their friends.

2. Integrity. Holders of public office should not place themselves under any financial or other obligation to outside individuals or organisations that might influence them in the performance of their duties.

3. Objectivity. In carrying out public business, including making public appointments, awarding contracts or recommending individuals for rewards and benefits, holders of public office should make choices on merit.

4. Accountability. Holders of public office are accountable for their decisions and actions to the public and must submit themselves to whatever scrutiny is appropriate to their office.

5. Openness. Holders of public office should be as open as possible about the decisions and actions that they take. They should give reasons for their decisions and restrict information only when the wider public interest clearly demands.

6. Honesty. Holders of public office have a duty to declare any private interests relating to their public duties and to take steps to resolve any conflicts arising in a way that protects the public interest.

7. Leadership. Holders of public office should promote and support these principles by leadership and example.

For central government in the UK, there is a code of good practice: 'Corporate governance in central government departments: Code of good practice 2011'. This Code sets out the composition and the role of the boards of central government departments.

In 2004, the Independent Commission for Good Governance in Public Service published the 'Good governance standards for public service'. This is a guide for everyone concerned with governance in the public services and applies to all organisations that work for the public using public money, whether they are in the public, private or not-for-profit sectors.

In 2007, The Chartered Institute of Public Finance and Accountancy (CIPFA) and Solace (the Society of Local Authority Chief Executives and Senior Managers) published a governance framework aimed at local government bodies called 'Delivering good governance in local government: Framework'. This framework was revised in 2016. It sets out principles of governance that local government bodies are encouraged to adopt and apply to their own particular circumstances.

The OECD published in 2005, and revised in 2015, its Guidelines on Corporate Governance of State-Owned Enterprises. These guidelines give 'advice to countries on how to manage more effectively their responsibilities as company owners, thus helping to make state-owned enterprises more competitive, efficient and transparent'.

10.2 Governance in the not-for-profit sector

The Charities Code was published in 2017. It replaced 'Good Governance: a Code for the Voluntary and Community Sector', which was first published in 2005 and revised in 2010. The Code is split into two, providing a set of guidelines and a diagnostic tool for larger charities, whose income is over £1 million a year, and a separate set for charities whose income is less than £1 million per year.

The Code is made up of principles, outcomes and recommendations under the following seven headings:

◆   Organisation purpose

◆   Leadership

◆   Integrity

◆   Decision-making, risk and control

◆   Board effectiveness

◆   Diversity

◆   Openness and accountability

The Code also explains the role of a trustee in a charitable context.

11. Governance for family-controlled companies

Many businesses start out as family businesses. The successful ones go through different stages in their lifecycles, each stage presenting its own challenges for the family owners.

In the first stage, the founder will probably be the owner of the company. In addition to being the owner, they will also be the decision-maker and the implementer (manager). Challenges with other family members who may have different views as to the future direction of the company will be non-existent at this stage. As the business passes to the next generation and the next, mechanisms will need to be found to manage what could potentially become value-destroying conflict between different family members.

Moving to future stages in the business's lifecycle, the organisation may want to consider the following governance in an attempt to keep conflict at a minimum.

At the shareholder level:

◆ Agreeing and documenting what the family's vision, mission and values for the organisation are. This allows those running the company, whether family members or outside managers, to be aware of the direction the business should be moving in and under what ethical framework.

◆ Setting up a structure through which family members can interact with those running the business. This may be a family assembly or council. The terms of reference for this body will have to be agreed and documented, in the company's articles of association, again so expectations can be set on this relationship.

◆ Agreeing the process for appointing and the number of family members to be on the company's board of directors. Again, this will need to be documented in the company's articles of association.

◆ A mechanism for family members to sell their shareholding and exit the company. Most company's articles of association include pre-emption rights, that is, the requirement that shares will need to be offered pro rata to the existing shareholders first before they can be sold to outsiders. Some family businesses establish a fund to allow family members to cash in their stock at a fair price. Where such a fund exists, a committee is usually established to manage this fund. The constitution and terms of reference of this committee will have to be agreed and documented.

At the board level:

◆ Where the board is made up wholly of family members, the board may decide to set up an advisory board comprising experienced and respected individuals known to the family that can support the family members in areas such as strategic planning, marketing, the development of human capital and expansion into new markets which may be international.

◆ Advisory boards are often seen as a stepping stone to opening up a board to independent directors.

At the management level:

◆ Some family businesses set up education programmes and career planning so that family members are developed to take up positions in management within the company to ensure it stays under the control of the family. Structure and processes around this will have to be set up: a committee to oversee the programme, criteria for who is chosen to participate and how much can be spent per individual are among them.

12. Global principles of corporate governance

12.1 G20/OECD Principles of Corporate Governance

The G20/OECD Principles of Corporate Governance help policy-makers, investors and other stakeholders assess and develop the legal, regulatory and institutional framework for corporate governance within a country. They do not provide detailed provisions on how the principles should be applied in practice.

As we have seen earlier in the chapter, many countries and bilateral organisations use the G20/OECD Principles as the basis for their corporate governance frameworks.

The Reporting on Observance of Standards and Codes (ROSC) for Corporate Governance, administered by the International Monetary Fund (IMF) and The World Bank, also uses the principles as the basis for their reports. ROSCs are also carried out in accounting, auditing and anti-money laundering.

The OECD Principles of Corporate Governance were first published in 1999 and revised in 2004. The latest version was endorsed by the G20 in November 2015 and so became known as the G20/OECD Principles of Corporate Governance.

The principles are made up of six chapters. Each chapter includes a principle and several sub-principles. The chapters each deal with a different aspect of corporate governance.

G20/OECD Principles of Corporate Governance
1. Ensuring the basis for an effective corporate governance framework:

    'The corporate governance framework should promote transparent and fair markets, and efficient allocation of resources. It should be consistent with the rule of law and support effective supervision and enforcement.'

2. The rights and equitable treatment of shareholders and key ownership functions:

    'The corporate governance framework should protect and facilitate the exercise of shareholders' rights and ensure equitable treatment of all shareholders, including minority and foreign shareholders. All shareholders should have the opportunity to obtain effective redress for violation of their rights.'.

3.   Institutional investors, stock markets and other intermediaries

'The corporate governance framework should provide sound incentives throughout the investment chain and provide for stock markets to function in a way that contributes to good corporate governance.'

4.   The role of stakeholders in corporate governance

'The corporate governance framework should recognise the rights of stakeholders established by law or through mutual agreements and encourage active co-operation between corporations and stakeholders in creating wealth, jobs and sustainability of financially sound enterprises.'

5.   Disclosure and transparency

'The corporate governance framework should ensure that timely and accurate disclosure is made on all material matters regarding the corporation, including the financial situation, performance, ownership, and governance of the company.'

6.   The responsibilities of the board

'The corporate governance framework should ensure the strategic guidance of the company, the effective monitoring of management by the board, and the board's accountability to the company and the shareholders.'.

12.2 Basel Corporate Governance Principles for Banks

The Basel Corporate Governance Principles for Banks were first issued by the Bank for International Settlements (BIS) in 2010 and revised in 2015. They provide 'a framework within which banks and supervisors should operate to achieve robust and transparent risk management and decision making and, in doing so, promote public confidence and uphold the safety and soundness of the banking system'.

The revised principles, according to BIS:

◆   expand the guidance on the role of the board of directors in overseeing the implementation of effective risk management systems;

◆   emphasise the importance of the board's collective competence as well as the obligation of individual board members to dedicate sufficient time to their mandates and to keep abreast of developments in banking;

◆   strengthen the guidance on risk governance, including the risk management roles played by business units, risk management teams, and internal audit and control functions (the three lines of defence), as well as underline the importance of a sound risk culture to drive risk management within a bank;

◆   provide guidance for bank supervisors in evaluating the processes used by banks to select board members and senior management; and

◆   recognise that compensation systems form a key component of the governance and incentive structure through which the board and senior management of a bank convey acceptable risk-taking behaviour and reinforce the bank's operating and risk culture.

The Basel Corporate Governance Principles for Banks

- Principle 1: Board's overall responsibilities
- Principle 2: Board qualifications and composition
- Principle 3: Board's own structure and practices
- Principle 4: Senior management
- Principle 5: Governance of group structures
- Principle 6: Risk management function
- Principle 7: Risk identification, monitoring and controlling
- Principle 8: Risk communication
- Principle 9: Compliance
- Principle 10: Internal audit
- Principle 11: Compensation
- Principle 12: Disclosure and transparency
- Principle 13: Role of supervisors

12.3 ICGN Principles

The International Corporate Governance Network (ICGN) was established in 1995. It is an international investor-led organisation aimed at promoting effective standards of corporate governance, in order to improve the efficiency of markets and economies globally. ICGN published in 2003, (and revised in 2014), the ICGN Global Governance Principles and Global Stewardship Principles which aim to enhance the dialogue between boards and investors by setting out the responsibilities of both parties.

13. Key issues in corporate governance

Many of the key corporate governance issues faced by UK companies today are relevant to both listed and unlisted companies. Some of them are listed below.

13.1 Composition of boards

The makeup of boards is a key issue in governance. The focus is on:

- More representative boards: there are quotas for women on boards and growing requirements for more social and ethnic diversity on boards and within the pipelines for board succession.
- Independence of board members to ensure that there is challenge to a dominant chairman or CEO: one of the key issues highlighted for 2019 AGM planning by Equiniti in its annual review of trends and developments from the 2018 AGM season was independence of directors.

13.2 Financial reporting

Every company under the CA2006 is required to keep accounting records which enable the directors to prepare accounts which that comply with the appropriate accounting standards. The accounts should show with reasonable accuracy the financial position of the company at that time.

Evidence shows, however, that directors and senior managers for many reasons produce accounts that disguise the true financial performance of their company. This may be to:

◆ enhance their own rewards;

◆ cover up a fraud; or

◆ cover up poor performance due to their own lack of experience and understanding of the business.

As we saw earlier in the chapter, it was concerns about misleading company financial information that led to the setting up of the first corporate governance committee, the Cadbury Committee, in 1992. It also led to the introduction in the US of the Sarbanes-Oxley Act in 2002. Despite all of the corporate governance regulations since then we still see corporate governance scandals that relate to accounting issues. One of the most recent, in October 2018, being the Patisserie Valerie case.

Case study 4.1

Serious Fraud Office (SFO)
An independent UK government agency that is responsible for investigating and prosecuting serious crimes involving financial wrongdoing and complex economic crimes, such as the Libor manipulation.

In 2014, Tesco reported that its half-year profits had been overstated by £263 million due to premature recognition of income and of anticipated cost savings. The report raised questions of whether the board was properly constituted as it lacked the retail experience necessary to effectively challenge the executive. The chairman resigned as a result of the incident. At the end of October 2014, the UK Serious Fraud Office (SFO) announced it was launching an investigation into the alleged accounting irregularities at Tesco. In 2016, three former Tesco executives were charged by the SFO with fraud and false accounting Two years later, following an initial court case being abandoned, all three former executives were acquitted at a retrial (at which the judge stated that the case was too weak against the individuals). Tesco was fined £129 million by the SFO, in addition to legal costs.

Case study 4.2

On 10 October 2018, Patisserie Valerie's (PV) shares were suspended from trading when it was announced that there was a material shortfall between PV's reported accounts and its true health. On 12 October 2018, PV's suspended finance director was arrested by the Serious Fraud Office for alleged accounting fraud.

PV's parent, Patisserie Holdings, owned by Luke Johnson, the founder of Pizza Express, is looking to raise capital to save around 2,500 jobs. Mr Johnson has loaned PV money so that it remains liquid until capital can be raised.

The company was valued at around £400 million prior to the reported accounting irregularities; its reported worth on 12 October 2018 was around £68 million.

13.3 Stakeholder relations

As we saw in Chapter 2, directors of all companies in the UK now have a statutory duty, under s. 172 of the CA2006, to take into consideration the interests of employees and foster business relationships with suppliers, customers and others. The Companies (Miscellaneous Reporting) Regulations 2018 have introduced reporting requirements for companies on their compliance with s. 172. Companies will have to disclose how their directors have engaged with employees and other stakeholders and how they have taken stakeholder interests into consideration in their decision making.

For listed companies, the UK Corporate Governance Code 2018 has suggested methods of workforce engagement that boards could adopt. They include:

◆ a director appointed from the workforce;
◆ a formal workforce advisory panel; or
◆ a designated non-executive director.

13.4 Corporate culture

There is a growing focus on corporate culture and the importance for the long-term sustainability of the company on getting the right culture embedded within the business practices of the company. The UK Corporate Governance Code 2018 has introduced for the first time a provision requiring boards to 'assess and monitor culture'. Guidance is provided by the FRC, in the 'Guidance on board effectiveness', on how boards may be able to accomplish compliance with this provision, but individual boards are still going to have to work out how they are going to do this and make disclosures about it effectively based on their individual circumstances and challenges. Corporate culture will be discussed further in Chapter 8.

13.5 Social responsibility and sustainability

The focus on an organisation's social responsibility activities has grown over recent years. One of the main reasons for this appears to be the millennialgeneration entering the workplace. Millennials want to be heard and have a voice in both contributing and making a difference in a broader community. They constantly share their views and opinions through social media platforms.

This characteristic of the millennial generation has led to an overwhelming demand for social responsibility as the potential workforce and consumer base look to do business only with those whom they feel are making a positive impact on society and pillorying those through social media who appear to be negatively impacting society.

An increase in non-financial reporting largely due to regulatory changes and the expectation of investors and stakeholders is also occurring. Boards are having to justify their activities more on the long-term sustainability of their organisations rather than the previous short-term view of meeting quarterly and half-yearly targets.

13.6 Sexual harassment in the workplace

The recent development of the 'Me Too' movement, which has now spread to corporates, has highlighted the issue of sexual harassment in the workplace.

The Equality Act 2010 states that sexual harassment is a behaviour that is either meant to, or has the effect of:

◆   violating your dignity; or
◆   creating an intimidating, hostile, degrading, humiliating or offensive environment.

Sexual harassment can include:

◆   sexual comments or jokes;
◆   physical behaviour, including unwelcome sexual advances, touching and various forms of sexual assault;
◆   displaying pictures, photos or drawings of a sexual nature; or
◆   sending emails with a sexual content.

Boards need to ensure that policies and procedures within the organisation create behaviours that do not leave them open to condoning sexual harassment.

13.7 Remuneration of directors and senior executives

The remuneration of directors and senior executives is still a major corporate governance topic in the UK. There is evidence, reflected in fewer remuneration policy and report voting rebellions, that companies are taking into account the guidance of institutional investor representative bodies when putting together the content of their remuneration policies. Feedback is also being sought from their major shareholders.

The issue of pay equality between men and women has again been in the news, with high-profile cases such as the pay practices of the BBC in 2017. Again, this poses a reputational risk for many organisations. Boards should be reviewing their pay policies and ensuring that their remuneration practices are fair. There have been examples where employees have taken their own decision to ensure equality in pay between genders. In January 2018, Johan Lundgren, the new easyJet CEO, offered to have his salary cut to the same level as his female predecessor, Dame Carolyn McCall, when the airline revealed its female staff were paid about half the rate of men on average.

13.8 Shareholder dialogue

There is a requirement for greater communication between a company and its shareholders. The amount companies are required to disclose to their shareholders appears to grow by the year. The challenge is that the profile of shareholdings in UK listed companies is changing with increased short-term holdings, a fall in retail shareholders and higher foreign ownership. It is therefore difficult for companies to have the dialogue intended through the UK's corporate governance framework of physical annual general meetings and engagement with institutional shareholders through one-on-one meetings with the chairman on governance or executive management on operational performance. Companies therefore appear to be exploring technology and electronic communications. More detail on this can be found in Chapter 15.

13.9 Performance of directors

The time commitment and capacity of directors to give the required attention to the companies whose boards they sit on is also becoming a topic of interest for investors. Institutional Shareholder Services (ISS) and Glass Lewis both recommend voting against 'overboarded' directors, which they define as:

◆ executive directors sitting on more then two public company boards; and

◆ non-executive directors sitting on more than five public company boards.

One of the key issues highlighted for 2019 AGM planning by Equiniti in its annual review of trends and developments from the 2018 AGM season was perceived overboarding by individual directors.

The 2018 Code recommends that executive directors should have no more than one FTSE 100 board non-executive directorship. There is no limit for board chairman or other non-executive directors. The 2018 Code only requires that non-executive directors should provide constructive challenge and strategic guidance to management in addition to holding them to account. To do this effectively, the directors need time.

Listed companies, in the FTSE 100, are also required to hold annual evaluations, using an external evaluator, of the whole board, its committees, the chair and individual directors. For FTSE 350 companies this should be at least every three years.

13.10 Risk management

Since the global financial crisis (2008–09) there has been a growing expectation that the boards of listed companies focus more on risk management. Previously this had been delegated to management and the board played a small role in it. The FRC 'Guidance on risk management, internal control and related financial and business reporting', issued in 2014, made it clear that the board has a primary role in the identification and management of risk.

13.11 Tax planning

The tax planning of organisations, especially multinationals, has been in the spotlight since the Starbucks tax avoidance case in 2012. Google, Amazon and Apple, among others, have all come under attack for their tax planning practices. Boards need to consider the reputational risk associated with their tax planning and other accounting policies.

13.12 Technology and information governance

The King III Corporate Governance Code, in South Africa, was one of the first to recognise the importance of 'technology and information governance' in 2009. Both aspects of governance are now receiving focus by boards of companies internationally.

Due to the ever-greater reliance on technology, organisations are required to manage the risks associated with technological disruptions within their organisations as well as an often 'insatiable' desire by management in many organisations to keep up with the latest technological developments. This requires governance.

The governance of information is also becoming critical for organisations. The management of both information and knowledge can offer competitive advantage, and many organisations are increasing their focus on both areas. Boards are increasing being expected to ensure that information and knowledge are managed effectively within their organisations and that they are protected.

Recent global cyber attacks have highlighted the importance of cyber security risk management for board directors. Companies no longer have a choice as to whether they mitigate against cyber attacks. In future, this should be an important part of their risk management process. Countries are starting to look at whether they need to regulate with respect to cyber security. For example, the SEC has expanded its focus on cyber security already, taking action against corporations for not protecting customer data against cyber attacks.

Stop and think 4.2

How is your organisation dealing with any of these issues?, Has it issued any statements or changed any of its structures, policies or procedures in response to them?

14. Corporate governance issues in developing and emerging markets

In many emerging markets the opposite phenomenon occurs to developed markets in that listed companies often have more concentrated ownership structures, where a small number of shareholders hold a significant portion of the companies' shares and therefore are able to exercise considerably more control over their boards and management. The corporate governance issue here is about protecting the minority shareholders.

Corporate governance issues are different in different countries and this is why countries should adopt governance practices to deal with their specific issues, not just cut and paste governance frameworks from other countries. This has been practiced in many developing and emerging market countries where practices designed in developed countries for large listed companies have been adopted in an attempt to attract foreign investment.

Regulatory institutions in both emerging and developing markets are often newer, less-experienced and under-funded in comparison to their counterparts in more developed markets. This leads to less enforcement of laws and regulations. In 2002, a World Bank Study found evidence that companies in countries with weak legal and regulatory systems could, by improving their corporate governance practices, have a proportionally greater impact on investor protection.

The term corporate governance often means that many organisations that could benefit from some aspects of corporate governance best practice dismiss it as not being applicable to them because they are not corporate. For example, much of the service and product delivery in developing countries is by organisations in the public and not-for-profit sectors, many of which are not accountable for or transparent about their activities. Non-corporates therefore lose out on the benefits of adopting good governance practices, such as sustainability, cheaper capital, less risk, and so on. For organisations in developing countries, this is particularly important since for sustainable economic development, organisations across all three sectors (private, public and not-for-profit) are needed.

Lack of transparency and disclosure is a red flag for investors in emerging markets according to a 2010 IFC Emerging Market Investor Survey. A company's willingness to disclose information is factored heavily into investors' decision making. A lack of disclosure is seen as being indicative of other problems.

Reliance on expatriate management, due to the lack of capability of local managers, can lead to a cultural issue and a lack of communication and trust between expatriate managers and local boards. An example of this led to the tobacco crisis in Malawi in 2011 (see case study 4.3).

Conflicts of interest arising from cross-share ownership (companies owning shares in each other), **cross-directorships** (where directors sit on each other's boards) and the influence of government or financial institutions over the affairs of companies are also issues that investors look out for.

cross directorships
Two or more directors on boards of the other.

Many organisations in developing and emerging countries are either state or family owned and/or not listed and this brings with it its own governance challenges:

◆   Lack of ownership control by government, no monitoring of management which is often lacking in capability and boards filled with inexperienced directors who would rather be somewhere else.

◆   Conflict in family-owned businesses between controlling family members, informal governance structures and often inexperienced boards and management teams.

Case study 4.3

Buyers of tobacco in Malawi introduced stricter quality controls on bales of tobacco bought from local farmers. As a result, according to buyers, 85% of bales submitted to buyers were rejected. This had a devastating impact on the economy of Malawi, which is one of the poorest countries in the world.

The decision to introduce the stricter quality controls came from an overseas holding company, which was part of a joint venture with a local Malawian company, and was implemented by the expatriate manager without recourse to the local board. It was claimed that the crisis may have been diverted if the expatriate manager had consulted the local board.

Chapter summary

◆   Corporate governance has developed in different ways in different countries to reflect their distinct legal systems and also the specific issues that they are dealing with.

◆   There is a convergence in governance practices – all countries recognise the importance of independent directors and the importance of the principles of corporate governance: responsibility, accountability, transparency and fairness.

◆   There is a growing recognition of the value of having a governance professional within the organisation.

◆   The corporate governance frameworks recognise the differing roles of the shareholder, director and manager and the relationship and dialogue between them.

◆   The adoption of corporate governance practices in other sectors such as the public and not-for-profit sectors is growing. There are, however, different challenges to be dealt with in these sectors so the focus is on different aspects of corporate governance.

◆   Many of the key issues in corporate governance are global issues.

Part two

The board of directors and leadership

Overview

The second part of this study text considers the knowledge and skills necessary for company secretary to advise the board on its governance role and the role its various participants. It also addresses best practice on composition, appointments and succession policies, and describes the behaviours and practices that can enhance board effectiveness.

Chapter 5 sets the scene by summarising the duties and powers of directors under the CA2006 and the general law, which form the foundation of the UK corporate governance regime.

Chapter 6 examines the practical role that the UK Corporate Governance Code expects boards to play in the management of the company's business and the specific roles of chair, CEO, executive directors, NEDs and the senior independent director.

Chapter 7 addresses issues regarding the composition and balance of the board (including diversity), the appointment process and succession policies, all matters which fall within the remit of the nomination committee.

Chapter 8 discusses other behaviours and practices that can enhance the effectiveness of the board and the Company secretary's role in promoting them. In particular it looks at decision-making processes, the supply of information, independent professional advice, board evaluations, induction and professional development.

Learning outcomes

Part Two should enable you to:

◆ advise the directors on their duties and on the possible consequences of any breach of those duties;

◆ advise the directors on their powers and the possible constraints on those powers, including when shareholder approval may be required;

◆ critically appraise and apply corporate governance principles and best practices on the role of the board;

◆ advise the board of the benefits of adopting a schedule of matters reserved for the board and to understand what such a schedule should cover;

◆ explain the role of the chair and how it should be separated from that of the CEO;

◆ explain the role of the CEO and how they exercise delegated powers;

◆ understand the role of non-executive directors and be able to advise the board on the criteria for independence and measures that can be taken to enhance their effectiveness;

◆ advise the board on the role of the senior independent director;

◆ advise the board on the role of the three main board committees required under the Code and the rules on their composition;

- explain the role of the company secretary envisaged under the Code;

- understand and advise the board on the factors that will affect the composition, size and balance of the board, including diversity;

- advise the board on best practices on diversity and the associated reporting requirements;

- explain the role of the nomination committee;

- identify best practices on the appointment and re-election of directors and succession planning;

- identify common failings in the decision-making process;

- understand the company secretary's role in the supply of high quality and timely information and the role of board portals in this regard;

- understand the board's role in monitoring and embedding a healthy corporate culture throughout the organisation;

- advise the board on the alternative procedures that could be adopted regarding independent professional advice;

- advise the board and the chair on what the annual board evaluation should cover and how it might be conducted; and.

- understand the objectives of induction and professional development programmes and the basic principles of their design.

Chapter five
Directors' duties and powers

CONTENTS

1. Introduction

This chapter sets the scene for considering the corporate governance role of the board and its members by outlining the position under the general law regarding the duties and powers of directors. In particular, it examines the general duties of directors under the CA2006, some of which lie at the heart of the UK corporate governance regime.

2. Powers of directors

In the UK, the directors of a company derive their powers from its **articles of association**, rather than anything in legislation. Although the Companies Act 2006 (CA2006) requires every company to have at least one director (or at least two for public companies), it does not really confer any management powers on them. It deliberately leaves the division of powers between the shareholders and the directors to be determined in the company's articles of association.

Almost without exception, articles of association delegate wide powers to the directors. If they did not do so, nearly all decisions would have to be taken by a majority vote of the shareholders, either by written resolution or at a general meeting. This would be impractical for most purposes even in a small owner-managed company, let alone a listed company with thousands of shareholders.

2.1 General management powers

Articles of association routinely make the directors collectively responsible for 'managing the company's business' and confer upon them (acting as a board) all the powers of the company necessary to do so. For example, article 3 of the CA2006 **model articles** for public limited companies states: 'subject to the articles, the directors are responsible for the management of the company's business, for which purpose they may exercise all the powers of the company.'

The wording in article 3 does not mean that each individual director can exercise these powers. The directors must exercise their powers collectively by a majority decision of the board, unless they are allowed under the articles to delegate those powers to someone else.

Provisions such as article 3 above are known as the 'general management clause'. They confer on the directors the powers necessary to manage the business and can only be used for those purposes. For example, the general management clause does not give the directors power to reject a share transfer. They need a 'special power' to do that.

In addition, the directors' general management powers can be subject to limitations which arise under:

◆ an objects clause, which limits the powers of the company, and therefore the powers of the directors (for example, if a company has an objects clause which limits the types of business the company may operate, the directors would be in breach of their duty to act within the company's powers if they decided to expand the business into an area not covered by the objects clause);

◆ an article imposing some sort of specific limit on the directors' powers, like a borrowing limit;

◆ an article allowing the members to give directions to the directors (see below);

◆ a shareholders' agreement – which could require shareholder approval for certain types of decisions which would normally fall within the directors' powers;

◆ the Companies Acts and other rules or regulations – which often impose a requirement for shareholder approval and may impose procedural conditions.

Company secretaries/governance professionals have to be alert to these potential restrictions and are expected to advise the board on whether matters are within the directors' powers.

model articles of association
Part of a companies constitution. Model articles are set out in CA2006 and automatically apply if a limited company is incorporated in the UK without registering its own articles.

2.2 Special powers

Invariably, articles of association also give the directors various special powers that they would not otherwise have under the general management clause. The power to delegate is one of those special powers. If a decision that the directors are proposing to make does not feel like a management decision and there are no special powers authorising them to make that decision, shareholder approval may be required. Share transfers are a good example of this. Rejecting a share transfer does not feel like a decision concerning the management of the business. It relates to the composition of the company's membership. Accordingly, directors need a special power in order to reject share transfers.

2.3 Power to delegate

Articles of association invariably allow the directors to delegate their powers and, in practice, this is what they do, recognising that a board which meets, say, once a month cannot possibly manage the business on a day-to-day basis.

For example, article 5 of the Model Articles for public limited companies states:

5. Directors may delegate

◆   Subject to the articles, the directors may delegate any of the powers which are conferred on them under the articles—

–   (a) to such person or committee;
–   (b) by such means (including by power of attorney);
–   (c) to such an extent;
–   (d) in relation to such matters or territories; and
–   (e) on such terms and conditions;
     as they see fit.

◆   If the directors so specify, any such delegation may authorise further delegation of the directors' powers by any person to whom they are delegated.

◆   The directors may revoke any delegation in whole or part, or alter its terms and conditions.

Boards usually delegate extensive management powers to the executive directors. These powers typically flow through the chief executive officer as the leader of the executive team. Executives are usually allowed to sub-delegate their powers to other people in the organisation. This does not necessarily happen by a literal chain of delegation down to the most junior employee. Most boards use a combination of formal delegation (e.g. to executive directors) and the adoption of company-wide policies and procedures, which set authority limits for the various tiers of management.

2.4 Shareholders' reserve power to give directions

As a general rule, where a company's articles confer a power on the directors, the shareholders cannot then exercise that power themselves unless the articles provide some sort of mechanism enabling them to do so. This is the case even though the shareholders are, in effect, the people who delegated those powers to the directors.

Most articles give shareholders a reserve power to issue directions to the directors but invariably require them to do so by passing a special resolution for these purposes. For example, article 4 of the Model Articles for public limited companies allows shareholders to instruct the directors by special resolution to take, or refrain from taking, specified action. However, it provides that a resolution of this nature has no effect on the validity of anything which the directors have already done before the resolution is passed. For example, there would be no point in the members passing a special resolution to prevent the directors from selling part of the business, if that sale had already taken place.

In practice, shareholders rarely use these powers. Shareholder activists sometimes do so as part of a campaign designed to put pressure on the company to change, say, its environmental policies. They typically do so more to gain publicity for their cause than in the expectation of victory. It is easier for shareholders who oppose the actions of management to seek the removal of the existing directors and to appoint new people in their place, both of which can be done by ordinary resolution, albeit one that requires special notice.

Test yourself 5.1

1. **Where might you find limitations on the directors' management powers?**

2. **Identify at least two special powers that are usually conferred by articles on the directors.**

3. **Is setting the company's strategy is a management decision?**

4. **Can shareholders interfere in the management of a company?**

3. General duties of directors under the Companies Act 2006

Directors have many duties under the CA2006. Most of these duties give rise to potential criminal sanctions. For example, the directors of a company can be prosecuted if it fails to file its accounts at Companies House on time. The Act usually places a cap on the financial penalties that can be imposed for each offence, which in the case of late filing of the accounts is £5,000. These financial penalties are paid into general government funds.

Directors also have a number of civil duties under the CA2006. These duties are set out in Part 10, Chapter 2, ss. 171–177 and are referred to as the 'general duties of directors'. Some people still refer to them as the common law or fiduciary duties of directors as they derive from common law and equitable principles developed by the courts over many years. The UK government decided to codify these duties in the CA2006 in order to make them more accessible and easier for directors to understand.

The general duties are owed by the directors to the company and concern the manner in which they carry out their functions as agents of the company. They set certain minimum standards of conduct and behaviour on the part of the directors. If they act in breach of these duties, they can be sued by the company in civil proceedings, which may result in them having to pay the company compensation for any losses that it suffered or account to the company for any **secret profits** they made. There is no limit to the amount of compensation that may be awarded in these civil cases.

As the duties are owed to the company, only the company can bring an action against the directors for a breach of the general duties. As an exception to this rule, shareholders can bring what is known as a 'derivative' action in the name of the company. However, if they win, any compensation is still paid to the company, rather than to the shareholders who brought the action.

secret profit
A profit that is not revealed. In the context of corporate governance, a director should not make a secret profit for his/her personal benefit and at the expense of the company.

3.1 Common law and fiduciary duties of directors

Section 170 of the CA2006 confirms that the general duties of directors set out in the Part 10, Chapter 2 (ss. 171–177) 'are based on certain common law rules and equitable principles as they apply to directors, and have effect in place of those rules and principles as regards the duties owed to a company by a director'. It goes on to say that the statutory general duties should be interpreted in the same way as the common law rules and equitable principles. Accordingly, most of the historic case law is still relevant today for the purposes of interpreting the relevant statutory provisions.

Most of the common law rules developed by the courts for directors were based on the rules that they already applied to trustees. This is why some of the duties are referred to as fiduciary duties.

fiduciary duty
A legal obligation of one party to act in the best interest of another.

A 'fiduciary' is a person in a position of trust. A **fiduciary duty** is therefore one owed by a person in a position of trust. A trustee is an obvious example of a person in a position of trust. The courts decided that company directors are also in a position of trust because they act as agents of the company, make contracts on its behalf and control the company's property.

The fiduciary duties that trustees owe to the beneficiaries of a trust include duties:

◆ to act in good faith in the interests of the beneficiaries;
◆ to act in accordance with the trust deed;
◆ not to make a profit from their position;
◆ not to place themselves in a position where their own interest conflicts with their fiduciary duties;
◆ not to act to their own advantage or the benefit of a third person without the beneficiary's informed consent;
◆ to properly invest trust property.

You will see close parallels between these duties and the general duties of directors which follow, subject to one notable exception. That exception relates to the duty of directors to exercise due skill, care and diligence. Strictly speaking, this duty does not derive from the fiduciary duties and was developed separately by the courts.

3.2 Summary of the general duties of directors

The general duties of directors under ss. 171–177 of the CA2006 are as follows:

◆ to act within their powers in accordance with the company's constitution (and to use those powers for proper purposes) (s. 171);

◆ to promote the success of the company (s. 172);

◆ to exercise independent judgement (s. 173);

◆ to exercise reasonable care, skill and diligence (s. 174);

◆ to avoid conflicts of interest (s. 175);

◆ not to accept benefits from third parties (s. 176); and

◆ to declare any interest in proposed transactions or arrangements (s. 177).

Section 170 confirms that these duties are owed by a director to the company and apply equally to any **shadow director**. It is also worth noting that the duties apply to both executive and non-executive directors.

shadow director
A person in accordance with whose instructions the directors of a company are accustomed to act and who has not been formally appointed as a director.

3.3 Consequences of a breach of the general duties

The CA2006 states that the consequences of a breach of a director's general duties are the same as if the corresponding common law rule or equitable principle applied, but it does not set out in detail what those consequences are. In practice, the remedies available to the company depend on the nature of the breach.

As a general rule, directors can be made to repay any illegal payments they have received or secret profits they have made. Where there is a breach of the duty of skill and care or the directors have acted beyond their powers, the company can be awarded compensation for any losses that it has suffered. Where the directors have acted outside their powers, the courts cannot normally declare the transaction void. However, where the directors have used their powers for improper purposes, the transaction can be declared void (see Section 4.1). Where a director has failed to disclose an interest in a transaction, the company can choose whether or not to treat that transaction as void.

Further details on these remedies can be found in the succeeding paragraphs for each of the general duties. It is, of course, part of the company secretary's job to ensure that the directors understand their duties, and it is a good idea to reinforce such training with practical examples from case law of the consequences of a breach.

Test yourself 5.2

1.   **Which of the general duties of directors arise from which of the fiduciary duties of trustees?**

2.   **What is a fiduciary?**

3.   **What are the remedies for a breach of the general duties?**

4. Duty to act within powers and for proper purposes

4.1   Duty to act within powers

Under s. 171, directors have a duty to act within their powers in accordance with the company's constitution and should only exercise powers for the purposes for which they are given.

A company's constitution is defined in s. 17 of the CA2006 as including:

◆   its articles of association (including any provisions in the memorandum of association of a company incorporated before 1 October 2009 that are treated as article provisions under s. 28); and

◆   any resolution or agreement that must be filed at Companies House in accordance with Part 3, Chapter 3 of the CA2006 (e.g., a shareholders' ordinary resolution authorising the directors to allot shares).

A breach of the duty to act within their powers may arise where:

◆   an individual director or the board does something that is beyond the company's powers; or

◆   an individual director or the board does something that is within the company's powers but not within their own powers.

As mentioned previously, the directors' general management powers under the articles may be subject to certain limitations in its constitution. For example, an objects clause may restrict the type of business activities the company may undertake or the articles could contain a borrowing limit.

If the directors act beyond the company's powers or their own powers and the company suffers a loss as a result of this breach of duty, the company can sue the relevant directors in order to recover that loss. Most cases in this area concern examples where the directors have acted outside the company's powers. Such a case could arise where, for example, a company has an objects clause which limits its business activities to, say, operating supermarkets in the UK. If the directors of this company sought to expand the business overseas and in the process the company suffered considerable losses, it could sue the directors to recover those losses. If the unlawful business venture had been successful, it would be pointless for the company to sue as there would be no losses capable of being recovered.

There have been surprisingly few cases of this nature against directors, probably because companies have always tended to adopt objects clauses that impose very few restrictions on what the company can do. Companies (other than charities) are no longer required to have an objects clause, and if they do not have one their objects are deemed to be unrestricted. If a company still has an objects clause, it still operates as a limitation on the company's powers. Given the choice, directors would probably prefer to operate without an objects clause. However, shareholders may prefer to have one in order to prevent the directors from expanding into areas in which both they and the company have no experience.

In the past, if the directors caused a company to enter into a transaction that was outside its powers, that transaction would be treated as void and could not therefore be enforced by third parties. The CA2006 now provides that:

◆ the validity of an act done by a company shall not be called into question on the ground of any lack of capacity by reason of anything in the company's constitution (s. 39); and

◆ in favour of a person dealing with a company in good faith, the power of the board of directors to bind the company is deemed to be free of any limitation under the company's constitution (s. 40).

Section 40 goes on to say that a person dealing with the company:

◆ is not bound to enquire whether there are any such limitations in the company's constitution;

◆ is presumed to have acted in good faith unless proved otherwise; and

◆ is not to be regarded as having acted in bad faith merely because they knew the act was beyond the powers of the directors.

This means that third parties will generally be able to enforce a contract against the company even though it was illegal for the directors to enter in that contract on its behalf.

These rules do not affect the potential liability of the directors to compensate the company for any losses arising from their breach of duty. In addition, a contract or arrangement entered into by the board with an individual director would not be protected because the director concerned would not be viewed as a person dealing with the company in good faith.

The duty under s. 171 to act in accordance with the company's constitution also means that the directors must comply with any procedural requirements set out in the articles. On its own, a breach of a procedural requirement will not necessarily give rise to any liability unless the company suffers a loss as a consequence of that breach. Cases of this nature are also surprisingly rare.

4.2 Duty to exercise powers for proper purposes

The second limb of the rule in s.171, that directors must only exercise their powers for the purposes for which they are conferred, means that they must not exercise their powers for any collateral purpose other than the purpose(s) for which the power was, on the true interpretation of the articles, conferred.

Cases under this second limb of s. 171 are much more common than under the first. Many of them concern abuses by directors of their power to allot and issue new shares. For example, in Hogg v. Cramphorn Ltd [1967] the directors, fearing a takeover bid, allotted shares to parties likely to support them and thereby enable them to continue in office. The court declared the allotment void. The primary purpose of any power to allot new shares is to raise new capital as and when required. The directors were found to have for an improper collateral purpose.

The duty to exercise powers for proper purposes has also been used to challenge directors' decisions:

◆   on the forfeiture of shares;

◆   on the approval of share transfers;

◆   to enter into a management agreement that effectively deprived shareholders of their constitutional right to appoint new directors; and

◆   to enter into a supplementary partnership agreement that exposed the company to a serious contingent liability.

The importance of this duty should not be underestimated. It is not sufficient for the directors of a company to act in what they consider to be the best interests of the company. They must also use their powers for proper purposes. This was demonstrated in a recent Supreme Court case, Eclairs Group Ltd and Glengary Overseas Ltd v JKX Oil & Gas plc [2016], in which the court overruled the exercise by the directors of JKX Oil & Gas of a power in the articles enabling them to impose restrictions on the shares held by the plaintiffs for failing to respond adequately to a s.793 notice (s.793 of CA2006 allows public companies to require shareholders to provide information about the beneficial ownership of the company's shares). The court held that the directors' primary motivation for imposing the restrictions was to prevent the plaintiffs from voting against certain resolutions at its 2013 AGM. Even though the directors were acting in what they considered to be the best interests of the company, this was held to be an improper purpose and therefore rendered their decision invalid.

Test yourself 5.3

1.   **Why are directors rarely sued for exceeding their powers?**

2.   **Why do you think there are a lot more cases about directors using their powers for improper purposes?**

3.   **What are the consequences of the directors exceeding their powers and how do these compare with cases where they have used their powers for improper purposes?**

5. Duty to promote the success of the company

Section 172 imposes a duty on the directors to exercise their powers in good faith in what they consider – not what a court may consider – would be most likely to promote the success of the company for the benefit of its members as a whole, and in doing so have regard (amongst other matters) to:

◆ the likely consequences of any decision in the long term;

◆ the interests of the company's employees;

◆ the need to foster business relationships with suppliers, customers and others;

◆ the impact of the company's operations on the community and the environment;

◆ the desirability for the company to maintain a reputation for high standards of business conduct;

◆ the need to act fairly as between members of the company.

It is important to note that this duty can only be enforced by the company and not by any of the stakeholders to whom the directors are meant to have regard.

Even though it does not appear first in the CA2006, the duty to promote the success of the company can be considered to be the primary duty of directors. This is reflected in the UK Corporate Governance Code, which uses very similar words to describe the overarching role of the board and makes reference to stakeholder interests.

When it was first introduced, many commentators thought that s. 172 represented a significant change to what was previously understood to be the position under the common law, in that it created a duty on the part of the directors to take into account the interests of other stakeholders. The previous formulation of this duty was usually summarised as being that the directors had a duty to act in good faith in what they consider to be the best interests of the company (as represented by the present and future shareholders).

Directors sometimes used this old formulation to argue that they could not, for example, legally spend any money cleaning up pollution caused by the company (unless required by law to do so) as it would not be in the best interests of its shareholders. This was never really the position under the common law, which has always allowed the directors to take stakeholders' interests into account. Under what became s. 307 of the Companies Act 1985, directors already had a duty to take into account the interests of employees. That duty was owed to the company and did not create any enforceable rights on the part of the employees. Similarly, the duties under s. 172 do not create any enforceable rights on the part of stakeholders such as employees, customers or suppliers.

Various bodies expressed concern that the new formulation may require boards to change their decision-making procedures so that they can show compliance with the duty to take into account stakeholder interests. This was denied by ministers during the passage of the CA2006. The GC100 Group has issued guidance on the practicalities of complying with s. 172 (Companies Act (2006) – Directors' Duties, 2007), which suggests that:

◆ Where the nature of the decision … is such that it is supported by a formal process, that process need only specifically record consideration of those duties where the particular circumstances make it particularly necessary or relevant. The default position should be not to include these references. The background papers put to the board is a key way of assisting directors in properly taking into account all relevant factors relating to their decision (the specified factors should be considered by those preparing the paper, while preparing the paper).

◆ Board minutes should not be used as the main medium for recording the extent to which the specified factors were discussed.

The duty to promote the success of the company can create problems for directors of subsidiaries. The principal duty of the directors of a subsidiary company is to promote the success of that subsidiary company. Under the CA2006t, directors are required to take the interests of other stakeholders into account. Those other stakeholders include the shareholders, which in the case of a subsidiary means its parent company. However, the interests of its stakeholders are not meant to override the interests of the company itself.

Case study 5.1

Charterbridge Corporation v. Lloyds Bank [1970]

In a case decided under the former common law rules, a subsidiary company mortgaged some land to secure the indebtedness of its parent. The directors of the subsidiary were sued for failing to act in the best interests of the subsidiary. The court ruled that the directors were not liable. The directors of a group company are required to have regard to the interests of the individual company and not to those of the group as a whole but this would not of itself involve a breach of duty if an 'intelligent and honest' person in the position of the directors could have reasonably believed the transaction to be in the interests of the individual company.

small company
In broad terms, a small company for accounting purposes is one which meets at least two of the following criteria: turnover of not more than £10.2 million; balance sheet total of not more than £5.1 million; or average number of employees must not exceed 50.

medium-sized company
In broad terms, a medium-sized company for accounting purposes is one which meets at least two of the following criteria: turnover of not more than £36 million; balance sheet total of not more than £18 million; or average number of employees must not exceed 250.

5.1   Section 172 statement in the strategic report

Section 414C of the CA2006 states that the purpose of the strategic report is to inform members of the company and help them assess how the directors have performed their duty under s. 172 to promote the success of the company.

Section 414CZA requires all large companies (whether quoted, unquoted, public or private) to include a s. 172 statement in the strategic report for financial years commencing on or after 1 January 2019. **Small-** and **medium-sized companies** are exempt from this requirement, unless in the latter case they are part of an ineligible group.

The s. 172(1) statement must describe how the directors have had regard to the matters set out in s. 172(1)(a) to (f) when performing their duty under s. 172 to promote the success of the company. These matters can broadly be summarised as the stakeholder interests.

Guidance on what the s. 172(1) statement should cover can be found in the latest 2018 edition of the FRC's Guidance on the Strategic Report. The GC100 Group also published further guidance for directors in 2018 on the stakeholder considerations associated with s. 172 (Guidance on Directors' Duties – Section 172 and Stakeholder Considerations). Further details on both guidance documents can be found in Chapter 14.

Test yourself 5.4

1. **According to the CA2006, what is the purpose of the strategic report?**

2. **What does 'promoting the success of the company' mean?**

3. **Do the directors need to consider stakeholder interests whenever they make a decision?**

6. Duty to exercise independent judgement

Section 173 of the CA2006 provides that a director must exercise independent judgement. This means that they must not fetter their discretion. For example, a director will be in breach of this duty if they make an arrangement with an outsider to vote in the outsider's interests on a particular transaction, thereby leaving themselves with no independent discretion to consider the company's interests in the matter (Re Englefield Colliery Co [1878]).

The duty applies to both executive and non-executive directors and does not depend on whether they are considered 'independent' for the purpose of the UK Corporate Governance Code.

The duty to exercise independent judgement does not prevent a director from acting in accordance with an agreement entered into by the company (which could include a shareholder agreement if the company is a party to that agreement) or from acting in a way authorised by the company's constitution (e.g. acting in accordance with a direction given by shareholders under the articles).

The duty can cause difficulties for directors who represent outside interests. The position under the law seems to be that a director, who, without any concealment and with the consent of the company, seeks to protect the interests of an outsider on the board will not be in breach of this duty as long as they preserve a substantial degree of independent discretion and do not allow the interests of the outsider to override the interests of the company.

It should be noted in this regard that directors are required to take into account the interests of other stakeholders under s. 172, but that their overriding duty is to promote the success of the company.

The ICSA guidance note on 'Directors' general duties' comments as follows on this duty.

◆ A director must not allow personal interests to affect his or her independent judgement. This means that if the board is considering a contract in which a director has a personal interest, ideally he or she should leave the meeting while the matter is being discussed. This is also relevant to the duty of directors to avoid any conflict of interest with the company.

◆ An executive director should not attend a board meeting to 'promote a collective executive line'. He or she should attend the board meeting in his or her own right and give the board the benefit of his or her independent opinion.

◆ Similarly, directors representing a particular interest should 'set any representative function aside and make final decisions on their own merits'. For example, a director who is a representative of a family interest in the company 'may consult his family but be clear that he will make the final decision'.

Finally, it should be noted that the duty to exercise independent judgement does not prevent a director from taking advice and acting on it.

Case study 5.2

Scottish Co-operative Wholesale Society v Meyer [1959]

A holding company deliberately and successfully 'starved out' its partly owned subsidiary by not providing it with business contracts on which its livelihood depended. Although the case was decided on other grounds, the House of Lords indicated that the three directors who were nominees of the holding company on the board of the subsidiary were in breach of their duty to exercise independent judgement through their failure to take any positive steps to protect the subsidiary against the oppressive policy of the holding company.

7. Duty to exercise reasonable skill, care and diligence

Directors have a duty under s. 174 to exercise reasonable skill, care and diligence in the performance of their duties. This was one of the common law duties that became a statutory duty under the CA2006. It does not derive from the fiduciary duties of trustees. Directors may be found to be in breach of this duty if they acted negligently.

For many years, the leading case in this area was Re City Equitable Fire Insurance

Co [1925], in which Romer J ruled that directors need not exhibit in the performance of their duties a greater degree of skill than may reasonably be expected from a person of their knowledge and experience.

Section 174(2) now sets a more rigorous and objective standard. It follows later cases, such as Re D'Jan of London Ltd [1993], in providing that the standards against which directors should be judged are those of:

'a reasonably diligent person with—

◆ the general knowledge, skill and experience that may reasonably be expected of a person carrying out the functions carried out by the director in relation to the company, and

◆ the general knowledge, skill and experience that the director has.'

The original Re City Equitable Fire Insurance test was wholly subjective. It could be summarised as saying that if you had the misfortune to appoint a fool as a director, you could only expect them to behave like one.

The modern formulation still includes a subjective test ('the general knowledge, skill and experience that the director has'). However, that test no longer acts as the lowest threshold for determining what is reasonable skill and care. This is set by the more objective test in which the director's conduct is compared against the general knowledge, skill and experience that may reasonably be expected of a person carrying out the same functions in relation to the company.

Under this objective test, a finance director would typically be expected to know more about finance than other directors. However, under the subjective test, a non-executive director with a financial background would be expected to bring that experience to bear and would be held to a higher standard on financial matters than those with no such financial background.

The duty of skill, care and diligence does not require directors to give continuous attention to the affairs of the company. Their duties are of an intermittent nature to be performed at periodical board meetings and at meetings of any committee of the board upon which they happen to be placed, although they ought to attend whenever, in the circumstances, they are reasonably able to do so (Re City Equitable Fire Insurance Co).

This requirement is probably best understood with regard to non-executive directors, who will typically only attend to the company's business at board or committee meetings and, possibly, the annual general meeting (AGM). The position is different for executive directors because they are also employees of the company with a contract of service. That contract will require them to attend to the company's business on a full- or part-time basis.

Unless there are particular grounds for suspecting dishonesty or incompetence, a director is entitled to leave the routine conduct of the company's affairs to the management. If the management appears honest, the directors may rely on the information they provide. It is not part of their duty of skill and care to question whether the information is reliable, or whether important information is being withheld.

The courts in the UK are generally reluctant to condemn business decisions made by directors that appear, in hindsight, to show errors of judgement. Directors can exercise reasonable skill and care, but still make bad decisions.

For a legal action against a director to succeed, a company would have to prove that serious negligence had occurred. It would not be enough to demonstrate that some loss could have been avoided if the director had been a bit more careful. For this reason, successful legal actions against directors for breach of this duty are relatively uncommon.

Case study 5.3

Dorchester Finance Co. Ltd v Stebbing [1989]

Dorchester Finance, a money-lending business, brought an action against its directors for negligence and misappropriation of the company's property. The company had three directors, S, H and P. S was a qualified accountant and acted as managing director; H and P were non-executives. One was an accountant. The other had considerable accountancy and business experience. S secretly arranged for the company to make loans to persons connected with him and persuaded P and H to sign blank cheques for this purpose. The loans turned out to be irrecoverable. It was held that all three directors were liable to pay damages to the company. S, as an executive director, was held to be grossly negligent. P and H, as non-executives, were held to have failed to show the necessary level of skill and care in performing their duties as non-executives, even though it was accepted that they had acted in good faith at all times.

Case study 5.4

Norman v Theodore Goddard [1991]

In this case it was held that a director was not liable for the theft of company money by a senior partner in a firm of solicitors as he had no reason to doubt that other person's honesty.

7.1 Delegation and the duty of skill and care

The case of Norman v Theodore Goddard above (case study 5.4) is an example of a director being allowed to trust the honesty of other company officials. However, in other cases, it has been ruled that delegation by the directors does not absolve them completely from the duty to exercise skill and care. They can be found to be in breach of that duty if they fail to exercise adequate supervision over those performing those delegated functions (see case study 5.5).

The power to delegate does not allow the directors to abdicate their functions in favour of some other person as manager. Nor does it allow them to place

unquestioning reliance upon others to do their job. They must retain the power
of overall control.

Case study 5.5

Re Barings plc and others (1998)

**Andrew Tuckey, the former deputy chairman of Barings bank, was
responsible for the supervision of Nick Leeson, the derivatives trader
whose unauthorised trading brought the bank close to collapse in 1995.**

**In a case concerning the disqualification of Tuckey as a director, it was
alleged that he had failed to exercise his duty of skill and care to the
company by failing to exercise adequate supervision over Leeson's
activities.**

**It was held that Tuckey had failed in his duties because he did not have
sufficient knowledge and understanding of the nature of the derivatives
markets and the risks involved in derivatives dealing (which led to the
collapse of Barings).**

**He was therefore unable to consider properly matters referred to the
committee he chaired, which was responsible for supervising Nick
Leeson's activities.**

Test yourself 5.5

1. **What tests should be applied in judging whether a director has
    breached the duty of skill and care?**

2. **To what extent can directors rely on other company officials?**

8. Duty to avoid conflicts of interest

Director have a duty under s. 175 of the CA2006 to avoid conflicts of interest.
Under this duty they must avoid a situation in which they have, or can have,
a direct or indirect interest that conflicts, or possibly may conflict, with the
interests of the company.

Section 175(2) clarifies that this duty applies in particular to the exploitation of
any property, information or opportunity. Section 175(3) clarifies that it does not
apply to a conflict of interest arising in relation to a transaction or arrangement
with the company in which a director has an interest. This type of conflict is
dealt with separately by ss. 177 and 182 of the CA2006.

Directors are liable as trustees if property under their control is misapplied, e.g.
applied outside their powers. This means that a director who wrongly makes a
profit by exploiting a business opportunity that belongs to the company can be
made to repay that profit. The courts may also rule that a third party acquiring
company property through a breach of duty by directors holds that property on

behalf of the company as a constructive trustee and, as a result, can be forced to return it.

Case study 5.6

Regal (Hastings) Ltd v Gulliver [1942]

Regal formed a subsidiary to take up the lease of two cinemas, but the owner of the cinemas insisted that the subsidiary have a paid-up share capital which, in the honest opinion of Regal's directors, was more than the company could afford. The directors accordingly subscribed for part of the balance themselves. The cinemas were eventually sold and the company sued the directors for the profits they had made through their investment in the subsidiary. They were held liable despite the fact that:

◆   **the directors were held to have acted honestly throughout;**

◆   **the company could not have completed the transaction without the additional investment;**

◆   **it had not suffered any loss as a result of the transaction;**

◆   **the directors probably could have secured shareholder approval for their involvement in the transaction; and**

◆   **none of the shareholders at the time of the proceedings was a shareholder at the time the profit was made;**

◆   **In effect, the court ruled that the only thing that would have saved the directors would have been for them to obtain authority from the company's shareholders for their participation in the transaction.**

Under s. 175 of the CA2006, the non-conflicted directors may now authorise conflicts such as the exploitation of business opportunities. This is the case for a private company unless the articles provide otherwise. In the case of a public company the articles must specifically allow the board to authorise such conflicts.

Irreconcilable conflicts of interest would arise if a director of a competitor joined the board. In the competing areas, any business opportunity could be viewed as a diversion of an opportunity from the other company. The directors who are conflicted in this regard cannot be counted in determining whether there is a quorum at the meeting on the matter and cannot vote on it. If they do vote, those votes must be ignored. If there are not enough non-conflicted directors to make a decision, only the members will be able to authorise the conflict.

Even though two companies may not necessarily compete directly in their main area of business, they may compete in some subsidiary areas of business. This is the reason why lawyers often suggest that all outside appointments should be authorised as a potential conflict of interest. Directors might be protected from liability in these circumstances by s. 175(4), which provides that the duty to avoid conflicts of interest is not infringed if the situation cannot reasonably be regarded as likely to give rise to a conflict of interest. However, it is very difficult to judge when this exception may apply.

Case study 5.7

Industrial Development Consultants Ltd v Cooley [1972]

The managing director of a design and construction company, who was an architect himself, failed in an attempt to win a valuable contract for the company. He was subsequently approached by the potential client with an offer to take up the contract in his private capacity. The client confirmed that it was still not prepared to offer the contract to the company. The managing director concealed this offer from the company and took it up himself. In order to do so he falsely represented to the company that he needed to retire on the grounds of ill health. He was held liable to account to the company for the profit he obtained from performing the contract on the basis that he put his own personal interest as a potential contracting party in direct conflict with his pre-existing and continuing duty as managing director of the company.

Test yourself 5.6

1. **What sort of conflicts does s. 175 of the CA2006 relate to?**

2. **What are the consequences of a breach of this duty?**

3. **Who can authorise conflicts of interest and what is the effect of authorisation?**

9. Duty not to accept benefits from third parties

Under s. 176 of the CA2006, directors must not accept any benefit from a third party, whether conferred by reason of them being a director or them doing (or not doing) anything as director.

A third party in this context means someone other than the company or any other member of the same group (including a person acting on their behalf). However, directors will not be in breach of this duty if their services (as a director or otherwise) are provided through a third party, such as an outside services company.

The duty not to accept benefits from a third party is clearly related to the duty to avoid conflicts of interest. By accepting such benefits, directors clearly put themselves in a position of potential conflict which may compromise their independent judgement and their duty to act in good faith to promote the success of the company.

The link between the duty to avoid conflicts and the duty not to accept benefits from a third party is reinforced by s. 176(4), which provides that the duty not to accept benefits will not be infringed if the acceptance of the benefit cannot reasonably be regarded as likely to give rise to a conflict of interest.

A clear and obvious example of a breach of the duty not to accept benefits would be for a director to accept a bribe in return for awarding a contract to a supplier (Boston Deep Sea Fishing and Ice Co Ltd v Ansell [1888]). Another example would be for a director to accept a secret benefit from a third party in connection with a takeover bid or reconstruction (General Exchange Bank v Horner [1870]).

It is almost inconceivable that a director could be found to be in breach of this duty for accepting an occasional invitation to lunch or dinner from a customer or supplier. These could not reasonably be regarded as giving rise to a conflict of interest. However, the acceptance of an all-expenses-paid trip to a high value corporate hospitality event (such as the Monaco Grand Prix) might conceivably be pushing the boundaries as to what might be acceptable.

In practice, the threshold as to what is or is not considered acceptable in this area will be influenced far more by the policies which the company adopts for the purposes of compliance with the Bribery Act 2010 (see Chapter 13). Directors are responsible for a company's arrangements concerning compliance with the Bribery Act. The Act made the giving or accepting of bribes illegal and introduced a corporate offence of failing to prevent bribery. Under that offence, a company risks prosecution for the illegal acts of employees or agents unless it can show that it had 'adequate procedures' in place to combat bribery.

Ministry of Justice guidance on the procedures that businesses need to put in place to provide a defence against prosecution under the Bribery Act suggests that companies need to adopt strict internal anti-bribery policies, including policies on matters such as the acceptance of gifts and corporate hospitality. Such a policy might preclude directors from accepting any gifts or allow them to accept small gifts but not to keep them. The policy may require directors to obtain clearance before accepting any benefits from third parties and/or require all instances of gifts or hospitality to be recorded in a register.

By their nature, anti-bribery policies should help to ensure that directors do not fall foul of their duty not to accept benefits from third parties. However, it is helpful to keep Companies Act compliance in mind as a subsidiary objective when designing such policies. For example, it might be a good idea to hold directors to higher standards than other employees.

10. Duty to declare interests in transactions

Directors have a general duty under s. 175 to avoid conflicts of interest. However, that general duty does not necessarily preclude them from having a direct or indirect interest in a transaction or arrangement that the company has entered into or is proposing to enter into. Section 175 specifically states that it does not apply to such interests.

10.1 Interests in proposed or existing transactions or arrangement

Instead, directors have a duty to declare any interests that they have in:

◆ any proposed transaction or arrangement with the company (s. 177); and

◆ any existing transaction or arrangement with the company (s. 182).

In the commercial world, it is almost inevitable that directors will have an interest in some transactions that the company enters into. This could, for example, arise because the individual is a director or shareholder of another company that is a customer or supplier. It could arise indirectly because their interest is held through a nominee or trust. The duty of directors under s. 177 to declare their interests in any proposed transaction or arrangement is an adaptation of one of the original fiduciary duties of directors under the common law. The original rule used to require directors to disclose such interests to the members in general meeting and for the potential conflict to be authorised by the members. This often proved to be impractical and companies began to adopt articles that modified these rules. The current duty under s. 177 is based on the typical provisions previously found in articles of association in this regard. As it is a civil duty, it gives rise to potential civil remedies in the event of a breach. These remedies are the same as those under the original common law rule. The company can force the director who failed to disclose the interest to repay any profits they made from the transaction. In addition, the company has the option to rescind the transaction. In these circumstances, the transaction is said to be voidable at the instance of the company. In other words, the company can choose whether or not to be bound by a contract.

The duty under s. 182 to declare interests in any existing transactions or arrangements is a statutory duty which gives rise to potential criminal penalties in the event of a breach. The maximum penalty is £5,000. It does not derive from the common law duties but could conceivably also lead to potential civil action for breach of statutory duty.

The basic position under the CA2006 now is that directors are allowed to have an interest in a proposed transaction or arrangement as long as they have declared that interest in accordance with the CA2006. Section 180 provides that, subject to any contrary provision in a company's articles, where s. 177 (duty to declare interest in proposed transaction or arrangement) is complied with, the transaction or arrangement is not liable to be set aside by virtue of any common law rule or equitable principle requiring the consent or approval of the members of the company. This was not the default position under the Companies Act 1985 or its predecessors. However, articles of association from that era usually included provisions that achieved the same outcome (see, for example, 1985 Table A, regulations 85 and 86).

It should be noted that, under the CA2006, it is not necessary for the board or the company to authorise any conflict of interest that may arise from a director's interest in a proposed or existing transaction or arrangement as long as the director has declared that interest in accordance with s. 177. By contrast, conflicts of interest arising under s. 175, such as the diversion of business opportunities, must be authorised by the non-conflicted directors in accordance with the procedures in that section or by the shareholders.

One could argue that by agreeing to enter into the transaction notwithstanding the fact that a director has declared an interest in it, the board has somehow authorised the interest.

10.2 Declarations of interest

Under s. 177, the declaration must be made to the other directors before the transaction is entered into. If there are no other directors, no declaration need be made. Declarations of interest can be made in a variety of ways, including at a meeting of directors, by general notice to the company or written notice to the other directors. The procedures for each method are designed to ensure that any declaration of interest is brought to the attention of the other directors before they or the company enters into the proposed transaction or arrangement.

It plainly makes sense that the other directors should be made aware of any potential conflicts of interest that their colleagues may have in this regard. It may, for example, help to explain why a particular individual has been promoting the transaction so enthusiastically or why the company does not appear to have put the proposed contract out to tender. Armed with this knowledge, the board might be more cautious about approving the proposal and might wish to review it.

Directors also need to declare their interests so that it can be decided whether they should be allowed to participate in the decision. Articles of association usually contain rules as to whether or not this is the case. In listed company articles the default position is usually that the interested directors cannot vote or be counted in the quorum on that matter, although they commonly make certain exceptions to that rule. One could also argue that disclosure is necessary to prevent directors from making secret profits.

It is easy to understand why the CA2006 requires directors to declare their interests in proposed transactions but less easy to understand why they are required to do so for existing transactions. One of the reasons is to ensure that the board is aware of any conflicts which may influence a director's opinion on whether, for example, the company should terminate an existing contract or seek to find a new supplier. In addition, it might not be sensible for the board to put a person who has a material interest in a contract in charge of managing that contract. If the company entered into the contract before the director joined the board, it would not otherwise know about these interests in existing transactions.

Another reason for the rule in s. 182 is that it creates a criminal sanction in the most serious cases where a director has failed to disclose an interest in a proposed transaction. There is no criminal penalty for failing to disclose an interest in a proposed transaction if the company never enters into that transaction. However, an offence is technically committed under s. 182 from the moment the company enters into the transaction if the director still has not made the necessary disclosure. It should be noted in this regard that notifications made for the purposes of s. 177 for a proposed transaction also serve as notice for the purposes of s. 182 if the company enters into that transaction.

Under both s. 177 and s. 182, directors are not required to make a declaration where they are not reasonably aware of the interest or where they are not reasonably aware of the transaction or arrangement in question.

In addition, they need not declare an interest:

◆ if it cannot reasonably be regarded as likely to give rise to a conflict of interest;

◆ if, or to the extent that, the other directors are already aware of it; or

◆ if, or to the extent that, it concerns the terms of their service contract.

However, if a declaration of interest under either s. 177 or s. 182 proves to be, or becomes, inaccurate or incomplete, a further declaration must be made.

10.3 Related party transactions

The Listing Rules include provisions that may require certain transactions in which one or more directors have an interest to be approved by shareholders in advance. These are known as the related party transaction rules. They are set out in LR 11 and only require shareholder approval if the result of any of the class tests for the transaction is 5% or more. However, details of all but the smallest transactions must also be announced (see Chapter 14).

Test yourself 5.7

1. **Do directors' interest in transactions and arrangement need to be authorised?**

2. **Why are directors required to disclose their interests in proposed transactions?**

3. **Why are they required to disclose their interests in existing transactions?**

11. Who can bring an action for a breach of the general duties

Section 170(1) of the CA2006 clarifies that the general duties of directors set out in ss. 171 to 177 are owed to the company. This means that only the company can bring an action against a director. In practice, boards of directors do not often relish the idea of suing themselves for a potential breach of duty, although they may be more inclined to do so with regard to a former director.

Most actions arise after a new board has been appointed or when a company is in liquidation. In the latter case, the decision whether to bring any legal action against existing or former directors will rest with the insolvency practitioner appointed to wind up the affairs of the company. The directors will have no say in the matter at this stage. Insolvency practitioners do not pursue every possible case as the costs can be prohibitive. They only tend to pursue those where there more than a reasonable prospect of success and the potential compensation outweighs the risks of losing.

11.1 Derivative actions

Recognising that directors rarely think it is a good idea to sue themselves, the CA2006 provides a procedure that allows shareholders to bring what is called a 'derivative action' in the name of the company against the directors. As mentioned previously, if the shareholders win such an action any compensation that is awarded is paid to the company, not to the shareholders. If the company is in financial difficulty, it is likely that other stakeholders, such as charge holders, creditors, preference shareholders, employees and pension schemes will be the main beneficiaries of any compensation awarded. Even if there is anything left for shareholders, those who brought the claim have to share the spoils with other shareholders who did not participate in bringing the claim. In view of these and other practical difficulties, it is hardly surprising that derivative actions are relatively uncommon.

The procedures for bringing a derivative action are set out in Part 11 of the CA2006. A derivative action can be brought in relation to an actual or proposed act or omission involving negligence, default, breach of duty or breach of trust by a director. There is no need to show that the company has suffered a financial loss. Minority shareholders are therefore able to bring actions against directors who have acted in a way that is preferential to a majority shareholder and has breached their duty to promote the interests of shares as a whole.

The procedures for making an application include safeguards designed to prevent shareholders from bringing unreasonable claims. One of the tests that the court must apply in deciding whether to allow a derivative action is whether a hypothetical director would consider it worth pursuing it in view of their duty under s. 172 to promote the success of the company. Where the act or omission has already occurred, the court must refuse permission if it was authorised by the company before it occurred or has been ratified after it occurred. For example, a conflict of interest may have been authorised under s. 175. Section 239 of the CA2006 deals with the procedure for ratification of directors' acts giving rise to liability.

The courts must also take into account any available evidence regarding the views of other members on whether the action should be pursued. Those other members must have no personal interest in the subject of the claim.

In practice, it is both expensive and time-consuming to pursue a derivative action. If the shareholders lose they will be liable to pay the other party's legal costs. Shareholders may sometimes threaten to initiate one in the hope that the directors or their insurers agree to settle the claim. If they refuse to do so, it may make more sense for shareholders to discuss their grievances with the company and to persuade the board to take measures to deal with the offending director or, where relevant, rely on the liquidator to do so.

Test yourself 5.8

1. **List the general duties of directors under Part 10, Chapter 2 of CA2006.**

2. **What is a derivative action?**

12. Fraudulent and wrongful trading

Where a company becomes insolvent, sanctions may be imposed on its directors under the Insolvency Act 1986. Fraudulent trading arises under s. 213 of the Insolvency Act 1986 where the directors have acted with intent to defraud creditors. In these circumstances, they may be required to contribute to the assets of the company. Fraudulent trading is also a criminal offence, even if the company does not go into liquidation (s. 993, CA 2006).

Directors may also be liable to contribute to the assets of the company if they are regarded as having authorised **wrongful trading** by the company under s. 214 of the Insolvency Act 1986. This liability will potentially arise where the directors allowed the company to continue trading even though they knew (or ought to have known) that there was no reasonable prospect that the company could avoid going into insolvent liquidation. It is a defence for a director to show that after becoming aware of the possibility of insolvent liquidation they took every reasonable step with a view to minimising the potential loss to creditors.

wrongful trading
Wrongful trading occurs when a company continues to trade when the directors are aware that the company had gone into (or would soon go into) insolvent liquidation.

The wrongful trading provision underlines the need for directors to insist on reviewing management accounts (including cash flow statements) at frequent intervals. Any director having doubts as to the continued solvency of the company should immediately take expert advice on their own and the company's position (immediate resignation is not necessarily the appropriate course).

13. Directors' and officers' insurance

In view of the heavy potential liabilities that directors (and other officers) face, it has become increasingly common for companies to effect and pay the premiums on an insurance policy (or policies) indemnifying directors and officers against such liabilities. This insurance is known as directors' and officers' insurance, or D&O insurance.

The UK Corporate Governance Code used to include a provision requiring listed companies to arrange such cover for directors (2016 Code provision A.1.3). This provision is no longer included in the 2018 Code or the 2018 FRC Guidance on Board Effectiveness, probably because the practice has become so well-established that it was no longer thought necessary.

Section 232 of the CA2006 generally renders void any attempt by a company to exempt its directors from any of their liabilities or to indemnify them against those liabilities. However, s. 233 specifically authorises companies to take out and maintain insurance policies on the directors' behalf as an exception to this rule.

One of the reasons why the CA2006 allows companies to take out such policies is that it is considerably cheaper to take out a group policy than for each individual director to arrange their own cover. If the directors had to take out their own policies and pay their own premiums, the company would still be paying for them indirectly. It would just cost more.

ICSA has issued a guidance note, 'Protection Against Directors' and Officers' Liabilities — Indemnities and Insurance', which was drawn up in 2015 with the assistance of the City of London Law Society, the ABI and the British Insurance Brokers' Association. The guidance note includes useful information on the types of cover available.

13.1 Indemnities

Section 232 declares that any provision (whether in a company's articles or in any contract) that purports to exempt or indemnify a director from any liability for negligence, default, breach of duty or breach of trust in relation to the company is void. Section 233 clarifies that this rule does not prevent a company arranging D&O insurance cover. Sections 234 and 235 provide two further exceptions to this rule. The exception in s. 234 allows (but does not require) companies to indemnify the directors against certain liabilities to third parties. These are known as qualifying third party indemnity provisions. These are defined (negatively) as excluding any indemnity:

◆ against any liability incurred by the director to the company or to any associated company;

◆ against any liability incurred by the director to pay a criminal or regulatory penalty; or

◆ against any liability incurred by the director:

– in defending criminal proceedings in which they are convicted;

– in defending any civil proceedings brought by the company, or an associated company, in which judgment is given against them; or

– in connection with any application for relief under s. 661(3) or (4) (acquisition of shares by innocent nominee) or s. 1157 (general power to grant relief in case of honest and reasonable conduct), where the court refuses to grant relief.

Indemnity provisions in articles or contracts often state that the directors are indemnified to the full extent allowed by law. In order to work out the scope of this type of indemnity you need to refer to the types of indemnities that are prohibited under ss. 232 and 234. Such an indemnity would not be effective against any liability for a breach of the general duties of directors under Part 10, Chapter 2 of the CA2006 because these duties are all owed to the company. However, it would be effective in a negligence case brought against a director by a third party that is not an associated company.

The exception in s. 235 permits companies to indemnify a director of a company acting as a trustee of an occupational pension scheme against liability incurred in connection with the company's activities as trustee of the scheme (a qualifying pension scheme indemnity provision).

Section 236 imposes disclosure requirements in relation to qualifying third party indemnity and qualifying pension scheme indemnity provisions. The directors' report must disclose whether any such provisions were in force at any time during the financial year covered by the report or at that time the directors' report was approved. In addition, ss. 237 and 238 require the terms of any such provisions to be made available for inspection and copying by members.

13.2 Funding of legal expenses

A company is not required to obtain members' approval (as would otherwise be required, in connection with loans to directors under ss. 197, 198, 200 or 201) for doing anything to provide a director with funds to meet expenditure incurred in defending any criminal or civil proceedings or an application for relief under s. 1157 (general power to grant relief in case of honest and reasonable conduct) or doing anything to enable a director to avoid incurring such expenditure (for example, insurance) (s. 205). Section 206 makes similar provision in connection with regulatory actions or investigations.

Chapter summary

◆ Directors derive their powers from a company's articles of association, rather than anything in legislation. Articles usually contain a 'general management clause' giving the directors all the powers necessary for the management of the business and confer certain special powers on the directors that they would not otherwise have under the general management clause.

◆ As a general rule shareholders cannot override decisions made by the directors under powers delegated to them by the articles. However, most articles include a reserve power enabling the shareholders to give binding directions by passing a special resolution.

◆ The general duties of directors under the CA2006 derive, for the most part, from common law rules and equitable principles developed by the courts for fiduciaries (people in a position of trust) or trustees.

◆ The general duties are owed to the company, which means that only the company can sue the directors in the event of a breach. Shareholders can bring a 'derivative action' in the name of the company but if they win any compensation is still awarded to the company, not the shareholders.

◆ The overarching duty of directors is promote the success of the company.

◆ Directors also have duties to:
  – to act within their powers and for proper purposes;
  – to exercise independent judgement;
  – to exercise reasonable care, skill and diligence;
  – to avoid conflicts of interest;
  – not to accept benefits from third parties; and
  – to declare any interest in proposed transactions or arrangements.

◆ The duty to avoid conflicts of interest in s. 175 deals mainly with the diversion of business opportunities by directors.

◆ Section 176 prohibits conflicts which could arise from a director accepting a benefit from a third party.

◆ Section 177 deals with the situation where a director has a direct or indirect interest in a transaction that the company is proposing to enter into.

◆ In the case of listed companies, certain transactions in which a director has an interest (known as related party transactions) must be approved by shareholders in advance.

◆ Directors also have a duty under s. 182 to declare any interest they may have in existing transactions and arrangements, including transactions that the company may have entered into before the director joined the company.

◆ As a general rule, directors can be made to repay any illegal payments they have received or secret profits they have made.

◆ Where there is a breach of the duty of skill and care or the directors have acted beyond their powers, the company can be awarded compensation for any losses that it has suffered.

◆ Where the directors have acted outside their powers, the courts cannot normally declare the transaction void. However, where the directors have used their powers for improper purposes, the transaction can be declared void. Where a director has failed to disclose an interest in a transaction, the company can choose whether or not to treat that transaction as void.

◆ Directors face considerable personal liability under the wrongful and fraudulent provisions of the Insolvency Act 1986 if they allow the company to continue trading while it is technically insolvent or act with deliberate intent to defraud creditors.

◆ Any provision in a company's articles or in any contract that purports to exempt or indemnify a director from any liability for negligence, default, breach of duty or breach of trust in relation to the company is void under CA2006, s. 232.

◆ However, s. 233 specifically authorises companies to take out and maintain insurance policies on the directors' behalf.

Chapter six
Role and membership of the board of directors

CONTENTS

1. Introduction

This chapter summarises the role of the board in the management of the business and the role of the various board participants, including the chair, chief executive, executive directors, non-executive directors and the senior independent director. It focuses, in particular on the roles that these different participants are expected to play under the UK Corporate Governance Code and the FRC Guidance on Board Effectiveness.

2. Role of the board

As mentioned in Chapter 5, articles of association routinely make the directors collectively responsible for 'managing the company's business' but allow them to delegate wide management powers to the executive management team led by the chief executive officer. In practice this is what the boards of most listed companies do and the question then arises over what residual role the board should play in managing the business.

2.1   Governance role under the Code

According to Principle A of the 2018 UK Corporate Governance Code (the Code) the overarching role of the board is to:

'...promote the long-term sustainable success of the company, generating value for shareholders and contributing to wider society.'

Although this wording is in keeping with the duty of directors under s. 172 of the CA2006, it obviously needs fleshing out if it is to be of any practical use to boards of directors. Accordingly, Principles B to E of the Code go on to say that the board should:

- establish the company's purpose, values and strategy, and satisfy itself that these and its culture are aligned (Principle B);
- act with integrity, lead by example and promote the desired culture (Principle B) – see Chapter 8 regarding corporate culture;
- ensure that the necessary resources are in place for the company to meet its objectives and measure performance against them (Principle C);
- establish a framework of prudent and effective controls, which enable risk to be assessed and managed (Principle C) – see Chapters 12 and 13;
- ensure effective engagement with, and encourage participation from, shareholders and other stakeholders (Principle D) – see Chapter 15; and
- ensure that workforce policies and practices are consistent with the company's values and support its long-term sustainable success (Principle E) – see Chapter 15.

With regard to Principle B, the FRC Guidance on Board Effectiveness states (at para. 11):

'An effective board defines the company's purpose and then sets a strategy to deliver it, underpinned by the values and behaviours that shape its culture and the way it conducts its business.'

A purpose statement is designed to encapsulate the company's purpose as far as the outside world is concerned, particularly from the perspective of existing and potential customers. A company that does not serve any purpose in this regard will probably not survive for very long. On the other hand, one could argue that a successful company must be serving some purpose. It is useful to identify what that purpose is, although it may not be easy to condense it into to a meaningful statement of around 20 words, particular for a group with diverse business activities. The values statement highlights the main qualities that the company views as being critical for achieving its purpose. The strategy statement sets out what the company is aiming to achieve and is supported by targets for measuring success.

Ensuring that the necessary resources are in place for the company to meet its objectives and measuring performance against them (the first part of Principle

C) will involve:

◆   approving annual operating and capital expenditure budgets;

◆   ensuring that any necessary financing is in place;

◆   appointing the right people in senior management positions; and

◆   setting targets for and reviewing management/operational performance.

Establishing a framework of prudent and effective controls (the second part of Principle C) will involve:

◆   approving delegated levels of authority, including the CEO's authority limits;

◆   establishing board committees and approving their terms of reference;

◆   adopting a schedule of matters reserved for the board;

◆   establishing internal control and risk management procedures; and

◆   setting the company's **risk appetite**.

The board's role in ensuring effective engagement with, and encouraging participation from, shareholders and other stakeholders (Principle D) reflects s. 172 of the CA2006, which requires the directors to promote the success of the company taking into account the interests of other stakeholders. The Code places primary responsibility on the chair for seeking engagement with shareholders and communicating their views to the board. However, the board is expected to establish structures to ensure that the views of other key stakeholders are heard (see Chapter 15).

risk appetite
The amount and type of business risk that the board of directors would like their company to have exposure to. Identifying risk appetite should be a part of strategic planning.

According to the FRC Guidance on Board Effectiveness (paras. 47 and 48), ensuring that workforce policies and practices are consistent with the company's values and support its long-term sustainable success (Code Principle E) will involve reviewing policies and practices – including remuneration policies, rewards and incentives – that have an impact on the experience of the workforce and drive behaviours.

2.2 Functions carried out through committees

The Code also requires boards to carry out certain functions through board committees comprised wholly or mainly of independent non-executive directors. These committees (audit, nomination and remuneration) usually make recommendations to the board on matters within their remit rather than make the final decision themselves. The only area in which the Code specifically states that a committee will make the final decision is on executive remuneration.

Accordingly, the board still retains ultimate control over various matters within the remit of its corporate governance committees, including:

◆   new appointments to the board (nomination committee makes recommendations);

◆   setting the directors' remuneration policy (by law the policy must be approved by the board, so the remuneration committee can only make recommendations);

- approving accounts and other financial statements (the audit committee's role is to review these prior to approval by the board);
- establishing a framework of prudent and effective controls, which enable risk to be assessed and managed (the audit committee's role is to review these matters and make recommendations); and
- proposing the appointment of auditors (audit committee makes recommendations).;

Placing responsibility on these board committees to review and make recommendations to the board enables the independent non-executives to set the agenda and reduces the influence that the executive directors may otherwise exert in these areas. Leaving the final decision to the board means that it still has a key role to play, for example, in the appointment and removal of directors. Appointing a new chief executive will still be one of the most important decisions that a board will make and is not something that the nomination committee will do in isolation.

2.3   Critical management decisions

Boards do not delegate the whole of their management responsibilities to the executive directors. As we have already seen, the Code expects boards to take certain critical management decisions, such as setting the company's strategy. In addition, most boards will insist on having the final say on other important management decisions, such as major capital investment projects or material contracts. The thresholds for whether board approval is required for these and other management decisions will typically be set out in a schedule of matters reserved for the board, which is the subject of the next section.

2.4   Matters required by law

Boards are also required by law to deal with certain matters (e.g., approval of the accounts, and the adoption of anti-bribery and health and safety policies). These should also be reflected in any schedule of matters reserved for the board.

3. Matters reserved for the board

The Code used to include a recommendation that boards of directors should adopt a formal schedule of matters specifically reserved for their decision. This recommendation can now be found in the 2018 FRC Guidance on Board Effectiveness (at para. 28), which states:

'Ensuring there is a formal schedule of matters reserved for its decision will assist the board's planning and provide clarity to all over where responsibility for decision-making lies.'

The recommendation that boards should adopt such a schedule was first made by ICSA in its Code on Good Boardroom Practice in 1991. That recommendation was subsequently included in the Cadbury Code on the Financial aspects of Corporate Governance in 1992, the first version of what we now refer to as the UK Corporate Governance Code.

Adopting a schedule of matters reserved for the board helps to clarify for board members (particularly new directors and non-executives) what the role of the board is. It also helps to clarify for the executive team which decisions need board approval. Without such a schedule, certain decisions that the board would expect to take might appear to fall within the delegated authority of an executive or a committee. The existence of a schedule of matters reserved for the board provides an internal safety net to ensure that those decisions are referred to the board.

Adopting such a schedule also simplifies the process of delegation. Broad powers can be delegated more easily if they are made subject to the exceptions set out in the schedule. There is no need to recite those detailed exceptions in the delegated authority if they are incorporated by reference. Adopting a schedule also allows company-wide changes to be made without having to alter the terms of delegation for each individual or committee.

Those who exercise delegated authority may not always be aware of the fine details set out in the schedule, particularly if it has recently been amended. The company secretary/governance professional will play a major role in ensuring that the schedule is observed through their participation in the executive committee and internal sign-off procedures and as the secretary of the various governance committees.

ICSA's Guidance on Matters Reserved for the Board (2013) includes a draft schedule of matters reserved for the board's decision. The draft schedule is not intended to be a definitive list but rather a reminder of the matters that may be relevant for consideration when a company is compiling its own schedule. It includes matters considered to be the preserve of the board under the Code and matters the board should attend to under the law. However, it also includes certain high-level management decisions where each individual board would be expected to set its own materiality thresholds (see 'Contracts' below).

The draft schedule includes matters related to:

- Strategy and management
    - approval of overall strategy and strategic objectives;
    - setting the company's values and standards;
    - approval of annual operating and capital expenditure budgets;
    - oversight of the group's operations (including accounting, planning and internal control systems);
    - reviewing management/operational performance;
    - extension of the group's activities into new business or geographic areas;
    - any decision to cease to operate all or any material part of the group's business;
- Structure and capital
    - changes to the group's capital structure;
    - major changes to the group's corporate structure;

- – changes to the group's management and control structure;
- – any changes to the company's listing or status as a plc;
- ◆ Financial reporting and controls
  - – approval of the annual and half-yearly report and accounts and any preliminary announcement of final results;
  - – approval of the dividend policy;
  - – declaring an interim dividend and recommending a final dividend;
  - – approving any significant change in accounting policies or practices;
- ◆ Internal controls
  - – ensuring maintenance of a sound system of internal control and risk management;
- ◆ Contracts
  - – approving major capital projects;
  - – approving contracts in the ordinary course of business which are material strategically or by reason of size;
  - – approving contracts not in the ordinary course of business;
  - – approving major investments;
- ◆ Communication
  - – approval of resolutions to be put to shareholders;
  - – approval of all circulars, prospectuses and listing particulars;
  - – approval of press releases concerning matters decided by the board;
- ◆ Board membership and other appointments
  - – appointment of directors to the main board and the boards of subsidiaries;
  - – appointment or removal of the secretary;
  - – appointment, reappointment or removal of the external auditor, taking into account the recommendations of the audit committee;
- ◆ Remuneration
  - – determining the remuneration policy for the directors, company secretary and other senior executives;
  - – determining the remuneration of the non-executive directors;
  - – the introduction of new share incentive plans or major changes to existing plans, to be put to shareholders for approval;
- ◆ Delegation of authority
  - – the division of responsibilities between the chair and the chief executive;
  - – approval of the delegated levels of authority, including the CEO's authority limits;
  - – establishing board committees and approving their terms of reference;

◆   Corporate governance matters
  –   such as determining the independence of non-executive directors and authorising conflicts of interest where permitted by the articles of association;

◆   Policies
  –   including policies on matters such as share dealing, bribery prevention; whistleblowing, health and safety policy, the environment and sustainability, corporate social responsibility and charitable donations

◆   Other matters
  –   including political donations, appointment of the group's principal professional advisers, material litigation, overall levels of insurance, major changes to group pension schemes.

The 1992 Cadbury Report recommended (at para. 4.24) that boards should establish procedures to be followed when, exceptionally, decisions are required between board meetings. The company secretary should promote the adoption of such procedures and will almost certainly have a critical role to play, together with the chair, in ensuring that they are followed. The procedures could provide for a variety of different approval mechanisms, depending on the nature of the decision. These could include having to obtain board approval by written resolution (or an equivalent informal procedure by email or telephone) or having to obtain the approval of a specified proportion or number of directors, including, perhaps, both the CEO and chair (or deputy chair). Failure to adopt or follow such procedures usually results in the board having to be asked to ratify decisions that can no longer be reversed. Although boards are sometimes prepared to do this, their patience can snap, particularly when they are being asked to ratify a decision they do not agree with.

The 2016 Code and its predecessors used to require annual reports to contain a statement of how the board operates, including a high-level statement of which types of decisions are taken by the board and which are delegated to management. This requirement has been removed from the 2018 Code, perhaps because these statements had become too generic and rarely revealed anything useful.

Test yourself 6.1

1.   **What is the overarching role of the board according to the UK Corporate Governance Code?**

2.   **Cite three examples of things that the Code expects boards to do in performing this role.**

3.   **List three functions that the board performs through its board committees on which it still has the final say.**

4.   **To what extent does the board manage the company's business?**

4. Composition of the board

The board of directors of a listed company will typically consist of:

◆ a chair and, possibly, a deputy chair;

◆ a chief executive officer (CEO);

◆ other executive directors (such as a finance director);

◆ non-executive directors (NEDs); and

◆ a senior independent director (SID) (who may also be the deputy chair).

The role of each of these different participants is considered in detail below. However in brief, the chair is responsible for leading the board and ensuring that it functions effectively. The chief executive leads the executive team and is responsible for the executive management of the company's operations. Other executive directors may bring specialist expertise to the table (such as the finance director) or owe their position on the board to their status as, say, head of operations or head of a major division.

Non-executive directors bring outside experience and expertise that may otherwise be lacking on the board (for example, experience of international operations for a company that is looking to expand overseas). They are expected to scrutinise and challenge management proposals and to perform important governance functions, such as setting the remuneration of the executive directors.

The senior independent director's function is to act as a conduit for shareholders and mediator in circumstances where the board fails to function properly. The deputy chair's role is to fill in for the chair where the person appointed to that position is unable to act.

4.1 Balance of executive and non-executive directors

UK Corporate Governance Code Principle G states:

'The board should include an appropriate combination of executive and non-executive (and, in particular, independent non-executive) directors, such that no one individual or small group of individuals dominates the board's decision-making.'

Code Provision 11 states:

'At least half the board, excluding the chair, should be non-executives whom the board considers to be independent.'

This requirement was introduced following the Higgs Review in 2003. Prior to that, the Code required just one-third of the board to comprise non-executive directors, and only half of those non-executives to be independent.

When the existing requirement was first introduced in 2003 a dispensation was included for smaller companies (i.e. those outside the FTSE 350 throughout the year immediately prior to the reporting year). Under this dispensation, smaller companies were only required to have at least two independent non-executive directors. This dispensation was removed from the 2018 Code and all companies are now expected to comply with the same rule.

The idea that at least half the board, excluding the chair, should be independent non-executive directors is plainly designed to ensure that no one individual or small group of individuals dominates the board's decision making. In practice, it means that the independent non-executives will often hold the balance of power.

If the independent non-executives number exactly half of the board, they may need to garner the support of at least one other board member in order to push something through. For example, the independent non-executives would be able to force the removal of the chief executive with the support of the chair or force the removal of the chair with the support of the chief executive.

If the independent non-executives number exactly one half of the board, they may be able to block proposals. However, this might depend on whether the chair has a casting vote at board meetings.

In all cases, the chair and the independent non-executives acting together will form a majority of the board and will outnumber the executive directors plus any non-executives who are not independent. It should be noted that under the Code (Provision 9), the chair is meant to be independent on appointment and might therefore be expected to be a natural ally of the independent non-executives.

Stop and think 6.1

In a company that has just enough independent NEDs to comply with Code Provision 11, will those NEDs be in a stronger position if the total number of directors is an odd or even number?

In order to answer this question you may find it helpful to calculate what the minimum number of independent NEDs should be for a board which comprises variously 8, 9, 10 or 11 directors.

4.2 Reporting on board composition

The CA2006 requires the names of those who have served as directors during the financial year to be disclosed in the directors' report. In practice this will typically form part of the corporate governance report.

The UK Corporate Governance Code used to require in addition that the annual report identify the chair, the deputy chair (where there is one), the chief executive, the senior independent director and the chair and members of the board committees. Even though this provision has been deleted from the 2018 Code it plainly remains good practice.

The Code requires the annual report:

- to identify the non-executive directors that the board considers to be independent together with any necessary explanations (Provision 10); and
- to set out the number of meetings of the board and its committees and individual attendance by directors (Provision 14).

The Code also requires:

- the responsibilities of the chair, chief executive, senior independent director, board and committees to be set out in writing and made publicly available (such as on the company's website) (Provision 14); and
- the board to set out in the papers accompanying any shareholder resolution to elect a director 'the specific reasons why their contribution is, and continues to be, important to the company's long-term sustainable success' (Provision 18).

5. Role of the chair

Principle F of the Code includes a statement which summarises the role that the chair of a listed company is expected to play. It states:

'The chair leads the board and is responsible for its overall effectiveness in directing the company. They should demonstrate objective judgement throughout their tenure and promote a culture of openness and debate. In addition, the chair facilitates constructive board relations and the effective contribution of all non-executive directors, and ensures that directors receive accurate, timely and clear information.'

The 2018 FRC Guidance on Board Effectiveness expands on this by suggesting that the chair's role includes:

- setting a board agenda primarily focused on strategy, performance, value creation, culture, stakeholders and accountability, and ensuring that issues relevant to these areas are reserved for board decision;
- shaping the culture in the boardroom;
- encouraging all board members to engage in board and committee meetings by drawing on their skills, experience and knowledge;
- fostering relationships based on trust, mutual respect and open communication – both in and outside the boardroom – between non-executive directors and the executive team;
- developing a productive working relationship with the chief executive, providing support and advice, while respecting executive responsibility;
- providing guidance and mentoring to new directors as appropriate;
- leading the annual board evaluation, with support from the senior independent director as appropriate, and acting on the results; and
- considering having regular externally facilitated board evaluations.

It goes on to say that the chair should ensure that:

◆ adequate time is available for discussion of all agenda items, in particular strategic issues, and that debate is not truncated;

◆ there is a timely flow of accurate, high-quality and clear information;

◆ the board determines the nature, and extent, of the significant risks the company is willing to embrace in the implementation of its strategy;

◆ all directors are aware of and able to discharge their statutory duties;

◆ the board listens to the views of shareholders, the workforce, customers and other key stakeholders;

◆ all directors receive a full, formal and tailored induction on joining the board; and

◆ all directors continually update their skills, knowledge and familiarity with the company to fulfil their role both on the board and committees.

5.1 Duties and powers of the chair under the law

Under the common law, the chair of any meeting has a duty to ensure that:

◆ the meeting is properly conducted;

◆ all shades of opinion are given a fair hearing;

◆ the sense of the meeting is properly ascertained and recorded; and

◆ order is preserved.

By electing a chair, the directors are deemed to have conferred upon that person all the powers necessary to fulfil the role. In particular, the chair is deemed to have authority to rule on points of order and on other incidental questions that may arise during the meeting.

In the unlikely event that a board meeting becomes disorderly, the chair has inherent power to take certain steps for the purposes of restoring order. This could include adjourning the meeting or ordering that somebody be ejected.

Articles of association usually give the chair:

◆ a specific power to make rulings on whether a director is entitled to vote on any matter which comes before the board (see article 16 of the Model Articles for public limited companies) – such a ruling may be required where a director has an interest in the transaction; and

◆ a casting vote at meetings of directors (see article 14 of the Model Articles for public limited companies). It is usually considered good practice for the chair to exercise any casting vote to 'preserve the status quo'. This means that the matter being voted on will not change and can be raised again at a later meeting;

◆ first right to chair board meetings; and

◆ first right to chair meetings of the members/shareholders.

5.2 Chair should be independent on appointment

Provision 9 of the Code states that the chair should be independent on appointment when assessed against the circumstances set out in Code Provision 10 regarding the independence of non-executive directors.

This implies that, thereafter, the chair need not be independent. There are two main reasons for this:

◆ some people argue that the time commitments of a non-executive chair and the fees they are paid automatically compromise their independence; and

◆ companies sometimes appoint an executive chair who will never satisfy the independence criteria in Code Provision 10.

This ambivalence regarding the independent status of even a non-executive chair is one of the reasons why the chair is excluded for the purposes of calculating whether at least half the board are independent non-executive directors. The Code generally envisages that the role of the chair is non-executive in nature but does not always treat the chair in the same way as the other non-executives. For example, it specifies that the chair may not serve as a member of the audit committee (even if considered by the board to be an independent non-executive director) and requires the fees paid to the chair to be set by the remuneration committee.

On the other hand, the FRC Guidance on Board Effectiveness recommends (at paras. 104 and 105) that the chair should be subject to similar length of service considerations as non-executive directors and should not stay in post longer than nine years. It suggests that the nine-year period should be calculated from when they were first appointed to the board. Accordingly, any time spent on the board prior to becoming chair must be included when considering their total length of service. As a concession, the Guidance states that a limited extension beyond nine years may be justified if, prior to being appointed, the chair served as a board member for a significant amount of time and the appointment supports the company's succession plan and diversity policy. This is a useful concession as many companies appoint an existing independent non-executive director as chair and that person often serves on the board for a total of more than nine years.

5.3 The chair's time commitments

The UK Code used to include a provision which stated that no individual should chair more than one FTSE 100 company. Although, this provision was deleted in June 2008, investors continue to express concern that certain individuals may not have enough time to devote to the role because of their other commitments.

Walker Report
A report published in the UK in 2009 about corporate governance in banks and other financial services organisations, following the banking crisis of 2007–2008.

The **Walker Report** on corporate governance in banks (2009) suggested that the chair of a large bank would need to spend about two-thirds of their time with the company, which would make it practically impossible to take on the post of chair at another FTSE 100 company.

The 2018 FRC Guidance on Board Effectiveness (para.s. 95) states:

'Directors are expected to undertake that they will have sufficient time to meet what is expected of them effectively. The role of chair, in particular, is demanding and time-consuming; multiple roles are therefore not advisable. The nomination committee may wish to consider whether to set limits on the number and scale of other appointments it considers the chair and other non-executives may take on without compromising their effectiveness. This could help deal with shareholder concerns that some directors may have too many commitments, sometimes referred to as "overboarding".'

It also recommends (at para. 96) that letters of appointment should set out the expected time commitment and be made available for inspection.

5.4 Appointment of the chair

Articles of association allow boards of directors to elect one of their number to act as the chair of the board and to remove that person from the office of chair (see article. 12 of the Model Articles for public limited companies). The person who becomes the chair of the board is sometimes referred to as the 'company chair'. This is not a separate position. The company chair will always be the person who was appointed as the chair of the board.

Under most articles you must already be a director to be elected as the chair of the board. This does not mean that an external candidate cannot be appointed. However, they will have to be appointed as director before they can be elected by the board to act as its chair. In practice, over three-fifths of FTSE chair appointments are made from external candidates (see the Russell Reynolds Associates study below).

The Code anticipates that the appointment process will be led by the nomination committee in the usual manner. This could present difficulties if the incumbent chair or potential candidates for the vacancy are members of the nomination committee. Neither should probably be involved in the appointment process. This may mean that the process ought to be led by someone else, such as the senior independent director or a bespoke committee of independent non-executive directors.

The final decision regarding the appointment must rest with the full board in view of the procedures in articles of association. Shareholders will not necessarily have any say in who the board appoints as chair. However, they can register their disapproval by voting against the chair's re-election at the AGM.

5.5 Typical background and characteristics of a FTSE chair

A study by Russell Reynolds Associates – 'FTSE chairs: The origins of the species' (2017) – found that:

◆ Companies with larger market capitalisations have a greater proportion of chairs with in-sector executive experience leading their board.

◆ Business leadership is the most popular functional background for FTSE chairs, with over one-third having previously served as a public company

CEO, followed by financial leadership, with former public company finance directors accounting for nearly one-fifth of FTSE chairs.

◆ Since 2015 there has been a significant increase in the number of FTSE chair appointments who have had executive experience in banking. Although the majority of these individuals chair boards of financial services companies, nearly one-third chair industrial and natural resources businesses.

◆ Individuals who have had executive experience in financial services account for over two-fifths of FTSE chairs, while nearly one-third of FTSE chairs have had executive experience in professional services.

◆ A majority of FTSE chairs have previous chair experience upon appointment to the role.

◆ Over one in ten FTSE chairs have served in the role for more than nine years, the point at which NEDs are not considered independent under the UK Corporate Governance Code.

◆ Nearly two-fifths of FTSE chairs were appointed internally, with over a third of these appointments coming through the senior independent director role, and over one-fifth having served as chair of the audit committee. Internal successors have served on average 6.6 years as an independent director before their promotion to chair.

◆ At the time of the study only 4% of board chairs were women. Three-quarters of those female chairs had been appointed internally.

6. Role of the chief executive officer

The Code does not define the role of the chief executive officer (CEO). However, the FRC Guidance on Board Effectiveness (paras. 70 to 73) suggests that the CEO, as the most senior executive director on the board, should be responsible for:

◆ proposing strategy to the board, and for delivering the strategy as agreed;

◆ setting an example to the company's employees, and communicating to them the expectations of the board in relation to the company's culture, values and behaviours;

◆ supporting the chair to make certain that appropriate standards of governance permeate through all parts of the organisation;

◆ making certain that the board is made aware, when appropriate, of the views of employees on issues of relevance to the business; and

◆ ensuring the board knows the executive directors' views on business issues in order to improve the standard of discussion in the boardroom and, prior to final decision on an issue, explain in a balanced way any divergence of view in the executive team.

For obvious reasons, the FRC Guidance focuses mainly on the CEO's role in the context of board governance and effectiveness. In practice, CEOs will spend the majority of their time 'delivering the strategy', i.e. managing the company's business with a view to meeting the strategic objectives and targets agreed by the board. The board will give the CEO wide delegated powers in order to allow them to perform this management function, with only major decisions having to be referred to the board in accordance with the schedule of matters reserved for the board.

Typically, the CEO will delegate most day-to-day management decisions to other members of the executive team but, like the board, will insist on having the final say on a variety of matters. These matters might be determined in a policy and procedure manual, an internal control manual or limits on the delegated authority of other members of the executive team.

Most CEOs establish a committee of senior executives to help them manage the business. This committee is typically referred to as the executive committee, but could be called something else. It will not normally be a committee of the board. Instead it will be constituted by the CEO and may include members who are not directors. It will usually consist of the executive directors who serve on the board and a range of senior executives just below board level, including any heads of major operations or divisions who do not serve on the board and the heads of certain administrative functions (such as HR or legal). Typically, the executive committee will not have any authority to take decisions itself. Its meetings will be chaired by the CEO, who will use them to take soundings from other senior executives and receive operational updates and progress reports. The committee may never proceed to a formal vote but, even if it does, that vote will be treated as merely advisory, with the CEO having the final decision.

7. Separation of the roles of chair and chief executive

The chair and the CEO are the two most powerful positions on the board of directors. The chair leads the board of directors. The CEO is the leader of the management team. Employees will look to the chief executive as their leader. Board members (particularly the non-executives) will look to the chair as their leader.

A person holding both positions could become an overly dominant influence on decision making in the company. In order to avoid this happening, Code Principle G states that:

'there should be a clear division of responsibilities between the leadership of the board and the executive leadership of the company's business'.

In practice, Code Provision 9 confirms that 'the roles of chair and chief executive should not be exercised by the same individual'.

When an individual holds the positions of both chair and CEO, they are likely to be able to exercise a dominant influence on the board, unless there are strong individuals, such as a deputy chair or a SID, to act as a counterweight. CEOs tend to be strong personalities with high levels of confidence in their own abilities. Although these characteristics may be desirable in a CEO, there is a risk that they may become overly domineering if their powers are left unchecked. A CEO who also acts as the chair is effectively allowed to mark their own homework, set their own targets and influence board appointments, thus reinforcing their own position. Over time, they may become less and less likely to listen to advice from board colleagues and the board may eventually cease to function as an effective body.

Without effective checks on their powers, an individual could ultimately try to run the company for their own personal benefit (and that of their acolytes) rather than in the interests of its shareholders (see further the discussion of agency theory in Chapter 1).

Code Provision 14 requires the responsibilities of the chair and chief executive to be clear, set out in writing, agreed by the board and made publicly available.

The FRC Guidance on Board Effectiveness states (at para. 70) that:

'When deciding the differing responsibilities of the chair and the chief executive, particular attention should be paid to areas of potential overlap.'

The definitions of the roles of the chair and CEO in the Code and the FRC Guidance on Board Effectiveness give some indication as to what this division of responsibilities should be. Areas of overlap are most likely to arise if the chair has executive management responsibilities. The role envisaged for the chair under the Code is essentially non-executive in nature. It is concerned with the leadership of the board rather than the management of the company's business. A chair with executive responsibilities is more likely to get embroiled in a clash with the chief executive. A dominant chief executive might seek to infringe on the chair's role as the leader of the board by manipulating the agenda for board meetings.

7.1   CEO should not become chair of the same company

As well as providing that the roles of chair and chief executive should not be exercised by the same individual, Code Provision 9 states that:

'A chief executive should not become chair of the same company.'

This used to be a relatively common practice where a successful CEO who had been in post for a long time was 'promoted' to the role of the chair. This was sometimes done as a way of retaining their expertise on the board. However, it was often seen as an unmerited reward for their long and distinguished service and as an inducement to persuade them to retire as CEO.

Investors usually oppose such promotions and rarely believe that a retiring CEO is the best person to fill the position of chair. Their principal objections are that:

◆   the outgoing CEO will not have been independent on appointment as the chair (as required by UK Code Provision 9);

◆   the outgoing CEO will often retain some of their executive responsibilities, effectively becoming an executive chair (the Code generally envisages the role of the chair as being non-executive in nature);

◆   as a consequence, the division of responsibilities between the chair and the CEO may become more blurred;

◆   the incoming CEO's freedom of action may be restrained by having their predecessor constantly looking over their shoulder;

◆   the outgoing CEO may view any changes proposed by the incoming CEO as implied criticism of what happened before under his or her watch.

7.2   Non-compliance with the UK Code on separation of the roles

Several companies have breached the Code by appointing the same person as chair and CEO and others by 'promoting' the retiring CEO to the chair (see case studies below).

In ordinary circumstances, companies are only required to explain their non-compliance with provisions of the Code at the end of the financial year in the report and accounts. However, in the case of the two recommendations regarding separation of the roles of chair and CEO, Code Provision 9 requires the board to consult major shareholders ahead of the appointment, set out its reasons to all shareholders at the time of the appointment and also publish these on the company website.

If you read Code Provision 9 literally, this requirement seems only to apply where a company promotes the retiring chief executive to the position of chair. However, investors expect companies to do likewise if they are proposing to appoint a person as both chair and CEO of the company.

Case study 6.1

In February 2000, Mr Luc Vandevelde was appointed as chair and CEO of Marks & Spencer, at a time when its business operations were in difficulty and the share price was falling sharply. The appointment attracted some criticism but appears to have been a successful short-term measure. By 2002, the company's fortunes had improved to the point where he relinquished the position of CEO, retaining his position as the part-time chairman.

However, in 2008 Marks & Spencer's CEO, Sir Stuart Rose, was also appointed as executive chairman for a limited period until a successor to the role of CEO could be found. This appointment attracted strong criticism from institutional investors, who argued that it would make it more difficult to appoint a successor to Sir Stuart as CEO. Shareholders could not prevent the appointment as it was within the powers of the board to elect one of their number as chairman. However, they were able to vote on Sir Stuart's re-election as director at the 2008 AGM, and 22% of them voted against or abstained on the resolution.

Case study 6.2

Polly Peck International, a FTSE 100 company during the 1980s, was effectively run by a single individual, Asil Nadir, who was both chair and CEO. The company collapsed without warning in October 1990. During the administration process, the system of internal controls at the company's London head office was found to be virtually non-existent. As a result, Nadir had been able to transfer large amounts of money from the company's UK bank accounts to personal accounts in Northern Cyprus, without any questions being asked. After the company collapsed, Nadir fled to Northern Cyprus. He returned to London in 2010 (20 years later) to face trial and was found guilty of 10 counts of theft totalling £29 million, for which he was sentenced to 10 years in prison.

Test yourself 6.2

1. **What is the role of the company chair?**
2. **What are the requirements of the Code with regard to the independence of the company chair?**
3. **Why should the role of chair and CEO be separate?**

8. Role of other executive directors

The Code makes provision about the balance of executive and non-executive directors on the board but has nothing else to say about the role of executive directors.

In addition to their responsibilities as directors, executive directors are full-time employees of the company, with executive management responsibilities. As directors they have the same duties as other members of a unitary board. These duties extend to the whole of the business, and not just that part of it covered by their individual executive roles.

The only constant on most boards is the presence of a CEO and a finance director. Many companies have deliberately reduced the number of executive directors that serve on the board in order to reduce the number of non-executive directors required and keep the overall size of the board down to manageable proportions.

In practice, there can be tensions for executive directors between:

◆   their role as members of the board, 'one step down from the shareholders'; and

◆   their role as senior operational directors, 'one step up from management'.

The executive directors, perhaps influenced by the CEO, will often want to present a united front to the rest of the board, perhaps to justify what the management team has done or what it would like to do. This means that they are unlikely to provide any effective challenge at board meetings to proposals made by the CEO and other members of the executive team. They may have argued against the proposals in prior discussions with the CEO but will often be reluctant to air these differences at board meetings. To do so would be seen as undermining the CEO.

Independent non-executive directors do not have these problems, which is why they are more free to provide effective challenge during board discussions, particularly where encouraged to do so by the chair. The problem for non-executive directors is that they do not normally know as much about the business as the executives.

If it is always the NEDs who challenge proposals and the executives who defend them;, this can create an 'us and them' mentality on the board. The executives may always be inclined:

◆   to support the views of the CEO on all matters, including strategy; and

◆   mistrust the views of NEDs as 'outsiders' who do not know much about the company and its business.

In order to address these potential problems, the FRC Guidance on Board Effectiveness (at paras. 69 and 74) recommends that executive directors should:

◆   not see themselves only as members of the chief executive's team when engaged in board business;

◆   broaden their understanding of their board responsibilities by taking up a non-executive director position on another board (although Code Provision 15 states that they should not take on more than one non-executive directorship in a FTSE 100 company or other significant appointment); and

◆   welcome constructive challenge from non-executive directors as an essential aspect of good governance, and encourage their non-executive colleagues to test proposals in the light of their wider experience outside the company.

Paragraph 72 of the FRC Guidance also states that it is the responsibility of the CEO to ensure the board knows the views of the senior management on business issues and to explain in a balanced way any divergence of view.

Test yourself 6.3

1.   **How does the FRC Guidance on Board Effectiveness expect the CEO to contribute to board effectiveness?**

2.   **How does the FRC Guidance on Board Effectiveness expect the executive directors to contribute to board effectiveness?**

3.   **What is the function of an executive committee?**

9. Non-executive directors – role and independence

Non-executive directors play a central role in the corporate governance process. They are expected to bring outside experience and independent judgement to bear on the major matters requiring decision by boards and to perform certain governance functions through their participation in board committees.

9.1   Role of non-executive directors

The Higgs Review, which gave rise to substantial amendments to the 2003 Code, was established principally to review the role and effectiveness of non-executive directors. One of the main changes to the 2003 Code arising from the Higgs Review was the inclusion of a new supporting principle outlining the role of non-executive directors. That supporting principle was removed from the 2018 Code. However, its contents are still reflected (with some modifications) in the 2018 Code, which provides that the non-executives should:

◆ provide constructive challenge, strategic guidance, offer specialist advice and hold management to account (Code Principle H);

◆ scrutinise and hold to account the performance of management and individual executive directors against agreed performance objectives (Code Provision 13);

◆ have a prime role in appointing and removing executive directors (Code Provision 13);

◆ through their participation in the nomination committee, lead the process for board appointments, succession planning and ensuring the development of a diverse pipeline (Code Principle J and Provision 17);

◆ through their participation in the audit committee, satisfy themselves on the integrity of financial information and that financial controls and systems of risk management are robust and defensible (Code Principles M and N); and

◆ through their participation in the remuneration committee, determine appropriate levels of remuneration for the chair, executive directors and senior management (Code Principle Q and Provision 13).

Some of these functions will be performed by the non-executives through their participation in full board meetings, others through their participation in board committees. However, the Code also envisages that:

◆ the non-executives will meet at least annually without the chair present in order to appraise the chair's performance (Code Provision 12); and

◆ the chair will hold additional meetings with the non-executive directors without the executive directors present (Code Provision 13). As this recommendation is included in the provision which sets out the non-executives' role in appointing and removing executive directors and holding management to account, it can be assumed that those issues are expected to be the primary focus of these meetings. However, there is no reason why they could not be used to raise other matters of concern.

9.2   Role of non-executive directors in transactions

The Investment Association's Transaction Guidelines make a number of recommendations regarding the role of non-executive directors in major and related party transactions (see Chapter 14). The Guidelines recommend that:

◆   Non-executive directors should be given sufficient time and information to give proper consideration to the merits of transactions, as well as the opportunity to provide their views to shareholders when they are first made insiders.

◆   Executive directors should inform the appropriate non-executive directors of the proposed transaction when an approach is received from a possible bidder or management first actively considers a transaction in respect of which a shareholder approval is to be sought.

◆   Non-executive directors should be kept informed of discussions between the company and the transaction counterparty.

◆   Non-executive directors should be given direct access to financial and legal advisers to the company on a transaction in order to ensure that information can be rapidly obtained and understood.

◆   Non-executives should have regular discussions about the transaction without the executives present. When considering a transaction, the non-executives' group should confirm to the chair, prior to publication of any circular or recommendation to shareholders, that they are satisfied they have received sufficient time and information.

◆   Non-executive directors should consider whether it is appropriate to seek separate, independent advice on the merits of the proposed transaction. In these instances, the adviser should be paid on a fixed fee (as opposed to a 'success' or 'incentive') basis.

◆   Where a company is subject to a management buy-out or similar transaction, or engaging in a transaction with a controller or a group of controllers, or where a conflict may otherwise arise, a special independent committee comprising only un-conflicted directors should be formed to consider the transaction.

9.3   Independent non-executive directors

As mentioned on page 140, Provision 11 states that at least half the board, excluding the chair, should be non-executives whom the board considers to be independent.

Code Provision 10 requires boards to identify in the annual report and accounts the non-executive directors they consider to be independent for the purposes of the Code. It sets out a non-exhaustive list of factors that may compromise the independence of a non-executive director. Where any of these or other relevant circumstances apply, and the board nonetheless considers that the non-executive director is independent, the Code states that 'a clear explanation should be provided'. It does not state specifically where or when this explanation should be provided. The obvious answer would be in the company's corporate governance report, together with any other explanations of non-compliance. However, shareholders might reasonably expect any independence issues that already exist on appointment to be explained at the time of that appointment.

The independence criteria in Code Provision 10 are as follows:

◆ The non-executive director is or has been an employee of the company or group within the last five years.

◆ The non-executive director has, or has had within the last three years, a material business relationship with the company either directly, or as a partner, shareholder, director or senior employee of a body that has such a relationship with the company.

◆ The non-executive director has received or receives additional remuneration from the company apart from a director's fee, participates in the company's share option or a performance-related pay scheme, or is a member of the company's pension scheme.

◆ The non-executive director has close family ties with any of the company's advisers, directors or senior employees.

◆ The non-executive director holds cross-directorships or has significant links with other directors through involvement in other companies or bodies.

◆ The non-executive director represents a significant shareholder.

◆ The non-executive director has served on the board for more than nine years from the date of their first election.

Despite the inclusion of criteria in the Code, it is still open to investors and corporate governance analysts to develop and apply their own criteria for assessing independence. One major institutional investor has stated that the final decision as to whether non-executive directors are independent lies with the shareholders who elect them and that there should be full disclosure in the annual report of any factors to be taken into account in judging an individual's independence.

In this regard, the 2016 Code used to require the names of directors submitted for election or re-election to be accompanied by sufficient biographical details and any other relevant information to enable shareholders to make an informed decision on their election (2016 Code provision B.7.1). By contrast, the 2018 Code Provision 18 merely requires the papers accompanying the resolutions to elect each director to set out 'the specific reasons why their contribution is, and continues to be, important to the company's long-term sustainable success'.

Test yourself 6.4

1.   **How are NEDs expected to contribute to the effectiveness of the board?**

2.   **What particular functions are independent NEDs expected to fulfil under the Code?**

3.   **List six circumstances in which a NED would not normally be considered independent.**

4.   **What should the board do if any of its NEDs do not meet these independence criteria?**

10. Non-executive directors – effectiveness

Non-executive directors are meant to bring outside experience and independent judgement to bear on the deliberations of the board. They may also bring specialist expertise that may otherwise be lacking on the board.

Principle H of the Code states:

'Non-executive directors should have sufficient time to meet their board responsibilities. They should provide constructive challenge, strategic guidance, offer specialist advice and hold management to account.'

The effectiveness of non-executive directors can be undermined by:

◆   a lack of knowledge about the company's business;

◆   insufficient time spent with the company;

◆   defects in the decision-making process; and

◆   ineffective challenge.

These potential weaknesses are all addressed to some degree in the FRC Guidance on Board Effectiveness, which suggests (at paras. 75 to 78) that, in order to be effective, non-executive directors should:

◆   on appointment, devote time to a comprehensive, formal and tailored induction in order to understand the culture of the organisation and the way things are done, and to gain insight into the experience and concerns of the workforce;

◆   have sufficient time available to discharge their responsibilities effectively;

◆   devote time to developing and refreshing their knowledge and skills to ensure that they continue to make a positive contribution to the board and generate the respect of the other directors;

◆   insist on receiving high-quality information sufficiently in advance so that there can be thorough consideration of the issues prior to, and informed debate and challenge at, board meetings;

◆ seek clarification or amplification from management where they consider the information provided is inadequate or lacks clarity; and

◆ take opportunities to meet shareholders, key customers and members of the workforce from all levels of the organisation in order to develop a good understanding of the business and its relationships with significant stakeholders.

Induction and training attempt to tackle the issue of insufficient knowledge about the business. The non-executives also need high-quality, accurate and timely information if they are to make a useful contribution to board deliberations. The Code places primary responsibility for ensuring this on the chair (Principle F). However, the FRC Guidance recognises that the CEO and other members of the executive team have a critical role to play, and exhorts non-executives themselves to insist on receiving high-quality information.

10.1 Time commitments

Non-executive directors may spend at most one or two days a month on the company's business, although this may be more for committee chairs. Many NEDs have executive positions in other companies or organisations, which take up most of their time. Some individuals have been accused of holding too many NED positions, with the result that they cannot possibly give sufficient time to any of the companies concerned.

Principle H of the Code states that:

'Non-executive directors should have sufficient time to meet their board responsibilities.'

One indicator that a non-executive director does not have sufficient time might be a patchy attendance record. This is one of the reasons why Code Provision 14 requires the annual report to set out the individual attendance by directors at board and committee meetings.

Code Provision 15 also requires the board to take preventative measures:

'When making new appointments, the board should take into account other demands on directors' time. Prior to appointment, significant commitments should be disclosed with an indication of the time involved. Additional external appointments should not be undertaken without prior approval of the board, with the reasons for permitting significant appointments explained in the annual report.'

The FRC Guidance on Board Effectiveness (at paras. 95 and 96) also tackles the issues of time commitments and 'overboarding'. Non-executive directors are expected to undertake that they will have sufficient time to meet what is expected of them effectively. Letters of appointment should set out the expected time commitment. Nomination committees are encouraged to consider whether to set limits on the number and scale of other appointments in order to address shareholder concerns about 'overboarding'.

10.2 Lack of effective challenge

One of the main criticisms of non-executive directors is that they do not provide effective challenge. Where a difference of opinion arises during a board meeting, the views of the executive directors are likely to carry greater weight, because they know more about the company. NEDs may be put under pressure to accept the views of their executive colleagues.

In 2002, Lord Young, the outgoing president of the Institute of Directors (IoD) argued in a speech to its annual conference that NEDs cannot hope to govern their company better than the executive directors, because they cannot know as much about the company as full-time executives. He said:

'The biggest and most dangerous nonsense is the role we now expect NEDs to perform. Even if they spend one day a week in the company, can the non-execs ever know the business as well as the execs? No, they can't. So why bother with non-execs at all?'

The Code places primary responsibility on the chair to facilitate 'constructive board relations and the effective contribution of all non-executive directors'. The 2018 FRC Guidance on Board Effectiveness expands on this by suggesting that the chair's role includes:

◆ shaping the culture in the boardroom;

◆ encouraging all board members to engage in board and committee meetings by drawing on their skills, experience and knowledge; and

◆ fostering relationships based on trust, mutual respect and open communication – both in and outside the boardroom – between non-executive directors and the executive team.

The FRC Guidance also states (at para. 74) that:

'Executive directors should welcome constructive challenge from non-executive directors as an essential aspect of good governance, and encourage their non-executive colleagues to test proposals in the light of their wider experience outside the company.'

It is possible that having a strong senior independent director could help to ensure that the opinions of the non-executive directors are properly considered. However, in the final analysis, the effectiveness of the non-executives will largely depend on their own calibre, the boardroom culture created and nurtured by the chair and the quality of information they are given. In a speech on corporate governance, Andrew Bailey, CEO of the Prudential Regulation Authority, commented:

'It is the job of the executive to be able to explain in simple and transparent terms… complex matters to non-executives. In doing so, you should understand the uncertainty around judgements, in what circumstances they could be wrong, and how there can reasonably be different ways to measure things like liquidity. Non-executives should not be left to find the answers for themselves, and they should not feel that they have to do so out of a lack of sufficient confidence in what they are being told.'

10.3 Delays in decision making

Boards that include a substantial proportion of non-executive directors may only meet on a monthly basis, or less. Where major decisions are reserved to the board, this may delay decision making, which could have a knock-on effect of stifling the 'entrepreneurial spirit' of the executive team. This can certainly be true in companies that were founded by entrepreneurs, who often find it difficult to adjust when their company goes public. Classic examples of this syndrome include Uber's CEO, Travis Kalanic and Tesla's CEO, Elon Musk.

Investors prefer public companies to take a more measured approach to decision making and for boards to exercise a measure of control over such characters, whose stars can burn very brightly but also have tendency to explode.

Test yourself 6.5

List the main criticisms regarding non-executive director effectiveness.

11. Senior independent director

The Code requires boards to appoint one of the independent non-executive directors as the senior independent director (SID) (Code Provision 12). The role of the SID should be 'should be clear, set out in writing, agreed by the board and made publicly available' (Code Provision 14). According to Code Provision 12, the SID's role is to:

◆ act as a sounding board for the chair and an intermediary for other directors and shareholders;

◆ take the lead in the non-executive directors' annual assessment of the performance of the chair.

The FRC Guidance on Board Effectiveness (paras. 66 to 68) suggests that the SID:

◆ might also take responsibility for an orderly succession process for the chair, working closely with the nomination committee;

◆ should also be available to shareholders if they have concerns that contact through the normal channels of chair, chief executive or other executive directors has failed to resolve or for which such contact is inappropriate;

◆ should work with the chair and other directors, and/or shareholders, to resolve significant issues when the board or company is undergoing a period of stress.

It calls on boards to ensure they have a clear understanding of when the SID might intervene in order to maintain board and company stability. Examples cited in the guidance include where:

◆ there is a dispute between the chair and chief executive;

◆   shareholders or non-executive directors have expressed concerns that are
    not being addressed by the chair or chief executive;

◆   the strategy is not supported by the entire board;

◆   the relationship between the chair and chief executive is particularly close;

◆   decisions are being made without the approval of the full board; and

◆   succession planning is being ignored.

The role of the SID is therefore likely to be more important at times when
the board is under stress or there has been a breakdown of communications.
Critics of the SID concept have argued that the chair should be able to resolve
difficulties between a company and its shareholders, and that the position of
SID should therefore be superfluous. However, the recommended role of the SID
is now much broader than simply dealing with dissatisfied shareholders.

Stop and think 6.2

**It may be tempting to think that the main role of the SID is to act as
a check on the chair, for example by providing an alternative channel
of communication for shareholders who are not satisfied with the
responses they have received from the chairman and CEO.**

**However, good corporate governance requires a united board. Board
members may have lively debates and occasional disagreements, but
the role of the SID, who may also be the deputy chair, is generally to
support the chair, and not oppose them. However, it should not be
forgotten that the SID is also expected to lead the process of evaluating
the chair, which could create some tension in the relationship.**

12. Board committees and NEDs

One of the features of the Code is that it expects certain board functions to be
carried out through committees comprised wholly of independent non-executive
directors or a majority thereof. It recommends that listed companies establish at
least three board committees:

◆   nomination committee;

◆   audit committee; and

◆   remuneration committee.

In the financial services sector boards are also expected to establish a risk
committee.

There is no statutory requirement in the UK for a quoted company to establish
a nomination committee or a remuneration committee, but, following the
implementation of the EU Statutory Audit Directive in 2008, quoted companies
are required to have an audit committee (see DTR 7.1).

The functions of the three main committees and the rules regarding their composition are summarised in Table 6.1 below.

Nomination committee	Audit committee	Remuneration committee
Function: leading the process for board appointments, ensuring plans are in place for orderly succession to both the board and senior management positions, and overseeing the development of a diverse pipeline.	Function: monitoring the integrity of financial statements, reviewing internal controls and risk management, ensuring the independence and effectiveness of internal and external audit functions.	Function: determining the policy for executive director remuneration and setting remuneration for the chair, executive directors and senior management.
Composition: majority of members should be independent NEDs. No minimum number specified.	Composition: all independent NEDs – in large companies, at least three, in smaller companies at least two.	Composition: all independent NEDs – in large companies, at least three, in smaller companies at least two.
There is no bar to the board chair serving on the nomination committee or chairing it.	The chair of the board should not be a member.	The chair of the board can only be a member if they were independent on appointment and cannot chair the committee.
The board chair should not chair the committee when it is dealing with the appointment of their successor.	At least one member of the committee should have 'recent and relevant financial experience'. The committee as a whole should also have 'competence relevant to the sector in which the company operates'.	Before appointment as chair of the remuneration committee, the appointee should have served on a remuneration committee for at least 12 months.

Table 6.1 Summary of the UK Code's recommendations regarding membership of board committees

If a company has a separate risk committee, it must also be comprised of independent NEDs. Such a committee will typically perform the risk management functions usually undertaken by the audit committee, including responsibility for oversight and advice to the board on the current risk exposures and future risk strategy, and the embedding and maintenance of a supportive culture in relation to the management of risk.

The roles of the various committees are explained in more detail in subsequent chapters.

The Code requires boards to establish the three main committees in order to ensure that certain important governance functions are undertaken exclusively by independent non-executives (or in the case of the nomination committee by a body on which they represent the majority). This is clearly designed to avoid conflicts of interest that may arise if executives were involved. The clearest example of this is with remuneration, where it would be wrong for any director to be involved in setting their own pay.

For the most part, the three committees are established to make recommendations to the board. The FRC Guidance on Board Effectiveness suggests (at para. 62) that the final decision on any matter within the remit of the three committees rests with the board. However, Code Provision 33 states that the remuneration committee should 'have delegated responsibility for determining the policy for executive director remuneration and setting remuneration for the chair, executive directors and senior management'. In practice, it may not be possible under some companies' articles of association for the directors to delegate these powers and the board may need to 'rubber stamp' the recommendations of the remuneration committee in this regard.

It is, however, true to say that most of the things that the audit committee is responsible for involve making recommendations to the full board (e.g., on the appointment of the auditors). Similarly, the final decision on any new appointment recommended by the nomination committee will rest with the board. Boards will rarely override the recommendations of the relevant committee. If they do so, the Code sometimes requires the difference of opinion to be made public (e.g., if the board ignores the audit committee's' choice of auditor). Whether or not this is the case, the FRC Guidance on Board Effectiveness recommends (at para. 62) that:

◆ the chair should ensure that sufficient time is allowed at the board for committees to report on the nature and content of discussion, on recommendations, and on actions to be taken;

◆ where there is disagreement between the relevant committee and the board, adequate time should be made available for discussion of the issue with a view to resolving the disagreement; and

◆ where any such disagreement cannot be resolved, the committee concerned should have the right to report the issue to the shareholders as part of the report on its activities in the annual report.

13. Role of the company secretary

Chapter 3 addresses the role of the company secretary in corporate governance. In this section, we highlight the provisions of the Code on the secretary and the related recommendations contained in the FRC Guidance on Board Effectiveness.

The Code has acknowledged since its inception in 1992 (in the form of the Cadbury Code) that the secretary has an important role to play in improving and maintaining standards of corporate governance. Through careful wording, the

Code has always sought to emphasise the secretary's role as an impartial adviser to the whole board, including both executive and non-executive directors alike.

Most of the things that the secretary does, or is expected to do, with regard to board governance have a critical impact on the effectiveness of the board. In pursuing these activities the secretary's main ally and main point of contact will be the chair, as the leader of the board.

13.1 Governance role of the company secretary

The UK Corporate Governance Code used to include a description of the company secretary's role in corporate governance. That description (in the supporting principles to B.5 of the 2016 Code) stated:

◆ Under the direction of the chair, the company secretary's responsibilities include ensuring good information flows within the board and its committees and between senior management and non-executive directors, as well as facilitating induction and assisting with professional development as required.

◆ The company secretary is responsible for advising the board through the chair on all governance matters.

The first part of this description of the secretary's role was removed from the 2018 Code and transferred to the 2018 FRC Guidance on Board Effectiveness (see, in particular, para. 81 of the Guidance). The second part was merged with another former code provision to create what is now 2018 Code Provision 16. That provision states that:

'All directors should have access to the advice of the company secretary, who is responsible for advising the board on all governance matters.'

This provision highlights the fact that the secretary is expected to act as an impartial adviser to the whole board on governance matters. This role as an impartial adviser is also protected by the requirement in the same Code provision that the secretary's appointment and removal should be a matter for the whole board (see below).

The company secretary is also mentioned in Principle I of the UK Corporate Governance Code, which states that:

'The board, supported by the company secretary, should ensure that it has the policies, processes, information, time and resources it needs in order to function effectively and efficiently.'

The description of the secretary's role in corporate governance is now set out in the FRC Guidance on Board Effectiveness, which states (at paras. 79 and 81 to 85):

'79. The company secretary is responsible for ensuring that board procedures are complied with, advising the board on all governance matters, supporting the chair and helping the board and its committees to function efficiently.

81. Under the direction of the chair, the company secretary's responsibilities

include ensuring good information flows within the board and its committees and between senior management and non-executive directors, as well as facilitating induction, arranging board training and assisting with professional development as required.

82. The company secretary should arrange for the company to provide the necessary resources for developing and updating its directors' knowledge and capabilities. This should be in a manner that is appropriate to the particular director, and which has the objective of enhancing that director's effectiveness in the board or committees, consistent with the results of the board evaluation processes.

83. It is the responsibility of the company secretary to ensure that directors, especially non-executive directors, have access to independent professional advice at the company's expense where they judge it necessary to discharge their responsibilities as directors of the company. Committees should be provided with sufficient resources to undertake their duties.

84. Assisting the chair in establishing the policies and processes the board needs in order to function properly is a core part of the company secretary's role. The chair and the company secretary should periodically review whether the board and the company's governance processes – for example, board and committee evaluation – are fit for purpose, and consider any improvements or initiatives that could strengthen the governance of the company.

85. The company secretary's effectiveness can be enhanced by building relationships of mutual trust with the chair, the senior independent director and the non-executive directors, while maintaining the confidence of executive director colleagues. They are in a unique position between the executive and the board, and well placed to take responsibility for concerns raised by the workforce about conduct, financial improprieties or other matters.'

Further discussion of the secretary's governance role can be found in Chapter 3.

13.2 Appointment and removal of the secretary

The Code provides that both the appointment and removal of the company secretary should be a matter for the board as a whole (Code Provision 16). This provision is designed to ensure that the secretary's initial appointment and continuing tenure is not dependent on the decision of a single director or group of directors. This helps to reinforce the secretary's position as an impartial adviser to the whole board. If the secretary could be appointed and removed by an individual director without recourse to the board, this impartiality could be compromised as they would inevitably feel under pressure to demonstrate greater loyalty to that person.

13.3 Reporting lines and remuneration

The FRC Guidance on Board Effectiveness recommends (at para. 80) that the company secretary should report to the chair on all governance matters but may also report to the CEO or some other executive director in relation to their other executive management responsibilities. Yet again, this recommendation is designed, in part, to protect the secretary's role as an impartial adviser to the board. It would, in any case, be inappropriate for the secretary to report to anyone else on governance matters. The chair and the secretary have to work very closely together on governance matters and the chair needs to be able to rely on the secretary to act impartially. If the secretary were to report, say, to the CEO on governance matters, this would potentially undermine the chair's position as the leader of the board.

Chapter 3 addresses the subject of reporting lines in more detail and considers the ICSA's guidance note, 'Duties and Reporting Lines of the Company Secretary', published in 2013.

That guidance note includes a long-standing recommendation that the secretary's remuneration and benefits should be fixed by the board or the remuneration committee. This recommendation has now effectively been adopted in Code Provision 33, which states that the remuneration committee should be responsible for setting the remuneration of 'senior management'. The term 'senior management' is defined for these purposes in a footnote to the Code as the executive committee or the first layer of management below board level, including the company secretary.

The FRC Guidance on Board Effectiveness also reiterates (at para. 80) that the remuneration of the company secretary should be determined by the remuneration committee.

Test yourself 6.6

1. **What is the governance role of the secretary?**

2. **Who should the secretary report to?**

Chapter summary

◆ Boards of directors do not delegate all of their management powers to the executive directors. One of the key powers that they retain is to set the company's strategy and its strategic objectives. The board is also responsible for establishing the company purpose and values and ensuring that these are aligned with the company's culture.

◆ The board is also expected under the Code to:
   - ensure that the necessary resources are in place for the company to meet its objectives and measure performance against them;
   - establish a framework of prudent and effective controls, which enable risk to be assessed and managed;
   - ensure effective engagement with, and encourage participation from, shareholders and other stakeholders; and
   - ensure that workforce policies and practices are consistent with the company's values and support its long-term sustainable success.

- The board performs various governance functions through committees which make recommendations to the board, e.g. on new appointments and succession, audit, risk and executive and workforce remuneration.

- It is good practice for boards to adopt a schedule of matters reserved for the board which will set out, among other things, the thresholds for high level management decisions that need board approval and matters which must be approved by the directors by law, such as anti-bribery policies.

- The chair is the leader of the board and is responsible for its overall effectiveness.

- The CEO is the leader of the executive team and is responsible for proposing and delivering the strategy agreed by the board.

- The Code recommends that the roles of chair and CEO should be clearly defined and should not be held by the same person. It also recommends that the CEO should not be 'promoted' to the role of chair.

- Non-executive directors bring outside experience and expertise to the board. They are expected to provide constructive challenge, strategic guidance, offer specialist advice and hold management to account. They also perform important governance functions through committees of the board, such as setting executive remuneration.

- The Code requires at least half the board, excluding the chair, to comprise non-executives determined by the board to be independent when judged against certain independence criteria set out in the Code. Most of the independent NEDs will serve on one or more of the board committees.

- The effectiveness of non-executive directors can be undermined by: a lack of knowledge about the company's business; insufficient time spent with the company; defects in the decision-making process; and ineffective challenge.

- The senior independent director's function is to act as a conduit for shareholders and mediator in circumstances where the board fails to function properly.

- The company secretary's is dealt with in Chapter 2, but can be summarised as being to act as an impartial adviser to the whole board and as a facilitator of good governance practices.

Chapter seven

Board composition and succession planning

CONTENTS

1. Introduction

As we saw in Chapter 6, the board of directors is the main decision-making body within an organisation. To ensure that the decision making is effective, it is important to have the right people on the board who work as a strong team.

Laurance Kuper (2006) said that a 'real team is a small number of good people with complementary skills who have equally committed to a common purpose, clear performance goals and a joint approach for which they hold themselves mutually accountable'.

In previous chapters we have looked at the importance of having:

◆ a clear purpose

◆ clear performance goals

◆ the board as a collective, that is being mutually accountable.

In this chapter we are focusing on how an organisation ensures it has the right people on the board who complement each other and work together as a team.

2. Board size

The Code makes no recommendation on the size of the board of directors. Previous versions of the Code used to include a supporting principle which stated that:

'The board should be of sufficient size that the requirements of the business can be met and that changes to the board's composition and that of its committees can be managed without undue disruption, and should not be so large as to be unwieldy.'

Although this supporting principle was deleted from the 2018 Code, it probably still represents the position that most companies aim for.

The size of boards varies depending on the size of the company, the complexity of the business and the industry or sector in which it operates. Unless a company's articles of association specify a minimum or maximum number of directors, it is left to the board itself to decide how big it should be.

In making this decision several factors need to be considered, including:

◆   the requirements for a balanced board;
◆   the requirements of the UK Code on the composition of the board;
◆   the need to service board committees;
◆   the ability of the board to hold productive, constructive discussions and make prompt rational decisions.

According to the Spencer Stuart 2018 Board Index, the average board of a top FTSE 150 company has 10.1 directors. The equivalent figure in 2007 was 10.8 directors, which means that the number has only decreased by 6.5% over that period. The average for the UK is very similar to the average in most other developed countries, including the US, although the average in both Germany and France is closer to 14, partly as a result of their worker participation rules (see Table 7.1).

According to the Spencer Stuart 2018 Board Index:

◆   22% of FTSE 150 companies have 8 or fewer directors;
◆   56% have 9 to 11 directors;
◆   18% have 12 to 14 directors; and
◆   4% have 15 or more.

For its 2017 Good Governance Report, the Institute of Directors and the Cass Business School ranked the 100 largest UK listed companies against a good governance index. Companies with fewer than eight and more than 15 directors were given a negative weighting. Anything between that was given a neutral weighting.

Country	Average size	Country	Average size
Belgium	10	Poland	8
Denmark	9.8	Russia	10.5
Finland	8.1	Spain	10.9
France	13.7	Sweden	10.6
Germany	13.8	Switzerland	10.4
Italy	11.5	UK	10.1
Netherlands	9.3	USA	10.8

Table 7.1 Comparison of average board sizes in other countries

Source: Spencer Stuart 2018 UK Board Index

2.1   Requirements for a 'balanced board'

The requirements for a balanced board include:

◆   separation of the roles of chair and CEO;

◆   an appropriate balance of executive, non-executive and independent directors;

◆   appropriate skills, experience and knowledge;

◆   gender balance; and

◆   diversity.

We deal with each of these issues separately below.

2.2   Requirements of the UK Code on composition

As we saw in Chapter 6, the Code requires:

◆   separation of the roles of chair and CEO; and

◆   balance between executive, non-executive and independent directors.

In practice, these rules require boards to comprise:

◆   a separate board chair (who must be independent on appointment);

◆   a separate chief executive officer (CEO); and

◆   a number of independent non-executive directors (NEDs).

The rule on the balance between executive, non-executive and independent directors is that at least half the board, excluding the chair, should be non-executive directors whom the board considers to be independent (Code Provision 11). In judging whether a company complies with this requirement, you compare the number of independent non-executives against the total number of executive directors and non-independent NEDs (remembering not to count the chair in either of these categories). Each additional executive director or non-independent NED must therefore be matched by at least one independent NED.

For example, a company that has five executive directors and two NEDs who are not independent will need at least seven independent NEDs to balance them out. Adding back the chair (assuming that the role of chair and CEO is not combined) means that the company must have a total of 15 directors.

Clearly, if you reduce the number of people on the right-hand side of the equation, you can reduce the number of independent NEDs required and therefore reduce the size of the board. However, there may be a limit to how far you can go with this because of the need to have sufficient independent NEDs to service the committees required under the Code.

The number of executive directors who serve on the board will be one of the biggest influences on overall board size. A large multi-national company with several diverse businesses may decide that it needs an executive director from each major division on the board. Smaller companies with less complex businesses often survive with just two executive directors – typically the CEO and a finance director. Having fewer executive directors means that the company needs fewer non-executives.

Banks and other financial services companies may need a larger board as they need additional non-executives to staff a separate risk committee. For example, in its 2017 annual report Barclays reported that it had a board of 15, comprising the chair, two executives and 11 non-executive directors. Those non-executives served on five different committees, including separate audit, nomination, remuneration, risk and reputation committees.

2.3 Servicing board committees

The Code requires listed companies to have at least three board committees (audit, nomination and remuneration). The rules on the composition of those committees under the Code (see Table 7.2 below) influence the number of independent NEDs that a company may require.

	Nomination committee	**Audit committee**	**Remuneration committee**
Code provision	17	24	32
Standard rule for larger companies	Majority of members should be independent NEDs.	At least three independent NEDs	At least three independent NEDs
Smaller companies	Same	At least two independent NEDs	At least two independent NEDs

Table 7.2 Rules on the composition of board committees under the Code

If each independent NED was only allowed to serve on one committee, you would need:

large company
For accounting purposes, a large company is one that does not qualify as a medium-sized company because it exceeds at least two out of the three size thresholds for determining whether a company as medium-sized. See also very large company.

◆ a minimum of eight independent NEDs in a **large company**; and
◆ a minimum of five in a smaller company.

The Code does not say that independent NEDs may serve on only one committee. However, the FRC Guidance on Board Effectiveness suggests (at para. 63) that the chair should ensure that individual independent NEDs are not over-burdened when deciding the chairs and membership of committees.

In practice, it is not unusual for independent NEDs to serve on more than one committee. In larger companies, it is rare for them to serve on more than two. However, in smaller companies, some NEDs may serve on all three committees. It should not be forgotten that under previous versions of the Code, smaller companies were only required to have a minimum of two independent NEDs. In a company that took full advantage of this dispensation, those two independent NEDs effectively had to serve on all three committees. In practice, what many smaller companies did in these circumstances was to merge some of the responsibilities of the usual board committees, enabling them to make do with just one or, maybe, two board committee to deal with corporate governance matters. As smaller companies are now subject to the standard Code provision on the balance of independent NEDs on the board, and can be expected to come under pressure to appoint more than two independent NEDs, it is less likely that any individual will need to serve on all three committees in the future.

2.4 Ability of the board to hold productive, constructive discussions and make prompt rational decisions

In theory, overly large boards can be unwieldy and difficult to manage. Research on optimal team numbers is not conclusive but seems to suggest that somewhere between five to 12 members is the optimal size. Teams of over 12 are difficult to manage. Allowing everyone to have their turn to contribute can lead to longer meetings. Some people may be less likely to contribute to their full capabilities feeling that someone else will make the contribution. More viewpoints also have to be dealt with and this can lead to ineffective decision-making as too many compromises are made.

According to a 2014 study by GMI Ratings for The Wall Street Journal, companies with fewer board members reap considerably greater rewards for their investors. An analysis of nearly 400 US companies with a market capitalisation of at least $10 billion, showed that typically those with the smallest boards (8–10 directors) produced substantially better shareholder returns over a three-year period between the spring of 2011 and 2014 when compared with companies with the biggest boards (12–14 directors). Companies with small boards outperformed their peers by 8.5%, while those with large boards underperformed their peers by over 10%. Some of the reasons cited were that:

◆ there is 'more effective oversight of management' by smaller boards;

◆   smaller boards are more likely to dismiss their CEOs for poor performance;

◆   and smaller boards are more likely to be 'decisive, cohesive and hands-on'.

Test yourself 7.1

1.   **If a board is comprised of a chair, three executive directors, one of whom is the CEO, and a non-executive director representing the major shareholder, how many independent directors will be required to comply with the UK Corporate Governance Code?**

2.   **List the factors that will typically influence the size of the board.**

3. Balance of skills, knowledge and experience

Principle K of the Code states that:

'The board and its committees should have a combination of skills, experience and knowledge.'

We have already dealt with how this principle translates into code provisions requiring a balance between executive, non-executive and independent directors. We also deal with the issues of gender and ethnic diversity separately in Section 4 of this chapter.

This issue can have an impact on the size of the board. Additional or replacement directors may be required to fill various skills or knowledge gaps on the board.

The FRC Guidance on Board Effectiveness (at paras. 87, 88 and 91) expands on Principle K by saying:

'87. Appointing directors who are able to make a positive contribution is one of the key elements of board effectiveness. Directors will be more likely to make good decisions and maximise the opportunities for the company's success if the right skillsets and a breadth of perspectives are present in the boardroom. Non-executive directors should possess a range of critical skills of value to the board and relevant to the challenges and opportunities facing the company.

88. Diversity in the boardroom can have a positive effect on the quality of decision-making by reducing the risk of group think. With input from shareholders, boards need to decide which aspects of diversity are important in the context of the business and its needs.'

Paragraph 91 of the FRC Guidance goes on to say that diversity of personal attributes is equally important. It suggests that the nomination committee should seek to ensure that the board is comprised of individuals who display a range of softer skills, such as:

- sources of intellect, critical assessment and judgement;
- courage;
- openness;
- honesty;
- tact;
- ability to listen;
- ability to forge relationships;
- ability to develop trust; and
- strength of character.

The FRC's 2015 discussion paper on UK board succession planning' suggested that nomination committees still needed to be more active in aligning board composition with company strategy. Its 2016 feedback statement revealed that many companies use skills and experience matrices, including personality-related versions, to help with cultural fit, and completed a gap analysis of board requirements in order to achieve a better link to strategy and company culture.

A skills matrix is a table that displays people's proficiency in specified skills, knowledge, competencies and aptitudes (see Table 7.3). It is likely that such a matrix will be prepared as part of an externally facilitated board evaluation. In such circumstances, the independent evaluator may come armed with a standard template of skills and aptitudes that could or should be evaluated. The nomination committee and chair (if not a member of the committee) should review whether that template includes all the skills and attributes that they consider desirable in view of the company's current and future strategy. This process of determining what should be evaluated may in itself reveal immediate and obvious skills gaps. The process of actually evaluating the skills and attributes of the existing directors may simply reinforce this. The evaluation process is often conducted using an anonymous survey in which the directors are asked to evaluate both themselves and their peers, with the results being weighted in favour of the latter.

The company secretary/governance professional will probably be responsible for keeping the skills matrix up to date. This will probably done as part of any internal annual board evaluation process and following any changes to the composition of the board.

A skills gap analysis will compare what skills and aptitudes the board now has against what it needs either now or in the future. For example, a company coming to the market for the first time may decide that it needs to recruit one or more directors with previous listed company experience. Similarly, a company seeking to expand overseas might need a director with previous international business experience.

Industry knowledge and experience	Directors (showing where relevant years left to serve)					
	CEO	CFO	NED A (5 yrs)	NED B (3 yrs)	Chair (2 yrs)	NED C (1 yr)
Business sector experience	x	x		x	x	x
International business experience						X
Dealing with government and regulators			x		x	
Technical skills						
Accounting		x	x			
Acquisitions & mergers						
Finance		X				
IT						X
Risk management	x		x	x		
Strategy development and implementation	x				x	
Personal attributes						
Ability to forge relationships					X	
Communication skills				x	x	
Courage	X					
Judgement		x			x	
Openness						
Integrity			x		x	
Listening skills					x	x
Mentoring skills		x			x	
Tact						
Willingness to challenge			x			x

Table 7.3 Example of a simple skills and attributes matrix

In Table 7.3 above, there is nobody with experience of acquisitions and mergers. In addition NED C, who has only one year left in office, has a number of skills which nobody else shares (e.g. on IT and international business experience). In our example you can see that we have positioned the directors in the table according to the number of years they have left to serve. This helps to highlight which skills may need to be replaced sooner rather than later. Our design also highlights certain critical skills held by only one person (using an uppercase 'X' instead of the usual lowercase 'x'). In our example we have made a binary decision as to whether a director has a particular skill or aptitude. This decision could be based on whether, on average, they exceeded a predetermined threshold in the anonymous survey by their peers. This method makes the matrix easier to interpret but hides the fact that some directors may have been judged to be on the cusp of this arbitrary threshold. For this reason, companies sometimes create a more detailed matrix showing the underlying figures for each director.

Stop and think 7.1

One of the consequences of having a smaller board and fewer executive directors may be that the board does not have the same breath of skills and knowledge. It may also result in the board becoming over-reliant on the skills and experience of just one board member in certain critical areas.

Test yourself 7.2

1. **What is a skills matrix?**
2. **What purpose would such a matrix serve in the process of appointing a new director?**

4. Diversity

4.1 Introduction

There has been no shortage of initiatives on diversity in the last 10 years.

In 2010, the FRC amended the UK Corporate Governance Code to state that appointments to the board should be 'made, on merit, against objective criteria and with due regard for the benefits of diversity on the board, including gender'. The FRC's intention was to encourage nomination committees to include diversity and gender mix in the factors that are taken into account when considering the need for new appointments.

The Code was amended again in 2012 to introduce several new requirements designed to promote gender diversity in the boardroom. The changes were made in support of proposals made by Lord Davies of Abersoch in the 2011 Women on Boards report, which set targets for female representation on boards. The Code changes required:

◆ companies to report on their diversity policies in the nomination committee's report; and

◆ board evaluations to cover the diversity of the board, including gender diversity.

In 2013, the CA2006 was amended to introduce for quoted companies a requirement that the strategic report should contain disclosures on gender diversity, not just on the board but also in senior management positions and the workforce as a whole. The FRC amended the UK Corporate Governance Code in 2018 to mirror some of these statutory requirements but also to clarify the definition of 'senior management' for reporting purposes.

In 2016, the FCA introduced a further disclosure requirement on diversity in the Disclosure Guidance and Transparency Rules in order to implement a requirement of the EU Non-financial Reporting Directive.

In November 2016, a committee chaired by Sir John Parker published a Report into the Ethnic Diversity of UK Boards.

4.2 Current Code principles and provisions

Principle J of the 2018 Code is now more explicit than the original 2010 code principle on diversity. It provides that:

'Both appointments and succession plans should be based on merit and objective criteria and, within this context, should promote diversity of gender, social and ethnic backgrounds, cognitive and personal strengths.'

Footnote 5 to the 2018 Code clarifies that the objective criteria applied should protect against discrimination for those with protected characteristics within the meaning of the Equalities Act 2010.

Principle L of the Code states that:

'Annual evaluation of the board should consider its composition, diversity and how effectively members work together to achieve objectives.'

Code Provision 23 requires the annual report to describe the work of the nomination committee, including:

◆ the process used in relation to appointments, its approach to succession planning and how both support developing a diverse pipeline;

◆ how the board evaluation has or will influence board composition;

◆ the policy on diversity and inclusion, its objectives and linkage to company strategy, how it has been implemented and progress on achieving the objectives; and

◆ the gender balance of those in the senior management and their direct reports.

Senior management is defined for the purposes of the 2018 Code in footnote 4 as 'the executive committee or the first layer of management below board level, including the company secretary'. This is deliberately not the same as the definition used in the CA2006 for the purposes of the statutory reporting requirements.

The FRC Guidance on Board Effectiveness suggests (at paras. 89 and 90) that:

'89. Developing a more diverse executive pipeline is vital to increasing levels of diversity amongst those in senior positions. Improving diversity at each level of the company is important if more diversity at senior levels is to become a reality. Greater transparency about the make-up of the workforce could support this. This might cover a range of different aspects of diversity, including age, disability, ethnicity, education and social background, as well as gender.

90. Working with human resources, the nomination committee will need to take an active role in setting and meeting diversity objectives and strategies for the company as a whole, and in monitoring the impact of diversity initiatives. Examples of the type of actions the nomination committee could consider encouraging include:

◆ a commitment to increasing the diversity of the board by setting stretching targets (such as the targets proposed by the Hampton-Alexander Review and the Parker Report);

◆ dedicated initiatives with clear objectives and targets; for example, in areas of the business that lack diversity;

◆ a focus on middle management;

◆ mentoring and sponsorship schemes;

◆ a commitment to more diverse shortlists and interview panels; and

◆ positive action to encourage more movement of women into non-traditional roles.'

Paragraph 94 of the FRC Guidance suggests that publicly advertising board appointments and working with recruitment consultants who have made a commitment to promote diversity are examples of ways in which the nomination committee can access a more diverse pool of candidates from which to appoint. It also suggests that attention needs to be paid to how the interview process is conducted so that candidates with diverse backgrounds are not disadvantaged.

4.3   Gender diversity – Women on Boards review

As mentioned above, many of the above changes were made in response to proposals made by Lord Davies of Abersoch in a report published in February 2011 entitled 'Women on Boards'. The report recommended that FTSE 350 companies should publicly adopt targets for the percentage of women on their boards and report on their compliance with those targets. Although these targets would be voluntary, it is suggested that FTSE 100 companies should be aiming for a minimum of 25% female board representation by 2015. In practice this target was achieved in 2015, and a new target was set in October 2015 of 33% representation by 2020 for all FTSE 350 companies.

The Women on Boards review also recommended that:

◆ Companies should periodically advertise non-executive board positions to encourage greater diversity in applications.

◆ Executive search firms should draw up a voluntary code of conduct addressing gender diversity and best practice which covers the relevant search criteria and processes relating to FTSE 350 board-level appointments. A large number of executive search firms subsequently signed up to comply with a Voluntary Code of Conduct for Executive Search Firms. The code sets out steps for search firms to follow across the search process, from accepting a brief through to final induction.

◆ In order to achieve these recommendations, recognition and development of two different populations of women who are well-qualified to be appointed to UK boards needs to be considered: (i) executives from within the corporate sector, for whom there are many different training and mentoring opportunities; and (ii) women from outside the corporate mainstream, including entrepreneurs, academics, civil servants and senior women with professional service backgrounds, for whom there are many fewer opportunities to take up corporate board positions.

4.4 Gender diversity – Hampton-Alexander Review

In February 2016, the Government appointed Sir Philip Hampton and the late Dame Helen Alexander to chair an independent review that would continue the work of the Women on Boards review. The Hampton-Alexander Review was tasked with increasing the representation of women on FTSE boards and in senior executive positions.

In November 2016, the Hampton-Alexander Review published a report which recommended:

◆ a 33% target for women on FTSE 350 boards by the end of 2020;

◆ a 33% target for women on FTSE 100 executive committees and direct reports to the executive committee on a combined basis by 2020; and

◆ that FTSE 350 companies increase the number of women in the roles of chair, senior independent director and into executive director positions on their boards.

In its 2017 report, the Review also called on FTSE 350 companies to comply with the second of these recommendations, as well as the first and third ones.

Figures published in the review's 2018 report reveal that FTSE 100 companies are on track to hit the 33% target with more than 30% of board positions occupied by women. This has risen from 12.5% in 2011.

According to the 2018 report, four companies in the FTSE 100 and six in the FTSE 250 already have 50% or more women on their boards. However, almost one in four FTSE 350 companies still only have one woman on their board, and there are still five all-male boards. The report suggests that in order to hit the targets set by the review, half the appointments to board positions in the FTSE 350 will have to be filled by women over the next two years.

The 2018 report also revealed an increase in the number of women in FTSE 350 leadership positions just below the board, with FTSE 100 executive committees at over 21% women for the first time.

The Spencer Stuart UK Board Index (2018), which studies the top 150 FTSE companies, reported that:

◆ the percentage of female board members rose to 27.5% in 2018, compared with 25.5% in 2017;

◆ in terms of non-executive directors (excluding chairs), women make up 38.5% of boards, rising from 34.7% in 2017; and

◆ in contrast the percentage of female executive directors decreased slightly in 2018 to 8.4%, from 8.9% in 2017, as did the percentage of female chairs which fell from 4.6% in 2017 to 4.0% in 2018.

The Spencer Stuart Board Index shows comparable figures for listed companies in other countries. These show that the UK still lags behind most other European countries, particularly Norway and France where the percentage of women on boards is over 40%, but is still ahead of the US, Russia and Spain.

UK companies have been meeting their gender diversity targets mainly by appointing more women as non-executive directors. The 2018 Hampton-Alexander Review expressed concern over the fact that this has not been reflected in a parallel increase in the number of women serving in the position of chair. This seems somewhat surprising in view of the fact that a 2017 study by Russell Reynolds Associates indicated that nearly two-fifths of companies recruit an internal candidate as chair. However, the same study showed that over half of company chairs had previous experience either as the CEO or finance director of a listed company (see Chapter 6). Clearly, the pool of women with this type of background is currently nowhere near as large as the pool of potential male candidates. According to figures in the 2018 Hampton-Alexander Report, between 2011 and 2018 the proportion of female executive directors in FTSE 100 companies nearly doubled from 5.5% to 10.2%. However, the underlying figures for the number of women in executive director posts during that period increased by less than 50% from 18 to just 26. The difference between these two figures reflects the fact that there are now fewer executive posts on FTSE 100 boards but that women hold proportionately more of those posts. This dichotomy is even more pronounced in the FTSE 250 where the percentage of women holding executive director posts increased from 4.2% in 2011 to 6.4% in 2018. Although this represents a 52% increase proportionately, the underlying figures show that the actual number of women serving as executive directors in FTSE 250 companies only increased over that same period from 27 to 30. Although this represents a 10% increase, there is no escaping the fact that there were only three more female FTSE 250 executive directors in 2018 than in 2011.

4.5 Ethnic diversity

In November 2016, the Parker Review (a committee chaired by Sir John Parker) published a Report into the Ethnic Diversity of UK Boards, which called for:

◆ an increase in the ethnic diversity of UK boards;

◆ companies to develop ethnic candidates for the pipeline and plan for succession; and

◆ greater transparency and disclosure on ethnic diversity.

The Committee's recommendations to increase the ethnic diversity of UK boards were that:

◆ Each FTSE 100 board should have at least one director of colour by 2021; and each FTSE 250 board should have at least one director of colour by 2024.

◆ Nomination committees of all FTSE 100 and FTSE 250 companies should require their human resources teams or search firms (as applicable) to identify and present qualified people of colour to be considered for board appointment when vacancies occur.

◆ The Standard Voluntary Code of Conduct for executive search firms should be extended to apply to the recruitment of minority ethnic candidates as board directors of FTSE 100 and FTSE 250 companies.

In order to help UK companies enhance the ethnic diversity of their boards, the Committee developed a series of Questions for Directors and a Directors' Resource Toolkit. These are set out in appendices A and B of its Report.

The Committee's recommendations on developing candidates for the pipeline and planning for succession were as follows:

◆ FTSE 100 and FTSE 250 companies should develop mechanisms to identify, develop and promote people of colour within their organisations in order to ensure over time that there is a pipeline of board capable candidates and their managerial and executive ranks appropriately reflect the importance of diversity to their organisation.

◆ Led by board chairs, existing board directors of FTSE 100 and FTSE 250 companies should mentor and/or sponsor people of colour within their own companies to ensure their readiness to assume senior managerial or executive positions internally, or non-executive board positions externally.

◆ Companies should encourage and support candidates drawn from diverse backgrounds, including people of colour, to take on board roles internally (e.g., subsidiaries) where appropriate, as well as board and trustee roles with external organisations (e.g., educational trusts, charities and other not-for-profit roles). These opportunities will give experience and develop oversight, leadership and stewardship skills.

The Committee's recommendations on transparency and disclosure are as follows:

◆ A description of the board's policy on diversity should be set out in a company's annual report. This should include a description of the company's efforts to increase, among other things, ethnic diversity within its organisation, including at board level.

◆ Companies that do not meet board composition recommendations by the relevant date should disclose in their annual report why they have not been able to achieve compliance.

The Pensions and Lifetime Savings Association (PLSA) has stated in its Corporate Governance Policy and Voting Guidelines that it expects listed companies to report on ethnic diversity and against the targets set out in the Parker Report.

4.6   Recruiting non-executives from diverse backgrounds

The Higgs Report (2003) recommended that the nomination committee should be tasked with considering candidates from a wide range of backgrounds. It recommended that boards:

◆   should draw more actively from areas such as human resources, change management, customer care and the professions where women tend to be more strongly represented;

◆   should also consider recruiting candidates from private companies, charities and public sector bodies;

◆   if operating in international markets, could benefit from having at least one international non-executive director with relevant skills and experience on their board; and

◆   should consider bringing onto the boards of subsidiary companies talented individuals from wider and more diverse backgrounds to give them exposure to the operation of a board as a possible stepping-stone to the board of a listed company (Higgs Report, para. 10.15–33).

At the invitation of the Government, Dean Laura D'Andrea Tyson of the London Business School agreed to chair a working group to take these proposals forward. The conclusions of the working group were published in The Tyson Report on the Recruitment and Development of Non-Executive Directors (2003).

The report highlighted how a range of different backgrounds and experiences among board members can enhance board effectiveness and explored how a broader range of non-executive directors can be identified and recruited::

◆   Factors such as a company's size and age, the makeup of its customer and employee base, the extent of its participation in global markets, its future strategies and its current board membership are important determinants of its NED requirements.

◆   Diversity in the backgrounds, skills and experiences of NEDs enhances board effectiveness by bringing a wider range of perspectives and knowledge to bear on issues of company performance, strategy and risk. Board diversity can also send a positive and motivating signal to customers, shareholders and employees, and can contribute to a better understanding by the company's leadership of the diverse constituencies that affect its success.

◆   Many UK companies would benefit from extending their searches for NEDs to new pools of talent. Possible sources of talented candidates that traditional, largely informal, search processes have tended to overlook include: the so-called 'marzipan' layer of corporate management just below board level; unlisted companies and private equity firms; business services and consultancies; and organisations in the non-commercial sector.

◆ Despite the increasing globalisation of business, the NEDs of UK companies tend to be domestic citizens rather than foreign nationals. Such board membership represents a potential mismatch between the international issues a company faces and the knowledge that its domestic board members can bring.

◆ Optimising board membership is vital for company performance and competitiveness. It can also play an important role in restoring shareholder and public trust in UK boardrooms.

4.7 Reporting on diversity

As mentioned previously, the Code (Code Provision 23) requires listed companies to disclose in the nomination committee's report:

◆ their policy on diversity and inclusion, its objectives and linkage to company strategy, how it has been implemented and progress on achieving the objectives; and

◆ the gender balance of those in the senior management and their direct reports.

The requirements in the first bullet point above are very similar to the requirements previously found in 2016 Code provision B.2.4.

Research conducted for the FRC by the University of Exeter Business School in 2018 found that the majority of listed companies have adopted policies on boardroom diversity but that their reporting to stakeholders needs to improve. The research, Board Diversity Reporting, assessed company reporting on diversity in annual reports published in the year to 1 March 2018. It found that:

◆ 98% of FTSE 100 companies and 88% of FTSE 250 companies have a policy on board diversity and that roughly a third of these policies refer to ethnicity as well as gender; but

◆ just 15% of FTSE 100 companies and 6% of FTSE 250 companies report against all four measures stated within provision B.2.4 of the 2016 Code.

The CA2006 requires quoted companies to include in their strategic report a breakdown showing at the end of the financial year the number of persons of each sex who were:

◆ directors;

◆ senior managers; and

◆ employees of the company (s. 414C).

For the purposes of the CA2006, a senior manager is defined as a person who is an employee and who has responsibility for planning, directing or controlling the activities of the company, or a strategically significant part of the company (s. 414C(9)).

The figures given by a parent company for the number of directors must be for its own board of directors. The breakdown given by a parent company for senior managers must include the number of people of each sex who were directors of undertakings consolidated in the group accounts (s. 414C(10)).

In the first few years of reporting under the statutory regime, companies did not always use the same criteria for determining whether a person qualified as a 'senior manager', making it difficult for users to make meaningful comparisons.

This is why the FRC adopted an additional reporting requirement in the 2018 Code covering the gender balance of those in senior management and their direct reports (2018 Code provision 23). Senior management is defined for the purposes of the Code in footnote 4 as 'the executive committee or the first layer of management below board level, including the company secretary'. This definition is a lot clearer than the one used in the CA2006.

It should also be noted that businesses, charities and certain public sector bodies with 250 or more employees must publish gender pay gap information in accordance with the Equality Act 2010 (Gender Pay Gap Information) Regulations 2017. This information must be published annually on both the employer's website and on a designated government website.

4.8 Diversity policy disclosures under the DTRs

Listed companies are also required to make disclosures in their corporate governance statement regarding their diversity policy under the Disclosure Guidance and Transparency Rules (DTR 7.2.8A). This rule was introduced in November 2016 and implements article 20(1)(g) of the Accounting Directive as amended by the Non-Financial Reporting Directive.

DTR 7.2.8A(1) requires listed companies to disclose:

◆ the diversity policy applied to the company's administrative, management and supervisory bodies with regard to aspects such as 'age, gender or educational and professional backgrounds';

◆ the objectives of the diversity policy;

◆ how the diversity policy has been implemented; and

◆ the results in the reporting period.

If no diversity policy is applied by the company, the corporate governance statement must contain an explanation as to why this is the case (DTR 7.2.8A(2)).

Companies that apply the UK Corporate Governance Code may already be meeting some of these requirements, although it should be noted that the rule in the DTR 7.2.8A covers a broader range of diversity criteria. It is, perhaps, somewhat surprising that the underlying EU legislation (and therefore DTR 7.2.8A) does not specifically mention ethnic diversity as one of the factors that should be covered by the diversity policy. Nevertheless, as we have already seen, this is something that the policies of UK listed companies are expected to cover and be reported on.

Test yourself 7.3

1.   **How does the 2018 UK Corporate Governance Code seek to promote diversity?**

2.   **List the types of disclosures listed companies are required to make on diversity.**

5. Nomination committee

Principle J of the Code states that:

'Appointments to the board should be subject to a formal, rigorous and transparent procedure and an effective succession plan should be maintained for board and senior management.'

In practice the Code requires the board to establish a nomination committee to lead the process for board appointments and succession planning (Code Provision 17).

The nomination committee is not expected to have the final say on these matters but to make recommendations to the board. The FRC Guidance on Board Effectiveness clarifies (at para. 62) that the final decision on all matters within the committee's remit will rest with the board (see Chapter 6, Section 11).

5.1   Membership of nomination committee

A majority of members of the nomination committee should be independent non-executive directors (2018 Code Provision 17). The 2016 Code used to state specifically that the committee can be chaired by the company chair or an independent non-executive director. This provision is not repeated in the 2018 Code, which implies that any member of the committee can chair it, including a person who is neither the chair or an independent non-executive. The 2018 Code still provides that the company chair should not chair the committee when it is dealing with the appointment of their successor. In practice, it is very common for the company chair to be a member of the committee and very unusual for anyone other than the company chair and independent NEDs to serve on it.

Although the Code does not provide any specific guidance on the matter, nomination committees rarely consist of more than three directors. If, as is often the case, the board chair is a member of the committee, this will be the minimum number required to comply with the requirement that the majority of members are independent NEDs. However, a nomination committee comprising just two independent NEDs would also comply with this requirement.

It is standard practice to identify the chair and members of the nomination committee in the annual report, even though the Code no longer specifically requires this.

The company secretary/governance professional will usually act as secretary to the committee and play a major role in assisting it in the performance of its duties.

5.2 Role of the nomination committee

Code Provision 17 suggests that the role of the nomination committee is to:

◆ to lead the process for appointments;
◆ ensure plans are in place for orderly succession to both the board and senior management positions; and
◆ oversee the development of a diverse pipeline for succession.

The Higgs Report (2003) suggested that, in addition to identifying and nominating candidates to fill board vacancies, the committee's duties could include:

◆ reviewing annually the time required from a non-executive director and making recommendations to the board regarding the reappointment of any non-executive director at the conclusion of their specified term of office;
◆ regularly reviewing the structure, size and composition (including the skills, knowledge and experience) of the board and making recommendations to the board with regard to any changes;
◆ keeping under review the leadership needs of the organisation, both executive and non-executive, with a view to ensuring the continued ability of the organisation to compete effectively in the marketplace;
◆ making recommendations to the board regarding plans for succession for both executive and non-executive directors; and
◆ making recommendations to the board concerning any matters relating to the continuation in office of any director at any time.

Most of these matters can be considered to follow on naturally from the role envisaged under the 2018 Code. We deal with each of the committee's three main roles separately below.

The FRC Guidance on Board Effectiveness suggests (at para. 63) that the committee's terms of reference should:

◆ set out its responsibilities;
◆ set out the authority delegated to it by the board; and
◆ be published on the company's website.

Specimen terms of reference for a nomination committee can be found in the ICSA guidance note 'Terms of Reference — Nomination Committee'.

5.3 Description of the work of the nomination committee in the annual report

Code Provision 12 requires the annual report to describe the work of the nomination committee, including:

◆ the process used in relation to appointments, its approach to succession planning and how both support developing a diverse pipeline;

◆ how the board evaluation has been conducted, the nature and extent of an external evaluator's contact with the board and individual directors, the outcomes and actions taken, and how it has or will influence board composition;

◆ the policy on diversity and inclusion, its objectives and linkage to company strategy, how it has been implemented and progress on achieving the objectives; and

◆ the gender balance of those in the senior management (executive committee or the first layer of management below board level, including the company secretary) and their direct reports.

Test yourself 7.4

1. **What are the three main roles of the nomination committee?**

2. **What are the membership requirements for the committee?**

6. Appointments to the board

6.1 Led by the nomination committee

Principle J of the Code states that:

'Appointments to the board should be subject to a formal, rigorous and transparent procedure.'

Code Provision 17 clarifies that this procedure should be led by the nomination committee. This does not mean that the nomination committee has the final say on board appointments. The FRC Guidance on Board Effectiveness clarifies (at para. 62) that the final decision on all matters within the nomination committee's remit, including appointments, will rest with the board. Accordingly, the nomination committee will be responsible for recommending suitable candidates for appointments to the board.

6.2 Appointment process

Principle J of the Code states that:

'Both appointments and succession plans should be based on merit and objective criteria and, within this context, should promote diversity of gender, social and ethnic backgrounds, cognitive and personal strengths.'

A footnote to Principle J clarifies that making appointments based on merit and objective criteria is intended to protect against discrimination for those with protected characteristics within the meaning of the Equalities Act 2010.

The Code states that open advertising and/or an external search consultancy should generally be used for the appointment of the chair and non-executive directors (Code Provision 20). It also provides that if an external search consultancy is engaged it should be identified in the annual report alongside a statement about any other connection it has with the company or individual directors.

The 2018 FRC Guidance on Board Effectiveness (paras. 92) states that:

'92. Board appointments should be made on merit against objective criteria. The nomination committee should evaluate the skills, experience and knowledge on the board, and the future challenges affecting the business, and, in the light of this evaluation, prepare a description of the role and capabilities required for a particular appointment. It should then agree the process to be undertaken to identify, sift and interview suitable candidates. It is important to build a proper assessment of values and expected behaviours into the recruitment process.'

It goes on to say (at paras. 93 and 94) that:

◆   skills matrices which map the existing skillset against that required to execute strategy and meet future challenges can be an effective way of identifying skills gaps (see Section 3 in this chapter);

◆   publicly advertising board appointments and working with recruitment consultants who have made a commitment to promote diversity are examples of ways in which the nomination committee can access a more diverse pool of candidates from which to appoint; and

◆   attention also needs to be paid to how the interview process is conducted so that candidates with diverse backgrounds are not disadvantaged.

The nomination committee is also expected to use the results of the annual board evaluation to perform this task. Board evaluations are an opportunity for boards to review skills, assess their composition and agree plans for filling skills gaps, and increasing diversity.

6.3   Time commitments

Code Provision 15 provides that:

'When making new appointments, the board should take into account other demands on directors' time. Prior to appointment, significant commitments should be disclosed with an indication of the time involved.'

The FRC Guidance on Board Effectiveness states that:

'95. Directors are expected to undertake that they will have sufficient time to meet what is expected of them effectively. The role of chair, in particular, is demanding and time-consuming; multiple roles are therefore not advisable. The nomination committee may wish to consider whether to set limits on the number and scale of other appointments it considers the chair and other non-executives may take on without compromising their effectiveness. This could help deal with shareholder concerns that some directors may have too many commitments, sometimes referred to as 'overboarding'.'

Code Provision 15 also states that:

'Additional external appointments should not be undertaken without prior approval of the board, with the reasons for permitting significant appointments explained in the annual report. Full-time executive directors should not take on more than one non-executive directorship in a FTSE 100 company or other significant appointment.'

6.4 Inspection of service contracts and terms of appointment

Section 228 of the CA2006 requires directors' service contracts (or if the contract is not in writing, a memorandum setting out its terms) to be made available for inspection by members at the company's registered office or SAIL (single alternative inspection location).

As non-executive directors do not have a service contract, the UK Corporate Governance Code used to require their terms of appointment to be made available for inspection by any person at the company's registered office during normal business hours and at the AGM (for 15 minutes prior to the meeting and during the meeting). This requirement has been deleted from the 2018 Code.

The FRC Guidance on Board Effectiveness still states (at para. 96) that 'the terms and conditions of appointment of the chair and non-executive directors must be available for inspection'. However, it cites the CA2006 as authority for this statement. It goes on to say that these letters of appointment should set out the expected time commitment and also indicate the possibility of additional commitment when the company is undergoing a period of particularly increased activity.

7. Accepting an offer of appointment

The Higgs Report (2003) on the role and effectiveness of non-executive directors recommended that before accepting an appointment, prospective non-executive directors should undertake their own thorough examination of the company to satisfy themselves that it is an organisation in which they can have confidence and in which they will be well suited to working.

ICSA subsequently published a guidance note for directors on how they might approach this task: 'Joining the Right Board — Due Diligence for Prospective Directors'.

The guidance recommends that prospective directors should conduct their own due diligence process prior to joining a board. This should include:

◆ looking at the company's annual report and website to see how it articulates its business model, governance, the market environment and dynamics, recent operational performance, strategy, risks and uncertainties, sustainability and financial performance;

◆ reviewing regulatory and media announcements issued since the last annual report was published and various other sources of information;

◆ arranging to meet the chair, CEO, CFO, company secretary and all members of the nomination committee, if not the entire board, before accepting an appointment;

◆ if joining with the intention of taking on the role of company chair or the chair of the audit or remuneration committees, arranging meetings with the auditors, the head of internal audit or the remuneration consultants as appropriate;

◆ taking the opportunity to talk with any other external advisers, senior management, employees, suppliers and customers; and

◆ checking scheduled board dates for the year ahead at an early stage in the due diligence process to ensure they will be able to attend.

The guidance accepts that published material 'is unlikely to reveal wrongdoing' but warns that 'a lack of transparency may be a reason to proceed with caution'.

Test yourself 7.5

1. **Outline the process for appointing a new NED.**

2. **How might that process differ when seeking to appoint a new chair or chief executive?**

8. Succession planning

Succession planning has long been considered to be one of the main weaknesses of boards. In October 2015 the FRC issued a discussion paper – 'UK Board Succession Planning' – which sought views on various issues surrounding board succession for both executives and non-executives.

The discussion paper suggested that listed company boards are not paying enough attention to succession planning, and cited as evidence the fact that succession planning was one of the issues most frequently highlighted in board evaluations.

The discussion paper focused in particular on whether the nomination committee's role in succession planning and ensuring a diverse pipeline should be made clearer and whether companies should be required to make further disclosures on these matters in the annual report. At the time the UK Corporate Governance Code stated as a supporting principle that boards should satisfy themselves that plans are in place for orderly succession for appointments to the board and senior management positions, but did not specifically task the nomination committee with any responsibility in this area. The clearest statement that the committee ought to play a role was made in the largely forgotten 2003 Higgs Report.

8.1   Succession planning in the 2018 Code

The FRC subsequently made changes to the 2018 Code to expand the remit of the nomination committee in this regard.

Principle J of the 2018 Code now states that:

'…an effective succession plan should be maintained for the board and senior management.'

Code Provision 17 recommends that the nomination committee should 'ensure plans are in place for orderly succession to both the board and senior management positions, and oversee the development of a diverse pipeline for succession'.

The definition of 'senior management' in the Code for these purposes includes 'the executive committee or the first layer of management below board level, including the company secretary'.

The FRC Guidance on Board Effectiveness envisages that the chair will play a major role in succession planning. Paragraph 97 states:

'The chair's vision for achieving the optimal board composition will help the nomination committee review the skills required, identify the gaps, develop transparent appointment criteria and inform succession planning. It is a good idea for the nomination committee to assess periodically whether the desired outcome has been achieved, and propose changes to the process as necessary.'

It should be noted in this regard that the company chair will often be a member of the nomination committee and may even chair it. Whether or not this is the case, the company chair will also be involved in succession planning as the leader of the board evaluation process. The FRC Guidance on Board Effectiveness suggests (at para. 109) that:

'Board evaluations should inform and influence succession planning. They are an opportunity for boards to review skills, assess their composition and agree plans for filling skills gaps, and increasing diversity. They can help companies identify when new board appointments may be needed and the types of skills that are required to maximise board effectiveness.'

Paragraph 110 goes on to say that:

'The outcomes from the board evaluation should be shared with and discussed by the board. They should be fed back into the board's work on composition…'

The FRC Guidance also suggests (at para. 101) that putting a succession plan in writing can help to ensure it is followed through.

Major shareholders sometimes expect to be consulted on a company's succession plans and new appointments. An Investment Association report produced in association with the accountancy firm EY, 'Board Effectiveness:

Continuing the Journey' (2015), highlighted:

◆   the benefits of having regular discussions about the CEO's tenure, not just when there are problems but when things are going well, and setting expectations around length of tenure at the time of appointment; and

◆   the value of involving investors in defining the attributes to be sought in new board appointments.

Any such discussions are likely to be led by the company chair.

8.2 What succession plans should cover

The FRC Guidance on Board Effectiveness suggests that succession plans should consider the following different time horizons:

◆   contingency planning – for sudden and unforeseen departures;

◆   medium-term planning – the orderly replacement of current board members and senior executives (such as retirement); and

◆   long-term planning – the relationship between the delivery of the company strategy and objectives to the skills needed on the board now and in the future.

It is obviously difficult to plan ahead for sudden and unforeseen departures. The post of CEO is particularly prone to sudden changes. These are often initiated by the board itself in response to poor performance, in which case there will normally be some warning in advance that a change may be necessary. However, executives sometimes move on to bigger and better jobs or may genuinely 'decide to spend more time with their family'. Where there is more than one internal candidate for the post of CEO, the ones who do not get the job may decide to leave.

Contingency planning for the sudden departure of the CEO will include assessing whether there are any internal candidates who would be capable of filling the role, whether on a permanent or temporary basis. For example, it is possible that the company chair could take on both roles while a replacement is found, although investors would normally prefer the roles to be kept separate.

Sudden departures by non-executive directors are much less common but may occur for personal or professional reasons. For example, a non-executive who also holds a full-time executive post may find that they can no longer commit the necessary time because of their other commitments. It is difficult to make any contingency plans to cater for the sudden departure of a non-executive director. For obvious reasons there is no pool of internal candidates to draw from. Replacement candidates will need to be selected, interviewed and appointed in the usual manner, which may take several months. This may mean that the company is temporarily unable to meet some of the requirements of the Code.

The starting point for medium-term planning will be the creation of a simple directors' succession timetable which shows in date order when each director's term of office is due to expire or when they are due to retire. A skills matrix (see Section 3) can then be used to determine whether a particular individual's departure will lead to a skills gap.

Long-term planning will be influenced mainly by the skills required to execute a change of strategy or to react to a changing business environment. For example, a traditional retailer may belatedly realise that in order to survive it needs an online platform but may not have the necessary skills to set one up.

The FRC Guidance on Board Effectiveness states (at para. 98) that: there 'are risks of becoming too reliant on the skills of one individual'. This is more likely to be an issue with regard to the CEO (see case study 7.1). It goes on to say (probably more in relation to non-executives, including the chair):

'Discussions on tenure at the time of appointment will help to inform and manage the long-term succession strategy. The needs of the company and the board will change over time, so it is wise to manage expectations and encourage non-executive directors to be flexible about term lengths and extensions. It is also a good idea to discuss board refreshment and succession with shareholders.'

The tenure of independent non-executive directors is effectively limited by the fact that they are not considered under the guidelines in Code Provision 10 to be independent after they have served for more than nine years.

The post of chair is not subject to the Code's independence test other than on appointment. Accordingly, this tenure limit does not strictly apply to the chair.

However, Code Provision 19 states that:

'The chair should not remain in post beyond nine years from the date of their first appointment to the board. To facilitate effective succession planning and the development of a diverse board, this period can be extended for a limited time, particularly in those cases where the chair was an existing non-executive director on appointment. A clear explanation should be provided.'

The FRC Guidance on Board Effectiveness expands slightly on this (at para. 105) by saying that there 'may be reasons for justifying a limited extension to the term of the chair beyond nine years if prior to being appointed chair, they have been a board member for a significant amount of time, and the appointment supports the company's succession plan and diversity policy'.

According to the 2018 Spencer Stuart Board Index, the average tenure for full-time chairs was about nine years (which means that about half of them must have served for more than nine years). By contrast, the average tenure for non-executive chairs was just 4.7 years, exactly the same as the average tenure of CEOs and slightly more than the average of 4.4 years for the finance director.

Case study 7.1

In April 2018, Sir Martin Sorrell resigned suddenly as CEO of the advertising group WPP after it was revealed that the company had launched an internal investigation into allegations of misconduct. Sir Martin had been one of the company's founders 33 years earlier and had been the driving force behind its expansion to become a global leader in advertising. Shareholders had previously expressed concern over the company's lack of a succession policy, particularly as Sir Martin was 73 at the time of his resignation. The company's initial response to his resignation was to appoint two existing executives as co-chief operating officers and to appoint the previously non-executive chair as CEO. It took the company a further five months to appoint one of the co-chief operating officers as the new chief executive after failing to find any suitable external candidates.

8.3 Overseeing the development of a diverse pipeline

The FRC Guidance on Board Effectiveness recognises that executive directors may be recruited externally, but suggests (at para. 99) that:

'…companies should also develop internal talent and capability. Initiatives to encourage this could include middle management development programmes, facilitating engagement between middle management and non-executive directors, as well as partnering and mentoring schemes.'.

It also suggests that:

◆ Talent management can be a strong motivational force for those who wish to develop their career within the company and achieve senior positions. It can provide the nomination committee with a variety of strong candidates. The nomination committee may find it worthwhile to take a more active interest in how talent is managed throughout the organisation (para. 100).

◆ Succession plans can also help to increase diversity in the boardroom and build diversity in the executive pipeline (para. 101).

8.4 Reporting on succession planning

The Code requires the annual report to contain a description of the nomination committee's work which must, amongst other things, set out the committee's approach to succession planning and how it supports the development of a diverse pipeline (Code Provision 12).

According to the 2018 Grant Thornton Corporate Governance Review, most companies (78%) already discuss senior management succession planning in the annual report. This tends to be limited in detail, however, with just 25% of the FTSE 350 doing any more than merely referring to the existence of a process of which only 6% give further detail.

With the 2018 Code's new concentration on succession planning and the nomination committee's enhanced responsibility below board level, one would expect the standard of reporting to get better.

Test yourself 7.6

1. **Briefly outline the three time horizons that a succession plan should cover.**

2. **Why is it more difficult to prepare a succession plan for executive directors?**

9. Refreshing board membership

The UK Corporate Governance Code used to provide that:

◆ non-executive directors should be appointed for specified terms subject to election and the Companies Act provisions relating to the removal of a director; and

◆ any term beyond six years should be subject to particularly rigorous review and should take into account the need for progressive refreshing of the board (2016 Code provision B.2.3).

This Code provision has been replaced in part by 2018 Code Principle K, which states that:

'Consideration should be given to the length of service of the board as a whole and membership regularly refreshed.'

This is obviously something that the nomination committee is expected to consider in consultation with the company chair as part of the company's succession planning.

The FRC Guidance on Board Effectiveness also states (at para. 63) that the chair should ensure that committee membership is periodically refreshed.

The independence criteria for non-executive directors in Code Provision 10 effectively set an upper limit of nine years' service. Code Provision 19 also recommends that the chair should not remain in post beyond nine years from the date of their first appointment to the board, although it allows this period to be extended in certain cases.

Most non-executive directors seem to serve for the full nine years. This can be seen from surveys showing the average tenure of non-executives. If every non-executive director served for exactly nine years, one would expect their average tenure at any one time (i.e. the average time they have spent in office) to be exactly 4.5 years. According to Spencer Stuart (2018), the average tenure of non-executive directors in 2018 was only slightly less at 4.3 years. This suggests that a significant proportion must serve the full nine years, although the average will also reflect some who have served for more than nine years and are no longer considered to be independent.

In view of the amount of time it takes for non-executive directors to gain the necessary knowledge required to contribute effectively, boards will often be reluctant to cut short their period office merely for the purposes of refreshment. However, refreshment could be used:

◆ as a cover to replace a non-executive who is not making an effective contribution;

◆ to meet diversity targets;

◆ to bring in a new director who has certain critical skills.

The recent increases in the number of women serving on listed company boards have almost certainly been achieved, in part, by a process of refreshment. According to Spencer Stuart (2018), the average tenure of non-executive directors in previous years consistently hovered around four years, compared to the latest figure of 4.3 years. This may reflect the fact that some companies were actively refreshing the board in order to meet their diversity targets and, possibly, that this period of refreshment is now slowing down as more and more companies meet their targets.

According to Spencer Stuart (2018), the average tenure of the chair also increased from 4.5 years in 2017 to five years in 2018, which reflects the fact that some serve more than nine years. However, the average tenure of CEOs fell from 5.5 years in 2017 to 4.7 years in 2018.

10. Annual re-election

10.1 Code requirements

Historically, articles of association used to require one-third of the directors to retire and offer themselves for re-election at the AGM. Early versions of the UK Corporate Governance Code included a requirement that directors should be subject to re-election at least once every three years.

In 2010, a provision was introduced requiring all directors of FTSE 350 companies to be re-elected on an annual basis. This was extended to all listed companies in the 2018 Code.

Code Provision 18 now states that 'All directors should be subject to annual re-election'. This requirement is intended to give shareholders an annual opportunity to express their views on the performance of the directors and to give boards an incentive to listen and respond to their concerns. The FRC hoped that this would in turn lead to ongoing engagement. Legally, annual re-elections mean that shareholders seeking the removal of a director do not need to propose their own resolution, which would involve giving special notice.

Investors use re-election resolutions to express their disquiet about various aspects of a company's behaviour. For example, if shareholders are unhappy about a company's remuneration policy, they may decide to vote against or withhold their vote on a resolution to reappoint the director who chairs the remuneration committee. Such rebellions rarely garner the necessary support to remove the director but might be considered a success if they reach the 20% threshold at which the company is required to respond to investors' concerns under Code Provision 4. Resolutions that receive this level of opposition are also added to the Investment Association's Public Register. When it launched the register in December 2017, the Investment Association revealed that over one in five (22%) listed companies featured on it, due to having at least one resolution that received over 20% dissent. Pay-related issues topped the list of shareholder concerns, with almost four out of ten (38%) resolutions listed. However, resolutions concerning the re-election of directors, came a close second at 32%.

10.2 Biographical details

The UK Corporate Governance Code used to require the names of directors submitted for election or re-election to be accompanied by 'sufficient biographical details to enable shareholders to take an informed decision on their election'. It also used to require the chair to 'confirm to shareholders when proposing the re-election of a director that, following formal performance evaluation, the individual's performance continues to be effective and to demonstrate a commitment to the role'. These provisions were deleted from the 2018 Code and replaced with one that, perhaps, seeks to combine the two ideas.

The Code now requires the board to set out in the papers accompanying the resolutions to elect each director the specific reasons why their contribution is, and continues to be, important to the company's long-term sustainable success (2018 Code Provision 18).

The Listing Rules (LR 9.8.8(9)) (but not the Code) require the annual remuneration report to include a statement of the unexpired portion of any service contract of a director who is being proposed for election or re-election at the forthcoming annual general meeting.

Test yourself 7.7

1. **Give three legitimate reasons why the nomination committee might propose a refreshment of the board.**

2. **Why does the Code require all directors to offer themselves for re-election on an annual basis?**

Chapter summary

◆ The size of boards varies depending on the size of the company, the complexity of the business and the industry or sector in which it operates.

◆ The minimum threshold in terms of board size is determined by the fact the Code expects the roles of chair and CEO to be separated and at least half the board (excluding the chair) to comprise of independent NEDs.

◆ In addition, listed companies need sufficient independent NEDs to service the various board committees required under the Code.

◆ Boards need a combination of skills, experience, knowledge and personal attributes. They should be comprised of individuals who display a range of softer skills, such as courage, tact, openness or integrity.

◆ The Code requires both appointments and succession plans to be based on merit and objective criteria and, within this context, to promote diversity of gender, social and ethnic backgrounds, cognitive and personal strengths.

◆ Boards are expected to adopt a policy on diversity and inclusion and make disclosures on that policy as part of the report of the nomination committee, including a summary of that policy, its objectives and linkage to company strategy, how it has been implemented and progress on achieving the objectives.

◆ As part of that policy boards are expected to adopt diversity targets for the board and senior management positions, particularly in relation to gender and race.

◆ These targets will probably be influenced by the recommendations of the Hampton-Alexander Review on gender diversity and the Parker Review on ethnic diversity.

◆ Quoted companies are required under the CA2006 to include in their strategic report a breakdown showing the number of persons of each sex who were directors, senior managers and employees of the company.

◆ In addition, businesses with 250 or more employees must publish gender pay gap information on their own website and a government website.

◆ The Code requires boards to establish a nomination committee comprising of a majority of independent NEDs to lead the process for board appointments and succession planning and oversee the development of a diverse pipeline.

◆ Board appointments should be made on merit against objective criteria.

◆ The nomination committee should evaluate the skills, experience and knowledge on the board, and the future challenges affecting the business, and, in the light of this evaluation, prepare a description of the role and capabilities required for a particular appointment.

◆ It should then agree the process to be undertaken to identify, sift and interview suitable candidates. This will result in a recommendation to the board, which will ultimately make the final decision on any new appointment.

◆ Before accepting an appointment prospective directors are expected to confirm that they are able to commit the necessary time. They are also expected to conduct their own due diligence on the company.

◆ Under the 2018 Code, the nomination committee is expected to ensure that plans are in place for orderly succession to both the board and senior management positions, and oversee the development of a diverse pipeline for succession.

◆ Succession plans should consider preparing for sudden and unforeseen departures, the orderly replacement of current board members and senior executives and the relationship between the delivery of the company strategy and objectives to the skills needed on the board now and in the future.

◆ The Code recommends that consideration should be given to the length of service of the board as a whole and its membership regularly refreshed.

◆ It requires all directors to be subject to annual re-election by shareholders at the AGM. This ensures that the shareholders have an annual opportunity to remove any director without having to propose such a resolution themselves and to register a protest vote against their re-election.

Chapter eight
Board effectiveness

CONTENTS

1. Introduction

Previous chapters in this part have dealt mainly with the structures and processes of the board. This chapter deals with behaviours and practices designed to enhance the effectiveness of the board, such as the decision-making process, corporate culture and annual board evaluations.

2. FRC Guidance on Board Effectiveness

The FRC publishes influential guidance in this area, which is known as the FRC Guidance on Board Effectiveness. The guidance was first published in March 2011 as a replacement for the Good Practice Suggestions from the 2003 Higgs Report (known as 'the Higgs Guidance'). However, the FRC published a new version of the guidance ('the 2018 FRC Guidance') to accompany the 2018 Code. The 2018 FRC Guidance is intended to come into force at the same time as the 2018 Code, i.e., for accounting periods commencing on or after 1 January 2019.

The stated purpose of the 2018 FRC Guidance is to stimulate boards' thinking on how they can carry out their role and encourage them to focus on continually improving their effectiveness. The guidance is not intended to be prescriptive. It contains suggestions of good practice to support directors and their advisors in applying the Code.

The core message behind the guidance is that boards need to think deeply about the way in which they carry out their role and the behaviours that they display, not just about the structures and processes that they put in place.

The 2018 FRC Guidance follows the layout of the Code and deals with the following topics:

◆ board leadership and company purpose;
◆ division of responsibilities;
◆ composition, succession and evaluation;
◆ audit, risk and internal control; and
◆ remuneration.

The 2018 FRC Guidance includes some of the procedural aspects of governance which were previously covered by the UK Corporate Governance Code, such as the 2016 Code provision A.1.1 on having a schedule of matters reserved for the board. According to the FRC, these former features of the Code are now well established as good practice, as evidenced by high levels of compliance. Transferring them to the FRC Guidance was intended to act as a reminder to boards and their support teams that good practice and procedure in these areas should continue to be followed.

3. Regular meetings

The UK Corporate Governance Code used to provide that the board should meet sufficiently regularly to discharge its duties effectively (2016 Code provision A.1.1). This provision has been removed from the 2018 Code and transferred to the 2018 FRC Guidance on Board Effectiveness (para. 28), which states that: 'Meeting regularly is essential for the board to discharge its duties effectively and to allow adequate time for consideration of all the issues falling within its remit.'

Code Provision 14 requires the annual report to set out the number of meetings of the board and its committees, and the individual attendance by directors. The Code previously specified that this information was only required in respect of the three main committees required under the Code. The 2018 Code extends this requirement to all board committees, which would include, for example, any risk committee.

According to the Spencer Stuart 2018 Board Index:

◆ top 150 FTSE companies held an average of just 7.3 scheduled board meetings in 2018, compared with 8.8 in 2017, although the average in 2018 was 8.7 if ad hoc meetings are included;

◆   two-thirds of companies held between six and eight scheduled meetings;

◆   although 22.6% held more than eight, only 10.7% held fewer than six;

◆   nearly a third of companies held at least one ad hoc meeting during the year;

◆   the average attendance rate at scheduled meetings was 98.2%; and

◆   attendance rates of at least 95% were recorded at 90.7% of companies.

The above results seem to suggest that the biggest listed companies are reducing the number of scheduled board meetings that they hold. The norm seems to be somewhere between six and eight meetings. It is likely that benchmarking conducted as part of the board evaluation process has caused companies to reconsider how many meetings they need.

4. Decision-making processes

Well-informed and high-quality decision-making is critical for board effectiveness. The FRC Guidance on Board Effectiveness suggests (at paras. 27 to 31) that many of the factors that lead to poor decision making are predictable and preventable, and that boards can minimise the risk of poor decisions by investing time in the design of their decision-making policies and processes.

Ensuring that there is a formal schedule of matters reserved for its decision is an essential part of this process that will assist the board's planning and provide clarity over where responsibility for decision making lies (see Chapter 6).

Paragraph 29 of the FRC Guidance states that:

'Most complex decisions depend on judgement, but the decisions of well-intentioned and experienced leaders can, in certain circumstances, be distorted. Factors known to distort judgement are conflicts of interest, emotional attachments, unconscious bias and inappropriate reliance on previous experience and decisions.'

Paragraph 30 states that boards also need to be aware of other factors that can limit effective decision making, such as:

◆   a dominant personality or group of directors on the board, inhibiting contribution from others;

◆   insufficient diversity of perspective on the board, which can contribute to 'group think';

◆   excess focus on risk mitigation or insufficient attention to risk;

◆   a compliance mindset and failure to treat risk as part of the decision-making process;

◆   insufficient knowledge and ability to test underlying assumptions;

◆   failure to listen to and act upon concerns that are raised;

◆   failure to recognise the consequences of running the business on the basis of self-interest and other poor ethical standards;

- a lack of openness by management, a reluctance to involve non-executive directors, or a tendency to bring matters to the board for sign-off rather than debate;
- complacent or intransigent attitudes;
- inability to challenge effectively;
- inadequate information or analysis;
- poor quality papers;
- lack of time for debate and truncated debate;
- undue focus on short-term time horizons; and
- insufficient notice.

The chair clearly has a critical role in ensuring that these factors do not impair the judgement of the board. The FRC Guidance suggests ways in which the chair can create conditions that support sound decision making. For example, para. 31 notes that some chairs favour a series of separate discussions for important decisions, covering steps like:

- concept;
- proposal for discussion; and
- proposal for decision.

Paragraph 32 suggests that, for significant decisions, boards may wish to consider extra steps, such as:

- describing in board papers the process that has been used to arrive at and challenge the proposal prior to presenting it to the board, thereby allowing directors not involved in the project to assess the appropriateness of the process before assessing the merits of the proposal itself;
- where appropriate, putting in place additional safeguards to reduce the risk of distorted judgements by, for example, commissioning an independent report, seeking advice from an expert, introducing a devil's advocate to provide challenge, establishing a specific sub-committee, and convening additional meetings; and
- ensuring that board minutes document the discussion that led to the decision, including the issues raised and the reasons for the decision.

Finally, the FRC Guidance suggests that after a significant decision has been made and implemented, the board may find it useful to review the effectiveness of the decision-making process, and the merits of the decision itself, maybe as part of the board evaluation process.

4.1 Dynamics at board meetings

Table 8.1 seeks to encapsulate the different roles played by the various participants in the decision-making process at board meetings. One could argue that executive and non-executive directors perform different functions. However, the FRC Guidance on Board Effectiveness suggests that executive directors should not see themselves only as members of the chief executive's team when engaged in board business. Although it will often be the executive directors who make proposals, which are then subject to scrutiny and challenge from the NEDs, it should not be forgotten that these roles can sometimes be reversed. Proposals will sometimes be made by an NED or a group of NEDs as a result of their participation in a board committee, in which case the executives will join in with the rest of the board in scrutinising and challenging that proposal.

Chair	Executive/Non-executive director	Company secretary
◆ Maintains control of proceedings, does not dominate ◆ Facilitates decision-making ◆ Stimulates debate, encourages all to contribute ◆ Encourages constructive duscussions ◆ Promotes airing and resolution of disagreements ◆ Steers towards consensus ◆ Ensures that decisions are understood and recorded ◆ Creates a positive environment ◆ Sets an example with respect to conflicts of interest	◆ Attends regularly, and prepares so as to be an effective decision-maker ◆ Acts objectively, and is open to other perspectives ◆ Does not dominate discussion ◆ Recognises collective decisions ◆ Fosters constructive challenge ◆ Evidences Independent enquiry ◆ Shares information ◆ Provides checks and balance ◆ Gives access to networks	◆ Registers attendance ◆ Determines quorum ◆ Maintains a record of the proceedings in order to produce the minutes and an action log ◆ Advises the chair on procedural matters ◆ Monitors climate of meeting ◆ Advises on governance issues

Table 8.1 Role of participants in board meetings

Table 8.2 sets out the characteristics of successful and painful meetings, according to Bernice McCarthy, About Learning, 1996. Painful in this context should be taken to mean unsuccessful.

PAINFUL MEETINGS	SUCCESSFUL MEETINGS
◆ The chair is insensitive to feelings ◆ There is a lack of trust among the group ◆ There are unresolved conflicts ◆ Consideration is not given to people who will be affected by the group's decision ◆ The meeting has no personal relevance	◆ Connections are made ◆ Honesty is encouraged ◆ Interests are elicited ◆ Time is allowed for discussion about feelings ◆ The chair provides for consensus building
◆ There is no agenda ◆ The chair does not understand the total picture ◆ There is no time for preparation ◆ There is insufficient time spent defining the problem ◆ No clarity is achieved as meeting progresses ◆ There is insufficient information for problem solving	◆ Issues and tasks clearly defined ◆ Information is based on facts ◆ There is adequate notice for preparation ◆ Pros and cons are weighed ◆ The group stays on task ◆ There is an objective perspective.
◆ There is a lack of focus, forays into side issues ◆ Emotions are vented ◆ Personalities are dealt with, not issues ◆ There is inattention to practical realities ◆ The chair does not move to closure	◆ There is a productive problem-solving climate ◆ Common sense is elicited ◆ Ideas are used ◆ Decisions aligned with the realities of existing structures and resources ◆ Closure is achieved
◆ There is rigid adherence to agenda and/or timetable ◆ People are tentative and cautious ◆ Strong, spirited interactions are not welcome ◆ There are long monologues ◆ There is only pretence at discussion, because in reality decisions have already been made	◆ There is a flexible agenda ◆ The participants look beyond stated objectives ◆ Energy is generated ◆ Actions are based on intuition ◆ Talk of possible creative action is encouraged

Bernice McCarthy (1996), About Learning

Table 8.2 Characteristics of meetings

Worked example 8.1

The board is in an all-day meeting called to discuss a new strategic plan. It is mid-afternoon. The meeting is supposed to end at 6 pm Board members are not paying attention to the CEO who has been showing a PowerPoint presentation for the last 30 minutes. Energy levels in the room are very low.

How can the chair get this meeting back on track?

Suggested answer

The chair suggests that, unless the presentation will draw to a close within, say, the next five minutes, they take a short comfort break.

During the break, the chair advises the CEO to assume that board members have read the background papers and to wrap up the presentation as swiftly as possible.

The chair negotiates a time limit with the CEO for wrapping up the presentation and devises a timetable that provides adequate time to allow board members to ask questions and discuss the proposals, with a view to reaching a decision before the end of the meeting.

When the meeting reassembles, the chair informs board members of the timetable, asks the secretary to act as impartial timekeeper and warns the board that unless a consensus is reached by 6 pm it may be necessary to hold a further meeting.

Stop and think 8.1

The board is discussing a proposed takeover of another company.

Opinions are divided, although it is not clear where the majority lies. The tone of the meeting is getting louder and more contentious by the minute. Those in favour of the takeover are accusing their colleagues of deliberately jeopardising an opportunity for growth, while those against say that the idea is rash and too risky. Old disagreements and issues are being raised by both sides.

What do you think the chair should do to get this meeting back on track?

Test yourself 8.1

1. Cite five factors that can limit effective decision making (excluding those relating to the supply of information).

2.   **What sort of significant decisions might the Guidance on Board Effectiveness have in mind when it suggests that boards may wish to consider extra steps?**

5. Supply of information

Principle F of the Code states that the chair should ensure that directors receive accurate, timely and clear information. The FRC Guidance on Board Effectiveness reiterates the role of the chair in this regard (at para. 61). However, it also states that:

◆   the chief executive is responsible for ensuring that management fulfils its obligation to provide the board with accurate, timely and clear information (para. 73);

◆   non-executive directors should insist on receiving high-quality information and should seek clarification or amplification from management where they consider the information provided is inadequate or lacks clarity (para. 77); and

◆   under the direction of the chair, the company secretary's responsibilities include ensuring good information flows within the board and its committees and between senior management and non-executive directors (para. 81).

These statements reflect the fact that all board participants have a role to play in improving the quality and timeliness of information, including the non-executive directors, who should demand that high standards are maintained.

The company secretary's role in this regard will be to implement processes that enable these objectives to be achieved and to be the facilitator, promoter and guardian of high standards.

5.1   Board packs

Agenda papers for board meetings (commonly known as board packs) are clearly the primary focus for these recommendations. An ICSA research report, 'Challenges to Effective Board Reporting' (December 2017), found that board packs are:

board pack
Consists of documents or board papers that are a source of information for a director prior to a board meeting.

◆   too backward-looking, internally focused and operational to enable board members to engage in forward-looking and strategic conversations; and

◆   time-consuming to produce.

Research conducted for the purposes of the report found that:

◆   there is a clear correlation between the average length of board packs and the size of the organisation, rising from 125 pages for organisations with a turnover of less than £10 million, to over 250 pages for those with a turnover of more than £500 million;

◆ board packs are typically longer in quoted companies and the public sector;

◆ 20% of respondents to a survey reported that their board packs were usually longer than 250 pages, with 1% reporting board packs of over 800 pages;

◆ taking into account the average number of board meetings annually, large organisations are producing an average of 2,000 pages of information for board members to absorb every year;

◆ even the smallest organisations in the survey produced on average 750 pages of information for their boards.

Following up on this report, ICSA published practical guidance for company secretaries and governance professionals on compiling board packs. The guidance, 'Effective Board Reporting' (2018), was produced in association with Board Intelligence, a firm of corporate governance advisers.

The introduction to the guidance sets the scene by saying that:

'Effective board decision making is not simply a matter of getting the right people around the table. They need to address the right issues and ask the right questions and to do these things they need the right information. Identifying those issues and questions and obtaining that information presents significant challenges, not only for boards and governing bodies, but also for those who advise and assist them.'

It suggests that the first challenge for boards is prioritising the issues on which they spend their time. The second is determining what information is most relevant to the decision or action that the board needs to take and then finding it. 'Some boards struggle to find it because it has not been provided, others because they cannot see the wood for the trees.'

The guidance addresses each of the four main stages in the development of a board pack:

◆ identifying the information the board needs;

◆ commissioning board papers;

◆ writing board papers; and

◆ collating and distributing the board pack.

It sets out the purpose and desired outcomes of each stage of the process, identifies who needs to be involved and then discusses some of the factors and questions that organisations should consider to achieve those outcomes.

The guidance poses 12 key questions in relation to board packs:

◆ Is the board clear about how it wishes to divide its time between strategy, operational performance and governance and compliance matters?

◆ Is the board clear about which decisions it needs to take and the criteria for determining when other matters are significant enough to be brought to their attention?

◆ Do the forward meeting plan and individual agendas reflect the board's priorities?

◆ Are responsibilities for commissioning, writing, reviewing and collating the board pack clear?

◆ Are authors properly briefed on why the board wants the paper, what information it needs and how it should be presented?

◆ Do the agenda and individual papers make clear what action or input is needed from the board?

◆ Do papers set out all the relevant considerations and implications of which the board should be aware?

◆ Do you have or need standard formats for different types of board papers?

◆ Is training and support available to authors?

◆ Is the board pack easy to navigate and readily accessible for board members?

◆ Are the methods by which the board pack is stored and distributed secure?

◆ Does the board give feedback on the clarity and usefulness of the papers it receives?

The company secretary's role in this process is critical and will include:

◆ facilitating discussion between the board and management on future priorities, the type and format of information the board requires and also for co-ordinating the planning process;

◆ planning a schedule of board meetings, maintaining a provisional agenda for those meetings which reflects the board's priorities and ensuring that those who will be required to submit board papers are kept informed about the practical consequences of that timetable and any changes to it;

◆ co-ordinating the preparation of the board pack, including commissioning papers, ensuring that authors and sponsors are clear about what the board requires, setting the timetable and tracking progress;

◆ supporting those writing and presenting board papers, e.g. by checking that the papers are understandable to a non-specialist;

◆ acting as the 'guardian' of the house style and format for writing board papers;

◆ ensuring that papers are submitted on time;

◆ co-ordinating the collation, storage and distribution of the board pack;

◆ reviewing with the chair and other board members whether the board papers met their needs.

Most boards set a target for distributing the board pack to board members of at least seven days before the meeting in order to give them time to digest its contents. The company secretary often needs the support of the chair in order to meet this target. People who submit board papers on an occasional basis are hardly ever late. Those who submit papers on a regular basis are much more likely to cause problems in this regard as, for them, it is not a special event. If the company secretary is always required to wait for these papers to be submitted before distributing the board pack, the target of seven days may become increasingly unobtainable. In order to meet the target, the chair has to be willing to allow papers that are ready on time to be distributed on time and order that the missing papers be distributed separately or tabled at the meeting. Many boards adopt this practice as a matter of policy, although such a policy may still require the chair to have the final say.

5.2   Other information

Board of directors increasingly need access to other information that may not be included in board packs. For example, it is good practice to make the most of the materials included in induction packs available to all the directors. This will include documents such as the company's articles of association, previous board papers and minutes.

An Investment Association report published in association with the accountancy firm EY in April 2015, 'Board Effectiveness: Continuing the Journey', suggested that:

◆ companies should consider making more internal company information available to directors, not necessarily as part of the board packs, such as reports of informal discussions about the business and formal stakeholder days; and

◆ companies should consider giving directors greater access to external information and reports on the general market in which the company operates and the competitive dynamics of that market, particularly where this might be useful to help them make better-informed long-term strategic decisions.

Companies are increasingly making this type of information available online through a secure portal.

6. Board portals and electronic board papers

Many companies now make use of bespoke software products, such as Diligent Boards and BoardEffect, to facilitate the production, distribution and storage of board papers. These board portals facilitate secure digital communication between board members and typically provide:

◆ secure tools to facilitate the distribution and use of electronic agenda papers and board packs for board and committee meetings;

◆ archiving facilities that enable directors to refer back to the papers and minutes prepared for previous meetings;

◆ secure tools which enable directors to annotate and make notes on the agenda papers;

◆ tools to enable secure access to additional papers of interest to board members;

◆ voting tools;

◆ tools to facilitate the circulation and approval of minutes, and

◆ messaging features.

Most companies that have adopted these board portals have managed to dispense with traditional hard-copy agenda papers. In the first few months of operation, some directors may still insist on receiving paper copies. However, most companies find that after using the software for a few months, those directors come to appreciate its advantages and are willing to give up receiving paper copies.

Using board portal software requires each individual director and committee member to have access to a laptop or tablet with an internet connection in order to access the board papers. The information that they need to access is stored either on the company's servers or in the 'cloud' and not on the director's own device. Any notes or messages are also stored centrally to reduce the risk of board papers and notes getting into the wrong hands.

Company secretaries and governance professionals usually find that using a board portal cuts the amount of time spent producing, collating and circulating board papers. Many companies now send out the agenda for the meeting before they send out the associated board papers. The software allows additional papers to be sent out late or tabled at the meeting and for replacement documents to be circulated. Non-executive directors particularly appreciate the facilities that enable them to refer back to the board packs from previous meetings.

Companies that do not use board portal software are increasingly using other ad hoc methods to circulate board papers electronically. For example, many circulate the papers as a pdf via email. Adding some sort of password protection to the pdf file (and regularly changing it) can provide a measure of security if this method is used. Although not as secure as board portal software, this would be preferable to distributing hard-copy agenda papers, which offer little or no security.

Test yourself 8.2

1. What are the four main stages in the development of a board pack?

2. What are the typical features of board portal software?

3. What are the advantages of board portal software over traditional hard copy agenda papers?

7. Use of social media by boards

Most board portals provide some sort of secure messaging functionality. However, boards of directors may sometimes prefer to use some of the more commonly available social media applications for these purposes. The independent NEDs could, for example, form a WhatsApp group to discuss matters that they do not want to share with the company or the other directors. This may or may not be possible with commercial board portals. The company might have concerns about the security of these methods of communications and over whether records of these discussions should be retained.

Companies have been using social media applications such as Twitter and Facebook for a long time now, mainly for corporate public relations purposes and customer engagement. Some CEOs are also famously active on social media, although the consequences are not always positive. For example, in 2018 Elon Musk, the CEO of Tesla, announced on Twitter overnight that he had finance in place to take the company private, which turned out to be false and resulted in him being fined by the US authorities for publishing misleading information.

Directors of listed companies clearly need to be careful not to release inside or misleading information through social media. The company might prefer to curate any social media account that they use for corporate purposes and it is probably best for them not to use their own personal social media accounts for corporate purposes. However, it may be the case that certain corporate messages would resonate more strongly with the target audience if they were put out under the name of the chair or CEO.

8. Corporate culture

In July 2016, the Financial Reporting Council (FRC) published the results of a study exploring the relationship between corporate culture and long-term business success in the UK and how it is being defined, embedded and monitored.

The report, 'Corporate culture and the role of boards: Report of observations' (2016), was the culmination of a collaboration with the Chartered Institute of Management Accountants, the City Values Forum, the Chartered Institute of Internal Auditors, the Chartered Institute of Personnel and Development and the Institute of Business Ethics.

The FRC stated in the report that it believes the UK governance model remains an efficient and effective means of meeting the objectives of, and arbitrating between, the many stakeholders in the market. The combination of legislation, regulation and codes provides a flexible framework for companies and their stakeholders to pursue their objectives and achieve long-term success. However, it said that 'success depends... on the spirit with which companies and investors apply the principles and use the flexibility they have'.

The FRC embarked on the corporate culture project to gain a better understanding of how boards are currently addressing culture, to encourage discussion and debate, and to identify and share good practice to help companies. The report sought to address how boards and executive management can steer corporate behaviour to create a culture that will deliver sustainable good performance.

The key findings of the study are as follows:

◆ A healthy corporate culture is a valuable asset, a source of competitive advantage and vital to the creation and protection of long-term value.

◆ Establishing the company's overall purpose is crucial in supporting and embedding the correct values, attitudes and behaviours.

◆ The board should determine the purpose of the company and ensure that the company's values, strategy and business model are aligned to it.

◆ The chief executive should ensure that the desired culture is embedded at all levels and in every aspect of the business.

◆ However, boards have a responsibility to monitor whether this has been achieved and to act where the desired culture has not been delivered.

◆ A culture of openness and accountability at every level is critical.

◆ The values of the company need to inform the behaviours which are expected of all employees and suppliers. Human resources, internal audit, ethics, compliance, and risk functions should be empowered and resourced to embed values and assess culture effectively. Their voice in the boardroom should be strengthened.

◆ Companies need to assess information from a wide variety of sources to gain an insight into the overall culture and sub-cultures of the organisation. Indicators and measures used should be aligned to desired outcomes and material to the business. The board has a responsibility to understand behaviour throughout the company and to challenge where they find misalignment with values or need better information.

◆ Boards should devote sufficient resource to evaluating culture and consider how they report on it.

◆ Particular attention should be paid to performance management and reward systems. These should support and encourage behaviours that are consistent with the company's purpose, values, strategy and business model.

◆ Companies should engage with stakeholders and improve the reporting on matters concerning corporate culture.

◆ Investors should challenge themselves about the behaviours they are encouraging in companies and to reflect on their own culture.

According to the study, integrity, respect and innovation are the three most commonly expressed values of FTSE 100 companies, followed by safety, transparency, excellence, teamwork, responsibility, trust and honesty.

The FRC's partners on the corporate culture project also published a series of associated reports, including:

◆ Chartered Institute of Personnel and Development – 'A duty to care? Evidence of the importance of organisational culture to effective governance and leadership';

◆ The Institute of Internal Auditors – 'Organisational culture: Evolving approaches to embedding and assurance';

◆ The Institute of Business Ethics – 'Stakeholder engagement: values, business culture and society';

◆ City Values Forum with Tomorrow's Company – 'Governing Values: risk and opportunity – a guide to board leadership in purpose values and culture'; and

◆ Chartered Institute of Management Accountants – 'Financial Management – Rethinking the business model'.

8.1   How corporate culture is reflected in the Code

Principle B of the Code states:

The board should establish the company's purpose, values and strategy, and satisfy itself that these and its culture are aligned. All directors must act with integrity, lead by example and promote the desired culture.

The FRC Guidance on Board Effectiveness puts this better (at para. 11) by saying:

An effective board defines the company's purpose and then sets a strategy to deliver it, underpinned by the values and behaviours that shape its culture and the way it conducts its business.

The behaviours that the directors display, both individually and collectively as a board, set the tone from the top.

Paragraphs 18 and 19 of the FRC Guidance state:

'18. The board sets the framework of values within which the desired corporate culture can evolve and thrive. Ownership of the values will be stronger if a collaborative approach is taken and both the leadership and the workforce are involved in a two-way process to define the company's values.

19. It is important for trust that companies avoid giving contradictory messages through their decisions, strategies or conduct. Directors can reinforce values through their own behaviour and decisions. To do this effectively, executive and non-executive directors may need to increase their visibility.'

To have an impact on behavioural outcomes and influence the way business is done, values need to be embedded at every level of the organisation. Boards will need assurance from management that it has effectively embedded the company's purpose and values in operational policies and practices. In particular, incentives, rewards and promotion decisions should be aligned to value.

8.2   Monitoring culture

Code Provision 2 provides that:

'The board should assess and monitor culture. Where it is not satisfied that policy, practices or behaviour throughout the business are aligned with the company's purpose, values and strategy, it should seek assurance that management has taken corrective action. The annual report should explain the board's activities and any action taken. In addition, it should include an explanation of the company's approach to investing in and rewarding its workforce.'

The FRC Guidance on Board Effectiveness suggests that the focus on culture needs to be continuous. Paragraph 21 suggests that the first step in assessing and monitoring culture for alignment with purpose and values is to establish a benchmark against which future monitoring can take place. A possible approach could be to identify and track core characteristics that are typical features of a positive culture – such as honesty, openness, respect, adaptability and reliability – and to link these to commitment to company values.

It is generally agreed that a common set of cultural measures or indicators for all companies would not be fit for purpose. The indicators that are used must be meaningful for the context and environment in which the company operates and the outcomes the company wants to achieve.

The FRC's 2016 report on 'Corporate culture and the role of boards', admitted that 'views are divided about the extent to which culture can be measured'. Only a minority of chairs were confident about the ability to measure culture. The majority felt that measuring culture is difficult and understanding it means drawing on information from a range of sources.

Site visits are one way for NEDs to experience the culture of a business. Other suggestions for monitoring corporate culture include:

◆ hosting town halls – open meetings with operational and frontline staff;

◆ becoming a customer/mystery shopper;

◆ talking to external stakeholders;

◆ holding meetings with junior managers without their bosses; and

◆ reviewing and following up customer complaints.

8.3 Values and culture in the Wates Principles

The first principle of the Wates Principles, the corporate governance code for large unlisted companies, also addresses the issue of corporate culture. It states that:

'An effective board develops and promotes the purpose of a company, and ensures that its values, strategy and culture align with that purpose.'

The guidance on this principle recommends that:

◆ a company's purpose and values should inform expected behaviours and practices throughout the organisation;

◆ values should be explained and integrated into the different functions and operations of the business, including internal assurance, employment practices, risk management and compliance functions;

◆ the board, shareholders and management must make and maintain a commitment to embedding the desired culture throughout the organisation;

◆ boards should consider how culture can be monitored effectively.

Test yourself 8.3

1. **How is corporate culture related to a company's strategy, values and purpose?**

2. **Why, in particular, might pay and performance structures lead to a bad corporate culture?**

9. Independent professional advice

The UK Corporate Governance Code used to require boards to ensure that directors, especially non-executive directors, have access to independent professional advice at the company's expense where they judge it necessary to discharge their responsibilities as directors. Compliance with this requirement was at such a high level that the FRC felt able to remove it from the 2018 Code and transfer it to the 2018 FRC Guidance on Board Effectiveness (para. 83), which now states:

'It is the responsibility of the company secretary to ensure that directors, especially non-executive directors, have access to independent professional advice at the company's expense where they judge it necessary to discharge their responsibilities as directors of the company.'

In reality, the secretary will not have any power to ensure that this happens unless the board has adopted policies and procedures in this area. ICSA has published a Guidance Note, 'Model Board Resolution on Independent Professional Advice for directors' (2015), which suggests how this could be done.

Under the ICSA Model Board Resolution:

◆   Directors of the company are given a right to consult the company's professional advisers and, if necessary, seek independent professional advice at the company's expense (e.g. where they are not satisfied with the advice received from the company's professional advisers).

◆   This right only applies if it is exercised in the furtherance of their duties as directors of the company.

◆   Directors must give prior notice to [the chair, the company secretary or the senior non-executive director] of their intention to seek independent professional advice under this procedure and must provide the name(s) of any professional advisers they propose to instruct together with a brief summary of the subject matter.

◆   The company secretary provides a written acknowledgement of receipt of the notification which states whether the fees for the professional advice sought are payable by the company under these procedures.

◆   A director must obtain the prior approval of [the chair, deputy chair or the senior independent NED] where the advisers' fees are likely to exceed a stated amount.

◆   Any advice obtained under this procedure must be made available to the board, if it so requests.

An alternative solution could be to authorise a member of the board to commit the company to pay or contribute up to a fixed amount to the costs of independent advice and to require the director to notify the chair or secretary whenever such expenditure has been authorised.

Pre-notification seems a reasonable requirement, but the choice of the recipient is more difficult. The obvious choice is the chair but this could cause embarrassment where the actions of the chair are the matter causing concern. An alternative would be to require notification to senior independent director. Some companies may be content with just requiring the matter to be discussed with another director. If the company secretary is the chosen recipient, the resolution should make it clear whether the secretary should then communicate the information to the chair or another director.

It appears to be prudent to place financial limits on the cost of the advice. However, this could be viewed as a fetter on the right to take independent advice. Rather than laying down arbitrary cost limits of general application, it may be better to require the cost limits to be agreed as part of the pre-notification procedure. The involvement of the company secretary in this aspect would be desirable as the secretary will usually be more experienced than most directors about the costs of obtaining professional advice and the methods of limiting and controlling costs.

In addition to passing a board resolution on this matter, it would be desirable for the right to take independent professional advice to be covered in directors' service agreements as a board resolution does not necessarily have contractual effect between the directors and the company.

9.1 Independent advice for board committees

The 2018 FRC Guidance on Board Effectiveness states (at para. 83) that board committees should be provided with sufficient resources to undertake their duties. Access to independent professional advice may be one of the resources that board committees may require. The terms of reference of each committee should include any delegated authority the committee needs for these purposes. For example, the remuneration committee will need to appoint remuneration consultants and the nomination committee will need to appoint recruitment consultants. It should be noted in this regard that Code Provision 35 states that the remuneration committee should be responsible for appointing any remuneration consultants.

Test yourself 8.4

How might the company secretary be involved in the procedures to enable the directors to obtain independent professional advice?

10. Performance evaluation

The Code requires boards to undertake a formal and rigorous annual evaluation of the performance of the board, its committees, the chair and individual directors (Code Provision 21).

The Code also provides that the non-executive directors, led by the senior independent director, should be responsible for performance evaluation of the chair and should meet without the chair present at least annually for this purpose (Code Provision 12).

Code Principle L states that:

◆ the annual evaluation of the board should consider its composition, diversity and how effectively members work together to achieve objectives; and

◆ each individual's evaluation should demonstrate whether they continue to contribute effectively.

The chair is expected to act on the results of the performance evaluation by recognising the strengths and addressing the weaknesses of the board (Code Provision 22). In particular, the evaluation is expected to feed into the company's succession policies by helping to identify any skills gaps.

Code Provision 22 also states that each director should engage with the process and take appropriate action when development needs have been identified.

Code Provision 23 requires the nomination committee report to state:

◆ how the board evaluation has been conducted;

◆ the nature and extent of an external evaluator's contact with the board and individual directors;

◆ the outcomes and actions taken; and

◆ how the evaluation has or will influence board composition.

10.1 General guidance

The FRC Guidance on Board Effectiveness (at paras. 106 to 110) makes the following suggestions regarding performance evaluations, whether internal or external:

◆ The evaluation process should aim to be objective and rigorous.

◆ Evaluation should be bespoke in its formulation and delivery.

◆ The chair has overall responsibility for the process, and should select an appropriate approach, involving the senior independent director as appropriate.

◆ The senior independent director should lead the process which evaluates the performance of the chair and, in certain circumstances, may lead the entire evaluation process (this could include where the chair also acts as the CEO).

- The chair should consider ways to obtain feedback from the workforce and other stakeholders – for example, the auditors – on the performance of the board and individual directors.

- Chairs of board committees should be responsible for the evaluation of their committees.

- Board evaluations should inform and influence succession planning. They are an opportunity for boards to review skills, assess their composition and agree plans for filling skills gaps, and increasing diversity. They can help companies identify when new board appointments may be needed and the types of skills that are required to maximise board effectiveness.

- The outcomes from the board evaluation should be shared with and discussed by the board. They should be fed back into the board's work on composition, the design of induction and development programmes, and other relevant areas.

- Companies should review how effective the board evaluation process has been and how well the outcomes have been acted upon.

- The chair should give a summary of the outcomes and actions of the board evaluation process in their statement in the annual report.

10.2 Externally facilitated board evaluations

Since 2010, the Code has required FTSE 350 companies to have an externally facilitated board evaluation at least every three years. This requirement was introduced because of the perceived benefits resulting from the greater objectivity that an external facilitator can bring to the evaluation process. The FRC decided not to extend this requirement to smaller companies outside the FTSE 350 mainly because of concerns about the cost and availability of external board evaluation services.

Code Provision 21 now states that:

'The chair should consider having a regular externally facilitated board evaluation. In FTSE 350 companies this should happen at least every three years.'

Despite the rather vague wording, this provision is still intended to require FTSE 350 companies to have an externally facilitated board evaluation at least every three years. It does not require non-FTSE 350 companies to do so, but requires the chair of such a company to consider every year whether the company should have one either now or in the future. Technically, in order to comply with this requirement, all the chair of a non-FTSE 350 has to do is think about it. If they decide not have one, they are not specifically required to explain their reasons in the annual report, although investors may very well expect them to do so.

The name of any external facilitator used should be identified in the annual report and a statement made as to whether they have any other connection with the company or individual directors (Code Provision 21).

According to the FRC's Annual Review of Corporate Governance and Reporting 2017/2018, a total of 11 FTSE 350 companies (including two FTSE 100 companies) reported in 2017/18 that they had not held an externally facilitated board evaluation in past three years.

The 2018 FRC Guidance on Board Effectiveness makes a number of recommendations (at paras. 114 to 116) on selecting an external board evaluator. In particular, it notes that different providers apply different methods and that costs vary greatly depending on the methods used. It suggests that the nature and extent of the external evaluator's contact with the board and individual directors will usually be defining factors in quality and that questionnaire-based external evaluations are unlikely to get underneath the dynamics in the boardroom.

It also suggests that companies should:

◆ be mindful of existing commercial relationships and other conflicts of interests, and select an evaluator who is able to exercise independent judgement;

◆ agree with the evaluator the objectives and scope of the evaluation, expected quality, value and longevity of service, and communicate this to the board;

◆ ensure full cooperation between the company and the evaluator, including full access to board and committee papers and information, to observe meetings, and meet with directors individually; and

◆ ensure that the evaluation is not approached as a compliance exercise.

An external evaluation is likely to be more valuable if:

◆ its recommendations are constructive, meaningful and forward-looking;

◆ there is a clear set of recommendations and actions, and a time period for review of progress against agreed outcomes by the evaluator with the board;

◆ it includes views from beyond the boardroom, e.g. shareholders, senior executives who regularly interact with the board, auditors and other advisors, and the workforce;

◆ it includes peer reviews of directors and the chair plus feedback on each director;

◆ good practice observed in other companies is shared;

◆ the evaluator observes the interaction between directors and between the chief executive and chair;

◆ there is a robust analysis of the quality of information provided to the board;

◆ feedback is provided to each individual board member; and

◆ the board is challenged on composition, diversity, skills gaps, refreshment and succession.

10.3 Internal evaluations

Internal evaluations are usually performed using a self-assessment questionnaire.

They are cheaper and easier to organise. Critics argue that they are not as effective as an external evaluation as those involved may not be able or willing to identify problems. If the board is suffering from interpersonal problems, an internal reviewer may prefer to avoid the issue. An external reviewer, who is well versed in boardroom behaviour, may find it easier to advise and deliver feedback on such issues.

Some companies use external advisers to help prepare the self-assessment questionnaires for internal evaluations, and may even do so to help analyse and report on the findings. Although this could be viewed as being an externally facilitated evaluation, it will not usually involve the sort of face-to-face contact one would normally expect for a full external evaluation.

10.4 What should be evaluated?

As mentioned previously, the Code requires the performance evaluation:

◆ to consider the composition of the board, its diversity and how effectively members work together to achieve objectives; and

◆ for each individual, to assess whether they continue to contribute effectively.

The FRC Guidance on Board Effectiveness suggests (at para. 113) the following non-prescriptive and non-exhaustive list of areas which may be evaluated:

◆ the mix of skills, experience and knowledge on the board, in the context of the challenges facing the company;

◆ clarity of, and leadership given to, the purpose, direction and values of the company;

◆ succession and development plans;

◆ how the board works together as a unit, and the tone set by the chair and the CEO;

◆ key board relationships, particularly chair/CEO, chair/senior independent director, chair/company secretary and executive/non-executive directors;

◆ effectiveness of individual directors;

◆ clarity of the senior independent director's role;

◆ effectiveness of board committees, and how they are connected with the main board;

◆ quality of the general information provided on the company and its performance;

◆ quality of papers and presentations to the board;

◆ quality of discussions around individual proposals;

◆ process the chair uses to ensure sufficient debate for major decisions or contentious issues;

◆ effectiveness of the company secretary/secretariat;

◆ clarity of the decision-making processes and authorities, possibly drawing on key decisions made over the year;

◆ processes for identifying and reviewing risks; and

◆ how the board communicates with, and listens and responds to, shareholders and other stakeholders.

10.5 Role of the company secretary

The company secretary will usually assist the chair in the selection of any external facilitator and, for internal evaluations, may also be involved in designing and performing the evaluation. Whether they are taking the lead or working with external consultants the company secretary will usually be involved in the analysis of the evaluations and framing the recommendations. Once the recommendations have been presented to the board, the company secretary should produce a matrix of the recommendations and the actions taken on them so that this can be monitored.

Test yourself 8.5

1. **Under the Code what should the annual performance evaluation cover?**

2. **What information should be disclosed in the annual report and accounts on the annual performance evaluation?**

3. **Under the Code, how often should a company have an externally facilitated evaluation?**

11. Induction and professional development

The UK Corporate Governance Code used to provide that all directors should receive induction on joining the board and should regularly update and refresh their skills and knowledge (2016 Code principle B.4). Although this principle has now been deleted from the 2018 Code, best practice on induction and professional development is still covered in the FRC Guidance on Board Effectiveness.

For example, para. 61 of the FRC Guidance states that the chair should ensure that:

◆ all directors receive a full, formal and tailored induction on joining the board; and

◆ all directors continually update their skills, knowledge and familiarity with the company to fulfil their role both on the board and committees.

Paragraph 81 states that, under the direction of the chair, the company secretary's responsibilities include 'facilitating induction, arranging board training and assisting with professional development as required'.

11.1 Induction

Paragraph 75 of the FRC Guidance on Board Effectiveness deals specifically with the induction of non-executive directors:

'75. Non-executive directors should, on appointment, devote time to a comprehensive, formal and tailored induction that should extend beyond the boardroom. Initiatives such as partnering a non-executive director with an executive board member may speed up the process of them acquiring an understanding of the main areas of business activity, especially areas involving significant risk. They should expect to visit operations and talk with managers and non-managerial members of the workforce. A non-executive director should use these conversations to better understand the culture of the organisation and the way things are done in practice, and to gain insight into the experience and concerns of the workforce.'

The 2016 Code used to provide that as part of their induction process, directors should avail themselves of opportunities to meet major shareholders (2016 Code provision B.4.1). As mentioned previously, all previous references to induction have now been deleted from the 2018 Code. Most of the former code provisions are now reflected in the 2018 FRC Guidance on Board Effectiveness. However, this particular recommendation is not. This is because the Code generally places responsibility for engaging with shareholders on the chair and expects the chair to communicate their views to the rest of the board.

11.2 ICSA guidance on induction

ICSA has produced a Guidance Note which makes suggestions for the design of an induction programme and sets out a list of materials that new directors may need as part of their induction process (see the ICSA Guidance Note: Induction of Directors – updated in May 2015).

The ICSA guidance suggests that:

◆ the way an induction programme is delivered will be an essential factor in its success;

◆ it is not possible to design a single programme to suit all circumstances, and that the programme should therefore be tailored to the needs of the specific individual; and

◆ the time taken to complete an induction will depend on the organisation, its size and complexity, but may take 12 months in order to cover a full board cycle.

The guidance states that the aim of the induction process should be to:

◆ build an understanding of the nature of the company, its business and the markets in which it operates;

◆ build a link with the company's people;

◆ build an understanding of the company's main relationships; and

◆ ensure an understanding of the role of a director and the framework within which the board operates.

The guidance suggests that the company secretary should:

◆   consult the new director before devising the induction programme;

◆   prioritise and schedule various elements of the programme over a reasonable period to avoid overloading the new director;

◆   vary the delivery of information, and limit the amount of data presented just as reading material (whether in hard copy or via a board portal or online reading room);

◆   organise site visits and make use of meetings with executives, advisers and stakeholders to cover off certain elements, and consider using external training courses;

◆   plan the induction programme with reference to the directors' training and development programme, as one should transition smoothly into the other; and

◆   review the induction programme with the director mid-way through, and at the end of, the process.

11.3 Professional development

As mentioned previously the FRC Guidance on Board Effectiveness states that:

◆   the chair should ensure that 'all directors continually update their skills, knowledge and familiarity with the company to fulfil their role both on the board and committees' (para. 61); and

◆   under the direction of the chair, the company secretary's responsibilities include 'arranging board training and assisting with professional development as required'.

It is likely that training needs will be one of the factors considered in the performance evaluation process. The 2018 Code provides that the chair should act on the results of any board evaluation and that each director should engage with the process and take appropriate action when development needs have been identified (Code Provision 22).

The FRC Guidance on Board Effectiveness suggests that the outcomes from the board evaluation should be shared with and discussed by the board, should be fed back into the board's work on composition, the design of induction and development programmes (para. 110).

With regard to non-executive directors, the FRC Guidance on Board Effectiveness states (at para. 76) that:

'They should devote time to developing and refreshing their knowledge and skills to ensure that they continue to make a positive contribution to the board and generate the respect of the other directors.'

The company secretary will be involved in identifying and fulfilling board training needs. Many company secretaries try to schedule ad hoc training sessions on important new developments before board meetings commence. Board 'away days' may also provide opportunities for short training sessions.

Company secretaries may be called upon to make some of these presentations themselves but should also consider inviting the company's professional advisers or a professional trainer to perform these tasks. More extensive in-house or external training courses may sometimes be required for particular individuals. In addition, online training, webinars and podcasts should be considered as potential training options.

11.4 Encouraging senior executives to take up a non-executive post

Taking up an outside position as a non-executive director is considered by some to be an essential part of the professional development of an executive director. The Code recommends that full-time executive directors should not take on more than one non-executive directorship in a FTSE 100 company or other significant appointment (Code Provision 15). Taking up a non-executive position on a non-competitor board enables executive directors to experience first-hand what it is like to be on the other side of the executive/non-executive divide. In theory, this should help them understand the concerns of the non-executives and make it more likely that they will cater for them. On the other hand, there is a danger that an executive director serving as a non-executive at another company may simply moderate their behaviour in that role to match what they would expect from their own non-executives, and in the process may (consciously or unconsciously) not offer sufficiently robust challenge.

Test yourself 8.6

1.   **What should the aims of an induction process be?**

2.   **How might a company benefit from having its executive directors serve as NEDs on other boards?**

Chapter summary

◆   Boards must meet regularly in order to discharge their duties effectively and allow adequate time for consideration of all the issues falling within their remit. In practice, FTSE 100 company boards meet on average about eight or nine times a year.

◆   Well-informed and high-quality decision making is critical for board effectiveness.

◆   Boards should consider adopting a more formal decision-making process for certain significant decisions.

◆   The chair's role in ensuring the effectiveness of the board is critical. However, all directors (and the secretary) should consider the contribution they make to the dynamics of the board.

◆   Effective board decision making is not simply a matter of getting the right people around the table. They need to address the right issues and ask the right questions and to do these things they need the right information.

- Companies are increasingly using board portal software to facilitate access to board packs and other information by directors. Such software enables companies to dispense with hard copy agenda papers and provide additional security features.

- Boards of directors may need to adopt policies on the use of social media applications for communications purposes.

- The 2018 Code introduced a renewed focus on corporate culture. A healthy corporate culture should be viewed as a valuable asset, a source of competitive advantage and vital to the creation and protection of long-term value.

- The Code recommends that the board should establish the company's purpose, values and strategy, and satisfy itself that these and its culture are aligned. It also requires all directors to act with integrity, lead by example and promote the desired culture, and requires the board to assess and monitor culture.

- Boards should adopt a procedures which enables directors to take independent professional advice at the company's expense on matters which concern them in the performance of their duties as directors.

- The Code expects boards to undertake a formal and rigorous annual evaluation of the performance of the board, its committees, the chair and individual directors.

- In the case of FTSE 350 companies, the evaluation should be externally facilitated at least once every three years.

- The chair is expected to ensure that all directors receive a full, formal and tailored induction on joining the board that all directors continually update their skills, knowledge and familiarity with the company. The company secretary will assist the chair in arranging such programmes.

Part three

Disclosure

Overview

Part 3 of this study text looks at financial and non-financial reporting by companies to their shareholders and different stakeholder groups. Accountability and transparency are two of the four principles of corporate governance and the chapters within Part 3 looks at how these principles work in practice through the disclosures companies make.

Chapter 8 focuses on the requirements for companies to report on their financial performance. It also examines the roles of the audit committee, external auditors and the company secretary in ensuring that the reporting is 'true and fair'.

Chapter 9 describes what is meant by corporate social responsibility (CSR), sustainability and business ethics, how the three are linked and how they influence risk management and strategy development within an organisation. It also considers what drives organisations to be more socially responsible. It also considers how corporate social responsibility, sustainability and ethics can be integrated into an organisation's strategy to achieve long-term sustainability for the organisation.

Chapter 10 looks at how companies report on non-financial matters such as their CSR and sustainable development initiatives. It also looks at the different reporting frameworks and how companies set and measure progress against CSR targets. Finally, it looks at the role of the company secretary in non-financial reporting.

Learning outcomes

Part 3 should enable you to:

◆ explain who the users of a company's financial reporting are and why they find it of interest;

◆ describe the different laws, regulations, standards and codes relating to financial reporting;

◆ understand the factors affecting investor confidence in a company's financial reporting;

◆ describe the role of the audit committee, external auditor, and company secretary in financial reporting;

◆ explain the importance of maintaining the independence of the external auditor and the measures that can be taken to protect their independence;.

◆ define CSR, sustainability and business ethics and show how they are different but linked;

◆ explain the business case for CSR and business ethics;

◆ describe the different CSR frameworks and guidelines;

◆ understand the concepts of integrated thinking and integrated reporting and why they are important to the sustainability of an organisation;.

◆ describe the role of the board and the company secretary in CSR, sustainability and business ethics;

◆ understand the limitations of financial reporting and the added benefits to the users of company information of supplementing it with non-financial reporting;

◆ explain the reasons for and the contents of the following

reports:

- audit committee report
- strategic report
- corporate governance report

- describe the mandatory and voluntary drivers for non-financial reporting; and
- explain the different reporting frameworks for non-financial information.

Chapter nine

Financial reporting to shareholders and external audit

CONTENTS

1. Introduction

The focus of this chapter is to describe the requirements for companies to report on their financial performance. It also considers the roles of the audit committee, external auditors and company secretary in ensuring that the reporting is 'true and fair'.

Corporate reporting was traditionally financial; in recent years there has been a move to also report on non-financial matters. The latter will be discussed in Chapter 11.

Financial reporting falls within the context of corporate governance as it involves the concepts of accountability and transparency.

2. Financial reporting

Limited companies are a form of corporate entity where the members (shareholders or guarantors) are only personally liable for the company's debts or liabilities to the extent of the amount of capital they have agreed to commit or the amount of their guarantee. Limited companies are of three types:

◆ Private companies limited by shares, where the shares are not to be issued to the public.

◆ Private companies limited by guarantee, usually used for charitable purposes.

◆ Public companies limited by shares – these are companies that are allowed to issue their shares to the public and usually do so through the stock market, that is as listed companies.

Although limited companies have the advantage of limited personal liability, they are required to make public disclosures requiring that books of accounts and records are kept in order to prepare the annual accounts. These accounts are filed at the Companies House so that they are available to the public allowing those dealing with the company to see that the company is financially stable.

Below is a list of other users of a company's financial reporting and why they find it of interest.

◆ Potential investors are interested in the ability of the company to generate net cash flows (for dividends, distributable profits) and/or an increase in the share price and to assist the decision to buy, hold or sell equities. They are also interested in assessing the stewardship or accountability of management.

◆ Creditors are interested in the amounts, timing and uncertainty of future cash flows that will give rise to interest, repayment of borrowings and/or increases in the prices of debt securities. They are interested in the security of their debt.

◆ Suppliers are interested in the fact that the entity may be able to pay a debt, when it becomes due, for goods or services provided to the entity. They will also be interested in the company's supplier payment practices and policies which now have to be reported under the Payment Practices and Performance Regulations 2017.

◆ Employees are interested in the stability, profitability and growth of their employer, which gives rise to the continuing ability to pay salaries, wages and other employment-associated benefits.

◆ Customers are interested in ensuring the continued supply of goods or services, especially if these customers have a long-term association with, or are dependent on, the company.

◆ Governments are interested in the efficient allocation of economic resources, and/or determining and applying taxation to the entity and/or for preparing national statistics.

◆ Regulators are interested in being able to assess that the company is complying with all of the laws, regulations, standards and codes applicable to it.

◆ The public has variable interests – including the assessment of the company's prosperity, activities and ability to continue participating in the local economy and in local activities.

As we will see below, the financial reporting requirements for listed companies are more rigorous than those for private companies. This is due to the fact that listed companies also have to be accountable and transparent to their shareholders. This is due to the separation of ownership and control between the shareholders and the board of the company whom the shareholders appoint to manage the company on their behalf. The separation of ownership and control is discussed in detail in Chapter 14.

The Financial Reporting Council (FRC) is the current regulator for auditors. Following a government review, the Kingman Review, conducted in 2018 following the collapses of high-profile companies such as Carillion and BHS, it was announced in March 2019 that, the government would be replacing the FRC with the Audit, Reporting and Governance Authority. The new authority would have stronger powers than the FRC, being able to intervene directly and make changes to company accounts and issue sanctions.

3. Requirements for financial reporting

The requirements for companies to report on their performance is contained within law, regulations, standards and codes in the UK dependent on the type, size and sector within which the company operates.

3.1 The Companies Act 2006

The Companies Act 2006 (CA2006) requires every company to keep adequate accounting records which are sufficient to:

◆ show and explain the company's transactions;

- disclose with reasonable accuracy, at any time, the financial position of the company at that time; and
- enable the directors to ensure that any accounts required to be prepared comply with the requirements of the CA2006 and, where applicable, International Accounting Standards (IAS).

The CA2006 further requires the directors of every company to prepare accounts for the company for each of its financial years. Such accounts should comply with IAS.

The financial year is determined by the company choosing an accounting reference date, which defaults to:

- in the case of a company incorporated before 1 April 1990, 31 March; and
- in the case of a company incorporated on or after 1 April 1990, the last day of the month in which the anniversary of its incorporation falls.

The accounts must comprise a balance sheet as at the last day of the financial year, and a profit and loss account, both of which should give a true and fair view of the company's financial affairs. The accounts must be approved by the board and signed on behalf of the board by a director.

Many people believe that it is the responsibility of the external auditors to give assurance that the financial statements of the company are free from material error and mis-statement and that they give a true and fair view of the company's financial affairs. In fact, under CA2006 it is the responsibility of the directors of a company not to approve and sign off accounts unless they are satisfied that they give 'a true and fair view' of the assets, liabilities, financial position and profit or loss; to do so is a criminal offence. The external auditor of a company in carrying out his functions is able to rely on this duty. This is why external auditors as part of their audit request the company to sign a letter of representation which attests to the accuracy of the financial statements that the company has submitted to the auditors for their analysis.

3.2 Listing, Disclosure Guidance and Transparency Rules

Listed companies, in addition to CA2006 requirements, as part of their accountability to shareholders are required by the Financial Conduct Authority and the London Stock Exchange to comply with certain continuing obligations to maintain their listing. These include provisions for voluntary preliminary statements and dividend announcements (LR 9.7) and annual report disclosures (LR 9.8). One of the requirements is that a statement should be included in the annual report on the appropriateness of adopting the going concern basis of accounting and on the directors' assessment of the prospects of the company. This is often referred to as the 'viability statement'. The Listing Rule requirements are in addition to the disclosures required under company law and international financial reporting standards, even though in many areas they overlap with them.

Listed companies are also required to comply with the Disclosure Guidance and Transparency Rules (DTRs), which also contain requirements for financial reporting. For example, Chapter 4 sets out the periodic financial reporting requirements, which include a requirement for these reports to be audited and for the auditors to be registered with the FRC's Professional Oversight Board.

3.3   Standards

The International Financial Reporting Standards, usually called IFRS, are standards issued by the IFRS Foundation and the International Accounting Standards Board (IASB) to provide a common global language for business affairs so that company accounts are understandable and comparable across international boundaries.

In the UK, IFRS are required for listed companies. The UK has also adopted the IFRS for SME standard FRS 102 with modifications. The components of financial statements complying with IFRS are as follows:

◆ Statement of comprehensive income – equivalent to the profit and loss statement required by the CA2006.

◆ Statement of financial position – equivalent to the balance sheet required by the CA2006.

◆ Cash flow statement.

◆ Statement of changes in equity.

◆ The notes to the accounts – the company secretary may be involved in the drafting of some of these such as notes relating to share capital and emoluments.

UK accounting standards require directors to satisfy themselves, based on the information available to them, that it is reasonable for them to conclude that the company is a going concern, so that the financial statements can be prepared on a going concern basis rather than a break-up basis, which is used when a company ceases business.

3.4   The UK Corporate Governance Code (2018)

The 2018 Code requires boards of listed companies, via their audit committees, to establish formal and transparent policies and procedures to satisfy themselves on the integrity of their company's financial statements and any formal announcements relating to the company's financial performance.

Directors are also required to explain in their annual report their responsibility for preparing the annual report and accounts, and make a statement that they consider that, taken as a whole, the annual report and accounts is 'fair, balanced and understandable, and provides the information necessary for shareholders to assess the company's position, performance, business model and strategy'.

The 2018 Code requires the board of a listed company to state, in both annual and half-yearly financial statements:

◆ Whether it considers it appropriate for the company to adopt a going concern basis of accounting when preparing the financial statements.

◆ Whether there are any material uncertainties, and if so, to identify them, to the company's ability to continue to do so over a period of at least 12 months from the date of approval of the financial statements.

◆ Taking into account the company's current position and principal risks, how it has assessed the prospects of the company, over what period it has done so and why it considers that period to be appropriate.

◆ Whether it has a reasonable expectation that the company will be able to continue in operation and meet its liabilities as they fall due over the period of assessment, drawing attention to any qualifications or assumptions necessary.

Companies are able within the framework of laws, regulations, standards and codes to explain in their own way their governance arrangements, strategic objectives, risks, performance and future prospects.

4. Investor confidence in financial reporting

Accurate financial statements create trust in a company. Investors need information on a company's performance before they invest in it. As was mentioned in Chapter 2, the Cadbury committee was constituted in the early 1990s due to the concerns about the quality of financial reporting in UK listed companies and the ability of external auditors to provide sufficient assurances to the investment community about the reliability of listed company financial statements. This led to the publication of the first corporate governance code in the UK, which looked at the financial aspects of corporate governance.

Over the last 25 years, the world appears to have become more concerned about accurate financial statements with governments making accounting and compliance rules ever more stringent, so that companies do not feel tempted to misreport their financial numbers.

A company can misreport their financial numbers to improve its financial position through:

◆ The adoption of accounting policies that give a more flattering picture of the company's position.

◆ Claiming that revenue or profits were earned earlier than it should have. This can happen when a company has a contract for several years. Revenue from the contract can be accounted for in the first year instead of being spread over the life of the contract.

◆ Taking debts off the company's balance sheet. This can be achieved by transferring these debts to other companies, special purpose vehicles. This was the case in Enron.

◆ Disguising money from loans as operating income so that the company's reported cash flow from operating activities is increased.

◆ Over-valuing the company's assets.

4.1   FRC review of corporate reporting and audit 2011

In 2011, the FRC produced a report 'Effectiveness of Company Stewardship: Enhancing Corporate Reporting and Audit', which was the outcome of a review by the FRC into the lessons that could be learned for financial reporting and audit from the global financial crisis 2007–09. The report made several recommendations:

◆   There should be higher quality narrative reporting, particularly on strategy and risk management.

◆   Directors should take full responsibility for ensuring that the information in the annual report as a whole gave a true and balanced view of their stewardship of the business.

◆   Directors should describe in more detail the steps that they had taken to ensure the reliability of the information contained within the annual report.

◆   Greater recognition should be given to the role of the audit committee in ensuring the integrity of the company's financial reporting. There should also be greater transparency in how the audit committee carried out its responsibilities, especially with regard to oversight of the external auditors.

One of the outcomes of the report was the introduction for listed companies of the audit committee report discussed below.

In December 2017, the FRC issued a report 'Audit Committee Reporting', which confirmed that reports from audit committees, which were introduced in 2012, were creating a higher level of trust and confidence among investors. 'Investors welcome that the interests of the company's shareholders are represented in matters of financial reporting,' the report states. However, the collapse of Carillion, the construction and outsourcing firm in January 2018 has dented investor confidence once again. The collapse has called into question once more the role of auditing firms in the financial reporting of companies, especially of the 'Big Four' – Deloitte, E&Y, KPMG and PwC. KPMG had signed off Carillion's accounts four months prior to its first profit warning. The FRC's enforcement powers have also come under scrutiny with calls for them to be strengthened.

Test yourself 9.1

1.   **In what way is financial reporting connected to corporate governance?**

2.   **What is the purpose of financial reporting and how is that purpose different in listed companies?**

3.   **How can a company mislead the market in its financial reporting?**

5. The role of the board in financial reporting

The board should satisfy itself about the integrity of the financial reports of the organisation by ensuring:

◆ Compliance with financial reporting standards. This responsibility is usually delegated to the audit committee and where this is done, the board should satisfy itself that the committee is adequately composed and able to fulfil its mandate. For example, the 2018 Code requires at least one member of the audit committee to have recent and relevant financial experience.

◆ Effective arrangements for oversight over the auditors. The audit committee should have primary responsibility for the appointment and removal of auditors.

◆ The independence and objectivity of the auditor are assessed periodically.

◆ Significant audit matters and how these were addressed are disclosed.

◆ The auditor's report to the shareholders and respond to any issues or queries raised in relation to their report. This is usually done at the company's annual general meeting.

More information on the above is given later in this chapter.

6. Role of the company secretary in financial reporting

According to ICSA, 'a company secretary has to be competent in financial accounting and reporting as s/he needs to understand the significance and relevance of accounting information and the process by which it is acquired'. The reason for this is that the company secretary's role in financial reporting would typically include:

◆ Ensuring that the board complies with the legal, regulatory, standards and codes relating to financial reporting for the type of organisation they work for and the sector within it operates. This will relate to the content and timing of disclosures.

◆ Interpreting in non-financial terms the financial performance and disclosures for the board, shareholders and other stakeholders. This may be in terms of advice or in some companies the company secretary is called upon to actually draft the disclosures, many of which fall within the narrative reporting requirements discussed in Chapter 11.

◆ Reading the notes to the financial statements to ensure that they clearly and transparently explain the figures in the financial statement, where they do not asking for further clarification to be provided. The company secretary should also check that the narrative reporting section of the annual report and accounts is consistent with the financial statements and notes to them.

window dressing of accounts

Applying accounting policies that are just within the limits of permissible accounting practice, but which have the effect of making the company's performance or financial position seem better than it would if more conservative accounting policies were used. For example, accounting policies might be used that recognise income at an early stage in a transaction process, or defer the recognition of expenses.

◆   Advising the board on the implications and potential reputational risk of the financial performance and disclosures. This will include the potential reaction of shareholders, shareholder representative groups and other stakeholder groups to the financial performance and disclosures.

◆   Providing advice and oversight, on behalf of the board, for the preparation of financial reporting documentation, annual and half yearly reports. This responsibility may be as either the leader or a member of the production team. The company secretary should ensure that the information disclosed is:

–   transparent;

–   balanced between the positive and the negative information, properly reporting everything of relevance and not 'window dressing' bad news;

–   presented in a fashion that non-financial people can understand – this will include a narrative explanation beneath tables of figures as well as explanation in the narrative reporting portions of the documentation.

◆   Overseeing the distribution/circulation of the documentation/disclosures.

Stop and think 9.1

What role do you play in the production of the annual report and accounts? Should you be playing a wider role?

7. Audit committee requirements

The audit committee is key to ensuring that an organisation has robust and effective processes relating to financial reporting, internal controls, risk management and ethics. The committee is also the main oversight body for the internal and external auditors.

Listed companies are required to have audit committees as are some financial institutions. For other types of companies, audit committees are optional, and it is up to the board of the company to decide how to manage risk and audit matters. An example of how the board of one private company decided to deal with the matter is given in case study 9.1.

Case study 9.1

A private company providing lines of credit and a guarantee loan scheme to financial institutions to encourage the provision of loans to individuals in the agricultural sector in a developing country did not have to have an audit committee.

The board of four individuals agreed for the first five years of its existence that the board itself could deal with the responsibilities

usually delegated to the audit committee.

As the business of the company matured the board realised that this position was unsustainable, especially as there was a feeling among board members that the risk and audit skills and experience on the board could be strengthened. However, as there were only four board members, they felt that forming an audit committee, which would have consisted of three members of the board, was not appropriate.

What the board did was to engage an accountant who was skilled and experienced in audit and risk matters to work with one of the board members to review all of the audit and risk matters prior to them being presented to the board. When the items came up for consideration on the board agenda the board member briefed the full board on any issues that they should consider when dealing with the matter.

This approach continued for a couple of years until there was a board evaluation. One of the findings of the evaluation was that the board's agenda was becoming very full and the audit and risk issues which were usually at the end of the agenda were not getting the focus they should for a quasi-financial company. The recommendation from the evaluator was to establish an audit committee.

The board took the advice of the evaluator and established an audit committee consisting of two board members, one of whom became chair of the audit committee, and a non-board member who was an expert in risk and audit matters.

7.1   Requirements for an audit committee

◆   Disclosure Guidance and Transparency Rules. Listed companies are required under the Disclosure and Transparency Rules (DTR 7.1) to establish an audit committee. The DTRs are mandatory, unlike the 2018 Code which operates 'a comply or explain' regime described in Chapter 1.

◆   UK Corporate Governance Code 2018. Principle M of the 2018 Code requires the board of a listed company to 'establish formal and transparent policies and procedures to ensure the independence and effectiveness of internal and external audit functions and satisfy itself on the integrity of financial and narrative statements.' In the provisions forming part of Section 4: Audit, Risk and Internal Control of the 2018 Code, the board is required to:

   –   establish an audit committee with the main roles and responsibilities listed in the UK Code; and

   –   describe in the company's annual report the work of the audit committee.

In addition to the above requirements, the FRC Guidance on Audit Committees states that the main role and responsibilities of the audit committee should be set out in written terms of reference tailored to the particular circumstances of the company and that the audit committee and board should review annually the effectiveness of the audit committee.

7.2 Composition of the audit committee

◆ Disclosure Guidance and Transparency Rules. DTR 7.1 requires that audit committees of listed companies be comprised of:

 – a majority of independent members, including the chair;

 – at least one member who has competencies in accounting or auditing, or both;

 – members who as a whole have the competencies relevant to the sector in which the listed company is operating in.

◆ UK Corporate Governance Code 2018. The 2018 Code has stricter requirements for listed companies as it requires audit committees to be comprised of:

 – a minimum of three independent directors, two for companies below the FTSE350;

 – one member should have recent and relevant financial experience;

 – members who as a whole have the competencies relevant to the sector in which the listed company operates.

The chair of the board should not be a member.

The FRC Guidance on Audit Committees provides that appointments to the audit committee should be made by the board on the recommendation of the nomination committee, in consultation with the audit committee chair.

8. Role and responsibility of the audit committee

The FRC in their Guidance on Audit Committees (April 2016) provides information about the role and responsibilities of the audit committee. These include:

◆ Annual reports and other periodic reports. The audit committee should review, and report to the board on, significant financial reporting issues and judgements made in connection with the preparation of the company's financial statements, interim reports, preliminary announcements and related formal statements. The guidance notes that it is the responsibility of management, and not the audit committee, to prepare complete and accurate financial statements and disclosures in accordance with accounting standards and other regulations. The audit committee should consider:

 – whether the company has adopted appropriate accounting policies, and any changes to them;

 – the methods used to account for significant or unusual transactions where the accounting treatment is open to different approaches and the judgements made as to the methods chosen;

 – the clarity and completeness of disclosures in the financial statements and consider whether the disclosures made are set properly in context;

- the related information presented with the financial statements, including the strategic report, and corporate governance statements relating to the audit and to risk management;

- the content of the annual report and accounts and advise the board on whether, taken as a whole, it is fair, balanced and understandable.

◆ Internal control and risk management systems. The audit committee should review the company's internal financial controls; that is, the systems established to identify, assess, manage and monitor **financial risks**, as part of their expected roles and responsibilities in the 2018 Code. If a separate risk committee has not been established, the audit committee should also review the company's risk management system. More information on internal controls and risk management is provided in Part 4. The company's management has day-to-day responsibility for the risk management and internal control systems, including the financial controls, and these should form an integral part of the company's day-to-day business processes. The audit committee should receive reports from management on the effectiveness of the systems they have established, and the conclusions of any testing carried out by internal or external auditors. It should consider whether the level of assurance it is receiving is enough to help the board in satisfying itself that the internal controls are operating effectively.

financial (reporting) risks
A risk of a failure or error, deliberate (fraud) or otherwise, in the systems or procedures for recording financial transactions and reporting financial performance and position, or the risk of a failure to safeguard financial assets such as cash and accounts receivable.

◆ Internal audit. The audit committee should regularly review the need for establishing an internal audit function. More detail on internal audit is provided in Part 4. In the absence of an internal audit function, the audit committee will need to assess whether other processes need to be put in place to provide sufficient and objective assurance that the system of internal control is functioning as intended. Where there is an internal audit function, the audit committee should:

- review and approve the role and mandate of the internal audit function;

- approve the annual internal audit plan and budget ensuring that sufficient resources are available to permit internal audit to carry out its role effectively;

- monitor and review the effectiveness of the work of the internal audit function;

- review and annually approve the internal audit charter to ensure that it is appropriate to the current needs of the organisation;

- approve the appointment or termination of appointment of the head of internal audit.

◆ External audit. The audit committee is responsible for overseeing the company's relations with the external auditor. This role includes:

- Initiating a tender process, negotiating the fee and scope of the audit and making formal recommendations to the board on the appointment, reappointment and removal of the external auditors.

- Annually assessing, and reporting to the board on, the qualification, expertise and resources, and independence of the external auditors and the effectiveness of the audit process, with a recommendation on whether to propose to the shareholders that the external auditor be reappointed.

- Developing and recommending to the board for approval a policy in relation to the provision of non-audit services by the external auditor. Once the policy is approved, the audit committee should be responsible for approving or recommending to the board for approval any non-audit services to be carried out by the external auditor within that policy.

- Meeting with the external auditors prior to the start of each annual audit cycle, to ensure that appropriate plans and resources are in place for the audit. The audit committee may also wish to hold an initial discussion without the auditor to consider factors that could affect audit quality and discuss these with the auditor.

- Review the audit representation letters before signature and give particular consideration to matters where representation has been requested that relate to non-standard issues. These letters confirm that all the information provided to the auditors for during the audit process is complete and appropriate based on the board's own knowledge.

- Following the audit, reviewing with the external auditors, in a timely manner, the findings of their work and the auditor's report.

- Review and monitor management's responsiveness to the external auditor's findings and recommendations.

- Assessing the effectiveness of the audit process.

- Investigating, if the external auditor resigns, the issues giving rise to such resignation and consider whether any action is required.

The FRC Guidance on Audit Committees states that the audit committee should deliberate on its agenda on its own initiative rather than relying solely on the work of the external auditor. This requires the audit committee to decide what information and assurance it requires in order to properly carry out its roles to review, monitor and provide assurance or recommendations to the board and, where there are gaps, how these should be addressed.

9. Meetings of the audit committee

The audit committee chair, in consultation with the company secretary, should decide the frequency and timing of audit committee meetings. There should be as many meetings as the audit committee's role and responsibilities require. The FRC Guidance on Audit Committees recommends there should be no fewer than three meetings during the year, held to coincide with key dates within the financial reporting and audit cycle.

In a perfect world, there should be a sufficient interval between the audit committee meetings and main board meetings to allow any work arising from the audit committee meeting to be carried out and reported to the board as appropriate. For many companies this may not be possible as board members may have to travel so the meetings are held together. In this case, the company secretary should assist the audit committee chair in preparing a report for the board covering the issues and recommendations which need to be considered by the them at the board meeting.

The FRC Guidance also recommends that no one other than the audit committee chair and its members should be present at a meeting of the audit committee unless they are invited by the committee to attend for a particular meeting or a particular agenda item. It is to be expected that the finance director, head of internal audit and external audit lead partner will be invited regularly to attend meetings.

The audit committee should meet the external and internal auditors, without management, at least annually, to discuss any issues arising from the audits.

10. Audit committee relationship with the board

The FRC Guidance on Audit Committees states that the audit committee should report to the board on how it has discharged its responsibilities. This would usually be done through a report from the audit committee chair at each board meeting following and audit committee meeting. The issues to be raised with the board would be:

- any significant issues that the audit committee considered in relation to the financial statements and how these issues were addressed;
- the audit committee's assessment of the effectiveness of the external audit process and its recommendation on the appointment or reappointment of the external auditor;
- the audit committee's assessment of the effectiveness of the internal audit function;
- feedback on the audits carried out by internal audit; and
- any other issues on which the board has requested the committee's opinion.

When reporting to the board, the audit committee should identify any matters it considers that action or improvement is needed and make recommendations as to the steps to be taken.

If there is disagreement between the audit committee and the board, the FRC guidance states that adequate time should be made available for discussion of the issue with a view to resolving the disagreement. Where any such disagreement cannot be resolved, the audit committee should have the right to report the issue to the shareholders as part of the report on its activities in the annual report.

11. Audit committee relationship with shareholders

The FRC Guidance on Audit Committees states that the audit committee has a role in ensuring that shareholder interests are properly protected in relation to financial reporting and internal control. In carrying out this role, the audit committee should:

◆ consider the clarity of its reporting and be prepared to meet investors;

◆ develop for inclusion in the annual report a separate report describing the work of the audit committee in discharging its responsibilities, which should be signed by the chair of the audit committee.

The chair of the audit committee should be present at the annual general meeting to answer questions on the separate section of the annual report describing the audit committee's activities and matters within the scope of the audit committee's responsibilities.

12. Audit committee report

The FRC Guidance on Audit Committees recommends that the audit committee report to be included in the annual report should include the following matters:

◆ a summary of the role and work of the audit committee;

◆ how the audit committee composition requirements have been addressed, and the names and qualifications of all members of the audit committee during the period, if not provided elsewhere;

◆ the number of audit committee meetings;

◆ how the audit committee's performance evaluation has been conducted.

◆ an explanation of how the committee has assessed the effectiveness of the external audit process;

◆ the approach taken to the appointment or reappointment of the external auditor; the length of tenure of the current audit firm;

◆ the current audit partner name, and for how long the partner has held the role;

◆ when a tender was last conducted and advance notice of any retendering plans;

◆ if the external auditor provides non-audit services, the committee's policy for approval of non-audit services;

◆ how auditor objectivity and independence is safeguarded;

◆ the audit fees for the statutory audit and for audit related services and other non-audit services, including the ratio of audit to non-audit work;

◆ for each significant engagement, or category of engagements, explain what the services are and why the audit committee concluded that it was in the interests of the company to purchase them from the external auditor;

◆ an explanation of how the committee has assessed the effectiveness of internal audit and satisfied itself that the quality, experience and expertise of the function is appropriate for the business;

◆ the significant issues that the committee considered, including: issues in relation to the financial statements and how these were addressed, having regard to matters communicated to it by the auditors; the section need not repeat information disclosed elsewhere in the annual report and accounts, but could provide signposts to that information;

◆ the nature and extent of interaction (if any) with the FRC's Corporate Reporting Review team.

Test yourself 9.2

1. **What is the purpose of the audit committee?**

2. **Briefly describe the four areas over which the audit committee would typically have responsibility?**

3. **What is the audit committee's relationship with shareholders?**

4. **What matters should be included in the audit committee report?**

13. Role of the company secretary in relation to the audit committee

The company secretary would typically be involved in:

◆ advising the board on whether it was appropriate to have an audit committee;

◆ developing the terms of reference for the audit committee to comply with FRC requirements and international best practice;

◆ advising the board on the appropriate composition for the committee;

◆ ensuring that board members with the appropriate skills and experience are included in the company's board succession planning;

◆ conducting an induction for new members of the audit committee;

◆ developing an annual calendar of activities for the committee based on the terms of reference to ensure that the committee covers all of its responsibilities;

◆ ensuring that the committee has sufficient resources to carry out its role. This may include advising the board on when it is appropriate to set up internal audit and risk functions. The company secretary usually has responsibility for developing the board and board committee annual budget. If an internal audit function exists, then the company secretary would liaise with it on this issue as the work of the internal audit function would also have to be catered for possibly in a separate budget;

◆ assisting committee members in their understanding of current and emerging issues, especially those from shareholders, regulators and other stakeholders that the company secretary may interact with;

◆ assisting the committee in sourcing advice of experts on issues under the committee's responsibility. This may be in liaison with the internal audit function;

◆ organising professional development for committee members either individually or as a group in those areas the committee is responsible for, such as, audit, risk and financial oversight;

◆ organising the annual evaluation of the performance of the committee and its chair;

◆ drafting (or at a minimum reviewing), in liaison with internal audit and the chair of the audit committee, the audit committee report to be included in the annual report;

◆ acting as secretary to the committee providing governance and procedural advice and logistical support to the committee, its chair and other members.

14. External auditor

Every company, with the exception of dormant companies, must have an independent external auditor who carries out the annual audit of the company which is published in the annual report and accounts. Investors, creditors and other stakeholders rely on the annual report and accounts for information about the company, so it is important that the external auditor can be trusted. Like other professionals, qualified accountants are expected to follow the code of ethics of their professional body.

To be eligible for appointment as a company's auditor, the person or firm must be a member of a recognised professional accountancy body. The board is responsible for ensuring that resolutions appointing the external auditor and giving the board the authority to set the remuneration of the auditors are placed before shareholders at the general meeting at which the annual financial statements are laid.

If shareholders are dissatisfied with the auditor, they have the power to remove them.

Auditors are able to resign as they wish. However, when doing so, they must give notice in writing to the company setting out why they have resigned and, if applicable, any circumstances that should be brought to the attention of the shareholders or creditors. If the auditor discloses circumstances surrounding the resignation, the company should bring these circumstances to the attention of the shareholders and creditors as soon as possible.

14.1 Auditor's liability to third parties

Auditor's owe a duty of care to their client company and its shareholders when conducting the audit and issuing their opinion. An area of uncertainty for auditors has been their potential exposure to third parties. Two legal cases have examined this potential liability.

The first was Caparo Industries plc v Dickman (1990). In this case the House of Lords held that the responsibility of auditors for mis-statements in a company's financial statements was owed to the company's shareholders as a body and not to any individual shareholder or the public at large who may have relied on the statements when deciding to invest in the company.

The second was the Royal Bank of Scotland v Bannerman Johnstone Maclay (2002) (the Bannerman case). In this case, the judge, Lord Macfayden, held that the third party could assume that a duty was accepted because it was not denied. Lord Macfayden found that it was open to the auditors to disclaim but in the Bannerman case they did not do so. If they had disclaimed, it would 'have been impossible to infer' a duty.

The focus in the Bannerman case on the absence of any disclaimer led the Institute of Chartered Accountants of England and Wales (ICAEW) to issue guidance in 2003, updated in 2010, on the auditor's duty of care to third parties. ICAEW recommended the inclusion of a disclaimer in audit reports which has become known as the 'Bannerman disclaimer'.

ICAEW guidance (2010) provides the following wording for the disclaimer:

'This report is made solely to the company's members, as a body, in accordance with Chapter 3 of Part 16 of the Companies Act 2006. Our audit work has been undertaken so that we may state to the company's members these matters we are required to state to them in an auditor's report and for no other purpose. To the fullest extent permitted by law, we do not accept or assume responsibility to anyone other than the company's members as a body, for our audit work, for this report or for the opinions we have formed'.

14.2 Criminal liability of auditors

Auditors are now able to limit their liability through entering into agreements with the companies they are auditing. The CA2006, through the Companies (Disclosure of Auditor Remuneration and Liability Limitation Agreements) Regulations 2008, requires companies to disclose fees receivable by their external auditors and to disclose any liability limitation agreements that they make with their external auditors as a note to the company's annual accounts.

In return for granting auditors limited liability for claims against them, which the audit firms had lobbied for, the government introduced a criminal offence to knowingly or recklessly cause an audit report to 'include any matter that is misleading, false or deceptive in any material particular' or to omit a statement that is required by the CA2006.

The offence, which is punishable by a fine, can be committed by an individual and applies to audit reports for financial years beginning or after 6 April 2008.

15. Role of the external auditor

The external auditor is responsible for carrying out each year, on behalf of the shareholders, an independent audit of the company to make sure that the financial statements of the company can be relied upon. After carrying out the audit, the external auditor is required to prepare a report (the audit report) for the shareholders which is included in the annual report and accounts. The audit report has two main purposes:

◆   to give an expert and independent opinion on whether the financial statements give a true and fair view of the financial position of the company as at the end of the financial year covered by the report, and of its financial performance during the year; and

◆   to give an expert and independent opinion on whether the financial statements comply with the relevant laws.

The external auditor of a listed company Is also required to review the company's compliance with the 2018 Code, and to obtain evidence to support the company's statement, included in the annual report and accounts, of its compliance with the 2018 Code.

The external auditors' report provides an opinion on compliance with the law and accounting standards and whether the accounts that have been prepared by the board present a true and (in some cases) fair picture of the financial reality of the company. They are not responsible for detecting fraud or errors in the organisation's financial statements. This is the responsibility of the board of directors.

The reports issued by the external auditors are either unmodified or modified. Most are unmodified, in that the auditors are stating that the company's financial statements do present a true and fair view of the financial position of the company. An unmodified report includes standard wording, shown in the following subsections.

Report on the financial statements
We have audited the accompanying financial statements of XYZ Company, which comprise the statement of financial position as at 31 December 20XX, and the statement of comprehensive income, statement of changes in equity, and cash flows for the year then ended, and a summary of significant accounting policies and other explanatory notes.

Management's responsibility for the financial statements
Management is responsible for the preparation and fair presentation of these financial statements in accordance with International Financial Reporting Standards. This responsibility includes: designing, implementing and maintaining internal control relevant to the preparation and fair presentation of financial statements that are free from material mis-statement, whether due to fraud or error; selecting and applying appropriate accounting policies; and making accounting estimates that are reasonable in the circumstances.

Auditor's responsibility

Our responsibility is to express an opinion on these financial statements based on our audit. We conducted our audit in accordance with International Standards on Auditing. Those standards require that we comply with ethical requirements and plan and perform the audit to obtain reasonable assurance whether the financial statements are free from material mis-statement.

An audit involves performing procedures to obtain audit evidence about the amounts and disclosures in the financial statements. The procedures selected depend on the auditor's judgement, including the assessment of the risks of material mis-statement of the financial statements, whether due to fraud or error. In making those **risk assessments**, the auditor considers internal control relevant to the entity's preparation and fair presentation of the financial statements in order to design audit procedures that are appropriate in the circumstances, but not for the purpose of expressing an opinion on the effectiveness of the entity's internal control. An audit also includes evaluating the appropriateness of accounting policies used and the reasonableness of accounting estimates made by management, as well as evaluating the overall presentation of the financial statements.

We believe that the audit evidence that we have obtained is sufficient and appropriate to provide a basis for our audit opinion.

Opinion

In our opinion, proper books of accounts were kept and the financial statements which are in agreement there with give a true and fair view of the financial position of XYZ Company as at 31 December 20XX, and of its financial performance and its cash flows for the year then ended in accordance with International Financial Reporting Standards.

Report on other legal and regulatory requirements

(Form and content of this section of the report will vary depending on the nature of the auditor's other reporting responsibilities.)

Signed: (Auditor)

15.1 Modified audit reports

If an external auditor has issued a modified audit report it is a serious issue, as it implies there are potentially grave concerns about the financial statements and the financial condition of the company. It also implies that the external auditor and the board of the company could not agree on the application of accounting policies and hence the content of the financial statements. There are three types of modified audit opinion:

1. A qualified audit opinion which is given when, in the opinion of the external auditor, the financial statements would give a true and fair view except for a particular matter, which the external auditor explains.

2. An adverse opinion which is given when the external auditor considers that there are material mis-statements in the accounts and that these are

risk assessment
An assessment of risks faced by an organisations. Typically, risks are assessed according to how probable or how frequent an adverse outcome is likely to be in the planning period and the potential size of the losses if an adverse outcome occurs. The greatest risks are those with a high probability of an adverse outcome combined with the likelihood of a large loss if this were to happen.

modified audit report
Audit report in which the auditors express some reservations about the financial statements of the company, because of insufficient information to reach an opinion or disagreement with the figures in the statements.

'pervasive'. In effect, the external auditor is stating that they believe that the information in the financial statements is seriously incorrect.

3. A disclaimer of opinion which is given in cases where the external auditor has been unable to obtain the information that they need to give an audit opinion. The lack of information means that the auditor is unable to state that the financial statements give a true and fair view, and that there may possibly be serious mis-statements that the external auditor has been unable to check.

16. Auditor independence

The external auditors should be independent from the organisation, so that the audit is not influenced by the relationship between the external auditor and the organisation.

16.1 Threats to auditor independence

The International Federation of Accountants (IFAC)'s Code of Ethics for Professional Accountants 2006 identifies the following ways that an accountant's independence may be compromised:

◆   If the auditor or audit firm have to rely on a single company for a large proportion of its income.

◆   If the auditor has a mutual business interest with the company or any of its directors or senior management

◆   If there is a close personal relationship between the auditor or audit firm and an employee of the company.

◆   If a partner of the audit firm holds a significant number of shares in the company.

◆   If the auditor performs any management functions in a company or takes any management decisions.

The audit profession has identified a number of potential threats that its members are required to watch out for when conducting audits. The company secretary should be aware of these and watch to make sure they are not happening within their company. The audit committee should be made aware as soon as possible if one of these threats exists.

◆   Self-interest threat. This is the threat that an auditor or audit firm is earning such a large amount of fee income from the audit and non-audit work that its judgement will be affected by a desire to protect this income stream.

◆   Self-review threat. This can arise when the audit firm does non-audit work for the company, and the annual audit involves checking the work done by the firm's own employees. The auditors may not be as critical of the work, or prepared to challenge it, because this would raise questions about the professional competence of the audit firm. For this reason, the accountancy profession has an ethical rule that firms must not take on non-audit work that may be the subject of future audit by its staff.

◆ Advocacy threat. This can arise if the audit firm is asked to give its formal support to the company by providing public statements or supporting the company in a legal case. The accountancy profession therefore has an ethical rule that firms should not take on any non-audit work in which they may be required to act as 'advocate' for the client as this means the auditor is being asked to take sides which will affect its independence.

◆ Familiarity threat. A threat to independence occurs when an auditor is familiar with a company or one of its directors or senior managers or becomes familiar with them through a working association over time. Familiarity leads to trust and a willingness to believe what the other person says, without carrying out an investigation into its accuracy or honesty. The auditor will also be unwilling to think that the other person is capable of making a serious error or committing fraud. A familiarity threat may also arise through personal association (for example, family connections) and through long association with the company and its management.

◆ Intimidation threat. An auditor may feel threatened by the directors or senior management of a company. For example, a company CEO or finance director may act aggressively and in a bullying manner towards audit staff, so that the auditors are browbeaten into accepting what the 'bully' is telling them. Both real and imagined threats can affect the auditor's independence. A company may also threaten to take away the audit or stop giving the firm non-audit work unless the auditor accepts the opinions of management.

Measures must be taken to limit the level and likelihood of the threat.

16.2 Measures to protect auditor independence

The organisation should ensure that suitable measures are in place to protect the independence of the external auditor. These measures may include the following:

◆ Appointment by shareholders. One of the most significant threats to auditor independence would be if they were reliant on management or the board for their reappointment as the company's auditor or future work with the company. The CA2006 therefore provides that the appointment of the company's auditors and their remuneration should be approved by the shareholders in general meeting.

◆ Restricting or prohibiting non-audit services. As we will see later in the chapter, it is assumed that if other arms of the accountancy firm, for example the consultancy department, are providing non-audit services, it will be difficult for the auditing department to take an independent view of the work conducted. In the case of Enron, Arthur Anderson, the company's auditors provided both non-audit services and audit work. In fact, Arthur Anderson were heavily reliant on the non-audit services provided to Enron for their income. It is argued that they may have gone along with Enron's financial reporting practices in order to retain the lucrative non-audit services; whichever way you look at it, their independence was clearly compromised.

◆   Assessment of independence of audit firm employees. The 2018 Code gives the audit committee the responsibility for reviewing and monitoring the independence and objectivity of the external auditors. The FRC Guidance on Audit Committees suggests various measures an audit committee should take in carrying out this role. These include the following:

–   The committee should seek reassurance that the auditors and their staff have no family, financial, employment, investment or business relationship with the organisation that could adversely affect their independence or objectivity.

–   The committee should annually seek information from the audit firm about its policies for maintaining independence and monitoring compliance with relevant requirements.

In practice, most audit firms make presentations to the governing bodies on their independence, without being requested to do so, when they present the annual financial statements.

◆   Rotation of audit partner or of audit firm. The company should consider, as another measure for protecting auditor independence, rotating auditors. This can be done in one of two ways:

–   rotation of audit partner;

–   rotation of audit firm.

◆   Requesting that the auditor make public statements on behalf of the company. The audit committee should monitor what statements, if any, the auditors are being asked to make on behalf of the company to ensure that the auditor or audit firm are not being asked to carry out an advocacy role on behalf of the company.

◆   Management intimidation. The audit committee should meet with the auditors at least one per year as part of the annual audit process without management present to ensure that the auditors are not being intimidated by management.

17. Non-audit services

As mentioned above, one area where the auditor's independence can be threatened is in the performance of non-audit services.

17.1 Restrictions

The accountancy profession does not prohibit its members from carry out non-audit work for their clients. ICAEW has made the following statements about non-audit work:

'A blanket prohibition on the provision of non-audit services to audit clients can be inefficient for the client and is neither necessary to ensure independence, nor helpful in contributing to the knowledge necessary to ensure the quality of the audit.'

In June 2016, the UK adopted into law the provisions of the 2014 EU Audit Directive and Regulations which related to non-audit work by audit firms. The regulations:

◆ restrict the amount of non-audit work that audit firms can undertake from these clients to no more than 70% of the average fees from audit work over the previous three financial years; and

◆ impose a ban by audit firms on certain types of non-audit work, including: tax advice; services involving management/decision making for the client; book-keeping; and designing or implementing internal controls relating to financial information.

Case study 8.2

In November 2018, accountancy firm KPMG announced that it was working towards no longer doing consultancy work for FTSE 350 companies if it was auditing them. This was due, the chair of KPMG, Bill Martin, said to 'remove even the perception of a possible conflict' of interest.

The big four accountancy firms have come under scrutiny since the collapse of the construction firm Carillion. Both the FRC and the Competition and Markets Authority (CMA) have been looking into banning them from doing both auditing and non-audit work.

17.2 Role of the audit committee

The FRC Guidance on Audit Committees states that the audit committee's objective should be to ensure that the provision of non-audit services does not impair the external auditor's independence or objectivity. The audit committee should apply judgement concerning the provision of non-audit services that are not prohibited by law, including assessing:

◆ threats to independence and objectivity resulting from the provision of such services and any safeguards in place to eliminate or reduce these threats to a level where they would not compromise the auditor's independence and objectivity;

◆ the nature of the non-audit services;

◆ whether the skills and experience of the audit firm make it the most suitable supplier of the non-audit service;

◆ the fees incurred, or to be incurred, for non-audit services both for individual services and in aggregate, relative to the audit fee, including special terms and conditions (for example contingent fee arrangements); and

◆ the criteria which govern the compensation of the individuals performing the audit.

The audit committee should set and apply a formal policy specifying the types of non-audit service for which use of the external auditor is pre-approved. Such approval should only be in place for matters that are clearly trivial. Reporting of the use of non-audit services should include those subject to pre-approval.

The audit committee needs to set a policy for how it will assess whether non-audit services have a direct or material effect on the audited financial statements, how it will assess and explain the estimation of the effect on the financial statements and how it will consider the external auditors' independence.

The 2018 Code requires an explanation in the annual report of how the auditor independence and objectivity are safeguarded, if the external auditor provides non-audit services,

18. Auditor rotation

It is argued that the independence of the audit is threatened by the personal relationship that builds up over time between the audit team and the company. Companies should therefore consider rotating either the audit partner or the audit firm to prevent this from happening.

18.1 Rotation of audit partner

The FRC Guidance on Audit Committees recommends that the normal rotation period for the audit engagement partner and key audit partners is five years. The audit committee, however, can decide that it is necessary to safeguard the quality of the audit without compromising the independence and objectivity of the external auditor, to extend the period. In such circumstances, the audit engagement partner may continue in this position for an additional period of up to two years, so that no longer than seven years in total is spent in this position. Where the period is extended, the audit committee should disclose this fact – and the reasons for it – to the shareholders as early as practicable.

18.2 Rotation of audit firm

public interest entities
(a) A Listed Entity; or
(b) An entity (i) defined by regulation or legislation as a public interest entity or (ii) for which the audit is required by regulation or legislation to be conducted in compliance with the same independence requirements that apply to the audit of listed entities. Such regulation may be promulgated by any relevant regulator, including an audit regulator.

In 2014, the EU introduced an Audit Directive and Regulation, requiring 'EU **public interest entities**' to change their audit firm at least every ten years. This rule came into force in the UK from 2016. There is an option, however, that mandatory rotation is necessary only every 20 years so long as the rules for annual tendering of the audit every ten years are complied with.

Whether audit firm rotation should be made mandatory is an issue that has been debated for almost five decades in the US and around the world. Proponents of mandatory audit firm rotation have argued that a new auditor would bring to bear greater scepticism and a fresh perspective that may be lacking in long-standing auditor–client relationships. They have also claimed that when a company has been a client of an audit firm for a number of years, the client can be viewed as a source of a perpetual annuity, potentially impairing the auditor's independence. Conversely, opponents of mandatory firm rotation have argued that audit quality would suffer under such a regime because the auditor would lack familiarity with the client and its industry. Furthermore, opponents have pointed to a higher incidence of problem audits in the early years of the auditor–client relationship than in the later years.

The Institute of Chartered Accountants in Australia responded in December 2011 to the US Public Company Accounting Oversight Board proposals to introduce mandatory audit rotation. The Institute outlined the following to the arguments against mandatory rotation:

◆ decreased audit quality due to the knowledge lost when the audit firm changes;

◆ increased audit costs due to high learning curve each incoming audit firm faces;

◆ increased client costs associated with the incoming audit firm becoming familiar with the business;

◆ difficulty for the audit committee in choosing a new audit firm that has the relevant industry experience and expertise; and

◆ difficulty for the audit committee in choosing firms for its non-audit services.

In countries where audit firm rotation is not mandatory, best practice requires leading partners to rotate off the client after five years and be subject to a five-year 'time out' period. Other audit partners should rotate every seven years and have two-year 'time out' periods. This, it is argued, prevents audit firms from getting too comfortable with the company, but still leads to continuity of knowledge.

Stop and think 9.2

How does your organisation protect the independence of the external auditor?

19. Role of the company secretary in relation to the external auditors

The company secretary would typically be involved in:

◆ The appointment and remuneration of the external auditor. This would usually be in liaison with the chief financial officer and finance department, who would probably carry out the tender for the audit firm. The company secretary would advise on the timelines for obtaining approval for the appointment as this would have to feed into the board meeting leading up to the annual general meeting. The board usually recommends the appointment of the auditors to the shareholders at the annual general meeting.

◆ As part of the appointment process and thereafter as part of the review of the auditor's performance, the assessment of independence of the auditor and advising the board or audit committee, if one exists on the amount and types of non-audit work that are acceptable.

◆ Liaising on behalf of the board with the external and internal audit function, if one exists, during the audit process.

◆ Ensuring that the external auditor attends the annual general meeting and is briefed about any questions that may be asked of them at that meeting.

◆ Advising the board, or audit committee if one exists on any auditor rotation requirements.

◆ Ensuring that an action plan is developed for the board for any recommendations for improvement in the internal control and risk management processes set out in the auditor's 'management letter'. The company secretary would also ensure that the management letter actions were on the agenda of the board until all items had been resolved.

Test yourself 9.3

1. **What is the purpose of an external audit?**
2. **Who is responsible for detecting fraud in a company?**
3. **How does an audit report become modified?**
4. **How can a company protect an external auditor's independence?**

Chapter summary

◆ Financial reporting requirements were first introduced with limited liability companies so that those doing business with the company could see that it was financially stable.

◆ As the separation of ownership and control became an issue in larger listed companies, requirements for the companies to become accountable and more transparent in their financial performance grew as shareholders were entrusting managers with their funds.

◆ Requirements for financial reporting can be found in the CA2006, the Listing, Disclosure Guidance and Transparency Rules, International Financial Reporting Standards and the 2018 Code. The applicability of the requirements differs depending on the type of company you are.

◆ Investor confidence which was growing following the corporate scandals in the early 1990s and the global financial crisis has been shaken by the recent collapse of Carillion.

◆ The board should satisfy itself about the integrity of the financial statements and are responsible for ensuring that frameworks are in place to detect fraud or errors in the company's financial statements.

◆ The audit committee is key to ensuring that an organisation has robust and effective processes relating to financial reporting, internal controls, risk management and ethics. It also oversees the work of the internal and external auditor.

◆ The audit committee is required to report on its activities in the annual report and accounts.

◆ It is important for the independence of the external auditor to be protected from the many threats that could potentially compromise their independence.

◆ Restrictions on the provision of non-audit services by the external auditor to the client company and requirements for auditor rotation are two ways that auditor independence can be protected.

◆ Auditors can protect themselves from liability to third parties by including a disclaimer known as the 'Bannerman disclaimer'.

◆ Auditors are now able to limit their liability through entering into agreements with the companies they are auditing. In return for granting limited liability auditors, the government has introduced a criminal offence of knowingly or recklessly causing an audit report to include any matter that is misleading, false or deceptive in any material particular or to omit a statement that is required by the CA2006.

◆ The external auditors' report provides an opinion on compliance with the law and accounting standards and whether the accounts that have been prepared by the board present a true and fair picture of the financial reality of the company. As stated previously, external auditors are not responsible for detecting fraud or errors in the organisation's financial statements. This is the responsibility of the board.

◆ The company secretary has a role to play in assisting the board and the audit committee in carrying out their responsibilities with regards to financial reporting and protecting the independence of the external auditor.

Chapter ten
Corporate social responsibility, sustainability and business ethics

CONTENTS

1. Introduction

This chapter describes what is meant by corporate social responsibility, sustainability and business ethics, how the three are linked and how they influence risk management and strategy development within an organisation. It also considers what drives organisations to be more socially responsible and how corporate social responsibility, sustainability and ethics can be integrated into an organisation's strategy to achieve long-term sustainability for the organisation.

2. Definition of corporate social responsibility

As with corporate governance, there appears to be no universally accepted definition of corporate social responsibility (CSR).

Examples of some of the definitions:

◆ The European Union has defined CSR as 'a concept whereby companies integrate social and environmental concerns in their business operations and in their interaction with their stakeholders on a voluntary basis'.

◆ The World Business Council for Sustainable Development defined CSR as 'the continuing commitment by business to behave ethically and contribute to economic development while improving the quality of life of the workforce and their families as well as of the local community and society at large'.

◆ King IV, the South African Corporate Governance Code, uses the term 'corporate citizenship' and defines it as 'the recognition that the organisation is an integral part of the broader society in which it operates, affording the organisation standing as a juristic person in that society with rights but also responsibilities and obligations. It is also a recognition that the broader society is the licensor of the organisation'.

As we will see in this chapter, some organisations understand it as pure charitable giving, others as an integral part of their business models and hence strategic planning. Others combine their environmental activities with CSR. The type of involvement in CSR by organisations will depend on their operational activities, their understanding of CSR, and the philosophy and values of their organisation.

Various terms are used to describe CSR. These include: corporate citizenship, responsible business, sustainable responsible business, corporate social performance, corporate moral responsibility and corporate sustainability. Not all of the terms have exactly the same meaning; for example, corporate citizenship and sustainability have subtly different meanings.

2.1 Corporate citizenship defined

The term 'corporate citizenship' was originally used in King II. It has a wider definition than CSR. Corporate citizenship describes how companies should act in the same way as the citizens of the countries in which they operate; that is, to meet the countries' legal, social ethical and economic responsibilities expected of its citizens. This requires companies to balance the financial needs of its shareholders with the societal need of the countries within which it operates.

2.2 Sustainability defined

The term sustainability refers to an organisation focusing on its long-term survival. It requires organisations to balance their current requirements for operating their businesses without compromising the needs of future generations. In doing this, CSR obviously plays a part in ensuring the long-term survival of the organisation this is often why the two terms are linked. Sustainability will be discussed further later in this chapter.

3. History of CSR

CSR is not a new phenomenon. In the late eighteenth and nineteenth centuries, following the Industrial Revolution in Britain, many entrepreneurs, including Robert Owen (New Lanark – cotton mills), the Lever Brothers (Port Sunlight – soap) and the Cadbury family (Bourneville – chocolate) developed what have become known as model villages around their factories, where workers had free housing, healthcare and education. These were the origins of CSR, which aimed at ensuring a fit, healthy and sober workforce focused on production.

Some believe that following World War II, the advent of free education and the National Health Service in the UK saw the state take over from companies the responsibility for the well-being of the workforce. This in turn led to companies focusing more on making profits and achieving growth to help economic recovery after the war than on acting in the interests of society at large.

By the late 1980s, society was becoming more and more concerned with the behaviour of corporations and their lack of concern for the communities within which they operated. There was a belief by some that short-term profits were being focused on to the detriment of long-term profitability and sustainability, not just of the organisations but also of society as a whole. In 1991, a theoretical debate on 'doing well by doing good' was started by the Porter hypothesis that the financial benefits from innovation induced by CSR more than offset the engagement and compliance costs. There has also been a growing recognition since the early 1990s that the reputational impact of a good CSR rating is positive to an organisation as the outside world sees the organisation as decent, trustworthy and good to its employees, the community and the environment. Evidence shows that this increases the financial returns for an organisation's investors.

As we have seen prior to the early 1990s, the focus of companies was on economic objectives, such as profitability and protecting and developing shareholder value. The introduction in 1974 of the Health and Safety at Work Act saw companies having to put attention on to their employees. It was still inward looking, however. Since the 1990s there has been a shift in emphasis with social and economic objectives becoming more important. Companies are now having to worry about the impact of their decisions and activities on different stakeholder groups and also on the environment. This in turn has led to a greater focus within the organisations on risk management and integrated thinking as they struggle to deal with the reputational risk aspects of a more transparent world. Figure 10.1 sets out the evolution of CSR since the 1990s.

	Economic	Social	Environmental
1990's	Occupational health & safety		
		Community development programmes	
		HIV/AIDS	Environmental protection
	Ethical business practices	Human rights	Water security
		Corporate social investment	Biodiversity
	Industry codes & standards		
			Climate change
	Energy efficiency		
		Employee wellness	
	Integrated thinking and reporting		
	Risk management		Green growth
	Diversity: gender & ethnicity	Political correctness	Food security
	Higher standards for suppliers		
	Data privacy & protection		
	Reputational risk management – Brand protection		
	Sexual harassment – #metoo movement		Climate resilience
2020's	Workers representation		

Figure 10.1 CSR through the decades

Test yourself 10.1

1.   Explain the difference between CSR, corporate citizenship and sustainability.

2.   Why did companies give up responsibility for the welfare of their employees?

3.   What changed to create an interest in the social responsibility of companies?

4. The business case for CSR

Certain aspects of CSR are required by law and regulations, such as those that provide for health and safety at work, employee protection and environmental laws. However, many CSR activities carried out by organisations are voluntary. This has been driven from four different sources: the organisations themselves, governments and bilateral organisations, investors and customer demand.

4.1   Organisations themselves

Organisations have realised that they can use CSR activities for the following:

◆ To obtain competitive advantage. For example:

– Cadbury announced that all cocoa in Dairy Milk chocolate would be certified by Fairtrade.

– BP, in the late 1990s, committed the company to reducing its emissions of greenhouse gases that contributed to global warming. The initial process cost to BP was about $20 million but by 2007 the company had saved $2 billion.

– In 2002, Unilever commenced a five-year programme, Swasthya Chetna, in Indian rural communities aimed at hygiene education. Working in partnership with parents, health educators, teachers, community leaders and government agencies, the aim was to educate 20% of the population (200 million people) about basic hygiene habits, including washing hands with soap. In 2005 alone, sales of Lifebuoy soap in India increased by 10%.

◆ To reduce risk, especially reputational risk. However, as we shall see later, organisations should use these activities not to cover up wrongdoing, which may antagonise stakeholders, but to help mitigate the risks or prevent them from happening.

◆ To attract human capital. Evidence seems to suggest that organisations that have a strong reputation for pursuing CSR activities find it easier to attract and retain talented employees. This is more relevant with the millennial generation. Employees also seem to perform better in organisations pursuing CSR policies.

◆ For innovation. Mobile phone banking in Africa was developed originally by Vodafone for Safaricom, a Kenyan-based telecommunications company, in 2007 to provide individuals in rural areas with money transfer, financing and microfinancing services. The idea came from research funded by the Department of International Development (DFID) in 2002, at Gamos and the Commonwealth Telecommunications Organisation. They documented that in Uganda, Botswana and Ghana, people were spontaneously using airtime as a proxy for money transfer.

◆ For sustainability. The shift in thinking by many in the corporate world to long-term thinking has led to a realisation that to be sustainable, an organisation has to focus more on its CSR activities, which are seen to be vital for the long-term sustainability of the organisation. When defining their strategies, organisations have to consider the challenge of sourcing the different resources they need, recognising that these resources are becoming scarcer and hence more expensive. This challenge is only going to get worse in future years. Pressure is on organisations therefore to develop strategies for utilising their resources more effectively and efficiently. This pressure has led to more and more organisations adopting the concept of 'integrated thinking' as part of their strategy development. Integrated thinking is discussed later in this chapter.

Case study 10.1

Unilever is known for its 'green credentials'. In 2016, Unilever launched its 'Bright Future' campaign, which aimed at showing consumers how Unilever's brands were making a positive impact on the world. TV and digital media campaigns showed how Domestos was helping 5 million people to access toilets, how Persil had helped 10 million children get and education and how Dove was helping 19 million young people to build positive self-confidence.

Keith Weed, Unilever's chief marketing and communications officer said 'Our Bright Future campaign shows people that when they buy our products they're not just purchasing a bar of soap, they're enabling children to live past the age of five by helping to teach handwashing and they're helping children access education'.

4.2 Governments and bilateral organisations

The governments of many countries have become interested in CSR due to the pressure from their citizens to protect the environment and improve the quality of life for those citizens, and for companies to take responsibility for the impacts of their business. The governments need to balance this desire of their citizens with economic success. Laws and regulatory requirements have therefore been introduced in many countries to set minimum standards for the protection of the environment and society at large. Examples of such laws and regulations include environmental, health and safety at work, protection of employee rights, the UK Modern Slavery Act, payment practices reporting, consumer rights and anti-discrimination (gender, race, religion, sexual preference or age), among others.

The Organisation for Economic Co-operation and Development has issued guidelines for multinationals on sustainable development, human rights, employee rights, human capital development, compliance with laws and regulations, and protection of the environment.

The World Bank Group, including the International Finance Corporation and the United Nations, has also issued guidance in areas such as human rights and good corporate governance practices. These include social and environmental practices as good corporate citizens. More information on bilateral organisation guidelines can be found in Section 6.

4.3   Investors

Many investors recognise the impact of CSR issues on success and therefore take a company's CSR practices into consideration in their investment decision making. Factors such as the company's record on human rights, child labour, impact of the company's activities on the environment, and the nature of business are taken into account. Some investors would not invest in companies whose practices are considered to go against the values espoused by the investors or to be violating laws, regulations and the principles of human rights. This also includes any products that are considered harmful to society, such as tobacco, arms and ammunitions. This type of investment is referred to as socially responsible investment (SRI) and it will be discussed further in Chapter 14.

Case study 10.2

On 4 January 2012, one of the world's largest pension funds, the Dutch civil servants and teachers pension fund ABP, announced it would no longer invest in US retailer Walmart and the Chinese oil company, PetroChina. ABP did not make this decision based on the poor financial return on its investment but because both companies had persisted in behaviour that ran contrary to the UN Global Compact principles which covered human rights, labour, the environment and anti-corruption, that ABP had adopted.

Walmart was excluded over its personnel policy, 'which violated international directives, particularly with regard to working conditions and the opportunity for employees to unionise', according to APB.

PetroChina was excluded due to alleged activities of its parent company CNPC in Sudan and Burma.

4.4   Shareholder trade associations

Many shareholder trade associations have issued guidance on socially responsible investment for their members. These include, among others:

- UK – Pensions and Lifetime Savings Association (formerly NAPF);
- UK – Investment Association (formerly ABI and IMA);
- US – CalPERS, which has integrated since 2011 environmental, social and governance issues into its investment decision-making; and
- International Corporate Governance Network (ICGN), which issued its Global Stewardship Principles in 2016.

Some countries have introduced Indexes to rank organisations on their CSR activities – for example, the FTSE 4 Good Indices in the UK and the Dow Jones Sustainability Indices in the USA.

4.5 'Greenwashing'

Despite evidence of CSR's benefits to organisations, some sceptics of CSR claim that most organisations are involved in CSR because of what they expect to gain from it and question the motive behind CSR activities. They believe that the major motive behind the practice is advertisement or superficial window-dressing, as such activities are often accompanied by photo opportunities and publicity activities in the press. It has even been postulated that some organisations use CSR activities to cover up unethical or harmful practices that their core operations are involved in.

'Greenwashing' is the practice of making an unsubstantiated or misleading claim about the environmental benefits of a product, service, technology or company practice. An example of greenwashing is an organisation committing to reduce the environmental impact of its product line before the products are even ready.

An organisation's stakeholders, especially the media, will be looking out for organisations that are not delivering on the promises they make. If found out, organisations risk a drop in brand value and trust, loss of sales and, where those organisations are listed on a stock exchange, a drop in the share price.

4.6 Impact of the millennial generation

The focus on an organisation's CSR activities has grown over recent years. One of the main reasons for this appears to be the millennium generation entering the workplace. Millennials want to be heard and have a voice in both contributing and making a difference in a broader community. They constantly share their views and opinions through social media. This characteristic of the millennial generation has led to an overwhelming demand for CSR as the potential workforce and consumer base look to do business only with those whom they feel are making a positive impact on society and pillorying those through social media who appear to be negatively impacting society. According to a 2015 Cone Communications Millennial CSR Study, 'more than 9 in 10 millennials would switch brands to one associated with a cause' and take a pay cut to work for a responsible organisation (see Table 10.1).

Action	% millennials	% general population
Switch brands to one associated with a cause	91	85
Use social media to engage around CSR	66	53
Purchase a product with a social or environmental benefit	87	83
Tell friends and family about CSR efforts	82	72
Voice opinions to a company about its CSR efforts	70	60
Volunteer for a cause supported by a company they trust	74	56
Pay more for a product to have an impact on issues they care about	70	66
Share products rather than buying to have an impact on issues they care about	66	56
Take a pay cut to work for a responsible company	62	56
Use social media to share positive information about companies and issues they care about	38	30
Use social media to learn more about specific companies and issues	33	27
Use social media to share negative information about companies and issues they care about	26	21
Use social media to communicate directly with companies about issues	18	14
Use social media to contribute directly to an effort led by a company	17	12

Table 10.1 2015 Cone Communications Millennial CSR Study

5. Categories of CSR activity

This section looks at the different categories of CSR activity and how companies are participating in CSR.

5.1   Different categories of CSR activity

Figure 10.2 shows the four main categories of CSR. It is based on a McKinsey article written by Keys et al. (2009).

Figure 10.2 The CSR landscape

Pet projects

These are the projects most closely associated worldwide with CSR. They frequently reflect the personal interests of board members or senior executives within the organisation. These activities often get a lot of press coverage for the organisation, but usually offer minimal benefits to society or the organisation. They are also very dependent on the individual whose interest it is for their sustainability. In hard times, these projects are often the first to be dropped, as their value to the organisation is low. Examples of such projects are sponsoring an art exhibition, a local theatre production, a local sports club event, and so on.

Philanthropy

Philanthropy usually takes the form of large charitable donations to groups of people, institutions or individuals. These donations can be in the form of money, equipment and other materials, or even staff time where the company has the expertise to assist others who need their input. Examples of these activities include large donations to charitable organisations, educational projects, healthcare projects, scholarships for students who cannot afford to pay their fees and sponsorships for needy people to receive medical attention. This category of CSR activities confers the majority of the benefit on society. There is often little noise and fanfare with these donations and therefore often questionable reputational benefits to the organisation.

Propaganda

Activities in this category are focused primarily on building the organisation's reputation. They have little real benefit to society. They include sponsoring large sporting events, renovating and covering properties in advertising, sponsoring an international event, and so on.

Organisations need to be careful when pursuing this category of CSR activity. If it is perceived that there is a gap between the organisation's words and actions, this may be dangerous to the reputation of the organisation.

Partnerships

CSR activities that create significant shared value creation for both the organisation and society fall within the category of partnerships. Such activities usually create value for the organisation by addressing major strategic issues or challenges faced by the organisation. This in turn leads to a long-term sustainable benefit for society, as it is in the best interests of the organisation to continue the activity. It makes business sense.

Case study 10.3

The Satemwa and Médecins Sans Frontières Partnership in Malawi. Satemwa is a certified FairTrade producer of tea. HIV was having a negative impact on the company, and the in-house clinical services on the estate were insufficient. Satemwa therefore entered into a partnership with Médecins Sans Frontières for the provision of voluntary counselling and testing services to employees and local communities.

Case study 10.4

In 2004, Unilever created the Dove Self-Esteem Project (DSEP). This project was aimed at helping girls and young women to develop a positive relationship with the way they looked. The project has helped millions of young people around the world to build body confidence and self-esteem. By 2015, the project had reached 20 million young people. Unilever/Dove aims to reach another 20 million by 2020.

The DSEP includes the following components:

'Confident Me', a series of courses for teachers to conduct in schools;

'Uniquely Me', for parents to discuss with girls of all ages; and

'True to Me', a step-by-step activity guide for youth leaders and mentors to encourage mindfulness with girls aged 10–14.

As part of the DSEP, Unilever/Dove has partnered with the Girl Guides and Girl Scouts associations with the aim of reaching 3.5 million girls across 125 countries by the end of 2016. The programme is to be extended from 2017 to 2020, with an aim of reaching an additional 3 million girls.

In 2016, Unilever/Dove expanded their formal education reach by partnering with the governments of France, Argentina and the UK to disseminate self-esteem education in schools.

Unilever's data shows that as well as raising awareness about body confidence, the project has helped to 'drive Dove loyalty and growth'.

Case study 10.5

Walmart has partnered with Yvon Chouinard, the Founder of Patagonia, the outdoor-clothing brand. The two companies have created the Sustainable Apparel Coalition, inviting other major brands, such as Levi Strauss, Nike, Gap and Adidas to join them in crafting clear, quantifiable standards for environmentally responsible clothing production.

Stop and think 10.1

What CSR activities does your organisation carry out? How would you categorise them? Are there any win-win partnerships you can identify?

5.2   Creating CSR partnerships

In July 2004, Marco Albani and Kimberly Henderson published the findings of their research into what makes partnership collaborations work long term. They identified the following seven essential principles:

1.   Identify clear reasons to collaborate – when choosing a partner or agreeing to enter into a partnership, it is important for both organisations to understand why they are collaborating and identify strong incentives for the partnership. Entering a partnership just because you don't want to be left out is not a good reason and will usually lead to a weak partnership.

2.   Find a 'fairy godmother' – it is important for both organisations to identify a core group of people totally committed to the partnership. There is often a lot of risk associated with getting these partnerships started, so commitment to the cause is essential.

3.   Set simple, credible goals – it is important for the organisation to have a simple, achievable goal, especially where the partners are unlikely bedfellows. For example, Unilever and the World Wildlife Fund (WWF) had different motives for collaborating in the Marine Stewardship Council (MSC) but the same objective: ensuring sustainable fish stocks. Unilever at the time was the world's largest fish retailer. The WWF received a lot of criticism for collaborating with a multinational. It was seen as compromising their values by other NGOs.

4.   Get professional help – most partnerships need help to get started, especially where the cultures of the organisations clash; for example, a private sector organisation and NGO. The facilitator should be independent and be able to drive the project forward, especially at the start while the partner organisations are getting set up for the project. As the project matures, it may be possible to phase out a facilitator.

5.   Dedicate good people to the cause – if the partnership is seen to be strategic, both organisations will dedicate good people to the collaboration. Tying incentives and career progression to the success of the partnership is also important in ensuring that it is successful.

6.   Be flexible in defining success – don't be too ambitious in what you are trying to achieve, as projects often depend on many issues to succeed. Achieving something may be moving in the right direction. The first time Unilever disclosed its environmental targets, it disclosed that it had not met all the targets but had made progress towards them. The organisation received a lot of kudos for trying and what it had achieved, and virtually no criticism for not having achieved the targets.

7.   Prepare to let go – organisations should plan an exit strategy for the partnership. It may be winding down the project or spinning it off into a separate organisation.

Test yourself 10.2

1.   **Give three reasons why companies initiate CSR activities.**

2.   **Describe what is required for a win-win CSR partnership.**

6. CSR frameworks

6.1   UN Guiding Principles on Business and Human Rights

The UN Guiding Principles on Business and Human Rights were established in 2011 and recognised that there was a role to play for businesses in the protection of human rights. There were existing obligations for member states of the UN to respect, protect and fulfil human rights and fundamental freedoms and these were extended to businesses. The principles apply to all businesses regardless of their size, sector, location ownership or structure. Countries are required to put in place effective remedies for those who suffer from business-related human rights abuses.

6.2   UN Global Compact

The United Nations (UN) Global Compact was launched in 2000 with the aim of encouraging companies to align their strategies and operations with the 10 principles covering human rights, labour, the environment and anti-corruption, as set out below.

Human rights
Principle 1: Businesses should support and respect the protection of internationally proclaimed human rights; and

Principle 2: make sure they are not complicit in human rights abuses.

Labour
Principle 3: Businesses should uphold the freedom of association and the effective recognition of the right to collective bargaining;

Principle 4: the elimination of all forms of forced and compulsory labour;

Principle 5: the effective abolition of child labour; and

Principle 6: the elimination of discrimination in respect of employment and occupation.

Environment
Principle 7: Businesses should support a precautionary approach to environmental challenges;

Principle 8: undertake initiatives to promote greater environmental responsibility; and

Principle 9: encourage the development and diffusion of environmentally friendly technologies.

Anti-corruption
Principle 10: Businesses should work against corruption in all its forms, including extortion and bribery.

The ten principles of the UN Global Compact are derived from:

◆ The Universal Declaration of Human Rights

◆ The International Labour Organisations Declaration on Fundamental Principles and Rights of Work

◆ Rio Declaration on Environment and Development

◆ United Nations Convention against Corruption

By September 2017, there were 9,500 companies and 3,000 other organisations which had signed up to the UN Global Compact.

6.3 The SIGMA Project

The SIGMA Project – Sustainability – Integrated Guidelines for Management – was launched in 1999 by the British Standards Institution (a leading standards body), Forum for the Future (a leading sustainability charity and think-tank) and AccountAbility, (the international professional body for accountability), with the support of the UK Department of Trade and Industry (DTI, now BEIS).
Its purpose was to develop a set of guidelines 'to provide clear, practical advice to organisations to enable them to make a meaningful contribution to sustainable development'.

The SIGMA Guidelines, which were published in 2003, consist of:

◆ A set of Guiding Principles that help organisations to understand sustainability and their contribution to it. Five capitals similar to those used in the integrated reporting framework make up the guiding principles:
  – natural;
  – human;
  – social;
  – manufactured;
  – financial.

◆ A Management Framework that integrates sustainability issues into core processes and mainstream decision making. It is structured into phases and sub-phases. The framework includes the efficient use of natural resources, protection of the environment, and the protection of employee and citizen rights.

The SIGMA Guidelines link into existing management systems and frameworks such as ISO 14001, Investors in People, the ISO 9000 series, OHSAS 18001 and AA1000 Framework, thus enabling compatibility with existing systems and helping organisations to build on what organisations already have in place.

6.4 The Equator Principles

The Equator Principles (EPs) is a risk management framework, adopted by financial institutions, for determining, assessing and managing environmental and social risk in projects and is primarily intended to provide a minimum standard for due diligence and monitoring to support responsible risk decision making.

At the time of writing there were 94 Financial Institutions in 37 countries which had officially adopted the EPs, covering the majority of international project finance debt within developed and emerging markets.

According to the EP website, 'the EPs have greatly increased the attention and focus on social/community standards and responsibility, including robust standards for indigenous peoples, labour standards, and consultation with locally affected communities within the Project Finance market. They have also promoted convergence around common environmental and social standards'.

6.5 OECD Guidelines for Multinational Enterprises

The OECD issued in 2001, and revised in 2011, Guidelines for Multinational Enterprises, the aim of which was to encourage 'the positive contributions that multinational enterprises can make to economic, environmental and social progress and to minimise the difficulties to which their various operations may give rise'.

Some of the Guidelines are listed below.

General policies
The OECD Guidelines suggest several general policies that multinationals should adopt. These include having policies that:

◆ contribute to economic, social and environmental development with a view to achieving sustainable development;

◆ respect the human rights of those people affected by their activities;

◆ encourage the development of local business through cooperation with local communities;

◆ encourage the development of human capital in those communities, by creating employment and providing training;

◆ refrain from seeking or accepting exemptions from local laws on the environment or health;

◆ support and promote good corporate governance practice; and

◆ avoid improper involvement in local politics.

Employment policies

The OECD Guidelines include more specific policy guidelines on employment and industrial relations. These include requirements for multinationals to:

◆ respect the right of employees to be represented by trade unions;

◆ contribute to the abolition of child labour;

◆ contribute to the abolition of forced labour;

◆ avoid discrimination on the grounds of race, gender, religion or political opinion;

◆ observe standards of employment that are not less favourable than those provided by comparable employers in the host country;

◆ take adequate steps to ensure occupational health and safety;

◆ as much as possible, use local labour and provide them with skills training; and

◆ in negotiations with trade union representatives, avoid using the threat of moving all or part of the company's operations to another country or region.

Environment policies

The OECD Guidelines on the environment include requirements for multinationals to:

◆ establish and maintain a system of environmental management that includes the collection of adequate information about the environmental and health and safety effects of their activities, targets for improvements in environmental performance and regular monitoring of actual performance in comparison with the established targets;

◆ provide the public with adequate information about environmental and health and safety matters, and engage with communities that are directly affected by the environmental and health and safety policies of the company;

◆ consider the long-term environmental, health and safety-related consequences when making decisions;

◆ continually seek to improve environmental performance through encouraging environmentally friendly technologies and developing environmentally friendly products; and

◆ maintain contingency plans for dealing with unforeseen environmental, health and safety damage arising from their operations, including accidents and emergencies.

There are other policies in the Guidelines, such as the requirement that multinationals should avoid the use of bribery of officials to obtain contracts and revenue.

7. Integrated thinking

Integrated thinking is a process that takes into consideration in a balanced way the effective and efficient utilisation of each of the following six capital resources available to an organisation when developing strategy or decision-making.

◆ Financial capital – money, equity, bonds, monetary value of assets, etc. that an organisation needs to operate.

◆ Human capital – the collective skills and experience of the people that work for the organisation.

◆ Manufactured capital – physical means and infrastructure needed for an organisation to provide its products and services, e.g. fixed assets.

◆ Intellectual capital – patents, copyright, designs, goodwill, brand value and knowledge accumulated, i.e. intangible assets.

◆ Natural capital – natural resources and energy that the organisation depends on to produce its products/services.

◆ Social capital – value added to an organisation of the social relationships with individuals and institutions that an organisation has developed through its stakeholder engagement.

For organisations to have effective integrated thinking, they need information about how effectively they are using the above types of capital. This information is provided through 'integrated reporting', discussed in Chapter 11.

The company secretary should be watching out for what is known as the 'silo effect' when each of these capitals is managed separately: financial in the finance department, human in the HR department, intellectual in the legal department and so on. This tends to happen as organisations get larger. It can be countered by:

◆ the CEO having regular senior management meetings especially before board meetings so that proposals can be discussed with the heads of all departments present;

◆ the company secretary reading proposals being submitted to the board to check that a holistic view across all of the capitals has been taken within a proposal;

Some companies have a sign-off form which has to be signed by key departments before the proposal can be submitted to the CEO and/or the board.

8. Advising the board on being socially responsible

The company secretary should ensure that CSR is on the board's agenda. Matters that should be brought to the board's attention are as follows:

◆ Highlighting the risk of non-compliance with the ever-growing mandatory requirements of laws and regulations for CSR related activities and the reporting requirements on these activities. The chair and CEO should be advised that this should be an agenda item.

◆ During the discussion of the legal and compliance requirements the commercial benefits of carrying out CSR activities should also be discussed.

◆ These benefits will come from management where they see competitive advantage in adopting CSR initiatives within the organisation's strategic planning and risk management processes.

◆ The possibility of meeting some of the s. 172 requirements relating to stakeholder engagement – employees, customers and suppliers – could be met through CSR activities. Further information on s. 172 requirements can be found in Chapters 5, 11 and 15.

◆ Once the board has bought into the need for and benefits of CSR activities, developing a policy(ies) and criteria to govern their CSR activities. These should be aligned with the organisation's ethical values.

◆ Appointing a board champion to make it clear that the board is supporting any CSR initiatives.

◆ Communicating to employees the CSR policies and expectations for CSR initiatives.

◆ Requesting management to carry out an analysis as to where there are gaps between the organisation's current position and where it wants to be and also what opportunities have been identified for CSR initiatives as part of the strategic planning and risk management processes. An action plan can then be developed.

◆ Requesting management to develop and recommend CSR activities, strategies and targets to enable the organisation to meet its social and environmental objectives. These should have clear timelines and individual responsibility.

◆ Linking management's rewards, remuneration and other benefits, to the achievement of CSR targets.

◆ Receiving regular reports back to the board which should be included on agendas so that progress against targets can be monitored.

◆ Informing key stakeholders about the CSR initiatives and targets and keeping them up to date on progress. The board should ensure that stories are shared in a balanced way showing successes and also challenges in meeting targets explaining what those challenges are and what the organisation is doing to overcome those challenges.

◆ The board carrying out an evaluation of the effectiveness of the CSR initiatives on an annual basis.

9. Sustainability

As mentioned earlier, sustainability is about ensuring the long-term survival of the organisation. A key aspect is the management of the organisation's economic, social and environmental impacts, whether negative or positive. Sustainability planning recognises the effect of the interactivity of these impacts on strategic planning and risk management in the organisation.

Sustainability requires the balance of current needs against future needs. The challenge with this is determining:

◆   What are current and future needs? Are these just survival needs, or is the expectation that they are/will be greater? Different stakeholder groups will have different views on this. The company, shareholders, the board and management may have one view as they have financial targets to meet against environmentalists and other social activist groups who are trying to preserve the environment and natural resources.

◆   What is the time period to be considered when looking at future generations? Is it 20, 50, 100 years or more? Companies and governments often plan for shorter timeframes. Others may consider longer periods.

◆   Should sustainability be for the company alone, the country(ies) within which that company operates or all people in all countries globally.

10. Advising the board on planning for sustainability

Principle A of the 2018 Code states that the board's role 'is to promote the long-term sustainable success of the company, generating value for shareholders and contributing to wider society'. So how does the board do this?

◆   The first step is to determine what the organisation's sustainability needs are. This can be done by examining the resources, assets and processes that are critical for the organisation's sustainability. A starting point for this will be the organisation's strategic objectives and the risk management process which should highlight short- and medium-term requirements.

◆   Once the critical resources, assets and processes are determined the potential threats to the supply and maintenance of them can be identified. Remember that some threats can become opportunities if managed effectively.

◆   Sustainability objectives and policies should be developed in conjunction with management.

◆   A sustainability or business continuity plan (BCP) should be developed based on the sustainability objectives and policies. The BCP should align with the ethical values of the organisation. Wherever possible, the BCP should be integrated into the strategic planning process.

◆   Sometimes the company secretary is asked to take the lead by the board in developing the BCP. Once it is completed it should be recommended to the board.

◆ Often people associate BCPs with information technology (IT) but a true BCP actually plans for the long-term sustainability of the organisation. It will include **disaster recovery plans** for IT, buildings and equipment, among others.

◆ The board and/or management will have to decide which parts of the BCP to communicate to whom, internally and externally. This will depend on the type of business the organisation does and the level of confidentiality that needs to be maintained around certain aspects of the organisation's operations.

◆ The channels for communication will also have to be agreed – this will depend on the recipient and the technology available to the organisation. For example, social media could be used or email or town hall meetings.

◆ Sustainability indicators should be developed and monitored by management so that the organisation can assess whether the plans are effective.

◆ The board should evaluate the BCP annually to ensure that it is still the right plan and operating as expected.

◆ Key stakeholders should be informed about sustainability planning, which will include strategic planning and risk management.

disaster recovery plan
Plans to be implemented, in the event of a disaster that puts normal operational systems out of action, to restore operational capability as quickly as possible.

Case study 10.6

VINCI Construction UK Ltd's overarching sustainability objectives set out in its sustainability policy, published in February 2018, are as follows:

Offer career development, supporting our teams to be diverse, engaged, motivated and competent – together working towards the sustainable success of our business.

Engage positively with civic projects and the local communities in which we work, both through specific project engagement and through company-wide initiatives.

Deliver sustainable profitable growth while satisfying our ethical, legal and contractual obligations.

Improve resource efficiency, sustainable consumption, and production, throughout the whole supply chain from design through to operation.

Encourage ideas and innovation, internally and with our supply chain, which can create financial savings and benefit our customers, society and environment.

Actively promote sustainability in our industry through the industry associations, partnerships and organisations we support, including Build UK and the Supply Chain Sustainability School.

Demand sector-leading health, safety, environmental and quality performance from our own teams and our subcontractors.

Integrate our sustainability goals throughout our operations.

Commit to measuring our impact through health, safety, environmental and quality performance data, employee engagement surveys, customer satisfaction feedback and our financial performance.

Test yourself 10.3

1. Why is it important for companies to think in an integrated way?

2. What are the six capitals that companies need to manage effectively and in an integrated way?

3. What are the challenges with determining a company's sustainability?

4. Why is there a greater focus on the longer term in organisations?

11. Business ethics

The Institute of Business Ethics (IBE) defines business ethics as:

'the application of ethical values to business behaviour. Business ethics is relevant both to the conduct of individuals and to the conduct of the organisation as a whole. It applies to any and all aspects of business conduct, from boardroom strategies and how companies treat their employees and suppliers to sales techniques and accounting practices. Ethics goes beyond the legal requirements for a company and is, therefore, about discretionary decisions and behaviour guided by values.'

Principle B of the 2018 Code states:

'The board should establish the company's purpose, values and strategy, and satisfy itself that these and its culture are aligned. All directors must act with integrity, lead by example and promote the desired culture.'

Principle E of the 2018 Code states:

'The board should ensure that workforce policies and practices are consistent with the company's values and support its long-term sustainable success. The workforce should be able to raise any matters of concern.'

Principle One of the Wates Corporate Governance Principles for Large Private Companies 2018 states:

'A company's purpose and values should inform expected behaviours and practices throughout the organisation. The values should be explained and integrated into the different functions and operations of the business. This may include internal assurance, employment practices, risk management and compliance functions.'

So how does the board achieve this?

◆   Develop ethical values.

◆   Reflect the ethical value in a code of conduct/ethics.

◆   Ensure that the values and code are communicated to the board, management and employees.

◆   Implement a training programme to ensure that the values and code are embedded within the organisation's behaviours and functions.

◆   Ensure that the organisation rewards behaviour in line with the values and code.

◆   Ensure that there is an environment within the organisation that employees feel they can raise unethical practices.

◆   Ensure that the code of ethics is reviewed from time to time to take into account changes in societal norms.

12. The role of the company secretary in building an ethical culture

Evidence shows, for example at Enron, that just having a code of ethics is not sufficient. A company needs to embed the code within the organisation's businesses behaviours and practices. In 2016, Sir Winfried Bischoff, the chair of the FRC, in the foreword to the FRC's publication 'Corporate culture and the role of boards', said 'A healthy culture both protects and generates value. It is therefore important to have a continuous focus on culture, rather than wait for a crisis.'

The recognition that ensuring that the right ethical culture is created within an organisation is not new. Bob Bauman, the former CEO of SmithKline Beecham said about ethical cultures in the late 1990s, 'Culture is an accepted way of doing things around a company. Every organisation has a culture. A culture happens either by design or default, we are going to design ours.'

The UK Corporate Governance Code, Provision 2 requires the board to monitor culture and take corrective action if culture is not what was anticipated by the company's values or code of ethics. The IBE has issued a board briefing, 'Culture Indicators: understanding corporate behaviours', to help boards with this task. The briefing includes the results of a survey carried out by the IBE into the information boards receive on culture, how they consider it and how they report on culture to the outside world. The survey found that 82% of the respondents to the IBE survey said their boards monitored data related to culture. Despite this, many boards did not take into consideration when monitoring culture items such as customer complaints, supply chain data, social media records and exit interviews. The top 10 culture indicators used by respondent boards are set out in Table 10.2.

The company secretary has a role to play in assisting the board to establish and maintain an ethical culture by:

◆   suggesting that discussions about corporate culture are on the board's agenda;

◆   suggesting that culture indicators are selected based on the expectations of the organisation's key stakeholders;

◆   developing a dashboard for the culture indicators that should be reviewed from time to time by the board;

◆   ensuring that information is drawn from a variety of sources to support and monitor perceptions of performance for the selected indicators;

◆   organising site visits so that members of the board can get out and about and meet employees to assess for themselves the culture embedded within the organisation;

◆   assisting in developing the reporting to stakeholders on the organisation's culture.

In some organisations, the company secretary may work with the HR function to organise training sessions on ethics and other aspects of culture creation.

Indicator	% of boards receiving information
Speak up and whistleblowing data	100
Results of employee surveys	88
Taxation policy	85
Diversity	85
Regulatory infringements	85
Health and safety record	77
Financial indicators	76
Customer satisfaction data	62
Engagement with charities	58
Code of ethics sign off rate	58

Table 10.2 Top 10 culture indicators

12.1 Speaking out against bad governance and unethical behaviour

The company secretary, as we saw in Chapter 3, is often known as the 'conscience of the company' due to their governance role. They therefore have a direct role in liaising with the board and/or management to ensure that that the board and/or company carry out the organisation's operations according to the values set by the organisation. The company secretary should speak out against bad governance and unethical practices, and remind the board and senior executives of the appropriate course of conduct and principles of good governance that they should apply to protect the reputation of the organisation and ensure that the company is sustainable in the long term. Company secretarys have a responsibility to ensure that the organisations they work for 'do the right thing'. Often this may be going beyond what is required in law. Traditionally, ethics was often described as the grey area between the law and the realities of acceptable behaviour. Today, many ethicists prefer to see ethics as legal activities that are interpreted according to the values of the company or individual.

The company secretarys have to develop skills, policies and procedures to ensure that they are able to test the acceptability of a certain course of action to external stakeholders and advise the board and management accordingly of the impact on the organisation of implementing the decision they are about to make. Again, this is not always easy, but by engaging with stakeholders, listening to their opinions and views, and enlightening the board and senior management to legitimate concerns and interests of key stakeholder groups a company secretary should be able to carry out this role.

12.2 Ensuring that the board sets standards of ethical business.

One of the key roles of the board is to set standards of ethical behaviour that it and the owners of the company expect the board and all the company's employees to follow. This entails creating ethical values and principles for the company. The company secretary is often asked by the board to work with senior management to develop the ethical values of the company.

Ethical principles are statements that:

◆ provide guidance and direction for behaviour;

◆ relate to issues such as fairness, equity and justice;

◆ are universal; and

◆ set boundaries that should be respected.

Ethical values:

◆ shape the context in which ethical principles are implemented;

◆ guide choices made by the board, management and other employees;

◆ frame norms of behaviour within the organisation applied to daily decisions; and

◆ are incorporated into the organisational culture.

The company secretary should advise the board and senior management to select ethical values for the company that are appropriate to that company. To achieve this best practice is to develop ethical values and standards of behaviour from the bottom up. Employees should be asked for their opinions, and the values and standards of behaviour should be developed including their input.

Company secretaries/governance professionals should be wary of plucking values from the internet with little thought and plastering them on the walls of the company. Employees, and often the board, struggle to associate with them and in many cases to even remember them. Being able to embed within a company its ethical values is very important to the success of the company.

Company secretaries/governance professionals should be careful when choosing 'integrity' as a value, which many companies do. In itself, integrity does not have a meaning; it needs to be combined with other values. It is an assurance that the values will be lived up to, as integrity means we will do what we say we will do. When choosing integrity as a value, many associate their own values with it and so assume that it means being honest, truthful, and so on. In reality, people who are dishonest can be so with integrity if they make it clear it is their intention to be so.

Stop and think 10.2

What are the ethical values of the organisation you work for? Do you feel that they are reflected in the behaviours of employees within your organisation?

12.3 Developing a code of ethics

The company secretary is often asked by the board to develop a code of ethics. When drafting the code of ethics, as with the company's values, the company secretary should avoid recommending the adoption of someone else's code. Every company is different and has different ethical issues to deal with. Time should be taken to develop a code specifically for the company.

Once a code has been drafted, the company secretary should take time to consult with employees on the draft code and share feedback with the board. The board would then approve the code, which should then be piloted for about six months to ensure that it is appropriate for the organisation.

The company secretary should work with the HR and internal audit functions to pilot the code, collect input from employees, give feedback to the board on the success of the pilot, and suggest amendments that arise from the pilot. This is to ensure buy-in by employees.

The company secretary should work with the HR function to roll out the code throughout the company. This will include posters, workshops and information on the company's intranet site.

Once the code is operational, the company secretary should work with the internal audit function to monitor compliance with the code. The board should have established a whistleblowing policy and procedure, discussed in Chapter 13, so that any breaches of the code can be reported to the board via the audit committee (if one exists).

The company secretary should recommend any amendments required to the code based on breaches and/or societal changes to the board for approval, via the audit committee if one exists. Once the revised code has been approved by the board, with the help of the HR function, the changes should be communicated to employees. Amendments to the code should only be made when absolutely necessary, as constant changes will confuse employees.

Contents of a code of ethics

A code of ethics would usually contain the following:

◆ Company values.

◆ Company ethical principles – honesty.

◆ Company ethical standards towards:

  – employees;

  – customers;

  – suppliers and other business partners;

  – government; and

  – community, society and the environment.

◆ Implementation of the code:

  – statement of responsibility for complying with the code;

  – means to obtain advice; and

  – training.

The Institute of Business Ethics suggests that, to help with the assimilation of the Code of Ethics into the organisation's business practices, the code should be given 'a more accessible title, such as 'The Way We Work Around Here' or 'The XP Way'.

12.4 Communicating the expected standards of ethical behaviour

It is important for companies to indicate to the board and its employees the standards of behaviour expected, because, as with individuals, each company will have its own ethical values and standards of behaviour. To honour these values, those connected with the company need to know what the values are and how the company expects them to act in certain circumstances. Sometimes the approach to governance adopted by the company can influence the expected action. For example, if the company has a shareholder approach to corporate governance, its values may indicate that it puts the interests of shareholders ahead of the interests of anyone else. If the company adopts a stakeholder approach, its values may indicate that the board and its employees should take into consideration the needs and concerns of a wider stakeholder group than just shareholders. These indications will result in different behaviours. When disseminating the values, the company secretary should ensure that the reason why the value is so important for the company is also communicated. This will help employees identify with the importance of living up to the value.

12.5 Alerting the board and management to the professional ethical standards of advisers and others

Company secretaries/governance professionals should also be aware of any professional ethical standards of people within the company or those dealing with it, and they should ensure that the board and management are alerted to them when developing the company's standards. This is to ensure that the company does not develop standards that are contradictory to the professional standards. For example, auditors are required to comply with certain professional standards when carrying out an audit.

12.6 Ensuring that compliance with the values and the code of ethics is monitored and breaches are reported to the board.

The company secretary should ensure that management and internal audit are monitoring compliance with the values and code of ethics. Any breaches should be reported to the board via the audit committee (if one exists). The company secretary should review the breaches and advise the board on whether changes are needed to the values and/or code of ethics.

12.7 Ensuring that ethical values and the code of ethics are reviewed from time to time

A good company secretary will also be aware that ethical values change over time. This can often be detected from the types of issues that are raised through the whistleblowing procedure, reported in the press, and received in information from professional bodies and advisers. At least annually, the company secretary should review the company's values and standards of behaviour and propose amendments to the values and code of ethics, when necessary, to the board.

12.8 Ensuring that the board approves and monitors implementation of whistleblowing policies and procedures

To assist boards in monitoring adherence to codes of ethics, many companies adopt whistleblowing policies. Company secretaries/governance professionals often get involved in drafting these policies and working with either internal audit or the HR function to implement them.

Case study 10.7

Bauman, Jackson and Lawrence (1997) tell the story of how SmithKline Beecham (SB) went about creating a joint culture from an American company SmithKline Beckman and a British company Beecham plc. Due to the success of the methodology used, it has become the basis of many models since.

One of the main pillars for creating a joint culture was to come up with a set of values that both sets of employees could buy into.

The executive management team met to discuss the values for the new company. They started by considering the cultures of the two previous companies and identifying the attitudes they wanted to keep from them, such as, being highly ethical, and those they wanted to eliminate, such as 'we've always done it that way' and then looked at the values that would drive SB's competitive advantage in the future. They came up with the following values, which were linked to SB's strategy:

Performance	Most efficient producers
Innovation, discovery and development	Leader in new product
Customer-orientated	More effective marketeers
People/integrity	Best managed company

It was important to SB's management that employees brought the values to life and it was agreed that as part of their annual appraisal all employees would be assessed on their application of the values. To assist with this SB developed nine statements that described the values in practice.

1.   Find opportunities for constantly challenging and improving his/her personal performance.

2.   Work with his/her people individually and as a team to determine new targets, and to develop programmes to achieve higher standards of performance.

3.   Identify and continuously implement improved ways to anticipate, serve and satisfy internal and external customer needs.

4.   Stress the importance of developing and implementing more effective and efficient ways to improve SB procedures, products and services through quality analysis.

5.   Initiate and display a willingness to change in order to obtain and sustain a competitive advantage.

6.   Reward and celebrate significant and creative achievements.

7.   Develop and appoint high-performing and high potential people to key positions.

8.   Help all employees to achieve their full potential by matching their talents with the jobs to be done and through quality performance feedback and coaching.

9.   Communicate with all constituents open, honestly, interactively and on a timely basis.`

13. Difference between business ethics, corporate responsibility and sustainability

Hopefully you will have realised that the three topics are different but interlinked.

◆ Business ethics is about integrating the company's ethical values into all business behaviours and functions. It's about an organisation doing the right thing. It relates to the conduct of individuals within the organisation as well as how the organisation itself conducts its business.

◆ Corporate responsibility, on the other hand is about doing good deeds, having a positive impact on communities and environment and lessening negative impacts. An organisation should integrate its corporate responsibility initiatives into its strategy and business operations, it should also reflect the organisation's ethical values.

◆ Sustainability is about the long term. The term often gets associated with corporate responsibility and business ethics as it could be argued that for an organisation to be around for the long term it needs to be seen by its stakeholders as being trustworthy, ethical and exercising strong corporate responsibility.

Chapter summary

◆ There is no universally accepted definition of CSR.

◆ Although people use the terms corporate social responsibility, corporate citizenship and sustainability interchangeably, there are subtle differences between the terms.

◆ Organisations face an increasing pressure to conduct their operations in a socially and environmentally friendly manner. This pressure is likely to continue with the millennial generation entering the workplace.

◆ Evidence shows that organisations that integrate their CSR activities into their business model and strategies have higher performance and are more likely to be sustainable.

◆ Many benefits of carrying out CSR activities comes from communicating their impact to stakeholders. This has led organisations to focus on CSR reporting.

◆ It is important for organisations to conduct their affairs in an integrated way to maximise the effective use of their resources.

◆ Boards are required to consider in their decision making the sustainability of their organisation and plan for the longer term.

◆ It is important not just to create a set of ethical values and develop a code of ethics for our organisation – both have to be assimilated into the organisation's business practices so an ethical culture is created.

◆ Business ethics, sustainability and corporate social responsibility should all be linked with the strategy of the organisation.

◆ The company secretary has a role to play in advising the board on its responsibilities with regard to corporate social responsibility, sustainability and business ethics.

Chapter eleven

Corporate responsibility and reporting on non-financial issues

CONTENTS

1. Introduction

Chapter 9 described the nature of corporate social responsibility and sustainable development. This chapter looks at how companies report on non-financial matters such as their CSR and sustainable development initiatives. It also looks at the different reporting frameworks and how companies set and measure progress against CSR targets. Finally, it looks at the role of the company secretary in CSR reporting.

2. Non-financial reporting

Companies have been reporting their financial information for well over 100 years and it is now heavily regulated. Over the last 20 years or so, organisations have started to report on their non-financial information. This is because there has been a recognition that financial reporting tells only half the story and the annual reports that are being produced are not fit for purpose.

King and Roberts (2013) argue that there are a number of problems with traditional corporate reporting. Some of the major problems they highlight are listed below:

◆ Too heavy for the postman – annual reports, due to ever-increasing regulation and reporting requirements, have become so detailed and extensive that many are totally inaccessible to the average reader.

◆ Yesterday's story – annual reports present the historic performance and activities of the company over the previous financial year.

◆ The financial picture only – as we have discussed annual reports have tended to focus on the financial performance of the company excluding information on non-financial matters.

◆ Some intangibles are excluded – due to the focus on financial information, intangibles, such as good corporate governance, brand recognition, good reputation and sound risk management are not included in the performance metrics of annual reports. This is because it is difficult to assign them accurate monetary values. The market value of many companies is heavily based on these intangibles, so an increasing portion of a company's worth is actually off its balance sheet.

◆ Some costs are excluded – the environmental costs of using up natural resources that can never be regenerated and of the impact of carbon emissions on climate change are excluded from financial accounting.

◆ Different reports are prepared for different users, for example the sustainability report and the corporate governance report. Each of these reports tries to meet the demands of a particular stakeholder group. These reports are often not connected as they are developed by different departments within the organisation that are not talking to each other – the so-called 'silo effect'. The result is that they end up showing each stakeholder group a different aspect of the organisation.

◆ By focusing on financial reporting only, organisations have been pushed into short-termism as they strive to meet the requirements on a quarterly or six-monthly basis of the markets.

2.1 Narrative reporting

In response to these problems there has been a move by companies and other stakeholder groups to report more on non-financial issues. This is usually done through 'narrative reporting'. Narrative reporting describes the additional non-financial information which is included in companies' annual reports, providing a wider and, some would argue, more meaningful picture of the company's business, its strategy and future prospects. Historically this included the chair's statement and directors' report. The directors' remuneration report, to be discussed in Chapter 16, and the corporate governance report, were added in the 1990s. More recently the strategic report and further narrative reporting on risk were added in 2014. The upcoming requirement for companies reporting after 1 January 2019 on s. 172 CA2006 on how companies take into consideration in their decision-making the interests of employees and other key stakeholders will add to amount of narrative reporting companies are required to do.

The major players demanding that organisations report on the economic, social and environmental impact of their operations are, among others:

◆ shareholders/investors, to assist in their investment decision making;

◆ governments who are dealing with social and environmental issues and looking for economic development;

◆ consumers, who are looking to buy products from sustainable resources;

◆ other businesses, such as suppliers, who may have to meet the sustainability criteria of the organisation or who may be imposing sustainability criteria on businesses they engage with;

◆ employees, who want to work for companies that have good reputations based on their corporate responsibility practices;

◆ banks, who are looking to lend money to organisations with good corporate responsibility practices;

◆ stock market analysts if the company is listed; and

◆ social and environmental activists.

2.2   Corporate governance report

The UK Listing Rules require listed companies to make a statement in their annual report and accounts, usually in the way of a corporate governance report, of how they have:

'Applied' the Principles within the 2018 Code. The statement should not be boilerplate in nature but should 'cover the application of the Principles in the context of the particular circumstances of the company and how the board has set the company's purpose and strategy, met objectives and achieved outcomes through the decisions it has taken'.

'Complied' with the Provisions within the 2018 Code. Where a company is unable to comply with the provision, an explanation should be provided which 'should set out the background to the non-compliance, the rationale for it, the impact of the non-compliance and if, time limited the date when the company will comply'.

In addition to the 2018 Code requirements, listed companies are also required to comply with certain mandatory disclosures set out in the Disclosure Guidance and Transparency Rules and the compliance with them should be incorporated into the corporate governance report.

The contents of the corporate governance report should be consistent with and complement the strategic report, mentioned below, and any other information provided on governance related issues in the annual report and accounts. The FRC Guidance on Board Effectiveness was published in 2018 to support companies in their application of the 2018 Code. Guidance on other topics within the 2018 Code has also been issued by FRC, such as on audit committees risk management and internal controls which are discussed elsewhere in this study text.

2.3 Strategic report

In 2013, the UK through the Companies Act 2006 (Strategic and Directors' Reports) Regulations 2013 introduced new narrative reporting legislation by requiring companies (other than those subject to the small companies regime) to produce annually a strategic report which should be separate from the directors' report. The FRC issued 'Guidance on the Strategic Report' in 2014, which was updated in 2018.

The purpose of the strategic report, according to the FRC, is 'to provide information for shareholders and help them to assess how directors have performed their duty, under section 172 of the CA2006, to promote the success of the company'.

The strategic report should:

◆   describe the company's strategy, objectives and business model;
◆   provide an explanation of the main trends and factors affecting the company;
◆   describe the company's principal risks and uncertainties;
◆   include an analysis of the development and performance of the business, including key performance indicators (KPIs);
◆   include information about the environment, social, community, human rights, anti-corruption and anti-bribery matters when material; and
◆   include information on gender diversity.

In doing the above, the strategic report should:

◆   be fair, balanced and understandable;
◆   be concise, only including information that is 'material' to shareholders so that key messages are not obscured;
◆   include company-specific information; and
◆   link related information in different parts of the annual report.

It is a criminal offence for a director to approve the strategic report knowing that it does not comply with the requirements of the CA2006.

Section 463 of the CA2006 introduces a new safe harbour in relation to directors' liability for the directors' report, the strategic report and the directors' remuneration report. Directors are only liable to compensate the company for any loss it suffers as a result of any untrue or misleading statement in, or omission from, one of these reports if the untrue or misleading statement is made deliberately or recklessly, or the omission amounts to dishonest concealment of a material fact.

This safe harbour addresses the concern of directors over liability for negligence when making, for example, forward-looking statements in the reports, in particular, the strategic report. The directors' liability is limited to the company rather than to third parties.

Test yourself 11.1

1.   **What are some of the major problems with traditional corporate problems?**

2.   **Define narrative reporting.**

3.   **What parts of an annual report and accounts are examples of narrative reporting?**

4.   **What is a safe harbour?**

3. CSR reporting and the law

In recent years the requirements for mandatory CSR reporting, known also as sustainability reporting and environmental, social and governance reporting (ESG) have increased. This reflects the growing desire by different stakeholder groups, including shareholders and potential investors, to know about an organisation's CSR policies and track record. Many ethical studies, among them the Edelman Barometer, show that people have lost trust in their leaders and in big business. They do not trust that they have genuine ethical, social and environmental concerns and believe that if they are not regulated and monitored, they will act in their own self-interest with the resultant damage to society and the environment.

In the UK, there are three sets of regulations which have introduced mandatory annual CSR reporting by companies in their annual report and accounts.

3.1   Companies Act 2006 (Strategic and Directors' Reports) Regulations 2013

The Companies Act 2006 (Strategic and Directors' Reports) Regulations 2013 imposed a new duty on listed companies to report on their greenhouse gas (GHG) emissions as part of their directors' reports. The directors' report should contain the annual quantity of emissions in tonnes of carbon dioxide equivalent, in respect of:

◆   emissions produced by activities the company is responsible for, including fuel usage; and

◆   emissions resulting from the purchase of electricity, heat and steam cooling by the company.

Companies must also, under the regulations, disclose the method of calculating the amounts disclosed including, for future years, comparative information.

The GHG information can be disclosed as part of the company's strategic report, instead of in the directors' report, if the company deems the information to be strategic in nature.

3.2   The Companies, Partnership and Groups (Accounts and Non-Financial Reporting) Regulations 2016

The Companies, Partnership and Groups (Accounts and Non-Financial Reporting) Regulations 2016 implemented into UK law the European Union Directive on disclosure of non-financial information and diversity information. They resulted in changes to both the strategic report and the Disclosure and Transparency Rules for listed companies.

The regulations apply to companies with:

◆ more than 500 employees which are:

- – traded companies, which include those companies with debt securities;
- – banking companies;
- – authorised insurance companies; and
- – companies carrying on insurance market activity.

◆ financial years beginning on or after 1 January 2018, so reporting using the new regulations commenced in 2018.

Strategic report

Companies are required, under the regulations, to disclose information relating to environmental, employee, social, respect for human rights, anti-corruption and bribery matters, to the extent needed for shareholders to have an understanding of the company's development, performance, position and the impact of the company's activities on those matters in their strategic reports.

This includes a description of:

◆ the company's business model;
◆ the policies pursued by the company in relation to the matters;
◆ due diligence on the implementation of the policies;
◆ the outcome of the policies;
◆ the principal risks relating to the matters arising out of the company's operations;
◆ how the company manages the principle risks; and
◆ non-financial key performance indicators.

Disclosure Guidance and Transparency Rules

In addition to the requirements of the Companies, Partnership and Groups (Accounts and Non-Financial Reporting) Regulations 2016, listed companies are required under the amended DTRs to disclose in their corporate governance statements the following in relation to diversity:

◆   the diversity policy of the company;

◆   the objects of the diversity policy;

◆   how the diversity policy has been implemented; and

◆   progress towards achieving the objectives during the financial year

If no diversity policy is adopted or applied by the company then an explanation as to why this is the case should be made.

3.3   Companies (Miscellaneous Reporting) Regulations 2018

Section 172 of the CA2006 requires directors to have regard to employee interests and fostering relationships with customers, suppliers and others. The Companies (Miscellaneous Reporting) Regulations 2018 includes the following provisions for companies to report on the adoption of s. 172 requirements in their strategic and directors' reports:

◆   Strategic report: Companies will have to include a 'Section 172(1) statement' on how directors, when carrying out their duties, have had regard to the interests of employees and how they have fostered relationships with customers suppliers and others. This statement will also have to be made available online. This should not be a problem for listed companies who already make their annual report available online. Non-listed companies, however, are going to have to think about how they meet this requirement. If they do not have a website, they will have to consider if there is non-company website that could be used for this purpose.

◆   The directors' report has been amended to require companies to explain how they have engaged with employees, and how directors have regard to employee interests, and the effect of that regard. Large private companies are also required under the Wates Corporate Governance Principles for Large Private Companies 2018 to explain how they have engaged with suppliers, customers and others in a business relationship with the company.

The new regulations will apply to companies reporting on financial years starting on or after 1 January 2019, so actual reporting by companies on them will be in 2020.

The Department for Business, Energy & Industrial Strategy has provided extensive guidance on how the regulations should be applied by companies, and the FRC has also issued guidance about stakeholder reporting.

The FTSE 100 General Councils (GC100) has also published guidance to provide practical help to directors on the performance of their duties under section 172. They are advising directors to consider:

◆   reflecting stakeholder issues and how they are monitored in the next round of strategic planning and risk management for their company;

◆   training for existing directors and inclusion in future induction programmes information on the new requirements;

◆ information flows to the board on stakeholder issues. Is the information they currently receive too focused on financial performance? Are they aware of stakeholder interests and factors relevant to their company?

◆ reviewing existing policies and processes and, where necessary, putting in place new policies and processes specifically aimed at meeting the s. 172 provisions and reporting requirements;

◆ engaging with stakeholder groups on their experience and views of the company; and

◆ how to embed the appropriate culture of care and stewardship for the environment and focus on social issues.

4. Drivers for voluntary CSR reporting

As we saw in Chapter 10, organisations can derive competitive and other advantages from their CSR initiatives. In order to do so they need to report on them so that different stakeholder groups are aware of what the company is doing. This is why, prior to the introduction of mandatory requirements for CSR reporting, companies were voluntarily reporting.

Since 1993, KPMG has been tracking the drivers for CSR reporting in the Global 250 companies. In 2011, 67% said that a driver was their reputation, and 58% cited ethical considerations. Among the least popular drivers were improved relations with the government and saving money.

With what appears to be many benefits in favour of CSR reporting, why would companies not choose to report? The following are some reasons:

◆ The company may not have performed as well as they were hoping against their CSR targets and may be concerned that stakeholders will express disapproval in the lack of performance resulting in reputational risk.

◆ The board may not be aware of the CSR initiatives being conducted by the company. This may be due to insufficient information flows from management or a disinterest by the board in these types of activities.

◆ The cost of collecting and disclosing the information on CSR activities may be prohibitive against the perceived value of doing so.

◆ The company may not have set up their management information systems to produce the information on progress against non-financial targets at the time needed to report on it with the financial information.

◆ The company may feel that the information gives them competitive advantage so wants to keep it secret.

5. Measuring CSR initiatives

To be able to report on their CSR activities, organisations need to be able to set non-financial targets and measure their progress against targets. An organisation, when deciding what targets and measurement to use, should consider the following:

◆ Focus on outcomes. Organisations should not just measure the quantifiable such as number of hours used, the cost of the initiative or the number of employees engaged in the initiative. They also need to measure the outcome: that is, how the initiative changed the lives of the beneficiaries of the initiatives and/or helped create a better planet.

◆ Measuring the outcome is not as simple as measuring quantifiable targets. Qualitative measurement can be more subjective. For example, a river basin is to be cleaned, bringing a health benefit to communities living within it. How can the organisation measure whether it is the cleaning up of the river basin or some other factors that have led to the health benefits? There are methodologies that try to measure the performance of non-financial indicators to organisations, but they are not 100 per cent absolute when doing so. They can be challenged.

◆ Listen to stakeholders. By taking the time to understand the motivations, goals and needs of their stakeholders, organisations are not only able to develop initiatives that best serve those interests, they can also be smarter about selecting the metrics, data and stories that align with what the organisation's stakeholders value most. Engagement can be through one-on-one meetings, small focus groups, or even social media polling.

◆ Do not undervalue stories. So often, organisations think that reporting should only be communicated through numbers – percentages, hours, pounds, increases, decreases, and so on. As mentioned earlier, often CSR activities cannot be quantified so stories and qualitative observations are just as important as data when it comes to communicating your impact. Stories can be incredibly powerful, for instance how an individual's life has been changed by the organisation's initiative.

◆ Learn from others. Organisations can learn to improve their impact measurement by reviewing the sustainability reports of other companies that have been applauded for them.

◆ Identify and measure the risks. As well as measuring the progress towards achieving the targets, organisations should also identify and manage the risks associated with their CSR initiatives and put in place metrics to measure the effectiveness of their risk management of those risks.

◆ Measure, refine, modify, measure again. Organisations who appear to have the most impact on their communities, their participants and their businesses do not look at a one-time endeavour. As we saw in Chapter 10 they see their CSR initiatives as an integral part of their business model.

Over the period of the initiative, the board and management of the organisation will be evaluating the activities to find out what works best for the organisation and its stakeholders, so more of it can be done, and what doesn't work, so that management can intervene to either cease the activity or tweak and continuously improve it. To enable this to happen, the metrics used to establish whether the desired outcome has been achieved may also need to be modified.

The organisation will also have to evaluate its risk management around the initiative and tweak it if circumstances change.

In June 2018, the Financial Reporting Lab published 'Performance metrics – an investor perspective', which was the outcome of a study carried out by the Lab into whether the recent regulations and initiatives on non-financial reporting were meeting investor needs. The study concluded that investors were looking for performance metrics 'to be aligned to strategy, transparent, in context, reliable and consistent'. These requirements have been turned into the five Principles in the guidance for companies on the presentation of performance metrics in their reporting published by the Lab in November 2018, 'Performance metrics – Principles and practice'. The guidance considers both financial and non-financial metrics.

In addition to the five Principles, the guidance provides examples of how companies have applied the Principles in their reporting. For example, Vodafone in their Annual Report 2018, pages 2 and 20, have shown the progress and performance of a series of KPIs linked to strategy.

The guidance also provides a series of questions that a company's boards and management should ask themselves.

Stop and think 11.1

Read the performance metrics online. Do the performance metrics reported on by your company meet the Lab Principles?

Review the examples of best practice in the guidance and highlight areas where your organisation's performance metrics and reporting on them could be improved.

5.1 CSR and senior executive remuneration

Some organisations are starting to use CSR targets or achieving a certain status on a CSR Index as part of the performance criteria in bonus and incentive schemes for senior executives. For example, Royal Dutch Shell, which has been reporting on its environmental and social performance since 1997, tracks a range of environmental and social indicators as part of its performance appraisal system.

Boards should consider whether it is appropriate for their company to set CSR targets for their senior executives. Targets should only be set where organisations have developed clearly articulated business cases for CSR initiatives outlining how the initiative helps secure the overall sustainability of the organisation. As we have seen above investors will be looking for the performance metrics to be well-defined and tied to concrete measurable plans, otherwise senior executives may be able to take advantage of vague targets with the potential consequence of reputational and **business risk**.

business risk
Risks (and opportunities) facing the organisation. Consists of strategic risk, operation risk, financial (reporting) risk and compliance risk.

Boards, in the absence of CSR metrics, have retained the right to reduce incentive awards in cases of substantial damage to the company's business or reputation resulting from an event that has had a negative effect on the environment, society or the organisation's long-term sustainability. For example, an oil spill where inadequate precautions tied to the activities of senior executives can be shown.

5.2 Sustainable development goals

The sustainable development goals (SDGs) are a collection of 17 global goals set by the United Nations General Assembly in 2015 as 'a universal call to action to end poverty, protect the planet and ensure that all people enjoy peace and prosperity'. All 193 countries of the UN have accepted them and the aim to achieve them by 2030.

The private sector is critical in achieving the SDGs and have been tasked to ensure that their businesses contribute to achieving SDG targets as well as raising awareness about them. Several organisations, Coca Cola and Unilever among them, are measuring their CSR performance against the SDGs.

UN Sustainable Development Goals
- No poverty
- Zero hunger
- Good health and well-being
- Quality education
- Gender quality
- Clean water and sanitation
- Affordable and clean energy
- Decent work and economic growth
- Industry, innovation and infrastructure
- Reduced inequalities
- Sustainable cities and communities
- Responsible consumption and production
- Climate action
- Life below water
- Life on land
- Peace, justice and strong institutions
- Partnerships for the goals

Case study 11.1

Unilever, in its Annual Report and Accounts 2017, states: 'Our scale and reach mean we are well placed to capture value from the global Goals. The SDGs are fundamental to future economic and business growth.

The Business & Sustainable Development Commission ... concluded that successful delivery of the SDGs will create market opportunities of at least USD 12 trillion a year.' Unilever's progress against the SDGs is outlined in its online 'Sustainable Living Report', disclosed on the Unilever website.

6. Triple bottom line reporting

Triple bottom line is an accounting framework which includes information about a company's social and environmental performance as well as the traditional financial performance when evaluating the overall performance of an organisation. The term was first used by John Elkington in 1994 in an article in the California Management Review on win-win business strategies, in which he argued that companies, in addition to disclosing profit and loss, should disclose how socially and environmentally responsible they had been throughout their operations during the year. Elkington argued that it was only by taking into account all three elements of what he called 'profit, people and planet' that an organisation could calculate the full cost of doing business. It was further argued that by measuring the social and environmental elements companies, and in particular their boards and management teams, were more likely to pay attention to them and thus create more socially and environmentally responsible organisations. Evidence of this is the discovery through the requirement to collate information of corporate malpractices, such as Nike child labour issues with suppliers, which in turn have led to greater oversight by companies into the practices of their suppliers. It has also led, it is argued, to the growth of global initiatives such as the Fairtrade Foundation, which adds its brand to products that have been produced and traded in an environmentally and socially fair way.

Despite the positives associated with triple bottom line reporting, there are challenges with it.

◆   You cannot add up the three separate disclosures of financial, social and environmental information. This is because it is often very difficult to quantify social and environmental initiatives and impacts in monetary terms. For example, the impact of cleaning of a river basin or an oil spill from a tanker is far wider than the financial costs involved. This has led to organisations presenting separate reports for each element: financial statements, social report and environmental report. It is argued that this then defeats the object of having triple bottom line reporting. We will see later that the concept of integrated reporting has developed to counter this.

◆   There has until recently been no widely accepted set of standards for triple bottom line reporting or measuring social and environmental impacts as is the case for financial reporting. This makes it difficult to compare the performance of one company with that of another. In July 2018, the Global Reporting Initiative issued the GRI Sustainability Reporting Standards, which it claims are the first global standards for sustainability reporting. More on these standards can be found later in this chapter.

triple bottom line reporting
Reporting on the economic, social and environment performance of the company.

◆ There are no requirements to independently audit social and environmental measures as there are with financial measures. Some companies, such as IKEA, do carry out external assurance programmes to verify the impacts of their CSR initiatives.

◆ There is a lack of trust in the image presented by companies through triple bottom line reporting as many companies present good news whilst withholding the bad news. Fleming and Jones (2013) argue that, of the companies that have embraced CSR reporting, most are companies that are in businesses that, it could be argued, create the greatest harm, such as tobacco companies or oil companies. These companies, they argue, carry out the reporting of their CSR initiatives as a branding and marketing exercise.

7. Integrated reporting

The recognition that it is important for a company's long-term sustainability for it to measure and report on social and environmental performance as well their financial performance together with the greater desire for accountability by an organisation's stakeholders has led to the development of the concept of integrated reporting.

The South African Corporate Governance Code was the first to include provisions on integrated reporting in King III in 2009. Since then the understanding of the concept has evolved. The latest version, King IV, defines integrated reporting as 'a process founded on integrated thinking that results in a periodic integrated report by an organisation about value creation over time. It includes related communications regarding aspects of value creation.' An integrated report is defined as 'a concise communication about how an organisation's strategy, governance, performance and prospects, in the context of its external environment, lead to the creation of value in the short, medium and long-term'. King III had stated that 'integrated reporting' reflected the challenge that organisations faced to make sustainability issues mainstream in their operations and to integrate social, environmental and economic issues into the way that the organisation operates. King IV assumes that sustainability issues are now mainstream for most organisations and that integrated reporting is an outcome of integrated thinking by the organisation's governing body.

The economic value of a company includes its balance sheet and profit and loss statement, an assessment of future earnings, brand, goodwill, the quality of its board and management, reputation, strategy and other sustainability aspects. All of these elements are found in an integrated report. Integrated reporting is, therefore, seen as essential to enable all stakeholders (internal and external) to make informed assessments of the economic value of a company.

The integrated report should record how the company has impacted (both positively and negatively) the economic life of the community in which it operated during the year, and how in the coming year it can improve the positive and eradicate or reduce the negative aspects.

Principle 5 of King IV states: 'The governing body should ensure that all reports issued by the organisation enable stakeholders to make informed assessments of the organisation's performance, and its short, medium and long-term prospects.' Recommended practice 12 under this principle goes on to say:

'The governing body should oversee that the organisation issues an integrated report at least annually, which is either:

A standalone report which connects the more detailed information in other reports and addresses, at a high level and in a complete, concise way, the matters that could significantly affect the organisation's ability to create value; or

A distinguishable, prominent and accessible part of another report which also includes the annual financial statements and other reports which must be issued in compliance with legal provisions.'

In August 2009, His Royal Highness the Prince of Wales, through his Accounting for Sustainability Project (A4S) convened a meeting of investors, standard setters, companies, accounting bodies and UN representatives, which established the International Integrated Reporting Committee. The Committee was chaired by Mervyn King, the namesake of the King Reports. The Committee's purpose was to oversee the creation of a globally accepted integrated reporting framework. In 2011, the International Integrated Reporting Committee was renamed the International Integrated Reporting Council (IIRC).

7.1 The importance of 'integrated thinking' to integrated reporting

As discussed previously, 'integrated thinking' is important to integrated reporting as this enables an organisation to understand better the relationships between its various operating and functional units and the capitals the organisation uses and affects. Integrated thinking should take into account the connectivity and interdependencies between all those factors that have a material effect on an organisation's ability to create and preserve value in the short, medium and long term, including (but not limited to):

◆ the capitals the organisation uses and affects, including the critical interdependencies of financial, manufactured, human, intellectual, natural and social capitals;

◆ the external context in which the organisation operates;

◆ the opportunities and risks faced by the organisation and how it tailors its strategies to manage them;

◆ activities, results and performance – past, present and future; and

◆ financial and non-financial information.

An integrated report should enhance transparency and accountability, which are essential in building trust and resilience, by disclosing:

◆ the nature and quality of the organisation's relationships with key stakeholders, such as customers, suppliers, employees and local communities; and

◆   how their issues are understood, taken into account and responded to.

7.2   Responding to stakeholder issues

An integrated report should show how an organisation is responding to stakeholder issues. How organisations respond to stakeholder issues is demonstrated through decisions, actions and performance, as well as ongoing communication with stakeholders. An integrated report is an important part of the communication process with stakeholders. This does not mean that the report should attempt to satisfy all the information needs of all stakeholders. Rather, by focusing on matters that are most material to long-term success, an integrated report will often provide relevant information in itself, as well as a clear reference point for other communications, including compliance information, investor presentations, detailed financial information, sustainability reports and communications directed to specific stakeholders who have particular information needs. Much of this more detailed information is likely to be placed online.

In the introduction to Philips' 'Annual Report 2008: Financial, Social and Environmental Performance', the organisation explained why it had combined all of the financial, social and environmental information into a single report. In summary, the two main reasons were as follows:

◆   It is a key element of taking sustainability seriously. An organisation should create a truly sustainable strategy responding to the risks and opportunities created by the need to ensure a sustainable society. Once this has been achieved the only way to report on it is in an integrated fashion. To try to split it back into 'silos' of financial and non-financial information does not make business sense.

◆   One report can give a single simplified message to an organisation's stakeholders. It helps improve transparency in corporate reporting.

Eccles and Krzus (2010) describe the four major benefits to an organisation that has adopted integrated reporting:

1.   Greater clarity about relationships and commitments. Integrated reporting helps companies identify the most important financial and non-financial metrics for the company. Management is also able to describe what it believes the relationship between financial and non-financial metrics should be. Most companies still have a lot of work to do on this. A 2008 KPMG CSR survey found that only 16% of the Global250 companies had quantified the value of corporate responsibility for their analyst and investor stakeholders. As management develops a better understanding of the relationships between financial and non-financial performance, it can re-evaluate what is included in its categories of risks, opportunities and choices. This will lead to better decisions.

2.   Better decisions. As management attempts to be more explicit about the relationships between financial and non-financial outcomes, integrated reporting will help management strengthen or develop better metrics. In

some cases, better information comes from simply combining data that already exists in the firm but may be being collected in different parts of the business. Kaplan and Norton's work on the Balanced Scorecard provides compelling evidence for how better measurement leads to better management decisions.

3. Also, when information is reported externally, the standards for its reliability are especially high. The higher-quality metrics required for external reporting demand higher-quality internal information, and this results in higher-quality decisions. The external transparency of the results of these decisions adds an incentive for making them good ones.

4. Deeper engagement with all stakeholders. In today's world, where companies are facing the demands of many stakeholders, it is essential that every stakeholder understands how its interests are related to those of others and to the factors that contribute to the level of performance that is being met. Integrated reporting therefore helps both companies and stakeholders take a more integrated view about how their interest relates to those of others.

5. Integrated reporting also helps eliminate the artificial distinction between shareholders and stakeholders. It can help shareholders focus in a more holistic way on a company's ability to earn profits and grow in the long term. A single integrated report ensures that there is a coherent and consistent message going out to all stakeholders. It creates a platform for one conversation in which all stakeholders can participate.

6. Through engagement, companies remain aware of the interests of their different stakeholders and how those interests are in alignment or conflict with each other. Companies should also encourage engagement among their stakeholders so that consensus can be reached on society's expectations for the company.

7. Lower reputational risk. An integrated view of the company's financial and non-financial performance, it is argued, will help identify areas at risk, since it will make clearer the areas where company's reputation is based on overlapping performance outcomes. It can also help company's monitor trends, social attitudes and the media and so improve awareness of how social norms and values are changing, helping the company become more aware of early-stage changes in expectations that will become more widely held and supported in the future.

7.3 Difference between sustainability reports and integrated reports

Sustainability reports describe the organisation's non-financial performance, both positive and negative, in areas such as the environment, society and governance. They are targeted at different stakeholder groups.

Integrated reports, on the other hand, combine financial and non-financial information and are usually targeted at investors.

Test yourself 11.2

1.   Give three examples of why a company would choose to voluntarily report on its CSR activities.

2.   Why is it important to set CSR targets and link them to executive pay?

3.   What is the difference between triple bottom line reporting and integrated reporting?

8. Global Reporting Initiative

The Global Reporting Initiative (GRI) was established in 1997 as an independent international organisation to help 'businesses and governments worldwide understand and communicate their impact on critical sustainability issues such as climate change, human rights, governance and social well-being'. GRI believe that the 'practice of disclosing sustainability information inspires accountability, helps identify and manage risks, and enables organisations to seize new opportunities'.

Since its inception, GRI has published a voluntary sustainability framework intended to introduce some standardisation into sustainability reporting. In 2015, GRI established the GRI Global Sustainability Standards Board (GSSB) as an independent entity under GRI. The GSSB has sole responsibility for setting globally accepted standards for sustainability reporting.

The GRI Sustainability Reporting Standards were introduced for reports and other materials published on or after 1 July 2018. The GRI Standards are the first and most widely adopted global standards for sustainability reporting.

GRI states on its website (3 November 2018) that the 'GRI Standards create a common language for organisations and stakeholders, with which the economic, environmental and social impacts of organisations can be communicated and understood. They have been designed to enhance the global comparability and quality of information on these impacts, thereby enabling greater transparency and accountability of organisations.'

The GRI Standards can be used in one of two ways:

◆   to prepare a sustainability report in accordance with the GRI Standards; or

◆   to report on specific sustainability information, where selected standards or part of the standards are used to produce this information.

In both cases the fact that the GRI Standards have been used should be referenced.

GRI has made available resources and tools to support organisations in the use of the GRI Standards. These are available on the GRI website. The GRI Standards are presented in modules which are interrelated. They are designed to assist organisations to prepare their sustainability reports. The GRI Standards consist of three universal standards to be used by every organisation that prepares a sustainability report and a series of topic-specific standards, which an organisation can select from depending on the economic, environmental or social factors that are applicable for their type of organisation.

8.1 GRI Universal Standards

GRI 101: Foundation

This standard is divided into three sections:

◆ Section 1 describes the Reporting Principles for determining the report's content and quality.

◆ Section 2 explains the requirements for applying the Reporting Principles, and for identifying and reporting on topic-specific standards.

◆ Section 3 sets out the ways that the GRI Standards can be used and the specific claims, or statements of use, which are required for organisations using the Standards.

GRI 102: General Disclosures

This standard requires the organisation to provide contextual information about an organisation and its sustainability reporting practices, under the following headings:

◆ organisation's profile;

◆ strategy;

◆ ethics and integrity;

◆ governance;

◆ stakeholder engagement practices;

◆ reporting process.

The information in this standard is important to help stakeholders understand the nature of the organisation and its economic, environmental and social impacts. More detailed reporting on these matters is provided in the topic-specific standards.

GRI 103: Management Approach

This standard sets out the reporting requirements for an organisation to explain how it manages the economic, environmental and social impacts related to a topic-specific standard. An organisation preparing a report in accordance with the GRI Standards is required to report its management approach for each topic-specific standard selected by the organisation as the disclosures under this standard provide context for the information reported using the topic-specific standards.

8.2 Topic-specific GRI Standards

Each standard includes:

◆ Requirements – mandatory instructions presented in bold font within the standard and indicated with the word 'shall'.

◆ Recommendations – encourage a particular course of action but are not required. They are indicated in the standard by the use of the word 'should'.

◆ Guidance – background information, explanations and examples to help organisations understand the requirements.

Series 200 – Economic
GRI 201 Economic Performance

GRI 202 Market Presence

GRI 203 Indirect Economic Impacts

GRI 204 Procurements Practices

GRI 205 Anti-corruption

GRI 206 Anti-corruption behaviour

Series 300 Environmental
GRI 301 Materials

GRI 302 Energy

GRI 303 Water and Effluents

GRI 304 Biodiversity

GRI 305 Emissions

GRI 306 Effluents and waste

GRI 307 Environmental compliance

GRI 308 Supplier Environmental Assessment

Series 400 Social
GRI 401 Employment

GRI 402 Labour/management relations

GRI 403 Occupational Health and Safety

GRI 404 Training and education

GRI 405 Diversity and equal opportunity

GRI 406 Non-discrimination

GRI 407 Freedom of association and collective bargaining

GRI 408 Child labour

GRI 409 Forced or compulsory labour

GRI 410 Security practices

GRI 411 Rights of indigenous peoples

GRI 412 Human Rights Assessment

GRI 413 Local communities

GRI 414 Supplier social assessment

GRI 415 Public policy

GRI 416 Customer health and safety

GRI 417 Marketing and labelling

GRI 418 Customer privacy

GRI 419 Socioeconomic compliance

Stop and think 11.2

Does your organisation report against the GRI Standards? Which topic-specific GRI Standards are relevant to your organisation and why?

9. Sustainability Accounting Standards Board

The Sustainability Accounting Standards Board (SASB) is an independent organisation that develops and maintains global reporting standards for companies wishing 'to identify, manage, and communicate financially material sustainability information to their investors'. SASB standards are used by companies and investors to implement principles-based frameworks, including integrated reporting and the recommendations of the Task Force on Climate-related Financial Disclosures.

10. IIRC integrated reporting framework

The IIRC has developed an international integrated reporting framework and issued guidance on integrated reporting in an attempt to build consensus among governments, listing authorities, businesses, investors and accounting bodies on the future shape of corporate reporting.

The IIRC 2013 guidance on integrated reporting establishes guiding principles and content elements for an integrated report. It does not set benchmarks for assessing such things as the quality of the organisation strategy or the level of its performance. This is because assessments of this kind are the role of the report user, based on the information provided by the company in its integrated report.

The IIRC guiding principles are:

◆ strategic focus and future orientation;

◆ connectivity of information;

◆ responsiveness and stakeholder inclusiveness;

◆ materiality and conciseness;

◆ reliability; and

◆ comparability and consistency.

The IIRC content elements for an integrated report are:

◆ organisational overview and business model;

◆ operating context, including risks and opportunities;

◆ strategic objectives and strategies;

◆ governance and remuneration;

◆ performance; and

◆ future outlook.

These content elements are not mutually exclusive and are fundamentally linked to each other. How a company presents the information in the integrated report should show this interconnectedness, rather than presenting the information in standalone 'silos'. Historically, information has often been reported by department or function and it is therefore difficult to assess the impact of one area on another in the organisation. According to the IIRC, integrated reporting should lead to a more accurate picture about what is going on in an organisation. This in turn should:

◆ promote change in corporate behaviour, decision making and thinking with a focus on long-term, in addition to medium- and short-term value creation and preservation;

◆ inform resource allocation by investors, again creating a focus on long-term as well as the short- and medium-term value creation and preservation;

◆ catalyse a more cohesive and comprehensive approach to corporate reporting that communicates the full range of factors that materially affect the ability of an organisation to create and preserve value over time; and

◆ enhance accountability and stewardship with respect to a broader base of capitals than just financial capital (including manufactured, human intellectual, natural and social [and relationship] capitals) and promote understanding of the interdependencies between them.

According to the IIRC there are, at the time of writing, 1,500 businesses worldwide using integrated reporting to communicate with their investors, 300 of which are in Japan. Regulators in Japan, India and the UK are among those taking a greater interest in integrated reporting as a route towards more cohesive reporting and financial stability.

11. The Corporate Reporting Dialogue

In June 2014, the Corporate Reporting Dialogue was convened by the International Integrated Reporting Council to create dialogue and alignment between the key sustainability standard setters and framework developers. Its members include CDP, the Climate Disclosures Board (CDSB), the Global Reporting Initiative (GRI), the International Accounting Standards Board (IASB), the International Organisation for Standardisation (ISO), the sustainability Accounting Standards Board (SASB) and the International Integrated Reporting Council (IIRC). The Financial Accounting Standards Board (FASB) has been invited to participate as an observer.

The Corporate Reporting Dialogue has already adopted a statement of Common Principles of Materiality, developed a common map of the reporting landscape and taken a common position in support of the Financial Stability Board Task Force on Climate-related Financial Disclosure (TCFD). In November 2018, the Corporate Reporting Dialogue announced a project aimed at:

◆ aligning all current sustainability standards with the TCFD recommendations published in June 2017;

◆ identifying the similarities and differences between the current standards and frameworks to create even greater alignment taking into account the different requirements of each set of standards and frameworks; and

◆ continuing dialogue with financial reporting standard setters towards integrating financial and non-financial reporting.

12. CSR benchmarking

The demand for information from different stakeholder groups on the CSR and sustainability initiatives of global companies has led over the last 20 years to the development of benchmarking indexes. Three examples are given below.

12.1 Dow Jones Sustainability Indexes (DJSI)

The DJSI was established in 1999 to provide the investment community with information on global sustainable companies. It was the first CSR index. A number of investment funds base their investment policy on holding a portfolio of shares of companies listed on the DJSI. The DJSI selects companies by evaluating information from:

◆ Sustainable Asset Management Questionnaire compiled by the company.

◆ Other company documentation, which include sustainability reports, environmental reports, health and safety reports, social reports, corporate governance statements and employee relations information.

◆ Media and stakeholder reports, which include press releases, news articles about the company and stakeholder commentary.

◆ Meetings with company management – this may be face to face or by telephone.

12.2 FTSE4Good Indexes

FTSE4Good was established in 2001 and provides a series of indexes and benchmarks for investors, fund managers, asset owners, investment banks and consultants, among others, interested in social responsible investment. The indexes are used for asset allocation, investment analysis, portfolio hedging, tracking funds and performance measurement.

In June 2018, 82 new companies were added to the FTSE4Good Developed Index and 34 new companies were added to the FTSE4Good Emerging Index; six companies were removed from the FTSE4Good Developed Index and five companies were removed from the FTSE4Good Emerging Index for no longer meeting the FTSE4Good criteria.

12.3 Business in the Community (BiTC) Corporate Responsibility Index

The BiTC corporate responsibility index was launched in 2002. It takes the form of an online survey which allows companies to self-assess their management and performance of responsible business practices, using the following framework:

- Corporate Strategy looks at the main corporate responsibility risks and opportunities to the business and how these are being identified and then addressed through strategy, policies and responsibilities held at a senior level in the company.

- Integration is about how companies organise, manage and embed corporate responsibility into their operations through KPIs, performance management, effective stakeholder engagement and reporting.

- Management builds on the Integration section looking at how companies are managing their risks and opportunities in the areas of community, environment, marketplace and workplace.

- Performance and Impact asks companies to report performance in a range of social and environmental impacts areas. Participants complete three environmental and three social areas based on the relevance to their business.

All submissions require board-level sign-off to ensure board commitment to the process and to responsible business practices.

13. External assurance

Many organisations are obtaining external assurance for their CSR initiatives and sustainability reports. These assurances provide a measure of credibility as they are performed by third parties. In 2008, according to KPMG, 80% of the Global 250 largest companies issued a sustainability report, and of these 70% engaged major accountancy firms to provide external assurance of their reports.

Other organisations have pulled together panels or committees of experts to give credence to their reporting. For example, Royal Dutch Shell, which has been reporting on its environmental and social performance since 1997, has established an external review committee of independent experts to help the organisation evaluate and improve the quality and credibility of its sustainability reporting.

The International Organisation for Standardisation (ISO) has established standards against which organisations can receive certification. For example, ISO 14001 for Environmental Management Systems and ISO 26000 for social responsibility.

14. Environmental Profit & Loss Accounts

The Environmental Profit & Loss Account (EP&L) was created by Puma, the sports lifestyle company and first published in 2011. Other companies such as Puma's parent Kering, Novo Nordisk and Stella McCartney have since released EP&Ls.

Kering have stated that 'an EP&L allows a company to measure in euro value the costs and benefits it generates for the environment, and in turn make more sustainable business decisions'.

In 2015, Stella McCartney, the fashion house, released its first EP&L which was estimated to be €5.5 million. Stella McCartney described the EP&L as 'a form of natural capital accounting that measures and monetises the negative and positive impacts on the environment generated by a company's activities – not just within its own operations, but also across all of its supply chains'.

Test yourself 11.3

1. **What are the GRI Standards and why are they important?**

2. **Why was the Corporate Reporting Dialogue established?**

3. **Why do companies have external assurance of their CSR initiatives?**

4. **What is an environmental profit & loss account?**

15. The company secretary's role in CSR reporting

In some companies, it is the responsibility of the company secretary to head up the process for preparing a company's CSR reporting. Even in those companies where the company secretary does not head up the process they have a role to play. This will include some, if not all, of the following:

◆   Ensuring that the board has ownership of the reporting process.

This can be achieved by liaising with management to ensure that a presentation is included on the board's agenda to explain:

- the reporting framework to be adopted, for example the GRI standards or the UN Global Compact. This should also be disclosed and agreed with the board;

- how the non-financial information is to be presented: as part of the annual report and accounts, in a separate sustainability report or in an integrated report;

- how the reporting will meet the differing needs of the different audiences for the reporting.

◆ The company secretary should also make a presentation explaining the director's duty for describing how they are promoting the success of the company and how it is expected to be reported within the company's documents.

◆ Ensuring that KPIs for non-financial matters are developed and approved by the board.

◆ A discussion is held at board level about the types of future-orientated information that is to be included in the reporting and how a balance is to be struck between the information to be disclosed and maintaining confidentiality of competitive and commercially sensitive information.

◆ Information flows should be maintained between the board and management covering:

- The company's value creation story; that is, how the company creates value not just for shareholders but also for other stakeholder groups.

- Views and interests of key stakeholders and their perceptions of how the company is performing from a non-financial perspective.

- What peer companies and companies from other industries are doing, the KPIs they are using, the type of future-orientated information they are including in their reports and how they are responding to stakeholder issues.

- Progress against the approved non-financial KPIs should be reported to and discussed by the board on a regular basis. The company secretary should ensure that this is on the board's or the appropriate board committee's agenda. If the board or board committee is not asking the types of questions suggested by the FRC Lab, then circulate them and organise some training on the board's responsibility with regard to overseeing performance measurement.

- Ensuring that the principle risks associated with CSR activities are known and are being managed and reported on in the appropriate company documents. Again, the board should be receiving regular updates on this at its meetings and the company secretary should ensure that it is on the agenda of the board or the appropriate board committee.

-   Liaising with internal audit to ensure that the management information systems being used to collect the data used for non-financial reporting is audited and the appropriate assurances are being provided to the board on them.
-   Being a member or team leader of the multi-departmental team responsible for delivering the CSR or integrated report.
◆ Following the reporting cycle, ensuring that a review of the annual process is conducted and presented to the board highlighting gaps and areas for improvement and any feedback received from different stakeholder groups.

Chapter summary

◆ Financial reporting tells only half the story about the performance of the company and the impact of its operations on society and the environment.

◆ Narrative reporting has been introduced to give a broader view of a company's business, its strategy and future prospects.

◆ Narrative reporting is included in the chair's statement, directors' report, strategic report, corporate governance report and directors' remuneration report.

◆ A strategic report provides information to shareholders on how directors have performed their duty under s. 172 of the CA2006, to promote the success of the company.

◆ Organisations report on their CSR activities for the following reasons: benefits of doing so to their brand and reputation; stakeholder interest; and increasing mandatory requirements.

◆ To ensure that organisations embed their corporate social and environmental responsibilities into their operations it is important for targets to be developed and for these targets to be linked to an employee's performance appraisal and remuneration.

◆ Triple bottom line reporting and integrated reporting combine both financial and non-financial reporting. This differs from sustainability and CSR reports which only provide information on the organisation's impact on society and the environment.

◆ There are initiatives to produce a globally accepted set of standards for sustainability reporting. This will make it easier for stakeholders to compare companies and also for companies to report on their activities.

Part four

Risk management and internal control

Overview

The fourth part of this study text considers the knowledge and skills necessary for the company secretary to act as the chief adviser to the board and other stakeholders on best practice in the area of risk management and internal control. It also describes the operational role of the company secretary in ensuring that the structures, policies and procedures approved by the board are operating effectively.

Chapter 12 explains the role of the company secretary in advising the board on their responsibility for risk management and for ensuring that the internal control system is effective. It describes the risk management process and outlines the different structures, policies and procedures which should be in place.

Chapter 13 examines the company secretary's role in operationalising the risk and internal control structures, policies and procedures and in how compliance with them is achieved. The chapter looks at internal audit, risk committees, whistleblowing, information governance, conflict prevention and resolution, business continuity, and disaster recovery planning and how reward systems within an organisation should ensure compliance with the risk management and internal control system.

Learning outcomes

By the end of Part Four, students should be able to:

◆ define risk and explain the different types of risk differentiating between business and governance risks;.

◆ critically appraise and apply corporate governance principles and best practices in risk management;

◆ advise the board on the benefits of applying the principles of risk management;

◆ explain the two main risk and internal control frameworks – the UK system based on Turnbull and the USA COSO frameworks;

◆ identify common failures of boards in risk management and advise the board on how they might avoid them;

◆ advise the board on the content of a long-term viability statement;

◆ advise the board and other stakeholders on the structures that should be in place for effective risk management;

◆ identify when it is of benefit for an organisation to have a separate board risk committee;

◆ explain the benefits of having an internal audit function;

◆ describe the typical role of the company secretary in risk management;

◆ advise the board and other stakeholders on the policies and procedures that should be in place for effective risk management, such as those regarding whistleblowing, cybersecurity, information and disaster recovery;

◆ operationalise the structures, policies and procedures required for effective risk management;

◆ advise the board on the implications of the UK Bribery Act 2010 and actions to be taken to ensure its provisions are not breached; and

◆ explain how conflict can be minimised in the boardroom.

Chapter twelve
Systems of risk management and internal control

CONTENTS

1. Introduction

Corporate governance best practice following the global financial crisis has become more focused on a board's role in risk management and in ensuring that an organisation has an effective internal control system. Best practice in this area is now concentrating on the creation of risk cultures within an organisation not just on compliance with policies and procedures. As the chief governance adviser to the board, the company secretary therefore has an important role to play in supporting the board and other stakeholders in this role.

2. Corporate governance, risk and internal controls

2.1 The relevance of risk management and internal control systems for corporate governance

The management of risk in an organisation is considered as part of corporate governance. This is because it requires the development of structures, policies and procedures which, when operationalised effectively, should create a culture that leads to a better performing organisation, more likely to weather the shocks of the environment within which it operates leading to its continued sustainability.

The board as part of its role in governing an organisation has a responsibility to manage the risk that the organisation is prepared to take in achieving the strategic objectives it has set itself. How successful the board is in doing this can affect the performance of the organisation and in some cases where risk is not successfully managed can lead to the insolvency of the organisation.

Part of the risk management process is to develop an internal control system. Corporate governance best practice refers to a board's responsibility for ensuring the effectiveness of the organisation's risk management and internal control systems.

The company secretary should advise the board on the significance of risk management to corporate governance and the board's responsibilities regarding risk management and the internal control system.

2.2 The UK corporate governance code requirements: internal control and risk management systems, and internal audit

The 2018 Code applies only to UK listed companies.

Principle O of the Code states that:

'The board should establish procedures to manage risk, oversee the internal control framework, and determine the nature and extent of the principal risks it is willing to take in order to achieve its long-term strategic objectives.'

The Principle is supported by the following Provisions:

'28. The Board should carry out a robust assessment of the company's emerging and principal risks. The board should confirm in the annual report that it has completed this assessment, including a description of its principal risks, what procedures are in place to identify emerging risks, and explanation of how these are being managed or mitigated.

29. The board should monitor the company's risk management and internal control systems and, at least annually, carry out a review of their effectiveness and report on that review in the annual report. The monitoring and review should cover all material controls, including financial, operational and compliance controls.'

In practice, the company secretary should advise and facilitate the board to:

◆ Develop a set of strategic objectives for the company.
◆ Identify the principal risks it is willing to take to achieve its strategic objectives and those that could threaten the company's 'business model, future performance, solvency and liquidity'.
◆ Carry out a 'robust' assessment of the principal risks.
◆ Explain how the principal risks are being managed or mitigated.

◆ Monitor the risk management and internal control systems.

◆ At least annually, carry out a review of the effectiveness of the risk management and internal control systems.

◆ Annually carry out an assessment of the future viability of the company for a period to be determined by the board considering the organisation's current position and the principal risks. This provision is instead of the current going concern statement made by companies in their annual report and accounts which only covers a 12-month period. The change has been introduced as a period of 12 months may not be appropriate for every company; allowing the flexibility for boards to determine their own time periods was seen as beneficial.

◆ Report on the above in the company's annual report and accounts.

The 2018 Code (Provision 25) requires that the audit committee should review the company's internal financial controls. The review of the company's internal control and risk management systems could be done by the board itself, the audit committee or by a separate board risk committee. The company secretary should advise and facilitate the board to consider how this might best be done in their company.

2.3 FRC guidance on risk management, internal control and related financial and business reporting

In September 2014, the FRC published 'Guidance on Risk Management, Internal Control and Related Financial and Business Reporting' to assist listed companies in complying with the requirements in Section C of the 2014 version of the UK Corporate Governance Code. The guidance applied to companies with accounting periods beginning on or after 1 October 2014.

The guidance, in its introduction, makes clear that when developing an organisation's risk management and internal control systems boards 'should not inhibit sensible risk taking that is critical to growth'. The risk management process should support decision making in the organisation and be part of the normal business processes within the organisation. This is discussed further in Chapter 13.

The guidance, in addition to stating that the board has ultimate responsibility for risk management and internal control, also stated that the 'board is responsible for ensuring that an appropriate culture has been embedded throughout the organisation'. This change in approach from the traditional mechanical compliance with previous risk and internal control requirements was in response to the global financial crisis where organisations had elaborate structures, policies, procedures and reporting in place, but they were not embedded in the culture of the organisation. Failure to embed them in the culture of the organisation is perceived by many to be the cause of the failure of many organisations. Boards are now expected to take responsibility for ensuring that appropriate culture and reward systems have been embedded throughout the organisation.

In addition to giving guidance on the board's responsibilities under the Code, the guidance also provides information on how the board may exercise those responsibilities under the following points:

◆ The culture the board wishes to embed within the organisation and whether this has been achieved.

◆ How the board ensures that there is adequate discussion at board level on risk management and internal controls.

◆ Consideration of the skills, knowledge and experience of the board and management in risk management.

◆ The flow and quality of information to and from the board.

◆ What the board has agreed to delegate and to whom.

◆ What assurances the board requires on risk management and how this is to be obtained.

2.4 FRC guidance on the strategic report

In July 2018, the FRC published its revised 'Guidance on the Strategic Report', which defines principal risks as risks which 'are not necessarily limited to, those risks that could result in events or circumstances that might threaten the entity's business model, future performance, solvency or liquidity, or result in significant value erosion. In determining which risks are the principal risks, entities should consider the potential impact and probability of the related events or circumstances arising and the timescale over which they may occur.'

3. Risk

Risk refers to the possibility that something unexpected or not planned for will happen. This could be something bad happening, which in many cases is the perception, but it could also be that things turn out better than expected. These two situations are referred to as **downside risk** and **upside** or opportunity risk respectively. Many organisations plan for downside risk but fail to take into account upside risk in their decision-making processes. For an organisation to manage risk effectively it should have processes in pace to manage both downside and upside risk.

Examples of downside risk are fires, consequences of bad weather systems, earthquakes, IT breakdowns, etc.

Examples of upside risk would be sales volumes being higher than planned, an investment decision could lead to higher than anticipated returns, take-up of a product or service being more than anticipated etc.

downside risk
A risk that actual events will turn out worse than expected. Downside risk can be measured in terms of the amount which profits could be worse than expected. The expected outcome is the forecast or budget expectation.

upside risk
A risk that actual events will turn out better than expected and will turn out better than expected and will provide unexpected profits. Some risks, such as the risk of a change in interest rates, or a change in consumer buying patterns could be 'two-way' with both upside and downside potential.

Stop and think 12.1

What upside and downside risks can you identify in an organisation you are familiar with?

The International Standard ISO31000 defines risk as 'the effective of uncertainty on objectives, whether positive or negative'. The key point here is that risks to a specific organisation are only those that affect the achievement of the objectives of that organisation, one of which will be the continued existence of that organisation.

Boards should, therefore, when considering proposals look at both the downside and upside risks associated with that proposal and consider the effect they will have on the objectives of the organisation. The company secretary should ensure that this information is provided when the proposals are submitted for consideration.

3.1   Business risk versus governance risk

◆   Business risk is the possibility a company will have lower than anticipated profits or experience a loss rather than taking a profit. Business risk is influenced by numerous factors, including sales volume, per-unit price, input costs, competition, the overall economic climate and government regulations.

◆   Business risk is often broken down into the following categories:

–   Reputational risk: the risk of loss in customer loyalty or support due to an event that has damaged the company's reputation.

–   Competition risk: the risk that business performance will be affected because of the actions of the company's competitors. An example of this is RIM (the manufacturer of the BlackBerry) and Nokia, who failed to anticipate new entrants and product categories in the smartphone market and were caught flatfooted by Apple's iPhone and Samsung's Galaxy phones.

–   Business environment risks: the risk that the business environment in which the company operates will change significantly. This may be due to political factors, regulatory factors, economic factors, social and environmental factors or technological factors.

–   Liquidity risk: the risk that the company will have insufficient cash to settle all of its liabilities on time, so will be forced out of business.

◆   Governance risk relates to the risks associated with the following:

–   Structure – from boards and steering groups to business models and policy frameworks.

–   Processes – from new product processes and communication channels to operations, strategic planning and risk appetite.

–   Information – from financial performance and audit reporting to management, risk and compliance reporting.

–   People and culture – from leadership at the top to accountability and transparency throughout the organisation, including relationships with regulators.

Case study 12.1

An example of an organisation managing a potential reputational risk was ABC cancelling the sitcom Roseanne in May 2018, after Roseanne Barr, the star and creator of the show posted an alleged racist tweet about former President Obama's senior advisor, Valerie Jarrett.

ABC issued a statement which said: 'Roseanne's Twitter statement is abhorrent, repugnant and inconsistent with our values and we have decided to cancel her show.'

Bob Iger, the CEO of Disney, ABC's parent company, added: 'There was only one thing to do here, and that was the right thing.'

Roseanne was the top comedy show of 2017, making $45 million in advertising dollars for ABC with a projected $60 million advertising dollars for the next season. The cast and others on the show amounting to around 200 individuals also lost their jobs. Cable channels who showed re-runs will also lose out on millions in advertising dollars.

Roseanne Barr was also dropped by her agency.

Different risks are faced by each industry and company. The board and senior management should therefore ask themselves the following questions when assessing the risks for their company:

◆ What risks does the company face?
◆ How can these risks be measured?
◆ What is the worst-case scenario for the company for each of the risks?
◆ What is the likelihood of a bad outcome from each of the risks?
◆ What is the company's risk appetite?
◆ What is the company's risk tolerance?
◆ What should the company be doing to manage the risks?

Case study 12.2

In May 2018, Cambridge Analytica, the political consultancy firm, announced that it was to close and declare bankruptcy following the Facebook data row. This announcement followed several months of intense media and regulatory scrutiny in several countries.

In March 2018, information about Cambridge Analytica's business practices, some of which it has been claimed were nefarious, were reported by various global media outlets. These reports led the UK's Information Commissioner to seek and obtain a warrant to search the company's servers.

Cambridge Analytica collected data to be used during electoral campaigns.

It used the data to gain knowledge about target audiences, with a view to changing that audiences' behaviour through targeted highly personalised advertising.

The company harvested information from around 87 million Facebook users, which it used to build psychological profiles on large portions of the electorate in several countries, including the UK and US. It has been claimed that their services which were used in the Brexit referendum and in recent elections in India, Kenya, Malta, Mexico and the US influenced the outcome of those elections. This has, however, been disputed by many politicians and by political scientists.

The company said it had been 'the subject of numerous unfounded accusations' and was 'vilified for activities that are not only legal, but also widely accepted as a standard component of online advertising in both political and commercial arenas'.

Cambridge Analytica's business practices raised both ethical and privacy issues due to the fact that:

◆   the users were unaware that their data was being collected without their permission; and

◆   their data was being used to change their behaviour without their knowledge.

The case is further complicated by the fact that what Cambridge Analytica did was not illegal in the US but was in Europe which has stricter privacy laws.

No legal action was taken against Cambridge Analytica whose business failed due to the damage to the company's reputation. No one wanted to be connected with the company.

Facebook, on the other hand, in addition to suffering some reputational damage from the Cambridge Analytica scandal, was also fined £500,000 for breaching the UK Data Protection Act 1998.

4. Internal controls

An internal control system is made up of all of the structures, policies and procedures within an organisation related to the management of financial, operational and **compliance risks**, often known as business risk.

compliance risk
Risk of failure to comply with laws or regulations and the consequences of such a failure if discovered.

Internal controls form that part of the internal control system which manages business risk. They can be classified into three main types:

◆   Preventative controls intended to prevent an adverse risk event from occurring, e.g. fraud by employees.

◆   Detective controls for detecting risk events when they occur, so that the appropriate person is alerted, and corrective action taken.

◆   Corrective controls for dealing with risk events that have occurred and their consequences.

Internal controls and the internal control system are, according to the Committee of Sponsoring Organisations of the Treadway Commission (COSO), aimed at providing 'reasonable assurance' regarding the achievement of objectives in the following categories:

◆ effectiveness and efficiency of operations;

◆ reliability of financial reporting; and

◆ compliance with applicable laws and regulations.

Case study 12.3

In 2008, French bank Société Générale's (SocGen) independent directors identified 'weaknesses' in the bank's controls that led to the biggest fraud in banking history. The losses of nearly €5 billion were triggered by junior trader, Jérome Kerviel. The independent directors identified 75 'warning signals' on Kerviel's trading that the bank failed to follow up. Kerviel's supervisor accepted explanations that he gave without verifying them, and in spite of warnings about Kerviel from derivatives exchange Eurex. There were also no controls on cancelled or modified trades, which Kerviel used extensively. Within the bank, there may have been a culture of deference by risk managers to successful traders.

Subsequent investigations by internal and external auditors for the bank found that traders and their superiors at SocGen frequently flouted the rules, giving Kerviel an opportunity to take €50 billion in unauthorised trades. There was a low appreciation of the risk of fraud, a strong entrepreneurial culture and the emergence of unauthorised practices with trading limits regularly exceeded.

Neither the 2018 Code nor the FRC guidance call for disclosure of failures in internal controls or weaknesses in the internal control system or the measures that have been taken to deal with them. The DTRs which govern listed companies include a requirement for the disclosure in the annual report of a description of the main features of the company's internal control and risk management systems relating to the financial reporting process. Boards of directors may also consider that they have obligations under the DTRs to report significant internal control weaknesses when they occur if the company's financial performance or position would be adversely affected as a result.

4.1 Internal control risks

'Internal control risks' are risks that internal controls will fail to achieve their intended purpose, and will fail to prevent, detect or correct adverse risk events.

These risks can occur because:

◆ they are badly designed, and so not capable of achieving their purpose as a control; or

◆ they are well-designed, but are not applied properly, due to human error or

operational risk
Risk of an error, deliberate
or otherwise, in operating
system design, the risk
of failures due to weak
organisational structure,
or risks due to weak
organisational structure;
or risks due to human
error including inefficient
management. Includes
health and safety risks,
environmental risks.

oversight, or deliberately ignoring or circumvention of the control (a form of **operational risk** event).

An internal control system needs to have procedures for identifying weak or ineffective internal controls. This is one of the functions of monitoring the effectiveness of the internal control system which is discussed in more detail in Chapter 13.

5. Elements of a risk management and internal control system

Warren Buffet, who many consider to be the most successful investor in the world, said that 'Risk comes from not knowing what you are doing. Never invest in a business you do not understand'. To understand a business, you need to know and manage its risks.

The most commonly used 'models' for risk management and internal control systems are those developed in the UK in the Turnbull Report and in the USA by the Committee of Sponsoring Organisations (COSO).

5.1 The Turnbull Report

The Turnbull Report or Turnbull Guidance provided additional guidance to boards on their responsibilities for the systems of risk management and internal control within their companies. The Guidance was introduced following the inclusion in the 1998 UK corporate governance code of principles and provisions relating to risk management and internal control.

The Turnbull Guidance suggested that there should be financial, operational and compliance controls to deal with the financial, operational and compliance risks identified by the company.

Financial controls
Financial controls are internal accounting controls that are sufficient to provide reasonable assurance that:

◆ transactions are made only in accordance with the general or specific authorisation of management;

◆ transactions are recorded so that financial statements can be prepared in accordance with accounting standards and generally accepted accounting principles;

◆ transactions are recorded so that assets can be accounted for;

◆ access to assets is only allowed in accordance with the general or specific authorisation of management;

◆ the accounting records for assets are compared with actual assets at reasonable intervals of time; and

◆ appropriate action is taken whenever there are found to be differences.

The maintenance of proper accounting records is an important element of internal control.

Effective financial controls should ensure:

◆ the quality of external and internal financial reporting, so that there are no material errors in the accounting records and financial statements;

◆ that no fraud is committed (or that fraud is detected when it occurs); and

◆ that the financial assets of the company are not stolen, lost or needlessly damaged, or that these risks are reduced.

Operational controls

Operational controls are controls that help to reduce operational risks or identify failures in operational systems when these occur. They are designed to prevent failures in operational procedures, or to detect and correct operational failures if they do occur. Operational failures may be caused by:

◆ machine breakdowns;

◆ human error;

◆ failures in IT systems;

◆ failures in the performance of systems (possibly due to human error);

◆ weaknesses in procedures; and

◆ poor management.

operational controls
Internal controls to prevents or detect errors resulting from operational risks.

Operational controls are measures designed to prevent these failures from happening or identifying and correcting problems that do occur. Regular equipment maintenance, better training of staff, automation of standard procedures, and reporting systems that make managers accountable for their actions are all examples of operational controls.

Compliance controls

Compliance controls are concerned with making sure that an entity complies with all the requirements of relevant legislation and regulations. The potential consequences of failure to comply with laws and regulations vary according to the nature of the industry and the regulations. For a manufacturer of food products, for example, food hygiene regulations are important. For a bank, regulations to protect consumers against mis-selling and regulations for detecting and reporting suspicions of money laundering are important.

The Turnbull Guidance has now been replaced by the FRC's Guidance on Risk Management, Internal Control and Related Financial and Business Reporting (2014), the contents of which are described elsewhere in this chapter.

The FRC guidance on risk follows a similar 'model' to COSO, however it considers risk management and internal control systems jointly and not as two separate systems.

5.2 COSO

The COSO guidance on risk management and internal controls is published in two sets of documents, the most recent versions being:

◆ COSO Enterprise Risk Management – Integrating with Strategy and Performance (2017);

◆ COSO Internal Control – Integrated Framework (2013).

Links to both of these documents can be found in the resources section at the back of this text.

COSO Enterprise Risk Management – Integrating with Strategy and Performance (2017)

In 2017, COSO updated its Enterprise Risk Management Framework to highlight the importance of considering risk in both the strategy-setting process and in driving performance. The revised Framework consists of five interrelated components:

1. Governance and culture: which COSO defines as 'governance sets the organisation's tone, reinforcing the importance of, and establishing oversight responsibilities for, enterprise risk management. Culture pertains to ethical values, desired behaviours, and understanding of risk in the entity'.

2. Strategy and objective-setting: which COSO defines as 'enterprise risk management, strategy, and objective-setting work together in the strategic-planning process. A risk appetite is established and aligned with strategy; business objectives put strategy into practice while serving as a basis for identifying, assessing, and responding to risk'.

3. Performance: which COSO defines as 'risks that may impact the achievement of strategy and business objectives need to be identified and assessed. Risks are prioritised by severity in the context of risk appetite. The organisation then selects risk responses and takes a portfolio view of the amount of risk it has assumed. The results of this process are reported to key risk stakeholders'.

4. Review and revision: which COSO defines as 'by reviewing entity performance, an organisation can consider how well the enterprise risk management components are functioning over time and in light of substantial changes, and what revisions are needed'.

5. Information, communication and reporting: which COSO defines as 'enterprise risk management requires a continual process of obtaining and sharing necessary information, from both internal and external sources, which flows up, down, and across the organisation'.

There are 20 principles which underlie these components. COSO believes that the 20 principles describe practices that can be applied in different ways for different organisations regardless of size, type, or sector, 'adhering to these principles can provide management and the board with a reasonable expectation that the organisation understands and strives to manage the risks associated with its strategy and business objectives'.

COSO Internal Control – Integrated Framework (2013)
The updated COSO Internal Control Framework maintains the following five components and the COSO cube:

1. The control environment is a set of standards, processes, and structures that provide the basis for carrying out internal control across the organisation.

2. Risk assessment is the process for identifying and analysing risks to achieve the company's objectives. The assessment should form the basis for determining how risks should be managed.

3. Control activities are 'actions established by the policies and procedures to help ensure that management directives to mitigate risks to the achievement of objectives are carried out'. Control activities should be performed at all levels of the organisation and at various stages within the organisation's business processes. They should include, wherever possible, the segregation of duties.

4. Information and communication – information is necessary for the organisation to carry out its internal control activities to achieve the organisation's objectives. Communication occurs both internally and externally and provides the organisation with the information needed to carry out the day-to-day internal control activities.

5. Monitoring activities – the organisation should carry out evaluations and other monitoring activities to ascertain whether each of the five components of the internal control system are present and functioning. Any deficiencies in the internal control system should be communicated to management and the board in a timely manner.

The revised framework adds 17 principles to support the five components.

Test yourself 12.1

1. What is the responsibility of a board of directors for risk and internal controls?

2. Explain the difference between downside and upside risk?

3. What is the difference between the UK and US models of risk management and internal control systems?

6. Developing a risk management system

6.1 Risk identification

The board has ultimate responsibility for determining the nature and extent of the principal risks it is willing to take to achieve its strategic objectives. The board carries out this role with the assistance of management. Some risks are easy to recognise as they are always present, and an organisation or particular sector have a lot of experience of dealing with them, for example credit risk (the risk that customers will not pay what they owe). Other risks are more difficult to identify and anticipate. An organisation's ability to deal with these types of risks is often what gives it competitive advantage over other organisations in the same sector. An example of this is typewriters becoming obsolete with the word processor.

Risks change over time so identification should be an ongoing activity within an organisation.

6.2 Risk categories

Risks can be divided into the following categories:

◆   Financial risks are internal risks such as:
   –   risk of errors or fraud in accounting systems, or in accounting and finance activities within the organisation
   –   failure to protect cash
   –   failure to record financial transactions
   –   processing financial transactions without the proper authorisation
   –   misreporting in the financial statements intentionally or unintentionally.
   –   Liquidity risk – the lack of cash in the business so it is unable to settle its liabilities on time.
   –   Credit risk – customers failing to pay what they owe on time.
   –   Operational risks arising out of the failure of organisational processes and systems, for example,
      –   breakdown in a system due to machine failure or software errors;
      –   theft of information from the organisation;
      –   a terrorist act;
      –   inefficient or ineffective use of resources;
      –   errors and omissions by staff.
      –   Within some countries, such as South Africa, the operational risks associated with IT and information are categorised separately.
◆   Compliance risks are that important laws or regulations will not be complied with properly leading to legal action and/or fines.

◆ **Strategic risks** tend to be external risks occurring or arising in the business environment in which the organisation operates. Examples are:

- people risks;
- marketplace risks;
- ethical risks;
- reputational risks;
- supplier/outsourcer risks;
- stakeholder risks;
- environmental risks;
- political risks.

strategic risk
Risk from unexpected events or developments in a business or in the business environment which are outside the control of management. Business risks should be managed and kept within acceptable limits.

The first three categories – financial, operational and compliance risks – are those, according to the COSO model, which are managed by the internal control system. The board should be aware that internal controls themselves can create risk when they fail to achieve their intended purpose. This can occur when the internal controls are badly designed or when they are well-designed but not applied properly.

When identifying a risk, it is important that it is defined as specifically as possible to ensure that when it is assessed and responded to, it is correctly managed. Often management identify a business problem, e.g. 'the foreign exchange rate is killing us', rather than identifying the risks to the organisation's strategic objectives associated with the problem. They then put a lot of time and resource into managing what they perceive is a financial risk whereas they may have another type of risk, such as people risk (as they have to pay their staff in US dollars instead of a local currency).

Stop and think 12.2

What could be the risk to an organisation of a higher or lower foreign exchange rate?

Case study 12.4

Following the September 11 2001 terrorist attacks on the World Trade Centre, several financial institutions, including Goldman Sachs and Morgan Stanley, identified terrorism as a principal operational risk. Many of these organisations were located in the same area and shared power and telecommunications systems. Their back-up facilities were also shared on the basis that not all of them would need the facilities at the same time. Many employees turned up at contingency facilities to find employees from another financial institution sitting in their allocated desk or using their allocated facilities. This experience led

these financial institutions to decentralise their facilities and to ensure that their IT systems could be operational from other sites, often in other states or countries.

6.3 Methods of identifying risk

◆ Mind mapping: this is the simplest method and involves thinking of all the risks to the organisation. It is very random and will throw up all kinds of risks which need to be categorised and then assessed. However it may miss risks which are identified in a more systematic or scientific way. An example of this method is a company secretary asking board members to write what they believe are the top three risks to the organisation on a piece of paper. These are then collated and analysed.

◆ Process mapping: this method involves mapping every process within an organisation to identify interdependent, critical and vulnerable functions and activities within the organisation. The related risks can then be managed.

◆ Stress testing: organisations assess their ability to withstand extreme 'shocks' or unexpected events in the business environment within which they operate. The findings of the stress testing would indicate areas of risk to be managed.

◆ Use of internally generated documents: examples of these types of documents are:

– business impact studies;

– market research reports;

– internally generated reports which describe historical experiences, lessons learned etc.; and

– expert reports on areas such as health and safety, research and development, etc.

◆ These types of documents would be reviewed to see if any risks can be identified.

6.4 Risk assessment

Once a risk has been identified, it should be assessed to see if it qualifies as a principal risk of the organisation. A procedure should be established to assess:

◆ the likelihood or probability of the occurrence; and

◆ the potential size of the impact of the occurrence.

In the simplest forms of assessment, criteria should be developed to assess likelihood as high, medium or low and impact as significant, moderate or minor. Some organisations, such as those in the financial sector, will model risk in detail and so will have established more complicated systems that divide risk likelihood and impact to greater degrees.

In establishing the criteria for risk assessment, the board, on management's recommendation, should consider the risk appetite and tolerance of the organisation.

Risk appetite is the level of risk that an organisation is willing to take in the pursuit of its objectives. It should be set by the board, who should review its level regularly as the business environment changes.

Risk tolerance is the amount of risk that an organisation is prepared to accept in order to achieve its financial objectives. It is expressed as a quantitative measure; for example, in banks, the value at risk (VaR) for a portfolio.

The Institute of Risk Management issued guidelines in 2011 on 'Risk Appetite and Tolerance'.

Once the risks have been assessed they should be ranked so that they can be prioritised. This is often done in one of two ways:

◆ By plotting the assessed risks on a matrix. This is where every risk is placed on a the same matrix, which plots the probability of a risk occurring against the severity of the consequences of that risk.

◆ By multiplying the likelihood ratings against the impact ratings. For example, likelihood ratings of high, medium and low would be rated as three, two and one respectively. The impact ratings of significant, moderate and minor would also be rated as three, two and one respectively. This would produce a ranking of one to nine:

   – nine to seven being considered high or red risks;

   – four to six being considered medium or amber risks; and

   – one to three being considered low or green risks.

One of the lessons from the global financial crisis was that when using a risk management system, the order in which you conduct the different elements is very important. Many organisations assessed risk following the response to the underlying risk. For example, risks were ranked less severe because of the presence of insurance. This meant that catastrophic risks were treated as less severe than they actually were. It is critical to ensure that the underlying risk as well as the effectiveness of the response to that risk is assessed.

6.5 Risk response

Once the principal risks have been identified, the board can agree a response to them. There are four main responses to risk:

1. Avoidance: responses which reduce the likelihood of the risk occurring. This usually means that the organisation shuts down or sells that part of the business that is causing the risk. For example, the Shell Petroleum Development Company stopped production of oil in part of Nigeria and withdrew from the area due to violence against its staff and facilities by a local activist group.

2. Reduction: responses that reduce the negative impact or take advantage of opportunities for positive impact.

3.   Transfer: responses that transfer the risk somewhere else, e.g. insurance or outsourcing.

4.   Acceptance: responses that retain the risk because it is deemed to be not a significant threat or the organisation has no control over it, e.g. regulatory risk.

When reducing or transferring risk, the risk is not entirely eliminated. There is usually some residual risk which the board should ensure is within the limits the board is prepared to tolerate.

6.6   Selecting a response

The selection of an appropriate response to a risk is a complex process and may involve one or more of the available responses:

When determining the response, the board should consider:

◆   The 'exposure' to the risk – is it high, medium or low? Greater effort and resources should be put into responding to higher ranked risks.

◆   Any negative consequences of the response(s). Organisations often respond to a risk and fail to assess the impact of the response — which may create its own risks that may be greater to the organisation than the original risk.

◆   Whether they are adding responses to existing ones rather than formulating new response to the risk. This can lead to ineffective use of resources and the creation of new risks.

Worked example 12.1

Example: fire in a warehouse

Avoid: No lighters, open flames or flammables in warehouse

Reduce: Sprinklers (but beware risk of water damage)

Transfer: Insurance to cover losses

Accept: Loss of some consumables (excess on insurance)

Stop and think 12.3

Bomb disposal experts reduce their risk by:

◆   **gathering intelligence;**

◆   **working in teams;**

◆   **wearing protective clothing;**

◆   **using specialised equipment;**

- **having a certain 'mindset';**
- **training;**
- **following set processes and procedures; and**
- **communicating effectively with other team members.**

How could you manage risk in your workplace using some of the methods described above?

Disaster recovery planning, business continuity planning and crisis management are all responses to risk and would form part of an organisation's risk management system.

6.7 Risk monitoring

A process for monitoring the effectiveness of the responses to the risks should be established. Examples of widely used methods are:

- Stress testing – the organisation assesses the robustness of the risk response by modelling extreme situations to see how effective the response is in reducing the risk.
- Developing measures to monitor the effectiveness of the risk response. When developing measures, the board should ensure that they are SMARTER, i.e. specific, measurable, achievable, relevant, time bound, ethical and rewarded.
- Use of internal audit

The outcome of the monitoring would be fed through to the board in the regular risk reports from management.

6.8 Risk reporting

Management to the board
The board needs information from management on the principal risks and the effectiveness of how they have been managed. This enables the board to evaluate the effectiveness. Management may use a risk register or dashboard to report to the board on the principal risks faced by the organisation, the actions taken to deal with the risks and the effectiveness of those actions.

Description of the risk	Assessment rating (Traffic light or ranking)	Risk response or control	Effectiveness rating (Traffic light)	Comments on further action needed

Figure 12.1 Sample risk register

The board to shareholders

As we saw in Chapter 11, the company's strategic report must contain a description of the principal risks and uncertainties facing the company, together with an explanation of how they are to be managed or mitigated. Additional reporting requirements exist for large public interest entities (PIEs). These entitites should include in their strategic report, where relevant and proportionate: a description of the company's business relationships, products and services which are likely to cause adverse impacts on principal risks related to environmental matters, the company's employees, social matters, respect for human rights and anti-corruption and anti-bribery matters.

Case study 12.5

The bankruptcy of the US mining giant Peabody in April 2016 is an example of why companies need to take their financial and narrative reporting seriously. Peabody was investigated by the Attorney General of New York for failures to report honestly about known risks to the company's business model.

It was alleged that the company hid bad news by:

◆ **claiming that it could not predict the impact of government policy on coal sales when in fact its own internal projections had predicted a fall in coal sales of 33%; and**

◆ **using the least pessimistic hypothetical scenario presented by the International Energy Agency (IEA) in their reporting.**

The alleged outcome of this was that the market was misled about the risks to the company's performance of the change in government policy by the company's corporate reporting.

Test yourself 12.2

1. **What is risk appetite and risk tolerance?**

2. **What are the main categories of risk?**

3. **List the responses to risk.**

4. **You are the company secretary of a clothing retail business. As the person responsible for risk, you have been asked to complete the risk register for the following risk which has been assessed as high – theft of clothes from the store. Please propose a treatment and a method of measuring the effectiveness of the treatment.**

7. Benefits of risk management

For operational performance

◆ Increases (reduces) the likelihood of (not) achieving business objectives.

◆ Uses incidents to highlight the risk environment and helps management to enhance risk awareness and develop performance indicators or risk indicators to improve business performance and processes.

◆ Facilitates monitoring and mitigation of risk in key projects and initiatives.

◆ Provides a platform for regulatory compliance and building goodwill.

For financial performance

◆ Protects and enhances value by prioritising and focusing attention on managing risk across an organisation.

◆ Contributes to a better credit rating, as rating agencies are increasingly focusing on the risk management of organisations.

◆ Builds investor, stakeholder and regulator confidence and shareholder value.

◆ Reduces insurance premiums through demonstrating a structured approach to risk.

For decision making

◆ Shares risk information across the organisation, contributing to informed decisions.

◆ Facilitates assurance and transparency of risks at board level.

◆ Enables decisions to be made in the light of the impact of risks and the organisation's risk appetite and tolerance.

8. The role of the board in risk management and internal control

The board has overall responsibility for risk management. Even though most boards delegate this responsibility to management they keep the following responsibilities:

◆ Deciding the organisation's risk appetite.

◆ Ensuring that management manage risk within the board's guidelines for risk appetite.

◆ Monitoring the performance of management, to ensure that the business is being managed within the risk guidelines set by the board.

◆ Monitoring the risk management system to ensure that it is effective and achieves its purpose.

To enable the board to carry out these responsibilities effectively board members should have an understanding of risks and risk management. Training is very important in this area. There should also be a risk management system in place that the board as a whole or the appropriate board committee can review.

At board level, the responsibility for reviewing the effectiveness of the risk management and internal control systems can be delegated by the board to either an audit or risk committee.

In February 2017, the Association of Insurance and Risk Managers in Industry and Commerce (Airmic) published a report 'Ensuring Corporate Viability in an Uncertain World'. The report followed a series of roundtables hosted by the Chair's Forum, the Chartered Institute of Management Accountants (CIMA) and consulting firm Alvarez & Marsal, which were held to assess how boards viewed risk management.

The report concluded that boards were concerned about the growing complexity of global risk and cared about risk management.

The following issues may explain why boards are becoming more interested in risk management:

cyber risks
Any risk that leads to financial loss as a result of disruption or damage to the reputation of an organisation from some sort of failure of its information technology systems.

◆ The increased speed of change within the environments which companies were operating required a greater speed of response in terms of risk management.

◆ The increased transparency occasioned by social media, the internet and the insatiable needs of 24-hour traditional media meant that companies were operating in a 'glass bubble' with its associated risks.

◆ The change in the type of risks from tangible measurable risks to intangible risks, such as reputational and **cyber risks**, which required new methods of assessment and mitigation.

◆ Risks are becoming more interconnected and therefore need to be managed in a more holistic and integrated approach than the traditional silos.

◆ An increasing recognition that risk management is not just a compliance discipline. It is more about building relationships between different parts of the business and developing behaviours and a culture of risk management which require a different skill set.

◆ A growing awareness that risk management should support better decision making and strategy development.

◆ An appreciation that the board has a role in ensuring that the appropriate risk management systems are in place to support the integration of risk management in the company and to foster collaboration in the management of risk both vertically and horizontally around the organisation.

Case study 12.6

An example of the complexity of risk management and how companies are having to deal with the risks associated with the interconnectedness of their businesses is the Volkswagen (VW) emissions scandal, which has become known as 'Dieselgate'. Some 13 years after it came to light, 'Dieselgate' is still rumbling on.

VW learned in 2005 that its diesel vehicles could not meet US emissions standards, so in order to meet these standards, they deployed a software 'fix' that reported dramatically lowered emissions levels during testing to meet emission requirements. Vehicles in fact emitted up to 40 times more pollutants on the road than were allowed by regulation. The software was installed on at least 11 million vehicles worldwide before a team from West Virginia University discovered the deception and reported it.

What went wrong? According to commentators, the publicly announced goal of VW for many years was growth: the goal was to make VW the largest car maker by sales in the world, which it ironically achieved in the first half of 2005. Its remuneration policies which consisted of high-powered incentives in the form of heavily performance-related pay were deployed to reward the achievement of this goal. Executives' variable pay was also linked closely to several metrics including operating profits, sales growth etc., not to the share price. In 2014, VW's CEO, Martin Winterkorn, took home €16m ($18.3m), of which only €2m ($2.3m), or 12.5%, was fixed compensation.

The scandal has already cost a number of top VW executives their jobs, not the least of which is former CEO Martin Winterkorn. As of May 2018, it has cost more than $30 billion in settlements, fines, fixes and compensation. Several former senior executives, including Martin Winterkorn, have been charged with misleading regulators and obstruction of justice.

VW's once impeccable reputation has also been damaged.

9. Common failures of boards

The most common failures boards tend to make in relation to risk management are as detailed below.

Failure to take responsibility for risk at the board level

Many boards outside regulated companies (listed or financial institutions) still see risk as something that they delegate to management with little or no real oversight from the board. This is often because the board members do not have the capacity to challenge management on the risks associated with the submissions they are receiving or on the operational risks of the business. The boards are then caught out when a crisis occurs, having to be reactive rather than having been proactive in managing the risk.

The company secretary can support the board to avoid this mistake by identifying the capacity gaps and discussing with the chair training opportunities to help fill them. It could also be that a board member with experience in risk could be appointed to help strengthen the board's capacity in this area. Strengthening the board through independent advice for certain potential risk advice is another action that could be taken.

Failure to see the importance of risk to the organisation as a whole.
Even when boards do take an interest in risk they often delegate it to a board committee, such as the audit committee or a risk committee. As a result, the whole board does not see the importance of risk to the organisation, they only receive soundbites. The board is also not sending the message to management that managing risk is important.

The company secretary can ensure that all proposals to the board contain a section on the risks associated with the proposal and those associated with not approving the proposal. These risks should be discussed by the board and the company secretary should ensure that these discussions are minuted. They should also ensure that the board has a regular agenda item to discuss risk.

Failure to capture the major risks of the organisation
The review of the risk register, if one is even presented at board level, can be a mechanical rather than a qualitative discussion on the real risks for the business. The major risks faced by the organisation are often missed by this exercise.

The company secretary can help the board avoid this mistake by suggesting to the chair that he ask the CEO 'What is currently keeping them awake at night?' This gives recognition to the fact that risks can continually change. They are not always static. The chair could also ask board members to brainstorm what risks they think are relevant to the organisation and compare them to those in the risk register. The board could also ask for a consultant to advise them on the major risks the organisation may be facing.

Failure to consider the integrated nature of risk
Some boards fail to understand how a potential risk affects the operations of the organisation as a whole. They split risk up into 'silos'. Financial risks are dealt with by the finance department, human resource risks by the HR department and legal risks by the legal department, for example. This means that the board can make decisions silo by silo rather than treating risk as being inter-related across the whole business. A risk in one part of the business could be an opportunity elsewhere, or mitigating a risk in a certain way in one part of the business could create a far bigger risk elsewhere.

For example, mitigating the risk of fire by putting in water sprinklers could be more damaging to the business (for example, to stock/products being held) than using another form of fire prevention. This would only come to light if the mitigation was discussed holistically across the business. Risk therefore needs to be integrated into the organisation's strategic planning processes and decision making.

The company secretary can help the board avoid this mistake by highlighting the connections between different proposals and departments. Part of the role of the company secretary is to be the conduit for all information flowing to the board. By reading and listening to what management is proposing, they should be in a position to advise the board on the integrated risk picture.

Failure to put in place the appropriate control or other mitigants for risk

This is often a by-product of the board failing to understand the true nature of risk in their organisation.

The company secretary can help the board avoid this failure by ensuring that both they and the board are exposed to information on the type of risks that may affect the business. These risks, as mentioned above, change as the environment within which the organisation operates changes. Recent risks organisations are having to come to terms with are those related to data protection, cyberattacks, Brexit and climate change. The impact of each will vary depending on the business of the organisation. Exposure can be gained through training and seeking the advice of experts in the field. The company secretary should ensure that time is allocated within the board's agenda for these types of discussions. These could be held during a board meeting or at a separate information session for the board and management.

The company secretary could also work with the internal audit function, where this exists, to help the board to identify whether the appropriate internal controls and mitigants are in place. Internal audit should check, as they carry out their audits, whether the three types of controls (preventative, detective and corrective) are in place.

Internal audit should also carry out annually an assessment of the adequacy of the risk management and internal control systems within the organisation. This should create a wealth of information for the board to work with on improving both systems.

Failure to manage reputational risk

Reputational risk can be one of the most damaging risks for an organisation and requires careful management. A reputation takes years to build but can be damaged in a second. Boards should discuss the reputational impact and potential risks to their reputation of the decisions they make.

The company secretary can assist the board by making sure information that can support these discussions is made available to the board. This could be examples of what has happened with other companies, for example the recent tax planning cases involving Apple, or getting advice from external parties.

Boards should engage with major shareholders and other stakeholders to get feedback on actions the board is planning to take. Management should support this through surveys and impact studies, and the company secretary should be prompting management where this information is lacking within a proposal.

Failure by the board to map out clearly who has responsibility for what, at different level of the organisation

For individuals or bodies within the organisation to be held accountable it is important for their roles to be clearly defined. By carrying out this exercise, gaps in responsibility can be identified and resolved. For successful risk management there needs to be a combination of strong oversight by the board and assessment, management and monitoring by management. This can only occur if everyone within the organisation plays their part; they can only do this if they know what is expected of them.

All employees should be aware that they have a responsibility for risk management. It is not just the responsibility of the risk officer or senior management team. Processes should be in place where different departments discuss their risks and the interrelated nature of them across the business on a regular basis. This process should be set out in a risk manual which should be approved by the board.

The company secretary can assist the board and management by ensuring that a risk manual is put in place and that the process it describes is actually implemented within the organisation. Feedback on its implementation should be provided to the board and the company secretary can ensure that time is made available on the board's agenda for this to occur. The risk manual should also be reviewed at least annually.

Failure to consider, decide or articulate effectively the risk appetite for the organisation

The expectations of shareholders and other stakeholders, such as employees, customers and suppliers, should be taken into consideration when making decisions about risk appetite.

Even where risk appetite is considered by the board, there is often no follow through as far as other policies and procedures are concerned to ensure that they encourage behaviours in line with the risk appetite. For example, are the remuneration and reward practices within the organisation supporting the risk appetite? A financial institution may have agreed a conservative approach to risk. It pays its staff in branches performance-related pay heavily based on the number of loans they issue. An outcome of this could be a poor loan portfolio as employees find ways of issuing loans to clients who in other circumstances would not be eligible just to meet their monthly pay requirements. The financial institution is therefore actually working at very high-risk levels despite the board feeling their level of risk is low.

The company secretary should ensure that discussions about risk appetite are on the board's agenda. They should also advise the board to consider the impact on risk appetite of any policy and procedural changes that are submitted to them for approval. The company secretary should also advise the board to seek assurance from internal audit that the risk appetite in the organisation is reflective of the levels agreed by the board. The company secretary should watch out for examples of where policies and procedures may be creating a different outcome as far as risk appetite is concerned than was anticipated by the board when introducing them and advise the board and/or management accordingly.

Failure to obtain and share timely and good quality information

This can lead to heightened risk within an organisation. This is an important part of the company secretary's role, as the position has responsibility for ensuring that the board receives all the relevant information for effective decision-making and then communicates to management and other stakeholders the decisions made by the board. The company secretary should ensure that they have the processes, networks and resources to ensure this happens. Examples of these are as follows:

◆ Build relationships with members of the management team and staff in key positions to enable the company secretary to build a network to help them understand the nature of the business and obtain information about the business and particular projects.

◆ Read and query where information is not clear in submissions to the board. The company secretary should not be afraid to challenge management on the submissions and ask for additional information if this would assist the board in its decision making.
One of the respondents to the ICSA/Henley Business School study 'The Company Secretary: Building Trust through Governance' responded to a question on ensuring that the company secretary had relevant high-quality information: 'Give yourself time to think "What are the issues coming up?" and [to] pre-empt questions and constantly realign what it is that you do with the strategy [that] the company is leading on'. The study concluded that the role of the company secretary requires the ability to be intuitive and to know what types of information are important to the board to enable effective decision making.

◆ Supplement information during the board discussions if this would assist the decision-making process. This should always be done through the chair and wherever possible with the knowledge of management.

◆ Have a policy that board decisions are communicated from the company secretary prior to implementation so there are no misunderstandings as to what the board has decided.

◆ Failure of the board to appropriately challenge management on the proposals brought to the board can create risk. The role of the board is to ask questions and deliberate on issues with management until everyone is satisfied with the proposal. Some directors find this difficult to do.

The company secretary should be able to help the board by providing an environment where board members are encouraged to discuss issues. This can be achieved by, among other things:

◆ Encouraging the chair to ask all of the board members individually by name for their comments.

◆ The company secretary watching the body language of the board members and prompting the chair to ask them to comment. Alternatively, they could them in a break to see what their concerns were, either encouraging them to raise the issue or alerting the chair to the issue.

◆ Bringing in a facilitator to manage a discussion on a particular issue.

◆ Creating opportunities outside board meetings for the board members and management to get to know one another, such as dinners, board retreats and information sessions. This helps break down barriers and builds trust.

Stop and think 12.4

Is the board in your organisation exercising sufficient oversight of risk in the organisation?

Test yourself 12.3

1. **What are the benefits of risk management to an organisation?**

2. **List four common failures of boards in relation to risk management.**

10. Long-term viability statement

In addition to making a statement on the appropriateness of using the going concern basis of accounting, listed companies are also required under the 2018 Code to make a statement on the long-term viability of the company.

The 2018 Code (Provision 31) states:

'Taking account of the company's current position and principal risks, the board should explain in the annual report how it has assessed the prospects of the company, over what period it has done so and why it considers that period appropriate. The board should state whether it has a reasonable expectation that the company will be able to continue in operation and meet its liabilities as they fall due over the period of their assessment, drawing attention to any qualifications and assumptions as necessary.'

The 'reasonable expectation' is not certainty, so the board does not have to produce a detailed justification for their assessment in the statement. The statement should, however, be based on a robust assessment of the principal risks, future performance, solvency or liquidity of the company. The type of assessment will vary from company to company as it should be tailored to the company's position, performance, business model strategy and principal risks.

It is anticipated that the assessment period will be significantly longer than 12 months. According to the FRC's Guidance on Risk Management, Internal Control and Related Financial and Business Reporting, the board should determine the period of the assessment taking account of a number of factors, including without limitation:

◆   the board's stewardship responsibilities;

◆   previous statements it has made, especially in raising capital;

◆   the nature of the business and its stage of development; and

◆   its investment and planning periods.

Any qualifications and assumptions should be company specific, not generic statements that are highly unlikely either to arise or have significant impact on the company.

Chapter summary

◆   The management of risk is considered as part of corporate governance as in addition to requiring structures, policies and procedures, it requires culture creation.

◆   The board has overall responsibility in managing the risks to the organisation in meeting its strategic objectives.

◆   Risk refers to the possibility that something unexpected or not planned for will happen and affect the organisation's ability to achieve its strategic objectives.

◆   It is important for organisations to manage both downside and upside risk if they are to maximise performance and remain sustainable.

◆   Boards should decide what level of risk the organisation is prepared to take, i.e. its risk appetite, and ensure that the appropriate culture is developed in line with the agreed appetite.

◆   A system of risk management should be introduced to ensure that the principal risks are identified, assessed and mitigated. The board should evaluate the effectiveness of the risk management system.

◆   An effective control environment should be developed within the organisation, including the embedding of financial, operational and compliance controls.

◆   The 2018 Code requires the board to review at least annually the effectiveness of the systems of internal control and risk management, and report to the shareholders that they have done so.

◆   There are two frameworks of risk management accepted globally: the UK system and the US COSO frameworks. The main difference is that the UK framework integrates risk management and internal control systems whereas the COSO framework deals with them separately.

◆   The role of the company secretary requires the ability to be intuitive and to know what types of information are important to the board to enable effective decision making.

Chapter thirteen

Risk structures, policies, procedures and compliance

CONTENTS

1. Introduction

For there to be effective systems of risk management and internal controls there needs to be a governance framework supporting both systems. As we saw in Part One, a governance framework consists of structures, policies and procedures. The company secretary has an important role to play in ensuring that the board is advised on the appropriate governance framework for the organisation and on also ensuring that it is operating effectively. In addition to a governance framework there are also some compliance requirements relating to reporting on risk and internal controls. The company secretary should have a role in ensuring that the board is aware of them and that they are met.

2. Structures

The board has overall responsibility for the systems of risk management and internal controls within an organisation. To enable the board to carry out this responsibility it needs to ensure that the appropriate structures are put in place at the proper levels within the organisation to manage risk. In deciding what these structures should be, the board needs to consider the following:

◆ Whether risk and internal controls should be considered by the whole board or be delegated to a committee of the board.

◆ If delegating to a committee, whether risk and internal controls should fall under one committee, the audit committee, or into two separate committees, the audit committee for internal controls and the risk committee for risk.

◆ The division of responsibility between itself and management for risk management.

The company secretary would usually play a role in advising the board on the above which will differ from organisation to organisation.

2.1 Board committees

As we saw in Chapter 6, boards set up committees to assist them in coming to informed decisions on specific areas which require monitoring, or detailed discussions of topics within the board's area of responsibility that the board as a whole does not have the capacity within its agendas to fulfil. Board committees do not usually have decision-making powers but recommend courses of action or inform the board about the matters within their remit.

Audit committee
In considering whether to establish an audit committee, a board should consider the following:

◆ Whether there is a requirement for the company to have an audit committee. This is the case for listed companies and financial institutions.

◆ The level of discussion and monitoring required on risk management and internal controls. If this is greater than what the whole board can realistically manage then it makes sense for a committee to be set up to do this on behalf of the board.

Many boards are deciding to delegate risk and internal controls to committees due to the complexity of risks facing the organisation and the level of interest shown by stakeholders in how the organisation is managing threats to its business and taking advantage of the opportunities created by risk.

The 2018 Code (Provision 25) states that the responsibilities of an audit committee, in the area of risk management and internal controls, should include:

◆ reviewing the company's financial controls;

◆ reviewing the internal control system and risk management system, unless this responsibility is given to a separate risk committee of the board or the board itself; and

◆ monitoring and reviewing the effectiveness of the company's internal audit function, or where there is not one, considering annually whether there should be one.

Provision 24 of the 2018 Code states that the audit committee should comprise:

◆ at least three independent directors or in the case of smaller companies, two; and

◆ at least one member who has recent and relevant financial experience.

The committee should have competence relevant to the sector in which the company operates. The chair of the board should not be a member of the audit committee.

Risk committee

In some cases, the audit committee may be overwhelmed by its other duties covering financial reporting and internal controls or may not have the necessary skill set required for the governance of risk. In these cases, the board may decide to establish a separate risk committee.

The size of the organisation and the sector the organisation is operating in may also determine whether responsibility for reviewing internal controls and risk management is dealt with in the same board committee, the audit committee, or whether two separate committees, one for audit and the other for risk, are established.

Banks and other large financial institutions normally have separate risk committees due to the complexity of their risk exposure. A growing number of listed non-financial companies, for example in the oil industry, are also finding it useful to establish a separate risk committee. The benefits of a separate risk committee are:

◆ It can focus solely on reviewing the organisation's risk management and providing assurance to the board that risk management and the processes for the control over risk are effective.

◆ It can give the board advice and make specific recommendations on risk appetite, the organisation's risk tolerance and strategies to manage risk.

◆ It can provide input into strategy formulation by helping the board to understand the key risks facing the organisation and the opportunities available to the organisation by managing those risks.

◆ The composition of the committee is not restricted by the requirements of the corporate governance code. An audit committee is required to be composed of all independent directors. A separate risk committee can have executive directors and non-board members to strengthen the skills and experience of the committee.

ICSA has issued a guidance note, 'Terms of reference for a risk committee', which makes the following suggestions:

◆ The risk committee should consist of a majority of independent directors, one of which should be the chair.

◆ The finance director/CFO should either be a member of the committee or attend committee meetings regularly.

◆ The chief risk officer should also attend committee meetings regularly.

◆ The CEO should attend committee meetings from time to time.

◆ As there may be overlap between the roles of the audit and risk committees it may be appropriate for the chair of the audit committee to be a member of the risk committee.

A risk committee will rely on information provided to it by risk managers and possibly also by internal auditors in the company. The role of a risk committee may include the following responsibilities:

◆ Providing assurance to the board that risk management and processes for control over risk are effective.

◆ Monitoring risk areas faced by the company by receiving period reports on them and their management and, making recommendations to the board where appropriate.

◆ Overseeing the CRO's role and responsibilities, and providing direction on them.

◆ Providing information to the board to help with strategy formulation, for example with regard to risk appetite in the company's strategy. This is achieved by helping the board to understand the key risks facing the company, its risk tolerances and its defences against those risks.

◆ Monitoring the behaviour of management to ensure that there is not excessive risk taking and take appropriate actions if such behaviours are discovered.

◆ Recommending to the board changes in the risk management policies.

The risks of setting up a risk committee are as follows:

◆ Conflict between the audit and risk committees. Where there is more than one committee with responsibilities for overseeing risk, it might create conflicts if the roles and responsibilities of each committee are not clearly defined and agreed upon at the outset. It is therefore important to have board-approved terms of reference for each of the committees and regular reports from the committees at board meetings.

◆ Danger of overlooking some risks. Each committee may think the other is considering a particular risk when in fact neither are. To promote cooperation between the two committees, it may be appropriate for the chair of each committee to also be a member of the other committee. The audit committee has responsibilities for audit and financial reporting, and even when a separate risk committee is established, the audit committee should therefore retain responsibility for monitoring financial risks and the effectiveness of internal controls relating to financial reporting.

◆ Message sent to senior management that risk is no longer their responsibility. To ensure this does not happen the organisation should have a risk manual which sets out clearly the roles and responsibilities of the board, committees and management. The contents of the manual should be communicated through training and through the implementation of the risk management framework by the CEO and CRO.

◆ Having sufficient directors with the required skills to constitute a separate risk committee. This may not be an issue for larger companies but small- and medium-sized companies with smaller boards do find it a challenge to source directors with the relevant experience to serve on these committees. To overcome this companies could source non-board members to sit on the committee. This may be the CFO or an advisor.

2.2 Risk management committee

Many organisations have a risk management committee consisting of senior executives, usually chaired by the CEO. This committee would be responsible for risk management at an operational level. It would normally report to the board committee responsible for risk. Reporting could be through the CEO, CFO or CRO. The Risk management committee is not a board committee.

2.3 Internal audit

According to the Institute of Internal Auditors, internal audit is 'an independent objective assurance and consulting activity designed to add value and improve an organisation's operations. It helps organisations accomplish their objectives by bringing a systematic, disciplined approach to evaluate and improve the effectiveness of risk management, control and governance processes'.

The FRC's Guidance on Audit Committees suggests that the need for an internal audit function depends on factors such as company size, diversity and complexity of activities and number of employees, as well as cost–benefit considerations. Based on the above an organisation's board, or audit committee, will have to decide whether they need to establish:

◆ An in-house internal audit function where the company maintains full responsibility for recruiting, developing, deploying and managing an internal audit team.

◆ A co-sourced internal audit function where the company hires a small core team of internal auditors and uses an outside professional firm to supplement the team or to provide strategic direction to them.

◆ Outsource the internal audit function where the company uses an external professional firm to provide all internal audit activities.

The benefits of an in-house internal audit function are that the team:

◆ understands the organisation, its culture, operations and risk profile and so should be able to add value to the organisation's internal control, risk management and governance processes;

◆ can build networks throughout the organisation, become integrated into the company's business and as such become the 'eyes and ears' of the board regarding those activities;

◆ provide assurance to stakeholders on the integrity of the organisation's systems of internal control and risk management;

◆ become an essential part of the checks and balances within the organisation's internal control system;

◆ could be a lower-cost option, depending on the make-up of the team.

The main benefits of co-sourcing or out-sourcing the internal audit function are that the organisation can leverage external resources, technology, skills and experience which may not be available to it with an in-house team.

Where an internal audit function exists, the 2018 Code (Provision 25) requires the audit committee to monitor and review the effectiveness of the internal audit function. Where there is no internal audit function, the audit committee should consider annually whether there is a need for one and make a recommendation to the board. The reasons why there is no internal audit function should be explained in the relevant section of the annual report.

The FRC's Guidance on Audit Committees comments:

'In the absence of an internal audit function, other processes may need to be applied to provide assurance to management, the audit committee and the board that the system of internal control is functioning as intended. In these circumstances, the audit committee will need to assess whether such processes provide sufficient and objective assurance.'

The objectivity and independence of internal auditors
Internal auditors ought to be objective, because they investigate the control systems of other departments and operations. However, they are also employees within the organisation and often report to someone in the organisational structure. If the internal auditors report to the finance director, they will find it difficult to be critical of the finance director. Similarly, if the internal auditors report to the CEO, they will be reluctant to criticise the CEO. In this respect, their independence could be compromised.

To protect the independence of the internal audit function, the FRC's Guidance on Audit Committees states that the audit committee should approve the appointment or termination of appointment of the head of internal audit. Internal audit should have access to the audit committee and board chair where necessary and the audit committee should ensure internal audit has a reporting line which enables it to be independent of the executive and so able to exercise independent judgement.

Review of the effectiveness of the internal audit function
The board or audit committee should review the effectiveness of the internal audit function each year. In its annual assessment of the effectiveness of the internal audit function the audit committee should:

◆ meet with the head of internal audit without the presence of management to discuss the effectiveness of the function;

◆ review and assess the annual internal audit work plan;

◆ receive a report on the results of the internal auditors' work; and

◆ monitor and assess the role and effectiveness of the internal audit function in the overall context of the company's risk management system.

The Institute of Internal Auditors also recommends that internal audit functions carry out an independent review of their performance every three years.

Stop and think 13.1

Every organisation is different and therefore needs different structures in place to manage risk. Are the structures that are in place within your organisation appropriate to manage the risks to its strategic objectives?

Test yourself 13.1

1. **What does the board need to consider when deciding what structures to put in place to fulfil its responsibilities for risk and internal control?**

2. **Why might an organisation decide to have a risk committee?**

3. Governance players

3.1 Company secretary/governance professional role

The company secretary is often in the best position to advise the board on the governance risks of the organisation. This can include risks to the reputation of the organisation caused by decisions and actions taken by the board or the board's inaction. All of these risks should be assessed, mitigated wherever possible, and the effectiveness of the mitigation evaluated by the board from time to time. The company secretary can carry out this role and present the risks to the board or they can ensure that these risks form part of the risks being managed and reported on by management.

The company secretary is usually the person who prepares the first draft of the agenda for a board meeting, discussing it with senior management and then with the chair, who would normally approve it. The company secretary should then ensure that the following items are on the agenda of either the main board or of the relevant board committee:

1. The approval of the organisation's internal control policies and framework. This would include:
   - risk management;
   - key financial, operational and compliance controls;
   - procurement and recruitment.
   - The approval of the organisation's risk appetite.
2. Reports from management on the implementation and effectiveness of the policies and framework.

3. Reports providing assurance from internal and external auditors and compliance officers on the effectiveness of management's implementation.
4. Reports from internal audit on suspected non-compliance or ineffectiveness of policies and frameworks.
5. Information on the key risks facing the organisation and how they have been managed effectively.
6. Evaluation of the risk management system which should occur at least annually.

The company secretary as part of the preparation for a board meeting receives all of the papers for that meeting. A template for board papers should have been created which includes a section on risk. Management should be requested to describe within this section the risks associated with doing (or not doing) the proposed item.

In addition, if the company secretary is secretary to the board committee responsible for risk, the company secretary would also ensure that:

◆ The committee has terms of reference.
◆ The committee follows the terms of reference by developing, along with the chair of the committee, an annual plan setting out the work of the committee at each of their meetings.
◆ The committee(s) follows its procedures and governance best practice. Advice should be provided to the chair of the committee(s) where this is not happening.
◆ A report is written for the chair of the committee(s) of the recommendations to the board for approval. This is usually written by the company secretary, especially where the time difference between the committee(s) meeting and the board meeting is very short.
◆ Minutes of the meeting are drafted and that a list of actions from the meeting is developed and monitored. Feedback should be given at the next meeting, usually by the company secretary on actions from the previous meetings.
◆ A regular evaluation of the effectiveness of the committee should be carried out.
◆ Agendas are drafted for each meeting reflecting the annual plan. Where there is a combined committee, the company secretary should ensure that the agenda alternates from meeting to meeting between risk and audit items being first on the agenda, so that the committee gives equal priority to both aspects of its role. The items should also be split on the agenda between those relating to audit and those relating to risk.

Example agenda items include:

Audit
◆ Review of performance against internal audit annual plan for the year.
◆ Review of internal audit reports on areas within annual plan and also

requested investigations to ensure effective internal control system.

◆ Reviewing the annual audit of risk management process. An organisation should ensure that internal audit do not become part of the risk process. If they do they will not be able to audit it. Their responsibility is to provide assurance to the board that the process is effective by auditing it.

◆ Recommending for approval accounting policies and finance manuals, and any subsequent changes to them.

◆ Annual financial statements and interim financial statements.

◆ Evaluation of performance of external auditors.

◆ Assessment of external auditor independence including the amount and type of non-audit work.

Risk

◆ Recommending for approval the risk policy and manual, and any subsequent changes to them.

◆ Recommendations on the risk appetite and risk tolerance of the organisation.

◆ Key risk dashboard and annual deep dive evaluation of risk within the organisation.

◆ Review of statements by the organisation on their risk appetite and risk management.

◆ The company secretary may be asked to write papers for committee review on areas such as:

    – the independence of the external auditor and the amount of non-audit work to be carried out by the external auditor; and

    – areas of risk and how they should be managed.

The company secretary may also be called upon to assist the board with its assessment of the effectiveness of the risk management system and internal controls. As part of preparing for board meetings the company secretary may be required to collect information and reports from management and internal audit on compliance with operational policies approved by the board, as well as on the effectiveness of the risk management process and the internal control system. In some organisations the company secretary may be requested by the board to:

◆ Draft or review statements in company reports such as the annual report and accounts which set out the organisation's attitude towards risk and the management of risks.

◆ Collate information from management and other staff within the organisation supporting the board's assessment that the system of internal control is effective. This can include individual certifications by staff and management that they have complied with all of the policies within the organisation that apply to them.

The company secretary, due to their knowledge of governance and board activities, would usually work closely with the internal and external auditors and the compliance officer.

The company secretary could also be asked to manage on behalf of the board the process for the production of the annual report and accounts. This would include collation, and in some cases drafting sections of the annual report and accounts. The company secretary would also oversee the verification of the information within the annual report and accounts and also other documents communicating information to the outside world to ensure that the information within them is correct.

Finally, the company secretary may be required to advise the board on business continuity (the long-term sustainability of the organisation). They may be called upon to draft the business continuity plan which will incorporate several disaster recovery plans, for instance concerning information technology and/or to communicate parts of the plan to the organisation's stakeholders both internally and externally. The company secretary is usually best placed to carry out this role due to the interaction and relationships they have with those contributing to the plan or needing to know about it.

In conclusion, the company secretary, being the person ensuring good governance within an organisation, has an important role to play in strengthening the control environment by:

◆ linking the various people, structures and processes within the control environment into a strong culture of control and risk management; and

◆ ensuring that the various structures and processes within the control environment are integrated effectively in the overall workflow and decision-making processes of the board.

3.2 CEO role

The CEO, who is accountable to the board, has the responsibility to ensure proper execution of the risk management strategies and policies laid down by the board. The CEO should ensure that the risk and internal control frameworks extend into the organisations and resources, both financial and human, are made available to ensure they work efficiently. The CEO should also ensure that a culture reflecting the risk appetite of the organisation is developed. This can be achieved through awareness sessions and through highlighting as an area to be assessed for reward performance in risk management.

3.3 CRO role

Some large companies, such as banks, other financial institutions and oil companies, have appointed specialist executive managers responsible for risk, usually known as the CRO.

The principal responsibilities of a CRO would usually include:

◆ creating an integrated risk framework for the entire organisation;

◆ appointing risk champions throughout the organisations;

◆ working with the risk champions to ensure that risks were identified, assessed, quantified and plans developed to mitigate risks wherever possible;

◆ ensuring that sufficient resources are made available for risk management;

◆ monitoring the progress of risk mitigation activities;

◆ developing and disseminating risk measurements, dashboards and reports;

◆ communicating to key stakeholders the risk profile of the organisation; and

◆ organising training in risk management for the organisation.

In carrying out their duties, CROs should normally work very closely with the company secretary and internal auditor.

The Walker Report recommended that (like the company secretary) the appointment and dismissal of the CRO should be a matter for the board. The remuneration of the CRO should be determined by the remuneration committee.

3.4 Internal auditors' role

The work done by any internal audit unit is not prescribed by regulation. It is decided by management or by the board (or audit committee). The possible tasks of internal audit include the following:

◆ Reviewing the internal control system. Traditionally, an internal audit department has carried out independent checks on the financial controls in an organisation, or in a particular process or system. The checks would be to establish whether suitable financial controls exist, and if so, whether they are applied properly and are effective. It is not the function of internal auditors to manage risks, only to monitor and report them, and to check that risk controls are efficient and cost-effective.

◆ Special investigations. Internal auditors might conduct special investigations into particular aspects of the organisation's operations (systems and procedures), to check the effectiveness of operational controls.

◆ Examination of financial and operating information. Internal auditors might be asked to investigate the timeliness of reporting and the accuracy of the information in reports.

◆ Value for Money (VFM) audits. This is an investigation into an operation or activity to establish whether it is economical, efficient and effective.

◆ Reviewing compliance by the organisation with particular laws or regulations. This is an investigation into the effectiveness of compliance controls.

◆ Risk assessment. Internal auditors might be asked to investigate aspects of risk management, and in particular the adequacy of the mechanisms for identifying, assessing and controlling significant risks to the organisation, from both internal and external sources.

Internal auditors are commonly required to check the soundness of internal financial controls. In assessing the effectiveness of individual controls, and of an internal control system generally, the following factors should be considered.

◆ Whether the controls are manual or automated. Automated controls are by no means error-proof or fraud-proof but may be more reliable than similar manual controls.

◆ Whether controls are discretionary or non-discretionary. Non-discretionary controls are checks and procedures that must be carried out. Discretionary controls are those that do not have to be applied, either because they are voluntary or because an individual can choose to disapply them. Risks can infiltrate a system, for example when senior management chooses to disapply controls and allow unauthorised or unchecked procedures to occur.

◆ Whether the control can be circumvented easily, because an activity can be carried out in a different way where similar controls do not apply.

◆ Whether the controls are effective in achieving their purpose. Are they extensive enough or carried out frequently enough? Are the controls applied rigorously? For example, is a supervisor doing their job properly?

Reports by internal auditors can provide reassurance that internal controls are sound and effective or might recommend changes and improvements where weaknesses are uncovered.

Stop and think 13.2

The company secretary has an important role to play in supporting the board with its risk management responsibilities. Is the role of the company secretary in your organisation appropriate in this regard or are there more areas in which they need to be involved to ensure that the systems of risk management and internal control are effective?

4. Policies and procedures

Policies set out what is required to be done by management and staff within an organisation. Procedures address how it should be done. Often the board is involved in approving the first (policies) and leaves it to management to design, implement and maintain the second (procedures). The board maintains an oversight role in regard to the procedures: this role is met through regular reporting and an annual evaluation of the procedures that have been put in place.

One could argue that all the policies and procedures in an organisation are aimed at managing risk. Set out here are the main policies and procedures that the board should ensure are in place with regard to risk and internal controls.

4.1 Risk policy and manual

A risk policy is a statement, approved by the board, of the extent and kind of risks an organisation is willing to take in pursuit of its objectives. This will vary from organisation to organisation.

A risk management manual sets out how risk will be managed within the organisation. In some organisations this manual is also approved by the board.

4.2 Procedure for monitoring and reviewing risk management and internal control systems

The existence of risk management and internal control systems does not, on its own, indicate that risk and internal controls are being managed effectively within an organisation. The board (or audit committee) should on an ongoing basis monitor and review the systems to ensure that they:

◆ remain aligned with the organisation's strategic objectives;
◆ address the risks facing the organisation; and
◆ are being developed, applied and maintained appropriately for the organisation.

The board is responsible for ensuring that the appropriate processes are put in place to allow them to carry out this review which will include reports from management and assurances from internal audit.

Code Provision 29 states that on an annual basis the board should undertake an annual review of the effectiveness of the systems of risk management and internal control. The company secretary and internal audit function should be able to assist in this process.

The FRC Guidance on Risk Management, Internal Control and Related Financial and Business Reporting, states that the annual review of effectiveness should consider:

◆ the company's risk appetite;
◆ the desired culture within the company and whether this culture has been embedded within the organisation;
◆ the operation of the risk management and internal control systems, covering design, implementation, monitoring and review and the identification of principal risks;
◆ the integration of risk management and internal controls with the company's business model, strategy and business planning processes;
◆ the changes in the nature, likelihood and impact of principal risks;
◆ the company's ability to respond to changes in its business and the external environment;
◆ the extent, frequency and quality of management's reporting on the organisation's risk management;
◆ the issues dealt with by the board throughout the year under review; and

◆   the effectiveness of the company's public reporting processes.

The Guidance also includes in an appendix a list of questions that the board should consider when conducting its annual review of the effectiveness of the organisation's risk management and internal control systems. Listed below are some of the questions:

Risk management and internal control systems

◆   To what extent do the risk management and internal control systems underpin and relate to the company's business model?

◆   How are authority, responsibility and accountability for risk management and internal control defined, co-ordinated and documented throughout the organisation? How does the board determine whether this is clear, appropriate and effective?

◆   How effectively is the organisation able to withstand risks, and risk combinations, which do materialise? How effective is the board's approach to risks with 'low probability' but a very severe impact if they materialise?

◆   What are the channels of communication that enable individuals, including third parties, to report concerns, suspected breaches of law and regulations, other improprieties or challenging perspectives?

◆   How does the board satisfy itself that the information it receives is timely, of good quality, reflects numerous information sources and is fit for purpose?

◆   How does the board ensure it understands the organisation's exposure to each principal risk before and after the application of mitigations and controls, what those mitigations and controls are, whether they are operating as expected?

Monitoring and review

◆   What are the processes by which senior management monitor the effective application of the systems of risk management and internal control?

◆   In what way do monitoring and review processes take into an account an organisation's ability to re-evaluate the risks and adjust the controls effectively in response to changes in its objectives, its business and its external environment?

◆   How are processes or controls adjusted to reflect new or changing risks, or operational deficiencies? To what extent does the board engage in horizon scanning for emerging risks accord with the FRC guidance?

The company secretary, in particular at the board meeting considering the annual report and accounts under International Financial Reporting Standards, would typically remind board members of the statements within the report and accounts which they were confirming, and any potential duties or liabilities they may have with regard to them. For example, board members are required to confirm in the 'statement of directors' responsibilities' that there is an effective system of internal control and that their organisation is a going concern for at least a year from the date of the document.

Test yourself 13.2

1. **Who are the main governance players that support the board with their risk management responsibilities?**

2. **Why should boards routinely monitor and review the organisation's systems of risk management and internal controls?**

3. **What matters should the annual review of the effectiveness of the systems of risk management and internal controls cover?**

5. Whistleblowing

Principle E of the 2018 Code states that 'the workforce should be able to raise any matters of concern'. Provision 6 expands on this, stating: 'There should be a means for the workforce to raise concerns in confidence and – if they wish – anonymously. The board should routinely review this and the reports arising from its operation. It should ensure that arrangements are in place for the proportionate and independent investigation of such matters and for follow-up action.' This is a whistleblowing procedure.

An effective whistleblowing procedure should allow for an employee to raise concerns about illicit behaviour usually in one of the following areas:

◆ fraud;
◆ a serious violation of a law or regulation by the company or by directors, managers or employees within the company;
◆ a miscarriage of justice;
◆ offering or taking bribes;
◆ price-fixing;
◆ a danger to public health or safety, such as dumping toxic waste in the environment or supplying food that is unfit for consumption;
◆ neglect of people in care; or
◆ in the public sector, gross waste or misuse of public funds.

The need for whistleblowing arises when normal procedures and internal controls will not reveal the illicit activity, because the individuals responsible for the activity are somehow able to ignore or get around the normal controls. This may be because the person to whom the individual reports may be involved in the suspected malpractice.

Although whistleblowing procedures are an internal control, they are not an embedded control within the company's regular procedures, and their effectiveness relies on the willingness of genuine whistleblowers to come forward with their allegations.

5.1   Introducing a whistleblowing procedure

The company secretary should ensure that the board approves and monitors implementation of a whistleblowing policy and procedures. Typically, a whistleblowing policy and procedures would cover the following:

◆   purpose, scope and coverage;

◆   procedures for reporting a matter;

◆   what happens when communication is received from a whistleblower;

◆   anonymity of the whistleblower;

◆   communication with the whistleblower; and

◆   protection of the whistleblower.

Issues the board should consider when introducing a whistleblowing procedure are as follows:

◆   Building a culture of trust and openness. This is essential for a whistleblowing policy and procedure to work. Evidence shows that the culture needs to start at the top of the organisation for it to be effective. The board should ensure that it is seen to be honouring the principle of whistleblowing.

◆   A statement that the organisation takes malpractice or misconduct seriously and is committed to a culture of openness in which employees can report legitimate concerns without fear of penalty or punishment. This is usually the opening paragraph of any whistleblowing policy and procedures.

◆   How are matters to be reported? There are many different methods of communicating matters ranging from a suggestion box to a hotline specifically for raising issues. The board will need to decide, with the advice of the company secretary, which is the most appropriate for the size and type of organisation. It is important that the employees have trust in the integrity of these methods. For example, putting a suggestion box in a reception area that is monitored by CCTV 24 hours a day may not be conducive for employees disclosing information.

◆   Who is going to be responsible for receiving issues? Again, there are many different models as to who is made responsible for receiving the information. Companies often stipulate in their whistleblowing policy who is the designated person; this could be the company secretary, the internal auditor, the chair of the audit committee or the legal/compliance manager. Some larger companies outsource this function to one of the firms offering such services. Employees need to have trust in the person receiving the reports.

◆   Anonymity versus non-anonymity. The board should decide whether it is prepared to accept anonymous reports of wrong-doing or whether for all reports the person submitting them must be named. It is argued that anonymous reporting causes more frivolous reports. Organisations, however, need to consider the real concerns of the whistleblower to their livelihoods if they are identified as the source of the report. Knowing the identity of the person submitting the report is often useful when it comes to investigating the report. The culture of the organisation is important in this aspect. Employees need to feel that there will be no downside to them being open and honest about a wrongdoing they have uncovered. Setting out in the policy that reprisals against whistleblowers will not be tolerated and the punishments for such reprisals can help in this regard. A whistleblower should be notified before their name is disclosed.

◆ Improprieties covered by the whistleblowing policy. The policy should be clear on what improprieties the organisation feels to be of sufficient seriousness that they should be reported. This will help pre-empt frivolous claims. The improprieties could be set out within the whistleblowing policy or within the company's code of ethics.

◆ Investigation, follow-up and reporting procedures. Organisations should ensure, when launching a whistleblowing policy, that the procedures for investigating follow-up and reporting for any complaints is in place. Boards (or audit committees) should receive reports on matters under investigation. Recommendations on changes to policies and procedures within the organisation based on lessons learnt from the matter reported should also be acted upon and linked to the matter so that employees see that any reports they make will be taken seriously. There should also be individual feedback to the whistleblower as to the action taken.

◆ Protection for genuine whistleblowers. The procedure should set out the protection for the genuine whistleblower but should make it clear that false or malicious allegations will result in disciplinary action against the individual making them. Procedures should state that victimisation for raising a concern will be a disciplinary offence.

Each employee should be given access to the whistleblowing policy, whether this is in hard copy or through the company's intranet site.

Some larger companies offer an external whistleblowing route in addition to the internal reporting procedure.

The board may request the company secretary to play a role in establishing an internal whistleblowing policy and procedures. If this is the case, the company secretary will need to ensure that there are trained people in the organisation to operate the procedure so that any matters raised under the procedure are dealt with effectively. If an employee does report a genuine concern in good faith, they must be supported and providing this support might be a role for the company secretary.

Case study 13.1

In May 2018, the CEO of Barclays, Mr Jes Staley, was fined £642,000 for attempting to unmask a whistleblower. This followed an investigation by the Financial Conduct Authority (FCA) and the Bank of England's Prudential Regulation Authority (PRA).

The case centred on a letter, signed 'John Q Public', allegedly sent by a Barclays' shareholder to the board making allegations of a personal nature against an employee who had been hired at Mr Staley's request. Mr Staley, after being questioned by the board, instigated an attempt through the firm's security department to track down the letter's author, discovering the date, time and location and cost of postage of the letter sent in the US.

The regulators felt that Mr Staley's behaviour had risked undermining confidence in Barclays' whistleblowing procedures. The Bank of England's Deputy Governor, Mr Sam Woods stated: 'protection for whistleblowers is an essential part of keeping the financial system safe and sound'.

The Barclays board, in response to the fine, docked part of Mr Staley's 2016 bonus.

5.2   Questions for boards

Questions boards should be asking themselves and checking to ensure that they have an effective whistleblowing procedure are as follows:

◆   Are employees aware of the whistleblowing procedures?

◆   Can employees raise concerns without risk of censure?

◆   Does the company act promptly on concerns?

◆   Are genuine whistleblowers protected?

◆   Do all managers understand the whistleblowing procedures and accept the principle of whistleblowing?

◆   Are all reports generated by the whistleblowing procedure submitted to the board (or audit committee)?

◆   Are all whistleblowing procedures known and available to all stakeholders, including the public?

6. Cybersecurity

Globally, there is an ever-greater reliance on technology. Organisations are required to manage the risks associated with technological disruptions within their organisations as well as an often 'insatiable' desire by management in many organisations to keep up with the latest technological developments. This requires governance. The King III Corporate Governance Code, in South Africa, was one of the first to recognise the importance of 'technology governance' in 2009. King IV has developed this further.

There is a growing recognition that cybersecurity should be high on the board's agenda. Recent global cyberattacks have highlighted the importance of cybersecurity risk management for board directors. Companies no longer have a choice as to whether they mitigate against cyberattacks. It should be an important part of their risk management process.

Countries are starting to look at whether they need to regulate with respect to cybersecurity. For example, the US Securities and Exchange Commission has expanded its focus on cybersecurity already, taking action against corporations for not protecting customer data against cyberattacks.

The consequences of a cybersecurity incident can be severe. The economic loss from an incident can be compounded by reputational damage, loss of trade secrets and the costs associated with implementing disaster recovery plans. Boards should ensure that the organisation's information and technology are protected. They do this through developing a cybersecurity policy and procedures.

The cybersecurity policy should inform employees and other authorised users of the company's technology, the requirements for protecting that technology and the information it contains from a cyberattack. The policy is usually made up of three parts:

1. Physical security of the technology. This section explains the importance of keeping the physical asset secure – locking doors, surveillance, alarms etc.

2. Personnel management. This section explains to employees how to conduct their day-to-day activities – password management, keeping confidential certain information, the use of the internet, the use of memory sticks etc. Some organisations go as far as restricting access to the internet and sealing the ports of computers for USB devices in an attempt to stop viruses and malware from being introduced into their systems.

3. Hardware and software. This section explains to the technology administrators what type of technology and software to use and how networks should be configured to ensure they are secure. Due to the technical nature of part of the policy, boards may wish to get independent advice on the recommendations of management in this area.

Boards should ensure that management is implementing the above policy. Internal audit can assist them in this role by auditing the compliance with the policy at least annually. Management can also be required to report to the board systems breaches.

In addition to the cybersecurity policy and procedures, boards should also consider the requirements for disclosure if a breach occurs. These fall under two sets of regulations – market abuse and general data protection.

6.1   Market abuse regulation

Listed companies are required to disclose any incident which was significant enough to be considered price sensitive, i.e. have a significant effect on the company's share price. The board, with the assistance of management, will need to ensure that there is a process in place to identify significant breaches and raise them to board level so that this reporting requirement is met. The company secretary should play a role in this process.

6.2 General Data Protection Regulation (GDPR)

These regulations came into effect in 2018 and apply to the processing of personal data for European citizens. If a cybersecurity incident occurs which leads to 'the accidental or unlawful destruction, loss, alteration, unauthorised disclosure of, or access to, personal data transmitted, stored or otherwise processed' a disclosure is required to the Information Commissioner's Office (ICO) without delay. If the cybersecurity incident is likely to result in a high risk to the rights and freedoms of natural persons, the GDPR requires the person to notify the affected individuals without delay. The threshold for notification to individuals is therefore higher than that for a notification to the ICO.

If the cybersecurity incident triggers both disclosures the company will have to ensure that the notifications required by both sets of regulations are released simultaneously. Again, the company secretary should play a role in this process.

6.3 Network and Information System (NIS) Regulations 2018

In May 2018, the Network and Information System Regulations 2018 came into force. These regulations are aimed at improving the security of network and information security systems of operators of essential services (OES) and relevant digital service providers (RDSP).

Operators of essential services are entities in the energy, transport, health, drinking water and digital infrastructure sectors. Relevant digital service providers are entities who provide their services to entities within the essential services sectors. Organisations, if they fall within the threshold criteria set out in the regulations, are covered by these regulations. Some organisations who do not meet the criteria can be required by the authorities to comply with the regulations.

The NIS regulations require the organisations which are subject to them to take appropriate and proportionate technical and organisational measures to manage the risks posed to their network and information systems and to minimise the impact of any incidents that occur. Where incidents do occur, which have had a significant impact on the essential service, the entity must notify their competent authority within the timescales provided.

Test yourself 13.3

1. What concerns should an employee raise though a whistleblowing procedure?
2. What areas should a whistleblowing policy and procedure cover?
3. What areas should be covered in a cybersecurity policy?

7. Governance of information

The governance of information is also becoming critical for organisations. The management of both information and knowledge can give competitive advantage and many organisations are increasing their focus on both areas. Boards are increasingly being expected to ensure that information and knowledge are managed effectively within their organisations and that they are protected. The King III Corporate Governance Code in South Africa, was one of the first to recognise the importance of 'information governance' in 2009. King IV has developed this further.

Boards should ensure that policies on information disclosure are developed and enforced by the management within the organisation. The CEO is usually the person within management responsible for ensuring the adherence and compliance with this policy.

An information disclosure policy should include the following:

◆ Objectives and principles of the disclosure. The main objective of disclosure is to keep stakeholders informed about the company to enable them to make informed decisions when dealing with the company. Information should therefore be accurate, accessible, timely, complete, balanced between the positive and the negative. Selective disclosure of information should be prohibited unless required by law.

◆ Authorised persons. The policy should set out who is authorised to disclose what information to which stakeholder group. Usually the CEO, CFO, investor relations officer and company secretary will be authorised to make disclosures. To ensure uniform and consistent disclosures it is important that these individuals co-ordinate the statements that they will be making to their audiences and this is often done either through a disclosure committee or the board.

◆ Public information. The policy will usually set out what information about the company is in the public domain. This will include company documents such as the articles of association, annual reports and accounts, press releases, information on the company's website, regulatory disclosures, etc.

◆ Confidential information. The policy should also set out what information should be kept confidential, for example trade secrets, who would normally be able to have access to that information and the steps to be taken to protect that information.

◆ Insider information. This is information that would, if disclosed, move the company's share price. The handling of this type of information would normally be set out in the policy.

Managing insider information is a major part of a company secretary role. The following are some of the matters that the company secretary may consider when handling insider information:

◆ Confidentiality of board papers. Extra care should be taken when distributing paper board packages. This might mean using double envelopes, anti-tear envelopes, and even hand delivery rather than email or courier. If documents are made available electronically though a board portal, the company secretary should make sure the system is as secure as possible, for example by encrypting documents.

◆ Careful consideration may have to be given to securing the computers used to prepare the papers to be included in the package. If shared drives are used or computers are networked, the company secretary should know who has access to these drives and networks. If a password is needed to access certain drives, the company secretary should know that usually the administrator of the system (often an IT person or sometimes an outsourced person) can access the drive/folder. It has been known in highly sensitive transactions for the papers to be prepared and kept on an offsite server usually maintained by the company's law firm.

◆ Confidentiality of board discussions. The company secretary should consider the following:

– Is the room in which the board is meeting soundproof?

– Can anyone see into the room from outside? Especially, if a PowerPoint presentation is made, will it be visible?

– Some listed companies even check for listening devices and coat windows so that no one can see in to ensure confidentiality.

◆ Insider lists. These lists are often required by regulators for listed companies, although they can be used by any company involved in a commercially sensitive project. To control the spread of confidential information, insider lists contain the names of people, internally and externally, who are aware of the project. Only those on the list can discuss the project. If someone else needs to be consulted, they have to be added to the list. The company secretary is often the holder of the insider lists. Insider lists are discussed in more detail in Chapter 14.

◆ The communication plan for the project. The company secretary may be asked on behalf of the board to work with management to produce a communication plan for the project. This will indicate who should be communicated to, how, and when. If the company is listed or is a regulated business, then any regulations for communications should be reflected in the plan. For example, a listed company may have to make a regulatory announcement before it can release information to others.

8. Disaster recovery plans

A disaster recovery plan is a plan of what needs to be done immediately after a disaster to recover from the event. The disaster is of a nature unconnected with the company's business and outside the control of management. Examples of disasters are:

◆ natural disasters, such as major fires or flooding or storm damage to key installations or offices;

◆ IT disruptions; and

◆ major terrorist attacks.

Disaster recovery plans are most needed in industries where a lengthy or widespread shutdown of operations could be catastrophic, such as in the banking industry, energy supply industry and airline industry. However, all companies should have such plans, which need to be kept under continual review and about which employees need to be kept fully aware and, where appropriate, trained.

Typically, a disaster recovery plan should do these things:

◆ Specify which operations are essential and must be kept going.

◆ Identify and analyse all potential threats to essential operations.

◆ Identify possible reactions to the threats to essential operations, for example:

– Where operations rely on IT systems, identify the computers or networks to which the system can be transferred in the event of damage to the main system.

– Specify where operations should be transferred to, if they cannot continue in their normal location. Make sure to check that the location will be available to you when you need it. On the day of the terrorist attack on the US World Trade Centre on 9 September 2011 (9/11) many companies arrived at their disaster recovery locations to find someone already sitting at their designated desk from another company. The owner of the building had rented out the building to several companies as their disaster recovery site, neither the company nor the building owner expecting a disaster that would require everyone to use the site at the same time.

– Identify key personnel who are needed to maintain the systems required to keep essential operations running.

◆ Identify who should be responsible for keeping the public informed about the impact of the disaster and the recovery measures that are being taken.

Wherever possible, disaster recovery plans should be tested periodically to ensure that they work effectively. Consideration should also be given to the realistic length of time the disaster recovery plan will need to be in operation. A company suffered flooding and had to move staff to a disaster recovery site. The site was fit for purpose for several days but did not have the facilities to be a longer-term solution. Repairs from the flooding took several months and an alternative site had to be found.

Disaster recovery planning and business continuity planning are terms which are often used interchangeably. They are, however, different. Business continuity planning goes beyond procedures that should be taken in an emergency, such as a fire or explosion in a building. It is intended to establish, in advance, a plan of what a company needs to do to ensure that its key products and/or services continue to be delivered in the longer-term, i.e. a plan for the sustainability of the business. A business continuity plan should be developed from the disaster recovery planning and the risk management process. It should seek to make the company ready to take advantage of the longer-term threats to the business thus giving the company competitive advantage over competitors who are not planning for the future sustainability of their business.

It is important for the board to be involved in both disaster recovery and business continuity planning as both are critical to the ongoing activity of the business.

The company secretary should ensure that there are opportunities during the board meetings and other events for the board to discuss with management arrangements that are being made for both.

A review of the disaster recovery plans and business continuity planning may also be a part of the annual review of the effectiveness of internal controls by the board or audit committee.

9. The UK Bribery Act 2010

The UK Bribery Act 2010 has made bribery a criminal offence. It has created three offences:

- Offering bribes (active bribery) and receiving bribes (passive bribery).
- Bribery of foreign public officials for business benefit.
- Failure to prevent a bribe being paid on the organisation's behalf.

The Bribery Act therefore makes bribery by businesses for commercial benefit (commercial bribery) a criminal offence, and it applies to UK businesses regardless of whether the act of bribery occurs inside or outside the UK.

A consequence of the Bribery Act is that UK companies must ensure that they have internal controls sufficient to prevent bribery by any of its employees or agents or detecting bribery when it occurs. However, the Act recognises that it is impossible to prevent bribery at all times, and a valid defence against a charge of failing to prevent a bribe being paid on its behalf will be evidence that procedures were in place to prevent bribery.

The Ministry of Justice has issued guidance on the Bribery Act, which in its introduction states: 'At stake is the principle of free and fair competition, which stands diminished by each bribe offered and accepted.'

This guidance promotes six principles:

1. Proportionate procedures. The procedures of a commercial organisation to prevent bribery by people associated with it should be proportionate to the risk of bribery that it faces and the nature and scale of its commercial activities.

2. Top-level commitment. Top-level management should be committed to preventing bribery and should foster a culture in their organisation in which bribery is considered unacceptable.

3. Risk assessment. There should be periodic, informed and regular assessment by organisations of the nature and extent of potential bribery by people associated with it.

4. Due diligence. There should be due diligence of third party intermediaries and local agents who will act on behalf of the organisation, with a view to identifying and mitigating bribery risk.

5. Communication (including training). Commercial organisations should seek to ensure that policies against bribery are embedded and understood, by means of communication and training that is proportionate to the bribery risk that the organisation faces.

6. Monitoring and review. There should be monitoring and review of the procedures designed to prevent bribery, and improvements should be made when weaknesses are detected.

A company could avoid conviction of failing to prevent bribery if it can show that, although bribery may have occurred, it has in place 'adequate processes' to prevent bribery. Having suitable whistleblowing procedures could be a sufficient defence against a criminal charge, provided that the company can demonstrate that the procedures work well in practice. It should not be sufficient simply to have a whistleblowing policy in existence, but which no one uses.

The adequate procedures defence was used for the first time in a recent case, R v Skansen Interiors Ltd, concluded in 2018. The former Managing Director of Skansen was found to have paid bribes to secure contracts. The company self-reported to the National Crime Agency (NCA), who is responsible for cases under the Bribery Act 2010, and the police. The company was prosecuted. It pleaded not guilty, relying on the adequate procedures defence. The jury convicted.

It appears from the case that size does not matter as Skansen was a small company which had become dormant. To win with the adequate procedures defence it would appear that a company needs to:

◆ demonstrate the steps taken since the introduction of the Bribery Act 2010;

◆ have a specific bribery policy and procedures in place;

◆ have evidence of communication and implementation of the policy and procedures to all staff, including any training that has been carried out. This should include evidence that the staff have read and understood the policy and procedures;

◆ conduct risk assessments both generally and on a transaction basis by country, if the company trades internationally, or by business partner;

◆ have a mechanism for staff and stakeholders to report breaches of the bribery policy and procedures;

◆ show evidence of changes introduced as a result of any breaches to strengthen either the policy and/or the procedures relating to bribery;

◆ show evidence of discussions on high-risk activities and relationships and the reasons for continuing, limiting or terminating such activities and relationships; and

◆ show evidence of how, when business is conducted outside of the UK, the risks of corruption have been addressed.

As of August 2018, the Serious Fraud Squad were investigating around 40 companies.

Case study 13.2

In 2013, Tullow Oil, Africa's largest independent exploration and production company, was forced to apologise to the President of Uganda, HE Yoweri Museveni, following allegations that he had received bribes from Tullow for the granting of oil exploration rights in Uganda. These allegations were made during a tax litigation case with Heritage Oil conducted in the UK courts.

The judge did not find any evidence that Tullow had engaged in any corrupt activities.

Aidan Heavy, Tullow's chief executive officer and founder, said: 'At no point has any allegation of corruption been substantiated in respect of Tullow's management.'

10. Conflict prevention and resolution

Boards should plan for conflict because once it arises it can have considerable impact on the company in terns of time spent resolving it, possible financial impact and also reputational impact. Conflicts can arise between:

◆ the shareholders and the company/board;

◆ the board and the CEO/senior management team;

◆ different board directors;

◆ board/senior management and the employees; and

◆ company/board and external stakeholders.

The types of conflicts vary depending on the groups involved. For each type of conflict, a different resolution may be required.

Boards should recognise what disputes are likely to arise and exercise the duty of care when dealing with situations which may result in a dispute. They should understand the risks posed by the dispute and if it crystallises be prepared to resolve the dispute as quickly and effectively as possible. This means that the board should:

◆ Plan ahead by anticipating potential disputes. These can be identified by assessing past and current disputes of the company and also other organisations involved in the same activities.

◆ Ensure that the company's policies, procedures, legal documents, such as articles of association, and disclosures are aimed at minimising the risk of conflict and include provisions to deal with conflict where it arises.

◆ Ensure that there is evidence that the company's policies, procedures etc., are actually integrated into the company's culture and not just documents on shelves.

◆ Identify a person to manage the dispute resolution process; this could be the company secretary or the company's lawyer.

◆ Review the effectiveness of the dispute resolution process following any dispute.

◆ Be prepared for mediation and as a backstop litigation to resolve conflicts.

One area where conflict can occur is in the boardroom itself. The company secretary can take the following steps to minimise boardroom disputes:

◆ Ensure that the roles of the board members have been set out in a clear and concise way in their appointment letter.

◆ On appointment a comprehensive induction programme should be held to ensure that there is no misunderstanding as to what is expected from the board members.

◆ There is a board charter/governance manual setting out what the roles of the board, board committees and senior management team are.

◆ Delegation of authority to the CEO is clearly documented.

◆ Proper flows of information to and from the board. The board requires sufficient information to make informed decisions. Management require prompt communication of board decisions.

◆ In agenda development, ensuring that there is plenty of time allowed for discussion, debate and deliberation of the matters brought to the board.

◆ Advising the chair to agree with the board ground rules for behaviour, attire and so on, during board meetings.

◆ Creating the right environment within the boardroom for calm, effective meetings and decision making. This can include:

  – Shape of the table – everyone being in eye contact with the chair.

  – Seating arrangements – non-executives on one side, executives on the other is like drawing battle lines. Mix them up so it is more like a team.

  – Lighting, heating, space etc., can all affect human behaviour.

- – Make sure there are plenty of breaks – two hours should be maximum time without a break. Stepping out of the boardroom can give new insights and perspectives as people have time to think.

◆ Being prepared to break a tense situation by advising the chair to take a break, asking for clarity for the minutes and so on.

◆ Encouraging the creation of a good culture within the board. This can be achieved by building relationships and trust between board members. Giving plenty of opportunity for board members to get to know each other through lunches or dinners, annual board retreats or board trainings etc.

Evidence that a company has done everything possible to plan for and resolve a conflict can help should a regulatory breach or litigation occur. As stated above, there needs to be evidence that the policies and procedures have been implemented and are operational for these defences to be successful.

Test yourself 13.4

1. **What matters should the company secretary consider when handling insider information?**

2. **What is the difference between disaster recovery planning and business continuity planning?**

3. **What are the six principles of the Ministry of Justice Guidance on the UK Bribery Act 2010?**

4. **What should the company secretary do to minimise boardroom disputes?**

11. Senior executive remuneration and risk

The 2018 Code (Provision 40) states that the remuneration committee, when determining remuneration policy and practices, should ensure that reputational and other risks associated with excessive rewards and the behavioural risks which can come from target-based incentive plans are identified and mitigated. The purpose of this provision is to reduce the likelihood of executives being paid large annual bonuses for achieving high levels of the performance in the short-term to the detriment of the long-term sustainability of the organisation. The 2018 Code (Provision 37) also provides that when developing performance-related remuneration, boards should include provisions that would enable a company to recover sums paid or withhold a payment of a sum where a senior executive has adversely affected the future performance and/or sustainability of the company.

To meet these requirements, boards can consider making bonus payments and other performance-related incentives over a period of time so that they are able to withhold or clawback payments should it be deemed necessary.

Stop and think 13.3

Corporate governance scandals have shown that the remuneration and reward systems within an organisation can affect the behaviour of the employees within that organisation. Do the remuneration and reward systems within your organisation encourage good or bad behaviours in relation to the risk appetite of the organisation?

Chapter summary

◆ The board is responsible for carrying out an annual review of the effectiveness of the internal control and risk management systems. The board may delegate this responsibility to the audit committee. In some cases, the delegation is to a risk committee. In the latter case, the audit committee would retain the task of reviewing the effectiveness of financial risk controls.

◆ The review of the effectiveness of the internal control system would rely on the regular risk and internal audit reports to the board or board committee responsible for receiving them. These may be supplemented by additional internal audit reports and the external auditors end of audit report on any weaknesses in the company's internal controls.

◆ A company may have an internal audit function, the key responsibilities of which vary but often include investigations into the operational effectiveness of financial, operational and compliance controls. Investigations can be at the request of the board, the audit committee or senior management.

◆ The internal audit function should be as objective and independent as possible. The head of the function should have a reporting line into the chair of the audit committee.

◆ The 2018 Code requires an annual review of the effectiveness of the internal audit function, and where there is not one, for the board to consider the need for one.

◆ An important part of the internal control system is an effective whistleblowing procedure. Many companies have whistleblowing policies but their procedures for whistleblowing are not very robust.

◆ The company secretary plays an important role in ensuring that risk is discussed at the board level by making sure that it features on the board's agenda at both full board and board committee level.

◆ Cybersecurity is becoming an important issue for many organisations and boards should be taking an interest in how it is being managed within the organisation.

◆ The governance of information is also critical for many organisations. This was first recognised in the King Code in South Africa. Boards should ensure that effective policies and procedures are in place to manage information flows both internal and external.

◆ Effective, well-documented and implemented procedures can assist in conflict prevention and resolution.

◆ The UK Bribery Act 2010 has made it a criminal offence to offer and receive bribes, to bribe foreign public officials for business benefit and for failure to prevent a bribe being paid on the organisation's behalf.

◆ The board should ensure that the organisation's reward system should be compatible with the risk management within the organisation.

Part five

Corporate governance systems, controls and issues

Overview

Part 5 of this study text examines a company's engagement with shareholders and other stakeholders, both from the perspective of the shareholder and of the board of directors on behalf of the company. It is important for the success of a company that there is a good dialogue between the company's board and its stakeholders.

Chapter 14 looks at the different types of shareholders, their rights and how those rights can be abused. It also examines the role the company secretary has in protecting the rights of shareholders particularly the minority shareholders and helping shareholders exercise the rights they have. The chapter also examines the responsibilities of institutional shareholders to oversee and monitor the companies in which they invest.

Chapter 15 examines the board's role in engaging with shareholders. It looks at the use of the annual general meeting in this process and the growing use by companies of technology as a means of engagement. The chapter also looks at how a board should engage with other stakeholders and the role of the company secretary in assisting the board with this process.

Chapter 16 looks at aspects of director remuneration and the elements of a remuneration package. It covers the principles and provisions on remuneration, and reports and policies that must be created. The chapter also covers the role of remuneration committee and compensation for loss of office.

Learning outcomes

Part 5 should enable you to:

◆ describe the most common types of shareholders in the UK;

◆ understand what is meant by the separation of ownership and control, and how it has led to the development of shareholder rights and protections;

◆ explain the different rights of shareholders and their sources;

◆ identify the different ways shareholders can be abused and how the company secretary can protect the different types of shareholders from these abuses;.

◆ describe the importance of institutional shareholders and their responsibilities set out in the UK Stewardship Code;

◆ explain the difference between responsible investment and socially responsible investment;

◆ understand the importance of the board's role in shareholder and other stakeholder engagement and how the feedback from this engagement should be fed in to the board's decision-making processes;

◆ explain the importance and limitations of the annual general meeting to the engagement process;

◆ describe the benefits to companies and their shareholders of electronic communication;

◆ explain the role of the company secretary in stakeholder engagement;

◆ identify the elements of a remuneration policy and package;

◆ know the role of the remuneration committee; and

◆ have an awareness of issues related to remuneration, including guidelines and disclosure.

Chapter fourteen
Shareholders' rights and engagement

CONTENTS

1. Introduction

This chapter describes the different types of shareholders, their rights, how those rights can be abused and how a company secretary can ensure that shareholder rights are not abused. It also looks at the shareholders' responsibility to oversee and monitor the companies in which they invest.

2. Definitions

Laymen think it is simple that the owners of a company are called shareholders. In practice it is not as simple as this and there are many types of individuals or groups termed shareholders, who are actually not the real owners of the company. Listed companies actually spend a lot of time, effort and money on trying to establish who their real owners are.

Below is a list of the most common types of 'shareholders'.

◆ Member – a person or organisation entered into the Register of Members of the company as the holder of the company's shares. It is the 'members' who normally have the rights and powers referred to as 'shareholder rights and powers' later in this chapter. The other types of shareholders or owners of shares are required to exercise their rights and powers through these members.

◆ Beneficial shareowner – a person or organisation that ultimately owns a share in a company. The shareowner may or may not be a 'member' of the company. Many of the recent Companies Act reforms have focused on giving these shareholders access to information and voting rights.

◆ Nominee/custodian – a person or organisation that holds shares as a 'member' on behalf of another person or organisation who may or may not be the ultimate owner of the shares.

◆ Retail shareholder – individual investors who buy and sell securities for their personal account, and not for another company or organisation. The individual usually registers the shares in the name of a nominee belonging to a stock broking firm, e.g. Barclays Nominees Limited.

◆ Institutional shareholder – a person or organisation that trades securities in large quantities or monetary amounts on behalf of multiple beneficiaries. It is assumed that institutional investors are more knowledgeable about the companies in which they invest and are therefore better able to protect themselves. Examples of institutional investors are banks, insurance companies, retirement or pension funds, hedge funds, investment advisors and mutual funds. Their role in the economy is to act as highly specialised investors on behalf of others. For instance, an ordinary person will have a pension from his employer. The employer gives that person's pension contributions to a fund. The fund will buy shares in companies, or some other financial product. Funds are useful because they will hold a broad portfolio of investments in many companies which spreads the risk, so if one company fails, it will be only a small part of the whole fund's investment, and minimises the cost of investment.

3. Separation of ownership and control

As far back as 1872, it was recognised that the separation of ownership from control brings with it difficulties that need to be managed. The owner of shares in a company has an intangible interest in an intangible entity. While the entity itself may have many tangible assets, the relation of those assets to the 'owners' is often questionable. It is argued that in many companies, a shareholder, in return for limited liability, gives up the right to control the use of the company's property by others. This right is delegated to the board of directors and management of the company, who in theory have the time and expertise, which the shareholder may not, to get the most out of these assets, in theory for the benefit of the company.

This separation of ownership and control has been the focus of companies and securities laws and regulations, and corporate governance best practices, which have developed to ensure that the rights and assets of the investors/owners of companies are protected from unscrupulous managers.

4. Powers and rights

Many of the powers and rights of shareholders are discussed elsewhere in this study text; for example, the rights to appoint and remove directors, appoint external auditors, and remunerate both directors and auditors. Some of the other powers and rights are discussed below.

4.1 Sources

The main sources of powers and rights for shareholders are as follows:

- Legislation – the two main areas of law that relate to shareholders are company laws and securities laws.
- Regulations – listed companies are subject to the requirements of the Listing Rules, Disclosure Guidance and Transparency Rules and the Takeover Code.
- Case law – some protection for minority shareholders can be found in common law rules which often operate when legislation is silent.
- Corporate governance codes and principles such as the OECD Principles of Corporate Governance.
- Articles of association of the company usually contain powers and rights of members, such as those for the holding of general meetings.
- Resolutions passed at general meetings of shareholders reinforce pre-emption rights, the rights to share by way of dividend in the profits of the company and the rights to elect the board of directors and the company's auditors.
- Shareholder agreements which may regulate:
  - the purchase and sale of shares;
  - the transfer of shares;
  - the preference to acquire shares;
  - the exercise of voting rights;
  - the exercise of control, including matters reserved to the board;
  - the company's policy on investments;
  - the company's budget;
  - the right of first refusal;
  - the tag along and drag along clauses; and
  - the preparatory meetings among the shareholders who executed the shareholder's agreement to decide how to vote in the general meetings of the company.

4.2 Shareholder rights

Ownership and the transfer

For shares to possess value to the shareholder there needs to be secure methods of registration so that the shareholder can prove that they have title to the shares they claim to hold. There also needs to be a mechanism for the shares to be transferred to another person or entity. The G20/OECD Principles of Corporate Governance state that secure ownership and the power to transfer a shareholding are basic rights of shareholders.

The company secretary is often responsible for maintaining the company's register of members and transfers for listed companies, overseeing the relationship with the company's share registrars.

Shareholders also have the right to protect the value of their shares. Some of the abuses affecting the value of shares and how shareholders can protect against them are discussed later in the chapter, for example dilution.

Equal Treatment

As a general principle, all shareholders of the same class of shares should be treated equally. This is reflected in the UK listing rules Principle 5 for listed companies.

The company secretary should be on the look-out for abuses against shareholders, especially minority shareholders. The G20/OECD Principles of Corporate Governance state: 'Minority shareholders should be protected from abusive actions by, or in the interest of, controlling shareholders acting either directly or indirectly, and should have effective means of redress.'

Some of the most common shareholder abuses are mentioned in Section 5.

Share in the profits

A company should have a dividend policy; these are usually displayed on the company's website. The company secretary may be involved in the drafting of this policy. As a minimum they should ensure that the board complies with the policy when deciding the level of dividend to be paid as either a final or interim dividend.

Receipt of information – shareholders should be kept sufficiently informed about the governance of an organisation and any fundamental changes occurring to or within the organisation. The G20/OECD Principles of Corporate Governance state that it is a basic right of shareholders to:

◆   within reasonable limits, be able to demand information from the company, whether by way of questions at general meetings or through requests to the chair of the board; and

◆   receive timely and regular disclosure of important information about the company.

For listed companies, Listing Rule Principle 6 states that a listed company must communicate information to shareholders and potential investors in a way as 'to avoid the creation of a false market' in the company's shares.

These days information for shareholders tends to be communicated electronically. More information on this can be found in Chapter 15.

Attend meetings and vote

It is a basic right of shareholders to be able to attend general meetings of the companies that they invest in and vote on resolutions affecting the governance and any fundamental changes to the company. They should also be given the opportunity to ask questions to the board and to propose resolutions, within reasonable limits.

In UK law, shareholders have a right to:

◆ require the directors to call a general meeting if together they hold at least 5% of the voting share capital; and

◆ propose a resolution to be voted on at the AGM of the company provided they hold at least 5% of the voting share capital. The request to include the item in the AGM must be received not later than six weeks before the date of the AGM, and if the request is received before the end of the company's financial year preceding the AGM, the company must bear the costs of circulating the details of the matter to the other shareholders.

Attempts by shareholders to call a general meeting or to put an additional resolution to the annual general meeting are not common in the UK. Shareholders will only seek to call a general meeting of the company in extreme circumstances, and possibly as a means of shaking the board of directors into re-thinking its attitude to the matter that is causing the shareholders extreme concern.

The CA2006 extended the statutory rights of shareholders to proxies. Shareholders are now able to appoint more than one **proxy** per shareholding, as long as each proxy represents a different part of the appointor's holding. Proxies are able to exercise all or any of the rights of shareholders to attend, speak and vote at a meeting on a show of hands or on a poll for the part of the holding they represent.

proxy
A person appointed by a shareholder to vote on the shareholder's behalf at a general meeting. In the UK, shareholders can appoint proxies electronically. They can either instruct a proxy how to vote on each resolution at a meeting, or can give the proxy freedom to decided how to vote on each resolution.

Enfranchising indirect shareholders

The CA2006 aims to assist indirect investors, i.e. shareowners who hold shares through one or more financial intermediary, to become more involved in the company's affairs through access to information, and the exercise of rights normally reserved for registered shareholders. The CA2006 seeks to achieve this through:

◆ enabling registered shareholders to nominate another person to exercise or enjoy all or any of the shareholder rights, including voting rights, so long as a provision to that effect is included in the company's articles. Few companies have changed their articles so the impact of this provision is not material; and

◆ giving beneficial shareholders direct rights to company information. The right is not automatic and requires the registered shareholder to nominate the indirect investor. Where this has happened, many listed companies do provide notifications of when information has been made available on the company's website direct to the indirect investor. Where a notice of a meeting is sent to an indirect investor, the company will usually alert the indirect investor to the fact that they may have the right to be appointed a proxy for the meeting.

Stop and think 14.1

How in your organisation do you enfranchise indirect shareholders? Are they treated equally to registered members?

5. Common abuses of shareholder rights

Many of the powers and rights of shareholders have been put in place to ensure that abuse of shareholders, or a group of shareholders, is prevented or controlled. The most common abuses are:

5.1   Market abuse and insider dealing

Market abuse

Market abuse is a civil offence that encompasses a wide range of unacceptable market practices and behaviours, including insider dealing. Under s. 123 of the Financial Services and Markets Act 2000 (FSMA), the Financial Conduct Authority (FCA) may impose an unlimited penalty on, or censure, any person who has engaged in market abuse. As it is a civil, rather than criminal, offence, it is only necessary for the FCA to prove that a person's behaviour was illegal 'on the balance of probabilities' as opposed to the 'beyond reasonable doubt' test applied in criminal prosecutions for insider dealing under the Criminal Justice Act 1993.

There are four types of market abuse:

◆ Engaging or attempting to engage in insider dealing, recommending that another person engage in insider dealing, or inducing another person to engage in insider dealing. Insider dealing arises where a person possesses inside information and uses that information to directly or indirectly acquire or dispose of financial instruments to which that information relates, whether in their own account or on behalf of a third party.

◆ Unlawfully disclosing inside information. The unlawful disclosure of inside information arises where a person discloses the inside information to someone else, except where the disclosure is made in the normal exercise of an employment, a profession or duties. Examples of unlawful disclosure would include:

–   disclosure of inside information by a director to somebody in a social context; and

–   selective briefing of analysts by a director or other PDMR (person discharging managerial responsibilities) of the issuer.

- The following would not involve unlawful disclosure:
    - the disclosure of inside information to a regulator, such as the Takeover Panel; and
    - the disclosure of inside information which is required or permitted by the Listing Rules (or any similar regulatory obligation).
- engaging in or attempting to engage in market manipulation. Market manipulation covers activities such as:
    - placing market orders which give false or misleading signals as to the supply of, demand for, or price of, a financial instrument; and
    - disseminating information through the media, including internet rumours, which give such false or misleading signals.

Insider dealing: criminal offence

Part V of the Criminal Justice Act 1993 makes insider dealing a criminal offence. The FCA is given power under s. 402 of FSMA, to institute criminal prosecutions for insider dealing offences under the Criminal Justice Act in addition to its powers to take civil action under the market abuse regime.

The criminal offence of insider dealing may take one of three forms:

- dealing in securities on the basis of inside information;
- encouraging another to engage in such dealing; and
- disclosing inside information otherwise than in the proper performance of one's employment, office or profession.

To be found guilty of the offence, the defendant must be an individual who has, as an insider, information affecting the securities concerned and must know that such information is inside information. The information must have been obtained by the defendant as a director, employee or shareholder of the company concerned or directly or indirectly from such a person.

'Inside information' is information that relates to particular issues of securities or to a particular issuer or issuers of securities, which is specific or precise and would be likely, if made public, to have a significant effect on the price of any securities. Information that relates to securities or issuers only 'generally' is not inside information. Information will also not be inside information if it has already been made public.

Information may be treated by the court as having been made public even if it can be acquired only by persons exercising diligence or expertise or by observation or if it is communicated only to a section of the public or is communicated only on payment of a fee or is published only outside the UK.

It is a defence to the 'disclosing' offence to show that the defendant did not, at the time of the disclosure, expect any person to deal because of the disclosure or alternatively that he did not expect any such dealing to result in a profit attributable to the price sensitivity of the information. It is a defence to the dealing offence to show that the defendant would have dealt in the same way even if he had not had the information. Thus, a director who is under financial pressure to sell securities may possibly not commit an offence even though he is in possession of inside information. This defence would also be of assistance to trustees acting on advice.

The insider dealing provisions over shares, debentures and loan stock, futures and options. Dealings are covered only if they occur on a regulated market or if the person concerned relies on or is himself a professional intermediary.

5.1.1 Disclosure of inside information

Listed companies are required to inform the public as soon as possible of inside information which directly concerns them as an issuer. The inside information must be disseminated though a Regulatory Information Service (RIS). However, if their RIS provider is not open for business, they must distribute the information as soon as possible to at least two national newspapers and two newswire services operating in the UK. The company secretary is often involved in the dissemination of inside information either directly or in liaison with the investor relations department.

Issuers are allowed to delay the disclosure of inside information where immediate disclosure is likely to prejudice their legitimate interests. This includes circumstances where the issuer is conducting negotiations whose outcome would likely be jeopardised by immediate public disclosure. Any such delay must not mislead the public and the issuer must be able to ensure the confidentiality of the information.

Case study 14.1

Mr Hannam, the Global Co-Head of UK Capital Markets at JP Morgan, was fined in April 2012 by the FSA £450,000 for disclosing to third parties inside information about a potential takeover of Heritage Oil PLC (Heritage) and about the results of Heritage's drilling for oil in Uganda. Both pieces of information were considered by the FSA as being inside information. Mr Hannam claimed that the disclosures were not inside information and that they had been made in the proper course of his employment. There was no evidence that anyone dealt in shares based on Mr Hannam's disclosures or that Mr Hannam made any personal gain.

Mr Hannam appealed the fine to the Upper Tribunal who upheld the £450,000 penalty, stating: 'We consider that it could never be in the proper course of a person's employment for him to disclose inside information to a third party, where he knows that his employer and the client would not consent to public disclosure of that information, unless the recipient is under a duty of confidentiality and that he knows that the recipient understands that to be the case.'

The FCA stated that it was 'very important to deter that sort of careless attitude to inside information' and warned of a 'floodgate' of appeals opening if the Upper Tribunal had overruled their decision in this case.

5.1.2 Insider lists and control of inside information

Listed companies should maintain a list of people who have access to any inside information (an 'insider list') and make that list available to their competent authority on request. The competent authority in the UK is the FCA. The company secretary is often the person responsible for keeping the insider list.

The insider list must include:

◆ the identity of any person having access to inside information;

◆ the reason for including that person in the insider list;

◆ the date and time at which that person obtained access to inside information; and

◆ the date on which the insider list was drawn up.

The insider list must be divided into separate sections relating to different inside information, although one of those sections can contain details of individuals who have access at all times to all inside information (known as 'permanent insiders').

The purpose of the insider list is to enable the FCA to conduct investigation regarding the source of any possible leaks.

Issuers must take all reasonable steps to ensure that any person on the insider list acknowledges in writing the legal and regulatory duties entailed and is aware of the sanctions applicable to insider dealing and unlawful disclosure of inside information. They must also establish effective arrangements to deny access to inside information to persons other than those who require it for the exercise of their functions within the issuer.

5.1.3 Dealings by directors and PDMRs

Persons discharging managerial responsibilities (PDMRs), as well as persons closely associated with them (PCAs), are required to notify the issuer and the FCA of any dealings in its traded securities no later than three business days after the date of the transaction. In practice, this notification will often be made by the issuer on their behalf. On receipt of such a notification, the issuer is required to make an announcement to the market no later than three business days after the transaction.

A PDMR is defined as a person within an issuer who is:

◆ a member of the administrative, management or supervisory body of that entity (e.g. a director); or

◆ a senior executive who is not a director but has regular access to inside information relating directly or indirectly to the issuer and power to take managerial decisions affecting its future developments and business prospects.

A PCA (person closely associated with a PDMR) is defined as:

◆ a spouse, or a partner considered to be equivalent to a spouse in accordance with national law;

◆ a dependent child, in accordance with national law;

◆ a relative who has shared the same household for at least one year on the date of the transaction concerned; or

◆ a corporate body, trust or partnership, the managerial responsibilities of which are discharged by a PDMR or family member, which is directly or indirectly controlled by such a person, which is set up for the benefit of such a person, or the economic interests of which are substantially equivalent to those of such a person.

PDMRs are prohibited from conducting any transactions in the company's securities on their own account or for a third party during a closed period of 30 calendar days before the announcement of the year-end results or any interim financial report which the issuer is obliged to publish.

In certain exceptional circumstances, an issuer can allow a PDMR to deal during a closed period, such as where a director is in severe financial difficulty. A PDMR must submit a written request to the issuer before being given permission to deal under these rules, which must explain why the sale of shares is necessary.

5.1.4 Dealing code and policy

Listed companies used to be required under the Listing Rules to ensure that their directors and other PDMRs complied with a code of dealing known as the Model Code. The requirement to apply the Model Code was abolished with effect from 3 July 2016 as it was thought to be incompatible with the requirements of the market abuse regulations.

Nevertheless, the FCA supported the adoption of a voluntary industry code in this regard, and in June 2016 a number of bodies (including ICSA, the GC100 Group and the Quoted Companies Alliance) jointly published specimen documentation for a dealing code and policy compatible with the requirements of the market abuse regulations.

The dealing code and policy document includes:

◆ a 'specimen' group-wide dealing policy which companies could issue to employees as an introduction to the concept of market abuse;

◆ a 'specimen' dealing code that companies would be expected to issue to PDMRs and other individuals whom they wish to be covered by the company's process;

◆ a 'specimen' dealing procedures manual for use by the company secretary or whoever else in the company is responsible for the implementation and management of the systems and procedures for the clearance of dealing by PDMRs and other individuals to whom dealing restrictions apply.

Test yourself 14.1

1.   **What are the four types of market abuse?**

2.   **Why might there be more successful prosecutions for insider dealing under the market abuse regime than under the Criminal Justice Act 1973?**

3.   **What is inside information and why are listed companies required to publish inside information so promptly?**

5.2   Dilution

Company secretaries/governance professionals are usually involved in the allotment of shares so they are best placed to monitor dilution.

Dilution can occur in three ways:

◆   Ownership percentage of voting control is reduced.

◆   Per-share earnings may be cut when disbursed among a greater number of shareholders.

◆   Share values may fall depending upon proceeds received from selling more shares to investors.

The CA2006 provides several protections for shareholders against dilution. The first of these is the requirement for directors to be authorised to allot shares in the company by the shareholders. This authority is usually given at the annual general meeting. There are exemptions, such as for private companies and for employee share schemes, though these exemptions may be disapplied in the company's articles of association.

Shareholders also have the right of 'pre-emption' in relation to the issue of new shares, that is to say, that the shares must be offered first to the existing shareholders in proportion to their existing holdings before they can be offered to others. This prevents dilution of a shareholder's value. Shareholders can by a resolution in general meeting waive this right. It is usual for listed companies to waive this right up to a certain amount each year at the company's annual general meeting.

The company secretary is responsible for ensuring that any resolutions relating to the allotment of shares or waiving of pre-emption rights are included in the agenda for the annual general meeting. The company secretary should also ensure that the authorities/waivers requested are in line with what shareholders expect. Many institutional shareholder representative bodies have rules about the level of dilution that is acceptable. In the UK, it is a maximum of 10% of the issued share capital for shares to be allotted non-pre-emptively each year.

Shareholders also have the right to approve long-term incentive schemes; this is because these schemes usually involve the allotment of new shares or the purchase of the company's existing shares in the market, the holding of these shares as treasury shares and then their redistribution. All of which can affect the value of the shares held by shareholders.

The company secretary will usually be involved in preparing the plan rules for the long-term incentive schemes and the resolutions to be placed before shareholders at the annual general meeting. They are also often involved in the maintenance of these schemes and in disclosures relating to their operation.

5.3   Tunnelling

Tunnelling occurs when the value of the shares held by a shareholder is reduced. This can happen when:

tunnelling
An illegal business practice in which a majority shareholder or high level company insider directs company assets or future business to themselves for personal gain.

- ◆ the company's assets are sold or transferred to third parties at non-market prices;

- ◆ value-destroying acquisitions and investments are made to help related companies;

- ◆ off-balance sheet loan guarantees are made;

- ◆ corporate opportunities are exploited by related companies and not the company itself;

- ◆ the articles are amended to give priority to one set of shareholders over another;

- ◆ the capital structure of the company is amended again to give one set of shareholders a priority over another; and

- ◆ changes, including mergers, acquisitions and disposals, are made which affect the fundamental legal and de facto bases of the company.

Chapter 10 of the Listing Rules: 'Significant Transactions', requires listed companies to notify their shareholders of certain transactions of more than 5% of the company's value calculated by a series of ratios. Where the transaction value is more than 25% a shareholder vote is required.

The company secretary should monitor the activities of directors and controlling shareholders to ensure that these types of abuses do not occur.

5.4   Related party transactions

International Accounting Standard (IAS) 24, Related Party Disclosures, defines a related party transaction as: 'a transfer of resources, services or obligations between a reporting entity and a related party, regardless of whether a price is charged.'

A related party is defined in IAS 24 as a person or an entity that is related to the company (reporting entity):

- ◆ 'A person or a close member of that person's family is related to a reporting entity if that person has control, joint control, or significant influence over the entity or is a member of its key management personnel.

- ◆ An entity is related to a reporting entity if, among other circumstances, it is a parent, subsidiary, fellow subsidiary, associate, or joint venture of the reporting entity, or it is controlled, jointly controlled, or significantly influenced or managed by a person who is a related party.'

If an entity has had related party transactions during the periods covered by the financial statements, IAS 24 requires it to disclose the nature of the related party relationship as well as information about those transactions and outstanding balances, including commitments, necessary for users to understand the potential effect of the relationship on the financial statements.

A company therefore needs to have a policy on related party transactions and a method of collecting information on related party transactions to meet the requirements of IAS 24.

The company secretary is involved in drafting, implementing and enforcing a policy on related party transactions. Where a related party transaction occurs, the company secretary will advise the director and the board about the consequences. These may range from disclosure in the annual accounts to obtaining shareholder approval.

The CA2006 sets out provisions in respect of substantial property transactions between a company and its director or a person connected to that director. The provisions state that a company may not transfer to a director, or a director to the company, non-cash assets, e.g. property if its value exceeds 10% of the company's net assets and is more than £5,000 or if the value exceeds £100,000, unless approved by the company in a general meeting.

If shareholder approval is required, then the company secretary will have to arrange for the general meeting and the appropriate documentation to be prepared for the meeting.

For listed companies, Chapter 11, Related Party Transactions, of the Listing Rules sets out safeguards which are intended to prevent a related party from taking advantage of its position and also to prevent any perception that it may have done so.

In the LR, a 'related party' means:

◆ a person who is (or was within the 12 months before the date of the transaction or arrangement) a substantial shareholder; or

◆ a person who is (or was within the 12 months before the date of the transaction or arrangement) a director or shadow director of the listed company or of any other company which is (and, if they have ceased to be such, was while they were a director or shadow director of such other company) its subsidiary undertaking or parent undertaking or a fellow subsidiary undertaking of its parent undertaking;

◆ a person exercising significant influence; or

◆ an associate of a related party.

In the LR, a 'related party transaction' means:

◆ a transaction (other than a transaction in the ordinary course of business) between a listed company and a related party;

- an arrangement (other than an arrangement in the ordinary course of business) pursuant to which a listed company and a related party each invests in, or provides finance to, another undertaking or asset; or

- any other similar transaction or arrangement (other than a transaction in the ordinary course of business) between a listed company and any other person the purpose and effect of which is to benefit a related party.

Case study 14.2

In April 2018, shareholders in Metro Bank were faced with media reports that the bank had paid £21 million to InterArch, a design and architecture company owned by the wife of its chair Mr Vernon Hill, including £4.6 million in 2017.

There was interest in the payments, which were related party transactions, due to the fact that Mr Hill had parted ways in 2007 with Commerce Bank Corp in the US, a bank he had founded, following investigations by American regulators into similar payments to InterArch. Mr Hill was re-elected with a 96.5% share of the vote despite shareholder advisory groups recommending that shareholders vote against his re-election.

Test yourself 14.2

1. **Briefly describe the most common types of shareholders.**

2. **What are the main sources of shareholder rights?**

3. **Give examples of shareholder rights.**

4. **Name four examples of shareholder abuse.**

6. Anonymity of shareholders

There are many reasons why listed companies, in particular, may not know who the owners of their shares are. Some are intentional, others are down to how the market works and people invest in shares.

In recent years several reasons have made it important for the identity of shareholders to be known, thus enabling them to:

1. Assert their rights.

2. Communicate with companies. The development of investor relations has led to companies often going beyond the statutory requirements for providing information to shareholders.

3. Monitor corporate governance best practice and hold management accountable.

4.   Join with fellow shareholders to overcome legal hurdles in the run-up to general meetings.
5.   React with management in a timely manner to threatened hostile takeovers.

Shareholders who have a substantial holding in a company are required to inform the company. This disclosure makes it clear to potential investors who owns the company or who aspires to secure control of the company. It also warns the company and allows them together with shareholders to prepare for an impending takeover. In the UK, the initial disclosure is triggered at 3% of total voting rights and a further disclosure is required for each whole percentage point change after that. There are exemptions for market makers holding less than 10% so long as they do not influence the management of the company or exert influence over the company. At 10% and over the entire holding is disclosable. Listed companies are required to make these notifications public.

Public companies can, under the CA2006 (s. 793), give notice to any person or entity whom the company believes to have an interest in the company's shares or to have had an interest at any time in the three years immediately preceding the date the notice was issued. The notice requires the shareholder to disclose whether or not they have had an interest and the nature of that interest. If the shareholder fails to provide the information the company is able to obtain a court order imposing certain restrictions on the shares it believes are held by the shareholder. If the shareholder fails to comply with a court order it is a criminal offence.

7. Institutional shareholder responsibilities

In theory, institutional investors should have a lot of influence in the management of companies, but many institutional investors do not see corporate governance as their responsibility. Many institutional shareholders have holdings in thousands of different companies and these holdings may only account for one quarter of 1% of a company. So, the expense and time spent entering into active engagement with a company is often not seen as beneficial to that organisation. In the *Financial Times*, 16 June 2003, Tom Jones, who at the time ran Citigroup's global investment management business, was quoted as saying 'he does not see himself as a do-gooder, so he does not see why his funds shareholders should spend money on an activity that benefits all investors'.

Some institutional shareholders, however, do actively engage with companies on their corporate governance, e.g. Hermes, CalPERS, The Teachers Insurance and Annuity Association – College Retirement Equities Fund (TIAA-CREF), APG (Dutch) and Norgist Fund and others. This dialogue is usually with the larger companies and will usually be with the company secretary.

Shareholder participation provides 'checks and balances' on the board of directors, thus helping the board monitor the management of the company. In corporate governance, the board is accountable to shareholders for how it uses the resources of the company. Despite delegating the running of the business to management, shareholders have kept certain decision-making powers to ensure that management acts in their interest and is subject to regular monitoring.

Institutional investors should take an interest in good corporate governance as:

◆   Investors expect a return on their investment. Most evidence suggests that well-governed companies deliver reasonable returns over the long term, and shareholders in these companies are less exposed to downside risk than shareholders in companies that are not so well governed.

◆   Institutional investors also have legal responsibilities (fiduciary duties) to the individuals on whose behalf they invest. For pension funds, these individuals are the beneficiaries of the funds. In fulfilling their responsibilities, institutions should try to ensure that they make a decent return on investment, and promoting good corporate governance is one way of trying to do this.

The courses of action institutional shareholders have available to them if they become concerned about the decisions taken by the board are as follows:

◆   Voice their concerns direct to the company.

◆   Escalate. If their concerns are ignored, they could escalate them to a wider group of shareholders possibly through a representative body.

◆   Vote. Shareholders can address their concern by either withholding their vote or voting against a particular resolution or the re-election of directors. They may also want to propose their own resolutions at a general meeting.

◆   Exit. In an extreme case a shareholder can sell their shares.

7.1   ICSA shareholder engagement

In July 2018, ICSA published 'Shareholder Engagement: The state of play' research into the participation of institutional shareholders in listed companies. The purpose of the research was 'to investigate the nature of engagement between issuers and investors, the extent to which it had changed over the last five years – whether in its frequency, the form it takes, the organisations and individuals involved, or the subjects being discussed'.

The research concluded that:

◆   There was clear evidence that the quality of and time devoted to the engagement had increased since 2013. Over 60% of respondents reported increased engagement with only a handful reporting reduced engagement.

◆   Companies and investors initiate equally the engagements. Engagements initiated by companies usually target large holders, potential investors or those they believe might take a hostile position towards the company. Investors focus on the value of their investments and concerns about performance and governance.

◆ Over 70% of company respondents considered the quality of the engagement with shareholders had improved over the last five years. The engagement was still predominantly event-driven, taking place around general meetings or the publication of financial results. There was some evidence that engagement was becoming an ongoing process.

◆ The issues discussed had not changed much over the last five years; still focusing on performance, strategy, capital structure, M&A activity and leadership. ESG issues and the impact of technological change had become more prominent issues for discussion over the period.

The reasons for the increased engagement, from the companies' perspective, were changes in the company's ownership base – more international so subject to international trends – and changes to the company's approach to engagement. Investors' engagement had increased due to the demand for discussions from the companies and the increased focus on ESG issues.

shareholder activism
A term that refers to: (1) the considered use by institutional investors of their rights as shareholders by voting against the board of directors at general meetings (or threatening to vote against the board); and (2) active dialogue with the boards of companies, to influence decisions by the board.

red top warning
A notice sent out by an institutional investor organisations to its members, advising the members who are shareholders to vote against a particular resolution at an approaching general meeting of a company.

7.2   Shareholder activism

The term 'shareholder activism' refers to activities by institutional investors to influence governance and strategy decisions in companies in which they invest. In most cases, activism is constructive, involving dialogue and discussion, and it is only when a board of directors fails to respond in an acceptable and appropriate way to shareholder concerns that more aggressive action may be considered. This further action will often involve withholding a vote at an AGM, or voting against a resolution at a general meeting, including votes against the re-election of certain directors. To do this successfully, they need a majority of the votes. Since most shareholders in large public companies hold a relatively small percentage of the total number of shares, organising a group of dissident shareholders into a voting majority is difficult, although voting guidelines on some issues are occasionally issued by institutional investor organisations or voting advisory firms, and such guidelines (such as a **red top**' notice advising members to vote against the resolution) may have the effect of persuading shareholders how to vote.

Shareholder activism therefore works through attracting publicity. Its potential strength is that it brings pressure to bear on companies from the negative publicity that shareholder opposition to the board can create.

Case study 14.3

In the run-up to the 2018 AGM of Sports Direct, shareholder advisory groups appeared to urge Sports Direct shareholders to vote against the re-election of the company's chair, Mr Keith Hellewell. This was due to his perceived approach to working practices and corporate governance, both of which were seen as being out-dated. This was reflected in his failure to appoint women to the board. It was argued that he had lost investor confidence evidenced by the fact that at the 2017 AGM 47% of investors had voted against his re-election. In September 2018, a week before the Sports Direct AGM, Mr Hellewell announced his retirement as

chair of the Sports Direct Board. The CEO and Founder of Sports Direct, Mr Mike Ashley accused institutional shareholders of 'hounding' Mr Hellewell out of office and not supporting him as CEO. 9.8% of investors voted against Mr Ashley's re-election at the 2018 Sports Direct AGM following shareholder advisory groups' recommendation to do so due to his excessive influence over the company.

Case study 14.4

SIG, the FTSE 250 building and materials group, suffered a shareholder revolt at its 2018 AGM when more than 78% of its shareholders voted against the re-appointment of Deloitte as the company's auditors. This followed SIG admitting months earlier that its profits in previous years had been overstated. The re-appointment of auditors is usually one of the least controversial resolutions proposed at company AGMs so the move was surprising.

Following the vote, SIG's board announced:

'The Board takes the views of shareholders extremely seriously and takes this opportunity to inform shareholders that it is committed to carrying out an EU audit regulation compliant audit tender for the role of external auditor, as soon as practicable...The Board intends to consult with shareholders over the coming weeks on timing of that audit tender and the resulting appointment of a new auditor'.

In July 2018, SIG announced that following a competitive audit tender process in line with EU audit regulations E&Y had been appointed as the company's external auditor with immediate effect.

Stop and think 14.2

How does your organisation engage with its shareholders?

8. UK Stewardship Code

Institutional shareholders first set out their responsibilities in 2002 in the Institutional Shareholders Committee's (ISC) 'The Responsibilities of Institutional Shareholders and Agents: Statement of Principles'. ISC turned this statement into a Code in 2009. Following the Walker Review of governance in financial institutions, published in 2009, the FRC was invited to take over responsibility for the Code which was renamed the Stewardship Code. The first version was published in 2010, a second in 2012. The FRC is currently consulting on a review of the 2012 Stewardship Code in light of changes to the UK Corporate Governance Code in 2018.

The UK Stewardship Code 2012 aims to enhance the quality of engagement between investors and companies to help improve long-term risk-adjusted returns to the providers of capital for companies. The Stewardship Code sets out the principles of effective stewardship by 'investors' not 'shareholders', so brings long-term debt holders under the purview of the Stewardship Code. The Stewardship Code also applies to service providers such as proxy advisors and investment consultants.

The Stewardship Code states:

'In publicly listed companies responsibility for stewardship is shared. The primary responsibility rests with the board of the company, which oversees the actions of management. Investors in the company also play an important role in holding the board to account for the fulfilment of its responsibilities.'

Like the UK Corporate Governance Code, the Stewardship Code is is applied on a 'comply or explain' basis. It consists of a set of principles and guidance on how the principles might be applied. Organisations that adopt the Stewardship Code provide a statement on their website describing:

◆   how the principles of the Stewardship Code have been applied;
◆   the specific information that is required by the Stewardship Code; and
◆   an explanation of any non-compliance with the Code.

The company secretary should monitor the websites of their major investors to assess whether there is anything in the content of these stewardship statements that can assist in their company's dialogue with the institutional investor or service provider. The outcome of this assessment should be shared with the board.

The Stewardship Code consists of seven principles, with some guidance for each principle.

Principle 1: Institutional investors should publicly disclose their policy on how they will discharge their stewardship responsibilities

The Stewardship Code assists institutional investors better to exercise their stewardship responsibilities, which in addition to voting include monitoring and engaging with companies on matters such as strategy, performance, risk, capital structure and corporate governance, including culture and remuneration.

As mentioned above, the institutional shareholder should make a public disclosure in a policy statement (or 'stewardship statement'), which should indicate how the institution applies stewardship with the aim of enhancing and protecting value for their ultimate beneficiaries or clients (such as pension fund beneficiaries and investors in unit trusts). The policy statement should reflect the institutional investor's activities within the 'investment chain', as asset owners or asset managers, and the stewardship responsibilities associated with those activities. Where the activities are outsourced, the policy statement should disclose what steps the institutional investor has taken to ensure that the activities are carried out in line with their own approach to stewardship set out in the policy statement.

Principle 2: Institutional investors should have a robust policy on managing conflicts of interest in relation to stewardship, which should be publicly disclosed

Institutional investors should take reasonable steps to act in the interests of their clients and/or their beneficiaries. The Stewardship Code recognises that conflicts of interest will arise from time to time and therefore requires that the institutional investor has a 'robust policy' on managing conflicts of interest in relationship to their stewardship responsibilities. This policy should be publicly disclosed.

Principle 3: Institutional investors should monitor their investee companies

Institutional investors should monitor regularly the companies in which they invest, in order to decide when it is necessary to enter into an active dialogue with their board of directors. Monitoring by institutional shareholders should include:

◆ keeping abreast of the company's performance and developments that affect the company's value and risks;

◆ satisfying themselves that the company has effective leadership;

◆ satisfying themselves that the board and its committees adhere to the spirit of the UK Corporate Governance Code: they can do this through meetings with the board chair and other board members;

◆ considering the quality of the company's reporting; and

◆ attending general meetings of companies in which they have a 'major' holding, where this is possible and appropriate.

The Stewardship Code suggests that investors should consider any non-compliance by a company with the provisions of the UK Corporate Governance Code, making a 'reasoned judgement' in each case of non-compliance. If they do not agree with the company's position, they should:

◆ give a timely explanation to the company, in writing where appropriate; and

◆ be prepared to enter into a dialogue with the company.

Institutional investors should also try to identify at an early stage issues that may result in significant loss in investment value. They should make sure that members of the company's board or its management are made aware of any concerns that they have.

By engaging in dialogue with a company, an institutional investor may become an insider, that is gain unpublished price-sensitive information about the company which would prevent them from buying or selling shares. The Guidance to the Stewardship Code suggests:

'Institutional shareholders may not wish to be made insiders. An institutional investor who may be willing to become an insider should indicate in its stewardship statement the willingness to do so and the mechanism by which this should be done.'

The company secretary should advise board members and management that are engaging with institutional shareholders what information can be shared with them and what information is unpublished price-sensitive information which requires the consent of the institutional shareholder before it is disclosed to them. Many companies and institutional shareholders require that their meetings be recorded so that there is proof of what information has passed between them at what stage.

Principle 4: Institutional investors should establish clear guidelines on when and how they will escalate their stewardship activities
Institutional investors should set out the circumstances when they will intervene actively, e.g. when they have concerns about the company's strategy, performance, corporate governance, remuneration or its approach to risks arising from environmental or social matters. They should also regularly assess the outcome of their interventions.

Initial discussions with the company should be on a confidential basis, but if the company's board does not respond constructively, the institutional investor should consider whether to escalate their action, for example by:

◆ holding additional meetings with management to express their concern;

◆ expressing their concern through the company's advisers, e.g. the company's investment bank and sponsor;

◆ meeting with the chair, or other board members;

◆ intervening jointly with other investment institutions on a particular issue;

◆ making a public statement in advance of an AGM or EGM;

◆ submitting resolutions to general meetings of the company (if sufficient support can be obtained from other shareholders, to get the 5% required) or speaking at an AGM or general meeting; and

◆ requisitioning a general meeting, possibly to propose changes to board membership.

The company secretary should monitor interactions with institutional shareholders, and having informed themselves of the published guidelines on when and how the institutional shareholder will escalate their stewardship activities, advise their board and management accordingly. Meetings should be held with institutional shareholders on 'sensitive' issues, such as board changes, remuneration matters and major strategic changes to ensure that the major investors are on-side with the changes prior to them occurring. The company secretary would normally be involved in arranging these meetings and would probably attend them with the chair. Records should be kept of these discussions and a feedback session to the board arranged as soon as practicable, so decisions can be made in light of the information gleaned at these meetings.

Voting advisories are issued either by the institutional investor or their representative bodies prior to AGMs/general meetings. The company secretary should obtain copies of the ones relevant to their companies and respond to them as appropriate, informing the chair and board where necessary. This may avoid the embarrassment of a resolution being voted down at, or requisitioned for, the meeting.

The company secretary mantra should be 'no surprises' so briefing the board and management on, and responding to, any issues raised by institutional investors is very important.

Principle 5: Institutional shareholders should be willing to act collectively with other investors where appropriate

Institutional investors should be willing to act collectively with other investors where appropriate. Collaborative engagement may be particularly appropriate at times when the company is under severe stress, or when risks threaten to 'destroy significant value'.

Institutional investors should disclose their policy on collaborating and how they intend to collaborate through formal or informal channels.

Again, the company secretary should be aware of the policies on collaboration of their major investors and brief the board accordingly. They should also keep a dialogue open with institutional investors during periods of potential conflict with institutional investors so that the company can head off negative activism from a collection of institutional investors.

Principle 6: Institutional investors should have a clear policy on voting and disclosure of voting activity

Institutional investors should seek to vote all the shares that they hold. They should not automatically support the board of directors. Where they have been unable to reach a satisfactory outcome through dialogue, they should consider withholding their vote on resolutions at a general meeting or voting against them. It is good practice to notify the company of an intention to vote against a resolution or withhold a vote in advance of doing so providing reasons for doing so.

The company secretary should inform the chair as soon as they are aware that an institutional investor who owns shares in the company has indicated that they may withhold or vote against a resolution at the company's general meeting. As mentioned earlier, a dialogue should be opened by the company with the institutional investor, as soon as possible, and any concerns should be addressed appropriately. The company secretary would normally be involved in arranging and attending any meetings with the institutional investor and also in organising any disclosures from the company relating to the matter.

Institutional investors should make public disclosure of their voting records at general meetings and disclose their use of proxy voting and/or voting advisory services.

Institutional investors should disclose their approach to stock-lending and recalling lent stock. Stock-lending, or 'Empty Voting' as it has come to be known, has been used by activists to alter the outcome of voting on a resolution at an annual general meeting. It is considered poor governance and frowned upon by public bodies and regulators. Famously in 2002, Laxey Partners, a boutique fund manager, borrowed 42 million shares in British Land (increasing its stake from 2.9% to 9%) to allow it to requisition resolutions at British Land's annual general meeting to return capital to shareholders and change some of British land's governance practices, including splitting the role of chair and CEO. More recently in July 2018, Oasis, a hedge fund, increased its stake in Premier Foods from 9% to 17%, of which according to the *Financial Times*, 4.5% was borrowed stock, to vote against the re-election of Mr Gavin Darby, Premier Foods CEO.

Principle 7: Institutional investors should report periodically on their stewardship and voting activities

Institutional investors should maintain a record of and report periodically on their stewardship and voting activities. Investment managers should report to their clients, and institutions that represent the interests of an end-investor or act as principals should report at least annually to those people to whom they are accountable.

The information that is reported may include both qualitative and quantitative information, but the particular information reported (including details of voting) are a matter for agreement between the agent and their client. Institutional investors should not make disclosures that are counterproductive or that compromise confidentiality which may be crucial to achieving a positive outcome.

Test yourself 14.3

1.   **What is a derivative claim? Who is able to bring it and when?**

2.   **In what ways does a company know who its interestedshareholders are?**

3.   **Why should institutional shareholders take an interest in good corporate governance?**

4.   **What are the seven principles of the Stewardship Code?**

9. Shareholder representative bodies

In the UK, there are two main shareholder representative bodies that provide guidance for their members on corporate governance issues of listed companies. These are:

◆   The Investment Association (incorporating guidance from the Association British Insurers (ABI)).

◆   Pension and Lifetime Savings Association (PLSA) (formerly the National Association of Pension Funds (NAPF)).

The company secretary should ensure they are aware of the view of these organisations so that they are able to advise their boards and management teams.

9.1   PLSA

The PLSA state on its website that:

'Members of the PLSA have a clear interest in promoting the success of the companies in which they invest. As a consequence of this, we have long considered that one of our prime functions is to support members in engaging with investee companies. Our efforts are directed towards maximising the long-term returns of pension schemes' assets, irrespective of the short-term discomfort.'

PLSA has issued a Corporate Governance Policy and Voting Guidelines 2017 which provides their members with examples of good stewardship practices and recommendations for voting at an investee company's AGM. The 2017 guidance also includes recommendations on the reporting of corporate cultures and working practices and emphasises the importance of boardroom diversity, with particular reference to targets on gender and ethnic diversity identified in the Davies and Parker reports respectively.'

9.2   The Investment Association

The Investment Association has a series of guidelines in which it sets out member expectations on issues such as corporate governance, share capital management, and other issues relating to capital markets.

Several of these guidelines were originally produced by the Association of British Insurers (ABI). Following the merger of ABI Investment Affairs with the IMA on 30 June 2014, the IA assumed responsibility for guidance previously issued by the ABI.

A list of the current guidelines which number over 20 can be found on the Investment Association's website. They include guidelines on the following topics:

◆   executive remuneration;
◆   long-term reporting;
◆   stakeholder engagement;
◆   audit tendering;
◆   virtual-only AGMs; and
◆   share capital management.

9.3   International shareholder advisory bodies

Due to the global nature of shareholdings, organisations such as Glass Lewis and International Institutional Shareholders also express opinions on UK companies. Company secretaries/governance professionals should be aware of the views of these companies as far as they affect their company. In turn, when the board is discussing issues they have an opinion on then this should be brought to the attention of the board and management if they are unaware.

10. Responsible investment versus socially responsible investment

Many investors, in addition to their views on corporate governance, are developing strong views about social and environmental issues. These views often affect their investment decision making.

PLSA, among other shareholder representative bodies, issued guidance in 2005, to its members on responsible investment. The guidance comments that:

'There is robust evidence that extra financial factors – often referred to as Environmental, Social or Governance (ESG) factors … can significantly impact a company's long-term value, reputation, brand, growth rate, margins, market share and borrowing costs.'

PLSA therefore recommends that investors take these factors into account when making investment decisions and consider whether the policies and actions of the company are consistent with value protection and enhancement.

The PLSA guidance differentiates between responsible investing, which it covers, and socially responsible investment (SRI), which it does not.

◆ Responsible or ethical investing means refusing to invest in 'unethical' companies and 'sin stocks', that is, companies that produce or sell addictive substances (like alcohol, gambling and tobacco) because the activities of the company are inconsistent with the investor's ethical, moral or religious beliefs.

◆ SRI investing goes further. It includes refusing to invest in 'unethical' companies, but SRI investors also encourage companies to develop CSR policies and objectives, in addition to pursuing financial objectives. SRI investors will seek out companies engaged in social justice, environmental sustainability and alternative energy/clean technology efforts. SRI investors may also be involved in shareholder activism when companies have social or environmental policies with which they disagree.

10.1 Pursuing an SRI strategy

There are several different ways in which institutional investors may pursue an SRI strategy:

◆ engagement;
◆ investment preference; and
◆ screening.

With an engagement strategy, the institutional investor acquires shares in which it wants to invest (for financial reasons) but then engages with the board of directors and tries to persuade the company to adopt policies that are socially responsible, or to make improvements in its CSR policies. Engagement may therefore involve expressing the views of the investor about telling what the CSR policies of the company should be and persuading it to change its policies in some areas (through regular meetings with its senior directors). If the company indicates its willingness to make changes, the investor may also offer to help with the formulation of new policies.

With an investment preference strategy, the investor develops a set of guidelines that companies should meet. The investor will then invest only in the shares (or other securities) of companies that meet the guidelines, some of which will be social, ethical or environmental in nature. With this strategy, its investment decisions need not be based entirely on SRI considerations. The investor can also consider the expected financial returns from an investment, and the selected investment portfolio can be a suitable balance of investments that are ethically sound and those that are not as ethical (or are 'riskier' in social or environmental terms) but should provide better financial returns.

With a screening strategy, investments are restricted to companies that pass a 'screen test' for ethical behaviour. Screening may be positive or negative. Positive screening means that companies must meet certain criteria for ethical and socially responsible behaviour; otherwise, the investor will not buy its shares. Negative screening means that an investor will identify companies that fail to meet certain minimum criteria for socially responsible behaviour and will refuse to buy shares in those companies. The screening process could make use of a published CSR index, such as the Dow Jones Sustainability Indices or the FTSE 4 Good indices. These are described in Chapter 11.

Investors that have an SRI strategy need information about the CSR performance of companies in which they invest in order to assess the success of their investment strategies. Company secretaries should ensure that sufficient information is provided through the company's publications for the institutional investor to make an assessment of the company's ESG activities. Methods of reporting CSR performance are described in Chapter 11.

Test yourself 14.4

1. **What is the difference between responsible investing and socially responsible investment?**

2. **What are the ways in which an investor can pursue an SRI strategy?**

Chapter summary

♦ Many individual shareholders believe they are shareholders of the company and call companies expecting to be treated as such. The company has no record of them as they are not registered members of the company. These individuals hold their shares through nominee companies for a variety of reasons including ease of transfer. The CA2006 included rights for these indirect shareholders.

♦ Institutional shareholders, such as banks, insurance companies and pension funds hold broad portfolios of listed company shares in an attempt to spread risk.

♦ The powers and rights of shareholders have developed to manage issues resulting from the separation of ownership and control in companies and also to protect minority shareholder rights.

♦ Shareholder rights cover the following:
  – ownership and transfer;
  – equal treatment;
  – share in the profits;
  – receipt of information; and
  – attend and speak at meetings and vote.

♦ Common abuses of shareholder rights include the following:
  – market abuse and insider dealing;
  – dilution;
  – tunneling; and
  – related party transactions.

♦ Shareholders are able to bring a cause of action on behalf of the company through a 'derivative claim' against a director for negligence, default or breach of duty.

♦ Institutional shareholders should take an interest in the companies in which they invest, however, sometimes the expense and time required to enter into a productive dialogue with the company may not be worth it for the level of investment, often less than 1% of the company.

♦ Evidence has shown that in the last five years engagement between shareholders and the companies has increased with interest in the impact of technological change and ESG factors.

♦ Shareholder activism is not always negative – it can be positive and constructive. It only becomes aggressive when companies fail to listen or engage properly with the institutional investor.

♦ The UK Stewardship Code aims to enhance the quality of engagement between investors and companies to help improve the long-term risk adjusted returns to the providers of capital for companies. The Code consists of seven principles with guidance for each.

◆ The company secretary plays an important role in ensuring that the engagement between companies and their shareholders happens effectively.

◆ There are two main UK shareholder representative bodies who engage in issuing guidance to institutional shareholders. These are:

– The Investment Association (incorporating guidance from the Associated British Insurers (ABI)).

– Pension and Lifetime Savings Association (PLSA) (formerly the National Association of Pension Funds (NAPF)).

◆ UK listed companies also communicate directly with some institutional shareholders, such as Hermes, who have their own corporate governance units.

◆ There are also international shareholder bodies who engage UK listed companies in discussions about ESG factors.

◆ There is a difference between responsible investing and socially responsible investing (SRI). The first means refusing to invest in companies that that produce or sell products that are inconsistent with the investors' ethical, moral or religious beliefs. The second, SRI, is wider in scope, with investors also encouraging companies to develop CSR policies and objectives, in addition to pursuing financial objectives.

◆ SRI investors will seek out companies engaged in social justice, environmental sustainability and alternative energy/clean technology efforts. SRI investors may also be involved in shareholder activism when companies have social or environmental policies with which they disagree.

◆ institutional investors may pursue an SRI strategy in the following ways:

– engagement;

– investment preference; and

– screening.

Chapter fifteen

Board engagement with shareholders and other stakeholders

CONTENTS

1. Introduction

The UK Corporate Governance Code 2018 (the 2018 Code) Principle D states that 'in order for the company to meet its responsibilities to shareholders and stakeholders, the board should ensure effective engagement with, and encourage participation from, these parties'. In the previous chapter we looked at the shareholders' side of the engagement; in this chapter we consider what the board can do to promote a successful dialogue. We also consider the board's responsibilities to the wider stakeholder group.

2. Shareholder engagement

It is important for the smooth running of companies for the shareholders and the companies in which they invest to be on good terms. This is usually achieved through a dialogue between the company and the shareholders.

The 2018 Code (Provision 3) and accompanying FRC Guidance on Board Effectiveness state that, in addition to formal general meetings:

◆ The chair should seek regular engagement with major shareholders in order to understand their views on governance and performance against the company's strategy.

◆   Chairs of board committees should also seek engagement with shareholders on significant matters related to their areas of responsibility. Where relevant, the chair of a board committee should make the whole board aware of shareholders' views on a particular matter.

◆   The senior independent director, when called upon, should meet a sufficient range of major shareholders to develop a balanced understanding of their views.

◆   Boards should consider additional ways to engage with smaller shareholders, for example by way of roundtables and webinars.

2.1   ICSA guidance on engagement

In 2013, ICSA published 'Enhancing Stewardship Dialogue', which provides guidance on the relationship between companies and their investors. The aim of the guidance is to improve the process of engagement between the company and its shareholders, by focusing conversations on 'the things that really matter in creating and destroying value, that is on strategy, risk and long-term comparative performance'.

The ICSA guidance recognises that companies may have difficulty in identifying which investors it should engage with (since the share register may continually change) and which individuals within large institutional investor organisations it should be speaking with.

There are four main elements to the ICSA guidance:

1.   Develop an engagement strategy. Companies should develop an investor engagement strategy and review it annually. This annual review should be referred to in the corporate governance section of the company's annual report. The strategy should consist of a combination of one-to-one meetings with the largest shareholders and group meetings for a number of smaller investors. Meetings should be ongoing – regular, and not driven by events or specific issues. The ICSA guidance also suggests that there may occasionally be merit in organising collective engagement for a number of the largest shareholders.

2.   Get the housekeeping right. The company should ensure that it invites the 'right people' to meetings. These will be mainly large shareholders and investors with a strong track record of engagement. The company should also ensure that individuals within the company attend who are best placed to speak on the issues that will be discussed at the meeting.

    From the investors' point of view, voting at the next annual general meeting should reflect the outcome of discussions at the meetings held as part of the engagement process. If shareholders intend to vote differently at the AGM, they should tell the company in advance, to give the board of directors time to work further on the engagement process.

3.   Strengthen the conversation. Meetings should discuss matters that are of direct relevance to the company's value. There should be at least one engagement meeting a year that focuses on the company's strategy and performance. Remuneration should not be allowed to dominate

discussions and should be discussed within the context of creating value. The ICSA guidance suggests that although executive directors may be invited to the strategy and performance meeting, they may be asked at some stage to leave the meeting, so that the shareholders can discuss the issues with the chair and other non-executive directors.

4. Provide feedback. There should be feedback in both directions. The procedures for providing feedback should be agreed and should relate to the matters discussed at meetings and the engagement process overall. From the company's perspective, feedback may consist of a series of questions from the company, such as:

    – Did you meet the right people?

    – Did the meeting cover all the topics that you expected?

    – Were there any aspects of the discussions that surprised you?

    – Have you learned anything from the meeting that might influence your view of the company as an investment?

Test yourself 15.1

What ways, in addition to general meetings, should boards use when engaging with their shareholders?

3. Annual general meetings

One of the most important ways companies communicate with their shareholders is through the annual general meetings (AGMs). Although the 2018 Code does not now refer to AGMs, the FRC Guidance on Board Effectiveness recommends that companies send out to shareholders at least 20 working days before the meeting, the notice of the meeting and related papers. This is to ensure that shareholders have sufficient time to consider any issues presented by the papers. The CA2006 requires a minimum of 21 calendar days.

Previous codes have suggested the following procedures for AGMs.

Giving shareholders an opportunity to ask questions.
There should be a formal question and answer session at the annual general meeting. Although this is supposed to only relate to the business of the meeting, that is the resolutions that are presented, most companies allow shareholders to ask questions on a wider range of issues. Companies manage questions at an AGM differently:

◆ some allow shareholders free range to ask questions using roving microphones;

◆ others require shareholders to walk to a fixed microphone to ask their question;

◆ some companies require shareholders to register their questions either before or at the meeting.

Whatever method is chosen, the company secretary should ensure that the chair is fully briefed on any potential questions that may arise. A book of Q&As is usually prepared based on recurring questions from previous years, questions that have been recently received by the chair's office and anticipated questions on the business of the meeting. Some company secretaries/governance professionals hold dress rehearsals of the Q&A session with the chair and the chairs of the board committees, requesting management to act as shareholders and fire questions at those who may be asked to answer questions at the AGM.

The board chair should arrange for the chairs of the audit, nomination and remuneration committees to be available to answer questions at the AGM, and for all directors to attend the meeting.

According to Equiniti's Registration Services, AGM Trends 2017, topics raised by shareholders include questions on:

◆ strategy, the annual report, dividend payments and results;

◆ executive and employee renumeration;

◆ governance and diversity;

◆ Brexit;

◆ corporate social responsibility including health and safety and the environment; and

◆ the AGM venue and arrangements.

Interestingly questions are rarely asked on specific resolutions.

Voting procedures

At the AGM, there should be a separate resolution for each substantially separate issue. This requirement is intended to prevent the practice of combining two or more issues, one 'popular' and the other more controversial, into a single resolution. Each issue will then be voted on separately.

The company secretary should check when the resolutions are drafted that issues are separated. For example, if there are to be changes to the articles of association these should all be separated and not presented as an all-encompassing single resolution to change the articles.

The company also needs to decide how the resolutions should be voted on – by poll or by a show of hands. Listed companies should vote by way of poll, that is by indicating on a voting card at the meeting how they wish to vote on each resolution. The advantage of voting by poll is two-fold:

◆ all the shares owned by the shareholder are counted not just one per person present as is the case on a show of hands; and

◆ votes sent in by proxy are included in the count.

The company secretary would usually liaise with a company's share registrars and the vote scrutineer to ensure that the process and systems are in place for the poll vote. Many companies now use electronic poll voting at the meeting.

vote withheld
A voting option for shareholders who appoint a proxy, as an alternative to voting for or against a may be instructed to abstain on a particular resolution at the general meeting. Votes withheld are 'positive abstentions' and the number of votes withheld should be counted and recorded.

Proxy voting forms should include a 'vote withheld' box.
This is in addition to the 'for' and 'against' boxes for each resolution. The 'vote withheld' box allows shareholders to indicate their displeasure about a company's proposals without actually voting against the resolution in question. However, a vote withheld is not a vote in law and so does not count towards the proportion of votes cast in favour of or against a resolution (for the purpose of deciding whether a resolution has been passed or rejected).

The number of resolutions which are not passed by shareholders at general meetings is very small. The UK Corporate Governance Code 2018 requires when 20% or more of votes have been cast against a board recommended resolution, the company should explain, when announcing the results, what actions it intends to take to consult shareholders in order to understand the reasons behind the result. The company should publish no later than six months after the general meeting, an update on the views received from shareholders and the actions taken by the company in response to them. A final report should be provided by the board in the company's next annual report.

proxy vote
A vote delivered by an individual (a proxy) on behalf of a shareholder, in the shareholder's absence.

Disclosure of information about proxy votes.
After a resolution has been dealt with on a show of hands, the company should indicate the level of votes lodged for and against the resolution, including proxy votes, and the number of shares in respect of which there was a specific instruction to withhold a vote. This information should be given at the meeting itself and made available as soon as practicable afterwards on the company's website. By announcing the number of votes including proxy votes, companies will give some recognition to the views of shareholders unable to attend the meeting, and will not be able to pass controversial resolutions simply on a show of hands of shareholders present and attending the meeting, when a vote on a show of hands differs significantly from what the results of a poll vote would have been.

If the results of a poll vote would have been different the company secretary should advise the chair to call for a poll.

There are limitations to the use of the AGM as a method for dialogue between companies and their shareholders. These include:

- The fact that the meeting is held only once a year.
- The location may make it difficult for shareholders to attend. Many AGMs are held in central London during the week so shareholders who live outside London or overseas may find it difficult to attend. Also, shareholders who work may not be able to get time off work to attend the AGM.
- AGMs often have a limited time duration imposed by the venue, the shareholders or the company. Chairmen wherever possible should allow all shareholders wanting to ask a question to do so.

This is why many companies seek other methods of engaging with their shareholders to make the interactions more meaningful and effective.

Case study 15.1

TV Presenter Noel Edmonds purchased one share at 67 pence in Lloyds Banking Group so that he could attend the 2018 AGM. He is seeking compensation after allegedly falling victim to a fraud by former staff at HBOS, which became part of Lloyds during the financial crisis. Mr Edmonds was also against pay plans for the top bosses.

3.1 Virtual AGMs

Section 360A of CA2006 permits a UK company to offer shareholders an electronic means for participating in a general meeting. The electronic means has to be real time, allow for two-way conversation and have a mechanism for shareholders to vote.

UK listed companies have done this by providing shareholders who could not attend the physical meeting access through either a web browser, conference call dial-in or satellite links. In 2016, Jimmy Choo held the first fully electronic AGM for a UK listed company.

Case study 15.2

Jimmy Choo PLC held the first fully electronic AGM for a UK listed company in 2016. It was different from previous AGMs that had used electronic means of participation as there was no physical place for the meeting. Shareholders were only able to participate through a conference call dial-in, to enable shareholders to ask questions, and an app and web browser so that shareholders could see the presentations made by management and vote. Shareholders were given a unique number and password so that the chair at all times knew who was participating in the AGM.

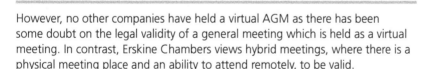

However, no other companies have held a virtual AGM as there has been some doubt on the legal validity of a general meeting which is held as a virtual meeting. In contrast, Erskine Chambers views hybrid meetings, where there is a physical meeting place and an ability to attend remotely, to be valid.

Things for companies to consider if they are planning to hold a virtual AGM:

Amendment of articles of association
Articles of association (AoA) will need to be amended so that the provisions do not imply that the general meeting must be held in a physical place, for example, historically, AoA have required notice of the time, date and place of the AGM, which implies a physical meeting. AoA should also cater for failures in technology whether this affects one person or a group of people, for example, by giving the chair the discretion to adjourn the meeting where the technology fails.

Views of their shareholders

Prior to deciding to hold a virtual AGM, the company should consult with their shareholders. It will depend on the make-up of a company's shareholder base and the number of retail shareholders who attend the AGM whether a company will get a favourable response to a proposal to hold its AGM virtually. Some individual shareholders who see AGMs as a day out where they meet old friends may not be too enamoured about the prospect of a virtual AGM which would deprive them of this opportunity.

Although many shareholders may have the tools to attend a virtual AGM, such as a web browser and smart phone, they may not feel comfortable in using them to attend a virtual meeting.

Mort and Wallace (2017) reported that no shareholder or shareholder representative body publicly objected to Jimmy Choo holding a virtual AGM.

Shareholder representative bodies, such as, the Investment Association (IA) and Pensions and Investments Research Consultants (PIRC) have, however, expressed concerns in their guidance materials about companies only holding virtual meetings.

The Investor Association in their Position Statement: Virtual-Only AGMs published in December 2017 stated:

'Our members believe that virtual-only AGMs are not in the best interests of all shareholders and should not be used by investee companies, as their use could be detrimental to board accountability. IA members are unlikely to be supportive of amendments to articles of association which allow for virtual-only AGMs.'

This is because the AGM is seen as the only opportunity that shareholders have to meet and question the whole board of a company. In reality, many institutional shareholders do not send representatives to attend AGMs unless there is a controversial issue. It is the retail shareholder in many FTSE100 companies who would be affected the most by this change in format of AGMS.

Technological considerations

Companies will have to engage with technology providers and make sure all of their requirements can be met. Participants will need to be able, in real time, to:

◆ hear the proceedings;
◆ see any presentations made;
◆ ask questions speak and hear responses; and
◆ vote.

The technology providers will in turn have to liaise with the company's registrars on voting requirements as it will remain the registrar's responsibility to count the votes.

The chair of the meeting needs to know who is speaking. The company secretary needs to know who is present at the meeting so they can establish that a quorum is always present.

Notice of meeting
Companies will have to redesign their notices of meeting. Instead of an address for the meeting, clear instructions on how to access, speak and vote at the meeting will have to be provided together with a helpline number for shareholders requiring assistance. All voting will have to be done on a poll and the notice should make this clear.

Proxy form
Companies will also have to alter their proxy forms which also usually contain information about the place of a physical meeting.

Helpline
A helpline will have to be established for any shareholders who require assistance in preparing for the meeting – acquiring apps and setting up for the meeting, accessing the meeting on the day or voting. The company will have to decide, in liaison with the technology provider and registrars, who the shareholder accesses via the helpline as this may differ based on the shareholder's query.

Preparing the chair and the board
As new procedures will be involved, the chair and board will need briefing. The company secretary may, with the help of the technology provider and registrars, prepare a detailed script for the chair. Rehearsals will also have to be held including preparing for questions and voting. The chair will also have to be prepared to answer questions from shareholders on the new arrangements.

Decisions will need to be taken as to how the board will attend the meeting. Certain members of the board, such as the chairs of the audit committee and the remuneration committee, will have to be available to answer questions if the company is a listed company as this is a requirement of the UK Corporate Governance Code. The board could attend from the company's boardroom or could be in separate locations. The former would probably be advisable as the chair, assisted by the company secretary, would be able to manage the meeting better if the board and senior management were in the same place. For multinationals, it may be that the board could consider two venues for the board joined by video conference.

On the day of the meeting, the company secretary should:

◆ Check that the technology is working. Contingency planning should have been put in place. If this also fails then the chair should adjourn the meeting, if there is a provision in the AoA to allow for this.

◆ Check that the legal and regulatory requirements are met for the holding of a meeting. These will include checking that a quorum is always present, that the process for counting the votes, by way of a poll, is followed and that the documents required to be on display are on display at the company's premises. Provision for the documents to also be available online will also have to be considered.

3.2 AGM trends

over boarding
These are directors who sit on excessive number of boards, hence failing to do their jobs thoroughly because of too many commitments.

Equiniti's Registration Services analysis of 2016/2017 AGMs published in a report 'AGM Trends 2017' gives the following advice on trends governance professionals should consider when planning for their next AGMs:

- There appears to be a widening of shareholder rebellions from just directors' remuneration issues to concerns over governance issues such as independence of directors and **over boarding**.
- Remuneration is a concern to shareholders where there is a perception that bonuses and pay rises are not warranted by performance.
- There is continued interest in electronic meetings
- There is a focus on non-financial reporting, largely due to regulatory changes and the expectations of stakeholders.
- Shareholders are willing to take action in specific cases of high-profile accounting or management irregularities.

Test yourself 15.2

1. **What are the limitations to the use of an AGM as a method of engaging with shareholders?**

2. **What is a virtual AGM and why do shareholder representative bodies have concerns about them?**

3. **What things should a company consider when planning to hold a virtual AGM?**

4. Electronic communication

4.1 Shareholder communications

The CA2006 introduced the following provisions into law relating to how a company communicates with its shareholders.

- Documents and information are now able to be sent by or to companies either in hard copy form or electronic form, i.e. email or fax. Under the Disclosure Guidance and Transparency Rules, listed companies need to obtain a shareholder resolution for communications to be sent by email and fax.
- Companies are also permitted, if a shareholder has not opted out, to communicate with their shareholders by means of a website. Notifications of any such communications will have to be sent in hard copy unless the shareholder has assented to receiving them by email or fax. The use of the company's website for shareholder communications requires the passing of a shareholders' resolution or permission in the company's articles.

- Shareholders always have the right to ask for a hard copy of the communications they receive electronically.

Many companies have adopted this method of communicating with their shareholders due to the benefits it presents to both the company and the shareholders.

- It should be much cheaper to produce documents in electronic form and use e-mails or a website for communicating with shareholders, than it is to print documents and send them out by post.
- There may also be environmental benefits, for large companies with many shareholders (less wastage of natural resources such as paper).
- For some shareholders, particularly foreign shareholders, communication should be much faster and possibly more reliable.
- Companies should also be able to provide more communication, such as posting the results of polls at general meetings on their website, so that shareholders are better informed.
- Large institutional investors may also benefit, because information sent or notified electronically is more likely to be seen by the key decision makers within large investor institutions: printed copies of annual reports and accounts are more likely to be handled by junior staff.
- The ability to appoint proxies electronically (or vote electronically) may also improve the probability that shareholders will participate in decision making by submitting proxy votes.

4.2 ICSA guidance on electronic communications

ICSA has issued a guidance note on 'Electronic communications with shareholders' (2013) which includes practical guidelines for best practice in communication in electronic form. These recommendations include the following suggestions:

- The facility to communicate in electronic form should be offered to all shareholders on equal terms.
- Shareholders should be able to retain a copy of any document or information sent to them in electronic form.
- Any electronic communication sent by a company giving notice of a general meeting and proxy voting should not include any electronic address unless the company intends that this address may be used by shareholders to respond to their communication.
- When information or notifications of availability (of information on the website) are sent to shareholders, the company should use a system for producing a list of recipients or a total number of messages sent, as 'proof of sending'.
- Shareholders opting to communicate electronically should be warned that if they file an electronic proxy voting form containing a virus, the company will not accept it.

◆ The company should alert shareholders to the fact that the company's obligation to communicate electronically ends with the transmission of the message, and the company cannot be responsible for failed transmissions that are outside their control. However, in the case of failed transmissions, the company should send a written communication to the shareholder within 48 hours of the failure.

5. Engagement with other stakeholders

As we have seen elsewhere within this study text, there is a greater focus in recent years for companies to engage with a wider stakeholder group. The 2018 Code (Provision 5) states that:

'The board should understand the views of the company's other key stakeholders and describe in the annual report how their interests and the matters set out in section 172 of the CA2006 have been considered in board discussions and decision-making. The board should keep engagement mechanisms under review so that they remain effective.'

The Oxford dictionary defines a 'stakeholder' as 'a person with an interest or concern in something, especially business'. CA2006 limits the stakeholder group to employees, suppliers, customers and others determined by the company. Companies will be required to report in their annual reports how the interests of stakeholders have been considered in board discussions and decision-making.

Larry Fink, the CEO of BlackRock, in his 2019 Letter to CEOs states: 'companies that fulfil their purpose and responsibilities to stakeholders reap rewards over the long-term. Companies that ignore them stumble and fail. This dynamic is becoming increasingly apparent as the public holds companies to more exacting standards.' The failure of governments to provide lasting solutions to pressing social and economic issues, among them, stagnant wages, the effect of technology on jobs, protecting the environment, gender and racial inequality, retirement and uncertainty about the future, has led society to look to companies to provide solutions to these issues. The pressure on companies to account for their activities in these areas will only continue to grow fuelled by social media. Company secretaries/governance professionals will have to be alert to these issues as far as they impact their organisations and make sure that information on them flows as appropriate to their boards as part of the decision-making process.

Stop and think 15.1

Who are your organisation's stakeholders? What is the interest they have in your organisation? How are you engaging with them?

5.1 Ways to engage with stakeholders

The following are ways that companies can interact with stakeholders.

Reactively
The organisation engages defensively, when forced to in response to a crisis and usually in an attempt to rebuild its reputation.

Proactively
The organisation tries to understand its stakeholders' concerns and issues. The company secretary could advise the board and management to:

◆ Carry out customer surveys, focus groups, shareholder surveys, competitor research, and so on. This information can then feed into the decision-making process.

◆ Engage directly with stakeholders to get their input before making decisions. This is often the case with shareholders and their representative bodies. Organisations will run a proposal or idea past some of their larger shareholders before making a final decision on an issue, such as remuneration packages for directors or senior executives.

◆ Involve stakeholders in the decision-making process. For example, an organisation could bring together groups of stakeholders (employees, the community, and so on.) and ask them to vote on an action. For example, LaFarge Cement involved people in the community in Morocco in the process of finding a new location for a cement plant.

Interactively
The organisation has ongoing relationships of mutual respect, openness, and trust with stakeholders. The organisation can do this through many of the channels mentioned under 'proactively' above.

Most engagements have fixed timetables to ensure that results are achieved. The company secretary may be asked to develop a timetable, which should be based on input from all parties. It is important to establish ground rules for public disclosure and for managing expenses related to the engagement. Organisations should avoid giving money to stakeholder groups as part of the engagement as this could be misconstrued as a bribe. Any money that is paid over should be documented and reported, giving the reason for the payment.

Communication to employees about the purpose of the engagement, and what the organisation seeks to achieve from it is also important and ensures that the organisation communicates a consistent message.

Where issues and concerns raised through a stakeholder engagement cannot be addressed, an organisation should be honest and transparent about why this is the case. For example, many pharmaceutical companies are asked by stakeholders to eliminate testing on animals, but many governments require such tests for product approval. Novo Nordisk, the world's largest maker of insulin products for diabetics, acknowledges that reducing its reliance on testing on animals is desirable, but notes that it cannot do so until governments change the approvals process. The company publicly reports on the number of animals used in testing and its progress in changing or influencing government policies on product testing.

5.2 Engagement with the workforce

The 2018 Code (Principle E) states that: 'The board should ensure that workforce policies and practices are consistent with the company's values and support its long-term sustainable success. The workforce should be able to raise any matters of concern.'

Provision 5 of the 2018 Code states that for engagement with the workforce, one or a combination of the following methods should be used:

◆ a director appointed from the workforce;

◆ a formal workforce advisory panel;

◆ a designated non-executive director.

If the board has not chosen one or more of these methods, it should explain what alternative arrangements are in place and why it considers that they are effective.

Provision 6 of the 2018 Code states that there should be a means for the workforce to raise concerns in confidence and – if they wish – anonymously. The board should routinely review this and the reports arising from its operation. It should ensure that arrangements are in place for the proportionate and independent investigation of such matters and for follow-up action.

5.3 ICSA: The stakeholder voice in board decision making

ICSA, in collaboration with the Investment Association, issued 'The Stakeholder Voice in Board Decision Making' which is aimed at helping company boards think about how to ensure they understand and weigh up the interests of their key stakeholders when taking strategic decisions.

The guidance sets out the following 10 core principles:

◆ Boards should identify, and keep under regular review, who they consider their key stakeholders to be and why.

◆ Boards should determine which stakeholders they need to engage with directly, as opposed to relying solely on information from management.

◆ When evaluating their composition and effectiveness, boards should identify what stakeholder expertise is needed in the boardroom and decide whether they have, or would benefit from, directors with directly relevant experience or understanding.

◆ When recruiting any director, the nomination committee should take the stakeholder perspective into account when deciding on the recruitment process and the selection criteria.

◆ The chair – supported by the company secretary – should keep under review the adequacy of the training received by all directors on stakeholder-related matters, and the induction received by new directors, particularly those without previous board experience.

◆ The chair – supported by the board, management and the company secretary – should determine how best to ensure that the board's decision-making processes give sufficient consideration to key stakeholders.

◆ Boards should ensure that appropriate engagement with key stakeholders is taking place and that this is kept under regular review.

◆ In designing engagement mechanisms, companies should consider what would be most effective and convenient for the stakeholders, not just the company.

◆ The board should report to its shareholders on how it has taken the impact on key stakeholders into account when making decisions.

◆ The board should provide feedback to those stakeholders with whom it has engaged, which should be tailored to the different stakeholder groups.

6. The Wates Corporate Governance Principles for Large Private Companies

Principle six of the Wates Principles states that 'directors should foster effective stakeholder relationships aligned to the company's purpose. The board is responsible for overseeing meaningful engagement with stakeholders, including the workforce, and having regard to their views when taking decisions'.

The boards of large private companies should consider how their company's activities may impact both current and future stakeholders, which, for example, could include impacts on the environment.

Dialogue with stakeholders will help boards of large private companies understand the effects of company policies and practices, predict future developments and trends and re-align strategy. Boards should identify and prioritise stakeholder relationships for those affected by company operations and are integral to its ability to generate and preserve value. These are likely to vary dependent on the size and nature of the company. Stakeholders include the workforce, customers and suppliers, but also other material stakeholders specific to company circumstances or sectors, such as regulators, governments, pensioners, creditors and community groups.

The board should present to stakeholders a fair, balanced and understandable assessment of the company's position and prospects and make this available on an annual basis. Boards should also ensure that there are channels to receive appropriate feedback from discussions with stakeholders. When explaining the company's impact on the community or environment, boards may want to refer to any recognised international standards or frameworks that the company follows. Further details on the recognised international standards and frameworks can be found in Part 3.

7. Impact of Section 172 duty to promote the success of the company on stakeholder engagement

As we saw in Chapters 5 and 11, directors have a duty to act in a way that promotes the success of the company and, under the Companies (Miscellaneous Reporting) Regulations 2018, to report on their adoption of the s. 172 requirements in their annual reporting. Boards are coming to terms as to what this means in relation to how they conduct their decision making as they may have to report in their s. 172 statements how regard was had to the matters set out in s. 172, including:

◆ the likely consequences of any decision in the long term;

◆ the interests of the company's employees;

◆ the need to foster business relationships with suppliers, customers and others;

◆ the impact of the company's operations on the community and the environment;

◆ the desirability for the company to maintain a reputation for high standards of business conduct;

◆ the need to act fairly as between members of the company.

The company secretary should review the governance framework of the organisation – structures, policies and procedures – to see if any changes are required to meet the reporting requirements for s. 172. They will also have to build into the board's calendar time for the board to engage with stakeholders or receive feedback from them prior to board meetings where decisions will be made on particular aspects of the organisation's business where a particular stakeholder may have an interest.

The company secretary will also be called upon to advise the board on what disclosures will be made and what engagement may be required with different stakeholder groups prior to the reporting to ensure that any reputational risk is minimised.

Complying with s. 172 may also require changes to the organisation's strategy, targets and risk management processes. The company secretary should ensure that the board considers stakeholder engagement as wider than just corporate social responsibility. There will obviously be a link to CSR but engagement with stakeholders should be considered in all decision-making. For example, the closure of shops in a retail business will have an impact on employees, customers and suppliers, and this impact should be considered as part of the decision making process related to this matter.

8. Role of the governance professional in stakeholder engagement

In many companies, the board looks to the company secretary or governance professional to assist with stakeholder engagement. The company secretary would typically do this in the ways described below.

8.1   Explaining to the board the business case for stakeholder engagement

The business case for stakeholder engagement is:

◆ Markets perceive them as less hostile to local values and ways of operating.

◆ Create value and wealth.

◆ Gain and retain loyal customers while avoiding boycotts or other undesirable consumer actions.

◆ Create the perception that the company is a desirable place to work and increase ability to recruit and retain talented staff members.

◆ Identify ways to increase efficiency and reduce costs in their operations.

◆ Show a more responsible approach to risk taking, which reduces risk.

◆ Become better able to leverage opportunities, giving the company competitive advantage as they are able to identify new ideas for products or services that address stakeholder needs. Effective stakeholder engagement promotes corporate learning and innovation.

◆ Be more readily welcomed into new markets, as companies embedded in those markets perceive them as less hostile to local values and ways of operating.

8.2   Assisting the board with stakeholder engagement

The company secretary may be called upon to assist and advise the board in the following areas:

◆ Identifying which stakeholders have legitimate expectations and interests.

◆ Mapping the power and interest of stakeholders or stakeholder groups, so that they can develop a strategy for engaging with them.

◆ Identifying, discussing and prioritising the key risks associated with changing societal expectations.

◆ Determining the board's financial and nonfinancial needs for decision making, management oversight, and monitoring with regard to key stakeholder relationships associated with creating value and long-term sustainability.

◆ Discussing and approving key performance indicators for social, environmental and financial performance.

◆ Approving a policy for external, financial, nonfinancial (sustainability) or integrated reporting.

◆ Looking to integrate stakeholder issues into annual shareholder meetings. This can be done through resolutions, presentations at meetings, and/or displays at the entrance or in the meeting room.

◆ Discussing the risks and impacts (positive and negative) of projects and operations and providing transparent disclosure information to stakeholders (including shareholders).

◆ Convening stakeholder forums and inviting key stakeholder representatives to address board meetings, so members of boards hear from stakeholders directly about their concerns and issues.

◆ Documenting the concerns and issues of stakeholders and lessons learned and feeding this into the risk management, strategic planning and business continuity processes, so that the company is able to leverage opportunities and lessen negative impacts.

◆ Recognising that different stakeholder groups may have different interests and ideas. Tailoring engagement and dialogue to better represent stakeholders' disparate interests to help them understand the reasons for board decisions.

◆ Developing policies on who within the organisation should be the prime communicator for each stakeholder group.

◆ Advising the board on any reputational risk aspects to stakeholder engagement.

◆ Coordinating with management to ensure that the board is advised on how to engage with different stakeholder groups.

8.3 Advising the board on reporting on stakeholder engagement

The company secretary advises the board on reporting – and ensuring that management make recommendations for reporting – to specific stakeholder groups, and where appropriate, develops reports to specific stakeholder groups. More information about the different tools for reporting can be found in Chapter 11.

8.4 Alerting the board and/or management to opportunities and risks associated with stakeholder engagements

The company secretary may be asked to work with management, compliance officers and investor relations officers to ensure that the correct strategies, policies and procedures are in place to manage risks, especially reputational risk, and to take advantage of the opportunities presented by particular stakeholders, particularly partnership opportunities that support the organisation's strategic objectives.

8.5 Advising the board on the setting up of a committee responsible for stakeholder issues

The company secretary should advise the board on whether a separate committee should be established to deal with stakeholder issues. These committees are often called the corporate responsibility committee, the ethics committee or the reputation committee, as they are often responsible for ethical and/or reputational issues. These committees often have members of management on them as well as the board members. The chair should be a board member, and the quorum should be a majority of board members. The company secretary typically would be the secretary of the committee.

Stop and think 15.2

1. What are the benefits of electronic shareholder communications?

2. What methods does the 2018 Code recommend for engaging with the workforce?

3. How can a company secretary assist the board in stakeholder engagement?

Chapter summary

◆ The 2018 Code recommends that companies should ensure effective engagement with and encourage participation from shareholders and other stakeholders,

◆ The main vehicle for shareholder engagement is the annual general meeting.

◆ In addition, the chair and other board members should seek, as appropriate, meetings with major shareholders to develop an understanding of their views.

◆ Small shareholders should be engaged through roundtables and webinars.

◆ The company secretary is usually involved in the annual general meeting and should ensure that:

  – shareholders are given the opportunity to ask questions;

  – resolutions are 'unbundled', i.e. voted on separately for each substantial issue;

  – shareholders appointing proxies are given the power to withhold their votes; and

  – information about the proxy votes is disclosed at the annual general meeting where voting is on a show of hands.

◆ The CA2006 permits virtual AGMs. However, the shareholder representative bodies are not in favour of total virtual AGMs they feel that there should be an opportunity for shareholders to meet the board face to face.

◆ Companies are, since CA2006, able to communicate electronically with their shareholders via email or by means of the company's website. Shareholders do have the right to request hard copy communications.

◆ There has been a greater focus in recent years for companies to engage with a wider stakeholder group. This is reflected in s. 172 of CA2006 which requires companies to include in their decision-making the interests of their employees, customers and suppliers and disclose in their annual reports how this has been done.

◆ The 2018 Code requires companies to chose one of the following methods for engagement with the workforce or explain what alternative measures have been put in place:

  – a director appointed from the workforce;

  – a formal workforce advisory panel; and

  – a designated non-executive director.

◆ Stakeholders can be engaged with reactively, proactively or interactively.

◆ The company secretary would typically have a role in advising the board on any engagement with stakeholders.

Chapter sixteen

Remuneration of directors and senior executives

CONTENTS

1. Introduction

Directors' remuneration has always been a difficult corporate governance issue because of the inherent conflicts of interest involved in directors being able to set or influence their own pay and the practical difficulties that shareholders face in having any realistic involvement in the decision-making process.

Standard articles of association, including the Model Articles, allow the board of directors to determine directors' pay. Most listed companies have articles which make similar provision. This does not necessarily mean that directors can participate in decisions on their own pay. Most articles provide that a director who has a material interest in any matter which comes before the board cannot vote on it or be counted in the quorum for that item.

In the nineteenth and early twentieth centuries, most listed company boards were comprised mainly of non-executive directors, some or all of whom had a significant stake in the company as shareholders. In some cases, the managing director of the company was not even a member of the board. As shareholders, the non-executives had a vested interest in ensuring that the company paid the managing director and other executives only what was strictly necessary in order to incentivise and retain them.

Over time, boards became increasingly professionalised. By the early 1980s they were typically dominated by executive directors who began to award themselves handsome pay increases and five-year rolling contracts, the maximum allowed under the law at the time.

In 1995, rising public disquiet over directors' pay eventually caused the Confederation of British Industry (CBI) to establish a special committee on directors' remuneration, chaired by Sir Richard Greenbury. The committee proposed a new code of best practice on executive remuneration (known as 'the Greenbury Code'). Its main innovation was to require listed companies to make detailed disclosures regarding the pay and benefits of individual directors to be made in a separate remuneration report within the annual report.

These measures had almost no effect in curbing increases in directors' pay. Indeed, many people now think they may have made matters worse. Everyone now knew what everyone else was earning and companies began to adopt pay policies based on this information. Most adopted a policy of paying their directors at least average or above average rates for their sector. Few adopted a policy of paying their directors below average rates. Basic economics suggests that the only possible result of this is that pay will continue to spiral upwards at an even faster rate, and this is what happened.

Between 1998 and 2015, the average total pay for CEOs of FTSE 100 companies increased over fourfold from about £1 million in 1998 to £4.3 million in 2015. This was largely accounted for by the growth in annual bonus and long-term incentive payments. In the same period, the ratio of average FTSE 100 CEO pay to the average pay of full-time employees in the UK increased from 47:1 in 1998 to 128:1 in 2015, according to the High Pay Centre. In 2017, the ratio increased yet further to around 145.

These pay increases for CEOs were not necessarily matched by increases in the long-term value of the companies they managed. Between 1998 and 2015, the FTSE 100 index increased only very slightly in value.

As disclosure was seemingly having no effect, the UK government introduced new rules in 2013 giving listed company shareholders more say over directors' pay. The new regime seems to have put the brakes on directors' pay, at least in its first few years of operation. However, the UK Government's Green Paper on Corporate Governance Reform (2016) noted that:

'There is a widespread perception that executive pay has become increasingly disconnected from both the pay of ordinary working people and the underlying long-term performance of companies. Executive pay is an area of significant public concern, with surveys consistently showing it to be a key factor in public dissatisfaction with large businesses.'

For example:

◆ research for PWC's 'Time to Listen' paper published in June 2016 found that two-thirds of respondents believe executive pay is too high; and

◆ a YouGov poll for the CIPD in September 2015 found that only 14% of respondents agreed that CEO pay is good value for investors.

2. Remuneration as a corporate governance issue

2.1 Why remuneration is an important corporate governance issue

The remuneration of directors is an important, but difficult, corporate governance issue for the following reasons.

◆ Companies need to attract and retain talented executives. Remuneration is one of the most important things that will help to achieve this.

◆ Remuneration incentives can be used to motivate executives to achieve better results for the company.

◆ Those incentives need to be aligned with the interests of shareholders and promote the success of the company. This is not easy to do.

◆ High salaries and performance-related pay are acceptable to investors if the executives are making good returns for shareholders. However, even investors can see the merit in having some sort of cap in place on what the executives can earn.

◆ Excessive remuneration for only moderate performance results in the company being run for the benefit of management rather than shareholders.

◆ In particular, directors should not be rewarded for failure.

◆ Directors should not be able to decide or influence their own remuneration. Where they are, this is likely to lead to a culture of excessive rewards.

◆ High levels of executive pay undermine public trust in large businesses.

◆ Remuneration committees should take into account the pay and conditions of employees when setting directors' pay. It does not look good if directors receive much larger pay increases than employees and looks even worse if they receive large pay increases after a round of redundancies.

◆ This may sometimes be unavoidable as directors' bonuses and incentives payments are based on past performance.

◆ Historically, shareholders have had very little influence over the remuneration of directors and senior executives. Although shareholders get to vote on the appointment and reappointment of directors, this happens after the company has entered into a service agreement with them.

◆   It would be impractical to require shareholders to approve each individual's remuneration package in advance.

◆   Shareholders can exercise greater control if they have a role in setting the company's remuneration policy for directors. Such a policy sets the boundaries within which executive remuneration will be structured.

◆   If shareholders are not happy with the way the policy has been implemented, they ought to be able take some action which forces the company to change its behaviour.

The remuneration of senior executives immediately below board level is also considered to be an important corporate governance issue as many of them will participate in the same sort of bonus and incentive arrangements as the directors.

2.2   Overview of the governance framework on directors' remuneration in the UK

In the UK, the governance framework on directors' remuneration for listed companies includes a mixture of statutory provisions, listing rule requirements and code recommendations. UK companies with a premium listing of equity shares have to comply with all these rules and report on their compliance with the UK Corporate Governance Code.

All UK companies are required under the CA2006 to make certain disclosures regarding directors' remuneration in their annual report and accounts. Quoted companies are required to publish much more detailed information in a separate report on directors' remuneration as part of their annual accounts and reports.

As mentioned previously, the CA2006 also gives shareholders a say in directors' remuneration by prohibiting quoted companies from making remuneration payments to directors unless they are in accordance with a directors' remuneration policy approved by shareholders. The policy must be approved by shareholders at least once every three years.

The Code plays an important part in establishing the processes by which directors' remuneration should be determined. It requires listed companies to establish a remuneration committee of independent non-executive directors to set the pay and benefits of the chair, executive directors and senior managers within the framework of the remuneration policy. The committee is also responsible for designing the policy for executive remuneration, which will form a substantial part of the policy that is put to shareholders. The CA2006 does not require quoted companies to establish a remuneration committee but, if there is one, requires various details about the committee to be disclosed in the directors' remuneration report.

The Code also includes some very broad recommendations on overall levels of pay and the design of performance-related incentives. This is supplemented by influential guidance issued by institutional investors and their representative bodies.

The Code also includes several measures that seek to prevent directors from being rewarded for failure, e.g. by restricting the length of service contracts and, therefore, the level of compensation that is awarded on termination.

The Listing Rules require UK companies with a premium listing to obtain shareholder approval for most long-term incentive schemes in which the directors may participate.

The Wates Corporate Governance Principles for Large Private Companies make a number of non-binding recommendations on directors' remuneration for large companies that are not subject to the UK Corporate Governance Code.

3. Elements of remuneration for executive directors and senior executives

Before we go on to look at the rules and code provisions on directors' remuneration in detail, it is useful to look at the basic elements of an executive directors' remuneration package. These are much more complicated than the arrangements for non-executive directors, who are simply paid directors' fees. In addition to being appointed as a director, executive directors are appointed under a service contract to perform executive management functions. Under that contract, the executives typically forego the payment of directors' fees and are paid a salary instead. Non-executive directors do not have a service contract. They are appointed using a relatively simple letter of appointment. Their fees are determined by the board.

3.1   Components of executive remuneration

The remuneration package for a director or senior executive is likely to consist of a combination of:

◆   basic salary;

◆   payments into a pension scheme for the individual (or payments in lieu);

◆   an annual bonus, usually linked to the annual financial performance of the company;

◆   long-term incentives, usually in the form of share options or share awards (sometimes called 'restricted stock awards'); and

◆   other benefits and perks, such as free medical insurance, a company car or accommodation.

Separate figures have to be disclosed in the annual remuneration report of a quoted company for each of these elements (see Section 9).

Remuneration can be divided into two elements – **fixed pay** and variable pay:

◆   The fixed element is the remuneration received by the director regardless of performance, such as their salary, benefits and any salary-related pension contributions.

fixed pay
The elements in a remuneration package that are a fixed amount each year, such as basic salary.

◆ The variable element consists of performance-related incentives, such as cash bonuses, share options and other long-term incentive schemes. Pay received under these elements is usually dependent on the performance of the company or the individual (or a combination of both).

It is not necessarily easy to decide the right balance between fixed and variable elements, or on the measures of performance for the variable elements. Some internet start-up companies give their directors and senior staff large share option awards and relatively low salaries. They are able to get away with this because the executives believe that by foregoing part of their salary, they will be able to reap even greater rewards in the future. By contrast, a director appointed to rescue a company in financial difficulty might expect a higher salary than usual but may still expect to have a generous incentive scheme that will pay out if they manage to turn the company around.

The variable elements of pay can be divided into:

◆ short-term incentives, often in the form of cash bonuses but maybe in the form of a grant of company shares; and

◆ long-term incentives, in the form of share options or share grants.

Short-term incentives are based on annual performance targets. Long-term incentives may be awarded each year, but are linked to performance over a longer period, typically three years or more.

Long-term incentive plans usually take the form of an award of either share options or fully paid shares in the company, although companies sometimes operate schemes under which equivalent cash rewards are paid.

performance-based incentives
Incentives to an individual, typically to an executive director and in the form of a cash bonus, that are achieved. Performance targets might be related to a rise in the share price, growth in sales or profits, growth in earnings per share, or to non-financial performance criteria.

3.2 Short-term performance-based incentives

Short-term performance-based incentives reward executives, usually with one or more cash bonus payments, if actual performance during a review period reaches or exceeds certain predetermined targets. Bonuses may depend on the achievement of both individual targets and the performance of the company as a whole. A threshold is normally set at which no bonus is paid. Thereafter, the bonus will increase in line with performance but may be subject to a cap.

The review period for short-term incentives is usually linked to the financial year, with the executive being rewarded according to the financial performance of the company in that year. There are many different ways of measuring financial performance.

All financial targets are liable to manipulation, including those which must be calculated in accordance with accounting standards. For example, Tesco famously agreed to pay a fine in 2017 of £129 million to avoid prosecution for overstating its 2014 profits. It reached what is known as a deferred prosecution agreement with the Serious Fraud Office after a two-year probe. Payments from its suppliers had been mis-booked and business costs had been glossed over.

The fact that a performance measure can be manipulated is not necessarily a good reason not to use it. One might reasonably expect the auditors and the audit committee to be on their guard to ensure that critical performance measures are not being manipulated and to pay particularly close attention to key judgement and estimates made by management in this regard.

What is probably more important is that the targets used are aligned with the interests of shareholders. This is not necessarily the case with certain profit targets. Higher annual profits do not necessarily guarantee higher dividends and higher share prices.

There are many different ways of measuring financial performance, including:

◆ earnings per share (profits after tax and any dividends paid on preference shares, divided by the total number of ordinary shares in issue);

◆ annual profit before interest and taxation (PBIT);

◆ total shareholder return (TSR) – this is a measure of the performance which combines share price appreciation and dividends paid to show the total return to the shareholder expressed as an annualised percentage. It is calculated by the growth in capital from purchasing a share in the company assuming that the dividends are reinvested each time they are paid;

◆ earnings before interest, taxation, depreciation and amortisation (EBITDA);

◆ return on capital employed (ROCE); and

◆ other key performance indicators – these are quantifiable values that the company uses internally to assess how effectively it is meeting its strategic objectives, such as cash conversion or net income.

Annual bonus schemes often measure performance against more than one target. Under this sort of arrangement, a director may not be entitled to receive a bonus unless both targets have been met. Alternatively, a company may operate more than one bonus scheme. One of the schemes could be linked to short-term financial results and the other, perhaps, to the achievement of individual or strategic objectives. Under this sort of arrangement, a director would usually be entitled to receive a bonus if only one of those targets was met.

A company might also offer a **deferred annual bonus scheme** whereby participants are entitled to use some or all of their annual cash bonus to buy shares in the company. These shares might then be held in trust for three years, after which the individual may be entitled to the award of additional free matching shares from the company, subject to a requirement that the company has met a target growth objective for the three-year period.

Even though annual bonuses can incentivise behaviour that is harmful to long-term success, they remain the most popular type of variable pay. According to the Grant Thornton Corporate Governance Review 2018:

◆ 96% of FTSE 350 companies have an annual bonus scheme.

◆ Some CEOs are potentially able to receive up to 435% of their salary. However, the median maximum bonus opportunity is 180% of salary for CEOs in the FTSE 100 and 150% in the FTSE 250.

◆ Specific financial measures based on the company's KPIs remain the most

deferred annual bonus scheme
An element in a remuneration package for directors or senior executives whereby the individuals are allowed to use some or all of their annual cash bonus entitlement to acquire shares in the company, which are then matched after several years (typically three years) by the award of additional free shares.

common performance measure for annual bonuses in the FTSE 350. They include total shareholder return, earnings per share, cash conversion, net income, return on capital employed, and profit before interest and tax.

◆   Only 23% of companies disclose specific non-financial targets.

Case study 16.1

In September 2002, the finance director of Anite plc (a UK software services company) resigned in the face of strong criticism from investors who were angry at the company's remuneration policy and acquisition strategy.

The individual concerned was one of the highest paid finance directors among UK technology companies, and his remuneration for the year to 30 April 2002 had risen 10% despite a collapse in the company's performance compared with the previous year.

Bonuses for the CEO and the finance director were based on profits before tax, exceptional items and goodwill, rather than earnings (profits after exceptional items, writing off goodwill and tax).

The company had a policy of growth through acquisitions and had made 17 acquisitions since April 2000. These resulted in large amounts of purchased goodwill. Writing off this goodwill reduced earnings, but not profits before goodwill.

The acquisitions were made with an open-ended purchase price. The final price depended on the performance of the purchased assets, with an 'earn-out' for the sellers of the acquired companies. All the purchases were paid for with new Anite shares.

The Anite share price fell by about 80% in the year to 30 April 2002, which meant that more shares had to be issued to pay for new acquisitions. The result was a big dilution in earnings per share. This reduction in earnings per share had no effect on the bonuses of the CEO and finance director. The new acquisitions added to profits before tax, exceptional items and goodwill, even though profits after exceptional items and goodwill fell.

The finance director, who was closely involved in the funding of the acquisitions, was therefore put under pressure to resign by shareholders. Had he not resigned, shareholders may well have voted to remove him at the next available opportunity.

3.3   Long-term incentives: share options

Share options may be given to executive directors and other senior managers as part of a long-term incentive scheme. The award of share options is usually conditional on the director or senior executive meeting certain performance targets. Each option gives the holder a right to buy a new share in the company at a fixed price on or after a specified date in the future (typically three years after the options were issued), provided that the individual still works for the company at that time. A director who is granted 2,000 options will have the right to subscribe for 2,000 shares.

The purchase price for the new shares under the option is known as the 'exercise price'. This will typically be the market value of the shares when the option was issued. Under the Listing Rules, the exercise price for options given to directors must not be less than the current market price for the company's shares on the date that the options are granted. If the market price of the company's shares goes up in the period between the issue of the options and the exercise date, the option holder will be able to make an immediate profit by exercising the options and selling the shares that they receive.

Options do not normally have to be exercised immediately. The executive can hold on to the share options and exercise them later, when the share price may have risen even further. However, they must be exercised within a maximum period after they have been granted, typically ten years, otherwise they will lapse.

3.4 Long-term incentives: grants of shares ('performance shares')

An alternative to a share option scheme is a grant of shares. These are sometimes referred to as performance shares. Directors and senior executives can be rewarded by the grant of existing shares in the company (which the company has bought back from other shareholders), provided that they are still in their job after a specified period of time, typically three years. At the time of grant, the director will not actually receive the shares or acquire ownership of them. This will not happen until the shares vest, which will be conditional on the achievement of certain performance targets during that time. For example, a scheme might award shares to a director provided that the company achieves targets for total shareholder return (TSR) over a three-year period relative to comparator companies. The individual might receive 30% of the available shares, say, if the company matches the TSR of comparator companies and 100% of the available shares if the company's TSR is comparable with the top quartile (25%) of comparator companies.

Grants of shares under such schemes are usually made on an annual basis.

With share options, the executive gets no benefit if the share price remains below the exercise price. With share grant schemes, however, the executive benefits even if the share price falls, because the shares still have some value.

3.5 Long-term incentive scheme performance measures

According to the Grant Thornton Corporate Governance Review 2018:

◆   97% of FTSE 350 companies reported in 2017 that they had some sort of long-term incentives scheme, with 74% using long-term incentive plans (LTIPs).

◆ The typical performance period under these plans was three years.

◆ TSR and EPS were the most common performance measures used for these incentive schemes. Most of those who used TSR, did so on a comparative basis against a peer group. Many companies use a broader range of metrics including other financial, strategic, personal and non-financial measures, such as customer service and employee engagement.

◆ The use of multiple performance measures remains widespread, with 71% of companies using more than one.

3.6 Problems with linking rewards to performance

The purpose of performance-related pay is to provide an incentive for executive directors and senior managers to improve the company's performance by linking their rewards to that performance. However, there are a number of practical difficulties in devising a satisfactory scheme, including:

◆ Selecting the right performance measures. For example, should short-term incentives be based exclusively on one or more financial targets, or should there be rewards for the achievement of individual non-financial targets?

◆ Setting the thresholds at which rewards are paid. These must be challenging but not so challenging that they appear unobtainable as they will no longer incentivise.

◆ Deciding whether to place a cap on any rewards under the incentive and determining the level of that cap.

◆ Ensuring that the targets used for short-term incentives like the annual bonus promote the long-term success of the company.

◆ Ensuring that the targets used for incentive schemes do not promote bad behaviour (such as the aggressive selling of PPI by banks).

◆ It is difficult to prevent executives who did not perform well from piggy-backing on the success of their colleagues. On the other hand, executives who did perform well may be dragged down by the performance of their colleagues.

◆ It is also difficult to prevent newly appointed executives from benefiting from the 'legacy effects' of their predecessors.

◆ Executives may develop an expectation that they should receive annual rewards regardless of the actual performance of the company.

◆ Designing a scheme that will be satisfactory to shareholders. Most listed companies consult major shareholders before proposing new long-term incentive schemes, either directly or indirectly through the Investment Association.

3.7 The use of benchmarks

Companies often use comparative pay data to decide the level of remuneration for directors and senior executives. This data is based on the rewards that are being paid to senior executives by companies in a comparator group. This information is usually provided by the company's remuneration consultant, who may also make recommendations on the choice of a suitable comparator group. The choice of the comparator group can have a significant effect on remuneration outcomes. For example, if it includes US companies (where directors' pay is usually higher), then the outcomes will be higher. Including companies from different sectors where average pay is higher will also have the same effect.

Even if an appropriate comparator group is selected, there is an inherent problem with this method of determining directors' pay. If every company in the comparator group decides that that they want to pay average or above average salaries, pay will begin to spiral out of control. The FRC Guidance on Board Effectiveness warns against this danger (at para. 134):

'It is important to avoid designing pay structures based solely on benchmarking to the market, or the advice of remuneration consultants, as there is a risk this could encourage an upward ratcheting effect on executive pay.'

3.8 Drawbacks of share option schemes

There are several drawbacks to using share options in a long-term incentive scheme. Rewarding executives with share options is intended to align the interests of shareholders and directors (and other senior executives rewarded with options). However, an excessive use of options can result in a serious misalignment of interests.

◆ Share options reward holders for increases in the share price. Although shareholders also benefit from a rising share price, some might prefer higher dividends. Option holders do not benefit from dividend payouts. Accordingly, if they hold share options, the executive directors may have a personal interest in keeping the dividends low.

◆ When stock markets have a bull run, share prices tend to rise regardless of the underlying strength of a company's business. In these circumstances, the profits that option holders can make may significantly outweigh any increase in performance.

◆ On the other hand, when the stock markets are in a bear run and prices are declining, share options lose value, and may even become worthless. This may happen even though the company performed well in comparison with its peers.

◆ If the market price of a company's shares falls below the exercise price for its share options, those options will have lost all their value, unless and until the share price recovers. It would be foolish for directors to exercise their options if they could buy the shares more cheaply on the market. In these circumstances, the options are often referred to as being 'under water' or 'out-of-the-money'. If it is clear that the share price will not recover during the life of the scheme, the options will no longer act as an incentive for the directors. In these circumstances, the remuneration committee may seek to re-price the options, or to issue replacement options at a lower exercise price. Institutional investors do not like companies doing this as it protects the directors against the downside risk of a falling share price, which shareholders themselves cannot avoid.

◆ Executive directors may prefer a long-term incentive scheme involving the grant of shares, since the shares will always have some value once they have vested.

◆ International Financial Reporting Standard 2 (IFRS2) Share-based Payment requires companies to recognise the award of share options as an expense, chargeable against the company's profits, from the time that the share options are granted. This may have discouraged some companies from using options as an incentive.

Test yourself 16.1

1. **What are the typical components of an executive director's remuneration package?**

2. **What company performance targets might be used as a basis for fixing annual bonus payments to a CEO?**

3. **What are the problems with linking rewards to performance for senior executives?**

4. **What company performance targets might be used as a basis for deciding how many shares should be granted to a senior executive as a long-term incentive arrangement?**

5. **What are the drawbacks to using share options for long-term incentive schemes?**

4. UK Corporate Governance Code principles and provisions on remuneration

4.1 No director should be involved in deciding their own remuneration outcome

The most fundamental principle in the Code is probably Principle Q. In order to avoid directors deciding their own remuneration outcome, Principle Q provides that 'a formal and transparent procedure for developing policy on executive remuneration and determining director and senior management remuneration should be established'. In practice this means setting up a remuneration committee, which we deal with in section 5.

4.2 Levels of remuneration

The UK Corporate Governance Code has always included a statement on overall levels of remuneration. It used to state that 'levels of remuneration should be sufficient (but not more than is necessary) to attract, retain and motivate directors of the quality needed to run the company successfully', and that a 'significant proportion of executive directors' remuneration should be structured so as to link rewards to corporate and individual performance'.

This original wording was thought to read like an apology for high pay and the relevant principle was amended in 2014 to provide that 'executive directors' remuneration should be designed to promote the long-term success of the company' and that 'performance-related elements should be transparent, stretching and rigorously applied' (2014 Code, Principle D.1).

Principle P of the 2018 Code now provides:

'Remuneration policies and practices should be designed to support strategy and promote long-term sustainable success. Executive remuneration should be aligned to company purpose and values, and be clearly linked to the successful delivery of the company's long-term strategy.'

This latest formulation is intended to ensure that directors' remuneration is more closely aligned with the interests of shareholders. This is also reflected in the revised 2018 Code provisions on performance-related remuneration (see below).

The 2018 Code differs from previous versions in that it no longer requires remuneration committees 'to judge where to position their company relative to others' in terms of executive remuneration. This used to be included as a principle in previous versions of the Code but has now been deleted. Indeed, the 2018 FRC Guidance on Board Effectiveness now cautions against designing pay structures based solely on benchmarking to the market, or the advice of remuneration consultants, as there is a risk this could encourage an upward ratcheting effect on executive pay.

Principle R of the 2018 Code states that:

'Directors should exercise independent judgement and discretion when authorising remuneration outcomes, taking account of company and individual performance, and wider circumstances.'

Code Provision 33 expands on what these wider circumstances may be:

'The remuneration committee should review workforce remuneration and related policies and the alignment of incentives and rewards with culture, taking these into account when setting the policy for executive director remuneration.'

Code Provision 38 also states that the pension contribution rates for executive directors should be aligned with those available to the workforce. Several listed companies have already come under pressure from institutional investors to comply with this recommendation in 2019.

Code Provision 35 expands on the 'independent judgement' concept in Principle R. It deals mainly with the appointment of remuneration consultants. However, the last sentence of the provision states:

'Independent judgement should be exercised when evaluating the advice of external third parties and when receiving views from executive directors and senior management.'

Due to its positioning, there is no doubt that this provision is directed towards members of the remuneration committee and that the 'third parties' that it has in mind are the remuneration consultants. To put it bluntly, it requires the remuneration committee not to blindly follow the recommendations of the company's remuneration consultants or the views of executive directors and senior management.

In relation to the chair and the non-executive directors, Code Provision 34 provides that

'Levels of remuneration for the chair and all non-executive directors should reflect the time commitment and responsibilities of the role. Remuneration for all non-executive directors should not include share options or other performance-related elements.'

4.3 Performance-related remuneration

As previously mentioned, Principle P of the Code requires executive remuneration to be 'aligned to company purpose and values', and to be 'clearly linked to the successful delivery of the company's long-term strategy'.

Code Provision 33 requires the remuneration committee to review and take into account workforce remuneration and related policies and the alignment of incentives and rewards with culture, for these purposes.

Code Provision 36 states that:

◆ Remuneration schemes should promote long-term shareholdings by executive directors that support alignment with long-term shareholder interests.

◆ Share awards granted for this purpose should be released for sale on a phased basis and be subject to a total vesting and holding period of five years or more.

◆ The remuneration committee should develop a formal policy for post-employment shareholding requirements encompassing both unvested and vested shares.

According to the Grant Thornton Corporate Governance Review 2018:

◆ 70% of FTSE 350 companies disclosed in 2017 that they had an additional holding period for shares awarded under long-term incentive plans. As the typical holding period was two years and the typical vesting period was three years, this means that most companies already comply with the new 2018 Code requirement that the total vesting and holding period should be five years or more.

◆ 93% of companies disclosed a shareholding requirement for the CEO. Of these, 49% reported a holding requirement of 200% of base salary, although five companies disclosed holding levels of between 500% and 800%.

Code Provision 37 states that:

◆ Remuneration schemes and policies should enable the use of discretion to override formulaic outcomes.

◆ They should also include provisions that would enable the company to recover and/or withhold sums or share awards and specify the circumstances in which it would be appropriate to do so.

The use of discretion is intended to help avoid situations where directors may be unjustifiably rewarded for performance improvements that are completely outside their control. For companies in oil production, this can happen, for example, when the price of oil rises on world markets.

The second sentence of Code Provision 37 refers to 'malus' and 'clawback' provisions, which enable incentives payments to be withheld or clawed back in light of subsequent events (such as when previous performance figures turn out to have been mis-stated). We deal with this subject in more detail in section 10.

Under previous versions of the Code, the remuneration committee was required to follow the provisions set out in a separate schedule to the Code (Schedule A) in designing schemes of performance-related remuneration. The guidance contained in that schedule has now incorporated in abbreviated form in 2018 Code Provisions 38 to 40.

Code Provision 40 now contains the main guidance on the design of performance-related remuneration, insofar as they relate to performance-related pay:

◆ Code Provision 38 states that only basic salary should be pensionable.

◆ Code Provision 39 seeks to prevent directors from being rewarded for failure by limiting notice and contract periods, and by requiring companies to be robust in reducing compensation to reflect departing directors' obligations to mitigate loss.

Code Provision 40 states that when determining executive director remuneration policy and practices, the remuneration committee should address the following:

◆ clarity – remuneration arrangements should be transparent and promote effective engagement with shareholders and the workforce;

◆ simplicity – remuneration structures should avoid complexity and their rationale and operation should be easy to understand;

◆ risk – remuneration arrangements should ensure reputational and other risks from excessive rewards, and behavioural risks that can arise from target-based incentive plans, are identified and mitigated;

◆ predictability – the range of possible values of rewards to individual directors and any other limits or discretions should be identified and explained at the time of approving the policy;

◆ proportionality – the link between individual awards, the delivery of strategy and the long-term performance of the company should be clear. Outcomes should not reward poor performance; and

◆ alignment to culture – incentive schemes should drive behaviours consistent with company purpose, values and strategy.

Test yourself 16.2

1. **What does the UK Corporate Governance Code say about the general level of executive remuneration?**

2. **What is the main guidance in the UK Corporate Governance Code on the design of performance-related pay?**

5. Remuneration committee

Code Principle Q states that:

'A formal and transparent procedure for developing policy on executive remuneration and determining director and senior management remuneration should be established. No director should be involved in deciding their own remuneration outcome.'

This principle was extended to cover the remuneration of senior management for the first time in 2018.

In practice, Code Provision 32 requires listed companies to establish a remuneration committee for these purposes.

5.1 Membership of the remuneration committee

Code Provision 32 states that the remuneration committee should consist exclusively of independent non-executive directors and should comprise at least three or, in the case of smaller companies, two such directors. Smaller companies are defined for the purposes of the Code as those that were outside the FTSE 350 throughout the year immediately prior to the reporting year.

The UK Code used to require the chair and members of the committee to be identified in the annual report. Although this provision has been deleted from the 2018 Code, it still remains good practice.

The 2018 Code still requires the annual report to set out the number of meetings of the board and its committees, and the individual attendance by directors (Code Provision 14). This information will serve to identify the members of the committee but not necessarily who chairs it.

The company chair is permitted to serve on the remuneration committee if they were considered independent on appointment as chair (although they are not allowed to chair the committee) (Code Provision 32). The 2018 Code introduced a new requirement that the chair of the remuneration committee must have served on a remuneration committee for at least 12 months before their appointment (Code Provision 32).

If the company chair serves as a member of the committee, care obviously needs to be taken to ensure that there is no breach of the principle that no director should be involved in fixing their own remuneration (Principle Q) as one of the committee's responsibilities is to set the remuneration of the chair.

The company secretary or deputy secretary will usually act as the secretary to the committee.

5.2 Duties of the remuneration committee

Code Provision 33 states that the remuneration committee should have delegated responsibility for:

◆ determining the policy for executive director remuneration; and
◆ setting remuneration for the chair, executive directors and senior management.

The term 'senior management' is defined in a footnote to the 2018 Code as the executive committee or the first layer of management below board level, including the company secretary.

Code Provision 33 also states that the committee should 'review workforce remuneration and related policies and the alignment of incentives and rewards with culture, taking these into account when setting the policy for executive director remuneration'.

The FRC Guidance on Board Effectiveness states (at para. 63) that the committee's terms of reference should be made available on the company's website and should explain its role and the authority delegated to it by the board.

For a sample set of terms of reference, see the ICSA guidance note 'Terms of Reference — Remuneration Committee'.

According to the Grant Thornton Corporate Governance Review 2018, FTSE 350 remuneration committees meet on average about five times per year. This average, which is nearly as many as some boards, may rise in future years in view of the committee's wider remit under the 2018 Code to review workforce remuneration (and related policies).

5.3 Delegated powers or recommendations to the board

The Code seems to envisage that the remuneration committee will have delegated authority to determine the policy for executive director remuneration and set the remuneration for the chair, executive directors and senior management (see Code Provision 33). However, the FRC Guidance on Board Effectiveness states (at para. 62) that:

'While the board may make use of committees to assist its consideration of appointments, succession, audit, risk and remuneration it retains responsibility for, and endorses, final decisions in all of these areas.'

In practice, the policy for executive director remuneration proposed by the remuneration committee will form a substantial part of the directors' remuneration policy that must be approved by shareholders at least once every three years. The CA2006 required the overall directors' remuneration policy to be approved by the board before it is put to shareholders (see section 8). In addition, it may not be possible under some articles for the board to delegate its power to fix the remuneration of directors. In practice, it may therefore be a legal necessity for the recommendations of the remuneration committee in these areas to be ratified by the board. Such a procedure would, however, raise questions as to whether the chair and the executive directors should vote on the recommendations of the remuneration committee with regard to their own remuneration.

5.4   Consultation with shareholders

The chair of the remuneration committee is expected to lead the process of consulting shareholders on matters within the committee's remit. These consultations will mostly take place prior to proposing a new directors' remuneration policy. The company will normally conduct these consultations through shareholder representative bodes, such as the Investment Association, but may also consult individual shareholders who hold a significant stake in the company.

5.5   Remuneration consultants

Companies usually appoint remuneration consultants to assist the remuneration committee in its work. In the recent past, there was a suspicion that remuneration consultants might be inclined to make recommendations that are favourable to the executive directors if it was the executive directors who appointed them. Accordingly, Code Provision 35 now provides that where remuneration consultants are appointed, this should be the responsibility of the remuneration committee.

It also provides that:

◆   The remuneration consultants should be identified in the annual report alongside a statement about any other connection they have with the company or individual directors (quoted companies also have an obligation to make certain disclosures about consultants and other advisers to the committee in the directors' remuneration report – see section 7).

◆   Remuneration committee members should exercise independent judgement when evaluating the advice of external third parties and when receiving views from executive directors and senior management.

These recommendations principally reflects concerns over the objectivity of remuneration consultants and the role that they may have played in promoting spiralling executive remuneration. These concerns arise from the fact that:

◆   Remuneration consultants may have conflicts of interest by virtue of the fact they are also engaged by the executives to advise the company on other aspects of remuneration or may have another connection with an individual director (e.g. an executive director who serves on another company's remuneration committee).

◆ In these circumstances, there is a risk that they will make recommendations which favour the executive directors and are not necessarily in the best interests of the company.

◆ Remuneration consultants may be inclined to recommend complex remuneration schemes in order to increase their fees and make it more difficult for the remuneration committee to dispense with their services in future years.

◆ Remuneration consultants may put pressure on the remuneration committee to accept their advice (e.g. by failing to come up with any credible alternative).

◆ Executive directors and senior management may also put pressure on the remuneration committee in this regard.

According to the Grant Thornton Corporate Governance Review 2018:

◆ 95% of companies that named their remuneration consultants appointed at least one of just six firms.

◆ Of these six firms, two audit firms acted as consultants to 42% of the FTSE 350, with one advising one-quarter of companies.

◆ Two audit firms, who acted as remuneration consultants to seven companies in 2017, became their auditors in 2018.

5.6 UK voluntary code of conduct for remuneration consultants

In 2009, a number of remuneration consultants established a representative body called the Remuneration Consultants Group (RCG), which then proceeded to publish a 'Voluntary Code of Conduct in Relation to Executive Remuneration Consulting in the United Kingdom' (the RCG Code).

The RCG Code, which was last revised in 2015, sets out a number of fundamental principles that consultants should apply when giving remuneration advice to listed companies. These principles cover transparency, integrity, management of conflicts, competence and due care, and confidentiality. It also includes guidelines on how these principles should be applied.

Where a remuneration committee, company or member firm believes that a consultant has breached the RCG Code, they are invited to report this to the member firm concerned. If the response is unsatisfactory, the RCG Code provides that the chair of the RCG 'will be available for consultation'. The articles of association of the RCG allow its board to terminate the membership of any remuneration consultant who has failed to meet the necessary standards of behaviour.

5.7 Remuneration committee report

The annual remuneration report of a quoted company is required, under the statutory disclosure regime, to include:

◆ Details regarding the membership of the remuneration committee and any advisers.

◆ A statement by the remuneration committee chair summarising the major decisions and changes made in relation to directors' remuneration during the year (including the exercise of discretion), and the context in which those changes or decisions occurred.

Code Provision 41 of the UK Corporate Governance Code also states that there should be a description of the work of the remuneration committee in the annual report, including:

◆ an explanation of the strategic rationale for executive directors' remuneration policies, structures and any performance metrics;

◆ reasons why the remuneration is appropriate using internal and external measures, including pay ratios and pay gaps;

◆ a description, with examples, of how the remuneration committee has addressed the factors in Provision 40;

◆ whether the remuneration policy operated as intended in terms of company performance and quantum, and, if not, what changes are necessary;

◆ what engagement has taken place with shareholders and the impact this has had on remuneration policy and outcomes;

◆ what engagement with the workforce has taken place to explain how executive remuneration aligns with wider company pay policy; and

◆ to what extent discretion has been applied to remuneration outcomes and the reasons why.

DTR 7.2.7 also requires a listed company's corporate governance statement to describe how each committee of the board operates.

Test yourself 16.3

1. **What are the principal duties of the remuneration committee?**

2. **Describe the recommendations of the UK Corporate Governance Code regarding the composition of the remuneration committee**

3. **What provisions are included in the UK Corporate Governance Code on remuneration consultants and why?**

6. Wates Principles for private companies on remuneration

Principle 5 of the Wates Corporate Governance Principles for Large Private Companies (the Wates Principles) states that:

'A board should promote executive remuneration structures aligned to the long-term sustainable success of a company, taking into account pay and conditions elsewhere in the company.'

For accounting periods commencing on or after 1 January 2019, certain very large companies (whether public or private) that are not subject to the UK Corporate Governance Code are required to report on their application of a corporate governance code and their compliance with any code provisions. Such companies can choose to report against the Wates Principles for these purposes, in which case they would need to report on how they have applied the above principle.

The Wates Principles do not actually include any code provisions. However, they do include non-binding guidance on remuneration, which suggests that:

◆ Remuneration for directors and senior managers should be aligned with performance, behaviours, and the achievement of company purpose, values and strategy.

◆ In setting director and senior manager remuneration, consideration should be given to remuneration throughout the organisation to reinforce a sense of shared purpose.

◆ The board should establish clear policies on remuneration structures and practices which should enable effective accountability to shareholders. This should take account of the broader operating context, including the pay and conditions of the wider workforce and the company's response to matters such as any gender pay gap.

◆ Such accountability can be supported by clear remuneration structures that are aligned with the company's purpose, values and culture, and the delivery of strategy to support long-term sustainable success. Policies may include robust consideration of the reputational and behavioural risks to the company that can result from inappropriate incentives and excessive rewards.

◆ Boards should consider the benefits of greater transparency of remuneration structures and policies which will build trust from wider stakeholders. Additional transparency could extend to commenting on how executive remuneration reflects general practice within the sector or voluntary disclosure of pay ratios.

◆ The establishment of a committee is a way some boards may wish to delegate responsibility for designing remuneration policies and structures for directors and senior management. Such a committee might benefit from the contribution of an independent non-executive director.

◆ Where directors' pay is controlled by a parent company, the subsidiary should explain this and cross-refer to information available elsewhere which explains the policy in relation to the subsidiary.

7. Directors' remuneration report

Quoted companies are required under the CA2006 to make detailed disclosures regarding directors' remuneration in a separate section of the annual report and accounts known as the directors' remuneration report (s. 420).

The directors' remuneration report must include:

◆ the directors' remuneration policy of the company if that policy is to be put to shareholders for approval at the **accounts meeting** (usually the AGM); and

◆ an annual remuneration report giving details of remuneration payments (and any payments for loss of office) made to directors in the relevant financial year under the policies that applied during that year or previous years.

accounts meeting
The general meeting at which the accounts are laid, which will usually be the AGM.

The definition of a quoted company for these purposes in s. 385 of the CA2006 includes any UK company whose equity share capital:

◆ has been included in the official list in accordance with the provisions of Part VI of the FSMA (this includes UK companies with either a premium or standard listing whose shares are traded on the main market of the London Stock Exchange);

◆ is officially listed in an EEA state (for example, a UK company whose shares are quoted on the Paris Bourse); or

◆ is admitted to dealing on either the New York Stock Exchange or the exchange known as Nasdaq.

It does not include UK companies which only have a listing of debt securities or any UK company traded on AIM or the NEX Growth Market. Such companies must comply with the Companies Act disclosure regime for unquoted companies and any other additional requirements in the relevant market rulebook (e.g. the AIM Rules for Companies).

The directors' remuneration report of a quoted company must be approved by the board of directors and signed on its behalf by a director or secretary (CA2006, s. 422).

The detailed content requirements are set out in Sch. 8 to the Large and Medium-sized Companies and Groups (Accounts and Reports) Regulations 2008, SI 2008/410 (the 2008 regulations). Sch. 8 to the 2008 regulations has been amended several times. Significant changes were made in 2013 to coincide with amendments made to the CA2006 designed to give shareholders of quoted companies more control over directors' pay. Further amendments to the content requirements in the 2008 regulations were made by the Companies

(Miscellaneous Reporting) Regulations 2018 as a consequence of proposals made in the 2016 Green Paper on Corporate Governance Reform. These changes came into force for accounting periods commencing on or after 1 January 2019 and are highlighted in the relevant paragraphs below by making reference to that implementation date.

7.1   GC100 and Investor Group Directors' Remuneration Reporting Guidance

A working group of investors and the GC100 Group has produced detailed guidance for quoted companies on the content and presentation of the directors' remuneration report and policy under the 2008 regulations (Directors' Remuneration Reporting Guidance (2016)) (the 'GC100 and Investor Group Guidance'). The Guidance was first published in September 2013 and was last updated in December 2018.

8. Directors' remuneration policy

8.1   General requirements regarding the remuneration policy

The directors' remuneration policy of a quoted company is required to form part of its directors' remuneration report if the company intends to move a resolution to approve a new policy or renew the existing policy at the next accounts meeting. The accounts meeting is the general meeting at which the company's accounts are laid, which will usually be the AGM. If the company does not intend to do so, the policy need not be included in the directors' remuneration report.

If the policy is included in the directors' remuneration report, it must be set out as a separate part of that report. If it is omitted for any reason, the directors' remuneration report must state when the current policy was approved and where a copy of that policy may be found (e.g. on the company's website).

A quoted company cannot make any payments to a director unless they are consistent with the latest policy approved by shareholders or the payment has been specifically approved by shareholders (CA2006, ss. 226A and 226B). The directors must invite shareholders to approve their policy at least once every three years whether or not it has been revised, and must obtain shareholder approval for any revised policy before they can make any payments under that new policy. In addition, if the annual advisory vote on the directors' remuneration report is defeated, the directors must put the directors' remuneration policy (which could be a new policy or the existing policy) to a vote either at the next meeting at which accounts are laid or an earlier meeting (CA2006, s. 439A).

The policy that shareholders are invited to approve must be a policy that has been approved by the directors either as part of the directors' remuneration report or separately as a revised policy (CA2006, s. 422A).

The directors' remuneration policy must be made available on the company's website, either as part of the company's annual report and accounts or, if it was revised separately, as a separate document.

One of the major issues that is addressed in the GC100 and investor guidance is the period for which any policy approved by shareholders should apply. The consensus at the moment appears to be that it should not apply retrospectively from the start of the financial year in which it is approved because of the danger of making payments under that policy before it has been approved. This means that the policy will only apply for part of the financial year in the year it is approved and in the year it is replaced. This can make it more difficult for shareholders to connect the information in the remuneration report with the policies that they approved because those payments may have been made under two different policies in some years. Investors rejected the idea of being asked to approve a policy for the following financial year, as they thought this would require them to look too far ahead.

8.2 Content of directors' remuneration policy

The detailed content requirements for the directors' remuneration policy are set out in Part 4 of Sch. 8 to the Large and Medium-sized Companies and Groups (Accounts and Reports) Regulations 2008 (as amended). In broad outline, it must contain:

◆ A table describing each component of the remuneration package that may be offered to directors under the policy – this must cover (but need not be limited to) the matters required to be disclosed in the single total figure table in the annual remuneration report (see Section 9).

◆ A statement of the principles which would be applied by the company when agreeing the components of a remuneration package for a new director.

◆ A description of any provisions contained in any director's service contract or letter of appointment which could have an impact on remuneration payments or payments for loss of office and details about where such contracts or letters of appointment can be inspected, including the address of any website on which they are made available.

◆ A bar chart which indicates the maximum and minimum amount which would be payable to each executive director under the policy in the first year and the amount that would be payable to them for on-target performance in the first year.

◆ An illustration, in relation to performance measures or targets, of the maximum remuneration of each executive director assuming share price growth of 50% during the performance period (for financial years commencing on or after 1 January 2019 only).

◆ The company's policy on notice periods under directors' service contracts and the principles on which exit payments will be made, including how they will be calculated, whether the company will distinguish between different types of leaver (e.g. good leavers and bad leavers) or the circumstances of exit and how performance will be taken into account.

◆   A statement on how pay and employment conditions of employees who are not directors was taken into account in setting the directors' remuneration policy, whether the company consulted employees on the directors' remuneration policy and whether any remuneration comparison measurements were used and, if so, what they were and how that information was taken into account.

◆   A statement on whether and, if so, how shareholders' views expressed to the company were taken into account in formulating the directors' remuneration policy.

The table setting out the key components of directors' pay must set out the following information for each component (e.g. for salary, fees, taxable benefits, bonuses, short-term incentives, long-term incentives, and pensions):

◆   how it supports the company's short and long-term strategic objectives;

◆   an explanation of how that component of remuneration package operates;

◆   the maximum potential value of that component (expressed in monetary terms or otherwise);

◆   where applicable, a description of any relevant performance measures, the relative weighting of each, the time period over which they are measured, and the amount that may be paid in respect of the minimum level of performance and any further levels of performance under the policy; and

◆   whether there are any provisions for the recovery of sums paid or the withholding of the payment of any sum (i.e. malus and clawback provisions).

The table must also be accompanied by notes which explain:

◆   why any performance measures were chosen and how any performance targets are set;

◆   the reasons for any changes to the components proposed in the new policy; and

◆   any differences between the directors' remuneration policy and the policy for employees generally.

9. Annual remuneration report

The rest of the directors' remuneration report will consist of detailed disclosures concerning remuneration payments made to directors in the previous financial year (including any payments for loss of office). We refer to this section of the report as the annual remuneration report in order to distinguish it from the directors' remuneration report, which could also include the directors' remuneration policy. The annual remuneration report can also be referred to as the 'implementation report' as it describes how the remuneration policies that were in force during the year were implemented.

Most of the information in the annual remuneration report must be audited.

By contrast, the information in the directors' remuneration policy need not be audited.

9.1   Advisory vote on the annual remuneration report

The annual remuneration report of a quoted company must be put to an annual vote by shareholders at the general meeting at which its report and accounts are laid (usually the AGM) (CA2006, s. 439). No entitlement to remuneration is made conditional on this resolution being passed (CA2006, s. 439(5)). However, if the resolution is defeated, the directors must put the existing directors' remuneration policy or a revised policy to a vote at the next meeting at which accounts are laid, if they have not already done so earlier (CA2006, s. 439A(2)).

9.2   Content of the annual remuneration report

The information required to be shown in the annual remuneration report is specified in Parts 1–3 of Sch. 8 to the Large and Medium-sized Companies and Groups (Accounts and Reports) Regulations 2008 (as amended). In broad outline, it must contain:

◆ Summary of major changes and the exercise of discretion – a statement by the remuneration committee chair summarising the major decisions and changes made in relation to directors' remuneration during the year, and the context in which those changes or decisions occurred. For accounting periods commencing on or after 1 January 2019, the statement must also include a summary of any discretion exercised by the remuneration committee in relation to the award of directors' remuneration.

◆ Single total figure table – showing for each director a single total figure for annual remuneration and its component parts, with comparative information for the previous year (see section 9.3 and Figure 16.1).

◆ Total pension entitlements for each director – the single total figure table above shows pension benefits that accrued during the financial year (e.g. contributions to a money purchase scheme in the year). This section shows each director's total pensions benefits as at the end of that year, their normal retirement date and a description of any additional benefit receivable in the event of early retirement.

◆ Scheme interests awarded during the financial year – a table showing, for example, any grant of options or shares during the year, the face value of those awards and a description of each scheme, including a summary of the performance measures and the percentage of scheme interests that would be receivable if the minimum performance was achieved.

◆ Payments made to past directors – including any pension benefits but excluding any payments for loss of office, which must be shown separately.

◆ Payments for loss of office – details of any payments made (or payable) to former directors for loss of office during the financial year, including an explanation of how each component was calculated and whether any discretion was exercised in respect of the payment.

◆ Director's shareholdings and share interests in the company – a table showing each director's interests in the company's shares (including those of connected persons) and scheme interests, together with various details about those schemes.

◆ Performance graph and table – a graph covering a period of 10 years which compares total shareholder return with a broad share index and a table showing a summary of the CEO's remuneration for each year covered by the performance graph.

◆ Percentage change in remuneration of the CEO – the percentage change in the following elements of CEO's pay compared to the employees of the company or group taken as a whole: (i) total salary and fees, (ii) all taxable benefits, and (iii) variable pay.

◆ Pay ratio information – for companies with more than 250 employees (and for accounting periods commencing on or after 1 January 2019 only), a table of pay ratio information comparing the remuneration of the CEO with the 25th, 50th and 75th percentile of the full time equivalent pay of the company's UK employees.

◆ Relative importance of spend on pay – a table or chart that shows for the relevant and preceding financial year the company's expenditure on (i) employee pay, (ii) dividends and share buy-backs, and (iii) other significant payments or uses of profit or cash flow.

◆ Description of how the company intends to implement the approved remuneration policy in the following year.

◆ Details regarding the membership of the remuneration committee and any advisers.

◆ Statement on voting – setting out the percentage of votes cast for and against (and the number of votes withheld) in respect of the last resolutions to approve the directors' remuneration report and directors' remuneration policy and, where there was a significant percentage of votes (e.g. 20%+) against either resolution, a summary of the reasons and any actions taken by the directors in response to those concerns.

9.3 Single total figure table

The single total figure table is perhaps the most important feature of the annual remuneration report. It must show for each person who was a director during the relevant financial year a figure for that year and the previous year in respect of:

◆ total salary and fees;

◆ all taxable benefits;

◆ bonuses and short-term incentives schemes that only relate to the relevant financial year;

◆ long-term incentive schemes where final vesting is determined as a result of the achievement of performance measures or targets relating to a period ending in the relevant financial year and not dependent on performance or targets achieved in any future financial year;

◆ all pension related benefits;

◆ a separate column (or row) for every other element of remuneration (other than a payment made to a past director) that is not required to be included in one of the above columns;

◆ the total amount of the sums set out in the previous columns.

The columns (or rows) do not need to be set out in the order specified in Sch. 8 and separate tables can be prepared for the executive and non-executive directors.

The table(s) must be followed by a detailed explanation of some of the components, including, for accounting periods commencing on or after 1 January 2019, the following new items:

◆ the amount of any variable award that is attributable to share price appreciation; and

◆ where any discretion has been exercised in respect of a variable award, particulars of how that discretion was exercised and how the resulting level of award was determined.

Director	Year	Salary £000	Benefits £000	Total bonus £000	LTIPs vested £000	Pension benefits £000	Total £000
Director A	2017/18	820	30	20	70	203	1,143
	2016/17	809	32	599	0	202	1,642
Director B	2017/18	590	15	20	70	150	845
	2016/17	590	20	500	0	150	1,260

Figure 16.1 Example of a single total figure table

9.4 Annual remuneration reports in practice

According to the Grant Thornton Corporate Governance Review 2018, the average FTSE 350 directors' remuneration report runs to about 20 pages. Somewhat surprisingly, Grant Thornton rated the remuneration report as the best explained section of the annual report:

◆ 96% included a personal introduction by the remuneration committee chair giving good or detailed insights, including clear overviews of company policy, with highlights of any changes and detailed accounts of matters considered during meetings.

◆ 94% discuss the connection between executive remuneration and company strategy. However, only 29% go further and reinforce the link between the execution of strategy and the creation of long-term sustainable value and rewards in the strategic report, with more detailed explanation on financial and non-financial KPIs ensuring that executives' and shareholders' interests align.

Test yourself 16.4

1. What are the two main component parts of the directors' remuneration report?

2. What is the purpose of the annual remuneration report?

10. Compensation for loss of office and rewards for failure

Most executive directors enter into a service contract with their company that provides for an annual review of their remuneration and a minimum notice period in the event of dismissal. When a company decides to dismiss a director, it will be liable to pay compensation in accordance with the terms of this service agreement. If a contract provides for a six month notice period, the director will be contractually entitled to six months' salary on being dismissed, subject to any obligations regarding mitigation.

10.1 Length of service contracts

The length of a director's service contract or notice period will be one of the most important factors determining compensation payable in the event of early termination. When the Cadbury Committee issued the first UK corporate governance code in 1992, five-year rolling contracts were relatively common and did not need shareholder approval under the Companies Act. Accordingly, the Cadbury Committee's recommendation that contracts of over three years' duration should be approved by shareholders appeared fairly radical.

In 1995, the Greenbury Committee recommended that the remuneration report should disclose and explain any service contracts providing for notice periods of more than one year. It also stated that there was a strong case for setting contract periods at, or reducing them to, one year or less.

CA2006 introduced a new legal threshold for directors' service contracts which now states that they must not exceed two years' duration without shareholder approval, compared to five years before (s. 188).

The UK Corporate Governance Code now provides in Code Provision 39 that:

◆ Notice or contract periods should be one year or less.

◆ If it is necessary to offer longer periods to new directors recruited from outside the company, such periods should reduce to one year or less after the initial period.

◆ The remuneration committee should ensure compensation commitments in directors' terms of appointment do not reward poor performance.

◆ They should be robust in reducing compensation to reflect departing directors' obligations to mitigate loss.

The obligation to mitigate loss means that a director should look for replacement work. If they find gainful employment, the company's obligation to compensate them may be reduced. In order to facilitate mitigation, compensation payments should not necessarily be paid in a lump sum. In practice, companies often prefer to negotiate a clean break and to take the negative publicity surrounding any termination payments on the chin.

Details of any payments made (or payable) to former directors for loss of office during the financial year must be disclosed in the annual remuneration report, together with an explanation of how each component was calculated and whether any discretion was exercised in respect of the payment. Discretion may, for example, be exercised to increase the termination payment beyond what the individual is contractually entitled to, perhaps to encourage the director to sign a gagging clause.

10.2 Disclosure of unexpired contract term in the annual report

The Listing Rules require companies with a premium listing to disclose in the annual report the unexpired term of any service contract for any director proposed for election or re-election at the AGM, and, if the director does not have a service contract, a statement to that effect (LR 9.8.8R).

10.3 Joint ABI/PLSA statement on executive contracts and severance

severance payment
Payment to a director (or other employee) on being required to resign (or otherwise leave the company).

In the UK, the ABI and PLSA (formerly NAPF) published a joint statement on best practice on executive contracts and **severance** (2008). The statement, which can still be found on the website of the Investment Association, was intended to assist boards and remuneration committees in negotiating contracts with senior executives and avoid situations in which departing executives are rewarded for failure. Nearly all of the recommendations in the statement are now reflected either in the Code or the statutory disclosure regime. It has also been superseded to a certain extent by the Investment Association's Principles of Remuneration. However, the statement still gathers together in one place the measures companies should take to avoid making payments which reward failure.

Case study 16.2

In August 2006, the Association of British Insurers wrote to FTSE 350 companies asking them to review their pension arrangements for senior executives. The letter asked the remuneration committees to look at the pension arrangements in executives' contracts, to make sure that they were in line with best practice. The specific matter of concern was that executives might have contracts that entitled them to a large increase in their pension fund, as part of any severance package.

What had prompted the letter was a payout to four former directors of Scottish Power, who had all retired with large increases in their pension

funds. **The former CEO had benefited from a doubling of his pension fund arrangements. The company admitted that the cost of the retirement benefits for the four directors had been £11 million. It stated that it was contractually obliged to make the pension increases, but was now reviewing its pension arrangements for senior executives.**

10.4 Use of discretion

The UK Corporate Governance Code provides that remuneration schemes and policies should enable the use of discretion to override formulaic outcomes (Code Provision 37).

This intended to allow remuneration committees to make certain adjustments to performance-related pay in certain circumstances, e.g. where there is an unjustified outcome.

Stop and think 16.3

In November 2018, Jeff Fairburn, CEO of the UK house builder Persimmon, was ousted from his job following controversy over a £75 million bonus.

The bonus became payable under an incentive scheme linked to the Persimmon share price, which had soared after a significant increase in the company's profits. Critics argued that most of that increase was attributable to the government's help-to-buy scheme for first-time buyers. About half of the homes that Persimmon built were bought with assistance under this scheme.

Legally, Mr Fairburn was entitled to receive a £110 million bonus under the scheme. He initially argued that he had earned and had 'worked very hard' to reinvigorate the housing market. He subsequently agreed to forego a substantial proportion (£35 million) of the bonus. However this was not enough to quell the critics and, he finally agreed to step down at the request of the company as the continuing controversy was beginning to have a negative impact on its business.

10.5 Malus and clawback provisions

Code Provision 37 provides that remuneration schemes and policies should include provisions that enable the company to recover and/or withhold sums or share awards and specify the circumstances in which it would be appropriate to do so.

This provision effectively requires listed companies to adopt 'malus' and 'clawback' provisions:

◆ 'malus' provisions allow the company, in specified circumstances, to forfeit all or part of a bonus or long-term incentive award before it has vested and been paid (also known as 'performance adjustment'); and

◆   'clawback' provisions allow the company to recover sums already paid.

The Investment Association's Principles of Remuneration recommend that the circumstances in which performance adjustment and clawback can be implemented should be:

◆   agreed and documented before awards are made;

◆   reviewed by the remuneration committee to ensure that they remain appropriate; and

◆   disclosed to shareholders.

The usual triggers for invoking malus and clawback are 'gross misconduct' and 'mis-statement of results'. However, the Principles of Remuneration now encourage companies to broaden these triggers. They call on remuneration committees to establish a more substantial list of specific circumstances in which the malus and clawback provisions could be used, and to disclose those circumstances to shareholders. They accept that performance adjustment (malus provisions) will probably apply to a broader range of circumstances than clawback.

The Principles also recommend that:

◆   remuneration committees should review the enforcement powers available to them to implement these provisions;

◆   executives should be required to sign forms of acceptance at the time of grant in order to set the expectations for malus and clawback applying to that award, and establish how and when they may be applied;

◆   any communication around the payment of bonuses or long-term incentive plans should also be consistent with the malus and clawback provisions; and

◆   remuneration committees should develop clear processes for assessing executives against either malus and clawback criteria and how they will exercise discretionary clawback.

The directors' remuneration policy of a quoted company is required to disclose whether incentive schemes make any provision for the recovery of sums paid or the withholding of the payment of any sum (i.e. malus and clawback provisions). If these provisions are ever invoked, details should be provided in the annual remuneration report.

According to the Grant Thornton Corporate Governance Review 2018:

◆   93% of FTSE companies reported having clawback provisions for bonuses or long-term incentives;

◆   about 87% of them had such provisions for annual bonuses; and

◆   89% for share performance plans;

◆   no company disclosed having invoked a clawback provision;

◆ some overseas companies explained that such provisions would not be enforceable under the national legislation of their country of incorporation, such as Russia or Germany.

Test yourself 16.5

1. **What are the principles and provisions of the UK Corporate Governance Code with regard to severance payments for senior executives?**

2. **What are 'malus' and 'clawback' provisions and where might you find them?**

11. Listing Rule provisions on long-term incentive schemes

The Greenbury Code recommended in 1995 that shareholders should be invited to approve all new long-term incentive schemes (including share option schemes), whether payable in cash or shares, in which directors and senior executives will participate (Greenbury Code, para. B12). These recommendations were implemented as continuing obligations under the Listing Rules for UK companies.

The UK Corporate Governance Code used to include a provision that effectively served as a reminder that these Listing Rule provisions exist. However, that provision has now been deleted from the 2018 Code.

11.1 Requirement for shareholder approval

The Listing Rules require all share option and long-term incentive schemes established by a UK company with a premium listing or any of its subsidiaries to be approved by an ordinary resolution of the shareholders (LR 9.4.1) unless the scheme falls within one of the exceptions set out in LR 9.4.2 for:

◆ schemes in which participation is offered to all or substantially all employees of the group; and

◆ schemes for individual directors established specifically to facilitate, in unusual circumstances, the recruitment or retention of the individual concerned.

In the latter case, detailed information on the special scheme must be given in the company's next annual report, including an explanation of why the circumstances were unusual.

11.2 Prohibition on discounted share options

The Listing Rules also provide that options, warrants or other rights over shares may not be granted without shareholders' approval to directors or employees if the exercise price would be less than the market value of the shares at the time the exercise price is determined (LR 9.4.4). Certain exceptions are made for employee share schemes open on similar terms to all or substantially all employees (e.g. SAYE schemes) and for replacement options following a takeover or reconstruction (LR 9.4.5).

12. Non-executive remuneration

Non-executive directors are not employees of the company, although are usually treated as such for tax purposes. They receive a fee for their services as an officer of the company, not a salary. They do not have a service contract with the company. The terms of their appointment are set out in a simple letter of appointment. If they are removed, there is no breach of contract and no compensation will usually be payable.

12.1 Procedure for setting NED fees

The Code provides that the remuneration of non-executive directors should be determined in accordance with the articles of association or, alternatively, by the board. It makes no specific provision allowing the board to delegate this matter to a committee (Code Provision 34).

Articles of association commonly used to place an overall cap on the fees that could be paid to non-executive directors. Subject to this cap, their fees could be determined by the board as a whole. The directors would need to obtain shareholder approval in order to increase the overall cap stated in the articles. Very few companies have such provisions in their articles of association any more. Most listed company articles simply allow the board to determine the fees of non-executive directors.

It would not be appropriate for the remuneration committee to be involved in this process as this would mean that some of the non-executive directors were involved in setting their own remuneration. In practice, the chair and/or the executive directors will usually take the lead on proposing the fees that should be paid to non-executives, probably after taking advice from the company's remuneration consultants.

The Code provides that the remuneration of the chair, whether executive or non-executive, should be determined by the remuneration committee (Code Provision 33). However, it also allows the chair to serve on the remuneration committee, if considered independent on appointment (Code Provision 32). This may appear to mean that a non-executive chair can be involved in setting their own remuneration. However, the statement in Principle Q that 'no director should be involved in deciding their own remuneration outcome' would still need to be respected. A non-executive chair who serves on the remuneration committee would need to recuse themselves when the committee is deciding their own remuneration.

12.2 Levels of NED fees

Under the Code, levels of remuneration for the chair and all non-executive directors should reflect the time commitment and responsibilities of the role. In addition, their remuneration should not include share options or other performance-related elements (Code Provision 34).

The Higgs Review (2003) endorsed the view that payment of part of a non-executive director's remuneration in shares (not share options) can be a useful and legitimate way of aligning their interests with those of the shareholders. However, this practice has not really been taken up.

Non-executive fees have risen appreciably in the last 20 years. Most of this increase can be attributed to the additional responsibilities and time commitments involved under the UK Corporate Governance Code. However, some of it may be attributable to the practice of everyone wanting to pay around the average rate.

12.3 Additional fees

Some non-executive directors may receive other forms of remuneration or rewards from the company, in addition to their basic fees (e.g. for acting as a consultant or specialist adviser). Although this is not prohibited, it will almost certainly compromise their independence under the criteria in Code Provision 10 which require companies to assess whether they:

◆ have received or receive additional remuneration from the company apart from a director's fee;

◆ participate in the company's share option or a performance-related pay scheme; or

◆ are a member of the company's pension scheme.

Engaging a non-executive director to provide consultancy services could therefore entail having to recruit an additional independent NED, unless the NED was already considered not to be independent.

12.4 Performance-related rewards for NEDs

As mentioned previously, the Code states that the remuneration of non-executive directors should not include share options or other performance-related elements (Code Provision 34).

It is not considered appropriate for the pay of non-executive directors to be based on the company's performance because:

◆ this would involve a conflict of interest for those serving on the remuneration committee who are responsible for designing these performance schemes;

◆ it would have the effect of aligning the interests of the non-executive directors more closely with those of the executive directors (rather than the shareholders) and make them more liable to allow the company to take bigger risks; and

◆ the company's performance is not as reliant on the things that non-executive directors do, although one could argue that their role in deciding the company's strategy could be critical in this regard.

Case study 16.3

In 2006, Coca-Cola in the USA announced major changes to the remuneration structure for its NEDs. Previously, NEDs had been paid a fixed annual fee of $125,000 ($50,000 in cash, and the rest in Coca-Cola stock), with extra fees for chairing board committees and attending board meetings and committee meetings. Under the new arrangement, NEDs would receive no remuneration unless earnings per share grew by at least 8% compound over three years. They would receive no interim fees until this target was reached. The stated aim of this scheme was to achieve greater alignment of the interests of NEDs with those of the shareholders.

Critics of the scheme argued that linking NED pay to company performance could compromise the independence of the NEDs and would effectively ensure that their interests were more closely aligned with the executive directors, rather than shareholders. In addition, it was argued that the scheme would make it more difficult for the company to recruit non-executive directors, but particularly those from less affluent socio-economic backgrounds.

Test yourself 16.6

1. **Who should set the fees of NEDs?**

2. **Why is it inappropriate for NEDs to participate in performance-related schemes?**

3. **Why might it be appropriate for some or all of their fees to be paid in shares?**

13. Other guidance on remuneration

13.1 Investment Association's Principles of Remuneration

The Investment Association publishes influential guidance on executive remuneration called the Principles of Remuneration (IA Principles). The Principles are usually updated once a year in either November or December. At the time of writing the last update was published in November 2018.

The IA Principles set out a number of over-arching principles on executive pay which are supported by more general guidance for remuneration committees on levels of pay, bonuses, pensions, long-term incentive schemes, contract terms and severance payments. They focus mainly on ensuring that levels of executive pay are appropriate and that performance conditions are challenging.

The IA Principles suggest, among other things, that:

◆ Remuneration committees should select a remuneration structure which is appropriate for the specific business, and efficient and cost-effective in delivering its longer-term strategy. The Principles do not seek to prescribe or recommend any particular remuneration structure.

◆ Shareholders prefer simple and understandable remuneration structures.

◆ Remuneration structures should be designed to reward sustainable business performance and therefore deliver long-term value to shareholders.

◆ Executives should build up a high level of personal shareholding to ensure alignment of interests with shareholders. The shareholding should be maintained for a period after they have left the company.

◆ Annual bonuses should be cancelled if the business has suffered an 'exceptional negative event', even if some targets have been met.

◆ Remuneration structures should be subject to 'malus' and 'clawback' provisions that allow the company, in specified circumstances, to withhold or claw back all or part of a bonus or long-term incentive award.

Recommendations made in the IA Principles are often adopted as either statutory provisions or Code requirements. This is one of the reasons why they are 'influential'. Another reason is that they represent the views of institutional investors in the UK, who still hold a significant stake in most listed companies. Accordingly, listed companies take the IA Principles very seriously.

The IA Principles include a section on shareholder consultation, which suggests that:

◆ Consultations needs to focus on the major strategic remuneration issues rather than the minor details of pay. However, companies should ensure that the final proposals do not contain any surprises. They should provide details of the whole remuneration structure, not just the proposed changes, so that investors are provided with a complete picture and sufficient information to make an informed voting decision.

◆ Companies should listen and respond to feedback from their shareholders to enhance their proposals. They should not anticipate that shareholders will always support their proposals. Consultation does not guarantee that they will be accepted.

◆ The consultation process can be improved by remuneration committees understanding the voting policies of the company's largest shareholders.

◆ Subsequent to the conclusion of the consultation process and prior to finalising details in the remuneration report, the remuneration committee should review the proposals in light of any subsequent events that occur between the consultation and the implementation of the policy, to ensure that the proposals remain appropriate.

The Investment Association also sends letters to listed companies highlighting current issues of concern to investors. For example, its November 2017 letter on executive pay highlighted:

◆ members' concerns over the general level of executive remuneration;

◆ the need to justify any disparity between executive director pension provision compared to the general workforce;

◆ the fact that shareholders expect full disclosure of threshold, target and maximum performance targets, either at the time of payment of the award, or within 12 months where the information is commercial sensitive; and

◆ the fact that shareholders expect an explanation if the metrics used to set targets for executive remuneration differ significantly from the company's headline key performance indicators.

13.2 PLSA Corporate Governance Policy and Voting Guidelines 2018

The Pensions and Lifetime Savings Association, formerly known as the NAPF, publishes and regularly updates a document called the PLSA Corporate Governance Policy and Voting Guidelines (the PLSA Policy).

On remuneration, it states that:

◆ Remuneration committees should expect executive management to make a material long-term investment in shares of the businesses they manage.

◆ Pay should be aligned to long-term strategy and the desired corporate culture throughout the organisation.

◆ Pay schemes should be clear, understandable for both investors and executives, and ensure that executive rewards reflect returns to long-term shareholders.

◆ Remuneration committees should use the discretion afforded them by shareholders to ensure that awards properly reflect business performance.

◆ Companies and shareholders should have appropriately regular discussions on strategy and long-term performance.

The PLSA Policy indicates the circumstances in which PLSA members (mainly pension funds) are likely to vote against the directors' remuneration policy or directors' remuneration report of a listed company. For example, it warns that the following circumstances might give rise to a vote against the remuneration policy:

◆ a shareholding requirement of less than 2x salary;

◆ inappropriate metrics or insufficiently stretching targets for annual bonus or LTIP;

◆ failure to disclose variable pay performance conditions for annual bonuses;

◆ an absence of malus and clawback provisions;

◆ any provision for re-testing of performance conditions;

- ◆ layering of new share award schemes on top of existing schemes; and
- ◆ excessively generous salary or performance-related pay awards.

It also warns that if the process of engagement prior to the AGM fails to produce a remuneration policy that shareholders can support, this will usually be viewed as a serious failure on part of the chair of the remuneration committee and is likely to result in shareholders voting against their re-election and, possibly, the re-election of other committee members.

13.3 PRA/FCA remuneration codes of practice

Companies in the financial services sector may also be subject to remuneration codes of practice found in the PRA Rulebook and the FCA Handbook. These remuneration codes establish principles that are used to assess the quality of a firm's remuneration policies and whether they encourage excessive risk-taking by its employees. Firms must apply the relevant code(s) to 'remuneration code staff', including senior management, risk takers, staff engaged in control functions and any employee receiving total remuneration that takes them into the same remuneration bracket as senior management and risk takers, and whose professional activities have a material impact on the firm's risk profile.

Test yourself 16.7

1. Why are the IA Principles of Remuneration and the PLSA Policy and Guidelines so influential?

2. Give two examples of things covered in the IA Principles and two examples of things covered by the PLSA Policy and Guidelines.

3. Why should companies consult the PLSA Policy and Guidelines when designing their directors' remuneration policy?

Chapter summary

◆ The corporate governance framework in the UK on directors' remuneration for listed companies includes a mixture of statutory provisions, listing rule requirements and code recommendations.

◆ A directors' remuneration package is likely to consist of a combination of fixed and variable pay elements. The fixed elements, which are not dependent on performance, include basic salary, pension payments (or payments in lieu) and other benefits and perks. The variable elements depend on performance and usually include short-term incentives, such as an annual bonus, and long-term incentives, usually in the form of share options or share awards which pay out for performance over a longer period.

◆ One of the fundamental principles of the Code is that no director should be involved in deciding their own remuneration outcome. In practice, the Code requires companies to establish a remuneration committee of independent NEDs to determine the company's remuneration policy for executive directors and to set the remuneration of the chair, executive directors and senior management. The committee is also expected to 'review workforce remuneration and related policies and the alignment of incentives and rewards with culture' and take these into account when setting the policy for executive remuneration.

◆ The Code provides that 'remuneration policies and practices should be designed to support strategy and promote long-term sustainable successes and that 'executive remuneration should be aligned to company purpose and values, and be clearly linked to the successful delivery of the company's long-term strategy'.

◆ The Wates Corporate Governance Principles for Large Private Companies state that boards should 'promote executive remuneration structures aligned to the long-term sustainable success of a company, taking into account pay and conditions elsewhere in the company'.

◆ The CA2006 requires quoted companies to put their directors' remuneration policy to a vote by shareholders at least once every three years and prohibits them from making any payment to a director unless it is consistent with that policy or has been approved by shareholders in some other way.

◆ Quoted companies are also required under the CA2006 to publish detailed information on directors' remuneration in a separate section of their annual reports and accounts, known as the directors' remuneration report. The information in this report is designed to enable shareholders to understand how the company has applied the approved policy during the financial year. The directors' remuneration report must be put to an annual vote by shareholders. Payments to directors are not contingent on the resolution being passed. However, if it is defeated, the company must put its existing remuneration policy (or a new policy) to a shareholder vote in the following year.

◆ The above regime gives shareholders in quoted companies far more say over directors' pay than they have ever had before. Most companies now consult their major shareholders (or bodies that represent them) before putting their directors' remuneration policy to the vote, and representative bodies (such as the Investment Association and the PLSA) publish detailed guidance on their expectations regarding remuneration policies and structures.

◆ The Code includes a number of measures designed to tackle the perception that directors are rewarded for failure. It provides that notice or contract periods for executive directors should be one year or less. It requires companies to be robust in reducing compensation to reflect departing directors' obligations to mitigate loss and requires them to adopt malus and clawback provisions that enable the company to recover and/or withhold sums or share awards in certain circumstances. In addition, the remuneration committee is expected to have general discretion to make adjustments to performance-related pay where there is an unjustified outcome.

◆ Subject to certain limited exceptions, the Listing Rules require all share option and long-term incentive schemes for directors and senior executives to be approved by shareholders.

◆ The remuneration of non-executive directors will be fixed by the board or under some other procedures determined by the articles. The articles of association of listed companies used to place an overall cap on the fees that could be paid to NEDs. This is now exceedingly rare. The current norm is for the board to have power to fix the remuneration of NEDs.

◆ The Code provides that the fees paid to the chair and NEDs should reflect the time commitment and responsibilities of the role they undertake. For example, those who serve on or chair committees will be paid a higher fee.

Test yourself answers

Chapter 1

Test yourself 1.1

1. What is the main difference between the agency and stakeholder theories?

Agency theory deals with the relationship between shareholders and directors where there is a separation between ownership: the shareholders playing the part of the principal and the directors and managers playing the part of the agent. Challenges associated with the agent-principal relationship occur. These relate to conflicts of inte est and the costs associated with avoiding/managing those conflicts

The stakeholder theory, in direct contrast to the agency theory, states that the purpose of corporate governance should be to meet the objectives of everyone that has an interest in the company.

2. How do they affect the objectives of the companies?

A company whose governance is based on the agency theory will be focusing on creating and maintaining shareholder value through managing conflicts of interest and the costs associated with avoiding/managing those conflicts. This is usually reflected in a focus on financial objectives such as eturn on investment, sales and profit targets. Objectives also tend to be short-term

In contrast, stakeholder theory requires boards to balance the interests of the different stakeholder groups when making decisions, deciding on a case-by-case basis which interests should take priority in a particular circumstance. This means that non-financial objectives, such as employee elations or limiting environmental impact would be considered. Objectives tend to be longer-term.

3. How can a company manage conflicts of interest between shareholders and directors and managers?

Agency theory says that companies should use corporate governance practices to avoid or manage these conflicts. Examples of how companies can achieve this are as follows:

◆ the use of long-term incentive share award or stock option schemes based on total shareholder return to align the interests of shareholders and management; and

◆   adoption of conflict of inte est and related party transaction policies.

Test yourself 1.2

1. What is the difference between the enlightened shareholder value and inclusive stakeholder approaches to corporate governance?
The enlightened shareholder value approach proposes that boards, when considering actions to maximise shareholder value, should look to the long term as well as the short- term, and consider the views of and impact on other stakeholders in the company, not just shareholders. The views of other stakeholders are, however, only considered in so far as it would be in the interests of shareholders to do so. This differs from the stakeholder and stakeholder inclusive approaches where boards balance the conflicting inte ests of stakeholders in the best interests of the company.

2. Which approaches see boards taking a longer-term view in decision-making?
Enhanced shareholder value, stakeholder, and inclusive stakeholder approaches tend to take a longer-term view than the shareholder value approach.

3. Which approaches put shareholders first?
The shareholder value and enhanced shareholder value approaches put shareholders first

Test yourself 1.3

1. What are the pros and cons of a rules-based approach versus a principles-based approach to corporate governance?
Critics of the rules-based approach argue that it only works:

◆   where the challenges faced by companies under the purview of the regulation are substantially similar, justifying a common approach to common problems; and
◆   if the rules and their enforcement efficiently and e fectively direct, modify or preclude the behaviours they are aimed at affecting.

The benefits of such a system is that it sends a message out to owners, potential investors and other stakeholders that the country takes seriously their protection from nefarious practices by those managing and overseeing the organisation's they are investing in or dealing with. In reality, it is the enforcement of the rules that achieves this and in many countries, enforcement is weak.

2. What is the 'comply or explain' rule for listed companies?
'Comply or explain' refers to the system whereby a company is asked to comply with a voluntary principles-based code of best practice. Where the company believes that it is not in its best interests to 'comply' with a provision of the code it is required to 'explain' to shareholders why they have not complied.

The company's shareholders and shareholder representative bodies are then expected to assess whether the explanation is acceptable or not. The UK corporate governance code works on the premise of a 'comply or explain' code.

3. How does it differ from the 'apply and explain' rule in King IV?
The term 'apply or explain' was adopted in the South African King Code for two main reasons.

Firstly, the code, for the first time, applied to all types of entities egardless of their form of establishment or incorporation. These entities under a 'comply or explain' regime would only have had the option of complying or not. As many of the entities were not listed companies, which the corporate governance practices had originally been designed for, it was felt that that regime would put off many entities from adopting good corporate governance. Asking them how they were 'applying' the principles within the code was a less harsh way of reporting on what they were doing as they did not have to give a yes or no answer, they could tell a story of how corporate governance was being adopted in their organisations.

Secondly, to avoid a 'mindless response' to the corporate governance recommendations contained within the code. There was a feeling amongst many stakeholders that the 'comply and explain' regime was leading to companies adopting a tick-box approach to corporate governance, adopting the provisions without considering whether they were suitable for their companies or not.

Test yourself 1.4

1. Why is knowing your purpose important for an organisation?
Knowing the organisation's purpose is very important as everything stems from it: the organisation's vision, mission, strategic goals and governance framework, including risk management. It is only through knowing the purpose of the organisation and focusing efforts and resources on achieving that purpose that organisations can be successful in the long run.

If an organisation has clarity of purpose then its employees know what they are working towards, investors know what they are investing in and boards and management know how to focus their resources and manage their risks.

For the company secretary, knowing the organisation's purpose helps set up the organisation's governance framework of structures, policies and procedures.

2. What is the difference between compliance and governance?
Compliance answers 'what is required'. It leads to an organisation adopting the appropriate structures, policies and procedures. On its own it is a purely box-ticking exercise.

Governance answers 'how do we make this effective'. The company secretary needs to ensure that the infrastructure is appropriate for the organisation, that people are focused and work well together, resources are used effectively, and information flows smoothl . Decisions are then made effectively, and this all contributes to a successful, sustainable organisation. If the infrastructure is not appropriate for the organisation, then the anticipated 'cultures' will not be developed. Those within the organisation will develop their own cultures which, as they are not being managed, often leads to bad practices, such as failure to follow policies, the misuse of resources, breakdown of important relationships, etc. This in turn threatens the performance and long-term sustainability of the organisation.

3. How can a business ensure it assimilates corporate governance practices into its culture?

If an organisation gets its governance right then it reaps the benefits of success. To ensure that this is happening an organisation should define what its critical success factors are so these can be measured. This will usually be done as part of the strategic planning process.

Chapter 2

Test yourself 2.1

1. What relevance does knowing the historical development of corporate governance have for advising on today's governance practices?

It is important to know the historical development of corporate governance as only by knowing why the practices have developed can a company decide whether to comply or explain with the practice, and also to know what structures, polices and processes to put in place to ensure the spirit of the practice is achieved.

For example, the practice of separating the roles of the chair and CEO is in response to individuals dominating decision-making and using the company's resources in their interests, not in the best interests of the company. It is assumed that by having two individuals in senior positions and separating the responsibilities between them this domination can be avoided. If a company decides to combine the roles, other checks and balances need to be put in place to ensure that one individual does not dominate. A senior independent director could be appointed, for instance.

2. What type of UK companies can be listed?

Only public limited companies can be listed.

3. What is the difference between a public and a private company in the UK?

The main difference is that public companies are able to offer their shares to the public whereas private companies are not.

Test yourself 2.2

1. What new requirements are included in the UK Corporate Governance Code 2018?
The 2018 UK Corporate Governance Code includes new requirements for boards to consider the needs and views of a wider range of stakeholders (employees, customers and suppliers), integrity and corporate culture, diversity and how the overall governance of the company contributes to its long-term success.

2. What is the difference between principles and provisions in the UK Corporate Governance Code?
The Principles state what a company should be aspiring to. The Provisions provide guidance on how the principles could be achieved.

Listed companies are required to make a statement in their annual report and accounts on how they have:

◆   applied the spirit of the Principles;
◆   complied with, or explain why they have not complied with, the provisions and supporting guidelines for the Code.

3. Who enforces the requirements of the UK Corporate Governance Code?
The company's shareholders enforce the requirements of the code through dialogue with the company and voting at general meetings.

Test yourself 2.3

1. Which corporate governance code(s) applies to:
◆   *UK listed companies;*
◆   *UK unlisted companies.*

The 2018 UK Corporate Governance Code applies to listed companies. Many AIM listed companies adopt as their corporate governance standards the Quoted Companies Alliance (QCA) Corporate Governance Guidelines 2018.

The Wates Corporate Governance Principles for Large Private Companies 2018 can be applied to any large private company.

Many private companies have selected to follow the Institute of Directors Corporate Governance Guidance and Principles for Unlisted Companies (2010) for their corporate governance arrangements. The guidance is voluntary and seeks to ensure the long-term survival and sustainability of the company as it develops and matures.

2. What are the arguments for and against the application of corporate governance codes of best practice to large private companies?
The owners of private companies are often their managers, so the issue of protecting the investor does not tend to exist. As corporate governance in the

UK was traditionally aimed at creating and protecting shareholder value where there was a separation of ownership and control, it was argued that it was not appropriate for private companies where this separation did not exist.

Recent high-profile corporate scandals, elating to large private companies, for example at British Home Stores (BHS), have raised a different concern to that of protecting the investor for private companies. This is the protection of a wider stakeholder group, which includes employees, former employees and suppliers of the company. The enhanced shareholder value approach to governance has led to arguments for large listed companies following corporate governance requirements.

Chapter 3

Test yourself 3.1

1. Why might a private company appoint a company secretary?
Although there is no requirement for private companies to employ a company secretary, in practice many still choose to do so. The important tasks that would normally fall to a company secretary, including shareholder administration and communication, corporate governance and statutory compliance, must still be done. In the absence of a company secretary, s.270 of the CA2006 states that directors must take on this responsibility. This is why many private companies continue to employ a company secretary: in order to reduce the administrative and corporate governance burdens which would otherwise be placed on their directors.

2. Why is the company secretary often referred to as a bridge for information, communications advice and arbitration?
The company secretary is often referred to as a 'bridge' for information, communications, advice and arbitration because they play an important role as the board's communicator. This will differ from company to company. However, best practice is that the company secretary should be the person responsible for:

◆ communicating all board decisions to the relevant members of the management team. Although CEOs often intend to do this, evidence shows that due to their other work commitments, CEOs are not very good at doing this in a timely manner;

◆ managing the disclosure of the board's decision's to regulators and other stakeholders. This is because they understand the requirements as far as content to be disclosed and the importance of timely and balanced disclosure;

◆ liaising between the board members and senior management on logistics for board and board committee meetings, training sessions, board retreats, board evaluation sessions and other board events; and

◆ facilitating good information flows, between the boa d, individual board members, the committees and senior management that foster effective working relationships between them;

◆ being the primary point of contact between the non-executives and the company, as a source of information and advice. Without this, management could be distracted by requests from non-executive directors, some of which may be for the same information. Also, non-executive directors could receive conflicting information or advice depending on whom they speak to. The company secretary can collate the information and/or advice in a format which is more appropriate for the non-executive directors;

◆ ensuring that the board keeps in contact with shareholder opinion and that shareholders are briefed on the reasons behind the board's adoption of certain governance practices and decision-making; and

◆ ensuring that relevant disclosures on corporate governance and directors' remuneration are made in the companies annual report and accounts and that the annual report and accounts is made available electronically on the company's website.

Test yourself 3.2

1. Why is it important for a company secretary to have interpersonal skills and commercial and business acumen?

Many company secretaries face the following key challenges:

◆ being considered traitors by the executive team;

◆ supporting chairs exhibiting poor performance;

◆ acting as the third person in a CEO-chair relationship;

◆ becoming a pivotal contact for unsurmountable problems; and

◆ maintaining independence from other executives and board members.

To overcome these challenges company secretaries, in addition to their technical skills, needed commercial and business acumen and interpersonal skills, which many considered the most important.

In 2012, a study by the All Party Parliamentary Corporate Governance Group criticised many company secretaries for not being 'commercially minded' or aware. They saw this as being an important feature of the job, especially as they advise the board on governance issues. To be commercially aware, an individual must understand the business they are in, and make good practical decisions as a result. In the case of the company secretary, this means being able to advise the board on this basis so that they can make the decisions.

'The Company Secretary: Building trust through governance' highlighted the importance that the majority of company secretaries acknowledged that 'commercial awareness and abilities are critical to ensuring their understanding of what is right for the organisation, what information means and to whom relevant questions need to be passed'.

2. Name five interpersonal skills a company secretary should have and explain why each one is important to the company secretary in fulfilling their responsibilities.

◆ Empathy and relationship management – it is important for company secretaries to be able to build relationships to enable them to remain independent and to carry out their roles as conscience of the company and the governance adviser.

◆ Respectful, diplomatic and effective communication – to build relationships, especially with senior people within an organisation, the company secretary will need to be respectful and diplomatic. The communications with these senior people will have to be brief and clear as they may not have the time for a long-winded explanation.

◆ Active listening – the company secretary should look interested in what they are being told. This is part of being respectful. It will also help the company secretary to build relationships and obtain the information they need to do they job.

◆ Bringing issues to the surface, especially those relating to reputational risk – managing reputational risk is now seen as an important part of governance. As the governance adviser, the company secretary will therefore be required to raise with the board, at meetings or on other occasions, matters that are relevant to the reputation of company.

◆ Personal and social awareness – company secretaries need to be able to read the body language of the board members to help with interpreting what is said and meant at board meetings. This enables them to write the minutes. Company secretaries also need to be personally aware of how their own behaviours may effect the decision making of the board.

◆ Being able to summarise common concerns and interests – the company secretary may have to summarise a decision within a board meeting so that it is clear to all board members what decision they have taken. They may also have to highlight the concerns of management or external stakeholders during a board meeting to ensure that the board has all the information to make an effective decision.

◆ Generating alternative solutions – in order to help the board make a decision, it may be necessary for the company secretary to come up with an alternative solution. For instance, they could suggest a decision is delayed whilst more information is collected, or that there is additional reporting on the implementation of a proposal to give the board members reassurance on a decision.

◆ Respecting confidences – the origin of the wo d 'secretary' is the keeper of secrets and confidentiality is still an important part of the ole. To be able to discuss and advise the board and management, the company secretary needs to be trusted with information.

◆ Independent mindset – the company secretary has to be impartial as they work between the board and management, and the board and shareholders. To ensure that these relationships between the different governance parties work effectively, the company secretary will have to work with an open mind and see both sides of the arguments.

- Strength of personality – the company secretary needs to have the strength to stand up to the strong personalities in the organisation and present good governance practices. Sometimes the board and management may not want to hear what the company secretary has to say, and the company secretary needs the strength to be persistent in a respectful way.
- Appreciating the views of all parties – as mentioned above, it is important that company secretaries keep an open mind and appreciate the views of all parties when carrying out their role.
- Effective team-working – company secretaries are often required to lead or be members of teams producing major company projects, whether this is production of the annual report and accounts, being part of an M&A team or in the event management of the annual general meeting.
- Disagreeing constructively – often the company secretary may have to inform the chair or the CEO that they cannot do what they want to do. Being able to do this in a constructive way, and offering alternatives is better than just saying no.
- Emphasising commercially minded approaches – the benefit of an in house company secretary is that they should know their business. They should therefore be able to suggest commercially-minded solutions and approaches to problems and issues that arise.
- Integrity – as the conscience of the company it is important that the company secretary has the highest levels of integrity.

Test yourself 3.3

1. Why does a company secretary's position need to be one of seniority?

In order for the company secretary to carry out their duties and responsibilities effectively, they need to hold a position of seniority within the organisation. It is debated whether they should be a member of the executive team. Some think this compromises their independence. Whether or not they are a member of the executive team, they should attend meetings of the executive team. This will enable them to advise the executives on governance issues arising out of any proposals as they are being formulated. They can also advise on how the board might react to a particular proposal and what questions the executive should be prepared to answer when the proposal is considered by the board. Attending executive meetings also helps the company secretary get an understanding of the executive's positioning and reasons for suggesting the proposal which may help the company secretary if the proposal needs to be 'sold' to the chair. Remember that the company secretary can often fill the ole of mediator or arbitrator between the CEO and the chair.

2. How can an organisation maintain the independence of the company secretary?

'Appointment of the company secretary' states that:

'Boards have a right to expect the company secretary to give independent, impartial advice and support to all the directors, both individually and collectively as a board.'

It is for this reason that best practice is that company secretaries should be appointed and dismissed by the board as a whole.

Test yourself 3.4

1. What are the major challenges to independence of the company secretary?

The two main challenges to the independence of the company secretary are caused by:

◆ reporting lines, especially when the company secretary reports to a member of management; and

◆ dual roles – there may be conflict between the esponsibilities of the other role with those of the company secretary.

2. Is it appropriate for the company's in-house lawyer to carry out corporate governance responsibilities?

If the company secretary role is combined with another role such as that of the in-house lawyer or accountant, care should be taken to see that the governance role is not compromised.

A general counsel who is also given the role of the company secretary, in fulfilling their legal ole will often have to take sides to represent the particular interests of the company. And although they may be complying with the letter of the law and in the interests of management, they may not be acting in the best long-term interests of the company. This would be inconsistent with the company secretary's governance role which requires impartiality when advising on governance issues.

It may also prevent a company secretary from speaking out against bad governance or unethical practices, or proposals that are not in the long-term interests of the company, especially if to do so was costly or against the wishes of the CEO. The company secretary, in their governance role, should also be considering the reputational impact of the board's decision. This again may require the board to consider more than just complying with the laws and regulations.

3. Explain why companies may not want to outsource the role of the company secretary.

◆ An in-house company secretary acquires an in-depth knowledge and understanding of the company and its history, and also develops relationships with the board and management that an external firm lacks.

◆ An in-house company secretary is available at all times to discuss corporate governance issues. A law firm may be much slower in p oviding assistance or responding to questions.

◆ A qualified in-house company sec etary offers a wide range of services and is able to take on other responsibilities in a start-up or smaller company.

◆ An in-house company secretary may provide support that is difficult for an external firm to p ovide; for example, assisting the chair to prepare for meetings.

◆ An in-house company secretary can truly act as the 'conscience of the company' and has no conflict, in that they do not do other work for the company such as providing legal or accountancy services.

◆ An in-house company secretary can be relied upon to maintain confidentialit . In-house corporate secretaries can in many cases be held liable for any breaches in confidentialit , whereas this may be problematic in cases of an outsourced service.

Chapter 4

Test yourself 4.1

Why have different countries' corporate governance best practices developed in different ways?
Corporate governance has developed in different ways in different countries to reflect their distinct legal systems and also the specific issues that they e dealing with.

Chapter 5

Test yourself 5.1

1. Where might you find limitations on the directors' management powers?
Limitations on the directors' general management powers can be found in:

◆ an objects clause;

◆ other article provisions, which may impose a borrowing limit or a require shareholder approval;

◆ article provisions allowing the members to give directions to the directors;

◆ a shareholders' agreement – which could require shareholder approval for certain types of decisions; and

◆ the Companies Act 2006 and the Listing Rules – which both impose requirements for shareholder approval.

2. Identify at least two special powers that are usually conferred by articles on the directors.
Examples of special powers given to directors include:

◆ the power to delegate;

◆ the power to reject transfers;

◆   the power to pay and fix di ectors' remuneration and fees;

◆   the power to forfeit shares;

◆   the chair's right to a casting vote.

3. Is setting the company's strategy is a management decision?

Setting the company's strategy is a management decision. It is one of several management decisions that, under the UK Code, must be performed by the board. Accordingly, it is wrong to suggest that the board delegates all management responsibility to the executive directors.

4. Can shareholders interfere in the management of a company?

Most articles of association provide a method by which shareholders can give directions to the board (typically by passing a special resolution). Those directions could cover matters regarding the management of the company. However, shareholders do not normally interfere in this way on management issues as it easier for them to secure their objectives by appointing and removing directors.

Test yourself 5.2

1. Which of the general duties of directors arise from which of the fiduciary duties of trustees?

Directors' general duties	Fiduciary duties of trustees
Duty to act within powers in accordance with the company's constitution (and to use those powers for proper purposes).	Duty to act in accordance with the trust deed.
Duty to promote the success of the company.	Duty to act in good faith in the interests of the beneficiaries
Duty to exercise independent judgement.	A combination of the duty to avoid conflicts of inte est and the duty to act in good faith in the interests of the beneficiaries
Duty to exercise reasonable care, skill and diligence (s. 174).	N/A
Duty to avoid conflicts of inte est (s. 175).	A combination of the duty not to place themselves in a position where their own interest conflicts with their fiducia duties and the duty not to make a profit f om their position.
Duty not to accept benefits f om third parties.	A combination of the duty not to place themselves in a position where their own interest conflicts with their fiducia duties and the duty not to make a profit f om their position.
Duty to declare any interest in proposed transactions or arrangements.	A combination of the duty not to place themselves in a position where their own interest conflicts with their fiducia duties and the duty not to make a profit f om their position.

2. What is a fiduciary?

A 'fiduciary' is a person in a position of trust, like a trustee.

3. What are the remedies for a breach of the general duties?

The remedies available for a breach of the general duties by directors vary depending on the nature of the breach. As a general rule, directors can be made to repay any illegal payments they have received or secret profits they have made. Where there is a breach of the duty of skill and care or the directors have acted beyond their powers, the company can be awarded compensation for any losses that it has suffered. Where the directors have acted outside their powers, the courts cannot normally declare the transaction void. However, where the directors have used their powers for improper purposes, the transaction can be declared void. Where a director has failed to disclose an interest in a transaction, the company can choose whether or not to treat that transaction as void.

Test yourself 5.3

1. Why are directors rarely sued for exceeding their powers?

Directors are rarely sued for exceeding their powers because:

◆ recent practice has been to draft any objects clause very widely so as not to constrain what the directors can do;

◆ companies are no longer required to have an objects clause and if they do not have one, their objects are deemed to be unrestricted;

◆ even if a company has a restricted objects clause, the company must have suffered a loss for it to be worth suing the directors.

2. Why do you think there are a lot more cases about directors using their powers for improper purposes?

There are probably more cases about directors using their powers for improper purposes:

◆ because this happens more often;

◆ directors are not aware of the underlying rule and believe, from a reading of the articles, that their powers are unrestricted in this regard;

◆ the remedies that the courts are willing to apply include declaring the improper transaction void.

3. What are the consequences of the directors exceeding their powers and how do these compare with cases where they have used their powers for improper purposes?

Where the directors exceed their powers, the transaction is still enforceable by third parties dealing with the company in good faith. However the directors can be sued for any losses that the company suffered as a result of the breach. Where the directors have used their powers for improper purposes, the transaction can be declared void.

Test yourself 5.4

1. According to the CA2006, what is the purpose of the strategic report?
According to the Act, the purpose of the strategic report is to inform members of the company and help them assess how the directors have performed their duty under s. 172, to promote the success of the company.

2. What does 'promoting the success of the company' mean?
The Act provides that directors have a duty to exercise their powers to promote the success of the company for the benefit of the members. In doing so, they must regard the likely consequences of any decision in the long term and various other matters. It would appear therefore that success can be equated with what is in the best interests the company's members/shareholders. Directors are allowed to take other interests into account. However, the interests of shareholders are paramount. The benefit to shareholders does not need to be immediate. A company may, for example, sustain a period of losses before it becomes profitable, as has been the case with most of today's big technology companies. The directors may not even be in breach of this duty if the company fails as long as they believed at the time that their actions would promote the success of the company. Section 172 also recognises that a successful company needs a contented and committed workforce, good relationships with its customers and suppliers, and a reputation for high standards of business conduct. It also recognises that a company's reputation may suffer if it has an adverse effect on the environment.

3. Do the directors need to consider stakeholder interests whenever they make a decision?
Where a decision may impact on the interests of stakeholders, directors must take those interests into account. Not all decisions will have an impact on stakeholders. Some may only have a very minor (or theoretical) impact. There is no need to record the fact that the board has taken into account the interests of stakeholders in these circumstances. It is much more important to do so in circumstances where the decision may have a major impact on stakeholders (e.g. shutting down a factory). The fact that such a decision might not be in the interests of factory workers does not prevent the company from making that decision.

Test yourself 5.5

1. What tests should be applied in judging whether a director has breached the duty of skill and care?
Under s. 174(2) the standard against which the duty of directors to exercise due diligence, skill and care is judged directors is that of:

'a reasonably diligent person with:

(a) the general knowledge, skill and experience that may reasonably be expected of a person carrying out the functions carried out by the director in relation to the company, and
(b) the general knowledge, skill and experience that the director has.'

2. To what extent can directors rely on other company officials?

Directors are entitled to trust people in positions of responsibility until there is reason to distrust them (Norman v Theodore Goddard [1991]). However, delegation by the directors does not absolve them completely from the duty to exercise due skill and care. They can be found to be in breach of that duty if they fail to exercise adequate supervision over those performing those delegated functions.

Test yourself 5.6

1. What sort of conflicts does s. 175 relate to?

The duty to avoid conflicts in s. 175 applies in particular to the exploitation of any property, information or opportunity. Section 175(3) clarifies that it does not apply to a conflict of interest arising in relation to a transaction or arrangement with the company in which a director has an interest. This type of conflict is dealt with separately by ss. 177 and 182 of the Act.

2. What are the consequences of a breach of this duty?

A director who wrongly makes a profit by exploiting a business opportunity that belongs to the company can be made to repay that profit. The courts may also rule that a third party acquiring company property through a breach of duty by directors holds that property on behalf of the company as a constructive trustee and, as a result, can be forced to return it.

3. Who can authorise conflicts of interest and what is the effect of authorisation?

Under s. 175 of the 2006 Act, the non-conflicted directors may now authorise conflicts such as the exploitation of business opportunities. This is the case for a private company unless the articles provide otherwise. In the case of a public company, the articles must specifically allow the board to authorise such conflicts. If a conflict has been properly authorised, the duty is not infringed, which means that the director cannot be sued on these grounds.

Test yourself 5.7

1. Do directors' interest in transactions and arrangement need to be authorised?

A conflict of interest that arises out of a director's interest in a transaction or arrangement with the company does not need to be authorised. The transaction itself may need to be authorised by the board if it is one of the matters reserved for its decision. However, the fact that the director has an interest in the transaction does not need to be authorised either by the board or the shareholders.

2. Why are directors required to disclose their interests in proposed transactions?

Directors are required to disclose any interest they may have in a proposed transaction or arrangement with the company to:

◆ ensure that the other directors are aware of that interest before entering into that transaction or arrangement; and

◆ ensure that the chair is able to rule on whether the director can participate in the decision on that matter.

3. Why are they required to disclose their interests in existing transactions?

Directors are required to disclose their interests in existing transactions because:

◆ they might otherwise be able to exert covert influence on the continuation or management of that contract or arrangement; and

◆ a failure to disclose an interest in a proposed transaction becomes a criminal offence under s. 182 as soon as it becomes an existing transaction, i.e. when the company enters into that transaction and the director's interest has still not been disclosed.

Test yourself 5.8

1. List the general duties of directors under Part 10, Chapter 2 of Companies Act 2006.

The general duties of directors under Part 10, Chapter 2 of Companies Act 2006 are:

◆ to act within their powers in accordance with the company's constitution (and to use those powers for proper purposes) (s. 171);

◆ to promote the success of the company (s. 172);

◆ to exercise independent judgement (s. 173);

◆ to exercise reasonable care, skill and diligence (s. 174);

◆ to avoid conflicts of interest (s. 175);

◆ not to accept benefits from third parties (s. 176); and

◆ to declare any interest in proposed transactions or arrangements (s. 177).

2. What is a derivative action?

A derivative action is a special court procedure which enables shareholders to bring a legal action in the name of the company against a director(s) for breach of duty. If the action succeeds, any compensation is awarded to the company rather than to the shareholders who initiated it.

Chapter 6

Test yourself 6.1

1. What is the overarching role of the board according to the UK Corporate Governance Code?
To promote the long-term sustainable success of the company, generating value for shareholders and contributing to wider society.

2. Cite three examples of things that the Code expects boards to do in performing this role.
Any three from:

◆ Establish the company's purpose, values and strategy, and satisfy itself that these and its culture are aligned.

◆ Act with integrity, lead by example and promote the desired culture.

◆ Ensure that the necessary resources are in place for the company to meet its objectives and measure performance against them.

◆ Establish a framework of prudent and effective controls, which enable risk to be assessed and managed.

◆ Ensure effective engagement with, and encourage participation from, shareholders and other stakeholders.

◆ Ensure that workforce policies and practices are consistent with the company's values and support its long-term sustainable success.

3. List three functions that the board performs through its board committees on which it still has the final say.
Examples include:

◆ making new appointments to the board;

◆ approving the accounts and other financial statements;

◆ establishing a framework of prudent and effective controls, which enable risk to be assessed and managed; and

◆ proposing the appointment of auditors.

4. To what extent does the board manage the company's business?
The board can be said to have a supervisory role in the management of the company's business. Responsibility for day-to-day management will be delegated to the executive team. However, the board will still retain control over key management functions, such as setting the company's culture, strategy, purpose and objectives and monitoring performance against those objectives. In addition, most boards will require certain critical management decisions to be referred to the board. The thresholds for when board approval is necessary will be set out in a schedule of matters reserved to the board.

Test yourself 6.2

1. What is the role of the company chair?
The chair leads the board and is responsible for its overall effectiveness in directing the company. The chair should demonstrate objective judgement, promote a culture of openness and debate, facilitate constructive board relations and the effective contribution of all non-executive directors, and ensure that directors receive accurate, timely and clear information.

2. What are the requirements of the UK Code of Corporate Governance with regards to the independence of the company chair?
The chair should be independent on appointment when assessed against the circumstances set out in Code provision 10 regarding the independence of non-executive directors. In addition, a chief executive should not go on to be chair of the same company.

3. Why should the role of chair and CEO be separate?
The chair leads the board of directors. The CEO is the leader of the management team. The Code requires there to be a clear division of responsibilities between these two functions to prevent one person from having an overly dominant influence on decision-making in the company.

Test yourself 6.3

1. How does the FRC Guidance on Board Effectiveness expect the CEO to contribute to board effectiveness?
The CEO is expected to contribute by:

◆ proposing strategy to the board, and for delivering the strategy as agreed;

◆ setting an example to the company's employees, and communicating to them the expectations of the board in relation to the company's culture, values and behaviours;

◆ supporting the chair to make certain that appropriate standards of governance permeate through all parts of the organisation;

◆ making certain that the board is made aware, when appropriate, of the views of employees on issues of relevance to the business; and

◆ ensuring the board knows the executive directors' views on business issues in order to improve the standard of discussion in the boardroom and, prior to final decision on an issue, explain in a balanced way any divergence of view in the executive team.

2. How does the FRC Guidance on Board Effectiveness expect the executive directors to contribute to board effectiveness?
The Guidance suggests that executive directors should:

◆ not see themselves only as members of the chief executive's team;

◆ broaden their understanding of their board responsibilities by taking up a non-executive director position on another board; and

◆ welcome constructive challenge from non-executive directors as an essential aspect of good governance, and encourage their non-executive colleagues to test proposals in the light of their wider experience outside the company.

3. What is the function of an executive committee?

The role of the executive committee is usually to act as a sounding board for the CEO and as a forum to receive and discuss operational updates and progress reports. It is not usually a formal committee of the board, but usually one that is established by the CEO to assist in the management of the business.

Test yourself 6.4

1. How are NEDs expected to contribute towards the deliberations of the board?

According to the UK Corporate Governance Code, NEDs are expected to:

◆ provide constructive challenge;

◆ provide strategic guidance;

◆ offer specialist advice; and

◆ hold management to account (2018 Code principle H).

2. What particular functions are independent NEDs expected to fulfil under the Code?

The UK Corporate Governance Code expects independent NEDs to:

◆ lead the process for board appointments, succession planning and ensuring the development of a diverse pipeline, through their participation in the nomination committee;

◆ satisfy themselves on the integrity of financial information and that financial controls and systems of risk management are robust and defensible, through their participation in the audit committee; and

◆ set the directors' remuneration policy and determine appropriate levels of remuneration for the chair, executive directors and senior management, through their participation in the remuneration committee.

3. List six circumstances in which a NED would not normally be considered independent.

Any six out of:

◆ is or has been an employee of the company or group within the last five years;

◆ has, or has had within the last three years, a material business relationship with the company either directly, or as a partner, shareholder, director or senior employee of a body that has such a relationship with the company;

♦ has received or receives additional remuneration from the company apart from a director's fee, participates in the company's share option or a performance-related pay scheme, or is a member of the company's pension scheme;

♦ has close family ties with any of the company's advisers, directors or senior employees;

♦ holds cross-directorships or has significant links with other directors through involvement in other companies or bodies;

♦ represents a significant shareholder; or

♦ has served on the board for more than nine years from the date of their first election.

4. What should the board do if any of its NEDs do not meet these independence criteria?
The board should identify, in the annual report and accounts, the non-executive directors it considers to be independent for the purposes of the Code. If a NED is not identified as being independent, the assumption must be that the board does not consider them to be independent. Boards can decide that a NED is independent even though that individual does not comply fully with the independence criteria. However, where this is the case, they must provide a clear explanation in the report and accounts.

Test yourself 6.5

List the main criticisms regarding non-executive director effectiveness.
The main criticisms of NEDs include:

♦ a lack of knowledge about the company's business;

♦ insufficient time spent with the company;

♦ defects in the decision-making process; and

♦ ineffective challenge.

Test yourself 6.6

1. What is the governance role of the secretary?
According to the UK Corporate Governance Code, the company secretary is 'responsible for advising the board on all governance matters'. It recommends that 'all directors should have access to advice of the company secretary' in this regard. The Code also envisages that the secretary will have a supporting role in ensuring that the board has the policies, processes, information, time and resources it needs in order to function effectively and efficiently. The Guidance on Board Effectiveness states that the company secretary is responsible for

ensuring that board procedures are complied with, advising the board on all governance matters, supporting the chair and helping the board and its committees to function efficiently.

2. Who should the secretary report to?

The FRC's Guidance on Board Effectiveness recommends that the company secretary should report to the chair on all governance matters, but points out that this does not preclude the company secretary from also reporting to the CEO or some other executive director in relation to any other executive management responsibilities.

Chapter 7

Test yourself 7.1

1. If a board is comprised of a chair, three executive directors, one of whom is the CEO, and a non-executive director representing the major shareholder, how many independent directors will be required to comply with the UK Corporate Governance Code?

Under the Code, at least half the board (excluding the chair) must be independent NEDs. Accordingly, the minimum number of independent NEDs required must balance out the three executive directors and the NED who is not independent. This means that there must be at least four independent NEDs.

2. List the factors that will typically influence the size of the board.

The main factors that will typically influence the size of the board are:

◆ the requirements for a balanced board;

◆ the requirements of the UK Code on the composition of the board;

◆ the need to service board committees; and

◆ the ability of the board to hold productive, constructive discussions and make prompt rational decisions.

Test yourself 7.2

1. What is a skills matrix?

A skills matrix is a table that displays people's proficiency in specified skills, knowledge, competencies and aptitudes.

2. What purpose would such a matrix serve in the process of appointing a new director?

A skills matrix can be used:

◆ to assess whether there are any areas in which the skills and aptitudes of the board as a whole may be lacking, or may become lacking as a result of the departure of one or more directors;

◆ to assess whether the board is over-reliant on the skills or aptitudes of certain individuals in any particular area;

◆ to map the existing skillset against that required to execute strategy and meet future challenges; and

◆ to draw up a profile of the ideal candidate for any board vacancies.

Test yourself 7.3

1. How does the 2018 UK Corporate Governance Code seek to promote diversity?

Code Principle J provides that both appointments and succession plans should be based on merit and objective criteria and, within this context, should promote diversity of gender, social and ethnic backgrounds, cognitive and personal strengths. In addition, Code Principle L states that the annual board evaluation should consider diversity.

However, the main tool used to promote diversity is to require disclosure in the report of the nomination committee on diversity issues.

These disclosure requirements effectively mean that the board must adopt a diversity and inclusion policy for board and senior executive appointments, which could include diversity targets, and succession policies that promote diversity. These policies could be part of an overall diversity and inclusion policy that covers the workforce as a whole or in addition to it.

2. List the types of disclosures listed companies are required to make on diversity.

Listed companies are required under the Code to make the following disclosures in the report of the nomination committee:

◆ the process used in relation to appointments, its approach to succession planning and how both support developing a diverse pipeline;

◆ how the board evaluation has or will influence board composition;

◆ the policy on diversity and inclusion, its objectives and linkage to company strategy, how it has been implemented and progress on achieving the objectives (this requirement is also mirrored by DTR 7.2.8A); and

◆ the gender balance of those in the senior management and their direct reports.

CA2006, s. 414C also requires quoted companies to include in their strategic report a breakdown showing at the end of the financial year the number of persons of each sex who were:

◆ directors;

◆ senior managers; and

◆ employees of the company.

Test yourself 7.4

1. What are the three main roles of the nomination committee?
The three main roles of the nomination committee are to:

◆ lead the process for appointments;

◆ ensure plans are in place for orderly succession to both the board and senior management positions; and

◆ oversee the development of a diverse pipeline for succession.

2. What are the membership requirements for the committee?
The Code provides that a majority of members of the nomination committee should be independent non-executive directors. This provision is effectively designed to enable the company chair to serve on the committee, even if not considered independent.

Test yourself 7.5

1. Outline the process for appointing a new NED.
The nomination committee should evaluate the skills, experience and knowledge on the board, the future challenges affecting the business, and, in the light of this evaluation, prepare a description of the role and capabilities required for a particular appointment.

It should then agree the process to be undertaken to identify, sift and interview suitable candidates, ensuring that a proper assessment of values and expected behaviours is built into the recruitment process. This will typically involve engaging recruitment consultants.

The nomination committee will interview a selection of candidates put forward by the recruitment consultants and use these interviews to narrow down the list of candidates or ask for further candidates to be proposed.

In the final stages of the process, the nomination committee may invite the final candidate(s) to meet other members of the board.

After taking soundings from other board members, the committee will make its final recommendation to the board, which will then make the final decision.

As the Code requires all directors to be re-elected annually, the shareholders will have the opportunity to confirm or reject the appointment at the next AGM.

2. How might that process differ when seeking to appoint a new chair or chief executive?

The appointment of a new chair or CEO may involve the consideration of internal candidates. An existing independent NED could be elected as the chair and an existing senior executive could be promoted to become CEO. In contrast, the appointment of a NED will always involve recruiting external candidates if they are to be considered independent.

Test yourself 7.6

1. Briefly outline the three time horizons that a succession plan should cover.

Succession plans should consider the following different time horizons:

◆ contingency planning – for sudden and unforeseen departures;

◆ medium-term planning – the orderly replacement of current board members and senior executives (e.g. retirement); and

◆ long-term planning – the relationship between the delivery of the company strategy and objectives to the skills needed on the board now and in the future.

2. Why is it more difficult to prepare a succession plan for executive directors?

There is no minimum term of office for executive directors. If the company is successful, the CEO may seek to avoid any discussion surrounding their eventual departure. If the company is not successful there may be sudden, forced departures. Senior executives may also be poached by other companies, leaving a sudden vacancy.

Test yourself 7.7

1. Give three legitimate reasons why the nomination committee might propose a refreshment of the board.

Refreshment could be used:

◆ to replace a non-executive who is not making an effective contribution;

◆ to meet diversity targets; or

◆ to bring in a new director who has certain critical skills.

2. Why does the Code require all directors to offer themselves for re-election on an annual basis?

According to the FRC, the annual re-election requirement was introduced to give shareholders an annual opportunity to express their views on the performance of the directors and to give boards an incentive to listen and respond to their concerns. The FRC hoped that this would in turn lead to ongoing engagement. Legally, annual re-elections mean that shareholders seeking the removal of a director do not need to propose their own resolution, which would involve giving special notice.

Chapter 8

Test yourself 8.1

1. Cite five factors that can limit effective decision making (excluding those relating to the supply of information).
Any five from:

- A dominant personality or group of directors on the board, inhibiting contribution from others.
- Insufficient diversity of perspective on the board, which can contribute to 'group think'.
- Excessive focus on risk mitigation or insufficient attention to risk.
- A compliance mindset and failure to treat risk as part of the decision-making process.
- Insufficient knowledge and ability to test underlying assumptions.
- Failure to listen to and act upon concerns that are raised.
- Failure to recognise the consequences of running the business on the basis of self-interest and other poor ethical standards.
- A lack of openness by management, a reluctance to involve non-executive directors, or a tendency to bring matters to the board for sign-off rather than debate.
- Complacent or intransigent attitudes.
- Inability to challenge effectively.
- Lack of time for debate and truncated debate.
- Undue focus on short-term time horizons.

2. What sort of significant decisions might the Guidance on Board Effectiveness have in mind when it suggests that boards may wish to consider extra steps?
Extra steps might be considered appropriate where the board is setting the company's strategy, purpose, culture and objectives and in situations where there appear to be strongly divergent views.

Test yourself 8.2

1. What are the four main stages in the development of a board pack?
The four main stages in the development of a board pack are:

- identifying the information the board needs;
- commissioning board papers;
- writing board papers; and
- collating and distributing the board pack.

2. What are the typical features of board portal software?
The typical features of board portal software are:

- secure tools to facilitate the distribution and use of electronic agenda papers and board packs;
- archiving facilities that enable directors to refer back to the papers and minutes prepared for previous meetings;
- secure tools which enable directors to annotate and make notes on the agenda papers;
- voting tools;
- tools to facilitate the circulation and approval of minutes, and
- secure messaging features.

3. What are the advantages of board portal software over traditional hard copy agenda papers?
The advantages of board portal software over traditional hard copy agenda papers are:

- reduced time spent producing, collating and circulating board papers;
- secure storage of those documents;
- easier access to and portability of those documents;
- easier navigation of papers during meetings;
- quicker distribution;
- ability to centrally store annotations and notes made by participants;
- ability to refer back to papers and minutes for previous meetings;
- secure messaging facilities.

Test yourself 8.3

1. How is corporate culture related to a company's strategy, values and purpose?
According to the Guidance on Board Effectiveness: 'An effective board defines the company's purpose and then sets a strategy to deliver it, underpinned by the values and behaviours that shape its culture and the way it conducts its business.'

A company's values and behaviours (its culture) should therefore be aligned with its purpose.

2. Why, in particular, might pay and performance structures lead to a bad corporate culture?

Pay incentives may reward employees for behaviour that is not in the best interests of the company's clients and customers leading to a breakdown of trust, e.g. the payment protection insurance mis-selling scandal in the UK.

Test yourself 8.4

How might the company secretary be involved in the procedures to enable the directors to obtain independent professional advice?

The secretary should propose that the board adopts a procedure to be followed by directors seeking to take independent professional advice. This could be done by way of a board resolution or as part of a board procedures manual. If that procedure sets certain conditions or imposes any financial limits, some sort of pre-approval mechanism will be required. The secretary could be the person whose approval is required. However, this could compromise the secretary's impartiality, particularly if the conditions require difficult judgement calls to be made. In these circumstances, it makes more sense for the chair or the senior independent director to be the person who makes the decision. Even if the secretary is not personally involved in the approval process, it may be sensible for the initial application by a director to be made through the secretary, who then forwards it on to the appropriate person for approval. Someone will need to record the fact that an application has been made and whether the necessary approval has been given (or refused). This information will also need to be reported to the board, particularly where approval has been given and advice has been obtained. Somebody also needs to authorise the payment of any invoices to the independent advisers. These task will typically fall to the secretary.

Test yourself 8.5

1. Under the Code what should the annual performance evaluation cover?

According to Principle L of the UK Code, the annual performance evaluation should cover:

◆ board evaluation: the composition of the board, its diversity and how effectively members work together to achieve objectives; and

◆ individual evaluation: should demonstrate whether each individual director continues to contribute effectively.

Code Provision 21 clarifies that the annual evaluation should extend not only to the performance of the board and individual directors, but also to board committees and the chair.

2. What information should be disclosed in the annual report and accounts on the annual performance evaluation?

Code Provision 23 requires the nomination committee report to state:

◆ how the board evaluation has been conducted;

◆ the nature and extent of an external evaluator's contact with the board and individual directors;

◆ the outcomes and actions taken; and

◆ how the evaluation has or will influence board composition.

A company that does not comply with Code Provision 21 on annual performance evaluation will also need to include an explanation in its corporate governance report.

3. Under the Code, how often should a company have an externally facilitated evaluation?

Code Provision 21 requires FTSE 350 companies to have an externally-facilitated board evaluation at least every three years. It requires chairs of other companies to consider having a regular externally facilitated board evaluation.

Test yourself 8.6

1. What should the aims of an induction process be?

Induction programmes should ultimately seek to enhance the effectiveness of new directors. According to the ICSA Guidance on Induction of Directors, they should aim to:

◆ build an understanding of the nature of the company, its business and the markets in which it operates;

◆ build a link with the company's people;

◆ build an understanding of the company's main relationships; and

◆ ensure an understanding of the role of a director and the framework within which the board operates.

2. How might a company benefit from having its executive directors serve as NEDs on other boards?

Executive directors serving as NEDs on other company boards will:

◆ gain experience of how other boards operate;

◆ be able to compare different practices and recommend the adoption of those that appear to be better; and

◆ experience first-hand what it is like to be a NED and what NEDs expect and require in order to perform effectively.

Chapter 9

Test yourself 9.1

1. In what way is financial reporting connected to corporate governance?
Financial reporting falls within the context of corporate governance as it involves the concepts of accountability and transparency.

2. What is the purpose of financial reporting and how is that purpose different in listed companies?
Below is a list of users of a company's financial reporting and why they find it of interest.

◆ Potential investors are interested in the ability of the company to generate net cash flows for dividends, distributable profits, or an increase in the share price, and to assist the decision to buy, hold or sell equities. They are also interested in assessing the stewardship or accountability of management.

◆ Creditors are interested in the amounts, timing, and uncertainty of future cash flows that will give rise to interest, repayment of borrowings, and/or increases in the prices of debt securities. They are interested in the security of their debt.

◆ Suppliers are interested in the fact that the entity may be able to pay a debt, when it comes due, for goods or services provided to the entity.

◆ Employees are interested in the stability, profitability, and growth of their employer, which gives rise to the continuing ability to pay salaries, wages, and other employment-associated benefits.

◆ Customers are interested in ensuring the continued supply of goods or services, especially if these customers have a long-term association with or are dependent on the company.

◆ Governments are interested in the efficient allocation of economic resources, determining and applying taxation to the entity and/or for preparing national statistics.

◆ Regulators are interested in being able to assess that the company is complying with all of the laws, regulations, standards and codes applicable to it.

◆ The public has variable interests – including the assessment of the company's prosperity, activities and ability to continue participating in the local economy and in local activities.

The financial reporting requirements for listed companies are more rigorous than those for private companies. This is due to the fact that listed companies also have to be accountable and transparent to their shareholders. This is due to the separation of ownership and control between the shareholders and the board of the company whom the shareholders appoint to manage the company on their behalf.

3. How can a company mislead the market in its financial reporting?

A company can misreport their financial numbers to improve its financial position through:

◆ The adoption of accounting policies that give a more flattering picture of the company's position.

◆ Claiming that revenue or profits were earned earlier than they were. This can happen when a company has a contract for several years. Revenue from the contract can be accounted for in the first year instead of being spread over the life of the contract.

◆ Taking debts off the company's balance sheet. This can be achieved by transferring these debts to other companies (special purpose vehicles).

◆ Disguising money from loans as operating income so that the company's reported cash flow from operating activities is increased.

◆ Over-valuing the company's assets.

Test yourself 9.2

1. What is the purpose of the audit committee?

The audit committee is key to ensuring that an organisation has robust and effective processes relating to financial reporting, internal controls, risk management and ethics. The committee is also the main oversight body for the internal and external auditors.

2. Briefly describe the four areas over which the audit committee would typically have responsibility?

The FRC in their 'Guidance on Audit Committees' provides information about the role and responsibilities of the audit committee. These include:

Annual reports and other periodic reports

The audit committee should review, and report to the board on, significant financial reporting issues and judgements made in connection with the preparation of the company's financial statements, interim reports, preliminary announcements and related formal statements. The guidance notes that it is the responsibility of management, and not the audit committee, to prepare complete and accurate financial statements and disclosures in accordance with accounting standards and other regulations. The audit committee should consider:

◆ whether the company has adopted appropriate accounting policies, and any changes to them;

◆ the methods used to account for significant or unusual transactions where the accounting treatment is open to different approaches and the judgements made as to the methods chosen;

◆ the clarity and completeness of disclosures in the financial statements and consider whether the disclosures made are set properly in context;

♦   the related information presented with the financial statements, including the strategic report, and corporate governance statements relating to the audit and to risk management; and

♦   the content of the annual report and accounts and advise the board on whether, taken as a whole, it is fair, balanced and understandable.

Internal control and risk management systems

The audit committee should review the company's internal financial controls, that is, the systems established to identify, assess, manage and monitor financial risks, as part of their expected roles and responsibilities in the UK Corporate Governance Code 2018. If a separate risk committee has not been established, the audit committee should also review the company's risk management system.

The company's management has day-to-day responsibility for the risk management and internal control systems, including the financial controls, and these should form an integral part of the company's day-to-day business processes. The audit committee should receive reports from management on the effectiveness of the systems they have established, and the conclusions of any testing carried out by internal or external auditors. It should consider whether the level of assurance it is receiving is enough to help the board in satisfying itself that the internal controls are operating effectively.

Internal audit

The audit committee should regularly review the need for establishing an internal audit function. More detail on internal audit is provided in Part 4.

In the absence of an internal audit function, the audit committee will need to assess whether other processes need to be put in place to provide sufficient and objective assurance that the system of internal control is functioning as intended.

Where there is an internal audit function, the audit committee should:

♦   review and approve the role and mandate of the internal audit function;

♦   approve the annual internal audit plan and budget ensuring that sufficient resources are available to permit internal audit to carry out its role effectively;

♦   monitor and review the effectiveness of the work of the internal audit function;

♦   review and annually approve the internal audit charter to ensure that it is appropriate to the current needs of the organisation; and

♦   approve the appointment or termination of appointment of the head of internal audit.

External audit

The audit committee is responsible for overseeing the company's relations with the external auditor. This role includes:

◆ initiating a tender process, negotiating the fee and scope of the audit and making formal recommendations to the board on the appointment, reappointment and removal of the external auditors;

◆ annually assessing, and reporting to the board on, the qualification, expertise and resources, and independence of the external auditors and the effectiveness of the audit process, with a recommendation on whether to propose to the shareholders that the external auditor be reappointed;

◆ developing and recommending to the board for approval a policy in relation to the provision of non-audit services by the external auditor. Once the policy is approved, the audit committee should be responsible for approving or recommending to the board for approval any non-audit services to be carried out by the external auditor within that policy;

◆ meeting with the external auditors prior to the start of each annual audit cycle, to ensure that appropriate plans and resources are in place for the audit. The audit committee may also wish to hold an initial discussion without the auditor to consider factors that could affect audit quality and discuss these with the auditor;

◆ review the audit representation letters before signature and give particular consideration to matters where representation has been requested that relate to non-standard issues. These letters confirm that all the information provided to the auditors for during the audit process is complete and appropriate based on the board's own knowledge;

◆ following the audit, reviewing with the external auditors, in a timely manner, the findings of their work and the auditor's report;

◆ review and monitor management's responsiveness to the external auditor's findings and recommendations;

◆ assessing the effectiveness of the audit process; and

◆ investigating, if the external auditor resigns, the issues giving rise to such resignation and consider whether any action is required.

◆ The FRC 'Guidance on Audit Committees' states that the audit committee should deliberate on its agenda on its own initiative rather than relying solely on the work of the external auditor. This requires the audit committee to decide what information and assurance it requires in order to properly carry out its roles to review, monitor and provide assurance or recommendations to the board and, where there are gaps, how these should be addressed.

3. What is the audit committee's relationship with shareholders?
The FRC Guidance on Audit Committees states that the audit committee has a role in ensuring that shareholder interests are properly protected in relation to financial reporting and internal control. In carrying out this role the audit committee should:

◆ consider the clarity of its reporting and be prepared to meet investors; and

◆ develop for inclusion in the annual report, a separate report describing the work of the audit committee in discharging its responsibilities, which should be signed by the chair of the audit committee.

The chair of the audit committee should be present at the annual general meeting to answer questions on the separate section of the annual report describing the audit committee's activities and matters within the scope of the audit committee's responsibilities.

4. What matters should be included in the audit committee report?
The FRC Guidance on Audit Committees recommends that the audit committee report to be included in the annual report should include the following matters:

◆ a summary of the role and work of the audit committee;

◆ how the audit committee composition requirements have been addressed, and the names and qualifications of all members of the audit committee during the period, if not provided elsewhere;

◆ the number of audit committee meetings;

◆ how the audit committee's performance evaluation has been conducted;

◆ an explanation of how the committee has assessed the effectiveness of the external audit process;

◆ the approach taken to the appointment or reappointment of the external auditor;

◆ the length of tenure of the current audit firm;

◆ the current audit partner name, and for how long the partner has held the role;

◆ when a tender was last conducted and advance notice of any retendering plans;

◆ if the external auditor provides non-audit services, the committee's policy for approval of non-audit services;

◆ how auditor objectivity and independence is safeguarded;

◆ the audit fees for the statutory audit and for audit related services and other non-audit services, including the ratio of audit to non-audit work;

◆ for each significant engagement, or category of engagements, explain what the services are and why the audit committee concluded that it was in the interests of the company to purchase them from the external auditor;

◆ an explanation of how the committee has assessed the effectiveness of internal audit and satisfied itself that the quality, experience and expertise of the function is appropriate for the business;

◆ the significant issues that the committee considered, including: issues in relation to the financial statements and how these were addressed, having regard to matters communicated to it by the auditors. The section need not repeat information disclosed elsewhere in the annual report and accounts, but could provide signposts to that information; and

◆ the nature and extent of interaction (if any) with the FRC's Corporate Reporting Review team.

Test yourself 9.3

1. What is the purpose of an external audit?
The purpose of an independent audit of the company is to make sure that the financial statements of the company can be relied upon.

2. Who is responsible for detecting fraud in a company?
The external auditors' report provides an opinion on compliance with the law and accounting standards, and whether the accounts that have been prepared by the board present a true and (in some cases) fair picture of the financial reality of the company. They are not responsible for detecting fraud or errors in the organisation's financial statements. This is the responsibility of the board of directors.

3. How does an audit report become modified?
If an external auditor has issued a modified audit report it is a serious issue, as it implies there are potentially grave concerns about the financial statements and the financial condition of the company. It also implies that the external auditor and the board of the company could not agree on the application of accounting policies and hence the content of the financial statements. There are three types of modified audit opinion:

◆ A qualified audit opinion which is given when, in the opinion of the external auditor, the financial statements would give a true and fair view except for a particular matter, which the external auditor explains.

◆ An adverse opinion which is given when the external auditor considers that there are material mis-statements in the accounts and that these are 'pervasive'. In effect, the external auditor is stating that they believe that the information in the financial statements is seriously incorrect.

◆ A disclaimer of opinion which is given in cases where the external auditor has been unable to obtain the information that they need to give an audit opinion. The lack of information means that the auditor is unable to state that the financial statements give a true and fair view, and that there may possibly be serious mis-statements that the external auditor has been unable to check.

4. How can a company protect an external auditor's independence?
The UK Corporate Governance Code gives the audit committee the responsibility for reviewing and monitoring the independence and objectivity

of the external auditors. The UK FRC Guidance on Audit Committees suggests various measures an audit committee should take in carrying out this role. These include the following:

◆ The committee should seek reassurance that the auditors and their staff have no familial, financial, employment, investment or business relationship with the organisation that could adversely affect their independence or objectivity.

◆ The committee should seek information annually from the audit firm about its policies for maintaining independence and monitoring compliance with relevant requirements.

The company should consider, as another measure for protecting auditor independence, rotating auditors. This can be done in one of two ways:

◆ rotation of audit partner; and
◆ rotation of audit firm.

The audit committee should also meet with the auditors at least one per year as part of the annual audit process without management present to ensure that the auditors are not being intimidated by management.

Chapter 10

Test yourself 10.1

1. Explain the difference between CSR, corporate citizenship and sustainability.
There is no one definition of CSR. Some organisations understand it as purely charitable giving, others as an integral part of their business models and hence strategic planning. Others combine their environmental activities with CSR. The type of involvement in CSR by organisations will depend on their operational activities, their understanding of CSR, and the philosophy and values of their organisation.

The term corporate citizenship has a wider definition than CSR. Corporate citizenship describes how companies should act in the same way as the citizens of the countries in which they operate, that is, to meet the countries' legal, social, ethical and economic responsibilities expected of its citizens. This requires companies to balance the financial needs of its shareholders with the societal need of the countries within which it operates.

The term sustainability refers to an organisation focusing on its long-term survival. It requires organisations to balance their current requirements for operating their businesses, without compromising the needs of future generations. In doing this, CSR obviously plays a part in ensuring the long-term survival of the organisation – this is often why the two terms are linked.

2. Why did companies give up responsibility for the welfare of their employees?

Some believe that following World War II, the advent of free education and the National Health Service in the UK saw the state take over from companies the responsibility for the well-being of the workforce. This in turn led to companies focusing more on making profits and achieving growth to help economic recovery after the war than on acting in the interests of society at large.

3. What changed to create an interest in the social responsibility of companies?

By the late 1980s, society was becoming more and more concerned with the behaviour of corporations and their lack of concern for the communities within which they operated. There was a belief by some that short-term profits were being focused on to the detriment of long-term profitability and sustainability, not just of the organisations but also of society as a whole. In 1991, a theoretical debate on 'doing well by doing good' was started by the Porter hypothesis that the financial benefits from innovation induced by CSR more than offset the engagement and compliance costs. There has also been a growing recognition since the early 1990s that the reputational impact of a good CSR rating is positive as the outside world sees the organisation as decent, trustworthy, and good to its employees, the community and the environment. Evidence shows that this increases the financial returns for an organisation's investors.

Test yourself 10.2

1. Give three reasons why companies initiate CSR activities.

Organisations have realised that they can use CSR activities for the following:

◆   To obtain competitive advantage.

◆   To reduce risk, especially reputational risk.

◆   To attract human capital.

◆   For innovation.

◆   For sustainability.

2. Describe what is required for a win-win CSR partnership.

There can be many factors which aid a win-win partnership, including: having clear reasons to collaborate, having core people entirely committed to the partnership, having simple and credible goals, having a facilitator, incentivising workers, flexibility and having a clear exit strategy planned.

Test yourself 10.3

1. Why is it important for companies to think in an integrated way?
Integrated thinking considers things in a balanced way to allow the effective and efficient utilisation of the capital resources available to an organisation when developing strategy or decision making. These capitals are growing rare and therefore costs to the organisation are growing. It is important for an organisation to manage resources in the most effective way.

2. What are the six capitals that companies need to manage effectively and in an integrated way?
◆ Financial capital – money, equity, bonds, monetary value of assets, etc. that an organisation needs to operate.
◆ Human capital – the collective skills and experience of the people that work for the organisation.
◆ Manufactured capital – physical means and infrastructure needed for an organisation to provide its products and services, e.g. fixed assets.
◆ Intellectual capital – patents, copyright, designs, goodwill, brand value and knowledge accumulated, i.e. intangible assets.
◆ Natural capital – natural resources and energy that the organisation depends on to produce its products/services.
◆ Social capital – value added to an organisation by the social relationships with individuals and institutions that an organisation has developed through its stakeholder engagement.

3. What are the challenges with determining a company's sustainability?
Sustainability requires the balance of current needs against future needs. The challenge with this is determining:
◆ The current and future needs.
◆ The time period to be considered when looking at future generations.
◆ Who the sustainability should be for (e.g. the company, the country or the world).

4. Why is there a greater focus on the longer-term in organisations?
By focusing on the long-term sustainable success of the company, organisations should generate value for shareholders and contribute to wider society.

Chapter 11

Test yourself 11.1

1. What are some of the major problems with traditional corporate reporting?
◆ Annual reports have become so detailed and extensive that many are totally inaccessible to the average reader.
◆ Annual reports present the historic performance and activities of the company over the previous financial year.
◆ Annual reports tend to focus on the financial performance of the company excluding information on non-financial matters.
◆ Some intangibles are excluded – such as good corporate governance, brand recognition, good reputation and sound risk management.
◆ Some costs are excluded – e.g. the environmental costs of using up natural resources that can never be regenerated, and of the impact of carbon emissions on climate change are excluded from financial accounting.
◆ Different reports are prepared for different users, for example, sustainability report and corporate governance report. Each of these reports tries to meet the demands of a particular stakeholder group. These reports are often not connected as they are developed by different departments within the organisation that are not talking to each other. The result is that they end up showing each stakeholder group a different aspect of the organisation.
◆ By focusing on financial reporting only, organisations have been pushed into short-termism as they strive to meet the requirements on a quarterly or six-monthly basis of the markets.

2. Define narrative reporting.
Narrative reporting describes the additional non-financial information which is included in companies' annual reports providing a wider, and some would argue a more meaningful, picture of the company's business, its strategy, and future prospects.

3. What parts of an annual report and accounts are examples of narrative reporting?
◆ the chair's statement;
◆ the directors report;
◆ the directors' remuneration report;
◆ the corporate governance report;
◆ the strategic report.

4. What is a safe harbour?

Section 463 of the 2006 Act introduces a new safe harbour in relation to directors' liability for the directors' report, the strategic report and the directors' remuneration report. Directors are only liable to compensate the company for any loss it suffers as a result of any untrue or misleading statement in, or omission from, one of these reports if the untrue or misleading statement is made deliberately or recklessly, or the omission amounts to dishonest concealment of a material fact.

This safe harbour addresses the concern of directors over liability for negligence when making, for example, forward-looking statements in the reports, in particular, the strategic report. The directors' liability is limited to the company rather than to third parties.

Test yourself 11.2

1. Give three examples of why a company would choose to voluntarily report on its CSR activities.

Any of the following could be given.

◆ reputation of brand
◆ ethical considerations
◆ innovation and learning
◆ employee motivation
◆ risk management or reduction
◆ access to capital/increased shareholder value
◆ economic considerations
◆ strengthened supplier relationships
◆ market position improvement
◆ improved relations with government
◆ cost savings

2. Why is it important to set CSR targets and link them to executive pay?

To be able to report on their CSR activities organisations need to be able to set non-financial targets and measure their progress against targets.

Using targets as part of the performance criteria in bonus and incentive schemes for senior executives ensures that CSR needs within companies are taken seriously and that targets are actively worked towards.

However, boards in the absence of CSR metrics have retained the right to reduce incentive awards in cases of substantial damage to the company's business or reputation resulting from an event that has had a negative effect on the environment, society or the organisation's long-term sustainability. For example, an oil spill where inadequate precautions tied to the activities of senior executives can be shown.

3. What is the difference between triple bottom line reporting and integrated reporting?

The difference is that triple bottom line reports describe the organisation's non-financial performance, both positive and negative, in areas such as the environment, society and governance.

Integrated reports, on the other hand, combine financial and non-financial information and are usually targeted at investors.

Test yourself 11.3

1. What are the GRI Standards and why are they important?

The GRI Sustainability Reporting Standards (GRI Standards) were introduced for reports and other materials published on or after 1st July 2018. The GRI Standards are the first and most widely adopted global standards for sustainability reporting.

GRI Standards create a common language for organisations and stakeholders, with which the economic, environmental, and social impacts of organisations can be communicated and understood. They have been designed to enhance the global comparability and quality of information on these impacts, thereby enabling greater transparency and accountability of organisations.

2. Why was the Corporate Reporting Dialogue established?

In June 2014, the Corporate Reporting Dialogue was convened by the International Integrated Reporting Council to create dialogue and alignment between the key sustainability standard setters and framework developers.

The Corporate Reporting Dialogue has already adopted a statement of Common Principles of Materiality, developed a common map of the reporting landscape and taken a common position in support of the Financial Stability Board Task Force on Climate-related Financial Disclosure. In November 2018, the Corporate Reporting Dialogue announced a project aimed at:

- aligning all current sustainability standards with the TCFD recommendations published in June 2017;
- identifying the similarities and differences between the current standards and frameworks to create even greater alignment, taking into account the different requirements of each set of standards and frameworks; and
- continuing dialogue with financial reporting standard setters towards integrating financial and non-financial reporting.

3. Why do companies have external assurance of their CSR initiatives?

Many organisations are obtaining external assurance for their CSR initiatives and sustainability reports. These assurances provide a measure of credibility as they are performed by third parties.

4. What is an environmental profit & loss account?

An EP&L allows a company to measure in euro value the costs and benefits it generates for the environment, and in turn make more sustainable business decisions.

Chapter 12

Test yourself 12.1

1. What is the responsibility of a board of directors for risk and internal controls?

Principle O of the UK Corporate Governance Code states that:

'The board should establish procedures to manage risk, oversee the internal control framework, and determine the nature and extent of the principal risks it is willing to take in order to achieve its long-term strategic objectives.'

The Principle is supported by the following Provisions:

'28. The Board should carry out a robust assessment of the company's emerging and principal risks. The board should confirm in the annual report that it has completed this assessment, including a description of its principal risks, what procedures are in place to identify emerging risks, and explanation of how these are being managed or mitigated.

29. The board should monitor the company's risk management and internal control systems and, at least annually, carry out a review of their effectiveness and report on that review in the annual report. The monitoring and review should cover all material controls, including financial, operational and compliance controls.'

2. Explain the difference between downside and upside risk?

Downside risk is the risk of something bad happening that affects an organisation's ability to meet its strategic objectives. Examples are a fire or an IT breakdown. Upside risk is where an organisation performs better than expected, which creates its own risks – for example, the take-up of a product being more than anticipated which could lead to a risk that the product will not be available, and the organisation may be seen as unreliable.

3. What is the difference between the UK and US models of risk management and internal control systems?

The US system separates the two systems whereas the UK model considers risk management and internal control systems jointly.

Test yourself 12.2

1. What is risk appetite and risk tolerance?

Risk appetite is the level of risk that an organisation is willing to take in the pursuit of its objectives. It should be set by the board who should review its level regularly as the business environment changes.

Risk tolerance is the amount of risk that an organisation is prepared to accept in order to achieve its financial objectives. It is expressed as a quantitative measure. For example, in banks, the value at risk (VaR) for a portfolio.

2. What are the main categories of risk?

◆ financial risks

◆ operational risks

◆ compliance risks

◆ strategic risks:
  - people risks
  - marketplace risks
  - ethical risks
  - reputational risks
  - suppliers/outsourcers risks
  - environmental risks
  - political risks

3. List the responses to risk.

◆ avoidance

◆ reduction

◆ transfer

◆ acceptance

4. You are the company secretary of a clothing retail business and as the person responsible for risk, you have been asked to complete the risk register for the following risk, which has been related high. Propose a treatment and a method of measuring the effectiveness of the treatment: theft of clothes from the store.

Treatment – security tags on each item.

Monitoring – stock auditors carrying out regular audits.

Test yourself 12.3

1. What are the benefits of risk management to an organisation?
For operational performance:

◆ Increases the likelihood of achieving business objectives.

◆ Uses incidents to highlight the risk environment and helps management to enhance risk awareness and develop performance indicators or risk indicators to improve business performance and processes.

◆ Facilitates monitoring and mitigation of risk in key projects and initiatives.

◆ Provides a platform for regulatory compliance and building goodwill.

For financial performance:

◆ Protects and enhances value by prioritising and focusing attention on managing risk across and organisation.

◆ Contributes to a better credit rating, as rating agencies are increasingly focusing on the risk management of organisations.

◆ Builds investor, stakeholder and regulator confidence and shareholder value.

◆ Reduces insurance premiums through demonstrating a structured approach to risk.

For decision making:

◆ Shares risk information across the organisation, contributing to informed decisions.

◆ Facilitates assurance and transparency of risks at board level.

◆ Enables decisions to be made in the light of the impact of risks and the organisation's risk appetite and tolerance.

2. List four common failures of boards in relation to risk management.

◆ Failure to take responsibility for risk at the board level.

◆ Failure to see the importance of risk to the organisation as a whole.

◆ Failure to capture the major risks of the organisation.

◆ Failure to consider the integrated nature of risk.

◆ Failure to put in place the appropriate control or other mitigants for risk.

◆ Failure to manage reputational risk.

◆ Failure by the board to map out clearly, often in a risk manual, who has responsibility for what at what level of the organisation.

◆ Failure to consider, decide or articulate effectively the risk appetite for the organisation.

◆ Failure to obtain and share timely and good quality information can lead to heightened risk within an organisation.

◆ Failure of the board to appropriately challenge management on the proposals brought to the board can create risk.

Chapter 13

Test yourself 13.1

1. What does the board need to consider when deciding what structures to put in place to fulfil its responsibilities for risk and internal control?

The board has overall responsibility for the systems of risk management and internal controls within an organisation. To enable the board to carry out this responsibility, it needs to ensure that the appropriate structures are put in place at the proper levels within the organisation to manage risk. In deciding what these structures should be, the board needs to consider the following:

◆ Whether risk and internal controls should be considered by the whole board or be delegated to a committee of the board.

◆ If delegating to a committee, whether risk and internal controls should fall under one committee, the audit committee, or into two separate committees, the audit committee for internal controls and the risk committee for risk.

◆ The division of responsibility between itself and management for risk management.

2. Why might an organisation decide to have a risk committee?

In some cases, the audit committee may be overwhelmed by its other duties covering financial reporting and internal controls or may not have the necessary skill set required for the governance of risk. In these cases, the board may decide to establish a separate risk committee.

The size of the organisation and the sector the organisation is operating in may also determine whether responsibility for reviewing internal controls and risk management is dealt with in the same board committee, the audit committee, or whether two separate committees, one for audit and the other for risk, are established.

Banks and other large financial institutions normally have separate risk committees due to the complexity of their risk exposure. A growing number of listed non-financial companies, for example in the oil industry, are also finding it useful to establish a separate risk committee. The benefits of a separate risk committee are:

◆ It can focus solely on reviewing the organisation's risk management and providing assurance to the board that risk management and the processes for the control over risk are effective.

◆ It can give the board advice and make specific recommendations on risk appetite, the organisation's risk tolerance and strategies to manage risk.

◆ It can provide input into strategy formulation by helping the board to understand the key risks facing the organisation and the opportunities available to the organisation by managing those risks.

◆   The composition of the committee is not restricted by the requirements of the corporate governance code. An audit committee is required to be composed of all independent directors. A separate risk committee can have executive directors and non-board members to strengthen the skills and experience of the committee.

Test yourself 13.2

1. Who are the main governance players that support the board with their risk management responsibilities?

The governance players responsible for risk are:

◆   The board.

◆   Audit and, if separate, risk committees.

◆   company secretary.

◆   CEO.

◆   Chief Risk Officer.

◆   Internal Auditor.

◆   All management and staff.

2. Why should boards routinely monitor and review the organisation's systems of risk management and internal controls?

The existence of risk management and internal control systems does not, on its own, indicate that risk and internal controls are being managed effectively within an organisation. The board (or audit committee) should, on an ongoing basis, monitor and review the systems to ensure that they:

◆   remain aligned with the organisation's strategic objectives;

◆   address the risks facing the organisation;

◆   are being developed, applied and maintained appropriately for the organisation.

3. What matters should the annual review of the effectiveness of the systems of risk management and internal controls cover?

The FRC Guidance on Risk Management, Internal Control and Related Financial and Business Reporting, states that the annual review of effectiveness should consider:

◆   the company's risk appetite;

◆   the desired culture within the company and whether this culture has been embedded within the organisation;

◆   the operation of the risk management and internal control systems, covering design, implementation, monitoring and review and the identification of principal risks;

◆   the integration of risk management and internal controls with the company's business model, strategy and business planning processes;

◆ the changes in the nature, likelihood and impact of principal risks;

◆ the company's ability to respond to changes in its business and the external environment;

◆ the extent, frequency and quality of management's reporting on the organisation's risk management;

◆ the issues dealt with by the board throughout the year under review;

◆ the effectiveness of the company's public reporting processes.

Test yourself 13.3

1. What concerns should an employee raise through a whistleblowing procedure?

An effective whistleblowing procedure should allow for an employee to raise concerns about illicit behaviour, usually in one of the following areas:

◆ fraud;

◆ a serious violation of a law or regulation by the company or by directors, managers or employees within the company;

◆ a miscarriage of justice;

◆ offering or taking bribes;

◆ price-fixing;

◆ a danger to public health or safety, such as dumping toxic waste in the environment or supplying food that is unfit for consumption;

◆ neglect of people in care; or

◆ in the public sector, gross waste or misuse of public funds.

2. What areas should a whistleblowing policy and procedure cover?

Typically, a whistleblowing policy and procedures would cover the following:

◆ purpose, scope and coverage;

◆ procedures for reporting a matter;

◆ what happens when communication is received from a whistleblower;

◆ anonymity of the whistleblower;

◆ communication with the whistleblower; and

◆ protection of the whistleblower.

3. What areas should be covered in a cybersecurity policy?

The cybersecurity policy should inform employees and other authorised users of the company's technology the requirements for protecting that technology and the information it contains from a cyberattack. The policy is usually made up of three parts:

◆ Physical security of the technology. This section explains the importance of keeping the physical asset secure – locking doors, surveillance, alarms etc.

◆   Personnel management. This section explains to employees how to
conduct their day-to-day activities – password management, keeping
confidential certain information, the use of the internet, the use of
memory sticks etc. Some organisations go as far as restricting access to the
internet and sealing the ports of computers for UBS devices in an attempt
to stop viruses and malware from being introduced into their systems.

◆   Hardware and software. This section explains to the technology
administrators what type of technology and software to use and how
networks should be configured to ensure they are secure. Due to the
technical nature of this part of the policy, boards may wish to get
independent advice on the recommendations of management in this area.

Test yourself 13.4

*1. What matters should the company secretary consider when
handling insider information?*
Managing insider information is a major part of the company secretary role.
The following are some of the matters that the company secretary may consider
when handling insider information:

◆   Confidentiality of board papers. Extra care should be taken when
distributing paper board packages. This might mean using double
envelopes, anti-tear envelopes, and even hand delivery rather than email
or courier. If documents are made available electronically through a board
portal, the company secretary should make sure the system is as secure as
possible, for example, by encrypting documents.

◆   Careful consideration may have to be given to securing the computers
used to prepare the papers to be included in the package. If shared drives
are used or computers are networked, the company secretary should know
who has access to these drives and networks. If a password is needed
to access certain drives, the company secretary should know that usually
the administrator of the system (often an IT person or sometimes an
outsourced person) can access the drive/folder. It has been known in highly
sensitive transactions for the papers to be prepared and kept on an offsite
server usually maintained by the company's law firm.

◆   Confidentiality of board discussions. The company secretary should
consider the following:

    –   Is the room in which the board is meeting soundproof?

    –   Can anyone see into the room from outside? Especially, if a
PowerPoint presentation is made, will it be visible?

    –   Some listed companies even check for listening devices and coat
windows so that no one can see in to ensure confidentiality.

◆   Insider lists. These lists are often required by regulators for listed
companies, although they can be used by any company involved in a
commercially sensitive project. To control the spread of confidential
information, insider lists contain the names of people, internally and
externally, who are aware of the project. Only those on the list can discuss

the project. If someone else needs to be consulted, they have to be added to the list. The company secretary is often the holder of the insider lists.

◆ The communication plan for the project. The company secretary may be asked on behalf of the board to work with management to produce a communication plan for the project. This will indicate who should be communicated to, how, and when. If the company is listed or is a regulated business, then any regulations for communications should be reflected in the plan. For example, a listed company may have to make a regulatory announcement before it can release information to others.

2. What is the difference between disaster recovery planning and business continuity planning?

A disaster recovery plan is a plan of what needs to be done immediately after a disaster to recover from the event. The disaster is of a nature unconnected with the company's business and outside the control of management. Examples of disasters are:

◆ natural disasters, such as major fires or flooding or storm damage to key installations or offices;

◆ IT disruptions; and

◆ major terrorist attacks.

Business continuity planning goes beyond procedures that should be taken in an emergency, such as a fire or explosion in a building. It is intended to establish, in advance, a plan of what a company needs to do to ensure that its key products and/or services continue to be delivered in the longer-term, i.e. a plan for the sustainability of the business. A business continuity plan should be developed from the disaster recovery planning and the risk management process. It should seek to make the company ready to take advantage of the longer-term threats to the business, thus giving the company competitive advantage over competitors who are not planning for the future sustainability of their business.

It is important for the board to be involved in both disaster recovery and business continuity planning as both are critical to the on-going activity of the business.

3. What are the six principles of the Ministry of Justice Guidance on the UK Bribery Act 2010?

◆ Proportionate procedures. The procedures of a commercial organisation to prevent bribery should be proportionate to the risk of bribery that it faces and the nature and scale of its commercial activities.

◆ Top-level commitment. Top-level management should be committed to preventing bribery and should foster a culture in their organisation in which bribery is considered unacceptable.

◆ Risk assessment. There should be periodic, informed and regular assessment by organisations of the nature and extent of potential bribery by people associated with it.

◆ Due diligence. There should be due diligence of third party intermediaries and local agents who will act on behalf of the organisation, with a view to identifying and mitigating bribery risk.

◆ Communication (including training). Commercial organisations should seek to ensure that policies against bribery are embedded and understood, by means of communication and training that is proportionate to the bribery risk that the organisation faces.

◆ Monitoring and review. There should be monitoring and review of the procedures designed to prevent bribery, and improvements should be made when weaknesses are detected.

4. What should the company secretary do to minimise boardroom disputes?

The company secretary can take the following steps to minimise boardroom disputes:

◆ Ensure that the roles of the board members have been set out in a clear and concise way in their appointment letter.

◆ On appointment, a comprehensive induction programme should be held to ensure that there is no misunderstanding as to what is expected from the board members.

◆ There is a board charter/governance manual setting out what the roles of the board, board committees and senior management team are.

◆ Delegation of authority to the CEO is clearly documented.

◆ Proper flows of information to and from the board. The board requires sufficient information to make informed decisions. Management require prompt communication of board decisions.

◆ In agenda development, ensuring that there is plenty of time allowed for discussion, debate and deliberation of the matters brought to the board.

◆ Advising the chair to agree with the board ground rules for behaviour, attire etc. during board meetings.

◆ Creating the right environment within the boardroom for calm, effective meetings and decision making. This can include:
  – Shape of the table
  – Seating arrangements
  – Lighting and heating
  – Make sure there are plenty of breaks
  – Being prepared to break a tense situation by advising the chair to take a break, asking for clarity for the minutes etc.

◆ Encouraging the creation of a good culture within the board. This can be achieved by building relationships and trust between board members. Giving plenty of opportunity for board members to get to know each other through lunches or dinners, annual board retreats, board trainings etc.

Chapter 14

Test yourself 14.1

1. What are the four types of market abuse?
The four main types of market abuse are:

◆ engaging or attempting to engage in insider dealing;

◆ recommending that another person engage in insider dealing or inducing another person to do so;

◆ unlawfully disclosing inside information; and

◆ engaging in, or attempting to engage in, market manipulation.

2. Why might there be more successful prosecutions for insider dealing under the market abuse regime than under the Criminal Justice Act 1973?
The market abuse offence of insider dealing is a civil offence. Accordingly, it is only necessary to prove that a person's behaviour was illegal 'on the balance of probabilities' as opposed to the 'beyond reasonable doubt' test applied in criminal prosecutions for insider dealing under the Criminal Justice Act 1993.

3. What is inside information and why are listed companies required to publish inside information so promptly?
Inside information is defined as:

◆ information of a precise nature;

◆ which has not been made public;

◆ relating, directly or indirectly, to one or more issuers or to one or more financial instruments; and

◆ which, if it were made public, would be likely to have a significant effect on the prices of those financial instruments or on the price of related derivative financial instruments.

Information is not inside information unless each of the criteria in the above definition is met.

Listed companies are required to publish inside information promptly in order to minimise the opportunities for insider dealing and the creation of a false market where the information has leaked.

Test yourself 14.2

1. Briefly describe the most common types of shareholders.
Below is a list of the most common types of 'shareholders'.

- Member – a person (or corporation) entered into the Register of Members of the company as a holder of the company's shares.
- Beneficial shareowner – a person or organisation that ultimately owns a share in a company. The shareowner may or may not be a 'member' of the company.
- Nominee/Custodian – a person or organisation that holds shares as a 'member' on behalf of another person or organisation who may or may not be the ultimate owner of the shares.
- Retail shareholder – individual investors who buy and sell securities for their personal account, and not for another company or organisation. The individual usually registers the shares in the name of a nominee belonging to a stock broking firm, e.g. Barclays Nominees Limited.
- Institutional shareholder – a person or organisation that trades securities in large quantities or monetary amounts on behalf of multiple beneficiaries.

2. What are the main sources of shareholder rights?
The main sources of powers and rights for shareholders are as follows:

Legislation –- the two main areas of law that relate to shareholders are company laws and securities laws.

Regulations – listed companies are subject to the requirements of the Listing Rules, Disclosure and Transparency Rules (DTRs) and the Takeover Code.

Case law – some protection for minority shareholders can be found in common law rules, which often operate when legislation is silent.

Corporate governance codes and principles such as the OECD Principles of Corporate Governance.

Articles of association of the company usually contain powers and rights of members, such as those for the holding of general meetings.

Resolutions passed at general meetings of shareholders reinforce pre-emption rights, the rights to share by way of dividend in the profits of the company and the rights to elect the board of directors and the company's auditors.

Shareholder agreements which may regulate:

- the purchase and sale of shares;
- the preference to acquire shares;
- the exercise of voting rights;
- the exercise of control;
- the company's policy on investments;
- the company's budget;
- the right of first refusal;

◆ the tag-along and drag-along clauses;

◆ the preparatory meetings among the shareholders who executed the shareholder's agreement to decide how to vote in the general meetings of the company.

3. Give examples of shareholder rights.

The following are examples of shareholder rights:

◆ ownership and transfer of shares;

◆ equal treatment;

◆ share in profits;

◆ receipt of information;

◆ attend and vote at shareholder meetings; and

◆ enfranchising indirect shareholders.

4. Name four examples of shareholder abuse.

◆ insider trading

◆ dilution

◆ tunnelling

◆ related party transactions

Test yourself 14.3

1. What is a derivative claim? Who is able to bring it and when?

CA2006 introduced the possibility of a 'derivative claim' by shareholders on the grounds that the company itself has a cause of action against the directors of the company. The cause of action must involve some negligence, default or breach of duty on the part of the director and may be brought against the director involved in the breach. There is no need to show that the company has suffered a financial loss. Minority shareholders are therefore able to bring actions against directors who have acted in a way that is preferential to a majority shareholder and have breached their duty to promote the interests of shares as a whole.

2. In what ways does a company know who its interested shareholders are?

Shareholders who have a substantial holding in a company are required to inform the company. This disclosure makes it clear to potential investors who owns the company or who aspires to secure control of the company. It also warns the company and allows them, together with shareholders, to prepare for an impending takeover. In the UK, the initial disclosure is triggered at 3% of total voting rights and a further disclosure is required for each whole percentage point change after that. There are exemptions for market makers holding less than 10% so long as they don't influence the management of the company or exert influence over the company. At 10% and over the entire holding is disclosable. Listed companies are required to make these notifications public.

Public companies can, under the CA2006, give notice to any person or entity whom the company believes to have an interest in the company's shares or to have had an interest at any time in the three years immediately preceding the date the notice was issued. The notice requires the shareholder to disclose whether or not they have had an interest and the nature of that interest. If the shareholder fails to provide the information the company is able to obtain a court order imposing certain restrictions on the shares it believes are held by the shareholder. If the shareholder fails to comply with a court order it is a criminal offence.

3. Why should institutional shareholders take an interest in good corporate governance?

Shareholder participation provides 'checks and balances' on the board of directors, thus helping the board monitor the management of the company.

Institutional investors should take an interest in good corporate governance as:

◆ Investors expect a return on their investment. Most evidence suggests that well-governed companies deliver reasonable returns over the long term, and shareholders in these companies are less exposed to downside risk than shareholders in companies that are not so well governed.

◆ Institutional investors also have legal responsibilities (fiduciary duties) to the individuals on whose behalf they invest. For pension funds, these individuals are the beneficiaries of the funds. In fulfilling their responsibilities, institutions should try to ensure that they make a decent return on investment, and promoting good corporate governance is one way of trying to do this.

4. What are the seven principles of the stewardship code?

◆ Principle 1: Institutional investors should publicly disclose their policy on how they will discharge their stewardship responsibilities.

◆ Principle 2: Institutional investors should have a robust policy on managing conflicts of interest in relation to stewardship, which should be publicly disclosed.

◆ Principle 3: Institutional investors should monitor their investee companies.

◆ Principle 4: Institutional investors should establish clear guidelines on when and how they will escalate their stewardship activities.

◆ Principle 5: Institutional shareholders should be willing to act collectively with other investors where appropriate.

◆ Principle 6: Institutional investors should have a clear policy on voting and disclosure of voting activity.

◆ Principle 7: Institutional investors should report periodically on their stewardship and voting activities.

Test yourself 14.4

1. What is the difference between responsible investing and socially responsible investment?

◆ Responsible or ethical investing means refusing to invest in 'unethical' companies and 'sin stocks', that is, companies that produce or sell addictive substances (like alcohol, gambling and tobacco) because the activities of the company are inconsistent with the investor's ethical, moral or religious beliefs.

◆ SRI investing goes further. It includes refusing to invest in 'unethical' companies, but SRI investors also encourage companies to develop CSR policies and objectives, in addition to pursuing financial objectives. SRI investors will seek out companies engaged in social justice, environmental sustainability and alternative energy/clean technology efforts. SRI investors may also be involved in shareholder activism when companies have social or environmental policies with which they disagree.

2. What are the ways in which an investor can pursue an SRI strategy?
There are several different ways in which institutional investors may pursue an SRI strategy:

◆ engagement;
◆ investment preference; and
◆ screening.

With an engagement strategy, the institutional investor acquires shares in which it wants to invest (for financial reasons) but then engages with the board of directors and tries to persuade the company to adopt policies that are socially responsible, or to make improvements in its CSR policies. Engagement may therefore involve the investor telling what the CSR policies of the company should be and persuading it to change its policies in some areas (through regular meetings with its senior directors). If the company indicates its willingness to make changes, the investor may also offer to help with the formulation of new policies.

With an investment preference strategy, the investor develops a set of guidelines that companies should meet. The investor will then invest only in the shares (or other securities) of companies that meet the guidelines, some of which will be social, ethical or environmental in nature. With this strategy, its investment decisions need not be based entirely on SRI considerations. The investor can also consider the expected financial returns from an investment, and the selected investment portfolio can be a suitable balance of investments that are ethically sound and those that are not as ethical (or are 'riskier' in social or environmental terms) but should provide better financial returns.

With a screening strategy, investments are restricted to companies that pass a 'screen test' for ethical behaviour. Screening may be positive or negative. Positive screening means that companies must meet certain criteria for ethical and socially responsible behaviour; otherwise, the investor will not buy its shares. Negative screening means that an investor will identify companies that fail to meet certain minimum criteria for socially responsible behaviour and will refuse to buy shares in those companies. The screening process could make use of a published CSR index, such as the Dow Jones Sustainability Indices or the FTSE 4 Good Indices.

Chapter 15

Test yourself 15.1

What ways, in addition to general meetings, should boards use when engaging with their shareholders?
The UK Corporate Governance Code states that in addition to formal general meetings:

- The chair should seek regular engagement with major shareholders in order to understand their views on governance and performance against the company's strategy.

- Chairs of board committees should also seek engagement with shareholders on significant matters related to their areas of responsibility. Where relevant the chair of the board committee should make the whole board aware of shareholders views on a particular matter.

- The senior independent director, when called upon, should meet a sufficient range of major shareholders to develop a balanced understanding of their views.

- Boards should consider additional ways to engage with smaller shareholders, for example, by way of roundtables, and webinars.

Test yourself 15.2

1. What are the limitations to the use of an AGM as a method of engaging with shareholders?
There are limitations to the use of the AGM as a method for dialogue between companies and their shareholders. These include:

- The fact that the meeting is held only once a year

- The location may make it difficult for shareholders to attend. Many AGMs are held in central London during the week so shareholders who live outside London or overseas may find it difficult to attend. Also, shareholders who work may not be able to get time off work to attend the AGM.

- AGMs often have a limited time duration imposed by the venue, the shareholders or the company. Chairmen wherever possible should allow all shareholders wanting to ask a question to do so.

This is why many companies seek other methods of engaging with their shareholders to make the interactions more meaningful and effective.

2. What is a virtual AGM and why do shareholder representative bodies have concerns about them?

Section 360A of the CA2006 permits a UK company to offer shareholders an electronic means for participating in a general meeting. The electronic means has to be real time, allow for two-way conversation and have a mechanism for shareholders to vote. These electronic meetings are also referred to as virtual AGMs.

Shareholder representative bodies, such as, the Investment Association (IA) and Pensions and Investments Research Consultants (PIRC) have expressed concerns in their guidance materials about companies only holding virtual meetings.

The Investor Association in their Position Statement: Virtual-Only AGMs published in December 2017 stated:

'Our members believe that virtual-only AGMs are not in the best interests of all shareholders and should not be used by investee companies, as their use could be detrimental to Board accountability. IA members are unlikely to be supportive of amendments to Articles of Association which allow for virtual-only AGMs.'

This is because the AGM is seen as the only opportunity that shareholders have to meet and question the whole board of a company. In reality though many institutional shareholders do not send representatives to attend AGMs unless there is a controversial issue. It is the retail shareholder in many FTSE100 companies who would be affected the most by this change in format of AGMS.

3. What things should a company consider when planning to hold a virtual AGM?

Things for companies to consider if they are planning to hold a virtual AGM:

- amendment of Articles of Association;
- views of their shareholders;
- technological considerations;
- notice of meeting;
- proxy form;
- helpline;
- preparing the chair and the board.
- to address board meetings, so members of boards hear from stakeholders directly about their concerns and issues.
- Documenting the concerns and issues of stakeholders and lessons learned and feeding this into the risk management, strategic planning, and business continuity processes, so that the company is able to leverage opportunities and lessen negative impacts.

◆ Recognising that different stakeholder groups may have different interests and ideas. Tailoring engagement and dialogue to better represent stakeholders' disparate interests to help them understand the reasons for board decisions.

◆ Developing policies on who within the organisation should be the prime communicator for each stakeholder group.

◆ Advising the board on any reputational-risk aspects to stakeholder engagement.

◆ Coordinating with management to ensure that the board is advised on how to engage with different stakeholder groups.

Chapter 16

Test yourself 16.1

1. What are the typical components of an executive director's remuneration package?
The remuneration package for a director or senior executive is likely to consist of a combination of:

◆ a basic salary;

◆ payments into a pension scheme for the individual (or payments in lieu);

◆ an annual bonus, usually linked to the annual financial performance of the company;

◆ long-term incentives, usually in the form of share options or share awards (sometimes called 'restricted stock awards');

◆ other benefits and perks, such as free medical insurance, a company car or accommodation.

2. What company performance targets might be used as a basis for fixing annual bonus payments to a CEO?
Bonus payments may depend on the achievement of both individual targets and the performance of the company over the previous financial year.

3. What are the problems with linking rewards to performance for senior executives?
It is difficult to design performance-related remuneration for the following reasons:

◆ selecting the right performance measures;

◆ setting the thresholds at which rewards are paid;

◆ setting a cap on any rewards under the incentive scheme;

◆ ensuring that the targets used promote the long-term success of the company;

◆ ensuring that the targets used do not promote bad behaviour;

◆ ensuring that executives who perform well are rewarded and preventing those that don't from piggy-backing on the success of their colleagues;

◆ executives may develop an expectation that they should receive annual rewards regardless of the actual performance of the company; and

◆ designing a scheme that will be satisfactory to shareholders.

4. What company performance targets might be used as a basis for deciding how many shares should be granted to a senior executive as a long-term incentive arrangement?

Most companies use total shareholder returns (TSR) or earnings per share (EPS) against a comparator group of companies.

5. What are the drawbacks to using share options for long-term incentive schemes?

The drawbacks of using share options as a long-term incentive are:

◆ Share prices are volatile. Option holders may be unjustly enriched in a bull market where prices are rising and inadequately rewarded in a bear market when prices are falling.

◆ If the market price of a company's shares falls below the exercise price for the share options, those options may no longer provide any incentive for the directors.

◆ It is more difficult to apply a holding period for shares acquired under a share option scheme as directors and senior executives may need to sell at least part of their holding in order to finance the exercise.

◆ International Financial Reporting Standard 2 (IFRS2) Share-based Payment requires companies to recognise the award of share options as an expense, chargeable against the company's profits, from the time that the share options are granted.

Test yourself 16.2

1. What does the UK Corporate Governance Code say about the general level of executive remuneration?

Principle P of the 2018 Code now provides:

'Remuneration policies and practices should be designed to support strategy and promote long-term sustainable success. Executive remuneration should be aligned to company purpose and values, and be clearly linked to the successful delivery of the company's long-term strategy.'

Principle R of the 2018 Code states that:

'Directors should exercise independent judgement and discretion when authorising remuneration outcomes, taking account of company and individual performance, and wider circumstances.'

2. What is the main guidance in the UK Corporate Governance Code on the design of performance-related pay?
Code Provision 40 recommends that:

◆ remuneration arrangements should be transparent and promote effective engagement with shareholders and the workforce;

◆ remuneration structures should avoid complexity and their rationale and operation should be easy to understand;

◆ remuneration arrangements should ensure reputational and other risks from excessive rewards, and behavioural risks that can arise from target-based incentive plans, are identified and mitigated;

◆ the range of possible values of rewards to individual directors and any other limits or discretions should be identified and explained at the time of approving the policy;

◆ the link between individual awards, the delivery of strategy and the long-term performance of the company should be clear. Outcomes should not reward poor performance; and

◆ incentive schemes should drive behaviours consistent with company purpose, values and strategy.

Test yourself 16.3

1. What are the principal duties of the remuneration committee under the UK Code?
Code Provision 33 provides that the remuneration committee should have delegated responsibility for:

◆ determining the policy for executive director remuneration; and

◆ setting remuneration for the chair, executive directors and senior management.

It also states that the committee should 'review workforce remuneration and related policies and the alignment of incentives and rewards with culture, taking these into account when setting the policy for executive director remuneration'.

2. Describe the recommendations of the Code regarding the composition of the remuneration committee.
Code Provision 32 states that the remuneration committee should consist exclusively of independent non-executive directors and should comprise at least three or, in the case of smaller companies, two such directors. The company chair is permitted to serve on the remuneration committee if they were considered independent on appointment as chair (although they are not allowed to chair the committee). The chair of the remuneration committee must have served on a remuneration committee for at least 12 months before their appointment.

3. What provisions are included in the Code on remuneration consultants and why?

Code Provision 35 provides that:

◆ Where remuneration consultants are appointed, this should be the responsibility of the remuneration committee.

◆ The consultant should be identified in the annual report alongside a statement about any other connection it has with the company or individual directors.

◆ Independent judgement should be exercised when evaluating the advice of external third parties and when receiving views from executive directors and senior management.

These provisions reflect concern about potential conflicts of interest remuneration consultants may have which may compromise their objectivity.

Test yourself 16.4

1. What are the two main component parts of the directors' remuneration report?

The two main components of the directors' remuneration report are:

◆ the directors' remuneration policy; and
◆ the annual remuneration report.

2. What is the purpose of the annual remuneration report?

The purpose of the annual remuneration report is to disclose to shareholders how the board has implemented the directors' remuneration policy during the financial year.

Test yourself 16.5

1. What are the principles and provisions of the UK Code with regard to severance payments for senior executives?

The UK Corporate Governance provides in Code Provision 39 that:

◆ Notice or contract periods should be one year or less.
◆ If it is necessary to offer longer periods to new directors recruited from outside the company, such periods should reduce to one year or less after the initial period.
◆ The remuneration committee should ensure compensation commitments in directors' terms of appointment do not reward poor performance.
◆ They should be robust in reducing compensation to reflect departing directors' obligations to mitigate loss.

2. What are 'malus' and 'clawback' provisions and where might you find them?
'Malus' provisions allow the company, in specified circumstances, to forfeit all or part of a bonus or long-term incentive award before it has vested and been paid (also known as 'performance adjustment'). 'Clawback' provisions allow the company to recover sums already paid.

Test yourself 16.6

1. Who should set the fees of NEDs?
Code provision 34 provides that the remuneration of non-executive directors should be determined in accordance with the articles of association or, alternatively, by the board. In practice the chair and the executive directors will take the lead on making a proposal to the board regarding the fees that should be paid to non-executives, probably after taking advice from the company's remuneration consultants. Remember that, under the Code, the remuneration of the chair (even if non-executive) must be determined by the remuneration committee.

2. Why is it inappropriate for NEDs to participate in performance-related schemes?
Non-executive directors are expected to play a role in setting the risk appetite of the company. Anyone whose remuneration is based on short- to medium-term performance has an incentive to take more risk in order to chase profits. Shareholders expect non-executive directors to act as a moderating influence in this regard. If they were allowed to participate in performance-related schemes, their interests would be more closely aligned with those of the executive team, rather than the interests of shareholders.

3. Why might it be appropriate for some or all of NED fees to be paid in shares? What are the practical difficulties with this proposal?
Some people argue that paying NEDs fees in shares would more closely align their interests with those of the shareholders, as it would force them to become shareholders themselves. However, if you want them to remain as shareholders, you would have to impose a minimum holding period. They could, for example, be required to hold the shares until they ceased to hold office. This would potentially mean that they did not receive any remuneration for their services until the end of their tenure. This would be likely to give rise to recruitment and retention problems. Accordingly, non-executives would probably have to be allowed to sell at least some of their shares. However, share sales by directors always send a negative message to the market. Setting up a system where these become a regular occurrence is not an attractive prospect for companies. A possible compromise might be for a minimum percentage of their fees to be paid in shares (say 20%), in which case a minimum holding period could also be applied. The minimum holding period could allow them to sell those shares after, say, three to five years. The average tenure of NEDs is around four years.

Test yourself 16.7

1. Why are the IA Principles of Remuneration and the PLSA Policy so influential?

The IA Principles of Remuneration and the PLSA Policy represent the views of institutional shareholders (e.g. investment managers and pension funds) who hold a significant stake in most listed companies. Most companies realise that shareholders will not support remuneration policies and structures that breach the guidelines issued by the two bodies. In addition, both bodies have a significant influence on government and regulatory policy in the field of corporate governance. Even if the majority of companies comply with the guidance, policy makers often give those recommendations more force by adopting them as legislative or code requirements.

2. Give two broad examples of things covered in the IA Principles and two broad examples of things covered by the PLSA Policy.

The IA Principles cover levels of pay, bonuses, pensions, long-term incentive schemes, contract terms and severance payments. A particular focus in recent years has been on 'malus' and 'clawback' arrangements.

The PLSA Policy covers a wide range of corporate governance issues of which remuneration is only one. It focuses more on matters that will be voted on by shareholders at the AGM. Accordingly, it focuses on the directors' remuneration policy and the annual remuneration report and explains the circumstances in which shareholders are most likely to vote against any resolution on those matters.

Directory of web resources

Companies House
https://www.gov.uk/topic/company-registration-filing

Department for Business, Energy & Industrial Strategy
https://www.gov.uk/government/organisations/department-for-business-energy-and-industrial-strategy

Financial Conduct Authority
https://www.handbook.fca.org.uk/handbook

Financial Reporting Council
https://www.frc.org.uk/

Information Commissioners Office
https://ico.org.uk/

Institute of Directors
https://www.iod.com/

Institute of Directors (South Africa)
https://www.iodsa.co.za/

Institute of Risk Management
https://www.theirm.org/

International Corporate Governance Network
https://www.icgn.org/

Pensions and Lifetime Savings Association
https://www.plsa.co.uk/

UK Legislation
http://www.legislation.gov.uk/

Glossary

Apply or explain rule – Similar to the 'comply or explain' rule. Companies should apply the principles of a code or explain why they have not done so.

Accountability – The requirement for a person in a position of responsibility to justify, explain or account for the exercise of their authority and their performance or actions.

Accounts meeting – The general meeting at which the accounts are laid, which will usually be the AGM.

Agency theory – A theory based on the separation of ownership from control in a large organisation and the conflict of interests between the individuals who direct the organisation and the people who own it. In a company, the directors act as agents for shareholders, and the conflict of interests between them should be controlled.

Annual general meeting (AGM) – A yearly meeting of the equity shareholders of a company. Public companies are required to hold an annual general meeting.

Articles of association – Effectively the company's constitution, together with certain shareholder resolutions.

Audit Committee – A committee of the board, consisting entirely of independent non-executive directors, with responsibility for monitoring the reliability of financial statements, the quality of the external audit and the company's relationship with its external auditors.

Audit firm rotation – Changing the firm of external auditors on a regular basis.

Audit report – A report for shareholders produced by the external auditors on completion of the annual audit and included in the company's published annual report and accounts. The report gives the opinion of the auditors on whether the financial statements present a true and fair view of the company's financial performance and position.

Balance of power – A situation in which power is shared out evenly between a number of different individuals or groups, so that no single individual or group is in a position to dominate.

Board committee – A committee established by the board of directors, with delegated responsibility for a particular aspect of the board affairs.

Board evaluation – The evaluation of the board, board committees, chair and other individual directors carried out by companies.

Board pack – Consists of documents or board papers that are a source of information for a director prior to a board meeting.

Board succession – The replacement of a senior director (typically the chair or CEO) when he or she retires or resigns.

Box ticking approach – An approach to compliance based on following all the specific rules or provisions in a code and not considering the principles that should be applied and circumstances where the principles are best applied by not following the detailed provisions.

Business risk – Risks (and opportunities) facing the organisation. Consists of strategic risk, operation risk, financial (reporting) risk and compliance risk.

Chair – Leader of the board of directors often referred to as the 'company chair' in companies and 'chair' in public bodies and voluntary organisations.

Chief executive officer (CEO) – The person who is the head of the executive management team in an organisation.

Claw back – The act of recovering sums paid or withholding payment to directors or senior executives where there has been deemed to be deliberate disclosure of misleading information to increase entitlement to bonuses.

Compliance controls – Internal controls to prevent or detect errors resulting from compliance risks.

Compliance risk – Risk of failure to comply with laws or regulations and the consequences of such a failure if discovered.

Compliance statement – A statement by a listed company of whether it has complied with the requirements of the national code of corporate governance, and if not, in what ways has it failed to do so.

Comply or explain rule – Requirement for a company to comply with a voluntary code of corporate governance (in the UK, the UK Corporate Governance Code) or explain any non-compliance.

Corporate citizen – A company acting with due regard for its responsibilities as a member of the society in which it operates. Corporate citizenship is demonstrated through CSR policies.

Corporate ethics – Standards of business behaviour, sometimes set out by companies in a code of corporate ethics.

Corporate governance – The system by which a company is directed, so as to achieve its overall objectives. It is concerned with relationship, structures, processes, information flows, controls, decision-making and accountability to the highest level in a company.

Corporate social responsibility (CSR) – Responsibility shown by a company or organisation for matters of general concern to the society in which it operates, such as protection of the environment, health and safety and social welfare.

Cross directorships – Two or more directors on boards of the other.

Cyber risks – Any risk that leads to financial loss as a result of disruption or damage to the reputation of an organisation from some sort of failure of its information technology systems.

Deferred annual bonus scheme – An element in a remuneration package for directors or senior executives whereby the individuals are allowed to use some or all of their annual cash bonus entitlement to acquire shares in the company, which are then matched after several years (typically three years) by the award of additional free shares.

Derivative action – Legal action taken against a director by shareholders in the company, alleging negligence or breach of duty.

Directors' report – A report by the board of directors to the shareholders, contained in the annual report and accounts of the company and containing a variety of reports and information disclosures, such as the business review and remuneration report.

Disaster recovery plan – Plans to be implemented, in the event of a disaster that puts normal operational systems out of action, to restore operational capability as quickly as possible.

Downside risks – A risk that actual events will turn out worse than expected. Downside risk can be measured in terms of the amount which profits could be worse than expected. The expected outcome is the forecast or budget expectation.

Enlightened shareholder approach – Approach to corporate governance based on the view that the objective of its directors should be to meet the needs of shareholders, while also showing concern for other major stakeholders.

Environment, social and governance (ESG) risks – Risks of adverse consequences to a company from circumstances or events relating to environmental, social or corporate governance issues.

EU Directive – An instruction devised by the European Commission and European Parliament. The contents of a Directive must be introduced into national law or regulations by all member states of the European Union.

European Commission – The managing and administrative body of the European Union.

Executive Director – A director who also has executive responsibilities in the management structure. Usually a full-time employee with a contract of employment.

External audit – Statutory annual audit of a company by independent external auditors.

Fairness – Impartiality, lack of bias. In a corporate governance context, the quality of fairness refers to things that are done or decided in a reasonable manner, and with a sense of justice, avoiding bias.

Fiduciary duty – A legal obligation of one party to act in the best interest of another.

Financial (reporting) risks – A risk of a failure or error, deliberate (fraud) or otherwise, in the systems or procedures for recording financial transactions and reporting financial performance and position, or the risk of a failure to safeguard financial assets such as cash and accounts receivable.

Financial controls – Internal controls to prevent or detect errors resulting from financial risks.

Fixed pay – The elements in a remuneration package that are a fixed amount each year, such as basic salary.

General meeting – A meeting of the equity shareholders of a company.

Going concern statement – A statement by the board of directors that in their view the company will remain as a going concern for the next financial year.

Induction – Process of introducing a newly-appointed director into their role, by providing appropriate information, site visits, meetings with management and (where necessary) training.

Insider list – A list of persons in a company who have access to inside information, which listed companies are required to prepare and maintain under the Market Abuse Regulation.

Insider trading – Dealing in the shares of a company by an 'insider' (such as a company director or professional adviser) on the basis of knowledge of price-sensitive information that has not yet been made available to the public.

Institutional investor – An organisation or institution that invests funds of clients, savers or depositors.

Integrated reporting – Reporting on all aspects of the company's activities that have relevance to the creation or loss of value in six areas of capital: financial, manufactured, human, intellectual property, natural and social. Similar to sustainability reporting, but directed at the company's shareholders.

Internal audit – Investigations and checks carried out by internal auditors of an organisations, internal auditors of an organisation. Internal audit is a function rather than a specific activity. However the programme of internal audit team might reduce the amount of work the external auditors need to carry out in their annual audit, provided the internal and external auditors collaborate properly.

Internal control – A procedure or arrangement that is implemented to prevent an internal control risk, reduce the potential impact of such a risk, or detect a failure of internal control when it occurs (and initiate remedial action).

Internal control risk – A risk of failure in a system or procedure due to causes that are within the control of management. They can be categorised as financial risks, operational risk and compliance risks.

Internal control system – A system of controls within an organisations. The system should have suitable control environment, and should provide for the identification and assessment internal control risks, the design and implementation of internal controls, communication and information and monitoring.

Large company – For accounting purposes, a large company is one that does not qualify as a medium-sized company because it exceeds at least two out of the three size thresholds for determining whether a company as medium-sized. See also very large company.

Majority shareholder – A shareholder holding a majority of the equity shares in company and so having a controlling interest in the voting power to remove directors from the board and so can control the board.

Management board – A board of executive managers, chaired by the CEO within a two-tier board structure. The chair of the management board reports to the chair of the supervisory board. The management board has responsibility for the operational performance of the business.

Market abuse – When an individual distorts a market in the investments, creates a false or misleading impression of the value or price of an investment, or misuses relevant information before it is published. Although it is similar to insider dealing, which is a criminal offence; this is a civil offence under the Financial Services and Markets Act.

Medium-sized company – in broad terms, a medium-sized company for accounting purposes is one which meets at least two of the following criteria: turnover of not more than £36 million; balance sheet total of not more than £18 million; or average number of employees must not exceed 250.

Minority shareholder – Shareholders holding a fairly small proportion of the equity shares in a company who could be at risk of having their interests ignored in favour of a controlling shareholder or group of large shareholders.

Model articles of association – Part of a companies constitution. Model articles are set out in CA2006 and automatically apply if a limited company is incorporated in the UK without registering its own articles.

Modified audit report – Audit report in which the auditors express some reservations about the financial statements of the company, because of insufficient information to reach an opinion or disagreement with the figures in the statements.

Money laundering – The process of transferring or using money obtained from criminal activity, so as to make it seem to have come from legitimate (non-criminal) sources. Companies are often used as cover for money laundering.

Nominations committee – A committee of the board of directors, with responsibility for identifying potential new members for the board of directors. Suitable candidates are recommended to the main board, which then makes a decision about their appointment.

Non-audit services/work – Work done by a firm of auditors for a client company, other than work on the annual audit, such as consultancy services and tax advice. In the context of corporate governance, the independence of the auditors might be questionable when they earn high fees for non-audit work.

Non-executive directors – A director who is not an employee of the company and who does have any responsibilities for executive management in the company.

Operational controls – Internal controls to prevents or detect errors resulting from operational risks.

Operational risk – Risk of an error, deliberate or otherwise, in operating system design, the risk of failures due to weak organisational structure, or risks due to weak organisational structure; or risks due to human error including inefficient management. Includes health and safety risks, environmental risks.

Over boarding – These are directors who sit on excessive number of boards, hence failing to do their jobs thoroughly because of too many commitments.

Performance-based incentives – Incentives to an individual, typically to an executive director and in the form of a cash bonus, that are achieved. Performance targets might be related to a rise in the share price, growth in sales or profits, growth in earnings per share, or to non-financial performance criteria.

Premium Listing – One of two categories of listing for companies in the UK. Companies with a premium listing are required to meet the highest standards of regulation and corporate governance.

Principles-based code of governance – A code based on general principles of best governance practice, rather than detailed rules and guidelines. A principle of best governance practice, rather than detailed rules and guidelines A principles-based code may include some practical provisions or guidelines, but these are not comprehensive.

Proxy – A person appointed by a shareholder to vote on the shareholder's behalf at a general meeting. In the UK, shareholders can appoint proxies electronically. They can either instruct a proxy how to vote on each resolution at a meeting, or can give the proxy freedom to decided how to vote on each resolution.

Proxy vote – A vote delivered by an individual (a proxy) on behalf of a shareholder, in the shareholder's absence.

Public interest entities – (a) A Listed Entity; or (b) An entity (i) defined by regulation or legislation as a public interest entity or (ii) for which the audit is required by regulation or legislation to be conducted in compliance with the same independence requirements that apply to the audit of listed entities. Such regulation may be promulgated by any relevant regulator, including an audit regulator.

Quoted company – For the purposes of the CA2006, a quoted company is defined in s. 385 as a UK company whose equity share capital: has been included in the official list in accordance with the provisions of Part VI of the FSMA (this includes UK companies with either a premium or standard listing whose shares are traded on the main market of the London Stock Exchange); is officially listed in an EEA state (for example, a UK company whose shares are quoted on the Paris Bourse); or is admitted to dealing on either the New York Stock Exchange or the exchange known as Nasdaq.

Red top warning – A notice sent out by an institutional investor organisations to its members, advising the members who are shareholders to vote against a particular resolution at an approaching general meeting of a company.

Related party transaction – A transaction by a company with a 'related party' such as a major shareholder, director, a company in which a director has a major interest or a member of a director's family.

Remuneration committee – A committee of the board of directors, with responsibility for deciding remuneration policy for top executives and the individual remuneration packages of certain senior executives, for example all the executive directors.

Remuneration – The payment packages offered to top company executives and all executive directors.

Responsible investment – Investing with due consideration for environmental, social and governance issues, because these can affect the value of the business.

Risk appetite – The amount and type of business risk that the board of directors would like their company to have exposure to. Identifying risk appetite should be a part of strategic planning.

Risk assessment – An assessment of risks faced by an organisations. Typically, risks are assessed according to how probable or how frequent an adverse outcome is likely to be in the planning period and the potential size of the losses if an adverse outcome occurs. The greatest risks are those with a high probability of an adverse outcome combined with the likelihood of a large loss if this were to happen.

Risk committee – A committee of the board that a company may establish, with the responsibility of monitoring the risk management system within the company, instead of the audit committee. A risk committee maybe established when the audit committee has so many other responsibilities to handle.

Secret profit – A profit that is not revealed. In the context of corporate governance, a director should not make a secret profit for his/her personal benefit and at the expense of the company.

Senior independent director – A non-executive director who is the nominal head of all the non-executive directors on the board. The SID may act as a channel of communication between in NEDS and the chairman, or (in some situations) between major shareholders and the board.

Serious Fraud Office (SFO) – An independent UK government agency that is responsible for investigating and prosecuting serious crimes involving financial wrongdoing and complex economic crimes, such as the Libor manipulation.

Severance payment – Payment to a director (or other employee) on being required to resign (or otherwise leave the company).

Shadow director – A person in accordance with whose instructions the directors of a company are accustomed to act and who has not been formally appointed as a director.

Share option – Rights given to an individual giving him (or her) the right but not the obligation to buy new shares in the company at a fixed (the exercise price) not earlier than a specified date and not later than a specified date in the future (typically not earlier than three years after the options are granted and not later than ten 10 years respectively.

Shareholder activism – A term that refers to: (1) the considered use by institutional investors of their rights as shareholders by voting against the board of directors at general meetings (or threatening to vote against the board); and (2) active dialogue with the boards of companies, to influence decisions by the board.

Shareholder value approach – Approach to corporate governance based on the view that the objective of its directors should be to maximise benefits for shareholders.

Short termism – This refers to the tendency for company management to take actions that maximise short-term earnings and stock prices at the expanse of the shareholders' objectives of long-term company performance.

Small company – In broad terms, a small company for accounting purposes is one which meets at least two of the following criteria: turnover of not more than £10.2 million; balance sheet total of not more than £5.1 million; or average number of employees must not exceed 50.

Smaller companies – For the purposes of the UK Corporate Governance Code, a smaller company is one is one that is below the FTSE 350 throughout the year immediately prior to the reporting year.

Social responsible investment – An investment by institutional investors that takes into consideration ethical issues and the CSR policies of companies when deciding which companies to invest in or whether to hold on to investment.

Stakeholder approach – Approach to governance based on the view that the organisations should aim to satisfy the needs of all stakeholders. Also called a pluralist approach.

Stakeholder theory – The view that the purpose of corporate governance should be to satisfy, as far as possible, the objectives of all key stakeholders.

Stakeholders – A stakeholder group is an identifiable group of individuals or organisations with vested interest. Stakeholder groups in a company include the shareholders, the directors, senior executive management and other employees, customers, suppliers, the general public and (in the case of many companies) the government. Stakeholders maybe categorised as financial or non-financial stakeholders and as an external or internal stakeholders (depending on whether The in the company) the nature of their interest differs between stakeholder group.

Statutory duties – Duties imposed by statute law.

Strategic risk – Risk from unexpected events or developments in a business or in the business environment which are outside the control of management. Business risks should be managed and kept within acceptable limits.

Supervisory board – A board of non-executive directors, found in a company with a two-tier board structure. The supervisory board reserves some responsibilities to itself. These include oversight of the management board.

Sustainability – Conducting business operations in a way that can be continued into the foreseeable future, without using natural resources at such a rate or creating such environmental damage that continuation of the business will eventually become impossible.

Total shareholder return – The total returns in a period earned by the company's shareholders, consisting normally of the dividends received and the gain (or minus the fall) in the share price during the period. The returns might be expressed as a percentage of the share value, e.g. the share price at the start of the period.

Transparency – Being clear about historical performance and future intentions, and not trying to hide information.

Triple bottom line reporting – Reporting on the economic, social and environment performance of the company.

Tunnelling – An illegal business practice in which a majority shareholder or high level company insider directs company assets or future business to themselves for personal gain.

Two-tier board – Board structure in which responsibilities are divided between a supervisory board of non-executive directors led by the chairman and a management board of executives led by the CEO.

Unitary board – A board structure in which decisions are taken by a single group of executive and non-executive directors, led by the company chairman.

Upside risk – A risk that actual events will turn out better than expected and will turn out better than expected and will provide unexpected profits. Some risks, such as the risk of a change in interest rates, or a change in consumer buying patterns could be 'two-way' with both upside and downside potential.

Very large company – A UK public or private company that is required to include a 'statement of corporate governance arrangements' in its directors' report. Subject to certain exceptions, this requirement applies to a company that satisfies one or both of the following criteria: has more than 2,000 employees; or has a turnover of more than £200 million and a balance sheet total of more than £2 billion.

Vote withheld – A voting option for shareholders who appoint a proxy, as an alternative to voting for or against a may be instructed to abstain on a particular resolution at the general meeting. Votes withheld are 'positive abstentions' and the number of votes withheld should be counted and recorded.

Walker Report – A report published in the UK in 2009 about corporate governance in banks and other financial services organisations, following the banking crisis of 2007–2008.

Window dressing of accounts – Applying accounting policies that are just within the limits of permissible accounting practice, but which have the effect of making the company's performance or financial position seem better than it would if more conservative accounting policies were used. For example, accounting policies might be used that recognize income at an early stage in a transaction process, or defer the recognition of expenses.

Wrongful trading – Wrongful trading occurs when a company continues to trade when the directors are aware that the company had gone into (or would soon go into) insolvent liquidation.

Index